To Stretch Our Ears

A DOCUMENTARY HISTORY OF AMERICA'S MUSIC

"[*My Father*] *would occasionally have us sing, for instance,*

a tune like The Swanee River *in the key of E♭, but play the*

accompaniment in the key of C. This was **to stretch our ears**

and strengthen our musical minds, so that they could learn

to use and translate things that might be used and translated

(in the art of music) more than they had been."

—CHARLES E. IVES

To Stretch Our Ears

A DOCUMENTARY HISTORY OF AMERICA'S MUSIC

EDITED BY

J. Heywood Alexander

W. W. Norton & Company

New York   London

For Bea

Epigraph on p. ii is from Charles E. Ives, *Memos*, ed. John Kirkpatrick (New York: W. W. Norton, 1972), 115. Epigraph on p. xxiii is from Randall Thompson, "The Contemporary Scene in American Music," *The Musical Quarterly* 18/1 (January 1932), 9.

The text of this book is composed in Minion with the display set in Optima
Composition by PennSet, Inc.
Manufacturing by Maple-Vail
Book design by Joan Greenfield

Library of Congress Cataloging-in-Publication Data
To stretch our ears : a documentary history of America's music / edited by J. Heywood Alexander.
    p. cm.
Includes bibliographical references and index.
ISBN 0-393-97411-1 (pbk.)
    1. Music—United States—History and criticism.   2. Music—United States—Sources.
I. Alexander, J. Heywood.

ML200 .T67 2002
780'.973—dc21

2001044816

ISBN 0-393-97411-1 (pbk.)
W. W. Norton & Company, Inc., 500 Fifth Avenue, New York, N.Y. 10110
www.wwnorton.com
W. W. Norton & Company Ltd., Castle House, 75/76 Wells Street, London W1T 3QT
1 2 3 4 5 6 7 8 9 0

CONTENTS

PART II: The Nineteenth Century 75

PART III: The Twentieth Century 319

PREFACE

Charles Ives had a lot of the "can do" American spirit about him. An independent and innovative experimenter, he composed in the evenings and on weekends while holding down a full-time insurance job in New York. Ives advised us "to stretch our ears"—a phrase that serves as the title of this book—"and strengthen our musical minds." We do both, as we listen directly to the voices of the men and women who created and performed America's music.

American music is multifaceted, as all recent studies have recognized. The earliest writers, however, reviewed a narrower scene. George Hood's *A History of Music in New England* (1846) concerns itself with sacred music exclusively, as does Nathaniel Gould's *Church Music in America* (1853). The first attempt at a more comprehensive history, Frederick Louis Ritter's *Music in America* (1890), is East-Coast oriented. Although it discusses activities primarily in New York and Boston, it also includes a chapter "Musical Development in the West" that deals principally with Milwaukee, Cincinnati, St. Louis, and the cultivation of popular music. John Tasker Howard's *Our American Music* (1931) emphasizes the development of classical music traditions.

Gilbert Chase's *America's Music* (first edition, 1955, with important second and third editions to follow) brought about a sea change in approach. Chase, in contrast to Howard, maintained that the most important developments in American music took place outside the classical realm, a point of view that has dominated histories of American music ever since. H. Wiley Hitchcock's *Music in the United States* (1969) brings full focus on a vernacular, popular tradition complementing a cultivated, classical one. Daniel Kingman's *American Music: A Panorama* (1979) likewise emphasizes traditions other than the classical.

Charles Hamm's *Music in the New World* (1983) presents a chronological, integrated view of American music history. Hamm explains that, first, music "was brought to the New World from elsewhere; in a second stage, new works were created here which resemble this imported music; finally, pieces gradually emerged with stylistic elements differing from those of the first two stages, usually as a result of acculturation of two or more national, racial, or ethnic groups in the New World." Also, Hamm emphasized performance through his enthusiastic acknowledgment of the *Recorded Anthology of American Music*, issued by New World records.

Historians need an organized approach and, in this sense, categorization is useful rather than arbitrary and academic. Richard Crawford's *America's Musical Life: A History* (2000) is oriented around performance, music that may or may not have been written down. Crawford recognizes three spheres of music: the classical, the popular, and the traditional (or folk), all coexisting and interacting.

Research in the field of American music has shown remarkable growth in the last quarter century, particularly since the American bicentennial. We now have at hand valuable reference works such as *Resources of American Music History* (1981), by D. W. Krummel et al., *The New Grove Dictionary of American Music* (1986), and Krummel's *Bibliographical Handbook of American Music*

(1987). William Billings is the first American composer to have had his complete works published (1977–1990). The substantial growth in the Society for American Music (formerly the Sonneck Society, incorporated 1975), which publishes the journal *American Music*, bears witness to scholarly interest in the field. Such continuing growth of scholarship means that a new, complete history will probably be written in every generation.

It became clear to me some time ago that a source readings book in American music that encompasses the entire field was needed. Thomas Riis had the same idea, and he and I discussed it on several occasions. He graciously provided four sections for this book. It was suggested that Crawford's *America's Musical Life: A History* become a frame of reference for the many diverse sections of *To Stretch Our Ears*, resulting in the present organization of the book. To a significant extent this book follows Crawford's approach, and many of the section headings match his. The two books are, in a sense, companion volumes, and they might well be consulted hand in hand.

To Stretch Our Ears is the first of its kind to cover such a wide spectrum. It keeps company with a number of collections devoted to smaller, specialized areas. Among these are Henry Cowell's *American Composers on American Music: A Symposium* (1933), Gilbert Chase's *The American Composer Speaks* (1966), Elliott Schwartz and Barney Childs's *Contemporary Composers on Contemporary Music* (1967), Eileen Southern's *Readings in Black American Music* (1971), Elwyn Wienandt's *Opinions on Church Music* (1974), Benjamin Boretz and Edward Cone's *Perspectives on Notation and Performance* (1976), Cole Gagne and Tracy Caras's *Soundpieces: Interviews with American Composers* (1982), Michael Mark's *Source Readings in Music Education History* (1982), Ruth Kate and Carl Dahlhaus's *Contemplating Music: Source Readings in the Aesthetics of Music* (1992), David Venney's *Source Readings in American Choral Music* (1995), William Duckworth's *Talking Music* (1995), Robert Walser's *Keeping Time: Readings in Jazz History* (1998), and William McKeen's *Rock and Roll Is Here to Stay: An Anthology* (2000).

To Stretch Our Ears may be compared with *4'33"*, John Cage's silent work that Cage, at age seventy, considered his most important piece. In both, ambient voices tell the story. The sounds are, as Allen Edwards called them in his conversation with Elliott Carter, both "flawed" and "stubborn," but they illuminate. Since there are so many sections to be covered in this book, necessity dictated that the readings be short. Many of them are extracts from longer works. Cuts made within the readings are indicated by three asterisks (***) or, within the same paragraph, ellipses. A source note is provided for each reading. Italics and capitalizations, so rampant in earlier material, are generally retained in readings prior to 1800.

To Stretch Our Ears presents voices from a variety of musical traditions. We meet Native Americans; Hawaiians, the first settlers in what is now the United States who brought their traditions with them; Americans who sought to uphold European values in the New World; musics of other cultures that influenced ours; our own classical, folk, and stage traditions; music for home use and for the concert stage; music as a business; our so-called popular traditions; and what may be our most important national heritage, music developed by African Americans, from ragtime and the blues to jazz. Many would agree with Anthony Philip Heinrich's sentiment, expressed in 1820, that "no one would ever be more proud than himself, to be called an *American Musician*."

J. Heywood Alexander
Hanover, New Hampshire
February 2001

ACKNOWLEDGMENTS

I especially acknowledge two colleagues who contributed material. Dr. Thomas L. Riis planned, provided the sources, and wrote the introductions to four sections: The Indians of Quebec; Music Afloat; Singing for Power and Wakaṇʼtaṇka; and The Spirituals after the War: Improvising Troubles into Art Forms. Dr. Riis is director of the American Music Research Center and professor of music at the University of Colorado at Boulder. Particularly interested in music by African Americans and in American musical theater, he won the ASCAP–Deems Taylor Award in 1995 for his book *Just Before Jazz*. Dorothy Lamb Crawford, who graciously contributed the section on "Evenings on the Roof," wrote an excellent book on the subject (University of California Press, 1995). She also contributed an interesting article, "Peter Yates and the Performance of Schoenberg Chamber Music" (*Journal of the Arnold Schoenberg Institute*, November 1989).

Much appreciation is due to those who provided interviews: John Duffy, Walter Holtkamp, Jr., Libby Larsen, and Robert Osmun. Their new material offers fresh insights.

Kellee Blake's talk before the Society for American Music (formerly the Sonneck Society) on birthday balls for George Washington inspired that section, and conversations with Richard Koloda at Cleveland State University prompted the section on the Mormons. Thomas Stoner advised with reference to Arthur Farwell. I thank Fard Johnson of Meet The Composer, and Ted Panken, who graciously allowed us to reprint part of his interview with Wynton Marsalis.

Special thanks to Michael Ochs, music editor at W. W. Norton, for his encouragement and fine editing, and his assistant, Claire McCabe, for her work in obtaining permissions.

Finally, I am grateful to a number of libraries and their librarians for their help: the American Antiquarian Society (Worcester, Massachusetts); Beinecke Rare Book and Manuscript Library, Yale University; Boston Public Library; Brown University; Case Western Reserve University (Cleveland); Cleveland Institute of Music; Cleveland Public Library; Cleveland State University; College Conservatory, Cincinnati; Dartmouth College Libraries, and in particular Sarah Hartwell, Patricia Carter, Kenneth Cramer, and Barbara Krieger (the latter two for material concerning John Hubbard); Detroit Public Library; Florida State University; Howe Library, Hanover, particularly Mary Hardy and Joanne Blais; Lee County Public Library; the New York Public Library; the Newberry Library (Chicago); Oberlin College; the San Francisco Public Library; Sanibel Public Library (Florida); Stephen C. Foster Memorial, with particular thanks to Deane Root; and the University of New Hampshire.

Are the dreams of yesterday the realities of today?

There is startling evidence of it in American music, for we have

only to read the past to decipher the present.

—RANDALL THOMPSON

PART I

The First Three Centuries

1 French Protestant Psalm Tunes in Florida

French Protestant psalm tunes and secular music were shared with the Indians in "La Floride" as early as 1562. The contacts predated the Spanish founding of St. Augustine, the oldest city in the United States (1565), Jamestown (1607), and the Pilgrims' landing at Plymouth (1620).

The first French attempt at colonization, in 1562–63 at Charlesfort, South Carolina, did not last. A year later, the French established a second colony, further south, at Fort Caroline, on the St. Johns River. The Timucan Indians greeted the new arrivals by singing psalms taught to them previously by the French. Secular music was represented among the colonists by several instrumentalists: a spinet player (the spinet is a small, domestic harpsichord, surely the first in Florida if not in what is now the United States), a horn player, four trumpet players, three drummers, and a fife player.

Despite the arrival of reinforcements in August 1565, the colony was soon destroyed by the Spanish. Only a handful escaped the massacre, but three of the survivors, Nicholas Le Challeux, René de Laudonnière, and Jacques Le Moyne de Morgues (d. 1588), set down their experiences in writing. Le Moyne, an artist, left a set of fascinating pictures as well.

A final French voyage in 1568 sought to avenge the massacre. Again the company sang Huguenot psalms en route and were met by Indians singing and dancing. The fort was retaken from the Spanish. Mission accomplished, the French returned to their native land.

NICHOLAS LE CHALLEUX

from *Brief Account of a Voyage . . . in Florida* (1579)

[The Indians] yet retain such happy memories that when someone lands on their shore, the most endearing greeting that they know how to offer is *Du fons de ma pensée*[1] or *Bienheureux est quiconques*,[2] which they say as if to ask the watchword, are you French or not? . . . The French while there taught them how to pray and how to sing certain psalms, which they heard sung so frequently that they still retain two or three words of those psalms.

Nicolas Le Challeux, *Brief Discours et histoire d'un voyage de quelques François en la Floride*, appendix to Girolamo Benzoni's *Histoire nouvelle du Nouveau monde* (Geneva: Eustace Vignon, 1579), 96; translation quoted from Robert Stevenson, *Protestant Church Music in America* (New York: W.W. Norton, 1966), [3].

---

[1]From the depths of my thought (Ps. 130).

[2]Happy is one to be a volunteer for God (Ps. 128).

3

JACQUES LE MOYNE DE MORGUES

from *Brief Narrative of What Occurred in the French Colony in Florida* . . . (1562–1565)

Some two hours before his arrival, Saturiba sent a chieftain with a hundred and twenty able-bodied men. They were armed with bows and arrows, clubs, and darts, and adorned, after the Indian fashion, with their riches: feathers of different kinds, necklaces of a special sort of shell, bracelets made of fish teeth, belts of silver-colored balls, round and oblong, and pearl anklets. Many of the men wore round, flat plates of gold, silver, or brass, which hung upon their legs, tinkling like little bells.

The chieftain announced the approach of his King and ordered the men to build a shelter for him. Using branches of laurel, mastic, and other sweet-smelling trees, they put up a hut on a nearby knoll. From this vantage point Saturiba could see whatever went on within our lines and examine the tents, supplies, and baggage we had not yet found time to get under cover. Our first concern had been to complete our fort rather than to put up huts, which could easily be built later.

When he received the Indian's message, M. de Laudonnière disposed his force. He was cautious, for he did not wish to be caught unawares. We would have been in a hopeless state if the natives had chosen to attack us, because our ammunition was not yet unloaded. As our commander had once before visited this place with Ribaut,[3] he had already met Saturiba, had learned a few words of the native language, and was familiar with the ceremony with which the chief expected to be received. And as one of the officers, Captain La Caille[4] had also been with Ribaut and understood the language of the natives, M. de Laudonnière decided it would be best if no one except himself, Ottigny, his second in command, and Captain La Caille approached the King.

Chief Saturiba came with seven or eight hundred handsome, strong, and well-built men, the best-trained and swiftest of his tribe, all armed as if on the warpath. In the van marched fifty youths with javelins and spears; behind these, and next to the chief, came twenty pipers making the wildest kind of noise, without any harmony or rhythm, each blowing with all his might as if to see who could blow the loudest. Their instruments were thick reeds, like organ pipes or whistles, with only two openings. They blew into the top hole, while the sound came out the other end. On the King's right hand limped his soothsayer, and on his left walked his chief counselor; Saturiba never made a decision without asking the opinion of these two.

Stephan Lorant, ed. *The New World: The First Pictures of America.* Made by John White and Jacques Le Moyne and Engraved by Theodore de Bry (New York: Duell, Sloan & Pearce, 1946), 38–40. First ed.: *Brevis narratio eorum quae in Florida Americae Provincia Gallis acciderunt* . . . (Frankfurt: Theodor de Bry, 1591).

---

[3] Jean Ribaut (Ribault) had been a leader of the first expedition in 1562.

[4] François de la Caille, who was really an elevated kind of sergeant.

THE HUGUENOT PSALTER
Psalms 128 and 130 (1547)

Psalm 128

Huguenot Psalter

Bienheureux est quiconques
Sert à Dieu volontiers
Et ne se lassa onques
De suivre ses sentiers.
Du labeur que sais faire
Vivras commodement
Et ira ton affaire
Bien et heureusement.

King James Version (1611)

Blessed *is* every one that feareth the Lord;
 that walketh in his ways.
For thou shalt eat the labor of thine hands:
 happy *shalt* thou *be*, and *it shall be*
 well with thee.
Thy wife *shall be* as a fruitful vine by the sides of
 thine house: thy children like olive plants
 round about thy table.
Behold, that thus shall the man be blessed that
 feareth the Lord.
The Lord shall bless thee out of Zion:
 and thou shalt see the good of Jerusalem
 all the days of thy life.
Yea, thou shalt see thy children's children,
 and peace upon Israel.

Psalm 130

Du fons de ma pensée
Au fons de tous ennuys,
A toy s'est adressée
Ma clameur jours et nuits:
Entens ma voix plaintive,
Seigneur, il est saison;
Ton aureille ententive
Soit à mon oraison.

Out of the depths have I cried unto thee,
 O Lord.
Lord, hear my voice: let thine ears be attentive
 to the voice of my supplications.
If thou, Lord, shouldest mark iniquities, O Lord,
 who shall stand?
But *there is* forgiveness with thee,
 that thou mayest be feared.
I wait for the Lord, my soul doth wait, and in his
 word do I hope.
My soul *waiteth* for the Lord more than they
 that watch for the morning:
 I say, more than they that watch
 for the morning.
Let Israel hope in the Lord:
 for with the Lord *there is* mercy,
 and with him *is* plenteous redemption.
And he shall redeem Israel from all
 his iniquities.

Pierre Pidoux, *Le Psautier huguenot du XVIe siècle: melodies et documents* (Basel: Barenreiter, 1962), 1:116, 118; and *The Holy Bible, Authorized, or King James* Version (New York: American Bible Society, 1934), 582.

2   The Indians of Quebec

Among the earliest records of the contact between Europeans and northern Native Americans were reports sent back to Paris by early-seventeenth-century French priests. These reports, which run to several volumes, tell many of the mundane details of life among the inhabitants of the St. Lawrence River valley and the Great Lakes region (including parts of the present-day United States). They frequently mention the Indians' involvement with music. Singing for recreation and celebration, in devotion, at funerals, at welcoming ceremonies, for success in hunting and war, and to cure illness are all amply attested. Even such details as the size and shape of drums and rattles are observed, as are the steps of the shamans' dances and their learning of songs through dreams. This cultural information has the ring of truth, even though it is conveyed indirectly in the form of ethnocentric comparisons filtered through the pious screen of churchmen dutifully addressing their superiors. It bolsters the obvious: that Native American music has an ancient history.

The words of the Indians themselves are often quoted or paraphrased, and their words for great gods or totemic animals, such as *manitou* and *moose*, are recorded and respected. The beliefs and customs reported in *The Jesuit Relations*, as the reports are called, accord to a remarkable degree with observations made by many later writers of the nineteenth and twentieth centuries.

What is most vividly illustrated by the Jesuit writers and many subsequent informants is the pervasiveness of song in Native American life. "They sing and beat drums in their feasts. . . . These poor wretches sing also in their suffering, in their difficulties, in their perils and dangers. . . . Their songs also play a part in the witchcraft of the sorcerers." As in the Old World, so in the New—right living required the right music.

—THOMAS L. RIIS

FATHER PAUL LE JEUNE

from Report on the Indians of Quebec (1634)

The Savages are great singers; they sing, as do most of the nations of the earth, for recreation and for devotion, which, with them, means superstition. The tunes which they sing for pleasure are usually grave and heavy. It seems to me that occasionally they sing something gay, especially the girls, but for the most part, their songs are heavy, so to speak, sombre and unpleasant; they do not know what it is to combine chords to compose a sweet harmony. They use few words in singing, varying the tones, and not the words. I have often heard my Savage make a long song with these three words, *Kaie, nir, khigatoutaounim,* "And thou wilt also do something for me." They say that we imitate the warbling of birds in our tunes, which they do not disapprove, as they nearly all take pleasure both in singing and in hearing others sing; and al-

Reuben Gold Thwaites, ed., *The Jesuit Relations and Allied Documents: Travels and Explorations of the Jesuit Missionaries in New France, 1610–1791,* trans. John Cutler Covert (Cleveland: Burrows Bros., 1897), 6:183–93.

though I told them that I did not understand anything about it, they often invited me to sing some
song or prayer.

As for their superstitious songs, they use them
for a thousand purposes, for which the sorcerer
and that old man, of whom I have spoken, have
given me the reason. Two Savages, they told me,
being once in great distress, seeing themselves
within two finger-lengths of death for want of
food, were advised to sing, and they would be relieved; and so it happened, for when they had sung,
they found something to eat. As to who gave them
this advice, and how it was given, they know nothing; however, since that time all their religion consists mainly in singing, using the most barbarous
words that come into their minds. The following
are some of the words that they sang in a long superstitious rite which lasted more than four hours:
*Aiasé manitou, aiasé manitou, aiasé manitou, ahi-
ham, hehinham, hanhan, heninakhé hosé heninakhé
enigouano bahano anihé ouibini naninaouai nanahouai nanahouai aouihé ahahé aouihé*; concluding
with *ho! ho! ho!* I asked what these words meant,
but not one could interpret them to me; for it is
true that not one of them understands what he is
singing, except in the tunes which they sing for
recreation.

They accompany their songs with drums. I
asked the origin of this drum, and the old man told
me that perhaps some one had dreamed that it was
a good thing to have, and thus it had come into
use. I thought it most probable they had derived
this superstition from the neighboring tribes; for I
am told (I do not know how true it is) they imitate
to a great degree the Canadians who live toward
Gaspé, a tribe still more superstitious than those of
this country.

As to this drum, it is the size of a tambourine,
and is composed of a circle three or four finger-
lengths in diameter, and of two skins stretched
tightly over it on both sides; they put inside some
little pebbles or stones, in order to make more
noise; the diameter of the largest drums is of the
size of two palms or thereabout; they call it
chichigouan, and the verb *nipagahiman* means, "I
make this drum sound." They do not strike it, as

do our Europeans; but they turn and shake it, to
make the stones rattle inside; they strike it upon
the ground, sometimes its edge and sometimes its
face, while the sorcerer plays a thousand apish
tricks with this instrument. Often the spectators
have sticks in their hands and all strike at once
upon pieces of wood, or upon hatchet handles
which they have before them, or upon their *oura-
gans;* that is to say, upon their bark plates turned
upside down. To this din they add their songs and
their cries, I might indeed say their howls, so much
do they exert themselves at times; I leave you to
imagine this beautiful music. This miserable sorcerer with whom my host and the renegade made
me pass the winter, contrary to their promise, almost made me lose my head with his uproar; for
every day,—toward nightfall, and very often toward midnight, at other times during the day,—he
acted like a madman. For quite a long time I was
sick among them, and although I begged him to
moderate a little and to give me some rest, he acted
still worse, hoping to find his cure in these noises
which only made me worse.

They make use of these songs, of this drum,
and of this noise or uproar, in their sicknesses. I
explained it quite fully last year; but since that time
I have seen so much foolishness, nonsense, absurdity, noise, and din made by this wretched sorcerer
in order to cure himself, that I should become
weary in writing and would tire your reverence, if I
should try to make you read the tenth part of what
has often wearied me almost beyond endurance.
Occasionally this man would enter as if in a fury,
singing, crying and howling, making his drum rattle with all his might; while the others howled as
loudly as he, and made a horrible din with their
sticks, striking upon whatever was before them;
they made the little children dance, then the girls,
then the women; he lowered his head and blew
upon his drum, then blew toward the fire; he
hissed like a serpent, drew his drum under his
chin, shaking and turning it about; he struck the
ground with it with all his might, then turned it
upon his stomach; he closed his mouth with the
back of one hand, and then with the other; you
would have said that he wanted to break the drum

to pieces, he struck it so hard upon the ground; he shook it, he turned it from one side to the other, and, running around the fire several times, he went out of the cabin, continuing to howl and bellow; he struck a thousand attitudes, and all this was done to cure himself. This is the way they treat their sick. I am inclined to think that they wish to conjure the disease, or to frighten the wife of Manitou; whom they hold as the origin and cause of all evils, as I have said above.

They sing and make these noises also in their sweating operations. They believe that this medicine, which is the best of all they have, would be of no use whatever to them if they did not sing during the sweat. They plant some sticks in the ground, making a sort of low tent, for, if a tall man were seated therein, his head would touch the top of this hut, which they enclose and cover with skins, robes, and blankets. They put in this dark room a number of heavy stones which they have had heated and made red-hot in a good fire, then they slip entirely naked into these sweat boxes. The women occasionally sweat as well as the men. Sometimes they sweat all together, men and women, pellmell. They sing, cry and groan in this oven, and make speeches; occasionally the sorcerer beats his drum there. I heard him once acting the prophet therein, crying out that he saw Moose; that my host, his brother, would kill some. I could not refrain from telling him, or rather those who were present and listened to him as if to an oracle, that it was indeed quite probable that they would find a male, since they had already found and killed two females. When he understood what I was driving at, he said to me sharply, "Believe me, this black robe has no sense." They are so superstitious in these uproars and in their other nonsense, that if they have sweats in order to cure themselves, or to have a good hunt, or to have fine weather, [they think] nothing would be accomplished if they did not sing, and if they did not observe these

superstitions. I have noticed that, when the men sweat, they do not like to use women's robes with which to enclose their sweat boxes, if they can have any others. In short, when they have shouted for three hours or thereabout in these stoves, they emerge completely wet and covered with their sweat.

They also sing and beat drums in their feasts, as I shall explain in the chapter upon their banquets. I have seen them do the same thing in their councils, mingling therein other juggleries. For my part, I suspect that the sorcerer invents every day some new contrivance to keep his people in a state of agitation, and to make himself popular. One day I saw him take a javelin and turn the point down and the handle up (for their javelins have a long stick for a handle); he placed a hatchet near this javelin, stood up, pounded on his drum, uttered his usual howls, pretended to dance, and walked around the fire. Then, concealing himself, he drew out a nightcap, in which there was a whetstone which he placed in a spoon made of wood, which had been wiped expressly for this purpose; then he lighted a bark torch, and passed from hand to hand the torch, the spoon, and the stone, which was marked with stripes,—all examining it attentively, one after the other, and philosophizing, as it seemed to me, over this stone, in regard to their chase, which was the subject of their council or assembly.

These poor wretches sing also in their sufferings, in their difficulties, in their perils and dangers. During the time of our famine, I heard nothing throughout these cabins, especially at night, except songs, cries, beating of drums and other noises; when I asked what this meant, my people told me that they did it in order to have a good chase, and to find something to eat. Their songs and their drums also play a part in the witchcraft of the sorcerers.

3   Spanish Catholic Missionaries

Once Spain established a beachhead in the West Indies in about 1521, Spanish exploration quickly followed. Balboa, Grijalva, and Cortés reached Panama, Mexico, and the Pacific Ocean. The Spanish discovery of California was not far behind: Fortún Jiménez came upon the California Peninsula in 1533, just forty-one years after Columbus's first voyage. Next, Juan Rodríguez Cabrillo, with his two ships the *San Salvador* and the *Victoria*, landed in 1542 at the site of present-day San Diego and proceeded to explore up the coast. As for New Mexico, the first Spanish settlement dates from 1598 and Santa Fe, its first permanent capitol, from 1610.

Religious conversion, with music an important ingredient, played a vital role in Spanish infiltration into the New World. The Spaniard Juan de Padilla (c. 1500–1542) and the Mexican Cristóbal de Quiñones (d. 1609) were probably the first to teach music in the United States. Padilla accompanied the explorer Francisco Vásquez de Coronado northward into New Mexico and beyond, beginning in 1540. Quiñones is said to have entered New Mexico with Juan de Oñate around 1598. A Franciscan, he learned the language of the Queres Indians, erected the church and monastery at San Felipe, installed an organ in the chapel there, and taught the Indians to sing. Fast on their heels was the Spaniard Bernardo de Marta (d. 1635), who came to America and settled in New Mexico about 1605.

Fray Alonso de Benavides arrived in January 1626 as the principal religious authority in the New Mexico area. Among his supplies were three large choir books, five bells each weighing eight arrobas (about two hundred pounds), five hand bells, one set of flageolet (a flute similar to a recorder) and bassoon, a set of trumpets, five antiphonal books, five choir books for Mass and Vespers, and one gross of little bells. He found Franciscans well entrenched, serving a large number of Indians and including music regularly in their instruction. Benavides prepared a report on his work in 1630 for the king. Clearly, it received a positive reception since within about four years it was translated into French, Dutch, Latin, and German (the German edition, a translation from the Latin, is undated). Benavides revised his *Memorial* in 1634 for the special use of Pope Urban VIII. From this important source we can piece together a picture of musical activity at that time in the New Mexico area.

FRAY ALONSO DE BENAVIDES

from *Revised Memorial* (1634)

The Queres Nation

Another four leagues farther on the Queres nation commences, with its first pueblo, San Felipe.[1] This nation, with its seven pueblos, extends for more than ten leagues, in which there must be more than four thousand souls, all baptized. It has three convents and churches, very spacious and attractive, in addition to the one in each pueblo, all of this achieved through the industry, courage, and care of Father Fray Cristóbal de Quirós, a great minister versed in the very difficult language of this nation. He has taught and trained these Indians well, not only in the things pertaining to our holy Catholic faith but in the ways of civilization, such as reading, writing, and singing, as well as playing all kinds of musical instruments.

*   *   *

The Tanos Nation

Turning another ten leagues to the north, we come upon the first and principal pueblo of the Tanos nation, called Galisteo.[2] It extends for another ten leagues, with five pueblos, where there must be more than four thousand baptized souls. It has one convent, and a fine church with three naves, and all use it for their service. They are very well instructed and ministered to, with their schools of reading, writing, singing, playing musical instruments, and praying, just like all the others.

*   *   *

The Zuñi Nation

Proceeding from the Peñol of Acoma toward the west another thirty leagues one arrives at the province of the Zuñi, which has eleven or twelve pueblos containing more than ten thousand souls. . . .

This conversion fell to the lot of Father Fray Roque de Figueredo, a learned and serious friar, very highly thought of and esteemed in the city of Mexico. In the year 1629, he entered New Mexico with great zeal for the conversion and salvation of those souls. . . .

He took with him a friar-preacher and another person, a lay-brother, men of ability and adapted to that conversion, where in a short time they studied and learned the language. They got those people into a state of much better living. The boys with the best voices especially, he at once taught organ chant,[3] which enhanced the mass and the divine service with much solemnity.

*   *   *

Conversion of the Navaho Apaches

Starting, then, from this province of the Xila Apaches, which extends for more than fifty leagues along the frontier of the pueblos of New Mexico toward the west, we reach the magnificent province and tribe of the Navaho Apaches. . . .[4]

[The chief of the Apaches] turned toward all the people in the church and exclaimed in a loud voice: "O, Teoas,[5] how greatly I envy you that you have one here who can teach you these things! So, from now on, I declare that I adore even more than

Alonso de Benavides, *Fray Alfonso de Benavides' Revised Memorial of 1634*, ed. Frederick Hodge, George Hammond, and Agapito Rey (Albuquerque: University of New Mexico Press, 1945), 65, 67, 73–75, 85, 88, 97–98.

[1]A Spanish league at this time was a distance of about three miles; the Queres nation extended along the Rio Grande.

[2]Twenty-two miles south of Santa Fe.

[3]That is, polyphonic music.

[4]Santa Clara pueblo, where Benevides established his tenth and last mission church, was about twenty-five miles north of Santa Fe.

[5]Tewa.

you this Lord, God, and Creator of all things. And again I vow in His name to keep this peace."

At this they all embraced one another. I ordered the bells to be rung and the trumpets and flageolets to be sounded, which greatly pleased the captain,[6] as well as those who had come with him, since they were hearing them for the first time.

* * *

Life and Happy Death of the Blessed Father, Fray Pedro de Ortega

The blessed father, Fray Pedro de Ortega, was a native of the city of Mexico in New Spain, the son of parents not only noble but so wealthy that, although there were numerous children, more than seventy thousand ducats fell to the share of Father Fray Pedro de Ortega alone. From childhood he was always a very good lad, and when he wished to become a Franciscan friar, his father, who wanted him to be a secular priest and had educated him to that end, opposed his plan. When his father died, he renounced all his possessions and immediately went to ask for a friar's habit, which was given him in the convent of San Francisco in Mexico. Soon after his ordination as priest, he dedicated himself to the conversions of New Mexico, where, with the greatest zeal, he converted the first Indians, and later nearly all those of Taos, amid very great hardships and personal dangers. He retained nothing of the vast fortune he had given up, for he was a very poor friar, possessing only his habit, a man of great humility and exemplary life. . . .

[Fray Ortega] was guardian for about two years in the villa of Santa Fe, where he maintained a general school for teaching reading, writing, singing, the playing of all kinds of instruments, and other matters. Here he taught the Spanish and Indian boys so effectively that, with their organ chants, they enhanced the divine service with great solemnity.

---

[6]The Navajo chief.

4 The *Ainsworth Psalter*

J ean Calvin, a French Huguenot, saw to the creation of metrical settings of all the psalms in the vernacular as part of the Protestant Reformation. This heritage from Geneva spread to the New World, at first abortively with the French in Florida, and later and more successfully with the Pilgrims.

While the Pilgrims were still in Holland, Henry Ainsworth produced for this exiled congregation *The Book of Psalmes: Englished both in Prose and Metre* (Amsterdam, 1612), which followed the Geneva model. It contained metrical versions of all 150 psalms and 39 monophonic tunes by which to sing them.

Ainsworth's book served the Pilgrims at Plymouth Colony from 1620 until the 1690s, when it was supplanted by the Bay Psalm Book. It was also used at Salem and Ipswich, Massachusetts, going through six editions to 1690. It served the colonists well and remains an important source of early religious music in America.

THE AINSWORTH PSALTER

Psalms 128 and 130 (1644)

Psalm 128

O Happy ev'ry one that in the LORDS fear-stands:
    that walketh, in his waies.
The labour of thy hands when thou shalt eate:
    O happie thou, and good unto thee
    shall be (it).
Thy wife, as fruitfull-vine by thy house sides
    thy children, shall be like the plants
    of th' Olive-tree, about thy board.
Loe sure thus, shall the man be blest,
    that feares the LORD.
The LORD will blesse thee, out of Sion:
    and see thou good of Jerusalem, all
    daies thy life thorow.
And doe thou see thy childrens children:
    peace *that shall* on Israel *be.*

Henry Ainsworth, *The Booke of Psalmes: Englished Both in Prose and Metre* (Amsterdam: Thomas Stafford, 1644), 152–153.

Psalm 130

Out of the deeps, I cal
    Jehovah unto thee.
LORD, heare my voice:
    O let thine ears attentive be,
    unto voice of my
    suits-that-doe-for-grace-request.
Iniquities, O Jah,
    observ if thou shouldest:
    O LORD, who shall subsist?
But with thee pardon *is:*
    that thou maist feared be.
I for Jehovah look;
    my soul looks-earnestly:
I also for his word,
    have hopefully-forborn.
My soul waits for the Lord:
    more-than watchmen for morn;
    than watchmen for the morn.
Let Israel wait for Jehovah hopefully:
    for with Jehovah *there is* bountifull-mercie;
    and with him plentifull
    redemption *there is.*
And he will Israel redeem:
    out of all his perverse-iniquities.

5   The *Bay Psalm Book*

The Puritans, brought up on Sternhold and Hopkins's *Whole Booke of Psalmes* (London, 1562), became dissatisfied with this source and wished for their own book. A group of some thirty ministers, notably Richard Mather (father of Increase Mather and grandfather of Cotton Mather), Thomas Weld, and John Eliot, undertook the work. They made use of a press and printing materials that had recently arrived in Cambridge, Massachusetts, brought over from Surrey, England, by a dissenting country minister named Jose (Josse? Jesse?) Glover. Since Glover died en route, the press arrived with his widow, who soon found herself installed in one of the larger houses in New-Town (Cambridge). On June 21, 1641, she married Henry Dunster, distinguished president of the recently established Harvard College. Mrs. Dunster died in 1643, at which point her husband took complete control of the press, which was now lodged in his house.

The first surviving book to come from this rudimentary press was also the first book printed in America, *The Whole Booke of Psalmes*, called the *Bay Psalm Book*, after its place of origin. Seventeen hundred copies were printed by Steven Daye, a locksmith Glover had brought with him from England. The book, containing 294 unnumbered pages in quarto (eight pages per printed sheet) and measuring five by seven and one-half inches in size, was roughly printed and had many compositional inconsistencies. The title page bears the date 1640 but lists no publisher, place of printing, or compiler.

The collection was quickly adopted in the Massachusetts Bay Colony. It was taken up in the 1660s at Salem and by 1692 had found its way into use at Plymouth. It went through seventy American editions to 1773, the date of the last one, and around forty English and Scottish editions as well.

The third edition of 1651, of which two thousand copies were printed, became the definitive one. The work of revision fell mainly to Henry Dunster and Richard Lyon. Versification was changed and alternative translations added. The number of unusual meters was reduced, so that 125 out of the 150 psalms now had versions in common meter, that is, verses comprising four lines of 8, 6, 8, and 6 syllables respectively. Thirty-six "scripture songs" were added. A preface "To the Godly Reader" appeared at the beginning, followed by three long texts, "The Song of Moses," "The Song of Deborah," and "David's Elegie," and the psalms, but no "Admonition to the Reader." This version became known as the *New England Psalter.*

It remained for the ninth edition of 1698, however, to include music: an eleven-page supplement contains thirteen psalm tunes, derived from John Playford's 1654 *A Brief Introduction to the Skill of Musick.* With this ninth edition, the history of American music printing in New England begins.

John Winthrop (1588–1649), whose journal is quoted below, served as governor of Massachusetts from 1629 to 1649.

JOHN WINTHROP

Journal Entry (1640)

Mo. 1 (*March*) A printing house was begun at Cambridge by one Daye, at the charge of Mr. Glover, who died on sea hitherward. The first thing which was printed was the freemen's oath; the next was an almanac made for New England by Mr. William Peirce, mariner;[1] the next was the Psalms newly turned into metre.

John Winthrop, *Winthrop's Journal: History of New England, 1630–1649*, ed. James Kendall Hosmer (New York: Scribner, 1908), 1: 293.

---

[1]Neither the freeman's oath nor the almanac is extant. The oath was a broadside of 222 words, to which colony members had to subscribe. The almanac was the work of William Peirce, captain of the *Lion* and other ships.

THE BAY PSALM BOOK, FIRST EDITION

"An Admonition to the Reader" (1640)

The verses of these psalmes may be reduced to six kindes, the first whereof may be sung in very neere fourty common tunes; as they are collected, out of our chief musicians, by *Tho. Ravenscroft.*[2]

The second kinde may be sung in three tunes as *Ps.* 25. 50. & 67. in our english psalm books.

The third. may be sung indifferently, as *ps.* the 51. 100. & ten cōmandements, in our english psalme books. which three tunes aforesaid, comprehend almost all this whole book of psalmes, as being tunes[3] most familiar to us.

The fourth. as *ps.* 148. of which there are about five.

The fift. as *ps.* 112. or the *Pater noster,* of which there are but two. *viz.* 85. & 138.

The sixt. as *ps.* 113. of which but one, *viz.* 115.

The Whole Booke of Psalmes (Cambridge, Mass.: Stephen Daye, 1640).

[2]Thomas Ravenscroft's *Whole Book of Psalmes* (London, 1621).

---

[3]That is, meters.

THE BAY PSALM BOOK, THIRD EDITION
"To the Godly Reader" (1651)

Wee know that these Psalms, and Hymns, & Spiritual Songs though in other languages, (& so consequently in other poetical measures) were inspired by the Holy Ghost, to holy men of old, for the edification, and comfort of the Church and people of God in all ensuing ages to the end of the world. And for those Holy ends we have with special care & diligence translated them into such Meeters as are most usual and suitable for such holy poems, in our own language, having a special eye, both to the gravity of the phrase of Sacred writt, and sweetness of the verse. And for fuller sat-

isfaction of the godly desires of all, we have added sundry interpretations, according to the latitude of the significations of the Hebrew text, commonly noted with an Asterism thus [*]. And some other various readings, though not so noted.

Exod[*us*]: 15.[19]

I to the LORD will sing, for hee
triumph'd in glory so:
The horse hee and his rider down
into the Sea did throw.[4]

The Psalms, Hymns, and Spiritual Songs of the Old and New Testament, 3rd ed. (Cambridge, Mass.: Samuel Green, 1651), [Preface].

---

[4]This long poem continues, with many references to scripture.

THE BAY PSALM BOOK, FIRST AND THIRD EDITIONS
Three Psalms (1640, 1651)

From the First edition (1640)

Psalme 100

[Long meter: 8.8.8.8.]

A Psalme of prayse.

[1]Make yee a joyfull sounding noyse
    unto Jehovah, all the earth:
2   Serve yee Jehovah with gladness:
    before his presence come with mirth.
3 Know, that Jehovah he is God,
    who hath us formed it is hee,
    & not ourselves: his owne people
    & sheepe of his pasture are wee.
4 Enter into his gates with prayse,

From the Third edition (1651)

Psalme 100

[Long meter: 8.8.8.8.]

A Psalme of prayse.

[1]Shout to Jehovah all the earth

2 With joyfulness. The LORD serve yee
    Before his presence come with mirth.
3 Know that Jehovah God is Hee;
    It's he that made us, and not wee,
    His folk, his pasture sheep also.

4 Into his gates with thanks come wee:

The Whole Booke of Psalmes (Cambridge, Mass.: Stephen Daye, 1640).

The Psalms, Hymns, and Spiritual Songs of the Old and New Testament, 3rd ed. (Cambridge, Mass.: Samuel Green, 1651), 267–68, 275, 280.

into his Courts with thankfullnes:
make yee confession unto him,
& his name reverently blesse.

5 Because Jehovah he is good,
for evermore is his mercy:
& unto generations all
continue doth his verity.

With prayses to his Court yards go.

5 Give thanks to him, bless ye his name,
Because Jehovah he is good:
His mercy ever is the same,
His trueth throughout all ages stood.

Psalme 121
[Common meter: 8.6.8.6.]
A song of degrees

[1]I to the hills lift up mine eyes,
from whence shall come mine aid.
2 Mine help doth from Jehovah come,
which heav'n & earth hath made.
3 Hee will not let thy foot be mov'd,
nor slumber; that thee keeps.
4 Loe hee that keepeth Israell,
hee slumbreth not, nor sleeps.
5 The Lord thy keeper is, the Lord
on thy right hand the shade.
6 The Sun by day, nor Moone by night,
shall thee by stroke *invade.*
7 The Lord will keep the[e] from all ill:
thy soule hee keeps alway,
8 Thy going out, & thy income,
the Lord keeps now & aye.

Psalme 121
[Common meter: 8.6.8.6.]
A *song* of degrees

[1]I to the hills lift up mine eyes,
from whence shall come mine ayd.
2 Mine help doth from Jehovah come,
which heav'n & earth hath made.
3 Hee will not let thy foot be mov'd,
nor slumber, that thee keeps.
4 Lo he that keepeth Israel,
he slumbreth not, nor sleeps.
5 The LORD thy keeper is, the LORD
thy shade on thy right hand.
6 Lest Sun by day, or Moon by night,
should thee by stroke offend.
7 The LORD will keep thee from all ill:
thy soule he keeps alway,
8 Thy going out, and coming in,
the LORD keeps now and ay.

Psalme 128
[Hallelujah meter: 6.6.6.6.4.4.4.4.]
A song of degrees

[1]Blessed is every one
that doth Jehovah feare:
that walks his wayes along.
2 For thou shalt eate *with cheare*
thy hands labour:
blest shalt thou bee,
it well with thee
shall be therefore.
3 Thy wife like fruitfull vine
shall be by thine house side:
the children that be thine
like olive plants abide
about thy board.
4 Behold thus blest

Psalme 128
[Hallelujah meter: 6.6.6.6.4.4.4.4.]
A *song of* degrees

[1]O Blest is every one
That doth Jehovah fear,
That walks his wayes along.
2 For thou shalt eat with chear
Thy hands labour:
Blest shalt thou bee,
It well with thee
Shall be therefore.
3 Thy wife like fruitfull Vine
Shall be by thine house side:
The children that bee thine
Like Olive plants abide,
About thy board.
4 Behold thus blest

that man doth rest,
  that feares the Lord.
5 Jehovah shall thee blesse
  from Sion, & shalt see
  Jerusalems goodnes
  all thy lifes dayes that bee.
6 And shalt view well
  thy children then
  with their children,
  peace on Isr'ell.

That man doth rest,
  That feares the LORD.
5 Jehovah shall thee bless
  From Sion, and thou shalt see
  Jerusalems goodness
  All thy lifes dayes that bee.
6 And shalt view well,
  Thy children *then*,
  With their children,
  Peace on Isr'el.

THE BAY PSALM BOOK, NINTH EDITION
"The Tunes of the Psalms" (1698)

Some few directions for ordering the Voice in Setting these following Tunes of the Psalms.

First observe of how many *Notes* compass the *Tune* is. Next, the place of your first *Note*; and how many *Notes* above & below that: so as you may begin the *Tune* of your first *Note* as [so that] the rest may be sung in the compass of your and the peoples voices, without *Squeaking* above, or *Grumbling* below. For the better understanding of which, take notice of the following Directions.[5]

The Psalms, Hymns, and Spiritual Songs of the Old and New Testament, 9th ed. (Boston: B. Green and J. Allen for Michael Perry, 1698), 419.

[5]The list of tunes and their uses follows.

6   Agitating for Regular Singing

At the heart of Massachusetts in the 1720s lay Boston, a city of twelve thousand, with four schools, eleven churches, and three thousand homes. The area included people of diverse backgrounds, a number of whom had come for reasons more economic than religious. Political strife, trouble with England, King William's War, Queen Anne's War, Indian raids, and other hardships had absorbed much of their energy.

All these factors contributed to a general erosion in learning, bringing with it a waning of musical skill. The expansion of the population into rural areas and the lack of paper and printed materials only exacerbated this trend. What had begun primarily as a written tradition of psalm singing became largely an oral one, with variant practices springing up everywhere.

The time was ripe for reform. Members of the clergy took the lead, advocating "regular singing" (singing by note). Indeed all the written rhetoric that survives supports their cause. On the other side were many average churchgoers who had become used to the status quo and preferred singing the "old way" (or "usual way"), in which each line of text was shouted out by a leader so that the congregants could hear what they were about to sing (a practice called "lining out"). The sounds of this "old way" of singing were not what we would judge today as pleasing, and they certainly offended the many who railed against the practice. But traditions die hard in churches and ordinary churchgoers felt strongly about their cause.

Two of the ministers who produced tracts arguing in favor of regular singing were Thomas Symmes (1678–1725) and Cotton Mather (1663–1728). Mather's *The Accomplished Singer* (1721) followed Symmes's *The Reasonableness of Regular Singing* by one year. Whereas Symmes designed his writing "chiefly for common Country People" and thus attempted to write plainly and clearly, Mather, the scholar, brought the full weight of biblical scripture to bear on the argument. Employing quotations from both Greek and Latin, Mather equates regular singing with the dictates of God: "The Skill of *Regular Singing*, is among the *Gifts* of God unto the Children of Men."

Thomas Symmes was the son of Rev. Zechariah Symmes, the first minister to settle at Bradford, Massachusetts. His grandfather had for forty years been pastor of the church at Charlestown. Having tutored locally, Symmes entered Harvard in 1694 and graduated as valedictorian four years later. He was ordained at Boxford in 1702 and served as parish minister there until his father's death in April 1708, when he succeeded at Bradford, remaining there until his death. He was married three times and was survived by six of his seven children. Symmes was described in 1726 as

> endowed and adorned with a healthy constitution; a comely and lively countenance and complexion, a very cheerful, free, affable, generous and courteous spirit and disposition; a very handsome genteel air and deportment; which rendered his company and conversation pleasant and entertaining. But withal he had a quick and hasty temper, which some too far improved to slur his other excellencies;

though to him 'twas matter of continual conflict, as may been seen afterwards, and indeed served to exercise and illustrate his good nature and grace.*

Symmes published two tracts on church music, *The Reasonableness of Regular Singing, or, Singing by Note* (1720) and *Utile Dulci; or a Joco-Serious Dialogue Concerning Regular Singing* (1723).

Cotton Mather was the son of Increase Mather, Puritan clergyman and president of Harvard College. Having himself received an M.A. degree from Harvard in 1681, he was ordained at the Second Church of Boston four years later. His work there and his outspokenness against English oppression soon made him one of the most respected members of the clergy in New England. He published voluminously, and although he has been criticized for his role in the famous Salem witch trials, he disapproved of much that went on, writing that his suggested reliance on fasting and prayer would have prevented a good number of the executions. Personally he was stalked by tragedy—his first two wives died, his third was mentally unbalanced, and all but six of his fifteen children died young—but his was one of the most important early voices in New England. An active force in the establishment of Yale University, he was a quintessential Puritan of great intellectual power who strove to realize lofty ideals which sometimes eluded him. In 1718 he wrote that "it is a thing to be observed, that all nations make singing to be one part of the worship which they pay unto their God (Introduction to his *Psalterium Americanum*).

---

*John Brown, *A Particular, Plain and Brief Memorative Account of the Rev. Mr. Thomas Symmes, Funeral Sermon*, 1725, appended to *Divine Help . . .* (Boston: T. Fleet, 1726), [1]–2.

THOMAS SYMMES,

from *The Reasonableness of Regular Singing* (1720)

The following Considerations, have occasioned many People to think, that the Publishing [of] something of the Nature of what is here offered, would be very serviceable, viz.

1. THE Total Neglect of *Singing Psalms, by many Serious Christians, for want of* Skill in *Singing Psalm Tunes*. There are many who never employ their Tongues in Singing GOD's Praises, *because they have not skill*. It is with great difficulty that this part of Worship is performed, and with great indecency in some Congregations, for want of Skill: It

---

Thomas Symmes, *The Reasonableness of Regular Singing* (Boston: B. Green for S. Gerrish, 1720), 3–15, 20–21.

is to be feared Singing must be wholly Omitted in some Places for want of Skill, if the Art is not revived. I was once present in a Congregation where Singing was for a whole Sabbath omitted, for want of a Man able to lead the Assembly in Singing.

2. THE imperfect *and irregular manner of Singing* Psalm Tunes *in most Places*. Some of the Tunes are varied much (and much more in some Congregations than others) from the Pattern or *Notes* in our own *Psalm Books*, and from the *Rules of Musick*.

3. *THE Difficulties and Oppositions which some Congregations have met withal, in their attempting and accomplishing a Reformation in their Singing.* These arose in a great Measure from the *Misappre-*

hensions and *Mistakes* of some honest and well-minded People among them. Thus it has happened in some, tho' not in all Congregations, where Singing has been Reformed. It is hoped, that as the Contentions of *Paul* and *Barnabas,* were overruled to the more effectual spreading of the Gospel; so the Oppositions which some have made against *Regular Singing,* will prove a means for the more speedy and successful Revising of the Duty of Singing Psalms and that in the most Decent, Regular Way.

4. *THE Success which has followed suitable Endeavours to remove those Cavils, which some* (while they laboured under their Prejudices to Singing by Rule) *have thought were unanswerable Reasons in their Favour.* Experience has sufficiently shewn, (in scores of instances) that the most vehement Opposers of Singing by Note, never fail of being convinced of their Mistakes, as soon as they gain a *Competent Knowledge* in the *Rules of Singing,* with Ability to Sing a small number of *Tunes* with some exactness. I have never known, (as I remember) or heard, of one Instance to the contrary. The Reasonableness of *Singing by Note,* and its excelling the *Usual Way,* cannot be fully understood by any, till they have attained some skill in the *Rules of Singing;* yet there is so much Reason for Singing according to *Note,* more than for the other Way, as may satisfy any Rational, unprejudiced Person, that is much rather to be chosen.

I SHALL now proceed in the plainest, most easy and popular Way I can, (for 'tis for the sake of common People I write) to show, that *Singing by or according to Note,* is to be preferred to the *Usual Way of Singing,* which may be evidenced by several *Arguments.*

I. THE first *Argument* may be taken from the *Antiquity of Regular Singing. Singing by Note* is the most *Ancient Way* of Singing, and claims the Preference to the other on that Account. . . .

1. IT was studied, known and approv'd of in our *College*[1] for many Years after its first Founding.

This is evident from the Musical *Theses,* which were formerly Printed, and from some Writings containing some *Tunes* with Directions for *Singing by Note,* as they are now Sung; and these are yet in Being, tho' of more than *Sixty Years* standing; besides no Man that Studied *Musick,* as it is treated of by *Alsted, Playford* and others, could be ignorant of it.[2]

2. IF *Singing by Note* was not designed, Why were the Notes plac'd in our *New-England* Psalm Books, and some General Directions there given about them? If they were designed for a Pattern for us to Sing by, either it was a true and exact Pattern or not; If it was not, either *Skill* or *Honesty* or both were wanting in our *Predecessors,* and surely you have so great and just a Veneration for them, as not to suspect either of these things of them; but if the Pattern was exact and was Sung by, then *Singing by Note* is of Ancient Date with us in this Land.

3. THERE are many Persons of Credit now Living, Children and Grandchildren of the *first Settlers of New-England,* who can very well remember, that their Ancestors Sung by *Note,* and they learnt so to Sing of them, and they have more than their bare Words to prove that they speak the Truth: for many of them can Sing *Tunes* exactly by Note, which they learnt of their Fore Fathers, and they say that they sang all the *Tunes* after the same manner; and these People now sing those *Tunes* most agreable to *Note,* which have been least practiced in the Congregation. . . .

Object[ion]. But some will say, if *Singing by Note* is the ancientest Way, How came it that it was not continued, when or by whom was it laid aside or altered?

Answ[er]. THE Declining from, and getting beside the *Rule was gradual* and *insensible.* Singing Schools and Singing Books being laid aside, there was no Way to learn; but only by hearing of *Tunes* Sung, or by taking the *Run of the Tune* (as it is

---

[1]Harvard.

[2]Henry Alsted, 1588–1638, was a renowned encyclopedist whom Symmes admired. John Playford, 1623–1686, was a well-known London music publisher whose *Introduction to the Skill of Musick* provided tunes for the ninth edition of the Bay Psalm Book.

phrased). The Rules of Singing not being taught or learnt, everyone sang as best pleased himself, and every *Leading Singer* would take the Liberty of raising any *Note* of the *Tune*, or lowering of it, as best pleased his Ear, and add such *Turns* and *Flourishes* as were grateful to him; and this was done so *gradually*, as that but few if any took Notice of it. One *Clerk* or *Chorister* would alter the *Tunes* a little in his Day, the next, a little in his, and so one after another, till in *Fifty* or *Sixty* Years it caused a *Considerable Alteration*. If the Alteration had been made designedly by any *Master* of *Musick*, it is probable that the Variation from our *Psalm Books* would have been alike in all our Congregations; whereas some vary much more than others, and 'tis hard to find *Two* that Sing *exactly alike*. The Alteration being so *gradual*, it is no wonder that People are ignorant when it was made, or that there is any at all: As *Weights* or *Measures* (which are sealed) with using them, *Seven* or *Ten* years, may alter considerably, and the Person using them not discern it, 'till he compares them with the *Standard*, and then he is presently convinced of it. We are well inform'd, that in other Countries, where *Singing Schools* are kept up, Singing is continued in the Purity of it: Where they are not, it is degenerated, as it is among us. Your *Usual Way* of Singing is handed down by *Tradition* only, and whatsoever is only so conveyed down to us, it is a thousand in one if it be not miserably corrupted in *Three* or *Fourscore* Years time.

II. Another *Argument for Singing by Note, may be taken from the MELODY of it*. The *Patrons* of the *Usual Way of Singing* plead, that it is the *Pleasantest*, therefore the *Best*, whereas the *Reverse* of this is the Truth. It does not make a *Tune* to be truly *Melodious*, because it pleases your Ear; the very same may be *unpleasant* in *another's* Ear; and who made your Ear a *Judge* of the *Controversy?* Why may not *another's* Ear determine when there is true *Melody* as well *as yours?* He only is a *prosecutor* in a Case who *understands* it: It is merely accidental, if any other passes a right Sentiment: and they only are proper Judges in the *Case* before us who have a *Right Understanding* of Singing both by *Note*, and

in the *Usual Way*, and can give a rational Account about them. Now I have never known or heard of *Two* Persons in us qualified, but what are of the Mind, that *Singing By Note* is the most *Melodious;* Nay, it cannot be otherwise, because when *Tunes* are Sung exactly by *Note*, in the several parts of them, there is such a perfect *Harmony* between the *Notes and Turnings* of the Voice, in which true *Melody* coexists as cannot be in the *Usual Way*. There is nothing but being us'd to the *Common Way* of Singing, and want of *Skill* in *Regular Singing*, that makes the *former* seem more delightful than the *latter*. As for those who exclaim against *Singing by Note*, when they understand but little, if any thing about it, *Solomon* hath left a *Sentence* upon Record for them to Meditate upon which they may find in *Pro*[*verbs*] 18:13.[3]

III. *THAT Way of Singing which is the most RATIONAL, is the best and most excellent;* but Singing by Note, *is the most Rational Way.* Therefore it is the *most excellent*. Singing by *Note* is Singing *according to Rule;* but the *Usual Way* of Singing is not *so*, any further than it agrees with *Singing by Note*, and *so far* there is no Controversy about it. Singing is as truly an *Art* or *Science*, as *Arithmetic*, *Geometry*, *etc*. It has certain and plain *Rules* by which it is taught, and without conforming to *them*, there is no true *Singing*. There is a Reason to be given why each *Note* in a *Tune* is placed where it is, *why* and *where* every *Turn* of the Voice should be made, How *long* each *Note* should be Sung, *etc*. Now, *Singing by Note* is giving every *Note* its proper *Pitch*, and *Turning* the Voice in its proper Place, and giving to every *Note* its true *Length* and *Sound*, *etc*. Whereas the *Usual Way* varies much from this: In it, some *Notes* are sung too *high*, others too *low*, and most too *long*, and many *Turnings* of, or *Flourishes with* the Voice, (as they call them) are made where they should not be, and some are wanting where they should have been: All contrary to the *Rules of Singing*, and create an *Ungrateful Jarr* in the Ears of those who can well *distinguish*

---

[3] "If one gives answer before he hears, it is his folly and shame."

Sounds, and have *Real Skill* in the *Rules* of Singing. It is most *Rational* in any *Art* or *Science* to practice according to the *Rules* of it, especially in that which is us'd in the *Joint Worship* of GOD; where every Man's following his own *Fancy,* and leaving the *Rule,* is an *Inlet* to great Confusion and Disorder, which is very contrary to Him, who is not the *Author of Confusion,* but the GOD of Order, as in all the Churches of the Saints. . . .

IV. IF Singing by Note, *is most agreeable in SCRIPTURE PRECEPT and PATTERN, then it is better than the* Vulgar or Usual Way; *but Singing by Note or Rule is so*; therefore Singing with *Skill* or by *Note,* which is the same thing, is most agreable to the General Institutions which we have in Scripture, about the *External* Part of Singing. Singing by *Note* agrees best with the Direction, *Play skilfully,* Psal[m] 33:3.[4] There is as much Reason why we should *sing faithfully* in GOD's Worship, as there was for the Jews *Playing faithfully.* It was writ for our, as well as *their* Instruction. *Still* in any Art or Science inspires a Knowledge of, and Conformity to the Rules of it; which they have not, who plead for and Sing in the Usual Way: a *Parrot* can imitate us in many Words and Sentences, yet has not Skill or Understanding in Speaking.

THERE was of Old great Care taken, that the Singers Sang skilfully; and in order to that, there was a *Singing Master* appointed to instruct them in Singing; it was a Man of Skill, I *Chron*[*icles*] 15:22,27.[5] And *this* was all for our Instruction. We may infer from the Text mentioned, that *faithful Singing Masters,* who instruct in Singing Psalm Tunes regularly, do that which is pleasing to GOD, and profitable to Men. *Jeremiah* (as Dr. *Edwards* observes, on 1 Chr. 15:22)[6] kept a Singing School, or

instructed about the Song because he was *faithful.* It implies that there was more to be learnt about Singing, to Sing with Skill, than could be learnt barely by hearing of the *Tunes* sung: The Understanding was to be enlightened and informed in this *Art,* by plain Rules and Instructions which is done where People are taught to Sing by *Note,* with the *Treble, Bass,* both which are in some of our *New England* Psalm Books, *etc.* Regular Singing is far more agreable than the *Usual Way,* to that Singing which is described, 2 *Chron.* 5:13.[7] There was but *One sound* to be heard, *i.e.* there was a perfect *Harmony* between the several Parts of the *Musick.* If an *Harmony,* or a pleasant and Regular Agreement of Sounds or Voices, and the avoiding all *Ungrateful Discords* were not to be required, the Holy Ghost would not have put this upon Record for an Example to us in Singing. They are greatly to Blame who carelessly, (they are much more so, who designedly) Sing so, as to make any Breach in the Singing and spoil the Harmony of it, and won't conform to the Congregation in regular Singing. That Singing by Note is far more *Harmonious* than the *Usual Way,* is evident to all that have real skill in Singing. If it should be said, that probably the Apostle *Paul* had some Respect to skill in Singing the *Tune,* when he spake of Singing *with Understanding,* it would not be contrary to the *Analogy of Faith.*

THUS have I shown, That Singing by Note is the most *Ancient, Melodious & Rational Way, & most agreeable to Scripture Precept & Pattern.* Much more might be said in favour of Regular Singing; as that it is most *Grave* and *Decent,* and *best answers the End* of Singing every way: And it is not without Reason that Regular Singing most nearly resembles the Singing which will be the Employment of Saints and Angels in the *Heavenly World,* of any Singing on Earth. And what follows is an Argument of no little *Weight* in it; it would give Regular

---

[4] "Sing unto him a new song; play skilfully with a loud noise."

[5] "And Chenaniah, chief of the Levites, was for song: he instructed about the song, because he was skilful. . . . And David was clothed with a robe of fine linen, and all the Levites that bare the ark, and the singers, and Chenaniah the master of the song with the singers: David also had upon him an ephod of linen."

[6] John Edwards's *A Discourse Concerning the Authority, Stile, and Perfection . . . of the Holy Scriptures* (1695), p. 178.

---

[7] "It came even to pass, as the trumpeters and singers were as one, to make one sound to be heard in praising and thanking the Lord; and when they lifted up their voice with the trumpets and cymbals and instruments of music, and praised the Lord, saying, For he is good; for his mercy endureth for ever: that then the house was filled with a cloud, even the house of the Lord."

Singing the *Preference*, if they were equal for *Age, Melody, Reasonableness* and Agreement with *Scripture precept* and *Pattern, viz.*

THAT a far greater Number of People can learn to Sing by *Note*, than can ever learn in the *Usual Way*. Both Reason and Experience prove this. . . .

I SHALL now conclude this Discourse with proposing several QUESTIONS.

* * *

Q. 9. *WOULD it not greatly tend to the promoting Singing Psalms,* if Singing Schools *were promoted*? Would not this be a Conforming to *Scripture Pattern*? Have we not as much need of them as GOD's People of Old? Have we any Reason to expect to be inspired with the Gift of *Singing*, any more than that of *Reading*? or to attain it without the use of suitable Means, any more than they of Old, when *Miracles, Inspirations, etc.* were common? Where would be the *Difficulty*, or what the *Disadvantages*, if People that want *Skill* in *Singing*, would procure a *Skilful Person to Instruct* them, and meet *Two or Three* Evenings in the Week, from *Five* or *six* a Clock, to *Eight*, and spend the Time in Learning to Sing? Would not this be an innocent and profitable *Recreation*, and would it not have a Tendency (if prudently managed) to prevent the unprofitable *Expence* of Time on *other Occasions*? Has it not a Tendency to divert Young People (who are most proper to learn) from Learning *Idle, Foolish*, yea, *pernicious Songs and Ballads*, and banish all such *Trash* from their Minds? Experience proves this. Would it not be proper for *School Masters* in *Country Parishes* to teach their *Scholars*? Are not they very unwise who plead against Learning to Sing by Rule, when they can't learn to Sing at all, unless they learn by Rule? Has not the grand *Enemy of Souls* a hand in this, who prejudices them against the best Means of Singing?

Q. 10. *WILL it not be very Serviceable in Ministers to encourage their People* to learn to Sing? Are they not under some Obligations by Virtue of their Office so to do? Would there not (at least in some Places) appear more of that *Fear of Man* which brings a snare, than of true *Christian Prudence* in Omitting *This*? And as Circumstances may allow, would it not be very useful and profitable if such Ministers as are capable would instruct their People in this *Art*?

THUS have I offered several Arguments to encourage Regular Singing, and answered the Principal Objections against it; which objections are so weak, that were it not for the sake of many, who have more Honesty than Strength of Reason, I should have passed them over in silence: what I have writ was designed chiefly for common Country People, and I have endeavoured to accomodate it to their Capacities, and have of choice used such Phrases and Similitudes, as have been most successful with them. If it had been designed for Men of Letters, some Arguments would have been fetched from some other Topicks, and proposed in another Method and Stile, but this is needless. And if what is written attains the end designed, the writer will esteem the good done unto others by it, a sufficient Reward for his Pains.

COTTON MATHER

from *The Accomplished Singer* (1721)

1. It is the Concern of every one that would enjoy *Tranquillity* in this World, or obtain *Felicity* in the World to come, to follow that Holy Direction of Heaven, *Exercise thyself in PIETY*. And there is no *Exercise* of PIETY more unexceptionable than that of *making a Joyful* Noise of SINGING in the Praises of our GOD; That of signifying our *Delight* in Divine *Truths* by SINGING of them; That of *Uttering* the Sentiments of Devotion, with the *Voice*, and such a *Modulation of the Voice*, as will naturally express the *Satisfaction* and *Elevation* of the *Mind*, which a Grave SONG shall be expressive of. 'Tis indeed a very *Ancient Way* of Glorifying the Blessed GOD; As *Ancient* as the Day *when the Foundations of the Earth were fastened*, and *the Corner-Stone thereof was laid*. The *Morning-Stars* then *Sang together* [Job 38:4–7]. And it is as *Extensive* an one; For it is Remarkable, That *All Nations* make SINGING to be one part of the *Worship* which they pay unto their GOD. Those Few *Untuned Souls*, who affect upon Principle to distinguish themselves from the rest of Mankind, by the Character of *Non-Singers*, do seem too much to divest themselves of an *Humanity*, whereof it may be said unto them, *Doth not Nature itself teach it you?* Be sure, they sufficiently differ from the *Primitive Christians*; For, though the *Eastern* Churches were at first Superiour to the *Western*, for the *Zeal of the house of* GOD in this matter, yet both betimes Concurr'd in it. Not only *Justin* the Martyr, and *Clemens* of *Alexandria*, as well as *Tertullian*, and several others of the *Primitive Writers*, but also Governour *Pliny* himself will tell us, what *Singers to their GOD*, the Faithful were then known to be; and how much they *Worshipped* Him in these *Beauties of Holiness*.

2. BUT this piece of *Natural Worship* is further Confirmed by a *positive Institution* of GOD our SAVIOUR for it. The *Sacred Scriptures* with which the Holy SPIRIT of GOD has Enriched us, have directed us unto this *Way* of Worshipping. In our *Old Testament* we there find it as a Command of GOD; but Calculated particularly for Times under the *New-Testament*: Psal. LXVIII. 32. *Sing Praises unto GOD, ye Kingdoms of the Earth, O Sing Praises unto the Lord.* And Psal. C. 1, 2. *Make a Joyful Noise unto the Lord, All ye Lands; Come into his Presence with Singing.* The *Ninety-fifth Psalm* in our Psalter, does according to the Interpretation of our Apostle *Paul*, an *Interpreter, One of a Thousand*, certainly to be relied upon! Prescribe the *Duties* of a *Sabbath* in the Days of the Gospel. But what is the *First* of those Duties? *O come, Let us sing unto the Lord, Let us with Psalms make a Joyful Noise unto Him.*

* * *

IT is Remarkable, That when the *Kingdom* of GOD has been making any *New Appearance*, a mighty Zeal for the *singing* of PSALMS, has attended it, and assisted it. And may we see our People grow more *Zealous* of this *Good Work*, what an hopeful *Sign of the Times* would be seen in it, That *the Time of Singing is come, and the Voice of the Turtle is to be heard in the Land.*[8] . . .

It has been found accordingly in some of our Congregations, that in length of Time, their *singing* has degenerated, into an *Odd Noise*, that has had more of what we want a Name for, than any *Regular Singing* in it; whereby the *Celestial Exercise* is dishonoured; and indeed the *Third Commandment* is trespass'd on. To take notice of the *Ridiculous Pleas*, wherewith some very weak People, go to confirm this Degeneracy, would indeed be to pay too much Respect unto them. And they must have strange Notions of the Divine SPIRIT, and of His Operations, who shall imagine, that the Delight

---

Cotton Mather, *The Accomplished Singer* (Boston, B. Green for S. Gerrish, 1721), 1–2, 21–24.

[8]*Song of Solomon*, 2:12; RSV translates "turtle" as "turtle-dove."

which their *Untuned Ears* take in an *Uncouth Noise*, more than in a *Regular Singing*, is any *Communion* with Him. The Skill of *Regular Singing*, is among the *Gifts* of GOD unto the Children of Men, and by no means unthankfully to be Neglected or Despised. For the Congregations, wherein 'tis wanting, to recover a *Regular Singing*, would be really a *Reformation*, and a Recovery out of an *Apostacy*, and what we may judge that Heaven would be pleased withal. We ought certainly to Serve our GOD with our *Best*, and *Regular Singing* must needs be *Better* than the confused Noise of a Wilderness. *GOD is not for Confusion in the Churches of the Saints*; but requires, *Let all things be done decently.* 'Tis a Great Mistake of some weak People, That the *Tunes* regulated with the *Notes* used in the *Regular Singing* of our Churches are the same that are used in the Church of *Rome*. And what if they were? Our *Psalms* too are used there. But the *Tunes* used in the *French Psalmody*, and from Them in the *Dutch* also,[9] were set by a famous Martyr of JESUS CHRIST;[10] And when *Sternhold* and *Hopkins* illuminated *England*, with their Version of the *Psalms*, the *Tunes* have been set by such as a Good Protestant may be willing to hold Communion withal. The *Tunes* commonly used in our Churches, are *Few*; T'were well if there were *more*. But they are also *Grave*, and such as well *become the Oracles of* GOD, and such as do Steer clear of the Two Shelves, which *Austin* was afraid of; when he did, *In cantu Sacro fluctuare, inter Periculum Voluptatis, et Experimentum Salubritatis*; in danger of too much *Delicacy* on the one side, and *Asperity* on the other.

THE *Musick* of the Ancient Hebrews, an Adjustment whereto seems to be all the *Measure* of their *Poetry*, (after all the Attempts of *Gomarus*, and other Learned Men otherwise to *Measure* it,) being utterly Lost; and as *Aben. Ezra* observes, of the *Musical Instruments* in the *Hundred and Fift[i]eth Psalm*, wholly Irrecoverable; we have no way Left us now, but with *Tunes* composed by the *Chief Musician* for us, to *do as well as we can.*

IT is desired, that we may see in the Rising Generation, a fresh and Strong Disposition to *Learn* the proper *Tunes*; that GOD may be Glorified, and Religion beautified, with a *Regular Singing* among us; And that, *To them that are His Servants, He may let His work be seen; His Glory also unto those that are their Children* here: *And that the Lovely Brightness of the Lord who is our GOD*, may with Conspicuous Lustre be seen shining *upon us.*

---

[9] *Genevan Psalter* and *Ainsworth Psalter*, which was based on Geneva.

[10] Loys Bourgeois (c. 1510–c. 1561) was responsible for the melodies of the French Psalter. Like Calvin, Marot, and de Bèze, he was harassed, but not martyred. The important French composer of psalm settings, Claude Goudimel, however, did perish in the massacre of the Huguenots at Lyons in 1572.

COTTON MATHER

from Letter to Thomas Hollis (1723)

A mighty Spirit came Lately upon abundance of our people, to Reform their singing which was degenerated in our Assemblies to an Irregularity, which made a Jar in the ears of the more curious and skilful singers. Our Ministers generally Encouraged the people, to accomplish themselves for a Regular singing, and a more beautiful Psalmody. Such Numbers of Good people, (and Especially young people,) became Regular Singers, that they could carry it in the Congregations. But, who would beleeve it? Tho' in the more polite City of *Boston*, this Design mett with a General Acceptance, in the Countrey, where they have more of the *Rustick*, some Numbers of Elder and Angry

---

Cotton Mather, *Diary of Cotton Mather* (New York: F. Ungar, 1957), 2: 693.

people, bore zelous Testimonies against these wicked Innovations, and this bringing in of Popery. Their zeal transported some of them so far (on the behalf of *Mumpsimus*)[11] that they would not only use the most opprobrious Terms, and call the Singing of these Christians, a worshipping of the Devil, but also they would run out of the Meetinghouse at the Beginning of the Exercise. The Parox-

ysms have risen to that Heighth, as to necessitate the Convening of several Ecclesiastical Councils, for the Composing of the Differences and Animosities, arisen on this occasion. And if such an Improbable occasion produce them, what is to be expected, when our Great Adversary getts a permission to start more hazardous Controversies? *O! Tell it not in Gath!*[12]

---

[11]Adherence to or persistence in an erroneous practice, out of habit or obstinancy.

[12]The Philistine city of Gath was a center of opposition to the Hebrews.

COTTON MATHER

from Letter to Thomas Bradbury (1724)

Very Lately, a Little Crue at a Town Ten miles from the City of Boston, were so sett upon their old Howling in the public Psalmody, that being rebuked for the Disturbance they made, by the more Numerous Regular Singers, they declared They would be for the Ch[urch] of E[ngland] and

would form a Little Assembly for that purpose, and subscribed for the Building of a Chapel; and expect a Missionary to be sent and supported from your Society (aforesaid) for the Encouragement of half a score such Ridiculous Proselytes. But we suppose, it will come to nothing.

Cotton Mather, *Diary of Cotton Mather* (New York: F. Ungar, 1957), 2: 797.

7 The Tunebooks of John Tufts and Thomas Walter

Two American tunebooks from 1721 served the cause of "regular singing." John Tufts's *Introduction to the Singing of Psalm-Tunes* has been called the first American music textbook.

Tufts's work went through eleven editions to 1744. All that remains of the first edition is an advertisement in the *Boston News-Letter* of January 2/9, 1721:

> A Small Book containing 20 Psalm Tunes, with Directions how to Sing them, contrived in the most easy Method ever yet Invented, for the ease of Learners, whereby even Children, or People of the meanest Capacities, may come to Sing them by Rule, may serve as an Introduction to a more compleat Treatise of Singing, which will speedily be published. To be Sold by Samuel Gerrish Bookseller; near the Brick Church in Cornhill, Price 6d.

The fifth edition, 1726, which includes thirty-seven tunes but no texts, became definitive, the contents remaining materially intact through the later editions. After a poem "On the Divine Use of Musick," a concise theoretical instructor begins: "A Short Introduction To the Singing of Psalm-Tunes. The Tunes which follow are set down in such a plain and easy Method, that a few Rules may suffice for direction in Singing of them." The introduction is an original work, not a paraphrase, but it is based on English models that had been circulating in the colonies. The tunes then appear with letter notation, *Fa (F), Sol (S), La (L), Mi (M)*, on the staff, without texts.

Tufts (1689–1750) lived his life in Massachusetts. A Harvard graduate in the class of 1708, he spent much of his time as minister of the Second Church in Newbury, Massachusetts. He was also a merchant, a composer, and probably a teacher of singing schools.

Thomas Walter (1696–1725), also a Harvard graduate, served the First Church (Congregational) of Roxbury, Massachusetts. It did not hurt him professionally that he was Increase Mather's grandson and Cotton Mather's nephew. He was ordained in 1718 and became assistant pastor to his father, Rev. Nehemiah Walter. Increase Mather delivered the ordination sermon.

Walter enjoyed a turbulent yet fascinating career. He helped introduce inoculations for smallpox, an activity that nearly cost him his life. Later, he survived a bomb tossed into a room in which he was sleeping.

Walter's *Grounds and Rules* provided a practical basis for regular singing. Eight editions appeared to 1764. The title page of the first edition (1721) is followed by "A Recommendatory Preface" signed by significant individuals including both Increase Mather and Cotton Mather. After a table of musical characters comes the instructor, "Some Brief and very plain Instructions For *Singing by* NOTE," and the twenty-four tunes themselves, in three parts with the melody in the middle voice (tenor), but without texts.

THOMAS WALTER

from *The Grounds and Rules of Musick Explained* (1721)

A Recommendatory Preface

An Ingenious Hand having prepared Instructions to direct them that would Learn to Sing PSALMS after a Regular Manner; and it being thought proper that we should signify unto the publick some of our Sentiments on this Occasion; We do declare, that we rejoice in *Good Helps* for a Beautiful and Laudable performance of that holy Service, wherein we are to Glorify God, and edify one another with the *Spiritual Songs*, wherewith he has enriched us.

And we would encourage all, more particularly our *Young People*, to accomplish themselves with Skill to *Sing the Songs of the Lord*, according to the *Good Rules* of Psalmody: Hoping that the Consequence of it will be, that not only the *Assemblies of Zion* will *Decently & in order* carry on this Exercise of PIETY, but also it will be the more introduced into private *Families*, and become a part of our *Family-Sacrifice*.

At the same time we would above all Exhort, That the *main concern* of all may be to make it not a meer *Bodily Exercise*, but *sing with Grace in their Hearts*, & with Minds Attentive to the *Truths* in the PSALMS which they Sing, and affected with them, so that in their *Hearts they may make a Melody to the LORD*.

[Signatures follow.]

*   *   *

Some Brief and Very Plain Instructions for Singing by Note

MUSICK is the Art of Modulating Sounds, either with the Voice, or with an Instrument. And as there are Rules for the right Management

---

Thomas Walter, *The Grounds and Rules of Musick Explained: or, an Introduction to the Art of Singing by Note* (Boston: Printed by J. Franklin, for S. Gerrish, 1721), i–iii, 1–5, 24.

of an Instrument, so there are no less for the well ordering of the Voice. And tho' Nature itself suggests unto us a Notion of Harmony, and many Men, without any other Tutor, may be able to strike upon a few Notes tolerably tuneful; yet this bears no more proportion to a Tune composed and sung by the Rules of Art than the vulgar Hedge-Notes of every Rustic does to the Harp of *David*. Witness the modern Performances both in the Theatres and the Temple.

SINGING is reducible to the *Rules of Art*; and he who has made himself Master of a few of these Rules, is able at *first Sight* to sing Hundreds of New Tunes, which he never saw or heard of before, and this by the bare Inspection of the Notes, without hearing them from the Mouth of a Singer. Just as a Person who has learned all the Rules of *Reading*, is able to read any new Book, without any further Help or Instruction. This is a Truth, altho' known to, and proved by many of us, yet very hardly to be received and credited in the Country.

WHAT a Recommendation is this then to the following Essay, that our Instructions will give you that knowledge in Vocal Musick, whereby you will be able to sing all the Tunes in the World, without hearing of them sung by another, and being constrained to get them by heart from any other Voice than your own? We don't call him a *Reader*, who can recite *Memoriter* a few Pieces of the Bible, and other Authors, but put him to read in those Places where he is a Stranger, cannot tell *ten Words in a Page*. So is not he worthy of the Name of a Singer, who has gotten eight or ten Tunes in his Head, and can sing them like a *Parrot by Rote*, and knows nothing more about them, than he has heard from the Voices of others; and shew him a Tune that is new and unknown to him, can't strike two Notes of it.

THESE Rules then will be serviceable upon a *Threefold* Account. *First*, they will instruct us in the right and true singing of the Tunes that are already in use in our Churches; which, when they first came out of the Hands of the Composers of them, were sung according to the Rules of the *Scale of Musick,* but are now miserably tortured, and twisted, and quavered, in some Churches, into an horrid Medly of confused and disordered Noises. This must necessarily create a most disagreeable Jar in the Ears of all that can judge better of Singing than these men, who please themselves with their own ill-sounding *Echoes.* For to compare small things with great, our *Psalmody* has suffered the like Inconveniences which our *Faith* had laboured under, in case it had been committed and trusted to the uncertain and doubtful Conveyance of *Oral Tradition.* Our Tunes are, for want of a Standard to appeal to in all our Singing, left to the Mercy of every unskilful Throat to chop and alter, twist and change, according to their infinitely divers and no less odd Humours and Fancies. That this is most true, I appeal to the Experience of those who have happened to be present in many of our Congregations, who will grant me, that there are no two Churches that sing alike. Yea, I have my self heard (for Instance) *Oxford* Tune sung in *three* Churches (which I purposely forbear to mention) with as much difference as there can possibly be between *York* and *Oxford,* or any two other different Tunes.[1] Therefore any man that pleads with me for what they call the *Old Way,* I can confute him only by making this Demand, *What is the* OLD WAY? Which I am sure they cannot tell. For, one Town says, theirs is the true *Old Way,* another Town thinks the same of theirs, and so does a third of their Way of Tuning it. But let such men know from the Writer of this Pamphlet (who can sing all the various Twistings of the old Way, and that too according to the *Genius* of most of the Congregations as well as they can any one Way; which must therefore make him a better Judge than they are or can be;) affirms, that the Notes sung according to the *Scale and Rules of Musick,* are the true *old Way.* For some body or other did compose our Tunes, and did they (think ye) compose them by Rule or

by Rote? If the latter, how came they pricked down in our *Psalm Books*? And this I am sure of, we sing them as they are there pricked down, and I am as sure the Country People do not. Judge ye then, who is in the right. Nay, I am sure, if you would once be at the pains to learn our Way of Singing, you could not but be convinced of what I now affirm. But our Tunes have passed thro' strange *Metamorphoses* (beyond those of *Ovid*) since their first Introduction into the World. But to return to the Standard from which we have so long departed cannot fail to set all to rights, and to reduce the sacred Songs to their primitive Form and Composition.

AGAIN, It will serve for the Introduction of more Tunes into the Divine Service; and these, Tunes of no small Pleasancy and Variety, which will in a great Measure render this Part of Worship still more delightfull to us. For at present we are confined to *eight or ten Tunes,* and in some Congregations to little more than half that Number, which being so often sung over, are too apt, if not to create a Distaste, yet at least mightily to lessen the Relish of them.

THERE is one more Advantage which will accrue from the Instructions of this little Book; and that is this, that by the just and equal *Timeing* of the Notes, our Singing will be reduc'd to an exact length, so as not to fatigue the Singer with a tedious Protraction of the Notes beyond the compass of a Man's Breath, and the Power of his Spirit: A Fault very frequent in the Country, where I my self have twice in one Note paused to take Breath. This *keeping of Time* in Singing will have this Natural effect also upon us, that the whole Assembly shall begin and end every single Note, and every Line exactly together, to an Instant, which is a wonderful Beauty in Singing, when a great Number of Voices are together sounding forth the Divine Praises. But for the want of this, I have observed in many Places, one Man is upon this Note, while another is a Note before him, which produces something so hideous and disorderly, as is beyond Expression bad. And then the even, unaffected, and smooth sounding the Notes, and the Omission of those unnatural Quaverings and

---

[1] YORK and OXFORD appeared in both Tufts's and Walter's books, as they do in John Playford's *Whole Book of Psalms* (London, 1677).

Turnings, will serve to prevent all that Discord and lengthy Tediousness which is so much a Fault in our singing of Psalms. For much time is taken up in shaking out these Turns and Quavers; and besides, no two Men in the Congregation quaver alike, or together; which sounds in the Ears of a good Judge, like *Five Hundred* different Tunes roared out at the same time, whose perpetual interferings with one another, perplexed Jars, and unmeasured Periods, would make a Man wonder at the false Pleasure which they conceive is that which good Judges of Musick and Sounds, cannot bear to hear.

THESE are the good Effects, which our Skill in the *Gamut* will produce. We shall then without any further Preamble, proceed to give the Reader some brief and plain Instructions for singing by Note and Rule.

The Instructions for Singing

*   *   *

Finally, observe that *Discords* are sometimes made use of in *Musick*, to prepare the Ear by their Harshness, to relish better the Sweetness, and Melody of a following *Concord*. Thus oftentimes, there will be an imperfect Concord, then a Discord, which is still more grateting; this serves to keep the Auditor in a longing Suspence, till all the Parts fall into a perfect Set of *Chords*, which finishes and compleats the Harmony, and strangely charms the Hearer.

Here follow the Notes for Tuning the Voice, and the Collection of Tunes fitted to our Psalms.

8   A Significant Tunebook

In its outward appearance, James Lyon's *Urania* resembles other books of contemporary Anglo-American psalmody. Its oblong shape houses an ornate title page, dedication, index, subscriber list, and a several-page theoretical instructor. Its format reminds us of the Tufts and Walter books. Like them, it is also based squarely on English material, although the instructor was not copied directly from other sources.

But *Urania* (the term alludes to the muse of astronomy, hence a book dealing with "celestial themes") is significant because it is the first American tunebook to include works by American-born composers, the first set primarily for four voices, the first to include "fuging tunes," and the first to contain music other than psalm tunes. Indeed, this uncommonly large collection is a first in its comprehensive sampling of current styles of English country psalmody.

James Lyon (1735–1794) graduated from Princeton in 1759. His musical activities sprang mainly from his early years, when he composed a little and taught singing-school. Ordained as a Presbyterian minister in 1764, he turned aside from any professional involvement in music and followed a career in the ministry, politics, and business. He moved about, spending much time in Nova Scotia, which the British had wrested from France. In 1772, Lyon accepted a call to become minister at Machias, Maine, where he remained under trying conditions for most of the rest of his life. *Urania*, published in Philadelphia (notably not in New England), was his only tunebook.

Among the ninety-six compositions in *Urania*, some with text and some without, five are by Lyon himself. Francis Hopkinson is represented with a *23rd Psalm Tune* arrangement, and John Tufts, probably, with *The New 100. Psalm Tune*. The fuging tune is represented in *The 12th Psalm Tune*, *The 15th Psalm Tune*, and *The V Psalm Tune*, each of which start homophonically and proceed by imitation. There are fifty-two hymns, thirty-two psalm tunes, and twelve anthems in all, with the melodies assigned to the tenor.

JAMES LYON

from *Urania* (1761)

To the Clergy of Every Denomination in *America*

Reverend Sirs,

RELYING on the evident Propriety of your patronizing this Publication, permit me to lay Urania at your Feet.

Should the following Collection of Tunes be so fortunate, as to merit your approbation; To please the Taste of the Public; To assist the private Christian in his daily Devotion; And to improve, in any degree, an important Part of Divine Service in these Colonies, for which it was designed: I shall think myself happy in being the Editor, notwithstanding the great Expence, Labour, and Anxiety, it has cost me to compleat it.

May you long continue Ornaments of your Profession: Daily see abundant Fruits of your Labour in the Reformation of Mankind: And incessantly enjoy those sublime Pleasures, which nothing, but a Series of rational and virtuous Actions, can create.

I am,
Reverend Gentleman,
Your most obedient,
and humble Servant,
JAMES LYON

*   *   *

Some Directions for Singing.

1. In learning the 8 Notes, get the assistance of some Person, well acquainted with the Tones & Semitones.

2. Chuse that Part, which you can sing with the greatest Ease, and make yourself Master of that first.

3. Sound all high Notes as soft as possible, but low ones hard and full.

4. Pitch your Tune so that the highest and lowest Notes may be sounded distinctly.

James Lyon, *Urania; or, A Choice Collection of Psalm-Tunes, Anthems, and Hymns* (Philadelphia: A. B. Hen[.] Dawkins, 1761), [1]–2, X.

9   William Billings, Singing Master

William Billings (1746–1800), foremost among American-born composers active at the time of the American Revolution, proudly identified himself in his first publication as "A Native of Boston, in *New-England*." Largely self-taught, he was a writer, teacher, tradesman, tunebook compiler, and composer. Reverend William Bentley described him in an 1800 diary entry as "a singular man, of moderate size, short of one leg, with one eye, without any address" although records show that in 1798, Billings owned a house at 89 Newbury Street. He also, according to Bentley, displayed "an uncommon negligence of person. Still, he spake & sung & thought as a man above the common abilities. He died poor & neglected & perhaps did too much to neglect himself."

Bentley's further comment in his diary (July 5, 1801) that Billings was "the first man to introduce original composition in Church Music" carries the ring of truth. In 1770, only a small number of American tunes were in circulation. Billings left a legacy of some three hundred compositions in six major collections.

Billings was a tanner, a trade he seems to have practiced for most of his life. He also served in a succession of minor municipal appointments: scavenger, hogreeve, and sealer of leather. His wife died in 1795, leaving him with six children under the age of eighteen. He ended his life in poverty and was buried in a pauper's grave.

The Singing Master's Assistant saw print as the fortunes of war were beginning to favor the Americans and the composer was near the height of his career. In a flurry of activity, he published three other tunebooks during the next three years, while *The Singing Master's Assistant* went through three editions (a fourth would come in the late 1780s). It contains seventy-one compositions, mainly psalm and hymn tunes, including fuging tunes and tunes with extension, but also nine large-scale compositions (anthems and a set-piece). Billings acknowledges authorship of as many as eleven texts of the sixty psalm tunes included.

In the thirty-two pages of front matter, Billings proves himself an entertaining and informative author, given to allegory and comedy. After a preface and advertisement, we find a tutor, organized by lessons, followed by rules for regulating a singing school, "An Historical Account of G. Gamut, as related by herself, taken in short hand by the Author," and a musical dictionary. Billings reaches his invective best as he addresses the Goddess of Discord and provides a Receipt ("Received by the Author, a piece of Jargon"). He winds down with "An Encomium on Music" ("That I am a Musical Enthusiast I readily grant").

Billings has at times been scoffed at and derided, but he continues to be lauded in our generation as a major figure at an important time in our national history. He represents an approach to life and music that is uniquely American in its originality and compositional approach.

WILLIAM BILLINGS
from *The Singing Master's Assistant* (1778)

The Preface

Kind Reader,

No doubt you (do, or ought to) remember, that about eight years ago, I published a Book entitled, *The New England Psalm Singer*. And truely a most masterly and inimitable Performance, I then thought it to be. Oh! how did my foolish heart throb and beat with tumultuous joy! With what impatience did I wait on the Book-Binder, while stitching the sheets and putting on the covers, with what extacy, did I snatch the yet unfinished Book out of his hands, and pressing it to my bosom, with rapturous delight, how lavish was I, in encomiums on this infant production of my own Numb Skull? Welcome; thrice welcome; thou legitimate off-spring of my brain, go forth my little Book, go forth and immortalize the name of your Author; may your sale be rapid and may you speedily run through ten thousand Editions; may you be a welcome guest in all companies and what will add tenfold to thy dignity, may you find your way into the Libraries of the Learned. Thou art my Reuben, my first born, the beginning of my strength, the excellency of my dignity, and the excellency of my power. But to my great mortification, I soon discovered it was Reuben in the sequel, and Reuben all over; for unstable as water, it did not excell: But since I have begun to play the Critic, I will go through with my Criticisms, and endeavour to point out its beauties as well as deformities, and it must be acknowledged, that many of the pieces are not so ostentatious, as to sound forth their own praises; for it has been judiciously observed, that the oftener they are sounded, the more they are abased. After impartial examination, I have discovered that many of the pieces in that Book were

never worth my printing, or your inspection; therefore in order to make you ample amends for my former intrusion, I have selected and corrected some of the Tunes which were most approved of in that book, and have added several new pieces which I think to be very good ones; for if I thought otherwise, I should not have presented them to you. But however, I am not so tenacious of my own opinion, as to desire you to take my word for it; but rather advise you all to purchase a Book and satisfy yourselves is that particular, and then, I make no doubt, but you will readily concur with me in this sentiment, viz. That the *Singing-Master's Assistant,* is a much better Book, than the *New-England Psalm-Singer*. And now Reader I have no more to say.

*   *   *

Lesson XIII

SING that part which gives you least pain, otherwise you make it a toil of a pleasure; for if you attempt to sing a part which is almost (or quite) out of your reach, it is not only very laborious to the performer; but often very disagreeable to the hearer, by reason of many wry faces and uncouth postures, which rather resemble a person in extream pain, than one who is supposed to be pleasantly employed. And it has been observed, that those persons, who sing with most ease are in general the most musical; for easy singing is a distinguishing mark of a natural Singer, and it is vastly more agreeable (at least to me) to hear a few wild uncultivated sounds from a natural Singer, than a Concert of Music performed by the most refined artificial singers upon earth, provided the latter have little or no assistance from nature.

ONE very essential thing in music, is to have the part properly proportioned; and here I think we ought to take a grateful notice, that the Author of Harmony has so curiously constructed our Organs, that there are about three of four deep voices

William Billings, *The Singing Master's Assistant; or Key to Practical Music, Being an Abridgement from the New-England Psalm-Singer* (Boston: Printed by Draper and Folsom, 1778), iii, 14–17, 25, 28–29, 102.

suitable for the Bass to one for the upper parts, which is about the proportion required in the laws of Harmony; for the voices on the Bass should be *majestic, deep,* and *solemn*; the tenor, *full, bold* and *manly*; the Counter *loud, clear* and *lofty*; the Treble *soft, shrill,* and *sonorous*; and if suitable voices cannot be had, to sing each part properly, some of the parts had better be omitted; for it is a Maxim with me, that two parts well sung are better than four parts indifferently sung, and I had rather hear, four people sing well, than four hundred almost well.

Lesson XIV

GOOD singing is not confined to great singing, nor is it entirely dependent upon small singing. I have heard many great voices, that never struck a harsh Note, and many small voices that never struck a pleasant one; therefore if the Tones be Musical, it is not material whether the Voices be greater, or less; yet I allow that there are but few Voices, but what want restraining, or softening upon high Notes, to take off the harshness, which is, as disagreeable to a delicate Ear, as a wire edged Raisor, to a tender Face, or a Smoaky House to tender Eyes. It is an essential thing, in a master, to propagate soft singing, in the School; because soft Musick, has a great tendency to refine the Ears of the Performers, and I know by experience, that a new piece may be learned with more ease to the master and scholars, where they practice soft singing, and in less than half the time, it would otherwise require. Here take a few hints, viz.

1. LET the low Notes in the Bass be struck full, and the high Notes soft.

2. LET not the upper parts overpower the lower ones.

3. LET each performer attend critically to the strength of his own Voice, and not strive to sing louder, than the rest of the company; unless he is in place of a leader.

4. LET each performer sing the part that is most suitable to his voice; and never stretch it beyond its proper bearing.

5. IF you are so unhappy, as to set a piece too high, it is best to worry through without lowering the pitch; because that has a tendency to take away the spirit of the performers; but if you set a piece too low you may raise it according to your judgment, and that will serve to animate the performers.

6. DO not set the pieces so high as to strain the voices; for that takes away all pleasure in the performance, and all Music from the composition.

7. FINALLY let every performer be fully qualified for a leader.

I would take this opportunity, to acquaint my younger Pupils, that it is deemed a point of ill manners to invade the province of another, by singing a Solo, which does not belong to your part, for it will admit of these two constructions, viz. that the persons to whom it is assigned, are not capable of doing justice to the piece, or at least, that you are more capable than they. It is also very degrading to the author to sing, when he (for reasons perhaps unknown to you) by presenting a number of empty Bars tacitly forbids your singing, and no doubt this invention of his, is to illustrate some grand point, in the plan of the composition; when, by your ill timed interuption, you not only destroy the sense, intended to be conveyed in the composition; but convey a very different sense to the audience: therefore for you to sing, when the author forbids your singing, is both unmannerly and ostentatious.

IT is also well worth your observation, that the grand contention with us, is, not who shall sing *loudest*; but who shall sing *best*.

* * *

Observe These Rules for Regulating a Singing-School

As the well being of every society depends, in a great measure, upon GOOD ORDER,[1] I here present you with some General Rules, to be observed in a Singing-School.

1st. Let the society be first formed, and the articles signed by every individual; and all those who are under age, should apply to their Parents,

---

[1] *I have heard it remarked that "Order was the first thing which took place in Heaven."* [Billings's note.]

Masters or Guardians to sign for them: the house should be provided, and every necessary for the school should be procured, before the arrival of the Master, to prevent his being unnecessarily detained.

2d. The Members should be very punctual in attending at a certain hour, or minute, as the master shall direct, under the penalty of a small fine, and if the master should be delinquent, his fine to be double the sum laid upon the scholars—Said fines to be appropriated to the use of the school, in procuring *wood, candles, etc.*

N. B. The fines to be collected by the Clerk so chosen for that purpose.

3d. All the scholars should submit to the judgment of the master, respecting the part they are to sing, and if he should think fit to remove them from one part to another, they are not to contradict, or cross him in his judgment; but they would do well to suppose it is to answer some special purpose; because it is morally impossible for him to proportion the parts properly, until he has made himself acquainted with the strength and fitness of the pupil's voices.

4th. No unnecessary conversation, whispering or laughing, to be practised; for it is not only very indecent; but very impolitic: it being a needless expence of time, and instead of acquiring to themselves respect, they render themselves ridiculous and contemptable, in the eyes of all serious people; and above all, I enjoin it upon you to refrain from all levity, both in conduct and conversation, while singing sacred words; for where the words *God, Christ, Redeemer, etc.* occur, you would do well to remember the third Commandment, the profanation of which, is a heinous crime, and God has expressly declared he will not hold them guiltless who take his name in vain, and remember that in so doing you not only dishonour God and sin against your own souls; but you give occasion, and very just ground to the adversaries or enemies of Music, to speak reproachfully. Much more might be said; but the rest I shall leave to the Master's direction, and your own discretion, heartily wishing you may reap both pleasure and profit, in this your laudable undertaking.

* * *

To the Goddess of Discord

DREAD SOVEREIGN

I HAVE been sagacious enough of late, to discover that some evil-minded persons have insinuated to your highness, that I am utterly unmindful of your Ladyship's importance; and that my time, as well as my talents, was wholly taken up in paying my divoto to your most implacable enemy and strenuous opposer, viz. the GODDESS of DISCORD, which representation is as false as it is ill-natured; for your Ladyship may believe me without hesitation, when I assure you on the word of an honest man, that knowing your Ladyship to be of a very captious disposition; I have always been very careful of trespassing on your grounds for fear of incuring your displeasure, so far as to excite you to take vengeance (which is well known to be your darling attribute.)

I have likewise been informed, that some of my most implacable enem[ies] are some of your Majesty's privy-council, and that your Majesty's Secretary at war, viz, Lord Jargon, was about to send some of your other Lords in waiting, viz. Lord second, Lord 7th, Lord 9th, alias Lord 2d, junior, with some others, to beat a tattoo upon the drum of my ear, with so great a number of contra-vibrations, without the intervention of a single coincidence, and with so much Forte as to dislocate my auditory; upon which information I called a court of Harmony, the result of which was, to repel force by force, and we had even proceeded so far as to order Lord Consonance, our Secretary at peace to furnish our life-guard with an infinite number of coincidences, without the intervention of one contra-vibration; and although we have the majority on our side, yet we held it in scorn to take any advantage from our numbers, therefore we had selected an equal number of those who had attained unto the first three, viz. Lord Unison, Lord Diapente, Lord Octave, alias Lord Unison, jun'r, and for their Aid de camps, we had chosen two twin brothers, viz. Major and Minor Trio, together with Major Sixth, etc. we had proceeded thus far, when in turning over a very antient history I met with the following passage, viz. "*by wise council thou shalt make thy war, and in multitude of councellors there is safety.*" Upon reading this passage I was resolved to enlarge the council, therefore we made choice of king Solomon, the son of David (but as he nor his father was never known to traverse your territories I suppose you have no knowledge of them). The result of our second council was to lay aside this enterprize and proceed in a very different manner; for by consulting this great councellor we were convinced "*that wisdom is better than weapons of war.*"

Therefore it was resolved, that I singly should begin the attack in the common form of dedications, and besiege you with flattery, and if that should fail, as we have brib'd over a number of your nobility, we are determined to turn their force against you, and then we assure ourselves of success; but perhaps I trespass on your patience in this ambiguous preamble: Know then dread Sovereign that I have composed the following p[ie]ce, out of such materials as your kingdom is made up of, and, without vanity, I believe you will readily grant that it is the best p[ie]ce that ever was composed: this I chearfully offer at your shrine; and I must take the liberty to tell your Majesty that I expect this one piece will fully compensate for my former delinquency and remissness to you ward; and that you will not be so unreasonable as to insist on another oblation from me; neither through time nor eternity; and let me tell you, that in this offering I followed the example of our native indians, who sacrifice to the angry God much oftener than to the good-natured one; not from a principle of love, but of fear; for although you could never excite my love, you have frequently caused me to fear and tremble; and I solemnly declare that I dread your extempore speeches more than I do the threats and menaces of all the crowned heads in Europe; and now madam, after this candid and honest confession, I must insist on your singing the following Receipt which for your honour and my security I shall always carry about me.

A Receipt

RECEIVED of the Author, a piece of Jargon, it being the best p[ie]ce ever composed, in full of all accounts

from the beginning of time, to and through the endless ages of eternity. I say received by me,
GODDESS OF DISCORD

GIVEN from our inharmonical Cavern, in the land of CHAOS; from the year of our existence, (which began at Adam's fall) Five Thousand Seven Hundred and Eighty Two.

Attest,
DEMON DREAD, Speaker
Haman Horrow, Secretary

And now Madam Crossgrain after informing you, that this receipt shall be my discharge, I shall be so condescending as to acquaint your uglyship, that I take great pleasure in subscribing myself your most inveterate, most implacable, most irreconcilable enemy.

The AUTHOR

In order to do this piece ample justice, the Concert must be made of vocal and instrumental Music. Let it be performed in the following manner, viz. Let an ass bray the Bass, let the fileing of a saw carry the Tenor, let a hog who is extream hungry squeel the Counter, and let a cart-wheel, which is heavy loaded, and that has been long without grease, squeek the Treble; and if the Concert should appear to be too feeble you may add the cracking of a crow, the howling of a dog, the squalling of a cat, and what would grace the Concert yet more would be the rubing of a wet finger upon a window glass; this last mentioned instrument no sooner salutes the drum of the ear, but it instantly conveys the sensation to the teeth; and if all these in conjunction should not reach the cause you may add this most inharmonical of all sounds, "*pay me that thou owest.*"

*   *   *

Jargon

Let horrid Jargon[2] split the Air;
And rive the Nerves asunder,
Let hateful Discord greet the Ear
As terrible as Thunder. . . .

---

[2]Defined in Billings's musical dictionary as "the worst of sounds, see Discord."

10   🌿   The Utopian Spirit

Utopian communities flourished in pre–Civil War America; some were founded in this country, others came from Europe seeking the promise of independence that the New World held. Three such groups stand out for their music making: the Ephrata Community founded in Pennsylvania by Conrad Beissel; the Moravians, who migrated from Europe to find a home in Pennsylvania; and the Shakers, who, under the leadership of Ann Lee (Mother Ann), came first to New York State and then spread out across the country. Idealistic, separatist, and communal, these groups pursued their own noble ideals of how to conduct their lives. They were attracted by the New World spirit of open-mindedness, freedom, and expansiveness, and for a time, at least, they fit well into the evolving fabric that would become America.

In 1732, German-born Conrad Beissel (1691–1768) led a group of followers from Germantown, Pennsylvania, to form a new semi-monastic community on the Cocalico River in what is now Lancaster County. The Ephrata Cloister practiced the ideals of spiritual purification as Beissel understood them. Converts took on new religious names—Beissel's was Father Friedsam (peaceful). Eventually known as German Seventh-Day Baptists, they donned habits in the style of Dominican monks. Although some members did marry, the sexes were separated and celibacy was encouraged. Baptism was performed by total immersion and the Sabbath was celebrated on Saturday.

This separatist community represents one of the earliest centers of musical creativity in America. Although only partially trained as a musician, Beissel did perceive music, along with writing, as an ideal pursuit for his community: "Who shall then sing? All the saints of God, whose hearts and mouths are full of praise, thanksgiving and prayer."

Beissel developed a unique harmonic system on which he based music for hundreds of hymns and anthems that he and his followers composed. The first major hymnal from the Ephrata press (and its most important publication) was *Das Gesäng der einsamen und verlassenen Turtel-Taube* (The song of the solitary and deserted turtle dove) of 1747. Of its 277 hymns, two-thirds were contributed by Beissel. Two other editions contain even more hymns.

In the *Turtel-Taube*, Beissel develops his ideas about composition and singing. The tones of the tonic triad of any tonality are called masters, the others servants. Harmony is based on the soprano voice, not the bass, leading to some surprising results. Rhythms follow word accentuation and show considerable metric flexibility.

The community declined after Beissel's death, and the unique nature of its music limited its acceptance elsewhere. In its own way the Cloister found what most immigrants sought in migrating to these shores: freedom to pursue their own way of life without interference.

The *Chronicon Ephratense* (Ephrata Chronicle) was written by two members of the order. It was begun by Brother Lamech (Jacob Gass?) and was continued and edited by Brother Jaebez (Johann Peter Miller, Agrippa in Latin).

Jacob Duché identifies himself on the title page of his *Observations . . .* (1774) as "a Gentlemen of foreign extraction, who resided some time in Philadelphia." In one printing, Duché used a pseudonym: "Written by Tamoc Caspipina," an acronym for "The Assistant Minister of Christ Church and St. Peter's in Philadelphia in North America." The letter quoted to the Lord Bishop of B——l is dated October 2, 1771, three years after Conrad Beissel's death.

JACOB GASS? AND JOHANN PETER MILLER
from *Chronicon Ephratense* (1786)

Now those of the Solitary, of whom about seventy of both sexes were in the Settlement, were selected who had talent for singing, and the above mentioned Ludwig Blum,[1] together with the Superintendent,[2] arranged a singing-school in the Settlement, and everything prospered for a time. But the Sisters at last complained to the Superintendent that they were sold to one man, and petitioned him to manage the school himself, saying that they would steal the whole secret of the school-master and hand it over to him. The Superintendent soon perceived that this advice came from God, for as the event proved, quite different things were hidden under it, for which the good school-master's hands were not made. And now the Sisters told the Superintendent everything they had learnt in the school, and as soon as they saw that he had mastered the art, they dismissed their school-master, at which he took such offence, that he left the Settlement, and did not walk with them any more. . . .

The singing-schools began with the Sisters, lasted four hours, and ended at midnight. Both master and scholars appeared in white habits, which made a singular procession, on which account people of quality frequently visited the school. The Superintendent, animated by the spirit of eternity, kept the school in great strictness and every fault was sharply censured. The whole neighborhood, however, was touched by the sound of this heavenly music, a prelude of a new world and a wonder to the neighbors. . . . [T]he school was re-commenced.[3] Soon after a choir of Sisters appeared in the meeting, and sang the hymn, "God, we come to meet Thee," with five voices, which was so well received in the Settlement, that everyone had his name entered for the choir, so that one did not know who should perform the outside work. But this heavenly art also soon found its enviers, for one of the house-fathers publicly testified and wrote against it, but the Brethren reprimanded him and said: The wisdom of God had ordered this school to their sanctification, they had sweated in it and endured school discipline, therefore they would not permit a stranger to interfere. After the Superintendent had with much trouble broken the ice, and taught the first principles of singing to the scholars, he divided them into five choirs with five persons to each choir, namely, one air, one tenor, one alto, and two bass singers.[4] The Sisters

Jacob Gass? and Johann Peter Miller, *Chronicon Ephratense: A History of the Community of Seventh Day Baptists at Ephrata, Lancaster County, Penn'a*, trans. J. Max Hark (Lancaster, Pa.: S. H. Zahm, 1889), ch. 24, 160–68.

[1]"House-father" and schoolmaster Blum, who served at Ephrata for only a short time, was a good singer and evidently knew a little about music.

[2]Conrad Beissel.

[3]Beissel's strictness had led to the temporary abandonment of the singing school.

[4]All but the bass parts were sung by women. Jacob Duché speaks of women taking the bass part also.

were divided into three choirs, the upper, middle and lower; and in the choruses a sign was made for each choir, when to be silent and when to join in the singing. These three choirs had their separate seats at the table of the Sisters during love-feasts,[5] the upper choir at the upper end, the middle at the middle, and the lower at the lower end; in singing antiphonally, therefore, the singing went alternately up and down the table. Not only had each choir to observe its time when to join in, but, because there were solos in each chorale, every voice knew when to keep silent, all of which was most attentively observed. And now the reason appeared which induced him to establish such choirs of virgins. It was with him as with Solomon, he was zealous to make manifest the wonderful harmony of eternity, in a country which but lately wild savages had inhabited; for God owed this to North America as an initiation into the Christian church, therefore these choirs belong to the firstlings of America. The contents of these songs were entirely prophetic, and treated of the restoration of the image of Adam before his division, of the heavenly virginity, the priesthood of Melchizedek, etc. The gift of prophecy overflowed the Settlement like a river at that time; and close observation showed that the beautiful sun of Paradise had then already reached its meridian, but afterwards inclined towards its setting, and was at last followed by a sorrowful night, as will be shown in its place. This wonderful harmony resounded over the country; whoever heard of it, wished to see it, and whoever saw it, acknowledged that God truly lived among these people.

And now let us tell for the information of those who are versed in this art, how he explained the first principles of singing so simply that even a child could understand them; therefore he did not care for the artificial terms of the masters, which rather obscure than enlighten the art. Accordingly, whenever he took a hymn in hand, in order to compose a tune to it, he was careful to represent the spirit of the hymn by the tune; then after he had composed a choral-song, he fixed the metre, not according to custom, but as the nature of the thing required it. He, however, soon found out that some of the melodies were very strained, and that notes occurred which did not belong there. Thus he discovered the key, for every key has its own peculiarity, and adopts only such notes as are natural to it, and this is the reason why the melodies of Lobwasser[6] have a strained sound, because the key to them was not understood, and notes were thus used which were not suitable. In order that he might not make mistakes in composing, he had for each key certain dominant notes, commonly four to the octave, which he called rulers, but the three other notes, servants. Thus in the *f* tunes, *f, a, c, f,* are the rulers, but *g, b, d* the servants, and although it sounds ill if a servant is made ruler, the composer, nevertheless, must know when it is proper to swerve into another key. This gives a very charming variation to the song, provided it resolves itself again into the original key before the end. The Superintendent was a master in this, but his scholars suspected that he had done it in order to find a cause for fault-finding with them; for as soon as they changed to another key their voices fell into disorder.

When he attempted to compose the bass and middle-voices he encountered new difficulties, for you must know that vocal music, as well as *mathesis,*[7] have their unalterable first principles, which angels even observe in their song. These he did not know, neither was he able, like masters in music, to find the concordance by means of instruments; at last he invented certain schedules, a special one for each key, in which he laid down the proportion between the soprano and the other voices, whereby composition was greatly facilitated. For instance, in the key of *f,* the *f* in the soprano corresponds to *a* in the tenor, and *c* in the alto; the bass, however, has the octave of the middle voices. All his tunes

---

[5]Simple services, including a meal, derived from the *agapae* of the Apostolic Church.

[6]Ambrosius Lobwasser (1515–1585), whose principal work was the popular *Psalter* printed in Leipzig in 1573.

[7]Acquisition of knowledge.

have two basses; but he also composed some for six voices, and even for seven, namely, two soprano, one alto, two tenor, and two bass; for that purpose, however, he after all had to use two octaves. His last work, by many masters declared the most important, were the choral-songs. They were brought to light, partly printed, partly written, Anno 1754, under the title: "Paradisiacal Wonder Music, which in these latter times and days became prominent in the occidental parts of the world as a prevision of the New World, consisting of an entirely new and uncommon manner of singing, arranged in accord with the angelic and heavenly choirs. Herein the song of Moses and the Lamb, also the Song of Solomon, and other witnesses out of the Bible and from other saints, are brought into sweet harmony. Everything arranged with much labor and great trouble, after the manner of singing of the angelic choirs, by a Peaceful one,[8] who desires no other name or title in this world."[9]

It is reported that the angels singing antiphonally appeared in a vision to St. Ignatius, and thus their methods found their way into the church. It is possible that in former ages they were more in use in the convents; now but little is known of them. Yet one of these tune-books came over the ocean, and we are informed that, being engraved on copper, it was printed at Augsburg; but we cannot answer for it.[10] When already half the Settlement was burdened with this work, the house-fathers, too, came to engage in the wonderful music, for the powers of eternity, which were embodied in it, had such an effect that whoever heard the song was forcibly attracted by the goodness of God. Some time during the night was fixed for the school-hour, and two Brethren were appointed teachers; but they showed such diligence in the school during winter that they neglected their domestic duties, which rendered it necessary to close the school. But the Superintendent, in consideration of the fact that such gray heads had paid so much honor to the work of God, in so far that they suffered themselves to be children again, had a music book for four voices written for them, which he presented to their Community. Their veneration for this music was so great that everyone wished to possess the book, and whoever had it accordingly fell under judgment, as happened yonder with the ark of the covenant. The book thus wandered from house to house, till at last nobody wished to have anything to do with it.

---

[8]Beissel's "church-name."

[9]Beissel's *Paradisisches Wunderspiel*, 1754, his last work, was the only one to include printed music. Since the press at Ephrata previously lacked music type, notation had been entered by hand. Of the forty-nine pieces in the book, most are for four parts, although some are for as many as seven parts.

---

[10]Possible Augsburg Psalters include that by Gregorius Sünderreiter (1574) and one by Narziss Rauner (1670).

JACOB DUCHÉ

from Letter to the Lord Bishop of B———l (1774)

We travelled through a thick-settled and highly-cultivated country, beautifully variegated with hills commanding extensive prospects, and vallies enriched with meadows, mills, farm-houses, and limpid streams of water. At length we arrived at *Lancaster*, a large and flourishing town, about sixty miles from hence. Its trade to this city is very considerable: But, as it is not situated on navigable water, this trade is carried on by means of large covered waggons, which travel in great numbers to Philadelphia (sometimes, as I have been informed, there being above one hundred in a company) carrying down the produce of the country, and returning with all kinds of stores and merchandize.

At *Lancaster* we tarried but one night; and the next morning pursued our journey to *Ephrata*, or Dunker-Town, as some call it, a small village situated on a beautiful little river or creek, in a most romantic and sequestered vale. This village and the adjoining lands are possessed by a religious sect called *Dunkers*, whose principles and manners are very singular. They are for the most part *Germans*. Their name, I am told, is taken from their mode of baptizing their new converts, which is by dipping them in a river, as the *Anabaptists* do among us. Certain it is, that they took their rise in this place about fifty years ago; and did not, as a sect, emigrate from any other country. Their society, however, at present, seems to be upon the decline, not exceeding one hundred members, though they have been heretofore more numerous. Both men and women are dressed in white linen for the summer, and woollen for the winter season. Their habit is a kind of long coat or tunic reaching down to the heels, having a sash or girdle round the waist, and a cap or hood hanging from one shoul-

der, not unlike the dress of the Dominican friars. The men do not shave the head or beard. They are in general industrious, cheerful and extremely sagacious.

The men and women have separate habitations and distinct governments. For these purposes, they have erected two large wooden buildings, one of which is occupied by the brethren, the other by the sisters of the society; and in each of them there is a banqueting room and an apartment for public worship: For the men and women do not meet together even at their devotions. The rest of the building is divided into a great number of small closets, or rather cells: each affording just room enough to accommodate one person.

They live chiefly upon roots and other vegetables: the rules of their society not allowing flesh, except upon particular occasions, when they hold what they call a *Love-feast*; at which time, the brethren and sisters dine together in a large apartment, and eat *mutton*, but no other meat. No member of the society is allowed a bed, but in case of sickness. In each of their little cells they have a bench fixed, to serve the purpose of a bed, and a small block of wood for a pillow. The *Dunkers* allow of no intercourse betwixt the brethren and sisters, not even by marriage. Nevertheless, some have broken through this restraint, and ventured upon the conjugal state. The married persons, however, are no longer considered in full communion, or suffered to live under the same roof, no, nor in the same village with the unmarried; but are obliged to remove to a place about a mile distant, called *Mount-Sion*. They continue indeed to wear the habit, and in other respects are deemed members of the society.

The principal tenet of the *Dunkers*, I understand, is this: "That future happiness is only to be obtained by penance and outward mortifications in this life; and that as JESUS CHRIST, by his meritorious sufferings became the redeemer of mankind in general; so each individual of the human race,

Jacob Duché, *Observations on a Variety of Subjects, Literary, Moral and Religious: In a Series of Original Letters, Written by a Gentleman of Foreign Extraction* (Philadelphia: John Dunlap, 1774), 69–74, 77–79.

by a life of abstinence and restraint, may work out his own salvation." Nay, they go so far, as to admit of works of supererogation, and declare, that a man may do much more than he is in justice or equity obliged to do, and that his superabundant works may therefore be applied to the salvation of others.

* * *

Beside the two large buildings above-mentioned, the *Dunkers* have several smaller ones, chiefly for the purpose of manufactures. They carry on several branches of business with great skill and industry. They have a convenient oil-mill, paper-mill, and printing-press. They make parchment, tan leather, and manufacture linen and woollen cloth, more than sufficient to serve their own society. The sisters are ingenious at making wax-tapers, curious paper-lanthorns, and various kinds of pasteboard boxes, which they sell to strangers who come to visit them. They likewise amuse themselves with writing favourite texts of scripture in large letters curiously ornamented with flowers and foliage. These seem to be rather works of patience than of genius. Several of them are framed and hung up to decorate their place of worship. Inclosed I send your Lordship a specimen of this writing, which you may, perhaps, think worthy of a place in your collection of foreign curiosities.

I shall at present remark but one thing more, with respect to the *Dunkers*, and that is, the peculiarity of their *music*. Upon an hint given by my friend, the sisters invited us into their chapel, and, seating themselves in order, began to sing one of their devout hymns. The music had little or no air or melody; but consisted of simple, long notes, combined in the richest harmony. The counter, treble, tenor and bass were all sung by women, with sweet, shrill and small voices; but with a truth and exactness in the time and intonation that was admirable. It is impossible to describe to your Lordship my feelings upon this occasion. The performers sat with their heads reclined, their countenances solemn and dejected, their faces pale and emaciated from their manner of living, their clothing exceeding white and quite picturesque, and their music such as thrilled to the very soul.—I almost began to think myself in the world of spirits, and that the objects before me were ethereal. In short, the impression this scene made upon my mind continued strong for many days, and I believe, will never be wholly obliterated.

By way of concluding this little narrative, I beg leave to transcribe a copy of verses.

11   The Moravians and Their Music

Moravian missionaries, members of the Moravian Church (Unitas Fratrem, or United Brethren), first reached the New World in the 1730s to work among African slaves in the West Indies. By 1741, they had found their way, via a short-lived stay in Georgia, to the Lehigh Valley of Pennsylvania, where they established a settlement called Bethlehem. The new community, isolationist and otherworldly, flourished. The Moravians, who had been persecuted in Europe, had found their promise in the expansive territory of the New World. Soon, other Moravian communities were founded in Pennsylvania at Nazareth and Lititz, and in 1753 at Salem (Winston-Salem), North Carolina.

The Moravians brought their musical culture with them from Europe, and each of these settlements became known for its music. But because of the Moravians' separatist nature, their music developed in isolation, unaffected by New England psalmody and other American traditions.

At Bethlehem, music played a vital role from the start. An Indian chief was buried to music in 1746, and a document from 1780 lists an orchestra consisting of violins, violas, cellos, French horns, flutes, trumpets, and oboes—an ensemble capable of performing solid literature. Church music was emphasized. Trombone choirs, a heritage from Europe, were a special feature, and organ building became a rich tradition. The early community was organized into choirs, with the sexes separated. This practice posed difficulties for performing mixed-voice choral music, but boys could always sing women's parts.

Music current in pre-classical Europe was performed, but Moravian composers such as Johann Friedrich Peter, Johannes Herbst, Jeremiah Dencke, and a host of others left us a rich vein of works composed in America. In 1811, Haydn's *Creation* was performed in Bethlehem's Nazareth Hall by the collegium musicum, a group organized just three years after the settlement's founding. The collegium was the first such ensemble in America, and this was the first performance of Haydn's work on these shores.

Visitors praised the quality of the music. In a travel account published in 1800, John D. Ogden expressed surprise at the number of instruments on hand and the Moravians' dedication to music. "In almost every room," he wrote "we saw some musical instrument—an organ, harpsichord or forte-piano. These are in many private families, in this settlement and other villages." Earlier, Benjamin Franklin, who visited in 1756, was impressed by the music for organ and other instruments performed at a church service. Henry Ellsworth, a Yale graduate and young son of a distinguished Connecticut general and signer of the Declaration of Independence, stopped at Bethlehem in 1811. He, too, commented on the Moravians' dedication to music.

In addition to a creative repertoire of enduring works, the Moravians gave us the first American collegium musicum, the first instruments built in America, the first chamber music written in America, and the first American performances of major European choral and orchestral works.

BENJAMIN FRANKLIN

Diary Entry (1756)

While at Bethlehem, I enquir'd a Little into the Practices of the Moravians. Some of them had accompanied me, and all were very kind to me. I found they work'd for a common Stock, eat at common Tables, and slept in common Dormitorys, great Numbers together. In the Dormitories I observ'd Loopholes at certain Distances all along just under the Cieling, which I thought judiciously plac'd for Change of Air. I was at their Church, where I was entertain'd with good Musick, the Organ being accompanied with Violins, Hautboys, Flutes, Clarinets, &c. I understood that their Sermons were not usually preached to mix'd Congregations, of Men Women and Children, as is our common Practice; but that they assembled sometimes the married Men, at other times their Wives, then the Young Men, the young Women, and the little Children, each Division by itself. The Sermon I heard was to the latter, who came in and were plac'd in Rows on Benches, the Boys under the Conduct of a young Man their Tutor, and the Girls conducted by a young Woman. The Discourse seem'd well adapted to their Capacities, and was delivered in a pleasing familiar Manner, coaxing them as it were to be good. They behav'd very orderly, but look'd pale and unhealthy, which made me suspect they were kept too much within-doors, or not allow'd sufficient Exercise. I enquir'd concerning the Moravian Marriages, whether the Report was true that they were by Lot? I was told that Lots were us'd only in particular Cases. That generally when a young Man found himself dispos'd to marry, he inform'd the Elders of his Class, who consulted the Elder Ladies that govern'd the young Women. As these Elders of the different Sexes were well acquainted with the Tempers and Dispositions of their respective Pupils, they could best judge what Matches were suitable, and their Judgments were generally acquiesc'd in. But if for example it should happen that two or three young Women were found to be *equally* proper for the young Man, the Lot was then recurr'd to. I objected, If the Matches are not made by the mutual Choice of the Parties, some of them may chance to be very unhappy. And so they may, answer'd my Informer, if you let the Parties chuse for themselves.—Which indeed I could not deny.

Leonard W. Labaree, et al., *The Autobiography of Benjamin Franklin* (New Haven, Conn.: Yale University Press, 1964), 236–37.

HENRY LEAVITT ELLSWORTH
Diary Entry (1811)

[June 5.] We arrived at *Bethlehem* about sunset. But being strangers to every body we cannot expect to gratify our curiosity in seeing the Moravians and learning their manners and customs. Whatever information I get must be by optical sense as I can understand no more from their conversation than the simple meaning of the two important words *yaw* and *nay.*

June 6th. Thursday morning. I am agreeably disappointed in not leaving the Moravians without gaining some information respecting the people. This sect came from Europe and settled here. The first house was built by them 70 years since and is now going to decay. They own 4,000 acres of land; their population is 500. They live very compact and pursue all kinds of employment though there is one man only who follows one kind of business; hence there is but one Tavern keeper, one druggist shop, one store, & &. The inkeeper has a stated salary and the p[r]ofits are weekly paid into the treasury. There is a neat simplicity in their dress which I admire. The men wear shoebuckles, and the old women, young women, and maidens we[a]re caps. Certain houses are alloted to the Clergy; others were allotted to the *widows* and called "widows houses"; others are aloted to unmarried ladies and these are called "single sisters houses." There is a small building back of the Church where the remains of deceased persons are laid for a considerable time lest they might be buried too soon.

Our guide and friend was Daddy Thomas,[1] a "*vary* coot *clavar* mon." We called him Daddy Thomas because he said that name delighted him most. He is superannuated and takes enjoyment in

showing strangers the curiosities of the town. By his assistance we gained admission into their great Church which I before mentioned they had embarrased themselves in building. It reminded me of the picture of St. Pauls church though it is nothing in comparison to it. It is 150 feet long and between 60 or 70 broad. It is 150 feet high, finished in the *neatest* but not most elegant stile. We first were introduced into the lower room where they hold public worship. The children all set [*sic*] on benches. The Pulpit is on the west side; on the east side is the singers' galery and two pews for strangers. But I must here remark that man and wife are not *one* but *twain* in the eyes of Moravians. No man must set with his wife but must be placed at the other side of the house with a great seperation. The music must be most excellent as the young men devote a great deal of attention to this subject. They have all kinds of instrumental music that will accord. Their organ cost 4,000 dolls. On the east side of this great room is the room where the ministers hold conferences among themselves. On the same side of the house is the "Childrens' room," a place where there is a stove for the comfort of the little folks in cold weather. On the north west side of this building were the meeting rooms, one for males, another for females. Here they meet to conver[s]e before the public service begins. The Moravians have their love feasts occasionally. These are nothing more than ordinary feasts the enjoyment of which consists in good eating and drinking. If they fill all the basketts which I saw with meat and cakes (and Daddy Thomas said they were for that purpose) *and eat it all* they certainly cannot be called *abstemious.* There are at present about 100 students in this school. They admit none after they have arrived at the age of 14. From the cupaloe we had a full view of this little town. We were not treated with particular attention by the Ladies—no, they shunned me as though I possessed *Pandora's box* and as

---

Phillip R. Shrifer, ed., *A Tour to New Connecticut in 1811: The Narrative of Henry Leavitt Ellsworth* (Cleveland: Western Reserve Historical Society, 1985), 34–36.

[1]The official guide appointed by the Elder's Conference of the Brethren's Church in Bethlehem.

though I were about to let out all the combined calamities of the Deities upon them. This you must know is the ladies school, the young gentlemen receive their education at Nazareth, another Moravian village north west of Bethlehem.

***

JAMES HENRY

from *Sketches of Moravian Life and Character* (1859)

In the chapel of Nazareth Hall, the teachers and citizens were wont to assemble in the evenings, and rehearse many of the symphonies of Haydn and other composers, together with an excellent programme of chamber music, in trios, quartettes and quintettes, and when engaged in the symphony, they employed as full an orchestra as they could muster. Each virtuoso, on his own favorite instrument, from the violincello to the kettle-drum, gave his whole soul to the subject, and if the performers, as a *tout-ensemble* [total ensemble], did not arrive at the proficiency of professed artists, they at least displayed the feeling, which is one of the first requirements of music, and often redeems the deficiencies of skill.

A favorite of these genial Haydn symphonies was the "Farewell,"[1] which was signalized by the successive disappearance of the lights. One performer after another, each as he closed his part, successively extinguished his taper, the music grew fainter, the sounds fell gradually into a pensive *andante*, another taper was extinguished, until the last survivor of that gay symphony was left alone, playing in his solitary position; and as the notes of his violin melted insensibly into feebler tones, and died away, he seemed, in extinguishing his own taper, to close the scene, and to drop the curtain on some fine dramatic act.[2]

As regards the other Moravian villages, music was industriously studied, although concert and chamber music were more successful in Bethlehem and Nazareth than elsewhere, for here there was a constant accession of proficients from Europe, who kept the flame alive, as the German Moravian student was, with rare exception, well trained in the art. Within recent years, as previously observed, the female Boarding-school at Bethlhem has taken up the cause of vocal music, performing the works of Haydn, Romberg, Mendelssohn, Rossini, and even Beethoven, in a very creditable style of execution and expression. . . .

The most characteristic of all music among the Moravians is that of the trombone, played usually in the open air, on the belfry, in the graveyard, at the church-door, and, at New Year's eve in the orchestra. Here the Moravian hymn is drawn out with wonderful expression, and in rendering its harmonies on these pensive wind instruments, we catch all its beauties in their fullest force. The trombones are generally played in quartette, and when the chorales are correctly executed by guiding the crescendo to its proper point, and imparting to the air its finest shades of meaning, the out-door impressions are deep and abiding. Many of these well-known chorales are very ancient, but their exquisite tone combinations never permit them to tire upon the cultivated ear, the long vibratory notes blending in beautiful accord when passing out of the sombre instrument. In their musical history of a past century the trombone has imparted solemnity to the opening and close of every anniversary; the quartette, with their thrilling tones, adding poetry to the transactions of life, as well as to the religious cultus. . . .

When music has been so fully incorporated with every form of a people's life, leading them

---

James Henry, *Sketches of Moravian Life and Character* (Philadelphia: J. B. Lippincott, 1859), 269–74.

[1]Symphony no. 45.

[2]All of this stage business appears in Haydn's score.

along by its irresistible power over the heart and soul, and making them familiar with its tone-visions—visions of a far higher order than all the materialistic associations of earth—we must conclude that it has left some marked results upon their character.

12 Yankee Doodle Rides into Town

Broadsides—single sheets printed on one side—containing text and music were a staple commodity in Colonial and Revolutionary America. One of the most famous songs to be printed in this form, *Yankee Doodle,* was also transmitted orally, in different versions. Its origin, though hazy, is probably American.

The earliest written source was most likely not a broadside but the libretto of an American comic opera, *The Disappointment; or, the Force of Credulity*, by Andrew Barton. The opera was published in New York in 1767, although the song was already well-known at the time. One of the characters, Raccoon, sings: "O! how joyful shall I be, / When I get de money, / I will bring it all to dee; / O! my diddling honey."

Parodies stemmed from both sides of the Revolutionary conflict. The early loyalist broadside, the text of which is included below, probably represents the first publication of the music together with the words. As its title, *The Lexington March,* suggests, the tune was used frequently as a march, but it also served for dancing. This version, which mocked the rebels, was printed in England, although the text originated in Boston.

The Yankee paraphrase that follows was reprinted a number of times and became standard. It may have been written by Harvard sophmore Edward Bangs, who served as a Minuteman on April 19, 1775.

Yankee Doodle was so sufficient a hallmark of the Revolutionary War that the *Massachusetts Spy or, American Oracle of Liberty* could report on May 10, 1775:

> When the second brigade marched out of Boston to reinforce the first, nothing was played by the fifes and drums but *Yankee Doodle* (which had become their favourite tune ever since that *notable exploit,* which did such *honour* to the troops of *Britain's King,* of tarring and feathering a poor countryman in Boston, and parading with him through the principal streets, under arms with their bayonets fixed:) Upon their return to Boston, one [loyalist] asked his brother officer how he liked the tune now,—"D—n them," returned he, *"they made us dance it till we were tired."*—Since which *Yankee Doodle* sounds less sweet to their ears.

In a similar vein, young patriot John Greenwood, who was George Washington's dentist and whose memoirs were eventually published in 1922, commented, "The war had begun, they told me; the British had marched out into the country to Lexington, to the tune of 'Yankee Doodle,' but they had made them dance it back again."

In the famous lines "Yankee Doodle came to town / Riding on a pony, / He stuck a feather in his hat / And called it macaroni," first mentioned in 1852, "doodle" means a trifler or shiftless fellow, "macaroni," a dandy or fop.

The third version below, written by English organist, violinist, conductor, and composer James Hewitt (1770–1827), was sung by English actor, singer, and theater manager John Hodgkinson (1765–1805). Both Hodgkinson and Hewitt moved to America in 1792, the one to Philadelphia and the other to Boston, where they continued their careers.

Numerous versions and parodies over time attest to the continuing popularity of "Yankee Doodle." It has been taken up and reused by many American composers, among them Benjamin Carr, Anthony Philip Heinrich, Louis Moreau Gottschalk, Charles Ives, and Virgil Thomson.

Text of *Yankee Doodle, or, The Lexington March*[1] (1775?)

Brother Ephraim sold his Cow
and bought him a Commission,
and then he went to Canada
to Fight for the Nation;
But when Ephraim he came home
he prov'd an arrant Coward,
He wou'd'n't fight the Frenchmen there
for fear of being devour'd.

Sheep's Head and Vinegar
Butter Milk and Tansy,
Boston is a Yankee town
Sing Hey Doodle Dandy:
First we'll take a Pinch of Snuff
And then a drink of Water,
And then we'll say How do you do
And that's a Yanky's Supper.

Aminadab is just come Home
His Eyes all greas'd with Bacon,
And all the news that he cou'd tell
Is Cape Breton is taken:
Stand up Jonathan
Figure in by Neighbour,
Nathen stand a little off
And make the Room some wider.

Christmas is a coming Boys
W'll go to Mother Cnases,
And there we'll get a Sugar Dram,
Sweeten'd with Melasses:
Heigh ho for our Cape Cod,
Heigh ho Nantasket,
Do not let the Boston wags,
Feel your Oyster Basket.

Punk in Pye is very good
And so is Apple Lantern,
Had you been whipp'd as oft as I
You'd not have been so wanton:
Uncle is a Yankee Man
'I faith he pays us all off,
And he has got a Fiddle
As big as Daddy's Hogs Trough.

Seth's Mother went to Lynn
To buy a pair of Breeches,
The first time Vathen put them on
He tore out all the Stitches;
Dolly Bushel let a Fart,
Jenny Jones she found it,
Ambrose carried it to Mill
Where Doctor Warren ground it.[2]

Our Jemima's lost her Mare
And can't tell where to find her,

Yankee Doodle, or, (as now Christened by the Saints of New England) The Lexington March / NB. The Words to be Sung thro' the Noise, & in the West Country drawl & dialect. (London: T. Skillern, 1775?).

[1] The title alludes to the battle of Lexington and Concord, April 18 and 19, 1775.

[2] "Doctor Warren" may be the famous patriot Joseph Warren, who practiced medicine in Boston starting in 1764 and was killed at the Battle of Bunker Hill, June 17, 1775.

But she'll come trotting by and by
And bring her Tail behind her
Two and two may go to Bed;

Two and two together,
And if there is not room enough,
Lie one a top o'to'ther.

Text of *The Farmer and His Son's Return from a Visit to the Camp* (1786?)

FATHER and I went down to Camp,
　Along with Captain *Goodin,*
And there we see the Men and Boys
　As thick as Hasty-pudding;

CHORUS

Yankey doodle keep it up,
　Yankey doodle dandy,
Mind the Musick and the Step,
　And with the Girls be handy.

And there we see a Thousand Men,
　As rich as 'Squire *David,*
And what they wasted every Day,
　I wish it had been saved.

The 'Lasses they eat every Day,
　Would keep an House a Winter;
They have as much that I'll be bound
　They eat it when they're a mind to.

And there we see a swamping Gun,
　Large as a Log of Maple,
Upon a ducid little Cart,
　A Load for Father's Cattle.

And every Time they shoot it off,
　It takes an Horn of Powder,
And makes a noise like Father's Gun,
　On'y a Nation louder.

I went as nigh to one myself,
　As '*Siah*'s Underpinning;

And Father went as nigh again,
　I tho't the Duce was in him.

Cousin *Simon* grew so bold
　I tho't he would have cock'd it;
It scar'd me so I shriek'd it off,
　And hung by Father's Pocket.

And Captain *Davis* had a Gun,
　He kind of clapt his Hand on't,
And stuck a crooked stabbing Iron
　Upon the little End on't.

And there I see a Pumpkin-Shell,
　As big as Mother's Bason,
And every Time they touch'd it off,
　They scamper'd like the Nation.

I see a little Barrel too,
　The Heads were made of Leather,
They knock'd upon with little Clubs,
　And call'd the Folks together.

And there was Captain *Washington,*
　And Gentlefolks about him,
They say he's grown so tarnal proud,
　He will not ride without them.

He got him on his Meeting-Clothes,
　Upon a Slapping Stallion,
He set the World along in rows,
　In Hundreds and in Millions.

The flaming Ribbons in his Hat,
　They look'd so taring fine ah,
I wanted pockily to get,
　To give to my *Jemimah.*

The Farmer and his Son Return from a Visit to the Camp
(n.p., n.d.), broadside.

I see another Snarl of Men,
  A digging Graves, they told me,
So tarnal long, so tarnal deep,
  They 'tended they should hold me.

It scar'd me so I hook'd it off,
  Nor stopt as I remember,
Nor turn'd about 'till I got Home,
  Lock'd up in Mother's Chamber.

Text of *Yankee Doodle* (c. 1798)[3]

Columbians all the present hour
as Brothers should Unite us,
Union at home's the only way
to make each Nation right us;
  Yankee doodle guard your coast
  Yankee doodle dandy,
  fear not then nor threat nor boast
  Yankee doodle dandy.

The only way to keep off war,
And guard 'gainst persecution,
Is always to be well prepar'd,
With hearts of resolution
  Yankee Doodle, let's Unite,
  Yankee Doodle Dandy,
  As patriots, still maintain our right,
  Yankee Doodle Dandy.

Great WASHINGTON, who led us on,
And Liberty effected,
Shall see we'll die or else be free—
We will not be subjected.

Yankee Doodle, guard your coast,
Yankee Doodle Dandy—
Fear not then nor threat nor boast
Yankee Doodle Dandy.

A Band of Brothers let us be,
While ADAMS guides the nation;
And still our dear bought Freedom guard,
In every situation.
  Yankee Doodle, guard your coast
  Yankee Doodle Dandy—
  Fear not then or threat or boast,
  Yankee Doodle Dandy.

May soon the wish'd for hour arrive,
When PEACE shall rule the nations—
And Commerce, free from fetters prove
Mankind are all relations.
  The[n] Yankee Doodle, be divine,
  Yankee Doodle Dandy—
  Beneath the Fig tree and the Vine,
  Sing Yankee Doodle Dandy.

Yankee Doodle (New York: J. Hewitt's Musical Repository, c. 1798), sheet music.

[3] This version relates to the undeclared war with France, 1798–1800; it was reissued for the War of 1812.

13 Philadelphia's Birthday Balls for George Washington

In Philadelphia society during the later 1770s, social dance was still heir to the Quaker philosophy, which held no place for worldly amusements. As Quaker influence waned, however, dance and music flourished increasingly. Dancing masters frequented the scene, also offering instruction in fencing, another social skill. As the century wore on, French influence increased with the arrival of numerous refugees from the revolutions in France and Haiti. Fencing, dancing, and music had been indispensable arts for French gentlemen of the old regime. John Durang, a fine professional dancer connected with the active theatrical life in Philadelphia, illustrates another important source of dance instruction: dancing masters connected with theatrical activities.

The social scene brightened when Philadelphia became the capital of the new country from 1790 to 1800. Following the pre-revolutionary precedent of birthday balls for the king, a regular series of dances was organized by the City Dancing Assembly in honor of George Washington's birthday. These were splendid events. One visitor to the city in the mid-1790s, the Duke de La Rochefoucauld-Liancourt, tells us, "I have seen balls on the President's birth-day where the splendor of the rooms, and the variety and richness of the dresses did not suffer in comparison with Europe; and it must be acknowledged, that the beauty of the American ladies has the advantage in the comparison."*

The *Daily Advertiser* of March 1, 1796 gave details about the birthday ball just held:

> There were seven sets of dancers, who took their stations in ranks from one centre, and verging toward the circumference, of which the dancers composed so many Radii. When the band of music struck up, which was composed of thirty capital performers, all the sets were put in motion at once, and dancing from the circumference toward one general centre, with so much elegance, and keeping such true time, it was the most enlivening sight that could possibly be conceived.

For a ball on February 22 (1797? the year uncertain), Washington offered a toast: "May the members thereof and the *Fair* who honor it with their presence long continue in the enjoyment of an amusement so innocent and aggreeable."

Accounts follow from two visitors to the city. The Englishman Henry Wansey (c. 1752–1827) was there in 1794. A second visitor to the United States, Julian Ursyn

---

*François-Alexandre-Frederic, duc de La Rochefoucauld-Liancourt, *Travels through the United States of North America, the Country of the Iroquois, and Upper Canada, in the Years 1795, 1796, and 1797* (London: R. Phillips, 1799), 2:385.

Niemcewicz (1758–1841), came to America from Poland in 1797 as the companion to Tadeusz Kościuszko (1746–1817). The leader of the Polish insurrection of 1794 against Russia, Kościuszko had distinguished himself on these shores as a volunteer in the American continental army. Niemcewicz's memoir describes the birthday ball in honor of George Washington on February 22, 1798.

HENRY WANSEY

from *The Journal of an Excursion* (1796)

[The Assembly Room of Oeller's Hotel] is a most elegant room, sixty feet square, with a handsome music gallery at one end. It was prepared after the French taste, with the Pantheon figures in compartments, imitating festoons; pillars, and groups of antique drawings, in the same style as lately introduced in the most elegant houses in London.

To help my reader to form some idea of the state of polished society there, I subjoin the Rules for regulating their Assemblies, which I copied from the frame hung up in the room.

Rules of Philadelphia Assembly at Oeller's Hotel.

1. The Managers have the entire direction.
2. The Ladies rank in sets, and draw for places as they enter the Room.[1] The Managers have power to place strangers and brides at the head of the Dances.
3. The Ladies who lead, call the Dances alternately.
4. No Lady to dance out of her set, without leave of a Manager.
5. No Lady to quit her place in the Dance, or alter the figure.
6. No Person to interrupt the view of the Dancers.
7. The Rooms to be opened at six o'clock, every Thursday evening, during the season; the Dances to commence at seven, and end at twelve precisely.
8. Each set having danced a Country Dance, a Cotilion[2] may be called, if at the desire of eight Ladies.
9. No Stranger admissible, without a Ticket, signed by one of the Managers, previously obtained.
10. No Gentleman admissible in boots, coloured stockings, or undress.
11. No Citizen to be admissible, unless he is a Subscriber.
12. The Managers only are to give orders to the Music.
13. If any dispute should unfortunately arise, the Managers are to adjust and finally settle the same; and any Gentleman refusing to comply, becomes inadmissible to the future Assemblies of that season.

Henry Wansey, *The Journal of an Excursion of the United States of North America, in the Summer of* 1794 (Salisbury, Pa.: J. Easton, 1796), 132–34.

[1] The room, being so wide, will admit two, or even three sets to dance at the same time. [Wansey's note.]

[2] Cotillion—for four or more couples, with one couple leading the steps.

JULIAN URSYN NIEMCEWICZ

Travel Diary Entries (1798; PUB. 1959)

City Assembly. One should see everything, even balls; one can catch there those features which portray the character of a nation. The 25th of Jan. [1798]. Mr. Montgomery got for me a ticket for the City Assembly. As a foreigner they could have invited me gratis, but no, I paid two piasters. The scene takes place in a hotel in a rather spacious hall lighted with 5 chandeliers of lamps. A full-length portrait of the founder of the dancing Society is the principal ornament of it. The hero is represented in a yellow suit with a black design, feet in the third position, with hat off and holding his sword in his hand. His memory is revered by the dancing tribe as is that of William Penn by the Quakers. On entering one sees the rules prescribed for the Society by the *Managers*. They are covered by a glass and encased in a gilded frame. The table of the twelve laws of Moses has not been more religiously observed. This love of order is met everywhere in this nation. They can neither eat, drink, nor dance without prescribing rules, without choosing officers who watch over the good order of the society. Is it possible that with this calm and systematic mind, this people could ever be seduced into disorder and anarchy? The Assembly was very splendid; one saw there more than 60 women. I saw some pretty ones, but none of striking beauty. This lack of brilliancy may perhaps be attributed to the absence of rouge, which the women in this country never use, unless in stealth, and then so little that one can not notice it.

Two things struck me in these beauties: their big feet and their bosoms, so lean that one could scarcely consider them as such. All the women were dressed in white with silver ruffles. They appeared to like to dance; perhaps it gave them pleasure, but they took care not to show it to the onlookers. Men and women both are very far from having that playfulness, that vivacity that one sees at our balls in Warsaw. They dance the quadrille of the English and French.[3] The newly-married ladies are at the head of the lines; at the least difficulty they hasten to the table of laws and the *Managers* decide. After ten o'clock they play Washington's March; everybody goes to supper, or rather the ladies, and the gentlemen eat the remains. The table is set with chocolate, coffee, tea, cold meats, *custards*, etc. The ball continues afterwards up to one o'clock in the morning. . . .

The 22nd Feb. [1798]. Washington Ball. This morning all the ships were decked out with flags and there was a general salute from their guns. It was the celebration of Washington's birthday. Mr. Adams, now President, was invited to it. Piqued by the fact that his predecessor, no longer in office, should be fêted and more thought of than he who was now actually filling the role of President, Mr. Adams answered the *Managers* on the spot in an ill-tempered note, that he would not come. This incident shows well a little man, envious, and quick tempered. The celebration was held in the *Circus*.[4] It is a rotunda painted horribly from top to bottom. The gray and black colors absorb completely the light from the hundreds of candles suspended in iron rings. The dress of the women in white and plumes, very elegant though it might be, did not appear in this gray light to an advantage. The musicians were on a little platform in the middle. Ropes radiating from the center partitioned the whole circumference into eight segments. It was within these partitions where one danced. No one was ill at ease but neither were they gay. Only

---

Julian Ursyn Niemcewicz, *Under Their Vine and Fig Tree: Travels through America in 1797–1799, 1805,* trans. and ed. Metchie J. E. Budka (Elizabeth, N.J.: Grassmann Pub. Co., 1965), 35, 44–46.

[3]A quadrille is related to a cotillion.

[4]Rickett's riding place, southwest corner Sixth and Chestnut Streets, which Washington called the "Pantheon" and which subsequently burned.

the Ambassadress of Portugal wore diamonds. The eyes of Mrs. Law née Custis, granddaughter of Mrs. Washington, shone far more brightly. . . .

Prudery. The 28 Feb. [1798] I was at a ball of Cl. Yruxo (Don Carlos de Irujo), the Spanish Minister. The women were dressed in everything of the very finest, in gauze, fine muslin, flowers, ribbons, and above all hoops and fringes of silver and ostrich plumes. This is indeed the height of luxury and the ruin of a good many husbands. How many barrels of flour and salt meat are necessary to clothe one of these ladies. What was most noteworthy at the fête were two busts of Venus de Medici and of Antinoüs, copies of ancient sculpture placed in two niches in the ballroom. On entering the hall we found them already covered with two cloaks of Indian muslin. The chaste eyes of our ladies were still offended. They were satisfied only when on top of the muslin the poor divinities were decked out with two blankets. I do not know whether covering them with such care is proof of much innocence.

14 Francis Hopkinson, Composer and Statesman

The versatile Francis Hopkinson (1737–1791) of Philadelphia, was a musician, statesman, lawyer, writer, artist, and inventor. He played the harpsichord and devised a new method for quilling the instrument. He was also the composer who is generally credited with leaving us the earliest surviving American secular composition, the song *My Days Have Been So Wondrous Free*. A patriot and pamphleteer on good terms with Washington, Jefferson, and Franklin, he represented New Jersey in the Continental Congress in 1776, and signed the Declaration of Independence.

Hopkinson's *Seven Songs*—actually an eighth was added after the title page had been engraved—were modeled on English compositions, among them pieces by Thomas Arne, popular composer of many stage works and song collections. Hopkinson wrote his own texts. Each song is set in two parts, melody and bass, with preludes that consistently begin with the first phrase of the sung melody. The songs are strophic, and the text setting is generally syllabic. The harpsichordist is expected to fill in the missing parts, much as one would realize a figured bass (there are no figures).

In his dedication to Washington, Hopkinson claims the credit "of being the first Native of the United States who has produced a Musical Composition." On the face of it, this is an exaggeration, but if we read the phrase to mean secular pieces, the statement is probably true.

On receiving a presentation copy of *Seven Songs*, George Washington wrote a letter to Hopkinson from Mount Vernon, dated February 5, 1789:

> I am sure that your productions would have had at least virtue enough in them (without the aid of voice or instrument) to soften the Ice of the Delaware & Potomack . . . what, alas! can I do to support it?—I can neither sing one of the songs, nor raise a single note on any instrument to convince the unbelieving.—But I have, however, one argument which will prevail with persons of true taste (at least in America)—I can tell them that *it is the production of Mr. Hopkinson*.*

Hopkinson's "A Camp Ballad" and his ode for the Fourth of July 1788 show the composer in his patriotic vein. "Make room for America, another great nation," he writes; "And let the people's motto ever be, / United thus, and thus united—FREE."

---

*Harold Milligan, preface to *The First American Composer: 6 Songs by Francis Hopkinson* (Boston: A. Schmidt, 1918), preface.

FRANCIS HOPKINSON

from *Seven Songs for the Harpsichord or Forte Piano* (1788)

To His Excellency
George Washington, Esquire

SIR,

I EMBRACE, with heart-felt satisfaction, every opportunity that offers of recognizing the personal Friendship that hath so long subsisted between us. The present Occasion allows me to do this in a manner most flattering to my Vanity; and I have accordingly taken advantage of it, by presenting this Work to your Patronage, and honouring it with your Name.

It cannot be thought an unwarrantable anticipation to look up to you as seated in the most dignified situation that a grateful People can offer. The universally avowed Wish of America, and the Nearness of the Period in which that Wish will be accomplished, sufficiently justify such an Anticipation; from which arises a confident Hope, that the same Wisdom and Virtue which has so successfully conducted the Arms of the United States in Times of Invasion, War, and Tumult, will prove also the successful Patron of Arts and Sciences in Times of national Peace and Prosperity; and that the Glory of America will rise conspicuous under a Government designated by the *Will*, and an Administration sounded in the *Hearts* of THE PEOPLE.

With respect to the little work, which I have now the honour to present to your notice, I can only say that it is such as a Lover, not a Master, of the Arts can furnish. I am neither a profess'd Poet, nor a profess'd Musician; and yet venture to appear in those characters united; for which, I confess, the censure of Temerity may justly be brought against me.

If these Songs should not be so fortunate as to please the *young* Performers, for whom they are intended, they will at least not occasion much Trouble in learning to perform them; and this will, I hope, be some Alleviation of their Disappointment.

However small the Reputation may be that I shall derive from this Work, I cannot, I believe, be refused the Credit of being the first Native of the United States who has produced a Musical Composition. If this attempt should not be too severely treated, others may encourage to venture on a path, yet untrodden in America, and the Arts in succession will take root and flourish amongst us.

I hope for your honourable Acceptance of this Mark of my Affection and Respect, and have the Honour to be

Your Excellency's most obedient, and
Most humble Servant,
F. HOPKINSON
PHILADELPHIA,
Nov. 20th, 1788

Song I

COME, fair Rosina, come away,
Long since stern Winter's storms have ceas'd;
See! Nature, in her best array,
Invites us to her rural Feast:
The Season shall her treasures spread,
Her mellow fruits and harvests brown,
Her flowers their richest odours shed,
And ev'ry breeze pour fragrance down.

At noon we'll seek the wild wood's shade,
And o'er the pathless verdure rove;
Or, near a mossy fountain laid,
Attend the music of the grove;
At eve, the sloping mead invites
'Midst lowing herds and flocks to stray;
Each hour shall furnish new delights,
And Love and Joy shall crown the day.

Francis Hopkinson, *Seven Songs for the Harpsichord or Forte Piano* (Philadelphia: Thomas Dobson, 1788), [Dedication], 1, 3–4.

Song III

BENEATH a weeping willow's shade
She sat and sang alone;
Her hand upon her heart she laid
And plaintive was her moan.
The mock-bird sat upon a bough
And list'ned to her lay,
Then to the distant hills he bore
The dulcet notes away.

Earth ne'er produc'd a gem so rare,
Nor wealthy ocean's ample space
So rich a pearl—as that bright tear
That lingers on Maria's face.
So hangs upon the morning rose
The chrystal drop of heav'n refin'd,
Awhile with trembling lustre glows—
Is gone—and leaves no stain behind.

Fond Echo to her strains reply'd,
The winds her sorrows bore;
Adieu! dear youth—adieu! she cry'd,
I ne'er shall see thee more.
The mock-bird sat upon a bough
And list'ned to her lay,
Then to the distant hills he bore
The dulcet notes away.

A Camp Ballad

Make room, oh! ye kingdoms in hist'ry renowned
Whose arms have in battle with glory been
    crown'd,
Make room for America, another great nation,
Arises to claim in your council a station.

Her sons fought for freedom, and by their own
    brav'ry
Have rescued themselves from the shackles of
    slav'ry,
America's free, and tho' Britain abhor'd it,
Yet fame a new volume prepares to record it.

Fair freedom in Briton her throne had erected,
But her sons growing venal, and she disrespected;

The goddess offended forsook the base nation,
And fix'd on our mountains a more honour'd
    station.

With glory immortal she here sits enthron'd,
Nor fears the vain vengeance of Britain disown'd,
Whilst Washington guards her with heroes
    surrounded,
Her foes shall with shameful defeat be
    confounded.

To arms then, to arms, 'tis fair freedom invites us;
The trumpet shrill sounding to battle excites us;
The banners of virtue unfurl'd, shall wave o'er us
Our hero lead on, and the foe fly before us.

On heav'n and Washington placing reliance,
We'll meet the bold Britton, and bid him
    defiance:
Our cause we'll support, for 'tis just and 'tis
    glorious,
When men fight for freedom they must be
    victorious.

An Ode for the 4th of July 1788

OH for a muse of fire! to mount the skies
And to a list'ning world proclaim—
Behold! Behold! an empire rise!
An Era new, Time, as he flies,
Hath enter'd in the book of fame.
On Alleghany's tow'ring head
Echo shall stand—the tidings spread,
And o'er the lakes, and misty floods around,
AN ERA NEW resound.

See! where Columbia sits alone,
And from her star-bespangled throne,
Beholds the gay procession move along,
And hears the trumpet, and the choral song—
She hears her sons rejoice—
Looks into future times, and sees
The num'rous blessings Heav'n decrees,
And with HER plaudit joins the gen'ral voice.

Francis Hopkinson, "A Camp Ballad," in *The Miscellaneous Essays and Occasional Writings of Francis Hopkinson, Esq.* (Philadelphia: Thomas Dobson, 1792), 3:174–75.

Francis Hopkinson, *An Ode for the 4th of July 1788*, (Philadelphia: 1788), broadside.

"Tis done! tis done! my Sons," she cries,
"In War are valiant, and in Council wise;
Wisdom and *Valour* shall my rights defend,
And o'er my vast domain those rights extend.
Science shall flourish—*Genius* stretch her wing,
In native Strains *Columbian Muses* sing;
Wealth crown the *Arts*, and *Justice* clean her scales;
Commerce her pond'rous anchor weigh,
Wide spread her sails,
And in far distant seas her flag display."

"My sons for *Freedom* fought, nor fought in vain;
But found a naked goddess was their gain:
Good government alone, can shew the Maid,
In robes of SOCIAL HAPPINESS array'd."

Hail to this festival! all hail the day!
Columbia's standard on her roof display:
And let the PEOPLE'S Motto ever be,
"UNITED THUS, AND THUS UNITED—FREE."

Alexander Reinagle

The career of Alexander Reinagle (1756–1809), an important musician of the Federal period, exemplifies what it meant to eke out a living in early America. Born in England, he came to the United States in 1786.

In New York, Reinagle gave concerts as a pianist, cellist, and vocalist. He was soon drawn to Philadelphia, where he presented successful concerts. In 1791, he teamed up with comic star Thomas Wignell (c. 1753–1803), himself an English émigré, to form a theatrical company in a new theater to be built on Chestnut Street. The New Company, as it was called, gave regular seasons in Philadelphia and Baltimore, beginning February 2, 1793, and Reinagle was its music director until his death. The company emphasized works from England, for which Reinagle composed or arranged the music.

Reinagle's activities ran the gamut of a professional musician's activities at the time. He gave concerts, taught pupils, worked with a theater company, and both published and sold music. In 1787, he began a fruitful relationship with a Scot, John Aitken (c. 1745–1831), America's first publisher of secular music. Reinagle's *A Selection of the Most Favorite Scots Tunes* appeared that year, and other pieces by the composer followed.

The anonymous article below points out the variety of activities for which Reinagle was known and by which he made his living. His unfinished oratorio, *Paradise Lost* (itself now lost), is mentioned, but his other serious works, such as his four unpublished piano sonatas written between 1786 and 1794, are not.

Boston's *Euterpeiad; or, Musical Intelligencer*, second among America's early literary journals devoted to music, was edited during its run from April 1820 to March 1823 by Boston music dealer and publisher John Rowe Parker (1777–1844). It served as an important model for some 350 American music magazines published during the nineteenth century.

"Mr. Reinagle" (1822)

Pianiste and composer, was born in Portsmouth, England, and commenced his early career in Scotland, where he received instructions in both the theory and practice of music from that scientific and valuable man Mr. Taylor, whose professional biography has already been noticed, and who at that time visited Scotland.[1]

Mr. Reinagle pursued the art with uncommon vigour, and paid at least two visits to the European

Euterpeiad; or, Musical Intelligencer, and Ladies' Gazette (January 19, 1822): 170–71.

[1]Rayner Taylor (1745–1825) also emigrated to America and was active in Philadelphia's musical life from 1793. One story has it that Taylor tossed his hat into Handel's grave.

continent for improvement; once for the sole purpose of hearing the great Bach,[2] whose extemporizing was reckoned among the wonders of the age.

Upon peace being concluded between America and Great Britain at the close of the revolutionary war, he emigrated to this country; spending some time in New York, but eventually settling in Philadelphia as a teacher of music, in which capacity he was employed by the most respectable families and the principal boarding schools in or near the city.

Not only the fashionable songs from England, as he received them, but others of a higher quality, and even Italian airs, did he arrange, in an easy and familiar style so as to make them attainable by his pupils. He also arranged several melodies with easy, yet very pleasing and rather showy variations, or made them into short rondos. These efforts, as few at that day gave sufficient attention to music to sing with a separate accompaniment, or to play a sonata, were highly laudable, inasmuch as it was introducing his students to at least some knowledge of celebrated authors, and gradually leading them into a love of good compositions, with which otherwise, they could not become acquainted. He also made a coalition of such talents as the city then afforded, and held subscription concerts every winter. Subsequently, he relinquished teaching, and joined Mr. Wignell[3] in the erection of the late elegant new theatre in Philadelphia. Mr. Reinagle, as a musical man, was anxious that their theatre should possess a complete orchestra, and also operatic performers, which his exertions accomplished; and this splendid edifice opened in 1791 with a band of several violins—two each of flutes, oboes, horns and bassoons, with trumpets and kettle drums, together with a grand piano forte and organ.[4] This collection gave for the first time, a full and complete orchestra to the American public and was the means of introducing the high talents of Gillingham and Menell, or Mrs. Oldmixon and

Miss Broadhurst for the gratification of the lovers of music.[5] Thus it will be readily perceived, that it is to Mr. Reinagle we are so much indebted for many improvements in musical acquirements.

His style of playing the piano forte, was peculiarly his own. He never aimed at excessive execution, but there was a sweetness of manner, nay, in the way he touched the instrument I might add, there was a sweetness of tone which, combined with exquisite taste and neatness, produced unusual feelings of delight.

His powers on the violin, though not equal to the latter, were nevertheless of the same nature. He could also take a part in a band on the flute, the trumpet, or violoncello.

As an author, both his style and subject were always rich and melodious. The songs of "I have a silent sorrow"—"Rosa"—"Cousin John" fully establish his character as a composer. To these might be added, his little book of lessons for young beginners, which has been in constant use for nearly thirty years and pronounced by numbers of experienced teachers to be the best work extant for that purpose. Many editors have republished it, and several have pilfered copiously from it, both in America and England.

During the latter years of his life, he was ardently engaged in composing music to parts of Milton's Paradise Lost, which he did not live to complete. It was intended to be performed in the oratorio style, except, that instead of recitatives, the best speakers were to be engaged in reciting the intermediate passages.

With a mind, well stored equally with various attainments and professional knowledge—with a disposition mild, amiable and conciliating—with manners bland, polished and engaging—an imagination lively and accurate—and a heart formed for tenderness and the charities of the world. Mr. Reinagle resigned his life at Baltimore in the year 1810.[6]

---

[2]Carl Philip Emanuel Bach.

[3]Thomas Wignell.

[4]No strings are mentioned.

[5]Wignell recruited these musicians while on a trip to London late in 1791. George Gillingham led the orchestra, and the company opened in February 1793.

[6]Recent sources give the date as 1809.

16 The Gospel Labors of Richard Allen

In 1784, Old St. George's Methodist Church in Philadelphia licensed two black men to preach, Absalom Jones and Richard Allen, the first African Americans so licensed by the Methodist Church in the United States. Black membership grew and, with it, increasing resentment among the whites. Eventually, the blacks splintered away to form the African Episcopal Church of St. Thomas, which was dedicated on July 17, 1794.

Richard Allen (1760–1831), a former slave, remained so uncomfortable with Episcopalianism, that he, in turn, led a group of followers to form yet another Methodist church, the African Methodist Episcopal Church (AME), which was dedicated on July 29, 1794. In the passage below, Allen rationalizes his allegiance to Methodism and describes the founding of this congregation.

Allen set about collecting hymns that he felt would have special appeal for his followers. His *Collection of Spiritual Songs and Hymns* of 1801 was the first book by a black author assembled for a black congregation. It consists of fifty-four hymn texts, without tunes, drawn from Dr. Watts, the Wesleys, the Baptists, and other sources, undoubtedly including church members and Allen himself. A unique feature of the book is what has been called a "wandering refrain": extra refrain verses or short choruses that are attached, seemingly at random, to hymn stanzas.

The two hymns below conclude with the same refrain: an affirmation of praise that is general enough to make sense for both texts. Undoubtedly memorized by Allen's congregation, the refrain might have served as a group response to one or more singers articulating the stanza, in a call-and-response performance. What Allen tells us about preaching was surely also true about music making: "Sure am I that reading sermons will never prove so beneficial to the colored people as spiritual or extempore preaching."

RICHARD ALLEN

from *The Life, Experience, and Gospel Labors* (c. 1793; PUB. 1887)

The Methodists were the first people that brought glad tidings to the colored people. I feel thankful that ever I heard a Methodist preach. We are beholded to the Methodists, under God, for the light of the Gospel we enjoy; for all other denominations preached so high-flown that we were not able to comprehend their doctrine. Sure am I that reading sermons will never prove so beneficial to the colored people as spiritual or extempore preaching. I am well convinced that the Methodist has proved beneficial to thousands and ten times thousands. It is to be awfully feared that the simplicity of the Gospel that was among them fifty years ago, and that they conform more to the world and the fashions thereof, they would fare very little better than the people of the world. The discipline is altered considerably from what it was. We would ask for the good old way, and desire to walk therein.

In 1793 a committee was appointed from the African Church to solicit me to be their minister, for there was no colored preacher in Philadelphia but myself.[1] I told them I could not accept of their offer, as I was a Methodist. I was indebted to the Methodists, under God, for what little religion I had; being convinced that they were the people of God, I informed them that I could not be anything else but a Methodist, as I was born and awakened under them, and I could go no further with them, for I was a Methodist, and would leave you in peace and love. I would do nothing to retard them in building a church as it was an extensive building, neither would I go out with a subscription paper until they were done going out with their subscription. I bought an old frame that had been formerly occupied as a blacksmith shop, from Mr. Sims, and hauled it on the lot in Sixth near Lombard street, that had formerly been taken for the Church of England. I employed carpenters to repair the old frame, and fit it for a place of worship. In July 1794, Bishop Asbury[2] being in town I solicited him to open the church for us which he accepted.[3] The Rev. John Dickins sung and prayed, and Bishop Asbury preached. The house was called Bethel, agreeable to the prayer that was made. Mr. Dickins prayed that it might be a bethel to the gathering in of thousands of souls.[4] My dear Lord was with us, so that there was many hearty "amen's" echoed through the house. This house of worship has been favored with the awakening of many souls, and I trust they are in the Kingdom, both white and colored.

Richard Allen, *The Life Experience and Gospel Labors of the Rt. Rev. Richard Allen* (Philadelphia: Lee and Yeocum, 1887), 19–20.

[1]Actually, Absalom Jones was licensed in the same year as Allen, also by Old St. George's; Jones remained pastor of the newly formed African Episcopal Church of St. Thomas.

[2]Francis Asbury (1745–1816), the first bishop of the Methodist Episcopal Church consecrated in America; born in England, lived in America after 1771.

[3]This church will at present accommodate between 3,000 and 4,000 persons. [Allen's note.]

[4]In a footnote, Allen refers to Genesis 28:17–19, "This is none other but the house of God, and this is the gate of heaven. And Jacob rose up early in the morning, and took the stone that he had put for his pillows, and set it up for a pillar, and poured oil upon the top of it. And he called the name of that place Bethel."

RICHARD ALLEN, ED.

Two Hymns (1801)

Hymn I

THE voice of Free Grace cries, escape to the
mountain,
For Adam's lost race, Christ hath open'd a
fountain,
For sin and transgression, and every pollution,
His blood it flows freely in plenteous redemption.

> Hallelujah to the Lamb who purchas'd our
> pardon,
> We'll praise him again when we pass over
> Jordan.

That fountain so clear, in which all may find
pardon,
From Jesus's side flows plenteous redemption;
Though your sins were increas'd as high as a
mountain,
His blood it flows freely in streams of salvation.

> Hallelujah to the Lamb, &c.

Oh! Jesus ride on, thy kingdom is glorious,
O'er sin, death and Hell, thou wilt make us
victorious:
Thy name shall be prais'd in the great
congregation,
And saints shall delight in ascribing salvation.

> Hallelujah to the Lamb, &c.

When on Zion we stand, having gain'd the blest
shore,
With our harps in our hands we'll praise him
evermore;
We'll range the blest fields on the bank of the
river,
And sing Hallelujah for ever and ever.

> Hallelujah to the Lamb, &c.

Hymn L

FROM regions of Love, lo! an Angel descended,
And told the strange news, how the Babe was
attended!
"Go Shepherds, and visit this wonderful Stranger,
"See yonder bright star—there's your God in a
manger."

> Hallelujah to the Lamb
> Who has purchas'd our pardon,
> We will praise him again
> When we pass over Jordan.

Glad tidings I bring unto you and each nation,
Glad tidings of Joy, now behold your salvation:
Then sudden a multitude raise their glad voices,
And shout the Redeemer, while Heaven rejoices.

> Hallelujah, &c.

Now glory to God in the highest is given,
Now glory to God, is re-echo'd thro' Heaven:
Around the whole earth let us tell the glad story,
And sing of his love, his salvation, and glory.

> Hallelujah, &c.

Enraptur'd I burn with delight and desire,
Such love, so divine, sets my soul all on fire:
Around the bright throne now hosannas are
ringing,
O, when shall I join them, and ever be singing?

> Hallelujah, &c.

Triumphantly ride in thy chariot victorious,
And conquer with love, O Jesu all-glorious:
Thy banners unfurl, let the nations surrender,
And own thee their Saviour, their God, and
Defender.

> Hallelujah to the Lamb
> Who has purchas'd our pardon,
> We will praise thee again
> When we pass over Jordan.

Richard Allen, *A Collection of Spiritual Songs and Hymns*
(Philadelphia: John Ormrod, 1801), [3]–4, 64–65.

17   American Tunebook Prefaces around 1800

Part of American music making from the beginning has been its relationship with European music, which at times was embraced and at other times defied. Music in America cannot be viewed as starting at the western edge of the Atlantic. What might be termed our "colonial sphere" has always been a part of our national artistic character.

Beginning in the early 1760s, the English on the East Coast began to include American-made sacred pieces in their tunebooks. The number of printed American compositions grew rapidly throughout the Revolutionary period.

About 1805, however, America took a right turn—right back to Europe. Reformers, under leadership of the clergy, who preferred the tried and true, decried native efforts and directed American attention abroad. We should learn European music written with "correct" taste, they said. We must emulate European models in our compositions if appropriate progress is to be made.

American tunebook prefaces from around 1800 reflect the tenor of the times. They nearly always include an apologia for the lack of musical training and culture on these shores. For example, Jacob Kimball wrote in 1793: "In a country where music has not yet become a regular profession, it cannot be expected that a composition of this kind can stand a rigid criticism." This sentiment is echoed across the period. Hezekiah Moors wrote in 1809: "In a country where Musick has not yet become a regular calling, it cannot be expected that a Composition of this kind can stand an inflexible criticism."

These prefaces speak of a lack of good models (presumably English), of insufficient vocal training, and of the proliferation in America of inferior compositions. Yet they carry the sense that "improvement" is under way, as one seeks the goal of "correct" musical taste. As Daniel Read put it in 1806, "Fashions are continually changing." Elias Mann spoke of the "daily improvement of taste in sacred music" (see below).

Fuging tunes, printed here in large numbers between 1760 and 1800, came in for particular ridicule. Samuel Holyoke's 1791 comments about fuging tunes, that "the parts, falling in, one after another . . . render the performance a mere jargon of words," were echoed almost word for word by Joel Harmon eighteen years later. Ironically, the concept of the fuging tune actually came from England, a country whose "correct taste" it was hoped American composers would emulate. Unlike English models, however, which were more varied, a single, uniform type developed in the United States. It consisted of a closed homophonic section of two to four lines, followed by a polyphonic one.

SAMUEL HOLYOKE

Preface to *Harmonia Americana* (1791)

THE advantages for studying the principles of harmony, being, in this country, so limited, it cannot be expected that a composition of this nature can stand the test of criticism. This circumstance considered, it is hoped that candid allowances will be made in the perusal of the following sheets, which are respectfully submitted to the public eye.

With respect to the design of the composition, it may be observed, that it is adapted, as far as possible, to the rules of pronunciation. Consequently, the music requires a moderate movement; for it is very difficult to follow the exact motion of the pendulum, and pronounce with that propriety and elegance, which the importance of the subject may *demand*. It may then be proper here to remark, that sentiment and expression ought to be the principal guide in vocal music.

Perhaps some may be disappointed, that fuging pieces are in general omitted. But the principal reason why few were inserted was the trifling effect produced by that sort of music; for the parts, falling in, one after another, each conveying a different idea, confound the sense, and render the performance a mere jargon of words. The numerous pieces of this kind, extant, must be a sufficient apology for omitting them here.

Samuel Holyoke, *Harmonia Americana* (Boston: Isaiah Thomas & Ebenezer T. Andrews, 1791),[4].

OLIVER HOLDEN

Preface to *American Harmony* (1792)

When the following pieces of Music were composed, it was not the intention of the Author to make them public; and no motive could have induced him to do it, but the request and patronage of his friends.

He is conscious that, in point of composition, they will not bear the test of criticism, especially with those whose advantages for acquiring the knowledge of so nice an art, have been greatly superior to those of the Author; but with a view to increase his own knowledge, and an humble reliance on the candour of the public, he has presumed to let them appear.

With respect to the manner of performing the Music, the Author wishes that the time in general might be slow, and the strains soft. Doubtless singing Choirs, in general, are too inattentive to these important parts of Music. By hurrying a piece of Music, performers are more likely to sing harsh; in consequence of which, good pronunciation is lost. To remedy this, it is necessary that the words be read, and the subject be well understood by every performer, before the notes are applied: In so doing, the importance of the words will become the surest guide.

Should this work continue to meet a favourable reception, additions will hereafter be made of such pieces of Music as will be calculated for divine Worship.

Charlestown, September 27, 1792

Oliver Holden, *American Harmony* (Boston: Isaiah Thomas and Ebenezer T. Andrews, 1792), [2].

WILLIAM COOPER
Preface to *The Beauties of Church Music* (1804)

The motives which induced the Compiler to publish this Collection of *The Beauties of Church Music,* arose from a conviction, that a book intended for the instruction of schools, should be perfectly correct in point of composition, in order that the learner may form his taste and establish his principles upon a system which is never departed from. Our present collections contain a medley of good and bad tunes, in continual contradiction to each other in point of composition, which leave no criterion whereby to determine the right from the wrong, and tend to involve genius in perplexity and error. Agreeably to the design of the Compiler, in this collection, he has been under the necessity of either excluding some pieces of music which he highly esteems, or to make some little alterations in the harmony. He has preferred the latter. They are now submitted to the public. To those persons to whom these alterations appear necessary and correct, no apology will be wanting; toward those who think differently, the Compiler has good nature enough to allow them the enjoyment of their opinions, without retracting his own till he is further enlightened.

It has become a general opinion among good singers, that the music in use before the revolution in 1775, is much better than that which has succeded. As the Compiler must confess, that he did as much as lay in his power, to produce this lamentable revolution in music, in contempt of the opinion of his fathers of better taste, he thinks it his duty in this selection to restore some of that music, which experience has taught him contains every thing that is beautiful in point of composition, delightful to the hearer; and which, above all, is calculated, from its solemnity and dignity, to raise our devout affections to Heaven.

William Cooper, *The Beauties of Church Music* (Boston: Manning & Loring, 1806), [iii].

From Preface to *The Salem Collection of Classical Sacred Musick* (1805)

It is a fact no less singular than undeniable, that while our country has produced very few authors of that kind of musick which for distinction's sake, may be called *profane* (by which we mean every species except *psalmody*) it has swarmed with men who have announced themselves as composers of *Sacred* Musick; and while the whole Union has scarcely afforded so much as a *song* of distinguished merit, almost every village has been able to boast of its original *anthems* and *oratorios*. Whether this has arisen from the peculiar genius of our musical composers—or from the fear of more certain detection and exposure in the one case than the other—or from a reliance on that well-meaning spirit of charity which has disposed Christian societies to admit into their service the productions of any author, who presents himself to them in a pious garb and with honest motives—it is not now material to inquire: the consequence is the same from any of these causes, in a country where the best *models* of composition are yet scarcely known; and it has been, what we blush to confess, a general and most deplorable corruption of taste in our church musick.

The present publication owes its existence to a long and serious reflection upon this humiliating fact; a fact which cannot fail of being the subject of

The Salem Collection of Classical Sacred Musick (Salem, Mass.: Joshua Cushing, 1805), [iii]–vi.

deep regret with every lover of harmony, as well as with the serious professor of Christianity; for it cannot be denied, that most of our modern psalmody is not less offensive to a correct musical taste, than it is disgusting to the sincere friends of publick devotion. . . .

Though the tunes here given to the publick may perhaps be found in the different compilations already made, yet they are so much dispersed, and so deeply buried under the crudities of half-learned harmonists, that a collection of them into one volume became in some measure requisite, as the first step to the speedy attainment of the desirable objects above mentioned:[1] for, in order to correct our taste in musick, as in the sister arts, we must, in the first place, have within our reach, and constantly before us, the best *models*; and not till after long contemplation of these, and unwearied study and labour, can we expect to see much progress made towards a reformation.[2]

---

[1]That is, "promoting a just taste in psalmody, as well as to further the purposes of publick devotion."

[2]We take pleasure in mentioning, as an honourable exception to these general remarks on the bad taste in our sacred music, the *Massachusett Compiler,* printed at Boston in 1795; and perhaps a few other Collections of some merit might be found [author's note].

Here the inquiry naturally presents itself— Why has the *ancient psalmody* fallen into such disrepute among us? On this subject we think the remarks of Dr. Miller so pertinent, that we cannot forbear introducing them.[3] As late as the year 1790 that author makes the same complaint of the neglect shown to the *antient melodies* in England. . . .

And yet how few societies do we find, where any but a professed singer is able to follow the choir through the rambling tunes that are now in common use! . . .

Before we quit the subject of the performance of church musick, we beg the reader's indulgence while we say one word upon the distribution of the *parts* of the tunes. It has been the usual practice to give the *leading part*, or *air*, under the denomination of *tenor*, to the *men's voices*. We think we are warranted by the authority of the most eminent composers (certainly by the authority of common sense, and of analogy in *instrumental* musick) in strongly urging that the *air* should be performed by *treble* voices.

---

[3]Edward Miller, Mus. Doc. [Author's note, refers to the English organist, composer, and author Edward Miller (1731–1807), who received his Mus.D. from Cambridge University in 1786.]

ELIAS MANN

Preface to *The Massachusetts Collection of Sacred Harmony* (1807)

The Compiler of this Work is decidedly of opinion with many of his musical friends, that the daily improvement of taste in sacred music calls for a collection which shall meet the wishes of the public, and promote correctness, simplicity, and sentiment, in this part of devotion.

Elias Mann, *The Massachusetts Collection of Sacred Harmony* (Boston: Manning and Loring, for the author, 1807), [iii].

In this Collection will be found none of those wild fugues, and rapid and confused movements, which have so long been the disgrace of congregational psalmody, and the contempt of the judicious and tasteful amateur. If the Compiler should be so fortunate as to lend any material aid, by the present Work, to the cause of reformation, he shall confidently expect the approbation and patronage of those who wish to share in this interesting part of public worship.

18 Andrew Law, Psalmodist

A major figure among the reformers, Andrew Law (1749–1821) clearly came down on the side of European music. The dedication to his *Musical Primer* states unequivocally: "Much of the music in vogue is miserable indeed. . . . The dignity and the ever varying vigor of Handel, of Madan, and of others, alike meritorious, are, in a great measure, supplanted by the pitiful productions of numerous composuists [*sic*], whom it would be doing too much honor to name."

In 1803, in a new edition of his comprehensive collection, *The Art of Singing*, Law advocated a staffless shape-notation that he had devised. Making it clear that his aim was to "correct" and "perfect" the taste in music, Law hoped to intrigue a wider public into the golden realm of better performance of better music. "Indeed there is nothing that will justify turning aside from the old way, unless it be, to walk in a new one, which is decidedly better." His promise was typically American—greater reward for less effort. Law, the teacher, sought "to take the bewildered learner, and conduct him along a smooth and gradual ascent in his way towards the summit of taste and general performance."

Law graduated from Rhode Island College (Brown University) in 1775 and immediately advertised himself as a singing master. Although he soon was studying theology and was eventually ordained into the ministry, his first love was music, and he pursued it as his main life's work. He traveled widely, using his published tunebooks in his classes. By the time he unveiled a new notational scheme in *The Art of Singing*, he could lean upon "more than twenty years experience" to support his argument. Indeed, the total collection, organized pedagogically from easy to hard, shows an experienced teacher at work.

Law's experiment in staffless notation, rather than being widely accepted, actually limited his cause. The Boston *Euterpeiad* rendered its judgment in 1820; "We cannot discover any advantage resulting from this system of notation."

Law's belief that works by American-born composers were crude and inferior served his need to reform and to teach. While doing so, however, he was the first to print a number of compositions by psalmodists from Connecticut and Massachusetts. His life story helps us define what it meant to be a professional musician at that time in America.

ANDREW LAW
from *The Art of Singing* (1803)

Dedication

To the Ministers of the Gospel, and the Singing Masters, Clerks and Choristers throughout the United States.

GENTLEMEN,

THE following work is addressed to you. It claims your candid and thorough perusal. It exhibits an Introductory Treatise and an Elementary Scale, possessing, it is believed, improvements of real and permanent worth; and it also presents specimens of that chaste and sober, that sublime and solemn Psalmody, which the friends of religion and virtue, as well as the friends of sacred song, would rejoice to see more generally improved in worshipping assemblies.

It will not, perhaps, have escaped the observation of any one of you, that very much of the music in vogue is miserable indeed. Hence the man of piety and principle, of taste and discernment in music, and hence, indeed, all, who entertain a sense of decency and decorum in devotion, are oftentimes offended with the lifeless and insipid, or that frivolous and frolicksome succession and combination of sounds, so frequently introduced into churches, where all should be serious, animated and devout; and hence the dignity and the ever varying vigor of Handel, of Madan,[1] and of others, alike meritorious, are, in a great measure, supplanted by the pitiful productions of numerous composuists, whom it would be doing too much honor to name. Let any one acquainted with the sublime and beautiful compositions of the great Masters of Music, but look round within the circle of his own acquaintance, and he will find abundant reason for these remarks.

The evil is obvious. Much of the predominating Psalmody of this country is more like song singing, than like solemn praise. It rests with you, Gentlemen, to apply the remedy. The work of reformation is arduous, but not impracticable, and the more difficult the task, the more praise worthy the accomplishment.

I will further add, that there are no description[s] of citizens in the community, who have it in their power to do half as much, as you, towards correcting and perfecting the taste in music, and towards giving to devotional praise its due effect upon our lives and conversation.

The cause of religion and virtue has therefore a claim upon your exertions. What remains then, but that every one who is convinced of the want, begin the work? Individual exertions, rendered unexceptionable, become universal, and the business is ended.

That you may criticise with the keenness and candor of real masters of music, and correct with the courage and conduct of irresistable reformers, is all that the fondest friends of sacred music would ask or wish; and if the following Book be found but an individual's mite, towards promoting so noble an undertaking as that, of improving the religious praise of a rising Empire, it will never become a subject of regret to one, who has devoted up the greater part of his life to the cultivation of Psalmody, and who is,

With all proper Respects,
THE AUTHOR

Advertisement

THIS Book exhibits a New Plan of printing Music. Four kinds of characters are used; and are situated between the single bars that divide the time, in the same manner as if they were on lines and spaces; and in every instance, where two char-

---

Andrew Law, *The Art of Singing, In Three Parts: I. The Musical Primer. II. The Christian Harmony. III. The Musical Magazine.* 4th ed. (Cambridge, Mass.: W. Hilliard, 1803), [3]–4, [5]–6, [9]–10, 22–23.

[1]English composer Martin Madan (1726–1790).

acters of the same figure occur, their situations mark, perfectly, the height and distance of their sounds; and every purpose is effected without the assistance of lines.

These four kinds of characters also, denote the four syllables, mi, faw, sol, law, which are used in singing. The diamond, has the name of mi; the square, of faw; the round, of sol; and the quarter of a diamond, of law.

The letters F and G, are used for cliffs.[2]

The letter R, is used for the repeat.

The long stroke of the Crotchet[3] is thrown out of this system, and the round part of it is the crotchet; the old crotchet, is the quaver;[4] and the old quaver, is the semiquaver.[5]

A few lessons are marked with figures over or under the notes, which show the degrees of the key.

A Book that may be obtained with little expence, and be suitable for learners at their first setting out, is frequently called for; such an one is the Musical Primer, the first part of the Art of Singing, independent of the rest of the work. The rules comprised in it are explained with the utmost conciseness and simplicity; and if the learner, upon perusing them and practizing upon the additional lessons and tunes, finds that he is like to succeed as a singer, he may safely venture to purchase other music; if not, he may relinquish his book and his undertaking together, without much loss of time or money.

Preface [to Part 1]

IN compiling the First Part of the following work, or the Musical Primer, I have endeavoured to compose an elementary system, which might open, at once, an improved pathway to the practise of music. I could not be at a loss in supposing, that such an acquisition would be very acceptable to all classes of singers, and especially to those on whom

the business of teaching devolves, as well as to all learners, during the first stages of their progress. To encompass my object, I have withholden no improvements, which patient industry, aided by more than twenty years experience in studying and teaching vocal music, could bestow; and I flatter myself, that the friends of Psalmody will find my Musical Primer an easier, and more eligible Book for beginners, than any one that has heretofore appeared.

In the Introductory Treatise immediately following, a number of the most important things relating to vocal music, are concisely explained and clearly enforced. Others of equal, or superior importance appearing to require it, are more critically and copiously treated.

But it is the Scale of Rules with which the labor, the actual task of the learner, more immediately commences. To render this task as easy as possible, neither time nor attention have been spared. As the readiest way to effect the purpose proposed, appeal has been uniformly made to the reason and nature of my subject, as presented in theory and practice. For the scale which follows, is not the offspring of a short and solitary attention to theory alone. On the contrary, it forms the result of those gradual improvements produced by repeated reflection and reiterated trials in the school of experience. European Gamuts in the mean while have not been overlooked. On the other hand, I have ever examined them with care and deference; but at the same time, without thinking myself obliged to be implicitly guided by them, merely, because they were already is use. For a thousand things are in use, which ought not to be copied. Hence, wherever I have discovered, that alterations might be made for the better, I have not scrupled to introduce them; and for such as are most material, have explained my reasons at large. Should the Reader be inquisitive enough to examine them, I have only to ask, that he will do it thoroughly and fairly, and then judge for himself.

All music is not, at present, printed upon this Plan, and according to the Rules of this Scale; but all music might be thus printed, and by that very means, be improved in point of simplicity. In re-

---

[2]Clefs.

[3]Quarter note.

[4]Eighth note.

[5]Sixteenth note.

gard to the music which is contained in the several parts of the Art of Singing, the rules which are thrown out of this system, are not wanted; and as to any other music, it may, in all cases, be rendered more simple, than by transcribing them into the Plan of the Scale. If any one should, however, choose to consult other music, as it stands, he will find the necessary directions with it. It will then be soon enough for him to attend to the rules for that purpose, when he actually finds, that he shall want them. And his attending to them at such after period, will rather be an alleviation to him, than otherwise; for he will then, probably, have fewer things to distract and divide his mind, than at his first setting out. At any rate, his attending to them, later, or by themselves, can be no additional burthen to him; for whatever is thrown out of this system, is knit into the body of common systems; and by adverting to them, he will only advert to some old rules, which, if music were printed as it might be, would be utterly useless.—As to the Tunes introduced into the Primer, they are principally of a kind, the most simple, plain and easy; calculated, not to entertain the accomplished performer, who is delighted with nothing short of refined and delicate airs; but to take the bewildered learner, and conduct him along a smooth and gradual ascent in his way towards the summit of taste and graceful performance. And at the same time, will furnish a considerable variety of solemn Church music.

As soon as learners have paid sufficient attention to the Rules and Tunes in the Primer and are in want of other music, they may find a supply in the second Part of the Work, or Christian Harmony. A great part of the music it contains, consists, not of long Pieces, but of short tunes; not of nice and difficult, but of plain and easy performance. To a large proportion of music of this discription preference has been given; and the tunes themselves have been suited to an uncommonly great variety of metres, on purpose that it might the better be calculated for answering two very important objects, to wit, that it might be suitable for singing schools and all learners immediately after having used the Musical Primer, and, that it might be rendered extensively servicable to all Christian Churches in the solemn exercises of humble devotional praise. The set Pieces and more difficult compositions introduced will be acceptable to Choirs of singers, who have arrived to more considerable accuracy and skill in performance.

The Third Part of the Work, or the Musical Magazine, enlarges the number of favorite Pieces. It may therefore accommodate accomplished and well taught schools, as well as the curious, who are desirous of possessing some of the most elegant and refined compositions, European and American.

Mean while, the whole work, collectively taken, may be useful to all classes of singers. To recapitulate its contents, it opens with an explanation of elementary principles. In its progress, it comprises an extensive variety of Psalm Tunes and plain productions, proper for singing schools and the solemn praise of sabbath devotion; and it also includes an interspersion and addition of set pieces and Anthems, suitable for all ordinary and particular occasions of public solemnity.

* * *

A VIEW of the new PLAN of printing MUSIC, and of the new METHOD of teaching the ART of SINGING. Upon this plan and method the knowledge of the Art will be easily obtained; music will be read in a short time with great facility; and the performance of it will be ready and familiar. The natural consequence of this will be, that the cultivation of the art will become more general; and the practice of it will be rendered more pleasing and entertaining.

It is sincerely and ardently wished, that the introduction of it may be of public utility; that our Psalmody may be improved by it; and that our devout acts of praise may become more delightful to the people of God, and more pleasing in the sight of Him, Who is the proper object of all worship, adoration and praise.

PART II

The Nineteenth Century

19 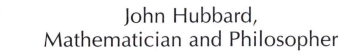 John Hubbard, Mathematician and Philosopher

In the early 1800s, Dartmouth College was a struggling institution. Established in Hanover, New Hampshire, under the leadership of the Rev. Eleazar Wheelock, it graduated its first class of four students in 1771. By the mid-1780s, its character was set as a men's college along English lines, educating its students in theology, teaching, medicine, or law. Bitter struggles between its second president, John Wheelock, son of the founder, and his board of trustees marred the Dartmouth atmosphere in the early 1800s. These difficulties erupted into both state and national politics and were not resolved until 1819 when "The Dartmouth Case" was argued successfully before the U.S. Supreme Court by Dartmouth graduate Daniel Webster. The decision reestablished the authority of the college and assured that it would remain a private institution.

John Hubbard (1759–1810), Dartmouth class of 1785, joined the Dartmouth faculty in 1805, during its difficult period, as professor of mathematics and natural philosophy. He remained there until his death. Hubbard, a scholar whose varied interests included music, was described by his student Nathaniel Gould (in *Church Music in America* [Boston, 1853]) as "a man of superior talent, knowledge and taste, in the science of music . . . at the time he lived, about the close of the last century, [he] had in his possession more means for acquiring a musical education than any other man in America, having more English publications and treatises on the science of music than any other individual."

In July 1807, Professor Hubbard and several undergraduates founded a new organization devoted to singing and studying sacred music, the Handel Society of Dartmouth College. Its constitution stated: "The object of this society shall be to cultivate true and genuine music, which is calculated to enkindle true devotion in the heart, and to discountenance that, which is trifling and unfinished." The Society prospered and continued until the early 1890s, only to be revived in the 1920s.

The weekly meetings of the Society, though centered on music making, were also social events. Frequently, they included an address. A talk in 1809 by Francis Brown, Dartmouth professor and later president of the College, underscored the Society's philosophy:

> Unhappily, the greater number of those in our country, who have undertaken to write music, have been ignorant of its nature. Their pieces have but little variety, and less meaning . . . Our best musicians, instead of being awakened to exertion by a call for splendid talents, have been discouraged by the increasing prevalence of a corrupt taste.*

---

*Francis Brown, *An Address on Music* (Hanover, N.H.: Charles and William Spear, 1810), 18–19.

The Dartmouth society, like its later cousin the Handel and Haydn Society of Boston, sprang from a rather narrow desire to "improve" musical taste on these shores by promoting the best traditions of European (principally English) music, as it understood them.

Nathaniel Gould became the first conductor of the Middlesex Musical Society, founded in 1805. Undoubtedly at his urging, his mentor, John Hubbard, was invited to deliver an address before the Society in September 1807. Hubbard seized the opportunity to lay out his ideals. He praised European composers, particularly Handel, while deprecating the Americans. The fuging tune came in for particular scorn. Hubbard's *Essay*, published the following year, became a major tract of musical reform.

JOHN HUBBARD

from *An Essay on Music* (1808)

To alleviate the innumerable calamities of human life, to soothe and calm the boisterous passions, to light up the emotions of love and friendship, to elevate and inspire the mind with true devotion, to give us some foretaste of those sublime pleasures enjoyed by the celestial choirs, is the office and effect of music:—

She, heavenly born, came down to earth,
When from God's eternal throne
The beam of all-creative wisdom shone,
And spake fair order into birth.
At wisdom's call, *she* rob'd yon glittering skies,
Attun'd the spheres, and taught consenting orbs to rise.
Angels wrapt in wonder stood,
And saw that all was fair, and all was good. . . .[1]

In treating upon music, we shall consider it both as an art and a science. As an art, it depends upon the powers, abilities, and genius of the writer. As an art, it cannot be limited, or restricted within any particular rules. The genius, the feelings, and the improved taste of mankind, must regulate every good writer. Like the painter, the sculptor, the architect and the poet, nature and propriety must direct the effusions of his mind. As a science, it is regulated by measure, harmony, cadence, accent, mode, etc. Science may invent good harmony, agreeable measure, flowing and easy cadence; but genius only can give force and energy to music.

We shall consider the essential part or divisions of music, as consisting of *melody, harmony, expression,* and *accent.* . . .

In the writers of music we find the same variety of style, as in poetry or prose, viz., the *sublime,* the *beautiful,* the *nervous,* the *concise,* the *dry,* and the *bombastic.*

Few writers have given us specimens of the sublime. Amongst these, Handel undoubtedly stands first.[2] His Grand Hallelujah, and his Chorus, "*Break forth into joy,*" in the Messiah, are excellent specimens of this style. Giardini[3] has

---

John Hubbard, *An Essay on Music* (Boston: Manning & Loring, 1808), 1, 4, 14–19.

[1]The Cure of Saul, a Sacred Ode, by Dr. Brown, Page 19. [Hubbard's note.] The English clergyman, writer, and amateur musician John Brown (1715–1766) wrote the libretto (London, 1763).

[2]"Handel stands eminent, in his greatness and sublimity of style." See Dr. Brown's dissertation on poetry and music. Page 214. [Hubbard's note refers to John Brown's *Dissertation on the Rise, Union, and Power, the Progressions, Separations, and Corruptions, of Poetry and Music* (London, 1763).]

[3]Italian violinist and composer Felice Giardini (1716–1796), who moved to England in 1750.

likewise given us some specimens in "Cambridge," especially on the words, "*Father, how wide thy glories shine,*" etc.; and on these, "*But when we view thy great designs,*" etc.[4] In performing such strains, the mind is lost in admiration. It is almost incapable of contemplating the great ideas thus presented. Like the sublime in nature, our astonishment incapacitates us for reflecting upon the object before our eyes. The sublime in music knows no medium. The writer who attempts this, must either reach sublimity, or sink to indifference. Sublime compositions must be simple, unstudied, expressive, and connected with some great and important idea.

The specimens we might produce of the *beautiful*, are very numerous. They ravish, they charm, they transport us beyond conception. In this style Handel is excellent. His air in the Messiah, "*I know that my Redeemer liveth,*" is perhaps, equal to any now extant. [Hubbard includes a music example.] Pergolesi, in his air, "*Eja, mater, fons amoris,*" in his "Stabat Mater," is beautiful beyond description. [Another music example.][5]

Passing over other styles, a discussion of which would afford very little amusement, we come to the *bombastic*. This style, in poetry and in prose, consists in attempting to magnify those subjects which are trifling or indifferent; or in using high sounding words and epithets without any great or noble ideas. In music it consists in laboured notes and strains, disconnected from any exalted ideas; or in attempting to communicate some low idea which cannot be expressed by notes. In this style, our unfortunate country has been peculiarly fruitful.[6] Almost every pedant, after learning his eight notes has commenced author. With a genius, sterile as the deserts of Arabia, he has attempted to rival the great masters of music. On the leaden wings of dullness, he has attempted to soar into those regions of science, never penetrated but by real genius. From such distempered imaginations, no regular productions can be expected. The unhappy writers, after torturing every note in the octave, have fallen into oblivion, and have generally outlived their insignificant works.[7] To the great injury of true religion, this kind of music has been introduced into our places of public worship. Devotion, appalled by its destructive presence, has fled from the unhallowed sound.

Among the most prominent faults of this style, we may reckon the common fuge [*sic*]. As the intention of vocal music is to communicate ideas, whatever renders those ideas indistinct or obscure, must be a perversion. Let us now examine music of the style last mentioned. We shall here find four parts, in harmonic order, each, at the same time, pronouncing different words. As a striking instance of this impropriety, we will mention a fuge in a piece of music called "Montague."[8] Beginning at the Bass, and proceeding up to the Treble, the bar, in the four parts, pronounced at the same time, will read thus; "*of brilliant light;*" "*Those spacious fields;*" "*Let the high heav'ns;*" and "*your songs invite.*" The four emphases will fall on the words, "*brilliant,*" "*spacious,*" "*the,*" and "*songs.*" [Music

---

[4]Were it necessary, we might exhibit several other instances of the sublime from A. Williams, from Dr. S. Arnold, H. Purcell, and many others. [Hubbard's note, referring to Aaron Williams, Samuel Arnold, and Henry Purcell, all English composers.]

[5]Many other examples might be produced from Dr. Arnold, from Worgan, Dr. Charles Burney, Millgrove, and others too numerous to mention. [Hubbard's note. Worgan is the London organist and composer John Worgan (1724–1790); Millgrove may be Benjamin Milgrove (1731–1810), presenter of the Countess of Huntington's Chapel at Bath.]

[6]This observation is not applicable to all the writers of music in this country. Several have composed music in an agreeable and appropriate style. Some have been so fortunate as to reach the sublime. [Hubbard's note.]

[7]No other proof of this fact need be adduced, than the ephemeral publications with which New England has been inundated. Many of these have never lived to see a second edition; and nearly all have become obsolete in a few years. Good music, good painting, good poetry, never grow old. [Hubbard's note.]

[8]*Montague* was one of the most popular fuging tunes in America. It appeared in about forty-five sources during the period 1783–1800.

example.][9] To catch any idea from such a chaos of words, uttered at the same instant of time, a hearer must be furnished with ears as numerous as the eyes of Argus.[10] Such fuges must be a perversion.[11] They cannot affect the heart, nor inform the understanding.[12] Though the performers may be admired for their dexterity, they can never excite any devout feelings in their hearers. Such music can never be of more consequence than an oration well pronounced in an unknown language.

But modern innovators have not stopped here. From the midnight revel, from the staggering bachanal, from the profane altar of Comus they have stolen the prostituted air, and, with sacrilegious hands, have offered it in the temple of JEHOVAH.[13] Such profanation must wound every feeling heart. Devotion ever assumes a dignity. It cannot delight in the tinkling bustle of unmeaning sounds.[14] The air of a catch, a glee, a dance, a march, or a common ballad is very improper for the worship of the MOST HIGH.[15]

As the taste and practice of music have a great influence on our religion and morals, every person is under the most solemn obligations to use all his exertions for the suppression of that which is improper. "Let me," said Voltaire, "write the common ballads for any nation, and I will make their religion what I please." If the common songs of a nation can thus influence their religion, how much more their sacred music? Many respectable clergymen in New England, have been almost determined to omit music in public worship. To their great sorrow, they have observed, that the effects of a most solemn discourse were often obliterated, by closing with improper music. We cannot doubt the correctness of this idea. Let every friend of religion use his utmost exertions to remove this Achan[16] from the sacred camp. Let not this Dagon[17] of impiety be permitted to stand in the presence of the holy ark.

---

[9]In a fuge like this, all the force of emphasis must be entirely lost; and, though the parts may be placed in harmonic order, yet their combined effect cannot exhibit any regular idea. When the parts of music move in unison with the words, the ideas are rendered more emphatical. When the different parts are pronouncing different words, the emphasis is diminished. [Hubbard's note.]

[10]Hundred-eyed monster of Greek legend.

[11]The fuge may be considered as very difficult to manage with propriety. Handel, Purcell, Croft, Dr. Arnold, and others have introduced it advantageously. They have generally practised the method of suspending one or more parts on long notes, while the others were jointly pronouncing short notes. Perfect specimens of the fuge may be seen in Handel's Grand Hallelujah, in Purcell's anthem, "*Blessed is he*," [music example] and in Dr. Arnold's Upton. [Hubbard's note.]

[12]"That the soul may be affected, it is necessary that the sound should imply, or bring before us, something which we can comprehend." Vossius on Poetry and Music. Page 72. [Hubbard's note, quoting Isaac Vossius (1618–1689), a prodigious scholar, born in Leyden, who lived in England from 1670. In his *De poematum cantu et viribos rythmi* (Oxford, 1673), he reviewed the ancient connections between poetry and music and advocated a traditional adherence to the rules of prosody.]

[13]If any person will take the trouble of examining the songs in the Beggars' Opera, he will find from what sources many of our modern tunes are derived. [Hubbard's note.]

---

[14]"There are also certain psalm tunes, which, with little merit as technical performances, are enabled to excite in the mind a great degree of devotional ecstacy. Those of the hundredth and the hundred and fourth psalms, are the most popular music in England; and they are no less adapted to excite a spirit of piety, than to soothe the ear with their simple melody." Knox's Essay on Music. Page 296. [Hubbard's note, referring to Vicesimus Knox (1752–1821), whose *Essays Moral and Literary* (London, 1778–79) were very popular.]

[15]It may, perhaps, be observed, that sound is only the vehicle we use to convey ideas; and that one tune is as good as another. But will any person say that a theatre is as proper for public worship as any place? [Hubbard's note.]

[16]Achan, a Biblical personage, was a troublemaker in the time of Joshua. He was stoned for stealing forbidden spoil from Jericho and concealing it in the Israelite camp.

[17]National deity of the ancient Philistines.

20   Nathaniel D. Gould and Sacred Music in New England

In 1818, Nathaniel Gould (1781–1864) gave a talk at the annual meeting of the Bethel Masonic Lodge in New-Ipswich, New Hampshire. In the audience were members of the recently established Hubbard Musical Society, of which Gould himself was the founder and conductor.

In this talk, Gould first discusses Masonic ideals, then considers the expulsion of Adam and Eve: "From universal harmony, in one fatal moment, all was turned to jargon . . . from that day to the present, have mankind been striving for *more light*, and man's invention has been on the stretch to restore a faint resemble of that perfect *harmony*, which was lost by the fall. . . ." Turning to music, Gould makes it clear that Masonry's highest ideals are consistent with sacred music, specifically that from Europe. "The moment the depraved heart becomes reconciled to God, it is *tuned* to sing the praises of the Giver of every good and perfect gift, and coincides with the principles of Masonry." "As civilization, morality and religion prevail," he writes, "so is the progress of Masonry and Sacred Musick."

Thirty-five years later, Gould published his major book, *Church Music in America*. After surveying sacred music from biblical times, he moves into a discussion of American sacred music. The topic becomes more lively as Gould reaches back into his own experience to discuss sacred music in the first half of the nineteenth century.

At the age of eleven, Nathaniel Duren Gould moved from Bedford, Massachusetts, to live with his uncle (his mother's brother) in New Ipswich and took his mother's family name as his own. Adept in music, Gould became conductor of the Middlesex Musical Society in 1805 and later the Hubbard Society. He also conducted a military band of good repute, participated in public affairs, served as a deacon in his church, and became a trustee of the New Ipswich Academy. He moved to Boston in 1820, where he continued as a teacher and conductor and joined the Boston Handel and Haydn Society.

NATHANIEL D. GOULD

from *An Address Delivered at New-Ipswich, N.H.* (1818)

Sacred Musick has a tendency to soften the impetuous feelings of man, and lead the mind to contemplate the peace, the joy, and the harmony of the heavenly hosts; who are represented as singing praise to God and to the Lamb, forever and ever.

It is one of the professed objects of the *Hubbard Society* to discountenance every species of that unmeaning, futile, *picture* of music, *called sacred,* set to solemn words, which is unfit to be applied to any words, of more consequence than the Bacchanalian's song. Also to assist in restoring to life the apparently *half murdered,* genuine musick, produced by taste and experience, by attempting to follow the directions and spirit of the composers in performing their sacred songs. How far we have succeeded, is not my province to determine; the good judgment of those who this day hear the performances, must determine this point. I am happy to state, however, that by the exertion of this and similar societies in this country—of which the *Middlesex* [Massachusetts] *Society* stands as *Father*—that host of insipid musick, which for many years seemed to threaten suffocation to that of worth, has been dispersed, and genuine musick is evidently convalescent.

Sacred Musick requires a natural taste, and a sacrifice of much time, in order to acquire enough of the art and science necessary to perform it; but more particularly, to *write* it, acceptably. In this country, until there is more encouragement given to promote it, we must be satisfied with performing those pieces of musick, which have been written in countries where the art and science of musick is made the business of an age. If it be asked why are not Americans capable of composing? the reason would be the same that the school-boy, who has just learned to read plain sentences, cannot write like Pope or Milton; and the same reason may be given, why those who have barely learned the distances of notes, cannot relish genuine musick; it is want of experience.

There is no doubt of the *natural,* and there are instances of *acquired* abilities, in this country, sufficient to write acceptably to the refined taste; and I can confidently state, that he whose name this society bears,[1] who was once an ornament of this town and state, but is now no more; was one. But in general, opportunities and perseverance have not been sufficient to qualify for writing musick scientifically. We need no further evidence than the productions of the multitudes who have attempted it. The great mass which has been written, filling the printing houses and crowding the shelves of almost every musician in New-England, have become insipid and worn "*thread* bare" by *once* using; while the musick of a Martin Luther or a Handel, have stood the test of ages, and by constant use has grown brighter and brighter. . . .

We can hardly doubt of the pleasing and interesting *talent* of Musick, being a gift of God to man, to be peculiarly employed to praise his great and holy name. But, alas! this noble talent, implanted in our natures by God himself, has been employed at all times and places and on all occasions. It would be in vain to attempt to trace it in its various grades, from the simplest *ballad* to the company of hundreds joined by the full toned *Organ.* We leave the Musick of the ball-room, the theatre, and the martial-field in their proper places: we do not view them as bearing any similitude to the *Heavenly Song.* We hope that the time will soon come when Musick shall no more be used to *kill time,* or hurry the warrior to the field of battle. The *object* of this Society is more noble; to enliven and raise the

Nathaniel Gould, *An Address, Delivered at New-Ipswich, N. H., May 16, 1818* (Amherst: R. Boylston, 1818), 13–16, 18, 20.

[1]John Hubbard, Professor of Mathematics and Philosophy at Dartmouth College. [Gould's note.]

drooping spirit above this unsatisfying world; to assist and animate the *devotion* of the pious soul; to aid in the worship of the temples of Jehovah, and celebrate the praises of the Father, Son and Holy Ghost. . . .

If then, Sacred Musick in its *effects*, has a tendency to improve the morals, assist devotion, and elevate the mind to superior realms, and is in itself pleasing, both to the hearer and performer; and when we consider its peculiar privilege of admitting hundreds and even thousands to join their voices at one and the same time; how ought our hearts to glow with gratitude to the great Author of our natures for this inestimable gift. And if any part of the human race are deprived of the means of grace, consequently of the sublime pleasures of Sacred Musick, how ought every one present, who considers it a privilege to sing or hear, to exert themselves to send the word of God to the destitute? . . .

If musick is of so great importance in publick worship, why such indifference in many places about encouraging it; either by practice, or defraying the expense unavoidable to acquire the art to perform with decency? Shall those who have a *talent* given them to sing, bury it? Has any one a license to use his talent when he pleases, and when he pleases, withhold it? Will any one say again, I have used this talent enough? Will any one say that this solemn part of divine service ought to be performed by the young? Will any one dare say that he is too old to sing; I have done my part in its expense and practice? What! too old to sing the praises of God? I have only to answer, when you have done receiving mercies; when you are too old to pray and give thanks for mercies received; then, and not till then, are you, in my opinion, at liberty to excuse yourself from singing the "Songs of Zion."

NATHANIEL D. GOULD

from *Church Music in America* (1853)

Chapter VIII
Progress of Musical Instruction

Change of Music, and Discussions

Soon after the commencement of the present century, when more just ideas of sacred music began to be entertained, and a few publications containing ancient music had been introduced to the public, the subject was canvassed at social meetings; animosities as bitter as in any political combat arose between the fugueing and Old Hundred singers, as they were called.

Old Hundred Seceders

The latter, who had seceded from the music that had prevailed for forty years, moved on calmly but decidedly; formed societies; sung in public;

had addresses from some of the worthiest of men in the community, setting forth the propriety and necessity of a change in the character of music in the churches. Although every attempt was made by their opponents to thwart the doings of the reformers, still they persevered, and the effect and influence of their doings spread from town to town, till all New England was more or less affected. It was, emphatically, "Old School" and "New School." And, in numerous towns, schools of each denomination were raised and put in operation, side by side. All this excitement, however unpleasant, tended to awaken an interest, and produce examination and practice in music; so that whatever the cause might have been that moved to action, the public were advancing in the art, and the cause was promoted.

Nathaniel D. Gould, *Church Music in America* (Boston: A. N. Johnson, 1853), 119–23.

Old School Prevailed

The result was, that in proportion to the amount of experience the more were there accessions to the ranks of the old school; so that in three or four years from the commencement of the reform, we could seldom hear of a congregation where the former popular music prevailed.

Struggle for the Possession of Seats

When schools of different character had been taught in the same town or parish, and had closed, then came the struggle for a place in the church. Sometimes the right was determined by numbers; sometimes neither party had strength and talent enough to proceed separately; then a compromise would, perhaps, take place; but they could no more mix than water and oil, and one or the other party must by and by prevail and control. The consequence was, that in most instances the music-books of the dark age were laid on the shelf, and the dust on them was seldom afterwards disturbed.

Reformation in Teaching and Music

The method of teaching continued much the same for many years, except that a natural progress resulted from experience in communicating instruction more fully in the theory of music; and every new publication attempted to improve their introductory lessons. About the year 1822, was the first appearance of "Templi Carmina,"[2] with the rudiments of music in the form of questions and answers, which was substantially what we had before published, in a pamphlet, for our own convenience in schools.

Attempt to Harmonize Correctly

The harmony of the tunes, where gross errors appeared, was cautiously corrected; but still,

those who did not know the difference, doubted the expediency of it, and even the competency of those who ventured to make any change.

The common saying that had prevailed, that "Americans did not, and could not, know anything of the science of music," had been so long sounded in the ear, that all were slow to believe that others knew better than themselves, and, therefore, could know little or nothing.

Public Interested

Singing-schools now assumed somewhat of a different character. The object and solemnity of church music began to be seriously contemplated. Ministers and officers of the church began to express their views and feelings on the subject. And the public generally began to be interested in the cause. As evidence of this, we could occasionally hear that an article was inserted in the warrant for town-meeting, to see if the *town* would raise money, some fifty to seventy-five dollars, for the encouragement and support of the music in the church. This was something new, and caused much altercation in towns and parishes, when first proposed. As might be expected, it was sometimes granted and sometimes refused.

Change of Books

It was a long time, however, before the habits and customs of schools could be materially changed. In addition to the books that we have mentioned, as being collected and published under the patronage of societies, there were many others, containing a variety of music designed to suit the tastes of all, with a sufficient number of tunes of different character for all practical purposes, such as "Bridgewater Collection," "Worcester Collection," "Village Harmony," with the arrangements of the parts much improved.

Tenor Voices Put in Place

One of the first steps that agitated the singing community, was that of giving the air or leading part of the tune, usually called *Treble*, or rather the *tune*, to the females; this was an interference with the rights of man, not readily acceded to, es-

---

[2] The first edition, issued by Bartholomew Brown and others, was called *Columbian and European Harmony: or, Bridgewater Collection of Sacred Music* (Boston, 1802). The title was changed to *Templi Carmina: Songs of the Temple, or, Bridgewater Collection in Sacred Music* with the fourth edition of 1816. The tenth edition was published in 1822.

pecially by those who had tenor voices and had always sung the air. They, of course, claimed it by possession. And, as in all other innovations, the question was asked with petulance, "What better is it? We have always sung the part, and the singing has been pronounced good by all." And the general want of information in regard to harmony rendered it difficult for any one to give reasons, so as to be understood, even if an explanation was desired; and if made to be understood, it was still more difficult to reconcile persons to practice. No teacher had previously enforced the rule and practice in schools but Andrew Law. This change commenced, practically, about a quarter of a century ago. For several years previously it had been agitated, and partially put in operation, but it was several years after, before it was fully adopted; and is not yet practised in many places in the country. Some individuals who had always sung the air, either could not or would not sing any other part. They did not, perhaps, go so far as some of our forefathers, who would debar females from singing in public altogether, regarding it as one manner of speaking; still, they were but little less consistent, for many claimed the part as their right, being men, to lead; and wrong for women to sing the governing part. But it is futile to take this ground; for the voice of woman is so constituted, that whatever part she sings will be heard, call it leading or what you please. In this one respect, if in no other, men must be led by women. At the time, there was much written on the subject; and we have seen a long and labored treatise to prove it to be wrong, on many accounts, to suffer the part to be sung by females, on the ground that it was contrary to Scripture, and of course a sin, for females to take the lead in singing, or any other religious service.

Example in a School

About this time, we were teaching in the vicinity of Boston; had a numerous school, and many good singers; but nothing could induce some of the gentlemen to relinquish the air or soprano. Some of the ladies chose to sing the tenor, as they had heretofore done. At length, a public exhibition came off. The editor of a musical publication was present. In his next number he praised the performance generally, but gave a severe and well-deserved censure for this single but obvious impropriety. We not only bore it patiently, but gladly; for it proved, as we hoped, a timely help to accomplish, by *publicly* exposing the error, what we and others had been trying to accomplish, for months and years, in private schools. This was a decisive blow. Singers, afterwards, generally kept their voices to their appropriate parts, in this region, but not through the country. We would not say that it is unnecessary for gentlemen to learn the air; for, in the absence of females, that part must be sustained by them, in order to make singing acceptable; for a tune is as unmeaning without the air as a sentence without a verb.

21   Lowell Mason, Music Educator

An astute businessman, organizer, administrator, popularizer, proselytizer, teacher, church musician, choral conductor, composer, compiler—all of these and more describe Lowell Mason (1792–1872), in his generation the most famous musician in America. Born into a musical family in Medford, Massachusetts, Mason's apprentice years from 1812 took him to Savannah, Georgia, where he held a number of minor positions, including clerking at the Planter's Bank. But he also studied music with German-born Frederick L. Abel and made a significant impact on local church music.

Mason's first real break came with the acceptance for publication of *The Boston Handel and Haydn Society Collection of Church Music*, issued by the Society in 1822. He soon moved to Boston to supervise the music of three Congregational churches and assumed, in addition, the posts of president and director of the Handel and Haydn Society itself. In 1831, he became choirmaster at Lyman Beecher's prestigious Bowdoin Street Church, leading a large choir of national standing.

Mason began to teach shortly after his move to Boston, and by 1830 had more than 150 pupils. He became converted to the merits of the Pestalozzian system, which he advocated throughout the remainder of his life.

Swiss educator and social reformer Heinrich Pestalozzi (1746–1827) developed a way of teaching in which children were guided to learn not through confrontation with the products of learning but through the exercise of their own powers. He regarded music as a most effective aid to moral education and as an important factor in engendering "the highest feelings" of which humans are capable.

The story of Mason's path-breaking involvement in music education in the Boston schools is well known. A major step was the establishment in 1832 of the Boston Academy of Music, which became the center for his teaching activities and for which he produced his best known written work, the *Manual of the Boston Academy of Music* (1834). Mason continued in public education until 1855.

In a real sense, Mason lived the American dream. Enormously successful, he was less an innovator than an organizer who implemented the ideas of others, less a pioneer than a popularizer. But he was skilled at working with people and was a good choral conductor, administrator, and teacher, and a competent composer. His ideas were based on strong religious impulses, which infused his work. His concern with education blossomed into the real beginnings of music education as we know it in this country.

Mason's *Pestalozzian Music Teacher* was written in the early 1870s with the assistance of his longtime disciple and colleague, Theodore Seward (1835–1902), then a public school music director. The book was mainly Mason's work, and it stands as a retrospective of a long and successful career in music.

LOWELL MASON

"Method of Teaching," from *The Pestalozzian Music Teacher* (1871)

Introduction

The Ability to acquire knowledge is more valuable than mere knowledge acquired, just as a living spring is of greater value than a vessel of water. The latter is limited, exhaustible; the former, limitless, inexhaustible. One is a possession; the other, the everlasting ability to acquire possessions. Hence the superior object of the right method of instruction is to secure to the pupil the power to acquire knowledge; the inferior object (however important) being to impart knowledge. In the acquirement of knowledge the pupil is so directed and trained to the constant and vigorous use of his powers that they may be developed, strengthened and made most efficient: thus accomplishing in the best manner the higher as well as lower end of school education.

For it is true that the right method of instruction secures best the inferior as well as the superior object; it tends to the most rapid possible progress in the attainment by the pupil of accurate and thorough knowledge. While being trained in the ability to acquire, he most rapidly and surely acquires. It is not, therefore, sacrificing the less object in any degree to the greater; both are advanced and promoted; the pupil obtains the greatest amount of real knowledge in a given time, while his powers are developed and trained in the best manner.

The following are characteristics of such a method of instruction:

1. The phenomena to be studied are brought under the actual observation of the pupil. Thus his powers of perception and observation are exercised and cultivated.

2. The pupil is guided to the attainment of general knowledge, first; then, by analysis, of particular knowledge. This is Nature's method; whole things are first observed and considered, and then the parts, which can be understood and comprehended only by their relation to the whole.

3. The teacher assists the pupil to combine the particulars which he has learned, in the whole from which they were taken.

4. The constant effect is to exercise the powers of the pupil; to interest him to observe with care and accuracy, and reason rightly from analogy and causality; thus it teaches and trains.

It may be said, familiarly, that the thing to be understood is to be first examined, then taken to pieces, then put together again,—the whole being done with interest, thought, understanding. The pupil is to investigate, learn and know; not merely to read, commit to memory, and take for granted without comprehending. The thing investigated and understood will be remembered. This process is not the mere committing to memory of words; it is the acquisition of knowledge, the enlarging of the understanding. It does not begin by giving signs, directions or rules for right action, but it investigates, searches into realities, and by so doing, ascertains *what* is right, and *why* it is so; thus it derives and establishes rules from whence signs follow.

These principles are more or less clearly recognized by those who nevertheless differ widely in the designations which they affix to their differing forms of giving instruction; indeed it is not easy to select a *name* for the method here so imperfectly described, at once appropriate and sufficient. The terms induction, deduction, analysis and synthesis are in very common use in relation to the process of teaching, but they are so differently understood and applied with such a diversity of meanings, that they seem not to be sufficiently definite or comprehensive to characterize as a whole, the true

Lowell Mason, *The Pestalozzian Music Teacher* (New York: C. H. Ditson, 1871), [7]–12.

method. The term Pestalozzian is in frequent and extensive use, and is appropriate since Pestalozzi was first in modern times to introduce and carry out in the ordinary process of common school teaching the method here advocated. But since the time of this distinguished teacher the system has made such progress, especially in this country, as probably to exceed the most sanguine expectations of its author, for it is now employed in the higher departments of mental and moral philosophy, and is steadily making its way up to the highest classical and professional schools. Hence the inadequacy, though not the inappropriateness of the appellation, Pestalozzian teaching.

But if the method of teaching be carried into the higher departments of study, it loses nothing of its original simplicity and truthfulness. Paradoxical as it may seem, so simple, and so natural is the method of instruction in its application that it not unfrequently seems difficult to be understood. Indeed it consists so little in *telling*, and so essentially in *doing*, that it is only by doing that a complete idea of the reality may be conveyed.

It has not been uncommon to mistake the mere adjuncts of the method for its reality, as, for example, the use of the numeral-frame, or blackboard, or other help. It has been supposed by some to consist in analysis, classification, or nomenclature; in "giving at the commencement a little at a time," "in well separating and simplifying the elements and rendering them familiar one by one," and "in advancing constantly, though by almost insensible degrees." These, indeed, are things which all must approve, but they do not touch the vitality of the system. It consists not in any one of these things, nor in all of them together. One may reject the use of the black-board, or in music the three-fold division of the subject, or the rhythmic classification of primitive and derived form of measure, or any peculiar use of syllables, or of syllables altogether, or of a new or old nomenclature, (although it naturally leads to the use of names arising from and descriptive of things named,) or of any particular order of subjects, or method for the voice, or of any particular method of notation, new or old, and yet, in general, pursue the right

method. Yet we can hardly conceive of any good teacher, or of one who really enters into the work of his profession in an intelligent and artistic manner, who will not be likely to adopt as helps most of these things. Still, there is great danger that in its application the mere outside may be taken, while its spirit is overlooked, or the body may be taken while the life and soul of the system is left out.

Again, it may be mentioned, the teacher who follows this method is not bound to any particular book or form of elementary treatise. He may use any book successfully which contains a clear statement of facts; while, on the other hand, no book of rules, formulas, definitions, or descriptions, however complete, can make a thorough teacher.

But if it does not consist in any of these things, the question may be asked again, In what does it consist? Before proceeding with the illustrations by which we hope in part to answer this question, we will, though it may seem quite inconsistent with the very principles advocated, attempt, in addition to what has been already said, to give some further description. The teacher, in pursuance of the right method, is guided by nature; he looks, on the one hand, to the intuitions, instincts, and opening faculties or active powers of his pupils, and on the other to the qualities, properties, or conditions of the object or subject, a knowledge of which he desires to communicate. In his attempts to communicate knowledge he depends not upon previously prepared books, rules, canons, or formulas as guides, but looking to the intuitive powers of his pupils, or to their ability to acquire a real knowledge of things through their own observation and experience, or action, he relies entirely upon *investigation and evidence*. He never allows either himself or the book-maker to attempt to teach by mere explanation, description, assertion, or declaration. That the book says so, or that the teacher himself says so, is not sufficient: present proof, the result of careful investigation and comparison, making its appeal to the capacities of the pupil, is positively required. The pupil must know a thing through his perceptive powers or because he sees it, or hears it; because it is self-evident, or is a logical deduction from well-ascertained facts; or if beyond the power of perception or reason, it is received on testimony, or as being conventional or of universal usage. These things may be regarded as the ground-work, or as embracing the philosophy of the true method of instruction; a few particulars which naturally grow out of this view of the subject may be mentioned.

1. The true teacher knows that he can not do much in a short time, or in a few lessons; and, *being honest*, he does not profess to do much. He does not look for any immediate striking results, but labors with reference to the gradual growth and future welfare of his pupils.

2. He always interests his pupils, and makes the path of knowledge pleasant. His teaching is so conducted as to employ both the *head* and the *heart*; and the training-exercises which necessarily follow instruction are always adapted both to secure to the pupil, as his own available property, the knowledge he has acquired, and to fasten it in the mind by some agreeable process.

3. He is not satisfied with the mere communication of knowledge, but, looking to the educational influence of his work, he constantly aims to call forth, develop, or enlarge the natural powers of his pupils.

4. He leaves the mind, unfettered by dogmas, free to pursue its own way of investigation, free to observe, compare, judge, and decide.

5. He looks at the substance; the reality, or the thing itself is always regarded by him as vastly more important than its mere sign or name, and is always presented first in order. His motto is: Things Before Signs; Principles Before Rules; Practice Before Theory.

6. His teaching-lessons are oral; when he teaches, or attempts to lead along his pupils in the pursuit of knowledge, he depends upon spoken words, having life and power, rather than upon mere written language, though in his reviews and in his trainings he finds a book a most valuable assistant.

In the illustrations which follow, in this work, the teacher is supposed to have before him a class of children of about ten or twelve years of age,

whom he attempts to teach, or with whom he carries on an elementary investigation of musical sounds, or of the things to be found in the "tone-realm." While the work is usually pursued in a conversational way, it is far enough, as will readily be perceived, from common catechetical instruction. The questions of the teacher are not addressed to the mere memory, but to the knowledge of his pupils, being such as naturally arise out of the instructions already given. He never asks a question, therefore, to which he has not good reason to suppose his pupils will be able to give a satisfactory answer; and yet his questions are so framed, or adapted to the condition of his pupils, as always to require thought on their part. His questions are addressed to his pupils themselves, for he wishes to know what they think, and not what they have read in a book, or what they have been told by himself, or by any other person.

The answers of the pupils, as here written down, are supposed to be substantially such as they will give if they really understand the subject; and, on the supposition that they are not deficient in mental capacity, and have given proper attention, if they do not understand, it must be the teacher's fault. It is hardly necessary to add, that it is by no means intended that these, or similar answers, should be put into the pupil's mouths from without, or that they should learn them from the book; on the contrary, they are always supposed to proceed from what is within, or from the knowledge which they have acquired in the exercise of their own powers.

The illustrations and explanations which follow are not intended as a pattern which the teacher must follow *verbatim*; he would be but poorly qualified for his work who should attempt to teach his class by saying over exactly these words, or to treat his subjects in exactly the same way, or in the same order. We have endeavored, indeed, to treat the whole subject in a natural way, and to introduce the different topics as they would be likely to come up in a class, but we may have gone, at one time too much, and at another too little into detail, for circumstances will often change the teacher's plans, and throw him quite on another track from that which he intended to pursue. Every teacher should have his own manner. There may be great diversity in the manner of those teachers who are controlled by the same leading principles or method of imparting instruction.

Finally, this and every other attempt to illustrate or explain the principles of this method of instruction must be very imperfect, or fall far short of the reality. One may not learn it from anything which can be written, or from any book whatever. To be fully understood, it must be wrought out or must have grown up in one's own practice and experience. One must positively do the actual work of a teacher, participating himself in the reality, before he can know the power and the beauty of teaching and educating the young according to these principles, which are nothing more or less than the principles of nature.

22 George F. Root, Songwriter and Music Publisher

George F. Root's *Autobiography*, published late in his life, provides an entertaining picture of one nineteenth-century musician's experiences. We follow him from his student days in Boston as his career develops as a teacher, compiler, and composer of parlor music and larger works. He also became a partner in the Chicago firm of Root & Cady, a major music outlet and publishing house.

George Frederick Root (1820–1895) was born in Sheffield, Massachusetts, the oldest of eight children. He moved to Boston at the age of eighteen to study piano with Artemas Nixon Johnson. A fateful moment arrived when he auditioned for Lowell Mason and was accepted into Mason's chorus at the Boston Academy. For the rest of his life, he remained an admirer and follower of Mason, whose name weaves through much of the narrative of Root's writing.

Root became an assistant in Mason's public school music classes and introduced his hero's methods to New York City. Later, when Mason moved to New York, Root helped him organize the first Normal Musical Institute for teacher training. He was instrumental in persuading the Chancellor of New York University to grant Mason an honorary doctorate, telling us that when he mentioned this to Mason, "he looked up, . . . but immediately resumed his usual manner . . . I mention this as illustrating the fact, well known to Dr. Mason's friends, that he never sought honors or distinctions any more than he did wealth. He gave himself wholly to his work, and if other things came they must come without any effort on his part."

In the excerpts below, we follow Root as he meets Mason for the first time. Root describes his own musical development, alluding along the way to his admiration for Wagner. He ruminates about public taste and musical standards, and he describes the beginnings of his association with Root & Cady. He relates the circumstances surrounding the composition and first performance of his phenomenally popular Civil War song, *The Battle-Cry of Freedom*. He also gives a first-hand description of the horror of the devastating Chicago fire of 1871, a conflagration that caused untold destruction and the bankruptcy of his company.

GEORGE F. ROOT

Text of *The Battle-Cry of Freedom* (1862)

Yes we'll rally round the flag, boys, we'll rally once again,
Shouting the battle-cry of Freedom,
We will rally from the hill-side, we'll gather from the
   plain,
Shouting the battle-cry of Freedom.

Chorus

The Union forever, Hurrah boys, hurrah!
Down with the Traitor, Up with the Star;
While we rally round the flag, boys,
Rally once again,
Shouting the battle-cry of Freedom.

George Frederick Root, *The Battle Cry of Freedom* (Chicago:
Root & Cady, 1862).

GEORGE F. ROOT

from *The Story of a Musical Life* (1891)

About this time Mr. Mason advertised that new members would be admitted to the Boston Academy's Chorus. Those who wished to join must be at a certain place at a certain time, and have their voices and reading ability tested. Mr. Johnson[1] said I had better go; that the Academy's work was more difficult than that of the Musical Education Society, and that the practice would be good for me in every way. I shook in my shoes at the suggestion, but Mr. Johnson's courage was equal to the occasion, and I went. That was my first sight of Lowell Mason, and also of Geo. Jas. Webb,[2] who did the trying of the voices, while Mr. Mason looked on. I passed, and was much surprised when Mr. Mason came to where I was sitting and asked me to join his choir—that famous Bowdoin Street Choir, the like of which has rarely been equaled, in my opinion, in this or any other country. I told him why I could not—that I was with Mr. John-

son, etc., but that invitation settled the voice question in my mind. I was going to sing. Lowell Mason had wanted me in his choir, and that was as good as a warranty that I could succeed.

* * *

During my first winter at Mercer Street Church I often said to the officers of the church that I could make the choir much better if they would have the key-board of the organ brought out to the front of the gallery so that the choir could be before me (between me and the organ), instead of behind me while I was playing—that my voice would help more, and my directions be better understood and observed, if I could see all the choir and they could see me. I also suggested that while they were about it they might make some much-needed improvement in the organ itself. This was done the next summer. A judicious expenditure of two thousand dollars made a great change in the fine old instrument. I was married during the vacation, and when I returned and put the new soprano and the other leading voices in front of me, with the remaining members of the choir, thirty or forty in number, at their sides, but all in sight, I felt like a king upon his throne, certain of his ability to control and take care of his entire kingdom.

And now my sisters came along, one after an-

George F. Root, *The Story of a Musical Life: An Autobiography* (Cincinnati: John Church, 1891), 14, 40–42, 52–55, 122–23, 132–33, 152–55, 157.

[1]Artemas Nixon Johnson, Root's teacher, a student of Lowell Mason.

[2]Boston organist and conductor who worked closely with Mason; an organizer of the Boston Academy of Music.

other, and went to school either at Rutgers or Abbott's, and under greater advantages pursued their musical studies. My brother, of whom I have previously spoken, and Mr. Henry T. Lincoln, a noble base [*sic*], who began his musical career in my first singing school at the "North End" in Boston, in '39, also came, both to sing in my choir and to assist me in my teaching. A little later my youngest brother, William A. Root, also came, and went to a commercial school and then into a business office. One of my sisters had an excellent contralto voice, and we now had a well-balanced home quartet—wife, sister, brother and self, and adding Mr. Lincoln, a good quintet. We took great delight in practicing some of the Mendelssohn part-songs, then comparatively new, and such old madrigals and glees as were set for soprano, alto, tenor, baritone and base. William Mason,[3] then a very young man, had written a serenade, entitled "Slumber Sweetly, Dearest," that we greatly delighted in

After a while we found we were singing with a balance and blending sometimes heard in very simple music by such singers as the Hutchinson family (then in the Zenith of their success), but rarely if ever (in our experience) in music of a higher grade, and this encouraged me to strive for the highest perfection possible in every point that I could think of for my quartet. In one of our summer vacations we all went to the old home in North Reading, and practiced together every day for six weeks—some days hours at a time on a repertoire of about five numbers. At last I, who was the leader, had no more to think of the others while we were singing together than if I had been singing alone. I could carry out every conception I had in the way of expression—increasing, diminishing, accelerating or retarding, sudden attack or delicate shading, with the utmost freedom, being sure that all would go exactly with me. I had for some time been feeling that a musical demonstration might have to be made in New York, and on their own ground, musically, to some of the chronic contemners of simple music, and of our

New England way of teaching it. I knew that as soloists none of us would be regarded as anything more than mediocre, but I believed that as a quartet, with the work we had done, we should at least close their mouths as to our musical competency.

* * *

Up to this time I had not written anything to speak of. I did put together some simple tunes while in Boston, one of which (Rosedale) has come along down in a modest way with its more popular companions, being occasionally sung and asked for at the present time. After I was well under way in New York Mr. Bradbury and Mr. Woodbury used to say: "Root, why don't you make books; we are doing well in that line,"—but I had no inclination in that way.[4] I am ashamed to say it, but I looked then with some contempt upon their grade of work. My ladies' classes and choirs were singing higher music, and my blind pupils were exciting the admiration of the best musical people of the city by their performances of a still higher order of compositions. There was a well-balanced choir of sixty good voices in this institution for the blind, and they worked with an interest and enthusiasm that was wonderful to see. . . .

How true it is that to every music lover and learner there is a grade of music in which he lives, so to speak—where he feels most at home and enjoys himself best. When he hears or studies music that is above that grade, if he is sensible he simply says: "That is above me; I am not there yet." If he is not sensible, he is liable to say: "There's no music in that." The conversation of two gentlemen at one of our recent Thomas [Theodore Thomas] concerts is a good illustration of that condition of things. One says: "Do you call that music?" The other answers: "Yes; and the best there is—it is a composition by Wagner." To which his friend responds: "Well, for my part, I think Wagner had better stick to his sleeping cars, and let music alone."

People change their musical homes, or rather add to them, as they progress in musical apprecia-

---

[3]William Mason, son of Lowell Mason, was a fine pianist.

[4]William Bradbury and Isaac Woodbury were students of Lowell Mason who carried on his work.

tion. At first they care only for the little way-side flowers and simple scenery of the land of tonic, dominant and subdominant. They regard the musical world outside of that boundary as a kind of desert, entirely unfit to live in, and I may add once more, what has often been said in substance, that many people remain in this musical condition all their lives. But those who progress, begin, by and by, to see some beauty in the sturdier growths and the more varied scenery, and after awhile realize that the still unexplored regions beyond may be yet more beautiful when they are reached.

But here there is a danger. People in this state are apt to grow conceited, and to despise the simple conditions they once enjoyed. "Unworthy, narrow and bigoted" are the proper terms to apply to such. The way-side flower has its place in the economy of God's creation as truly as the oak, and the little hill and the brooklet are as truly beautiful as the mountain and torrent are grand.

"But," some one says, "there is so much trash in the simple music of the day." There is trash at every musical grade, even to the highest. How much that is grotesque and senseless is seen in the ambitious attempts of those who follow Wagner, or would rival him in new paths, but have nothing of his transcendent genius. Such are usually among the despisers of the elementary conditions through which all must pass, and in which a majority of the music-loving world must always be. "Trash" of course; so there are offensive plants and flowers and disagreeable scenes, but the proportion is small, and I contend that most of the simple music that *lives* is no more trash than Mozart's "O dolce concento" or "Rousseau's Dream," than which nothing is written that is simpler or more perfect.

*   *   *

In 1858 my brother, E. T. Root, and Mr. C. M. Cady started a music business in Chicago—nearly the "far west" in those days—under the firm name of Root & Cady. My convention work brought me occasionally to their neighborhood, and it was an odd and very pleasant sensation to find in this new section a kind of business home. This was not so much on account of the small pecuniary interest I had in the enterprise as the great interest I took in

everything my brother did. This brother and myself were nearly of the same age. We had been much together all our lives. He had married the lovely "Lily" of the Rutgers Institute "Flower Queen," and was now preparing for himself a home in the comparatively new city of Chicago. So, whatever applications for conventions I declined, none from the West were refused, and I appeared more and more frequently at the little store.

It was very pleasant to see the new business grow, and it was not long before the partners said: "Come, put in some more capital, and join us; we need the capital, and your name will help us." I was delighted with the idea, not that I thought of giving up my professional work—I did not dream of that, nor of living in Chicago; but to have this connection with my brother, and this business for a kind of recreation, was extremely attractive. So it was soon brought about, and I became a partner in the house of Root & Cady.

*   *   *

I heard of President Lincoln's second call for troops one afternoon while reclining on a lounge in my brother's house. Immediately a song started in my mind, words and music together:

"Yes, we'll rally round the flag, boys, we'll rally once
    again,
        Shouting the battle-cry of freedom!"

I thought it out that afternoon, and wrote it the next morning at the store. The ink was hardly dry when the Lumbard brothers—the great singers of the war—came in for something to sing at a war meeting that was to be holden immediately in the court-house square just opposite. They went through the new song once, and then hastened to the steps of the court-house, followed by a crowd that had gathered while the practice was going on. Then Jule's magnificent voice gave out the song, and Frank's trumpet tones led the refrain—

"The Union forever, hurrah, boys, hurrah!"

and at the fourth verse a thousand voices were joining in the chorus. From there the song went into the army, and the testimony in regard to its use in the camp and on the march, and even on the field of battle, from soldiers and officers, up to generals, and even to the good President himself, made me thankful that if I could not shoulder a musket in defense of my country I could serve her in this way.

*　*　*

And now the memorable autumn of 1871 had come. Our presses had been at work all summer, and great piles of books filled the basement of the main building, ready for the fall trade. They would all be gone in a few weeks, so we did not take out a special insurance upon them, but assumed the risk for that short time ourselves. I lived then in Grove-land Park, near the Chicago University, about four miles south from our place of business. Between three and four o'clock in the morning of the ninth of October some one waked me and said Jerome Beardslee was at the door in a buggy and wanted to see me. What could Jerome want at that time in the morning, and why should he come in a buggy, since he lives next door but one? I got up and tried to light the gas, but there was none. I hurried on my clothes and went down. "What is the matter, Jerome?" "There's a great fire down town, and it is spreading fearfully. Our store is gone, but I got the books out, and have just brought them home. I am going back, and if you would like to ride with me you can. I think you'll be in time to see your place go." I went, and when we got within a mile of the fire we began to see signs of the great disaster. Groups of men, women and children (some scant-ily clad) were standing by such household goods as they had brought to where they supposed they were out of the reach of the flames. Team after team added to the number until the streets were lined with the fugitives and such of their belong-ings as they could save.

The wind blew fiercely from the south-west, so

the flames spread less rapidly our way, but on the north side nearly all the people who thought their goods were out of danger had to move again and again, and finally see them burn for the want of means to get them out on to the prairie beyond the farthest houses, four miles from the center. Some who placed their goods on the lake shore where there was a beach, not only had to see them burn, but had to get into the water to save their lives. The heat of the fire, maddened by the tornado it had caused, was beyond conception. . . .

I was in time to see the costly and elegant opera-house go. . . .

The days immediately following the fire were passed in anxious waiting to see if the vault and safes had protected our plates and account books. It was some days before they were cool enough to open; when they were, their contents were found to be safe, though some of the papers were scorched. . . .

One of Root & Cady's first acts was to sell the book catalogue, plates and copyrights to John Church & Co., of Cincinnati, and the sheet music plates and copyrights to S. Brainard's Sons, Cleve-land. These sales realized a large sum—in the neighborhood of one hundred and thirty thousand dollars, if I remember rightly—but so many insur-ance companies failed that they did not get half their insurance, and when the hard times, which followed the fire, came on, could not meet the great liabilities they had assumed, and were obliged to close up. With the assistance of a wealthy friend we purchased their stock. They went through bankruptcy, and Mr. Cady left the city. My brother E. T. and Mr. Lewis then started in again, under the firm name of Root & Lewis, and we (Geo. F. Root & Sons) formed a connection with John Church & Co., of Cincinnati.

23   The Music of Camp Meetings

The years following the American Revolution were relatively unchurched. Toward the close of the eighteenth century, however, the pendulum began to swing and the populace erupted in what has been called a Second Great Awakening. Itinerant ministers in the early 1800s carried the Gospel to the burgeoning frontiers of Kentucky, North Carolina, Georgia, and other southern states, and soon into New York, Connecticut, and Massachusetts as well.

Camp meetings became an advantageous way of spreading the word. Stands were erected from which preachers of various denominations sought to convert participants, calling on them to reject the evils of the world so that they might be assured of salvation and a place in Heaven.

Emotionalism ran high. Physical reactions to the process of conversion were often violent, the "mourners" being most affected. Dancing and "the jerks" were common, understood as an individual's recognition of his or her own wickedness and as a sign of God's mercy.

Blacks and whites participated together; music and rhythm were central to what went on, and hymn singing played a crucial part. Direct emotional involvement without written materials was paramount, although texts without music found their way into print in pocket-sized collections.

Verses were combined with simple choruses that could be easily grasped and performed by large crowds and that encapsulated the essence of the religious experience.

Two preachers who rode the circuit were Lorenzo Dow (1777–1834) and Peter Cartwright (1785–1872). Dow, born in Coventry, Connecticut, was educated by his parents and began preaching in 1794. Two years later he was accepted into a tentative connection with the Methodist ministry. His journal recounts his many travels alone on horseback, primarily in the South, although he also visited Ireland and England. Dow spent his declining years in Connecticut.

Peter Cartwright of Amherst County, Virginia, came from a large family that included a brother who was hanged for murder and a sister said to have lived a life of debauchery. About 1790, the family moved to a turbulent area in the wilds of Kentucky. Cartwright's education was sketchy, and, by his own report, he was "a wild, wicked boy, and delighted in horse-racing, card-playing, and dancing." Conversion came at a camp meeting in 1801. Cartwright then joined the Methodist Episcopal Church and became a circuit-rider on the frontier in the South and Midwest. He remained a major figure in Methodist life and served two terms in the Illinois legislature. In 1846, Cartwright ran for the United States Congress but lost to Abraham Lincoln. In the excerpt that follows, Cartwright describes a historic first camp meeting that took place at Cane Ridge, Kentucky, about 1801.

New York printer and publisher John C. Totten (c. 1776–1837) provides us with examples of camp-meeting hymnody in his *Collection* printed in 1809. This small volume, typical of such publications, contains 113 hymn texts without music.

LORENZO DOW

from *History of Cosmopolite* (1814)

I had heard about a singularity called the *jerks* or *jerking exercise* which appeared first near Knoxville, in August last [1803], to the great alarm of the people; which reports at first I considered as vague and false; but at length, like the Queen of Sheba, I set out, to go and see for myself; and sent over these appointments into this country accordingly.

When I arrived in sight of this town I saw hundreds of people collected in little bodies; and observing no place appointed for meeting, before I spoke to any, I got on a log and gave out an hymn; which caused them to assemble round, in solemn attentive silence: I observed several involuntary motions in the course of the meeting, which I considered as a specimen of the jerks.

* * *

Sunday, February 19th, I spoke in Knoxville to hundreds more than could get into the court house, the Governor being present: about one hundred and fifty appeared to have the jerking exercise, amongst whom was a circuit preacher, (Johnson) who had opposed them a little before, but he now had them powerfully; and I believe that he would have fallen over three times had not the auditory been so crowded that he could not, unless he fell perpendicularly.

Lorenzo Dow, *History of Cosmopolite; or, the Four Volumes of Lorenzo's Journal* . . . (New York: John C. Totten, 1814), 195, 197.

PETER CARTWRIGHT

from *Autobiography* (1856)

Somewhere between 1800 and 1801, in the upper part of Kentucky, at a memorable place called "Cane Ridge," there was appointed a sacramental meeting by some of the Presbyterian ministers, at which meeting, seemingly unexpected by ministers or people, the might power of God was displayed in a very extraordinary manner; many were moved to tears, and bitter and loud crying for mercy. The meeting was protracted for weeks. Ministers of almost all denominations flocked in from far and near. The meeting was kept up night and day. Thousands heard of the mighty work, and came on foot, on horseback, in carriages and wagons. It was supposed that there were in attendance at times during the meeting from twelve to twenty-five thousand people. Hundreds fell prostate under the mighty power of God, as men slain in battle. Stands were erected in the woods, from which preachers of different Churches proclaimed repentance toward God and faith in our Lord Jesus Christ, and it was supposed, by eye and ear witnesses, that between one and two thousand souls were happily and powerfully converted to God during the meeting. It was not unusual for one, two, three, and four to seven preachers to be addressing the listening thousands at the same time from the different stands erected for the purpose. The heavenly fire spread in almost every direction. It was said, by truthful witnesses, that at times more than one thousand persons broke out into loud shouting all at once, and that the shouts could be heard for miles around.

From this camp meeting, for so it ought to be called, the news spread through all the Churches,

Peter Cartwright, *Autobiography of Peter Cartwright, the Backwoods Preacher*, ed. W. P. Strickland (New York: Carlton & Porter, 1856), 30–31.

and through all the land, and it excited great wonder and surprise; but it kindled a religious flame that spread all over Kentucky and through many other states. And I may here be permitted to say, that this was the first camp meeting ever held in the United States,[1] and here our camp meetings took their rise.

---

[1] The first verifiable frontier camp meeting took place in Logan County, Kentucky, in July 1800; the meeting at Cane Ridge, Kentucky, in August 1801 soon followed.

Grace Reviving in the Soul, Hymn Text (1809)

1. I FEEL the work reviving,
    I feel the work reviving,
    I feel the work reviving,
        Reviving in my soul.
    I'm on my way to Zion,
    I'm on my way to Zion,
    I'm on my way to Zion,
        The new Jerusalem.
                CHORUS
    We'll shout and give him glory,
    We'll shout and give him glory,
    We'll shout and give him glory,
        For glory is his own.

2. O Christians will you meet me,
    O Christians will you meet me,
    O Christians will you meet me,
        On Canaan's happy shore?

There we'll shout and give him glory, &c.

3. *Quest.* O brothers will you meet me, &c.
    O brothers will you meet me,
    O brothers will you meet me,
    On Canaan's happy shore.
    Ans. By the grace of God I'll meet you,
    By the grace of God I'll meet you,
    By the grace of God I'll meet you
    On Canaan's happy shore.

There we'll shout and give him glory, &c.

4. *Quest.* O Sisters, will you meet me, &c.
    Ans.   By the grace of God I'll meet you, &c.

There we'll shout and give him glory, &c.

5. *Quest.* O mourners will you meet me, &c.
    Ans.   By the grace of God I'll meet you, &c.

There we'll shout and give him glory, &c.

6. *Quest.* O sinners will you meet me, &c.
    O will you try to meet me
    On Canaan's happy shore?
    I am sorry for to leave you, &c.
    I am sorry for to leave you,
    To leave you in your sins.

There we'll shout and give him glory, &c.

7. Fare you well my dearest brethren, &c.
    Fare you well my dearest brethren,
    Until we meet again.
    I am sorry for to leave you, &c.
    I am sorry for to leave you,
    To leave you all behind.

    But we'll shout and give him glory, &c.

John Totten, ed., *A Collection of the Most Admired Hymns and Spiritual Songs* (New York: John C. Totten, 1809), 7–9.

Shape notes were devised as part of a system for learning pitch. The *Bay Psalm Book*, in its ninth edition (1698), printed four letter names, *fa, sol, la, mi*, below the music, following British practice. John Tufts printed these four syllables on the staff itself (*Introduction to the Singing of Psalm-Tunes*, 1721). William Smith and William Little assigned each of the four syllables on the staff a particular shape (*The Easy Instructor*, 1801), thereby producing the first known shape-note tunebook. And Andrew Law, who claimed to have invented shape notes in the 1780s, devised similar characters for the fourth edition of *The Art of Singing* (1803), using the shapes alone without a musical staff (see No. 20, page 81).

Inevitably, a seven-note system was proposed, with one shape and syllable representing each pitch of the diatonic scale. The idea was put into practice in Jesse B. Aikin's *The Christian Minstrel* (Philadelphia, 1846) and gained wide acceptance. William H. Swan and his son Marcus Lafayette Swan soon brought out the seven-shape *The Harp of Columbia* (1848), published in Philadelphia but printed in Knoxville, Tennessee, where the system gained a foothold.

Such publications support a whole tradition of community singing that prevails to this day. The tradition also feeds directly into the heritage of denominational hymnals of Southern gospel music.

In 1816, Ananias Davisson (1780–1857), a Virginian, produced his *Kentucky Harmony*, the first tunebook to appear in the Shenandoah Valley. Five of its seventeen new tunes were composed by Davisson himself. A shape-note collection with music in four parts (the melody in the tenor), it was influenced by earlier shape-note tunebooks, notably John Wyeth's *Repository of Sacred Music, Part Second* and Little and Smith's *The Easy Instructor*.

Davisson's life remains partially in shadow. He spent most of his time near Harrisonburg, Virginia, where he was active as a composer, tunebook compiler, teacher, printer, and land speculator. A staunch Presbyterian, he is buried in the churchyard of what is now the Massanutten Cross Keys Church in Rockingham County.

Davisson's work as a printer leaves much to be desired. *Kentucky Harmony* is crudely printed, containing numerous typographical problems and a variety of grammatical and spelling errors. These are reproduced below, mostly without comment.

Davisson did not include sharps, flats, or naturals, except in key signatures. Probably some were added in performance, although the resulting modal flavor gives us a clue as to the actual sounds heard. Many of the hymns begin with long-note "gathering tones," a performance tradition.

Davisson was skilled in business, pouring his profits as a tunebook compiler and publisher into purchases of land, much of which he disposed of at a profit. An 1820 census showed him as a resident of Harrisonburg who owned one male slave and was engaged in manufacture. The census of 1840 had him prospering with a household of eleven—apparently one "free colored male" and ten slaves—six of whom were engaged in agriculture (his will contained a provision for the slaves' manumission). When he died, his widow's estate was sizable. So it was that one Southern musician made his living. Along the way he informed us about shape-note hymnody as he experienced it.

ANANIAS DAVISSON

from *Kentucky Harmony* (1816)

Preface

. . . It was [a] remark[1] of an eminent writer too applicable to the present day, "The worship in which we could most resemble the inhabitants of Heaven, is the worst performed upon earth." There appears too much truth in this observation, too often does a disgraceful silence prevail in our churches, too often are dissonance and discord substituted for the charms of melody and harmony. True it is, that there are individuals among us whom Providence has not blessed with singing faculties, but will not truth oblige the most of us to confess, that the fault rests not in a want of natural abilities? but in a great carelessness and neglect of our own.

*   *   *

Explanation of the Scale

Music is naturally divided into Melody and Harmony. Melody is the agreeable effect which arises from the performance of a single part of Music only. Harmony is the pleasing union of several sounds, or the performance of the several parts of Music together. The Notes which produce Harmony when sounded together, are concords, and their intervals, are called consonant intervals. Discords, are employed together in composition, are unison, third, fifth and sixth, with their octaves. The intervals or degrees called perfect cords, are the unisons, fifths and eighths. The intervals or degrees called imperfect cords, are the thirds, sharp fourths, flat fifths, and sixths. The intervals or degrees called discords, are seconds, flats fourths, sevenths, and ninths.

*   *   *

General Observations

A proper accent is a very essential ornament in singing, and should be carefully attended to, for if the poetry is good, and the music well adapted, accented syllable[s] will always fall on the accented parts of the measure. For instance: if the poetry begins with a trochee, the hand should fall on the first note, if with an iambus it should raise.[1] Some authors are opposed to two accents when the measure is divided into two parts, but in this case, I would ask what is to be done with a spondee,[2] where both the words or syllables are accented: but to be short, I would just observe, that when it so happens, that accented words falls on the unaccented part of the measure, language must predominate.

A genteel pronounciation is another excellence that should be inculcated; many who are otherwise excellent Singer, obscure the ideas the[y] utter in melody, by pronouncing ungramatically. Words terminating in ly, ny, &c. are apt to be pronounced as though they formed a seperate word, which not only destroys the beauty of the Music, but sense of the poetry; The best rule therefore that can be

---

Ananias Davisson, *Kentucky Harmony*, part 1 (Harrisonburg, Va.: A. Davisson, 1816), iii–xii.

[1]The text contains numerous grammatical and typographical errors; these have been faithfully transcribed but, for the most part, have been amended only when the sense would be unclear.

[1]A trochee is an accented syllable followed by an unaccented one; an iambus is the opposite.

[2]Two accented syllables.

given is, to pronounce according to the proper mode of speaking, so that what we sing may also be understood.

Youngsters should not be forgetful of the importance of the calling in which they are engaged, but remember that a becoming seriousness should at all time prevail when using sacred words, our thoughts ought always to correspond with the music and subject, and by these means we would find ourselves delighted with that solemnity, that should accompany the sacred worship of the Deity.

Young singers should be very industrious in acquiring a graceful manner of beating time, and should be careful not to contract any disagreeable habits, as they are hard to overcome.

All distortion of the limbs or features while singing, has a tendency to excite ridicule, and should be carefully avoided. Nothing is more disgusting in singers, than affected quirks and ostentatious parade, endeavouring to overpower other voices by the strength of their own, or officiously assisting other parts while theirs is silent. On the other hand, nothing is more praise whorthy in a choir of singers, than a becoming deportment, and a solemnity which should accompany an exercise so near a kin to that, which will through all eternity engage the attention of those who walk in "climes of bliss."

There should be no noise in time of singing, except the music alone, all whispering, laughing, talking, or struting about the floor, is ridiculous in time of school, and should not be suffered.

Young singers, should not join in concert, until each can sing their own part correctly. Too long singing at one time injures the lungs. A cold or cough, all kinds of spiritous liquors, long fasting, &c. &c. are destructive to the voice of one who is much in the practice of singing: A frequent use of spiritous liquors will speedily ruin the best voice.

Flat keyed tunes, should be sung softer than sharp keyed ones, and may be proportioned with a lighter bass, but for sharp keyed tunes let the bass be full and strong, but not harsh.

The proper proportion of the parts is generally said, to be 3 on the bass, 1 on the tenor, 1 on the counter, and 2 on the treble; but I think two on bass sufficient for the other proportions, particularly in flat keyed tunes.

Teachers of Music should be particular to inculcate soft singing, for a person who practises soft singing, will retain the power of hearing, and conforming to other voices, and may readily become master of such gestures and expressions as reason and propriety dictates: Soft singing is in fact the best expedient for refining the ear and improving the voice; "A good voice" says Mr. Lewis, "may soon be much injured by too loud singing."

Let the bass be sung full and bold, the tenor regular and distinct, the counter clear and plain, the treble soft and delicate.

"Teachers" says Little and Smith,[3] "commit an imperceptable error in singing to[o] much [to] their pupils, and allowing them to unite in concert before they can perform their parts seperately;" The best way therefore to improve scholars is, to exercise the parts seperately till they are capable of performing truly by themselves; The teacher should occasionally sing the part by himself, then after going over several times with the scholars; let them try it by themselves, and continue on in this way, frequently repeating the places where he discovers the greatest deficiency.

All solos should be sung softer than the parts when moving together.

Teachers should sing but few tunes at a time, and continue at them till they are well understood; to skim over 40 or 50 tunes of an evening is no way to improve scholars, it gives them a habit of raking [racing] through their books, and wishing to know something about every tune, before they understand one piece properly.

The high notes, quick notes, and slurred notes of each part, should be sung softer than the low, long, single notes of the same part.

As the performing of the several moods in their proper time, is a matter of great importance; I have thought advisable to give rules for the construction of a pendulum that will vibrate once for every beat in the several moods here laid down.

---

[3]Compilers of *The Easy Instructor*.

25   The Enduring Qualities of *Fasola*

Important shape-note collections that emphasized the ongoing tradition of *fasola* include William Walker's *Southern Harmony* (New Haven, 1835) and Benjamin Franklin White and E. J. King's *The Sacred Harp* (compiled in Georgia and printed in Philadelphia, 1844). Walker's collection was probably the most popular tunebook in the south before the Civil War. New editions of *The Sacred Harp* have been issued periodically and the work remains in print to this day.

"Singin' Billy" Walker (1809–1875), of Welsh descent, was born near Cross Keys, Georgia, but moved to the Spartanburg, South Carolina, area in his late teens. He became convinced that it was his calling to "perfect the vocal modes of praise." Walker, who habitually added the initials A. S. H. to his name ("Author of *Southern Harmony*"), operated a bookstore in Spartanburg and was active in the First Baptist Church and the Tyger River Baptist Association. He taught numerous singing schools in the Carolinas, Georgia, and the eastern part of Tennessee. According to legend, B. F. White, Walker's brother-in-law, collaborated in compiling the first edition of *Southern Harmony*, but when Walker took it north for publication, he took credit as sole author.

The original edition of *Southern Harmony* (New Haven, 1835) contains over two hundred pieces in three and four parts. Walker tells us that he served as arranger or composer for twenty-five of these. It is an eclectic collection from a variety of sources—the New England heritage, including "fuged tunes," plus folk hymns and revival songs—that was intended "to gratify the taste of all, and supply the churches with a number of good, plain tunes, suited to the various metres contained in their different Hymn Books."

Nine years after the publication of *Southern Harmony*, B. F. White (1800–1879) produced the first edition of *The Sacred Harp* (Philadelphia, 1844) in collaboration with his pupil, the short-lived Elisha J. King (c. 1821–1844). Both White, from South Carolina, and King, from Georgia, were singing-school teachers. White had little formal education, King perhaps had more. King, from a family of cotton planters, was reported to have been pious and promising. White moved to Georgia around 1840 and became mayor of Hamilton, county clerk, and a major in the militia. He edited a newspaper, *The Organ*, in which he published a number of songs, and he served as president of the Southern Musical Convention, which fostered the singing of sacred songs.

George Pullen Jackson (1874–1953), who provides a first-hand account of a *Southern Harmony* singing about 1930, was a major researcher of *fasola*. His *White Spirituals in the Southern Uplands* (1933) describes the Sacred Harp tradition and attests to its ongoing appeal.

WILLIAM WALKER

from Preface to *The Southern Harmony* (1835)

While those that are fond of fuged tunes have not been neglected, I have endeavoured to make this book a complete Musical Companion for the aged as well as the youth. Those that are partial to ancient music, will here find some good old acquaintances which will cause them to remember with pleasure the scenes of life that are past and gone; while my youthful companions, who are more fond of modern music, I hope will find a sufficient number of new tunes to satisfy them, as I have spared no pains in trying to select such tunes as would meet the wishes of the public.

I have also selected a number of excellent new Songs, and printed them under the tunes, which I hope will be found satisfactory.

Some object to new publications of music, because the compilers alter the tunes. I have endeavoured to select the tunes from original authors. Where this could not be done and the tune having six or seven basses and trebles, I have selected those I thought most consistent with the rules of composition.

I have composed the parts to a great many good airs, (which I could not find in any publication, nor in manuscript,) and assigned my name as the author. I have also composed several tunes wholly, and inserted them in this work, which also bear my name.

The compiler now commends this work to the public, praying God that it may be a means of advancing this important and delightful science, and of cheering the weary pilgrim on his way to the celestial city above.

William Walker
Spartanburg, S.C., September 1835

William Walker, *The Southern Harmony*, 5th ed. (Philadelphia: E. W. Miller, 1854), "Preface to the Former [first] Edition," iii.

B. F. WHITE AND E. J. KING

Preface to *The Sacred Harp* (1844)

Many efforts have been made to please the public with a collection of Sacred Music; and none but those who make the effort, know how difficult it is to accomplish this task. The Compiler of this work has spared no labour or pains in trying to accomplish this desirable object, having taught music for the last twenty years, and being necessarily thrown among churches of various denominations, and all the time observing their wants in that of a variety of church music, has in this work endeavoured to supply that deficiency which heretofore existed, by placing all the church music within his reach, in one book. That such a compilation is needed, no person of piety, observation, and taste, will deny. While the churches may be supplied from this work, others have not been forgotten or neglected; a great variety will be found suited to singing-schools, private societies, and family circles; in fact, the Sacred Harp is designed for all classes who sing, or desire to sing. The Compiler has not aimed at greatness or self-aggrandizement, but has desired, in his humble position, to benefit the public in general: and therefore has set out this work in a plain, easy, and familiar style;

B. F. White and E. J. King, *The Sacred Harp*, 3rd ed. (Philadelphia: S. C. Collins, 1859), 3. First ed., Philadelphia: T. K. and P. G. Collins for B. F. White and E. J. King, 1844.

and having passed the meridian of life, and entirely withdrawn from the business of teaching, is disposed to leave this work as a specimen of his taste, and recommend it to a generous public, praying God that it may answer in full the purposes intended.

B. F. White
Hamilton, Harris Co., Georgia, April, 1844

N. B. The *Harp* is a selection from the most eminent authors now extant; together with nearly one hundred pieces never before published, all of which have been harmonized and arranged under our immediate inspection expressly for this work.

B. F. White & E. J. King

GEORGE PULLEN JACKSON

from *White Spirituals in the Southern Uplands* (1933)

A Southern Harmony Singing

Armed with a camera and all my William Walker impedimenta, Mr. Douglas and I set out a few weeks later for Benton, a small county seat in western Kentucky where my companion had grown up and where, he told me, the yearly *Southern Harmony* singing had been going on, the fourth Sunday in every May, since long before he was born.

As we approached the place by motor, early on Sunday morning, everybody in the countryside seemed to be going our way, in autos, buggies, springless farm wagons, and on foot. The town was already crowded with visitors when we arrived at ten o'clock. Ropes kept the entire courthouse square free from vehicles and reserved it for the thousands of men, women, young folk, and children who covered the shady spaces under the trees surrounding the county building and the streets and sidewalks adjoining. A half dozen barrels of drinking water were placed here and there. An itinerant preacher was shouting at and entertaining highly one section of the crowd grouped around him, as he darted about in the manner of the Ital-

ian bandmaster of the one-time popular "athletic" type. Another group of a hundred or more was being entertained by a blind man singing religious ballads, strumming his own accompaniment on a guitar and playing interludes between stanzas on a mouth-harp that was held in playing position by a wire contraption around his neck, leaving his hands free for the guitar playing. The country girls in their gayest colors, shortest skirts, and tightest shoes were strolling around in twos and threes to the natural delectation of the sun-tanned swains. Old men and women were indulging in impromptu reunions and discussions of old times and new crops. The strains of choral singing came down faintly from the open court-room windows on the second floor. It was a big day in Benton.

Wedging our way into the court-room we found ourselves in the presence of thirty to forty singers occupying the space behind the chancel rail and as many listeners as could find seats or standing space in the court-room proper. The singers were old and very old men and women, and the tattered books from which they sang were, I saw at once, the old *Southern Harmony* that I had thought dead and gone. Some sang without books.

In talking with the listeners I found that a few of them were interested, as I was, in the event as a unique survival in cultural tradition, in listening to musical "antiques" as one of them called the songs. Most of the people, however, listened with a rapt

George Pullen Jackson, *White Spirituals in the Southern Uplands; The Story of the Fasola Folk, Their Songs, Singings, and "Buckwheat Notes"* (Chapel Hill: University of North Carolina Press, 1933), 64–67, 122–126.

expression which told me they were not thinking at all of any historical significance. To them it was just sweet music, "old-time singing" for which they had the same reverence and love as for its close kin, the "old-time religion," and for which the more recent makers of religious songs had brought them no satisfying substitute. It was this serious significance of the occasion, as it seemed, however much the out-door part of it might have reminded one of circus day, which put it beyond the criticism of the Lord's Day observationists and into the class of religious celebrations.

An elderly man with handle-bar moustache was leading in the most approved manner, holding his book in the left hand and beating time, down, left, right, up, with his right. And when the page of music called for a pause in the singing, he filled it out dutifully with his beats, calling them out audibly, "down, left." The singers first went through the song singing the notes, that is, the syllables *fa, sol, la,* and *mi.* If the leader was familiar with more stanzas than appeared in the book, he lined them out.

The response of the singers seemed to me pathetically weak, as I contrasted it to the vocal volume I had heard many times at *Sacred Harp* conventions and seven-shape gatherings farther south. (These will be described in appropriate environment below.) And they took the songs at a slow, draggy pace which reminded one strikingly of the primitive singing in some of the country churches of the Afro-Americans. The voices of the old singers were thin. Leaders were few. The memory of those singers who had no books was noticeably waning. The man, younger than the average, who shared my book and sang lustily, had lost his *Southern Harmony* when his house burned some time before. Some of the favorite songs were, "How tedious and tasteless the hours," "Salvation, Oh the joyful sound," "Oh, when shall I see Jesus and reign with Him above."

Because of the crowd which had come for the big holiday, the ancient institution of a general picnic "dinner on the grounds" to which all were to contribute and of which all were to partake, was out of the question. So at twelve the great throng left the court-room, gathered in little and larger groups in public eating places, in private homes, and on the grass under the trees, and opened their baskets.

It was during this period that I met Mr. George W. Lemon, who, with his brother, James Roberts Lemon, had started these Benton singings in 1884, and I heard from him about those early times. The Lemon brothers were little children in 1852 when their parents made the six-hundred-mile trek by covered wagon all the way from Guilford County, North Carolina, across the Blue Ridge, the Smoky, and the Cumberland Mountains to Marshall County in the western wedge of Kentucky. A copy of the *Southern Harmony*, widely used at that time in the Old North State, must have been tucked away somewhere in that prairie schooner. Anyway, young James Lemon used the Walker book later in "literary" schools and in singing schools which he taught, and when he and his brother George started the Benton singings it became the official song collection. The meager dozen copies of the William Walker book which the singers found at the start grew to a score as interest increased and as the singers inquired for further copies in the adjoining counties; until now the number of the precious volumes (last printed in 1854) in use at the Benton singings is about thirty, Mr. Lemon told me. Every year since 1884 the *Southern Harmony* singings have been held on the same day, the fourth Sunday in May, and always, excepting for a few times in the earlier decades, in the courthouse at Benton. James Lemon died about ten years ago. George W. Lemon, James K. Fields, and "Uncle Bud" Hunt are now the leading spirits in the continuation of the musical tradition.

The singers and listeners showed deep interest when I told them the story of William Walker's life and activities, and they responded with their best efforts when I led "Bound for Canaan," singing from a book that had been Walker's own copy and keying the song with Walker's own tuning fork, which its owner had lent me for the occasion. Afterwards a number of them wanted to examine the fork and listen to the clear "C" which had keyed unnumbered songs during the past century.

"Now I can say that I have held William Walker's tuning fork in my hand!" one old man exclaimed exultingly.

* * *

Songs for the Singers, Not for the Listeners

The effect of this singing on the singers is one thing, the most important thing indeed. But the impression made on the mere listener is quite another matter.

The person of standardized urban-musical background who hears casually his first *Sacred Harp* music is apt to judge it harshly. He will be impressed unfavorably by the shrill voices of some of the women, by the trotting movement of the songs, which will strike him as being at variance with their religious aspects, by the harmonic effects (he will call them "discords") that are strangely different from those to which his ear has been accustomed, by what seems to be an absence of melody or tune, and by the fact that all songs sound much alike to him.

As to the shrill voices, the Sacred Harpers will readily admit that a minimum of attention is paid to individual voice quality by the leaders. The song is the thing—the mass effect. And who is going to tell Sister So-and-so not to step on it quite so hard, or that she should place her tone differently, anyway? And why, in the name of good sense, should she bear the audience in mind when there is none? This is democratic music making. All singers are peers. And the moment selection and exclusion enter, at that moment this singing of, for, and by the people loses its chief characteristic.

The reason why some high female voices stand out with undue prominence is not, after all, primarily a matter of individual vocal quality. We are accustomed to hearing female voices predominate when they sing the melody part in mixed choruses. But here they sing, according to hoary tradition, a middle part corresponding roughly to the urban tenor of today. They call it treble and pronounce it "trible." Even when this part is taken by men, it *seems* to be pitched higher than the soprano melody. But when it is sung by women it is *actually* higher. So we have, under the circumstances that

obtain in *Sacred Harp* circles, a "middle part" in the harmony, sung very high and by the women, whose voices have normally greater carrying qualities than those of the men. And this female tenor part is exposed still more completely as the result of another ancient song custom of these singers, namely, the custom which gives the melody part into the keeping of the normal-voiced men, not exclusively but mainly. This means that the melody, while full, has not the carrying power that it would have if sung by female sopranos as we are accustomed to hearing it sung. And it is easy to see that with this partial submergence of the melody the prominence of the female tenor part becomes all the greater, a prominence which brings clearly to the ear of the listener all the vocal qualities, good or bad, of the singers of that part.

And it is, I am convinced, this same unique distribution of parts—men "sopranos" and women "tenors"—that is largely at the root of what strikes the novice-listener as "peculiar harmonic effects." There may be other reasons for the effects. My attention has been called also to the "successive fifths" in *Sacred Harp* songs as a factor in their harmonic character. Whit Denson, a *Sacred Harp* composer, doubts the importance of the "successive fifths" feature and calls attention to the frugality in the use of different chords. He points out that the *Sacred Harp* songs tend to specialize on the tonic and dominant chords and to neglect the subdominant and practically all others. As still further contributions to the unique musical character of these songs, it may be mentioned that many of them show pentatonic melodies, that very many of the songs are in minor keys, and that the fuguing songs are structural puzzles which demand a number of hearings and some study before the hearer can understand "what it is all about."

In the above paragraphs I have called attention to characteristics which have been at the bottom of the "peculiar harmonic effects," and which have contributed to the submergence of the melody. There is, however, still another reason why it is hard for the listener to identify the tune in *Sacred Harp* singing. In urban music of the usual simpler sorts the tune is paramount and the other parts are comparatively modest and subservient in their trend. This is not true for the *Sacred Harp*. There the melody part (they call it "tenor") is of hardly any greater import than any other. For the custom of the rural composers has been, from time immemorial, to make the parts, as nearly as possible, equally interesting to the singers. This objective seems to have been justified by the necessity, in the utter absence of instruments, for each of the four parts to be well manned. So we see treble, alto, and bass indulging in about as much running around as does the tune-carrying tenor. They even snatch a bit of the tune away from the tenor, here and there, forcing it to put up with the notes of a "middle part" or observe a "rest." The result of all this poaching of one part on the preserves of the others is confusion on the part of the listener who tries to identify the parts—soprano, alto, and tenor, the bass being more easily recognizable—to which his urban ear has become accustomed in choral church music *comme il faut.*

A word as to the trotting movement of practically all the *Sacred Harp* songs, that characteristic which usually impresses the city-dwelling listener as being inappropriate to the religious character of the words. The movement of these songs is, to be sure, uniformly sprightly, about the tempo of the march. And this condition often imposes on the singers the task of negotiating some very fast note and word sequences. But, after all, who has decreed that all sacred music should be slow? The old chorale type of music was slow, to be sure. The early American colonists dragged their tunes along. And modern city congregations pull back, despite the efforts of organ and quartet to overcome their phlegm. But does all that establish any immutable law? Certainly the congregations have found no scriptural injunctions against sprightly, glad music. On the contrary.

Another estranging rhythmic feature in the *Sacred Harp* singing is their common custom of not tolerating any dead spaces or long rests, those pauses which are found in instrumentally influenced music and even to some extent in the *Sacred Harp* pages—"waits" which are felt as needed to make the rhythmic form mathematically correct or quadratic, holes that are filled, in other environments, by instrumental inserts. But here, with no instrument to fill the melodic-rhythmic vacuum, the leaders and singers deliberately disregard the rest-beat and proceed as though it did not exist. This procedure naturally throws the leader's regularly alternating beat out of joint with the tune, making him beat "up" on a downbeat and vice versa, until he comes to another discarded pause that sets him straight again. With all this, it will be seen, much of the variation in accent heft is lost by the singer and to the hearer, and the rhythmic flow becomes mechanized.

It would seem, then, that the *Sacred Harp* type of music is to be sung and not listened to, and that the critic who makes his judgments from the false observation point of the twentieth-century hearer is pretty sure to draw unhappy and impertinent conclusions.

Joshua Leavitt (1794–1873), a Yale graduate who became a Congregationalist minister in New York City, was an influential figure in religious revivalism in the North. In 1831, he founded *The Evangelist*, a provocative periodical that reached twenty-six editions by 1842 and gained enormous popularity before the Civil War. Leavitt began printing revival hymns with tunes in the issues of this journal.

The Christian Lyre, which contains hymns from the periodical, was issued in 1831 to meet the needs of revival hymnody and ride the crest of the revival movement. Its popularity led to the publication of a *Supplement*, also in 1831, and a *Companion* two years later. A general advertisement lays bare Leavitt's purpose: "We want music here which is easy, yet effective; simple, touching, animating, moving; such as will, by its melody, affect the mind in correspondence with the language: music, in short, which will produce a religious effect, rather than that which is only calculated to please a musical ear." The preface to volume 1, a convenient, pocket-size hymnal, indicates that the work is not designed to please "scientific musicians" but that the words are uppermost in importance. Complete texts appear under or beside each hymn. Leavitt's claim that he possesses "no musical skill beyond that of ordinary plain singers" helps him communicate with the large public he is trying to reach.

In its appearance *The Christian Lyre* was ahead of its time, its format presaging the look of modern hymnals.

JOSHUA LEAVITT

from *The Christian Lyre* (1831)

Preface

Every person conversant with revivals must have observed, that whenever meetings for prayer and conference assume a special interest, there is a desire to use hymns and music of a different character from those ordinarily heard in the church. Nettleton's Village Hymns[1] in a good degree meets the first want. Jocelyn's Zion's Harp[2] partially supplies the other. But both are felt to be incomplete, as they are wanting in many pieces, which have proved of great use in revivals.

The usefulness also of many excellent hymns in all our modern collections, has been prevented by the inability of singers to find tunes adapted to the various subjects and metres. The "Christian Lyre" is undertaken with a view to meet both these deficiencies. It is intended to contain a collection of such pieces as are specially adapted to evening meetings and social worship, and chiefly such as are not found in our common collections of sacred music.

As the work is not designed to please scientific musicians, so much as to profit plain christians, reference will be had, chiefly, to the known popu-

---

Joshua Leavitt, *The Christian Lyre*, 5th ed., rev., 2 vols. (New York: Jonathan Leavitt, 1831), 1:[iii], 24–25.

[1]Asahel Nettleton, *Village Hymns for Social Worship* (Hartford, 1824).

[2]Engraved and published by Nathaniel and Simeon Smith Jocelyn (New Haven, 1824).

larity and good influence of what is selected. And it is intended to embrace the music that is most current among different denominations of christians.

As the number of parts is apt to distract the attention of an audience, or to occupy them with the music instead of the sentiment, the tunes here printed will generally be accompanied with only a simple bass, and sometimes not even with that. In a vast multitude of cases the *religious* effect of a hymn is heightened by having all sing the air only.

Possessing no musical skill beyond that of ordinary plain singers, I send out my work, without pretensions. If it aids the progress of Christ's cause, I shall be rewarded. If not, I shall be accepted according to what I had, and not according to what I had not. And it will prepare the way for some other person to do better.

* * *

Missionary Hymn Composed by Lowell Mason

FROM Greenland's icy mountains,
From India's coral strand;
Where Afric's sunny fountains
Roll down their golden sand;
From many an ancient river,
From many a palmy plain,

They call us to deliver
Their land from error's chain.

What though the spicy breezes
Blow soft o'er Ceylon's isle,
Though every prospect pleases,
And only man is vile;
In vain with lavish kindness
The gifts of God are strown;
The heathen in his blindness
Bows down to wood and stone.

Shall we, whose souls are lighted
With wisdom from on high,
Shall we to men benighted
The lamp of life deny?
Salvation! O Salvation!
The joyful sound proclaim,
Till earth's remotest nation
Has learn'd Messiah's name.

Waft, waft, ye winds, his story,
And you, ye waters, roll,
Till, like a sea of glory,
It spreads from pole to pole
Till o'er our ransom'd nature,
The Lamb for sinners slain,
Redeemer, King, Creator,
In bliss returns to reign.

27 Two Prima Donnas: Maria Malibran and Elizabeth Austin

Two performers toured America singing English opera repertoire to great acclaim during the period 1825–35. Maria Malibran (1808–1836), a Spanish mezzo-soprano, was the first genuine opera star Americans had seen. A highly popular successor was the radiant English soprano Elizabeth Austin (1800–after 1835), less of an actress, but America's reigning prima donna before she returned to England in 1835.

Maria Malibran, daughter of opera tenor, teacher, and impresario Manuel García, traveled with her father's opera company to New York. Italian opera was first heard there when García's company presented Rossini's *Barber of Seville* on November 29, 1825. After her marriage to French merchant Eugène Malibran, whom, it was believed, she married principally to get away from her domineering father, the singer remained in the United States, appearing in English roles. Her hopes for financial security were dashed when her husband went bankrupt. Malibran returned to Europe in 1827, where she continued to sing with great success.

Elizabeth Austin toured widely in America between 1828 and the mid-1830s, popularizing English opera adaptations. Theater actor and manager Francis Courtney Wemyss speaks both of her popularity in New York, where "she became a reigning favourite," and the brilliant style with which she executed the music.

The two articles below appeared in important nineteenth-century music journals. *The Musical World & Times*, a significant undertaking of the 1850s, existed under several titles and was edited by the impressive writer Richard Storrs Willis. The article on Elizabeth Austin, signed "Clio," comes from New York's short-lived *Euterpeiad: An Album of Music and Prose*, published 1830–31. Its editor, Charles Dingley, was hardly new to the publishing world, having been an editor of Boston's *The Euterpeiad; or, Musical Intelligencer* in 1823.

The article on Austin concludes by pointing out the tenuous situation for opera in New York in the early 1830s. Opera as an art form is expensive and complicated to produce, and the history of operatic production in New York—in whatever language—was fraught with turbulence during much of the nineteenth century. It reached a steadier base only in October 1883, when the Metropolitan Opera House opened at Broadway and 39th Street with Gounod's *Faust*.

RICHARD STORRS WILLIS?

from "Biography of Malibran" (1854)

Madame Malibran, Garcia by birth, belonged to a family which in varied gifts, and particularly genius for art, was a privileged one. She received her musical education from her father, the tenor Garcia, both a composer and singing master of the highest repute. From early childhood Maria evinced the most fortunate endowments of nature. But her sprightliness and indomitable petulance deterred her from all musical study. Nothing but the most strange and the most perilous exercises could captivate her imagination: such as running over the tops of houses, climbing up ladders and rocks. These were her favorite pastimes. Such eccentric habits displeased Garcia extremely, whose anger and dissatisfaction occasionally induced manual correction of the severest kind. It was only at the age of thirteen that she began to yield to her father's care. At this period her rapid progress and her abilities foretold a first-rate songstress.

At the age of fifteen, being in London with her family, she was requested unexpectedly to supply the place of the *prima donna* of the Italian Theater, who was to sustain the part of *Rosina* in the *Barbiere*.[1] She was familiar with all the pieces of the entire rôle. Her attempt and her performance was a triumph. When more deeply initiated in the mysteries of musical and dramatic art she continued her studies of the modern repertory, and was entrusted with the character of *Felicia* in *Crociato*,[2] by Meyerbeer. From London she followed her father to New York, where she enacted some characters of importance, such as those of *Trancredi*, of *Malcolm* in *Donna del' Lago*, of *Desdemona* in *Otello* &c.[3] In relation to the last work it is said, that her father performing the part of Otello, and finding her too cold in the first representation swore that he would really kill her did she not endeavor to be more spirited: which threat she took as serious, coming from so severe a master, and after the play was over, the father, not being able to restrain his satisfaction lavished upon his daughter eulogies and caresses, of which, till then, he had been too sparing. Mdlle. Garcia sang most successfully in the United States and Mexico. It was during her stay in America that a wealthy merchant wished to marry her, and, notwithstanding the disparity of age the suit was accepted and the marriage consummated. Madame Malibran withdrew from the stage. But, shortly after, her husband fell victim to a bankruptcy which deprived him of his fortune. The strangest reports were in circulation on this account; even, that Mr. Malibran had looked upon the talent of the young artiste as a means of retrieving again his affairs.—How much such rumors can be relied upon, is a matter of no importance for us to inquire. The fact is, that the ruin of the husband was irremediable, and that his wife reappeared on the stage she had unwillingly left. The creditors of Mr. Malibran then opposed the payment of her salary; domestic quarrels ensued, which led to a divorce. In 1827 Madame Malibran returned to Paris, where she had spent her youthful years. Her return was hailed earnestly by Parisian society, especially by the frequenters of Countess Merioni's saloon [sic], who assisted in getting her an engagement at the Italian Theater.

Her success in England and the United States secured her the most substantial offers. On the 14th of January, 1828, for the benefit of Galli,[4] she sustained with unanimous applause the character of *Semiramis*.[5] Shortly after she sang with equal

---

Richard Storrs Willis?, "Biography of Malibran," *Musical World & Times*, June 3, 1854: 53.

[1] Rossini's *Barber of Seville*.

[2] *Il Crociato in Egitto.*

[3] All three operas are by Rossini. Malcolm, a young warrior, is traditionally sung by a mezzo-soprano, as in *Trancredi*.

[4] Filippo Galli.

[5] Rossini's *Semiramide*. The subject, popular in the nineteenth century, was set by several different composers.

success in a concert at the Conservatory; lastly, on the 8th of April, of the same year, in the Italian Theater, with fifty thousand francs salary per year, and a benefit representation. She stamped her own genius on all the rôles she sustained; and though she had to fear such a rival as Mdlle. Sontag,[6] and the recollection of Mad. Mainvielle Fodor,[7] yet she evinced superior talent both as a witty comedienne and a consummate tragedienne. No artist ever possessed, to such a degree, that consummate grace and strength, that energy and delicacy, which give so much value to the productions of art. She obtained a brilliant ovation as *Desdemona*, and the warmest applause as *Rosina* in the *Barbiere*.

---

[6]German soprano Henriette Sontag (Gertrude Walpurgis Sonntag, 1806–1854) was a bitter rival.

[7]Joséphine Fodor-Mainvielle (1789–1870).

ANONYMOUS

"Mrs. Austin" (1830)

It is one of the most striking proofs that our pretensions to what we undertake are well grounded, when we extort from those who sit in judgment upon us, a gradually increasing approbation. This result has consecutively followed Mrs. Austin's various European professional engagements; it has attended her excursory visits to the various American Theatres, or (as the more familiar coloquial is) in starring it; and her progressive success in the Park Theatre in this city [New York] has been remarkable. Before giving any technical analysis of her vocal qualifications, or going into the particulars of her biography, we shall enumerate, en passant, a few points which have probably constituted the *accessories* to her success.

*   *   *

In the same summer [1827], she sang at several of the great festivals and from thence came to this country. She arrived in Philadelphia: the Press of that city speedily admitted her to be the best English singer that had ever appeared on this side [of] the Atlantic. From thence she proceeded to New-York, heralded by no puffs, without having the public mind prepossessed in her favor—a mode of proceeding adopted by managers, in this country, to a mischievous extent.[1] She played, at first, to scanty houses; but, on the appearance of Artaxerxes,[2] talent could no longer be kept back by circumstance, and she at once established her fame and exclusive right to the very first honors of her profession. And here we must pay a merited tribute of praise to the public of New-York: Mrs. Austin is a strong instance of their judgment and taste. They have adopted her from their own observation, and she has risen in their favor; in short, she is as much indebted to them, as is Mr. Forrest, whose deserving rise to eminence is attributable to the same source—and they form two instances of talent fostered, for its intrinsic merit, in this city. That this state of things has had an exciting effect on her energy, and leads to fresh exertion, there can be no doubt. In no theatre does she appear so thoroughly at home, as in the Park Theatre; and to hear Mrs. Austin to the greatest advantage it must be when exerting herself before a New-York audi-

---

[1]Her initial contract, with actor and manager Francis Courtney Wemyss, was for an appearance at Philadelphia's Chestnut Street Theatre. Her New York debut took place at the Park Theatre on January 2, 1828.

[2]F. C. Wemyss identifies the composer of this opera as "Dr. Ames," probably meaning Thomas Arne, whose *Artaxerxes* (1762) became well known.

"For The Euterpeiad. Portraits of Vocalists, Analytical and Biographical. Mrs. Austin," *Euterpeiad: An Album of Music, Poetry and Prose*, n.s., 1 (December 1, 1830): 147–48.

ence. We have now to speak analytically of Mrs. Austin, as a singer.

Mrs. Austin has a full soprano voice, of great compass and flexibility; but its most distinguishing attribute, is its equality; no division, no break, is perceptible throughout its range. In this country, in particular, an error seems to have crept into many persons' minds, that a lady or gentleman who sings a vast number of notes in a rapid manner, must have musical science; and when they speak of a lady being a great musician, their ideas are extremely indefinite on that head. We venture to lay down a definition of the term "good musician," as applicable to a female vocalist. She must have studied the Solfeggio, and founded on that study, she must be consequently capable of hitting with ease all the distances of the scales; she must read at sight, and she must be a good timeist, and have acquired a faultless intonation—this will entitle her to be called a good musician.—To merit the name of a fine singer, she must have very considerable natural qualities; voice of course being the primary one. . . .

We now venture upon some concluding remarks upon *audiences*. In the course of our attendance at the Park Theatre, during last October, we remarked, that Mrs. Austin, uniformly, in that month, obtained considerable applause from Southerners, or Southrons, as they have been called. Music is enthusiastically admired in the Southern States, and their taste is by no means *un-cultivated*. In all countries, *tuition in Music must precede full enjoyment*; and when such pains have been taken, as is the case in regard to a large portion of the population of Germany, the satisfaction derived from the musical drama, doubles: the musical auditor takes in the pleasures of sense through an intellectual medium. Respecting the inequality of the patronage bestowed upon the lyrical drama here, the following remark, from a popular print, in this city, is in point. "The fact is, our national character is so strongly marked with the love of novelty, variety, and singularity, that, like the men of Athens, we are perpetually in search of something *new*." On the continent of Europe, the most enthusiastic audiences, are musical; and for the reason above assigned. That taste, which is founded upon knowledge and science, never forsakes its possessor, but rather, on the other hand, is continually adding to his sources of enjoyment, by new discoveries made, and ideas imparted. Whether the regular Opera is to be maintained here, or carried back again to Europe, will be probably determined in the next six months: if the English Opera does not succeed, the Italian cannot, possessed, as the former is, of all the familiar avenues to the mind, and the passions of an audience, speaking the English tongue. Should the English Opera now be forced from the atlantic shores, one thing is certain, the attempt could not be rationally revived before 1930—viz: translated into words, *a century hence.*

28 Jenny Lind, the Swedish Nightingale

Most popular of all the prima donnas that came to America was Jenny [Johanna Maria] Lind (1820–1887), known as the "Swedish nightingale." One of her teachers was Manuel García, father of Maria Malibran. Not only did Lind sing well, but she came to America under contract with famed impresario and master showman Phineas T. Barnum, under whose management she gave ninety-five concerts in nineteen cities to great acclaim and financial reward. Like her predecessors Maria Malibran and Elizabeth Austin, she stayed in the United States for a short time only—from September 1850 to June 1852—but her impact was significant.

Under Barnum, Lind became the first musician to be promoted by a nonperformer. "Lindomania" swept the nation, as witnessed by an advertisement in a Washington paper for "Jenny Lind opera glasses from the optical institute in Munich and Vienna . . . more than one thousand have been sold during Jenny Lind's concerts in New York and Philadelphia." Indeed, her name was used to sell many more far-ranging products than that, including Jenny Lind hair gloss, pens, canes, and even Jenny Lind chewing tobacco. Commercialism coupled with significant charitable contributions helped seal her artistic success.

Lind's American tour took her to Washington, D.C. from Sunday, December 15, to Thursday, December 19, 1850. There she enjoyed an audience with President and Mrs. Millard Fillmore, who told her they were looking forward to her first concert in the New National Hall, which was still under construction.

The audience for the concert on December 16 included many national leaders. Lind's program, like most of her others, included the famous *Home, Sweet Home.* "Washington's *The National Era* commented on December 19, 1850: "We have heard many delightful singers, but none before that perfectly satisfied us." *The Daily Union* called the event "a noble gathering, worthy of her whose silvery tones called it together—and worthy, too, of the metropolis of a great nation." It commented further:

> It is not the vocal powers of Jenny Lind alone which call our people around her; nor is it her genius alone which commands their admiration; nor is it among the inhabitants of great cities alone, thirsting for excitement, that she is most esteemed. Her unobtrusive modesty—her meek virtues—her open-handed charity—were known among us before she ever saw the shores of the Western World. The people of America have been told these things. They have read her history, and they have seen how she has arisen from obscurity to fame; yet carrying all her homely virtues with her—clinging to them amidst scenes of splendor that have dazzled many and made them dizzy.*

---

*The Daily Union (Washington, D.C.), December 17, 1850: [4].

National leaders attended Lind's second and final Washington concert on December 18. Again the hall was filled, the program was a grand success, and the press was highly enthusiastic.

Although Lind's success lost some of its luster prior to her return to Europe, her visit to the United States can only be counted as remarkable. She brought a new kind of persona to the American concert stage, one of engaging artistry, yet projected by an individual of personal charm and appeal in tune with the American ideals of charity, modesty, generosity, and success against the odds. *The Musical World* editorialized upon her departure: "[A]nd we, America, with our million-fingered hand of religious honesty and world-loving freedom, this moment dread to give the farewell pressure to her who has for nearly two years blessed us with efforts such only as are prompted by a Charity that sits enthroned above Faith and Hope."†

†*The Musical World*, June 1, 1852: [1].

JENNY LIND

Letter to Her Parents (1850)

I have met with quite an astonishing reception and have given, already six concerts in New York, in a hall that holds 11,000 people.[1] It has been crowded each time, and we shall be able, most likely to give 40 or 50 concerts in New York alone. Here everything is done on a large scale. The first ticket sold here (Boston) for to-day's concert was sold by auction for as much as 625 dollars! It is amazing what heaps of money they seem to have here. My health, thank God, is excellent and my voice fresh and strong, and I am looking forward, when this tournée is over to a time of peace and rest. For indeed, in these two matters so precious to human beings, I seem to be given little share, torn and bothered as I am from morning to night. Still it is touching to see how much good-will and kindness I receive; people seem not to know how, enough, to show their favour and genuine interest. I wish I could send home to you some of the lovely fruit and flowers I continually receive. We have lovely warm weather, still, and ever a divinely blue sky. Time does pass; I shall soon be 30 years of age. How happy I am to become "an ould hag"! Every day I see round me numbers of new faces and I find it rather a bore, but I am trying to terminate my engagement perhaps in a year.[2] When we meet I shall have heaps to relate which I have now no time for.

It is already more than 3 months since I was dancing round the May-pole at home. Now pray take care of yourselves, and remember with tenderness your far-off daughter.

Jenny Lind, Letter to her parents, September 27, 1850, as quoted in Jenny M. C. Maude, *The Life of Jenny Lind* (London: Cassell, 1926), 162.

[1]The figure refers to her highly successful first concert in New York at the Castle Garden before a large audience on September 11, 1850. She was to give twenty concerts in all in that city.

[2]Lind broke with Barnum in May 1851.

CHARLES G. ROSENBERG
from *Jenny Lind in America* (1851)

On this evening, therefore, her first Concert in Washington took place. Mr. Bushnell had managed, by indefatigable industry, to get the Hall about one-half finished. The benches were of plain deal. The heat which they had been compelled to maintain during the last three or four days, in the interior, had warped at least one-half of them. The balustrades of the steps leading to the doors, were no more than some dozen of rough boards, hastily nailed together. Glasses had not been provided for one-half the jets of gas; and as for the gallery, that was left completely unfinished. Nevertheless, the public was not deterred by the state of the Hall, and it began to fill rapidly at an early hour. If rank be measured by intellect alone, the audience was essentially one of the very noblest before which Jenny Lind had ever yet sung in any part of the world. Here was the placid and quiet-faced President sitting with his family. Not far from him was Daniel Webster, his colossal brow rising boldly over the deep-set eyes which were ever and anon flashing fitfully around the scene before him. Indeed, of all the intellectual heads which I have ever seen, that of Daniel Webster impresses me the most. The character of the man is written tangibly and vividly upon it. A gigantic intelligence would seem imbedded in the capacious and magnificent forehead. The eye tells the tale of his eloquence and thought, and betrays, in conjunction with the marked and characteristic mouth, a slight propensity to irony. In addition to this, observe him when he stands listening to you. Would it not veritably seem as though the weight of his brow bent his neck, as his head, slightly declined forward, seems to listen to you? Again, here is General Cass, his broad, heavy and clever face, with its large features, betraying the impress of talent almost as clearly as does that of Webster. He avows frankly that he

cares not for music, and that it used to be an awful bore when he was obliged, while Ambassador at Paris, occasionally to show himself at the Opera; yet he is here with the intention of hearing the Nightingale, of whom so much has been said to him. Not far from him is Benton, and again, at no very great distance, is his antagonist, Foote. It would, however, be useless to fancy that I can reckon by name any thing like the number of remarkable men who were collected in the front of that audience. Suffice it that, not far from Webster, sits Crittenden, the Attorney General. A little to his right are the Secretaries of the Treasury and the Interior. Here is the Secretary of War, and near him is A. R. Hall, the Postmaster General.

However, it is already the hour for commencing the Concert. Benedict enters, and in a few moments the first notes of the orchestra are heard rising through the Hall.

Scarcely had the overture—if I remember rightly, that to *Massaniello*[3]—been half played through, than a murmur was heard from the end of the building. It was hushed instantly, and the overture was played to an end. Then burst out a long and loud shout of applause. For a moment Benedict looked around, somewhat astonished. He, however, saw immediately that this applause had not been called forth by the orchestra. The tall, slim—I should possibly have said, thin figure of an aged man was slowly advancing up the room. All made way for him, for the avenues had been almost completely blocked up. I no sooner saw the face than I recognized it, from the busts, engravings, and caricatures, which I had seen. It was that of Henry Clay. I must confess that it was not the character of face which I should have expected to have seen. The brow was not large. The greyish

Charles G. Rosenberg, *Jenny Lind in America* (New York: Stringer & Townsend, 1851), 88–92, 93–94.

[3]From the incidental music to Thomas D'Urfey's *The Rise and Fall of Massaniello* by Daniel Purcell (Henry Purcell's brother).

blue eye was, nevertheless, vivid and sparkling, and the capacious and broad mouth was the feature which most conveyed the idea of talent to my mind. It was singularly marked, and must, when he was younger, have possessed an immense power of expression.

As he advanced, the shouts and applause redoubled. He, bowing on every side, continued his path feebly, and somewhat cautiously. At length he reached his seat, and the applause ceased for a moment. Then a voice at the upper end of the Hall cried out:

"Three cheers for Harry Clay!"

And they were as heartily given by the whole audience as I had ever heard cheers given in my life.

Amongst those who had risen as Clay advanced down the Hall, was one man who stood well nigh a head taller than the rest of the audience. His head attracted my attention. It had a soldierly and marked countenance, expressing a good deal of energy and resolution. I asked the gentleman who was next me, to whom it belonged. It was the head of General Scott, who had entered the earliest of any of the distinguished men who were then present, with something more than the ordinary punctuality, even of a soldier.

The character of the audience seemed to inspire Jenny with more than her usual melody, and she sung far better than she had done since she last quitted New York. I, however, remarked that Daniel Webster adhered with praiseworthy pertinacity to his previous opinion, and expressed but trifling interest in her execution of Italian music. At length she came to the *Bird Song*, and when she commenced this charming morsel of German melody, I saw his eyes brighten, and am tolerably certain that I detected him endeavoring to beat time with his foot. Unfortunately, like Napoleon, his idea of time was not of the most correct class, which somewhat seriously interfered with the precision of his accompaniment to the melody.

During the latter portion of the concert, some young rascal on the outside of the building, indignant at having been cleared from the steps leading to the doors of the Hall by the police who were sta-

tioned there, flung a stone through one of the windows. Fortunately, none of the audience had their heads broken by this agreeable diversion. The police immediately endeavored to secure the delinquent, but this was useless. He had taken good care to abscond, without waiting to ascertain the effect of his missile.

Upon the following morning, Mademoiselle Lind received visits from most of the leading men who had been present at her concert on the Monday, while a note was brought to Mr. Barnum from Daniel Webster, requesting him to name a time when she could receive him, as he would be engaged in one of the Law Courts during the greater portion of the morning. With Henry Clay she had a long conversation, which she deeply regretted being compelled to terminate, in consequence of her intended visit to Mount Vernon at twelve o'clock. For this trip, a large party had been made, including, of course, M. Benedict and Signor Belletti, Mr. Barnum with his daughter, and Mrs. Lyman who had accompanied him upon this tour with the intention of visiting Havana. Max Hjortzberg and Mr. Seyton, with some few others, were also of the party. Colonel Washington accompanied her down the river to the estate and resting-place of his great ancestor. The day itself was beautiful, although the previous one had been wet in the extreme. The distance came clearly and crisply off the blue sky, and a fresh breeze just curled the breast of the broad Potomac, which laughed and played around the bows of the steamer, scattering its waters in the air in jets on either side. . . .

Meanwhile the public of Washington were beginning to feel anxious about her second appearance, which was to take place on the Wednesday evening. When the hour for which it was advertised, drew nigh, the hall was thronged with hearers. The President and Mrs. Fillmore were again present. So was Henry Clay and General Scott. Mr. Webster managed to arrive when the concert was about half over; and, indeed, all the remarkable men who had attended her first concert presented themselves on this occasion. Mr. Barnum had, as it seemed, been unfortunately induced to persuade Mademoiselle Lind to sing "Hail Columbia."

Knowing, as she must have done, how unsuitable the song would prove for the female voice, I am at a loss to conceive that she could have been persuaded to allow it to be announced for her. Of course it did not please the audience, brilliantly as she sung it. The preceding portion of the concert had, however, earned her as brilliant a triumph as that which had attended her on the Monday evening, and possibly she had no reason to regret this failure, as it subsequently offered a tangible and evident reason for Mr. Barnum's declining to suggest songs, in accordance with the desires of many well-meaning but injudicious friends, for her approval.

We were now to start for Richmond, whither Le Grand Smith had already preceded us, and on the Thursday morning we were on the bosom of the Potomac, on our way towards that city.

Two Reviews of Jenny Lind's Second Washington Concert (1850)

From *The National Intelligencer*, December 19, 1850

The success of Mad'lle Lind's second concert, last evening, establishes beyond question the unrivalled place she holds in the public esteem. The great crowd of high and humble which flocked to her first concert (notwithstanding the drawback of the unheard-of here, but necessary, prices of admission) might have been supposed to be moved chiefly by curiosity to hear one so renowned in song, and who had won so many hearts by her goodness. But when a greater crowd filled the vast hall a second time, and on the same terms, it could justly be ascribed to but one cause, and that one the unequalled attractions of the artiste combined with high esteem for the woman.

From *The Daily Union*, December 20, 1850

This unrivalled vocalist left us yesterday morning for Richmond, where she gives her only concert this evening. She has left thousands of admirers behind her, and many warm friends, whom her noble moral character has strongly attached to her. We have never seen such a person of "world-wide fame," who has been so much admired in every country which she has visited, so little affected and perverted by the triumphs she has won. Still simple in her habits; alive to all the purest touches of nature; warm of heart; cordial in her manner, when properly appreciated and treated; more fitted to grace even the domestic circle than to shine on the public arena—she realizes her own saying, when she observed to a lady on Tuesday evening in this city, "When I meet with a person of heart, my own melts."

For years we have held to the opinion—but paradoxical as it appears, it is nevertheless true—that "it is much easier to bear prosperity than adversity." Yet, though surrounded by the brightest triumphs of her art, followed as is by the applauses of the multitude, and possessed of immense wealth, out of whose store she liberally dispenses to the poor and the sufferer, we have never seen a person less changed or less corrupted by the prosperity she enjoys than Jenny Lind. Even calumny itself has not dared to attack her. She has passed through the fiery furnace unscathed. Indeed, she deserves to be admired and beloved not more for her musical talents than for the virtues which she possesses.

The National Intelligencer (Washington, D.C.), December 19, 1850.

The Daily Union (Washington, D.C.), December 20, 1850.

New England psalmody was kept alive in the North by nostalgic songfests featuring the "good old tunes." Other organized events and publications helped to perpetuate the repertoire. For example, the Billings and Holden Society, organized in Boston in the 1830s, published its *Ancient Psalmody* (1836) so that music "might not only be rescued from oblivion, but again be presented to the public in its original form."

This trend peaked during the 1850s and 1860s, with the concerts organized by shoe merchant "Father" Robert Kemp (1820–1897) riding the crest of the wave. His singers began to dress up as the old-time characters they represented. Touring widely, they presented a highly successful kind of entertainment bordering on the theatrical.

Kemp clearly enjoyed what he was doing, as he lets us know in the preface to his autobiography:

> I am under great obligations to the Pilgrim Fathers for landing so near Cape Cod. I thank them heartily. Had they gone farther South, their descendants would have dressed differently, sung different psalm-tunes, I might have been somebody else, and, consequently, "Father Kemp" would never have had a chance in the world.
> . . . No slight intended to the Puritans of the Massachusetts Colony, many of whose descendents were members of my choir.*

*Robert Kemp, *Father Kemp and His Old Folks* (Boston: The Author, 1868), v–vi.

ROBERT J. KEMP

from *Father Kemp and His Old Folks* (1868)

After the "dress rehearsals," I determined to appear in public, with my troupe, of whom I had began to feel somewhat proud. I saw that the entertainments pleased the "old folks," who did not belong to the choir. I felt also that a revival of the good music of former times, sung as our ancestors sung it, would be a novel experience to the present generation. Accordingly the evening of Dec. 6, 185- [1855] was set apart as the proper time for Father Kemp and his "Old Folks" to make their debut before the public. Extra pains were taken to

Robert Kemp, *Father Kemp and His Old Folks. A History of the Old Folks' Concerts* (Boston: published by the author, 1868), 27–34, 202, 226–27.

procure books, and we found it difficult to get a sufficient number. Doubtless more old garrets in Massachusetts were turned topsy-turvy for this purpose than for any object since the settlement of the colony. At the first entertainment the Lyceum Hall in Reading was literally packed with what Mr. Jenkins would call a "large and fashionable audience," although a very important number of the people present were noted for the scrupulous care which they took to discard everything of a fashionable nature. The timid ones feared a "break down;" but not such as one as our parents were wont to indulge in, in their moments of hilarity. Hundreds remained outside the building unable to gain admission, and listened to the music of the "Old

Folks;" and they thought, with the audience, that the voices of the fossils were remarkably fresh.

The people of Lynn had an awakening upon the subject of old music, and the company, which by this time had become quite well organized, received a cordial invitation to appear in that place. We started in teams for Lynn. A severe snow-storm came on, which rendered it impossible for us to get to the hall. As it has always been my principle never to postpone a concert on account of the weather, the Sagamore House was substituted for the hall, and those who heard the performance were anxious for a second trial, under more favorable auspices. We afterwards appeared in Lynn, with marked success. In the morning after the concert at the hotel we started for home. The roads were drifted and it was intensely cold, the thermometer being for the most of the day twenty degrees below zero. Several of the ladies were frostbitten. Shovels were procured to "clear the track," and thus we worked our passage back to Reading, where we arrived at 6 p.m. The distance from Lynn to Reading is ten miles. We were all day on the road. This was my first experience in going abroad to give concerts. Had I then forsaken the business, the facts in the case would have more than justified me in so doing.

The popular favor with which these unique entertainments had met, prompted me to consider the expediency of giving the citizens of Boston an opportunity to hear them. There was a natural shyness on my part, which was shared by my associates, as to the propriety of the undertaking. Having done business in the city for many years, I of course had many acquaintances, who would be influenced by the measure of my success. If I failed in giving satisfaction, I might as well also fail in the shoe business, and hereafter confine my operations to Reading and Lynn, where I was appreciated. But no man, in my vocation, can be completely discouraged at one failure. The motto of my customers, in purchasing boots, is, "Try, try again," until they find a pair which fits them; and I encourage the axiom. Why should it not apply to the concerts as well? I determined it should. I considered the matter carefully, and the more I considered the better I thought of it. When I had fully concluded to make the trial, I was convinced that the affair ought to assume the proportions of a demonstration,—a protest of the "Old Folks" against being ignored by their posterity. It was my desire to bring to the eye and ear of the citizens of the New England metropolis the customs of the good people of former generations—of whose characteristics as well as dress and behavior we all had read, but which none had been permitted to observe. To accomplish this there must be extensive labor and research, in which not one but scores of people must engage, and to the ardor with which the young "Old Folks" entered into the enterprise, in attending to the details and preparing for the occasion, is due the success of the first concert in Boston.

The Tremont Temple was secured, and I told the company we would try *one*; and if that "took," we would try another. An extra train was chartered to run from Reading to Boston, and return after the concert. The singers numbered about fifty ladies and gentlemen. Our friends turned out in round numbers, all dressed in the costume of "old folks," and those who went to the city to sing and sit on the platform were about two hundred. Such a collection of "nondescripts" was never seen in the Temple before. Arrived at the depot, we found a large crowd awaiting our coming. Twelve omnibuses conveyed us to the concert-room, which was packed with an audience, in which curiosity seemed to be the prevailing element. All the tickets were disposed of several hours before the time announced for the beginning of the entertainment; door-keepers had been knocked down, and the crowd held possession of the staircase and lobbies. The public were evidently aroused, and I felt somewhat aroused myself when I learned what had been going on.

As the members of the troupe and their friends slowly filed on to the platform before the immense audience the noise and disturbance ceased, and all were intently engaged in examining the queer, quaint, and curious costumes which covered the apparently venerable forms before them. One lady wore a dress brought to this country more than two hundred years ago, by Major Willard. His daughter, at her marriage, wore it, and three other ladies were afterwards joined in matrimony while wearing the same dress. The material was satin damask, very rich and brilliant. Other ladies wore dresses of antique fashion, none of which were less than fifty years old, and several were known to be upwards of two hundred years of age. Most of the gentlemen appeared in knee-breeches, buckles, and cocked hats; one had a coat which was worn by one of the first governors of Massachusetts; a hat worn at the battle of Bunker Hill by Lieut. Parker, of Reading, covered the head of another, and the coats, cloaks, etc., were generally venerable, but well preserved. Everything that could not count up a hundred years was considered modern.

The people in the vicinity of Reading were very kind in making presents of old relics, which were highly valued by us. In the way of bonnets, I believe this first concert at the Temple displayed more material on fewer heads than had ever been seen in the building before. One of my champion bonnets would make a score of modern "Fanchons," "Lamballes," and "Marie Antoinettes." One of these formerly belonged to a lady in Salem, and has been introduced at all my concerts. When it was first purchased, all the young ladies in the neighborhood sat in judgment upon it, and decided that the owner must carry it "right straight back," as it was too small for the fashion! She kept it however, in hopes that the fashions might change. This bonnet was as large as a flour-barrel!

Among the distinguished persons represented by the troupe were George and Martha Washington, John Hancock, General Putnam, Thomas Jefferson, Daniel Boone, and numerous others equally well known, besides Puritan fathers and mothers. A member of the company appeared in a check worn by one of the Salem witches. The audience were much interested and amused, and evidently awaited the opening chorus with great eagerness. The selections comprised a variety of sacred and secular music, the latter being of more modern composition. The orchestra was no mean affair, the most notable object being the big fiddle, of whose venerable owner we shall speak hereafter. "Auld Lang Syne" seemed to put the immense throng in the right humor to enjoy the concert. The "Anthem for Easter," "Greenwich," "Coronation," "Strike the Cymbal," the "Ode on Science," etc., followed in due time, all being received with applause. The concert closed with the singing of "Old Hundred," in which the audience were invited to join. They complied with the request with a hearty good will. Notice was given that the "Old Folks" would soon appear in another concert at the Temple. They did appear, and eleven were given in succession with the same éclat that attended the first performance. As an instance of the interest excited among the elder people to hear the company, I will mention a gentleman from Brookline, who, after being disappointed in gaining admission to the Temple on three different evenings, got indignant and entered a complaint at my store, that he had come to the city with his family in a carriage on these occasions, and had found the doors closed and the house full each evening. "Now," said he, with righteous indignation flashing from beneath his spectacles, "I am more than seventy years old, but I could manage these concerts better myself!" I took care of him and his family after that, notwithstanding the fact that half the tickets he had purchased were spurious. The following is one of the many very kind notices of this entertainment which appeared in the Boston papers, and to whose influence I attribute much of the fame which the "Old Folks" speedily acquired,—

"Half an hour before the performances of 'Father Kemp's Old Folks' were commenced last night, every inch of room within the Tremont Temple hall was occupied, and hundreds came afterwards. The excellence of this company was attested by this great desire to hear them, and we feel some local pride in chronicling this success, for they merit all the patronage bestowed upon them; they are capable singers, perform good music, and all of their actions are decorous and appropriate."

*   *   *

All Hail! The Power of Jesus' Name
[Coronation]

All hail! the power of Jesus' name;
Let angels prostrate fall;
Bring forth the royal diadem,
And crown him Lord of all,
Bring forth the royal diadem,
And crown him Lord of all.

Let every kindred, every tribe,
On this terrestrial ball,
To him all majesty ascribe,
And crown him Lord of all,
To him all majesty ascribe,
And crown him Lord of all.

Song of the Old Folks

Should auld acquaintance be forgot,
And never brought to mind;
Should auld acquaintance be forgot,
And songs of auld lang syne?
For auld lang syne we meet to-night,
For auld lang syne;
To sing the songs our fathers sang
In days of auld lang syne.

We've passed through many varied scenes,
Since youth's unclouded day;
And friends and hopes and happy dreams
Time's hand hath swept away.
And voices that once joined with ours,
In days of auld lang syne,
Are silent now and blend no more
In songs of auld lang syne.

Yet ever has the light of song
Illumed our darkest hours,
And cheered us on life's toilsome way,
And gemmed our path with flowers;
The sacred songs our fathers sang,
Dear songs of auld lang syne;
The hallowed songs our fathers sang
In days of auld lang syne.

Here we have met, here we may part,
To meet on earth no more;
And we may never sing again
The cherished songs of yore;
The sacred songs our fathers sang
In days of auld lang syne;
We may not meet to sing again
The songs of auld lang syne.

But when we've crossed the sea of life,
And reached the heavenly shore,
We'll sing the songs our fathers sang,
Transcending those of yore;
We'll meet to sing diviner strains
Than those of auld lang syne;
Immortal songs of praise, unknown
In days of auld lang syne.

30

Negro Minstrelsy

I n the 1820s, English stage productions were combined with African-American traditions to produce Negro minstrelsy, a new kind of spectacle that was uniquely American. It reached its heyday during the second and third quarters of the nineteenth century.

In the early stages of minstrelsy, individual white entertainers performed songs, dances, and comic sketches in blackface between acts of plays. By the 1840s, the genre had evolved into group performance, and the first of many minstrel companies was born. Instruments played on stage were the banjo, tambourine, violin, bones (bone castanets), and, frequently, accordion. At least one member of the company was expected to dance. As time passed, these shows began to stand by themselves as fully developed entertainments.

From behind the mask of blackface, white entertainers, representing stock characters, could overstep the conventional boundaries of social inhibitions to provide freer social commentary through stage business, song, and dance in an atmosphere of ecstatic pleasure. Beginning in the 1850s, even before the Civil War, black Americans themselves joined together in minstrel troupes. The first successful black company, the Brooker and Clayton's Georgia Minstrels, toured widely in the mid-1860s, to much acclaim. Thus, minstrelsy became a mixed-race tradition exploring interactions between black and white.

Minstrel shows enjoyed huge popularity, as the first article below shows: "[T]his entertainment has got strong hold of some secret chord in the popular heart." By the early twentieth century, however, changing traditions caused minstrelsy to evolve into new kinds of burlesque and musical theater, and blackface performances declined until World War II, by which time they had mercifully run their course.

The first article below, apparently by the editor of *The Musical World & Times*, Richard Storrs Willis, speaks to the popularity of minstrelsy. The second, which notes that black people themselves came to participate in the genre, illuminates what it was like to travel the Mississippi on a river steamboat in the early 1800s.

RICHARD STORRS WILLIS?

from "Negro Minstrelsy" (1853)

No one can doubt, we think, that this entertainment has got strong hold of some secret chord in the popular heart. People who turn their faces

Richard Storrs Willis?, "Negro Minstrelsy," *The Musical World & Times*, November 5, 1853: [69]–70.

against the theater and the opera, go to hear the "minstrels." Some families have their regular minstrel night; and it is a curious fact, that the most staid and sober-minded persons often frequent these performances.

In accounting for so paradoxical a taste, with

earnest, sober-minded people particularly, it has been suggested that it is the hidden *sarcasm* and *irony* beneath the burlesque of Negro Minstrelsy, which lend a certain dignity to it, and justify, to the person's own mind, the strong interest entertained. There may be something in this, and yet it seems to us, on the whole, somewhat far-fetched. For our own part, we think that it is nothing more or less than genuine *love of fun*—a latent feeling, after all, in most world-worn hearts—which crowds the hard benches of Negro Minstrelsy. There is so much real tragedy in life itself, as it passes, and so many high-wrought plots of Italian operas are constantly playing around us, that it is pleasant, now and then, to see the other and less dramatic side of the picture.

Who of us would not wish to be mischievous, frolicking, prank-loving children again, could we but drop the heavy mantle of our dignity, and behind a black mask extinguish our personality? Men are but grown up children. A great writer of our own day,[1] who says beautiful and true things in his "Friends in Council" and "Companions of my solitude," in speaking of providing entertainment for the people thus writes:—"Now do you suppose that the grown-up child does not want amusement, when you see children so greedy of it? Do not imagine we grow out of that: we disguise ourselves by various solemnities, *but we have none of us lost the child nature yet.*" And *this* we think the true reason, why we can well endure, occasionally, just such a foolish, mad-cap entertainment as that of the "Negro Minstrels."

So much for the *rationale* of the thing. But there are other collateral causes which contribute, doubtless, to the success of this entertainment: these are—its novelty—the marked peculiarity of the music—and the popular combination of song, dance and jest. No one will deny, that a disguised troupe of eight or nine persons, flanked at each end with a jester, with a musical equipment of bones, banjo, tambourine, accordion and fiddles, has at least the merit of novelty. There is a certain

primitive and traditional barbarism in it. Such an extraordinary defiance of all precedent in the formation of an *orchestra* and in combination of instruments, has something profoundly exciting in it to the learned and scientific musician. It is equaled by nothing except a college band we once conducted, where every instrument under the stars, from a fife and piccolo flute, down through guitars and all stringed instruments to a big drum, orphicleide and serpent, were huddled heterogeneously together, without regard to quantity or orchestral balance; the only consideration being the mass of instruments, and the number of "fellows" we could get into the "band." Minstrel music itself certainly has its strong characteristics; we mean the legitimate portion of it, not the foreign operatic trash. Genuine minstrel music is characterized by great freshness and simplicity of melody, combined with a harmony which consists only of the commonest chords, to the almost entire exclusion of discords. The tonic, dominant and subdominant, comprise nearly the entire wealth of minstrel harmony. These three chords, in fact, are the only ones appreciable by the ordinary ear. Their familiarity, moreover, adds to their charm, and the introduction of any less familiar chord rather diminishes the pleasing musical effect, to the untutored ear. A marked characteristic also of the music generally, is its great *vitality*. Whatever sentiment is to be expressed is given with the whole heart and soul. The merriment, the pathos, the mock-pathos—bathos—the joke and banter, are gone into with a perfect abandonment. Still another characteristic of the music is the strongly-marked and decided *rhythm*. The time is generally strictly kept, and so carefully *whipped-up*, as to appeal to that universal sense in even the commonest natures, a nice appreciation of *measure*. For where there is no appreciation of melody, still less of harmony, there is always a feeling for *time*—otherwise, not every man could be a soldier, and learn to march.

As regards the other accessory of "Negro Minstrelsy"—the jest—we would remark that it seems to us to be strongly stamped with our own nationality. We rejoice in anything that is *fast*, and wide-awake, and *knowing*. This is generally true in the

[1]Sir Arthur Helps (1813–1875).

present instance, and it is keenly appreciated by the masses. A sharp, cute, over-reaching style of talk and raillery is eminently Yankee.

Altogether, we think there is a certain charm even for the most cultivated ear in many of these negro melodies. They have one good quality—they are *complete in themselves*; which is not true of more learned, and perhaps more artificial melodies, depending for their effect upon an accompanying harmony. (A *true* melody should be, strictly speaking, independent of all collateral help.) Hence it is, that these simple airs so often recur to us in the ordinary occupations of life. We hum them alone to ourselves—we whistle them—we walk down Broadway to one of them—we have one in our mind and cannot get rid of it—our transient feeling, whatever it is, is often expressed by them, and the melody, found casually in the mind, generally suits the mood of the moment. Now, we think it high praise for any style of simple melody that it suits the *momentary mood*. A spontaneous, and unlabored expression of feelings in the breast at any moment, is a great luxury. What though the feelings are but transient and superficial, and the scraps of melody that express them necessarily of the same superficial and fragmentary character? Our life is made up of moments, and any music that makes a *moment* happy is quite beyond our contempt. . . .

While, therefore, our deeper, and holier, and more enduring feelings find expression only in the inspired strains of a Mozart, Beethoven or Felix Mendelssohn, for our every-day, transient, surface-feelings, we can sometimes find pleasant utterance in just such a simple little air as a minstrel melody.

ANONYMOUS
"Negro Minstrelsy on the Western Rivers, by One Who Has Been There" (1852)

The Negro Minstrelsy on our Western Rivers is not got up by white men, blackened for the occasion. It is not the spurious, imitative article, but the real, genuine "hoe-down," "shindig," juba,[2] jawbone stuff, simple as nature itself, as fresh as the water o'er which we glide, gleeful and joyous as the carol of the wild birds, with an occasional dash of pathos that goes straight to the heart of the listener. Sometimes the songs are so "jolly ludicrous" that a mummy, as old as the one that Gliddon unrolled before the assembled wisdom of Boston, could not keep its face in order—if it should hear 'em.

I am told that some of the Negroes on these

boats are free, and that others are slaves hired out to the Steamboat Companies; but it is impossible for a stranger to distinguish the slave from the freeman; all appear to enjoy "largest liberty." The waiters are quiet, industrious, respectful and attentive; but the firemen, that inhabit the Plutonic regions "away down below," are certainly the merriest, drollest, jolliest set of fellows I ever saw. Some of the firemen, I am sorry to add, are awfully profane; but their jests and witticisms, their songs and dances seem to be their life, day and night; and how, when or where they get there [their] rest is more than I can tell. The last sound one hears at night, and the first at break-of-day, is the merry peal of their stentorian voices. You are lulled to sleep by their melodies; you awake with the sounds still ringing in your ears.

In listening to the vocal performances of one of the waiters on a boat in which I performed a recent trip from Louisville to St. Louis, I was struck not

"Negro Minstrelsy on the Western Rivers," *The Musical World: An American and Foreign Record of Music, Literature, and Art,* May 15, 1852: 285.

[2]An elaborate form of hand clapping and body slapping performed as a rhythmic accompaniment to improvised dance, usually creating complex cross-rhythms.

only with his fine voice,—which was really clear and sonorous—but also with his poetical genius. He improvised his poetry, or, to use his own expression, he "made up his verses as he went along." The theme on the present occasion, was the steamboat in which we were rapidly gliding up the Mississippi, which bore the romantic name of *Cornelia*. The ebony improvisatore set forth, in his song, some of the most prominent merits of the beautiful *Cornelia*—her excellent accommodations, her great speed, and her superiority over all her rivals on the Western waters; always managing to work in an "invitation" to all travelers to "come on board." One of his songs was as follows:

Come all ob you passengers,
What want to ride fast,
Come on de Corneelyah,
You will nebber be passed;
De Corneelyah is a good boat,
She knows how to move.
But what will she do,
When her engines get smoothe?
CHORUS.—O, go it Corneelyah,
      She is de boat, I reckon.

She is a fast boat,
She never comes in late:
Leaves St. Louis at five,
And Cairo at eight;
But when she is comin',
De ladies dey will say,
'Behold, it is Corneelyah,
She has come before day.'
      O, go it Corneelyah,
        She is de boat, I reckon.

Come all ob you passengers,
Dat want to know your fare,
Jus' walk up to de office,
You'll find our clerk dare:
Our clerk he is a good man,
One ob de bery best,
He treats all ob de passengers
To de honest good jest.
      O, go it Corneelyah,
        She is de boat, I reckon."

As a specimen of spontaneous, unhewn poetry, I think the above should rank high.—That fearful interrogative in the last two lines of the first verse,

"But what will she do,
When her engines get smoothe?"

is pregnant with meaning, and can be interpreted as many different ways as a presidential aspirant's political letters.

Let us now go "below," among the noisy, fun-loving, hard-working firemen. These negroes, it will be observed, seem to have no idea of harmony; they all sing the same part, and that, of course, the melody or *tune*. After "wooding up," and "stirring up," the great fires, and closing the heavy furnace doors with an immense iron "long pole," one of the company turns his shiny face to his comrades, and with a tremendous open countenance, strikes up a sort of solo, *ad libitum*, with variations adapted to his taste or vocal powers, at the conclusion of which the whole company "join in," swelling the chorus to a most fearful extent by an *accumulation of power* on the same part. There they go, now, carrolling a strange melody—a sort of serio-comic strain, thus:

Solo   I saw my true love weep;
          I heard my true love cry.

Chorus
        Away down in Cairo,
        This nigga's gwine to die.

Here is another refrain, of rather less poetical pretensions; but it was given with a more grinning, shiny countenance which could not be withstood, even by Horace Greeley.[3]

"I wish I had some 'baccer,
Who'll give me a chaw tobaccer?
I want a chaw o' 'baccer so bad
I'm almost froze."

This song brought the " 'baccer," as I am told it invariably does. I could not withstand the appeal, but hastened to the saloon, purchased a roll of the

---

[3]Well-known editor and political leader.

"invigorator," as they call it out here, went back and supplied my entertainers with tobacco enough for the night, and immediately retired, to escape their profuse thanks. As I left their precincts they struck up a farewell song, something like the following, as near as I can remember. I hope the reader will observe the appropriateness of the invocation. The bursting of boilers is an ordinary occurrence on the Mississippi; and a passenger is liable to be disturbed at any moment by the intrusion of a "snag" into his berth or state-room, and if he happens to be "there" it is ten changes to one if he escapes being spitted like a widgeon, carried some ten or fifteen feet above the hurricane deck,

and held there as a warning to his fellow travelers not to be caught napping when snags are about. Premising that "*har*" means "*hair*," and "*dar*," "*there*," I give the firemen's farewell strain; leaving the reader to imagine the pleasing train of ideas it must have suggested. Here it is:

Good night, kind white man,
Good night, kind stranger,
May de Angels guard your sleep,
And keep you from all danger,
An' if de biler bust,
May he not singe your har,
An' when de snag pokes through your berth,
I hope you'll not be dar.

31

Jim Crow and *The Coal Black Rose*

Two individual performers represent minstrelsy in its early stages, Thomas Dartmouth ("Daddy") Rice (1808–1860) and George Washington Dixon (1808–1861). Both blackened their faces with burnt cork and wore stereotypical costumes in roles of the sort that would define minstrel characters for decades.

"Daddy" Rice was catapulted to fame when he created "Jim Crow," the first solo act by a blackface performer, probably in Louisville in 1828. Rice is reported to have modeled this character on the song and dance of an old black man working in a stable near the theater. Rice toured his entr'acte widely and to much acclaim, even taking it to England in 1836. The song, which saw a number of printings, accumulated numerous stanzas (there were nineteen in the original edition, c. 1829). From behind the mask, Rice, who was white, could poke fun at the whites and comment on political events as, in the song, the character travels around the country. Rice could thus satirize race relations while he explored what it meant to be black in America at that time.

Jim Crow was the first American song to achieve international prominence. The song's text ("For while de Crow are dancing," "jump Jim Crow," etc.) makes it clear that it was also a dance routine.

George Washington Dixon, also a solo performer, gained popularity through his entr'acte performances of the first blackface comic love song, *The Coal Black Rose*, and the first song representing a black dandy, *Long Tailed Blue*. He performed *The Coal Black Rose* in Albany in 1827 and brought it to New York shortly thereafter, where the song became very popular. Its straightforward, simple musical style set a standard for minstrelsy that remained in vogue for many years. Dixon subsequently expanded the song into a comic skit. The text does, indeed, lend itself to dramatic action, particularly as it takes a surprising turn midway.

THOMAS DARTMOUTH "DADDY" RICE
Text of *Jim Crow* (c. 1830)

Come listen all you galls and boys
I's jist from Tuckyhoe,
I'm goin to sing a little song,
My name's Jim Crow,
Weel about and turn about and do jis so,
Eb'ry time I weel about and jump Jim Crow.

Oh I'm a roarer on de Fiddle,
    And down in old Virginny,
They say I play de skyentific
    Like Massa Pagannini.

I git 'pon a flat boat,
    I cotch de Uncle Sam,
Den I went to see de place
    Wher dey kill'd Packenham.

I went down to de riber,
    I did'nt mean to stay,

Mr. T. Rice as The Original Jim Crow (New York: E. Riley, c. 1830).

But dere I see so many galls,
    I couldn't get away.

An den I go to Orleans
    An feel so full of fight
Dey put me in de Calaboose,
    An keep me dare all night.

When I got out I hit a man,
    His name I now forgot,
But dere was nothing left
    'Sept a little grease spot.

I wip my weight in wildcats
    I eat an Alligator,
And tear up more ground
    Dan kifer 50 load of tater.

I sit upon a Hornet's nest,
    I dance upon my head,
I tie a Wiper round my neck
    And den I goes to bed.

Dere's Possum up de gumtree,
    An Raccoon in de hollow,
Wake Snakes for June bugs
    Stole my half a dollar.

A ring tail'd monkey,
    An a rib nose Babboon,
Went out de odder day
    To spend de arternoon.

Oh de way dey bake de hoe cake
    In old Virginny neber tire,
Dey put de doe upon de foot,
    An hole it to de fire.

O by trade I am a carpenter,
    But be it understood,
De way I get my liben is,
    By sawing de tick oh wood.

I'm a full blooded niggar,
    Ob de real ole stock,
An wid my head and shoulder,
    I can split a horse block.

I struck a Jarsey niggar,
    In de street de oder day,
An I hope I neber stir,

If he didn't turn gray.

I'm berry much afraid of late
    Dis jumping will be no good,
For while de Crow are dancing,
    De Wites will saw de wood.

But if dey get honest,
    By sawing wood like slaves
Der'es an end to de busines,
    Ob our friend Massa Hays.

I met a Philadelphia niggar
    Dress'd up quite nice & clean
But de way he 'bused de Yorkers
    I thought was berry mean.

So I knocked down dis Sambo,
    And shut up his light,
For I'm jist about as sassy,
    As if I was half white.

But he soon jumped up again,
    An 'gan for me to feel,
Says I go away you niggar,
    Or I'll skin you like an eel.

I'm so glad dat I'm a niggar,
    An dont you wish you was too
For den you'd gain popularity,
    By jumping Jim Crow.

Now my brodder niggars,
    I do not think it right,
Dat you should laugh at dem
    Who happen to be white.

Kase it dar misfortune,
    An dey'd spend ebery dollar,
If dey only could be,
    Gentlemen ob colour.

It almost break my heart,
    To see dem envy me,
An from my soul I wish dem,
    Full as black as we.

What stuf it is in dem,
    To make de Debbil black
I'll prove dat he is white,
    In de twinkling of a crack.

For you see loved brodders,
  As true as he hab a tail,
It is his berry wickedness,
  What makee him turn pale.

I went to Hoboken,
  To hab a promenade,
An dar I see de pretty gals,
  Drinking de Lemonade.

Dat sour and dat sweet,
  Is berry good by gum,
But de best of lemonade is,
  Made by adding rum.

At de Swan cottage,
  Is de place I tink,
Whar dey make dis 'licious,
  An 'toxicating drink.

Some go to Weehawk,
  An some to Brooklyn hight
But dey better stay at home,
  If dey want to see de sight.

To go to de museum,
  I'm sure it is dare duty,
If for noting else,
  Jist to see de sleeping beauty.

An dare is daddy Lambert,
  An a skeleton on he hunkie,
An likeness of Broadway dandy
  In a glass case of monkies.

De Broadway bells,
  When dey carry full sail,
Around dem wear a funny ting,
  Just like a fox tail.

When you hear de name of it,
  I sure it make you roar,
Why I ax'd 'em what it was,
  And dey said it was a boar.

De great Nullification,
  And fuss in de South,
Is now before Congress,
  To be tried by word ob mouth.

Dey hab had no blows yet,
  And I hope dey nebber will,
For its berry cruel in bredren,
  One anoders blood to spill.

Wid Jackson at de head,
  Dey soon de ting may settle
For ole Hickory is a man,
  Dat's tarnal full ob mettle.

Should dey get to fighting,
  Perhaps de blacks will rise
For deir wish for freedom,
  Is shining in deir eyes.

And if de blacks should get free
  I guess dey'll fee some bigger,
An I shall concider it,
  A bold stroke for de niggar.

I'm for freedom,
  An for Union altogether,
Aldough I'm a black man,
  De white is calld my broder.

I'm for union to a gal,
  An dis is a stubborn fact,
But if I marry an dont like it,
  I'll nullify de act.

I'm tired of being a single man,
  An I'm 'tarmined to get a wife,
For what I think de happiest,
  Is de swee married life.

Its berry common 'mong de whites
  To marry and get divorced
But dat I'll nebber do
  Unless I'm really forced.

I think I see myself in Broadway
  Wid my wife upon my arm,
An to follow up de fashion,
  Dere sure can be no harm.

An I caution all white dandies,
  Not to come in my way,
For if dey insult me,
  Dey'll in de gutter lay.

FRANCIS COURTNEY WEMYSS

from "Mr. Thomas Rice" (1848)

Mr. Thomas Rice, better known as Jim Crow, made his appearance at the Walnut-Street Theatre. . . .

This gentleman, whose representation of the character of a negro raised him to affluence, made his first appearance in Philadelphia in the summer of 1832, at the Walnut Street Theatre. The roars of laughter with which his extravaganza of Jim Crow (the original of which was a negro of Pittsburgh, known as Jim Cuff,) was received, his excellent acting as well as singing, soon induced offers from managers, which filled *his* pockets and *their* treasury. He was for a time the "*lion*" of the minor theatres. With an innate tact for business, he improved the opportunity his popularity afforded, by collecting all the really beautiful airs which the negro sings while performing his daily labour, and writing himself the "libretto" to introduce a novel species of entertainment, with the imposing title of Ethiopian opera. His "Bone Squash" was an amusing affair, the music truly delightful, and ably exe-

cuted. The Virginny Cupids, although vulgar even to grossness, met a good reception. With this capital, Mr. Rice crossed the Atlantic, and turned the heads of the chimney sweeps and apprentice boys of London, who wheeled about and turned about and jumped Jim Crow, from morning until night, to the annoyance of their masters, but the great delight of the cockneys. That his financial affairs have been improved by the trip there is little doubt, but his popularity in his native country has been lost, by his endeavour to ingraft the English dandy with the American negro.

In London, where a black man is scarcely seen, it might be remarkably "*funny*," but the broad caricature of the American negro was the attraction of Jim Crow at home, who, when converted into an English gentleman, was a most insipid creature. As an actor, Mr. Rice's reputation depends upon his black face; and how he contrives to keep it white, might be a matter of grave debate, begrimmed as it has been for the last ten years, at least three hours in each of the twenty-four.

In private society, Jim Crow is a "*first-rate*" companion: full of anecdote, possessed of vocal abilities, and agreeable in conversation, he makes a valuable member of any social club.

Francis Courtney Wemyss, "Mr. Thomas Rice," *Theatrical Biography; or, the Life of an Actor and Manager* (Glasgow: R. Griffin, 1848), 178–79.

GEORGE WASHINGTON DIXON

Text of *The Coal Black Rose* (c. 1830)

Lubly Rosa' Sambo cum,
Don't you hear de Banjo tum, tum, tum.
Lubly Rosa' Sambo cum,
Don't you hear de Banjo tum, tum, tum,
Oh Rose de coal black Rose,

George Washington Dixon, *The Coal Black Rose* (New York: Bourne, c. 1830).

I wish I may be cortch'd if I don't lub Rose,
Oh rose de coal black Rose.

Dat you, Sambo? yes I cum,
Don't you hear de Banjo tum, tum, tum;
Dat you, Sambo? yes I cum,
Don't you hear de Banjo tum, tum, tum;
Oh, Rose, de coal black Rose,

I wish I may be burnt if I don't lub Rose,
Oh, Rose, &c.

Tay a little, Sambo, I cum soon,
As I make a fire in de back room:
Tay a little, Sambo, I cum soon,
As I make a fire in de back room;
Oh, Rose de coal black Rose,
I wish I may be burnt if I don't lub Rose,
Oh, Rose, &c.

Make haste, Rose, lubly dear,
I froze tiff as poker tandin here:
Make hast Rose lubly dear,
I almost froze a waitin here,
Oh, Rose I almose froze,
I wish I may be burnt if I don't lub Rose,
Oh, Rose &c.

Cum in, Sambo, don't tand dare shakin,
De fire is a burnin, and de hoe cake a bakin;
Cum in, Sambo, and top dat shakin,
De peas in de pot and de hoe cake a bakin;
Oh, Rose, bress dat Rose!
I wish I may be burnt if I don't lub Rose,
Oh, Rose &c.

Sit down, Sambo, an warm your shin,
Lord bless you, honey, for what make you grin;
Sit down, Sambo, an toast your shin,
Lord bless you, honey, for what make you grin
Oh, Rose, bress dat Rose;
I wish I may be burnt if I don't lub Rose,
Oh, Rose &c.

I laff to tink if you was mine, lubly Rose,
I'd gib you a plenty, the Lord above knows,
Oh possum fat and hominey, and sometime rice,
Cow heel an suger cane an ebery ting nice;

Oh, Rose bress dat Rose
I wish I may be shute if I don't lub Rose,
Oh, Rose &c.

What in de corner dare, Rose, dat I py?
I know dat nigger Cuffe by de white ob he eye;
Dat not Cuffee, 'tis a tick ob wood, sure,
A tick ob wood wid tocking on, you tell me dat,
      pshaw
Oh Rose take care Rose
I wish I may be burnt if I don't hate Rose,
Oh, Rose, you black snake Rose!

Let go my arm, Rose, let me at him rush,
I swella his two lips like a blacka balla brush;
Let go my arm, Rose, an let me top his win,
Let go my arm, Rose, while I kick him on de
      shin;
Oh, Rose, take care Rose
I wish I may be burnt if I don't hate Rose,
Oh, Rose, you blacka snake Rose!

I ketch hold of Cuffe, I take him by de wool;
I ketch hold of Cuffe, he try away to pull,
But I up wid a foot and kick him on de shin,
Which put him breafless on de floor an make de
      nigger grin
Oh, Rose, take care Rose
I wish I may be burnt if I don't hate Rose,
Oh, Rose, you blacka snake Rose!

He jump up for sartin, he cut dirt an run—
Now Sambo follow arter wid his tum, tum, tum;
He jump up for sartin, he cut dirt an run—
Now Sambo follow arter wid his tum, tum, tum;
Oh, Rose, curse dat Rose
I wish Massa Hays would ketch dat Rose,
Oh, Rose, you blacka snake Rose.

32

Dan Emmett and the Virginia Minstrels

Daniel Decatur Emmett (1815–1904) represents the next generation of negro minstrelsy. Joining up with three colleagues, all of whom had experience with blackface entertainment, principally in circuses, he formed the Virginia Minstrels, who made history when they appeared in New York on February 9, 1843, at the Bowery Amphitheatre. This was a *group* enterprise. Costumed in white trousers, striped calico shirts, and long blue calico tailcoats, the ensemble presented a full evening of music, dance, anecdotes, and oratory, reaping immediate success.

Although this appearance postdated a four-man show mounted by E. P. Christy in Buffalo in 1842, the Virginia Minstrels' performance was nonetheless the real beginning of the group minstrel show, and hence the start of the classic period of negro minstrelsy in America.

Emmett wrote the words for *The Fine Old Colored Gentleman* (1843). It was published in Boston as part of the collection *Old Dan Emmit's* [*sic*] *Original Banjo Melodies.* His *Old Dan Tucker* appeared as part of this set, as did *O Dance de Boatman Dance.* The cover illustration depicts a gleeful celebration under rather surprising circumstances (one person has caught his banjo around the tail of a bull that is butting into a tree stump; another, in the water, is using his banjo to fend off an alligator). Below this we read: "As sung by the Virginia Minstrels with enthusiastic applause at the principal Theatres and Concerts in the Union, being an entire new collection of pieces never before Published."

Emmett's most famous song, *I wish I was in Dixie's land,* was introduced in New York on April 4, 1859, by Bryant's Minstrels, with whom Emmett was then performing. It was published the following year. A Confederate band played *Dixie* for the inauguration of Jefferson Davis as president of the Confederacy and later, just a few days before his assassination, President Lincoln advanced its status as a national song by requesting a serenading band to play it.

DANIEL DECATUR EMMETT

Text of *The Fine Old Colored Gentleman* (1843)

In Tenn'see as I've heard say dare once did use to dwell,
A fine old Color'd Gemman and dis nigger knowed him well;

Dey used to call him Sambo or somethin near the same
De reason why da call dat was, becase it was his name;
For Sambo was a Gemman, One of de oldest kind.

Daniel Emmett, *The Fine Old Colored Gentleman* (Boston: Charles H. Keith, 1843).

His temper was very mild when he was let alone,
But when you get him dander up, he spunk to de
   back bone,
He whale de sugar off ye by de double rule of
   three
And whip his wate in wildcats, when he got on a
   spree,
For Sambo was a Gemman, One of de oldest kind.

When dis nigger took a snooze, it was in a nigger
   crowd,
He used to keep them all awake, because he
   snored so loud,
He drawed himself up in a knot, his knees did
   touch his chin,
De bedbugs had to clar de track, when he
   stretched down his shin.

He had a good old banjo so well he kept it strung,
He used to sing the good old song, of "go it while
   you're young;"
He sung so long and sung so loud, he scared the
   pigs and goats,
Because he took a pint of yeast to raise the highest
   notes.

When dis nigga stood upright an was'nt
   slantindicular
He measured about 'leven feet, he was'nt ver
   partic'lar,
For he could jump, and run a race, an do a little
   hoppin,
And when he got a goin fast the devil could'nt
   stop 'im.

Old Father Time kept rolling by and age grew on
   apace,
The wool all dropt off from his head, and
   wrinkled was his face,
He was de oldest nigger what lived on dat
   plantation,
He did'nt fear de debil den, nor all of his relation.

Old age came on, his teeth dropt out, it made no
   odds to him,
He eat as many taters and he drank as many gin;
He swallowed two small rail roads wid a spoonful
   of ice cream,
And a locomotive bulgine while dey blowin off de
   steam.

One bery windy morning dis good old nigger
   died,
De niggers came from odder states and loud for
   joy dey cried;
He layin down upon a bench as strait as any post,
De 'coons did roar, de 'possums howled when he
   guv up de ghost.

De niggers held an inquest when dey heard of his
   death,
De verdict of de jury was, he died for want of
   breath;
Dey went to work and skinned him and then they
   had it dried,
And de head of dis here banjo, is off dat old
   nigger's hide.

33   Pedee or Swanee?
Stephen Collins Foster

Stephen Collins Foster (1826–1864) was the first native-born American composer who sought to make a living solely from his craft. He was also one of the nation's most popular song writers. His legacy of over two hundred songs and instrumental arrangements, although uneven in quality, provides us with a national heritage, part of our shared experience as a people. Foster's synthesis of the popular and cultured traditions of his day, including the sentimental cast of parlor music, seized the American spirit in a unique way.

Foster's "Ethiopian melody" *Old Folks at Home* was entered for copyright on August 26, 1851 (the copyright deposit date was October 1, 1851). As Foster did for many of his songs, he wrote his own text, apparently between late July and mid-August of that year. The piece was one of a group of about thirty minstrel songs in "black dialect," composed with sympathy and understanding, yet from a northerner's point of view.

Perhaps because he lacked cash, Foster made the mistake of selling to Christy the credit for composing what is arguably his most popular song.* He even agreed to the omission of his name on the title page. Foster soon regretted this decision, but Christy would not forego the arrangement, scrawling across the back of Foster's request for acknowledgment, "vacillating skunk." It was not until the initial copyright ran out in 1879 that Foster's name began finally to appear on reprintings of the piece.

The song became enormously popular. *The Musical World* reported on September 11, 1852: "The publishers keep two presses running on it, and sometimes three; yet, they cannot supply the demand." When the demand did begin to wane, it was refueled through performances by the famous Swedish prima donna, Christine Nilsson, during the 1870s and 1880s. It has since been reprinted countless times, found its way into compositions by various composers, been used in political cartoons, become pantomimes, and been sung on such occasions as the arrival of General Joseph Stillwell and his troops in India during the Second World War, the wedding of Grace Kelly and Prince Rainier III of Monaco, and sessions held by the United States House of Representatives. In 1935, *Old Folks at Home* became the Florida state song.

A work like *Old Folks at Home* takes on life beyond what was given to it at its inception. Numerous editions, piano and instrumental arrangements, and parodies attest to its continued vitality. The song, which has by now passed into oral tradition, mirrors attitudes prevalent in its own day and important to ours. It has taken its place in our national stream of consciousness.

---

*Edwin P. Christy (1815–1862) was manager and perfomer with the noted Christy Minstrels.

STEPHEN FOSTER

Sketches for Text of *Old Folks at Home* (1851)

Sketchbook, 7v
Way Down Upon de Old Plantation
[original title]

> Way down upon de Pedee ribber
> > Far far away
> Dere's where my heart is turning ebber
> > Dere's wha my brudders play
>
> > Swanee
> Way down upon de / ~~Pedee~~ ribber
> > Far far away
> Dere's where my heart is turning ebber
> > Dere's where de old folks stay
> All up and down de whole creation
> > Sadly I roam
> Still longing for de old plantation
> > And for de old folks at home.

Sketchbook, 12v

> Oh take me to my kind old mudder
>
> Long time ago I left my fadder
> > Why tell me why,
> Oh take me to my kind old mudder
> > Dere let me lib and die
>
> Long time ago I left my fadder
>
> Den ebry day my heart grew sadder

Sketchbook, 13r

> Way down upon de Swanee ribber
> > Far, far away
> Dere's wha my heart is turning ebber

> Dere's wha de old folks stay
> All up and down de whole creation
> > Sadly, I roam
> Still longing for de old plantation
> > And for de old folks at home

> Chorus—All de world am sad and dreary
> > Ebry where I roam
> > Oh! darkeys how my heart grows weary
> > > Far from de old folks at home

> All round de little farm I wandered
> > When I was young
> Den many happy days I squandered
> > Many de songs I sung
> ~~Oh how I rambled wid my brudder~~
> When I was playing wid my brudder
> > Happy—~~Joyous~~ was I
> Oh take me to my kind old mudder
> > Dere let me lib and die

> One little hut among de bushes
> > All dat I love
> Still sadly to my memory rushes
> > No matter where I rove

> Way down upon de Swanee &c

Sketchbook, 12v

> When will I see de bees a humming
> > All round de comb
> When will I hear de banjo tumming
> > Down in my good old home

Stephen C. Foster, *Old Folks at Home* (sketchbook manuscripts), Foster Hall Collection, Stephen Foster Memorial, University of Pittsburgh. Cited with thanks to Deane L. Root.

STEPHEN FOSTER

Published Text of *Old Folks at Home* (1851)

Way down upon de Swanee ribber,
    Far, far away,
Dere's wha my heart is turning ebber,
    Dere's wha de old folks stay.
All up and down de whole creation,
    Sadly I roam,
Still longing for de old plantation,
    And for de old folks at home.

Chorus.
    All de world am sad and dreary,
        Ebry where I roam,
    Oh! darkeys how my heart grows weary,
        Far from de old folks at home.

All round de little farm I wandered
    When I was young,

Den many happy days I squandered,
    Many de songs I sung.

When I was playing wid my brudder
    Happy was I—
Oh! take me to my kind old mudder,
    Dere let me live and die.

Chorus. . . .

One little hut among de bushes,
    One dat I love,
Still sadly to my mem'ry rushes,
    No matter where I rove

When will I see de bees a humming
    All round de comb?
When will I hear de banjo tumming
    Down in my good old home?

Chorus. . . .

Stephen C. Foster, *Old Folks at Home* (New York: Firth, Pond, 1851).

MORRISON FOSTER

from *Biography, Songs, and Musical Compositions of Stephen C. Foster* (1896)

One day in 1851, Stephen came into my office, on the bank of the Monongahela, Pittsburgh, and said to me, "What is a good name of two syllables for a Southern river? I want to use it in this new song of 'Old Folks at Home.' " I asked him how Yazoo would do. "Oh," said he, "that has been used before." I then suggested Pedee. "Oh, pshaw," he replied, "I won't have that." I then took down an atlas from the top of my desk and opened the map of the United States. We both looked over it and my finger stopped at the "Swanee," a little river in Florida emptying into the Gulf of Mexico. "That's it, that's it exactly," exclaimed he delighted, as he wrote the name down; and the song was finished, commencing, "Way Down Upon de Swanee Ribber." He left the office, as was his custom, abruptly, without saying another word, and I resumed my work.

Just at that time he received a letter from E. P. Christy, of New York, who was conducting very popular Negro Melody Concerts, asking him if he would write a song for Christy which the latter

Morrison Foster, *Biography, Songs and Musical Compositions of Stephen C. Foster* (Pittsburgh: P. F. Smith, 1896), 19.

might sing before it was published. Stephen showed me the letter and asked me what he should do. I said to him, "Don't let him do it unless he pays you."

At his request I drew up a form of agreement for Christy to sign, stipulating to pay Stephen five hundred dollars for the privilege he asked.[1] This was forwarded to Christy and return mail brought it back duly signed by the latter. The song sent happened to be the "Old Folks at Home." It was in this manner that Christy's name came to appear on the first edition of the "Old Folks at Home." Stephen sent the manuscript to his publishers, Firth, Pond & Co., who paid him and his heirs the royalty. The publishers furnished Christy an advance copy of the song before publication.

[1] The actual amount was a mere $15.

STEPHEN FOSTER

Letter to Edwin P. Christy (1852)

May 25, 1852

Dear Sir:

As I once intimated to you, I had the intention of omitting my name on my Ethiopian songs, owing to a prejudice against them by some, which might injure my reputation as writer of another style of music, but I find that by my efforts I have done a great deal to build up a taste for the Ethiopian songs among refined people by making the words suitable to their taste, instead of the trashy and really offensive words which belong to some songs of that order. Therefore I have concluded to reinstate my name on my songs and to pursue the Ethiopian business without fear or shame and lend all my energies to making the business live, at the same time that I will wish to establish my name as the best Ethiopian song-writer. But I am not encouraged in undertaking this so long as "Old Folks at Home" stares me in the face with another's name on it. As it was at my own solicitation that you allowed your name to be placed on the song, I hope that the above reasons will be sufficient explanation for my desire to place my own name on it as author and composer, while at the same time I wish to leave the name of your band on the title page. This is a little matter of pride in myself which it will certainly be to your interest to encourage. On the receipt of your free consent to this proposition, I will if you wish, willingly refund you the money which you paid me on that song, though it may have been sent me for other considerations than the one in question, and I promise in addition to write you an opening chorus in my best style, free of charge, and in any other way in my power to advance your interests hereafter. I find I cannot write at all unless I write for public approbation and get credit for what I write. As we may probably have a good deal of business with each other in our lives, it is best to proceed on a sure basis of confidence and good understanding, therefore I hope you will appreciate an author's feelings in the case and deal with me with your usual fairness. Please answer immediately.

Very respectfully yours,
Stephen C. Foster

Stephen C. Foster to Edwin P. Christy, May 25, 1852; original at the Library of Congress.

News Item on *Old Folks at Home* (1852)

"Old Folks At Home" . . . is on everybody's tongue, and consequently in everybody's mouth. Pianos and guitars groan with it, night and day; sentimental young ladies sing it; sentimental young gentlemen warble it in midnight serenades; volatile young "bucks" hum it in the midst of their business and pleasures; boatmen roar it out stento-rially at all times; all the bands play it; amateur flute blowers agonize over it at every spare moment; the street organs grind it out at every hour; the "singing stars" carol it on the theatrical boards, and at concerts; the chamber maid sweeps and dusts to the measured cadence of *Old Folks at Home*; the butcher's boy treats you to a strain or two of it as he hands in the steaks for dinner; the milk-man mixes it up strangely with the harsh ding-dong accompaniment of his tireless bell; there is not a "live darkey," young or old, but can whistle, sing, dance, and play it. . . .

Albany State Register, September 1852. Quoted from Gilbert Chase, *America's Music*, 3rd ed. (Urbana: University of Illinois Press, 1987), 257.

ANONYMOUS

Text of *Great Democratic Song* (c. 1853)

AIR—"Old Folks at Home"

Way down upon the old Salt River,
    Far, far away,
There's where the Whigs are fixed forever,
    There's where they're doomed to stay.
All up and down its whole extension
    Sadly they roam,
Still groaning that the late Convention
    Sent them from the White House at home.
Chorus—All the Whigs are sad and dreary,
        Every where they roam,
        Singing, Brothers, how my heart grows
          weary,
        Far from the White House at Home.

All around the White House we have wandered,
    (Thus do they rave,)
Many a dollar for votes have we squandered,
Many an office we gave.
Then when we were a "cheerful giver,"
    Fillmore was their cry;
Now they've rowed us up Salt River,
    There to politically die.

Chorus—All the Whigs are sad and dreary, etc.

One little spot is all that's left us,
    Where we now stay;
Of all our pickings they bereft us,
    Then sent us far away.
When shall we have again our places,
    Live on the public comb,
When shall we dare to show our faces
    Down at the White House at home?

Chorus—All the Whigs, etc.

Great Democratic Song (c. 1853), broadside.

34

🦎 # Patriotic Songs

Patriotic music in the United States has a spotty history. Included here is one piece of patriotic intent, written in America, that did not survive popular judgment. Ironically, two others that did and that grew to become highly favored national music both use tunes that are English, not American. An American piece loses popularity, English music lives; the colonial tradition continues.

The composer of the first piece, Alexander Reinagle (1756–1809), was discussed earlier. The work, written in an accessible style to catch the public fancy, has a patriotic flavor to it. Introduced as part of a stage production, it served as a functional piece in the drama and fulfilled for a time, a role as entertainment for the home.

The music of *America, Commerce, & Freedom*, at least, was Philadelphia born. By comparison, many American national songs, including *The Star-Spangled Banner*, *America*, ("My Country, 'Tis of Thee"), and *Yankee Doodle*, had to cross the Atlantic before their use in the United States. The tune of our National Anthem began life as an English drinking song, and the melody of *America* started out as the English national anthem.

Both *America* and *The Star-Spangled Banner* were first printed in the New World as broadsides—texts without music—probably in 1764 and 1778 respectively. In the first publication of the tune of our future national anthem, believed to have been in 1798, the song was married to a patriotic text by Thomas Paine, "Adams and Liberty" (not the Thomas Paine who wrote *Common Sense* and *The Rights of Man*). Thus the tune of a British drinking song celebrating Venus and Bacchus was taken over by the Yankees. Its traditional American text was composed in 1814 by Francis Scott Key during the British bombardment of Fort McHenry. It was published immediately as a broadside, and was subsequently printed in two Baltimore newspapers. It became our national anthem more than one hundred years later, in 1931.

The English anthem *God Save the King* has served as a vehicle for numerous texts. One of these, "God Save the Right of Man," in praise of the other Thomas Paine's *The Rights of Man*, appeared in the *Providence Gazette* in 1793. Paine had published his text in defense of the French Revolution of 1789. The anonymous poet here refers to the French but underscores the universality of Paine's text.

The text of "My Country! 'Tis of Thee," set to the same tune, was written in 1831 by a young clergyman, Samuel Francis Smith, at the request of Lowell Mason. Smith claimed he did not know his words were being written to the English national anthem. The piece was first sung in 1831 at a children's Fourth of July celebration at the Park Street Church in Boston. The music and four stanzas of text appeared the following year in Lowell Mason's *The Choir: or Union Collection of Church Music*. Then it was published in sheet-music form.

Such is the history of patriotic music in America. Unfortunately, our forefathers' musical awareness did not keep up with their celebration of noble principles.

ALEXANDER REINAGLE
Text of *America, Commerce, & Freedom* (1794?)

How blest the life a sailor leads
From clime to clime still ranging
For as the calm the storm succeeds
The scene delights by changing.
Tho' tempests howl along the main
Some object will remind us
And cheer with hope to meet again
The friends we left behind us.

[Interlude]

Chorus
Then under full sail we laugh at the gale
And the landsmen look pale never heed em
But toss off the glass to a favorite lass
To America Commerce and freedom
To America Commerce and freedom.

[Interlude]

But when arriv'd in sight of land
Or safe in port rejoicing
Our ship we moor our sails we hand
Whilst out the boat is hoisting
With chearful hearts the shore we reach
Our friends delighted greet us

And tripping lightly o'er the beach
The pretty lasses meet us.

Chorus
When the full flowing bowl enlivens the soul
To foot it we merrily lead em
And each bonny lass will drink off her glass
To America commerce and freedom.

Our prizes sold the chink we share
And gladly we receive it
And when we meet a brother tar
That wants we freely give it
No free born sailor yet had store
But chearfully wou[l]d lend it
An when 'tis gone to sea for more
We earn it but to spend it.

Chorus
Then drink round my boys tis the first of our joys
To relieve the distress'd clothe and feed 'em
'Tis a duty we share with the brave and the fair
In this land of commerce and freedom.

Alexander Reinagle, *America, Commerce, & Freedom* (Philadelphia: Carr's Musical Repository, 1794?), sheet music.

THOMAS PAINE
Text of *Adams and Liberty* (1798)

Ye sons of Columbia, who bravely have fought,
For those rights, which unstain'd from your Sires
    had descended,
May you long taste the blessings your valour has
    bought

And your sons reap the soil, which your fathers
    defended.
    Mid the reign of mild peace.
    May your nation increase,
With the glory of Rome and the wisdom of Greece;

Thomas Paine, *Adams and Liberty*, (1798); sheet music.

And ne'er may the songs of COLUMBIA be slaves,
While the earth bears a plant, or the sea rolls its
waves.

In a clime, whose rich vales feed the marts of the
world,
Whose shores are unshaken by *Europe's*
commotion,
The *Trident* of Commerce should never be hurl'd,
To incense the *legitimate* powers of the ocean.
    But should *Pirates* invade,
    Though in thunder array'd,
Let your *cannon* declare the *free charter* of
TRADE.

For ne'er shall the sons of COLUMBIA be slaves,
While the earth bears a plant, or the sea rolls its
waves.

The fame of our arms, of our laws the mild sway,
Had justly ennobled our nation in story,
Till the dark clouds of *Faction* obscur'd our young
day,
And envelop'd the sun of American glory.
    But let TRAITORS be told,
    Who their *Country* have sold,
    And barter'd their *God* for his image in *gold*—

That ne'er will the sons of COLUMBIA be slaves,
While the earth bears a plant, or the sea rolls its
waves.

While FRANCE her huge limbs bathes recumbent
in *blood.*
And *society's base* threats with wide dissolution;
May PEACE, like the *Dove,* who return'd from the
flood,
Find an *Ark* of abode in our mild
CONSTITUTION!
    But though PEACE is our aim,
    Yet the boon we disclaim,
If bought by our SOV'REIGNTY, JUSTICE, or
FAME.

For ne'er shall the sons of COLUMBIA be slaves,
Whilte the earth bears a plant, or the sea rolls its
waves.

'Tis the fire of the *flint* each American warms;

Let *Rome's* haughty victors beware of *collision!*
Let them bring all the vassals of *Europe* in arms,
We're a WORLD BY OURSELVES, and disdain a
division!
    While, with patriot pride,
    To our Laws we're allied,
No foe can subdue us—no faction divide.

For ne'er shall the sons of COLUMBIA be slaves,
While the earth bears a plant, or the sea rolls its
waves.

Our mountains are crown'd with imperial *Oak,*
Whose *roots,* like our *Liberties,* ages have
nourish'd;
But long ere our nation submits to the *yoke,*
Not a *tree* shall be left on the field where it
flourish'd.
    Should *invasion* impend,
    Every *grove* would defend
From the *hill-tops* they shaded, our *shares* to
defend.

For ne'er shall the sons of COLUMBIA be slaves,
While the earth bears a plant, or the sea rolls its
waves.

Let our Patriots destroy *Anarch's* pestilent *worm,*
Lest our Liberty's *growth* should be check'd by
corrosion;
Then let clouds thicken round us, we heed not the
storm;
Our realm fears no *shock,* but the earth's own
explosion.
    Foes assail us in vain,
    Though their FLEETS *bridge* the main,
For our *altars* and *laws* with our lives we'll
maintain!

And ne'er shall the sons of COLUMBIA be slaves,
While the earth bears a plant, or the sea rolls its
waves.

Should the TEMPEST of War overshadow our
land,
Its bolts could ne'er rend FREEDOM'S *temple*
asunder;
For, unmov'd, at its *portal,* would
WASHINGTON stand,

And repulse, with his BREAST, *the assaults of the*
  THUNDER!
    His *sword*, from the sleep
    Of its *scabbard*, would leap.
And conduct, with its *point*, every *flash* to the
  deep.

For ne'er shall the sons of COLUMBIA *be slaves,*
While the earth bears a plant, or the sea rolls its
  waves.

Let FAME to the world sound America's voice;
No INTRIGUE *can her sons from their*

GOVERNMENT *sever;*
Her Pride *is her* ADAMS—*his* Laws *are her*
  CHOICE,
And shall flourish till LIBERTY *slumber forever!*
    Then unite, heart and hand,
    Like *Leonidas'* band,
And swear to the GOD of the ocean and land,

That ne'er shall the sons of COLUMBIA *be slaves,*
While the earth bears a plant, or the sea rolls its
  waves.

FRANCIS SCOTT KEY

Text of *Defence of Fort M'Henry* (1814)

The annexed song was composed under the following circumstances—A gentleman (*Francis S. Key, Esq, of Georgetown, District of Columbia.*) had left Baltimore, in a flag of truce for the purpose of getting released from the British fleet, a friend of his who had been captured at Marlborough.—He went as far as the mouth of the Patuxent and was not permitted to return lest the intended attack on Baltimore should be disclosed. He was therefore brought up the Bay to the mouth of the Patapsco, where the flag vessel was kept under the guns of a frigate, and he was compelled to witness the bombardment of Fort M'Henry, which the Admiral had boasted that he would carry in a few hours, and that the city must fall. He watched the flag at the Fort through the whole day with an anxiety that can be better felt than described, until the night prevented him from seeing it. In the night he watched the bomb shells, and at early dawn his eye was again greeted by the proudly waving flag of his country.

Francis Scott Key, *The Star-Spangled Banner*, autograph ms. (1814). Facsimile in *The Original Manuscript of "The Star-Spangled Banner": A Facsimile* (Baltimore: Maryland Historical Society, 1969).

***Tune*—Anacreon in Heaven**

O say can you see by the dawn's early light,
What so proudly we hailed at the twilight's last
  gleaming?
Whose broad stripes and bright stars through the
  perilous fight,
O'er the ramparts we watch'd, were so gallantly
  streaming?
And the rockets' red glare, the bombs bursting in
  air,
Gave proof through the night that our flag was
  still there;
O say does that star-spangled banner yet wave,
O'er the land of the free, and the home of the
  brave?

On the shore dimly seen through the mists of the
  deep,
Where the foe's haughty host in dread silence
  reposes,
What is that which the breeze, o'er the towering
  steep,
As it fitfully blows, half conceals, half discloses?
Now it catches the gleam of the morning's first
  beam,
In full glory reflected now shines in the stream,
'Tis the star-spangled banner, O long may it wave

O'er the land of the free and the home of the
brave!

And where is that band who so vauntingly swore
That the havoc of war and the battle's confusion,
A home and a country shall leave us no more?
Their blood has wash'd out their foul footsteps
pollution.
No refuge could save the hireling and slave
From the terror of flight, or the gloom of the
grave
And the star-spangled banner in triumph doth
wave
O'er the land of the free and the home of the
brave.

O thus be it ever when freemen shall stand,
Between their lov'd home, and the war's
desolation,
Blest with vict'ry and peace may the heav'n
rescued land,
Praise the power that hath made and preserved us
a nation!
Then conquer we must, when our cause it is just,
And this be our motto—"In God is our Trust;"
And the Star-spangled banner in triumph shall
wave,
O'er the land of the free and the home of the
brave.

Text of *A New Song* (1793)

GOD save—"THE RIGHTS OF MAN!"
Give him a heart to scan
Blessings so dear;
Let them be spread around,
Wherever Man is found,
And with the welcome sound
Ravish his ear!

See from the Universe
Darkness and clouds disperse:
Mankind awake!
Reason and truth appear,
Freedom advances near,
Monarchs with terror hear,
See how they quake!

Sore have we felt the stroke;
Long have we borne the yoke,
Sluggish and tame;
But now the Lion roars,
And a loud note he pours,
Spreading to distant shores
LIBERTY'S flame.

Let us with France agree,
And bid the WORLD BE FREE—
Leading the way:
Let tyrants all conspire;
Fearless of sword and fire,
Freedom shall ne'er retire;
Freedom shall sway!

Godlike and great the strife,
Life will indeed be life,
Should we prevail:
Death, in so just a cause,
Crowns us with loud applause,
And from tyrannic laws,
Bid us—ALL HAIL!

O'er the Germanic pow'rs
Big Indignation low'r
Ready to fall!
Let the rude savage host
In their long numbers boast,
FREEDOM'S almighty trust
Laughs at them all.

FAME! *let thy trumpet sound!*
Till all the world around!
Tell each degree!
Tell Ribbands, Crowns and Stars

A New Song, in *The Providence Gazette and Country Journal*.
(May 25, 1793): [4].

Kings, Traitors, Troops and Wars,
Plans, Councils, Plots and Jars,
FRENCHMEN *are* FREE.

God save—"THE RIGHTS OF MAN!"
Give him a heart to scan

Blessing so dear;
Let them be spread around,
Wherever Man is found,
And with the welcome sound
Ravish his ear!

SAMUEL FRANCIS SMITH

Text of *America* (1831)

My country! 'tis of thee,
Sweet land of liberty—
   Of thee I sing:
Land, where my fathers died;
Land of the pilgrim's pride;
From every mountain-side,
   Let freedom ring.

My native country! thee—
Land of the noble free—
   Thy name I love:
I love thy rocks and rills,
Thy woods and templed hills;
My heart with rapture thrills,
   Like that above.

No more shall tyrants here
With haughty steps appear,
   And soldier-bands;
No more shall tyrants tread

Above the patriot dead—
No more our blood be shed
   By alien hands.

Let music swell the breeze,
And ring from all the trees
   Sweet freedom's song:
Let mortal tongues awake—
Let all that breathes partake—
Let rocks their silence break—
   The sound prolong.

Our father's God! to thee—
Author of liberty!
   To thee we sing;
Long may our land be bright
With freedom's holy light—
Protect us by thy might,
   Great God, our King!

Samuel Francis Smith, *America*, in Lowell Mason, *The*
Choir: or Union Collection of Church Music (Boston: Carter,
Hendee and Co., 1832), 273.

35

The Brothers Chickering

Yankee ingenuity in nineteenth-century America proved that a profit could be made through the sale of sheet music and musical instruments, particularly pianos. Sales pitches targeted the home market, particularly women. Every home, the music industry declared, should be furnished with an elegant piano and with music to play and sing. The piano would become a status symbol for its owner, it was argued, proving the family a cultured one. It would become a valued heirloom for generations to come.

The firm Chickering & Sons of Boston rose to meet the need: its pianos became staples of many American homes during the nineteenth century. It did not hurt that such an impressive artist as Louis Moreau Gottschalk endorsed Chickering pianos highly and used one on his tours.

The Chickering firm was founded in 1823 by Jonas Chickering (1798–1853) in partnership with an Englishman, James Stewart. It occupied a dominant position in piano manufacture during the nineteenth century. Important improvements, particularly in the late 1830s and 1840s, included a patent for one-piece cast-iron frames. Awards and prizes followed, and sales increased steadily.

Unfortunately, the Boston factory on Washington Street that the firm had occupied for fourteen years was destroyed by fire in 1852. A lavish new establishment was soon under construction on nearby Tremont Street and its doors were opened in 1854. The *Boston Transcript* carried an account of the extravagant new premises, printed an engraving, and commented about the firm.

In applying savvy business leadership, Chickering & Sons solidified a path of success for itself, while also helping to create an atmosphere that encouraged everyone to participate in the joys of music.

News Item on the New Piano Factory (1854)

The annexed engraving gives a miniature view of the mammoth new Pianoforte Manufactory of Messrs. Chickering & Sons, located on Tremont street, Boston. It is probably the largest building in the United States, excepting only the National Capitol at Washington, and is unquestionably the most perfect and extensive pianoforte establishment in the world. Considered in this light alone, it is an object of attraction, ornament and pride for our city; but its general interest is doubly heightened by the reflection that the vast enterprise is one of an entirely private character, projected by one of our most celebrated and successful native pioneers in the mechanical departments applicable to the development of Music, and in its magnitude indicating the rapidly increasing culture of the "divine art" in this country.

This gigantic structure was put under contract May 16, 1853, the land upon which it stands and necessary grounds contiguous having been purchased of the City of Boston the month previous. The premises comprise an entire square of 206,000

Boston Evening Transcript, April 21, 1854, [1]; the article was picked up in *The Musical World & Times*, (May 13, 1854): [1].

feet, or about *five acres,* situated on the westerly side of Tremont, between Camden and Northampton streets. Such is the present state of forwardness of the building, machinery, &c., that it is calculated the new establishment will be under full operation by next autumn. Its novelty induces us to give a somewhat extended sketch of its details. . . .

The whole of the grand building is to be devoted exclusively to the manufacture of Pianofortes, and all the interior arrangements for the business are on a scale to correspond with what we have already described. The rough stock will be taken in at a lower door in one wing, and passing up this wing, through the main building, and down the other wing, will be delivered in the warerooms finished—so that almost literally "forests will enter at one end of the building, and come out perfect pianofortes at the other." The entire first floor will be filled with the requisite machinery, such as planers, lathes, all kinds of saws, &c., &c., and will probably exhibit the finest and largest display of machinery in any one building occupied by a single individual or firm in the country. This machinery was all made at Lowell, under the superintendence of Mr. L. A. Cutler, the experienced engineer and machinist of Chickering's establishment. In the evening the whole building will be lighted with gas from about 600 burners. Every known improvement will be introduced into the various departments of the manufactory, in order to make it and its work as near perfection as human skill, employed with the most ample means, can accomplish. . . .

The entire manufacturing business carried on in the establishment will be under the superintendence of the eldest of the late Mr. Chickering's sons, Mr. Thomas E. Chickering, who has since his father's death made all contracts, accepted all plans, and had the general direction of the building—also laid out the plans for finishing the interior and adapting it to the manufacture of pianos. In these important matters he has received the valuable assistance from Mr. Stephen R. Clapp, the foreman of the manufactory, Mr. L. A. Cutler,

the engineer and machinist, and Mr. E. Payson, the designer and superintendent of the contracted work.

The second brother of the firm, Mr. Charles F. Chickering, has the sole charge of the retail business, and the splendid warerooms in the Masonic Temple; while the third and youngest brother, Mr. George H. Chickering, is at present, as previous to the death of his father, engaged in the manufactory.

Mr. George H. Child, who has for the past ten years been the very efficient financier of the firm, still continues in that capacity.

The first piano made by the late lamented Jonas Chickering was in the year 1825, and sold to the late Mrs. Snelling Powell, the well known Boston actress. Mr. Chickering from time to time made valuable improvements in his instruments, until he finally brought them to that degree of superior excellence which has won for them a world-wide reputation. The demand for them has been constantly increasing from the first, and though for a long while the manufactory has turned out from 25 to 30 pianos weekly, yet during the past two years the firm have received some 300 orders beyond their ability to supply. The whole number of Chickering Pianos manufactured up to the present time is but a trifle less than *fifteen thousand!*

When the new manufactory shall be in full operation, (probably about six months hence,) an army of at least 400 workmen will be employed, and it is then calculated that the number of pianos finished each week will be about 60, or upwards of 3000 per year. With their enlarged and immense facilities the Messrs. Chickering will continue to do their full share towards increasing the popular taste for the refining and elevating art of Music.

There can be no better heir-loom in the family than a genuine "Chickering Piano," comprising as it does all the varied and fascinating qualities of this favorite instrument, and furnishing, from the stability of its construction, and its well known qualities of endurance, an enjoyment for its possessors which time has no power in lessening.

36 S. Brainard's Sons: The Model Music House of America

In 1834, Nathan Brainard brought his family of seven from New Hampshire to Cleveland, Ohio. The family soon opened a music store, described in the first Cleveland city directory as "Brainard & Mould, dealers in music and musical instruments, 34 Superior street." The firm bore the name of Nathan's son, Silas, during most of its Cleveland history, first as S. Brainard and later S. Brainard's Sons.

The fledging company began to publish music after 1845, using H. Tolman and Company plates. In a major move, it took over most of the catalog of Root & Cady, which suffered extensive damage in the Chicago fire of 1871. The company also sold instruments, manufactured cabinet organs, and held rehearsals and concerts in its piano warerooms.

During the course of its history, Brainard's established branch offices in other cities, becoming the second largest music house in the country, after Oliver Ditson of Boston. Riding the wave of westward expansion, it moved its headquarters to Chicago but maintained a presence in Cleveland as the H. M. Brainard Company through the early years of the twentieth century.

Beginning in January 1864, the company issued a monthly periodical, *Western Musical World: A Journal of Music, Art and Literature*. The publication carried local news, reports from correspondents, and music, generally of a light order, aimed primarily at women and the home market. It enjoyed an extraordinarily long run in the shaky world of nineteenth-century journalism. Karl Merz, author of the following article, served as editor of the publication from 1873 to 1890. The journal finally merged with *Etude* in November 1895, which in turn stayed in print into the 1950s.

A review of the pages of *Western Musical World* makes it clear that Brainard's looked up to the East Coast, particularly Boston, as the center of America's musical universe. It also admired the "Queen City," Cincinnati, which outshone Cleveland through most of the nineteenth century through its conservatory, the work of Theodore Thomas, and its May festivals. And yet the journal continually touted the "progress" being made in Cleveland and the Great West, describing its new Cleveland headquarters in 1876 as "a musical palace—the model music house of America." Brainard's shared in the booster spirit of a young country pushing west.

KARL MERZ

"Half a Century: S. Brainard's Sons' Golden Anniversary" (1886)

With the close of this year the firm of S. Brainard's Sons will have completed its fiftieth year. There are none in this country who are any way musical but know of this old and very successful firm of music publishers. A few facts concerning its history are therefore most timely and no doubt will be welcomed by our readers.

The business was founded by Mr. Silas Brainard, who was born in Lempster, N. H., on the 14th of Feb., 1814. He was noted for much sagacity and for remarkable clear judgment combined with an unusual degree of prudence. He had much mechanical genius and delighted in improving it in his spare hours, making many articles of usefulness and ornamentation. He was a great lover of music, and he practiced the art in various ways from his youth up. He played upon several instruments with a good degree of skill and wielded a ready pen as an arranger of music. He was the compiler of a number of books, all of which have a good sale. In 1824 Silas Brainard moved with his father to Washington, N. H., where he engaged in mercantile business. In 1827 he went to New Hampton, N. H., attending school, and after finishing his course, he entered his father's store, where he won for himself the good will of all by his obliging spirit and polite manners.

In 1834 Silas Brainard's parents came to Cleveland and both father and son started in the grocery business. For the year following a musical society was organized, and he became one of its leading members, making himself useful by arranging music for the orchestra and chorus, thus leading him into musical circles and practices. In 1836 he started the present business, beginning on a small scale. With prudent management it grew, assuming year after year greater dimensions, until in 1845 the publishing department was added. This brought the house prominently before the people of this country, and during these forty years its musical publications have carried the name of Brainard from one end of the land to the other.

In the year 1864 Silas Brainard took his two sons, Charles and Henry, into partnership and the firm name was S. Brainard & Sons. On the 8th of April, 1871, he suddenly died, leaving the business in the hands of his two sons, who remained at the old stand on Superior street until 1876, when they removed to the present very commodious buildings on Euclid avenue. The grand opening took place on the 18th of February, 1876, which was attended by a large number of people. The buildings were erected with a view to the music trade, and are pronounced the most perfect ever put up for this special business. The firm is the largest in this country with a single exception and has reached immense business proportions. In the main and adjoining building are located the publishing business, the main sales rooms, the imported goods department, the bindery, the electrotype foundry, the printing presses, the engraving rooms, and the retail music business. There is also a special department for the Musical World which is soon to begin its twenty-fourth volume, a publication which has found its way into all States and Territories, yes even into Europe and Asia. In the great fire proof vaults are stored away nearly 100,000 music plates, showing what an immense business in the publishing line the firm does. After the Chicago fire S. Brainard's Sons bought the plates of the old firm of Root & Cady, their catalogue containing most of the popular war songs, which since the close of the war, have reached immense sales. In order to accommodate their Western trade the firm established a branch house in Chicago in 1879, which has grown to great proportions and is doing an im-

Karl Merz, "Half a Century: S. Brainard's Sons' Golden Anniversary," *Brainard's Musical World* (December 1886): 475.

mense business. In the year 1884 the junior member withdrew from the firm, and his place was taken by Mr. Eugene L. Graves, the son-in-law of the founder of the firm, Silas Brainard.

Many changes have taken place in the music trade during the past fifty years. Many houses have changed names, others have entirely disappeared. The house of S. Brainard's Sons, however, stands upon such a solid basis that it has withstood all storms and survived every financial crisis. We feel satisfied that the name of S. Brainard's Sons will continue for another fifty years, and that the business will grow fully as fast as it has during the past half a century.

37 John Hill Hewitt: Writer, Publisher, and Composer

John Hill Hewitt (1801–1890), whose life spanned most of the nineteenth century, was a versatile and prolific dramatist, poet, historian, publisher, essayist, and composer, born into a family of musicians. His a father, a conductor, composer, and publisher, emigrated to America in 1792. The younger Hewitt, although born in New York, was a man of the South who settled finally in Baltimore and became a strong voice for the Confederacy.

Hewitt matriculated at the military academy at West Point but did not graduate. Instead, he joined his father on a theatrical tour of the Southeast, beginning a long career that emphasized newspaper work, musical activities, and theatrical productions. During his lifetime, he wrote more than three hundred songs, eight musical stage works, more than forty plays, as well as poetry, fiction, reminiscences, an autobiography, and numerous shorter pieces. "My fondness for the life of a journalist," he reported, "caused me to neglect, to a considerable degree, my sheet-anchor—music."

Musically, Hewitt is best remembered as a song composer. His first important piece, *The Minstrel's Return'd from the War*, was written in 1825 and published by his brother several years later. It became the most popular song by an American composer before Stephen Foster. The autograph copy contains the following penciled comments:

> This song, as crude as it is, was one of my first musical efforts. It was composed in 1825 in the village of Greenville, S.C., now a city of 20,000 souls. When I returned to the North, I took this book with me to Boston. My brother James was a musical publisher. I gave him a copy to publish—he did it very reluctantly—did not think it worthy of a copyright. It was eagerly taken up by the public, and established my reputation as a ballad composer. It was sold all over the world—and my brother, not securing the right, told me that he missed making at least $10,000.*

Thus Hewitt joined a legion of others, including Stephen Foster, who did not profit appropriately from their popular creations. Hewitt eventually penned a second version of the words to his popular melody.

The Bridesmaid represents a song of a different sort, combining chivalric romance with a new sense of Italianate melody. The text for this song, too, was published by Hewitt in one of his two volumes of poetry, this one from 1838, when he was in his thirties.

Hewitt composed the melody for a Civil War text, *All Quiet along the Potomac To-night*,† and this song, too, became highly popular. Written nearly forty years after *The Minstrel's Return'd from the War*, it shows that Hewitt's talent for songwriting continued strong.

---

*Charles Hamm, *Yesterdays* (New York: W.W. Norton, 1983), 103.

†For the text of *All Quiet along the Potomac Tonight,* see "No. 53."

JOHN HILL HEWITT

from *Shadows on the Wall* (1877)

Music and Musicians

Music has always been, and still is, my frailty. Since my earliest youth I have sought its gentle influence; and though in early days I prepared myself for another and quite a different pursuit, yet the fondness of it clung to me, and it finally became my profession, though my parents were solicitous that I should adopt any other honorable calling but that. I studied it as an art and as a science; but only for the sake of the accomplishment, never thinking that I should use it as the means of support. I was educated at the Military Academy at West Point, and prepared for the army, but never went into active service, for I resigned at the end of my fourth year, and commenced the study of law in South Carolina, thinking the law a less dangerous way of achieving honors than the sword. Whenever I failed in any enterprise I fell back on music; it was my sheet-anchor.

But I would avoid the charge of egotism. My ballads are (or rather *were*) well known throughout the country; for I have not published for many years. Why? the reader may ask. For the simple reason that it does not pay the author; the publisher pockets all, and gets rich on the brains of the poor fool who is chasing that *ignis fatuus*[1] reputation.

While editing or writing for various journals, I did not neglect my profession, during the practice of which I became acquainted with nearly all of my compeers.

John H. Hewitt, *Shadows on the Wall; or, Glimpses of the Past: A Retrospect of the Past Fifty Years* (Baltimore: Turnbull Brothers, 1877), 65–66.

[1] Foolish fire.

JOHN HILL HEWITT

Three Poems (1838)

The Minstrel's Return['d] from the War

THE minstrel's return'd from the war,
With spirits as bouyant as air;
And thus on his tuneful guitar,
He sings in the bow'r of his fair;
The noise of the battle is o'er,
The bugle no more calls to arms;
A soldier no more but a lover,
I kneel to the pow'r of thy charms!
    Sweet Lady, dear Lady! I'm thine,
    I bend to the magic of beauty;
    Tho' the helmet and banner are mine,
    Yet love calls the soldier to duty.

The minstrel his suit warmly prest,
She blush'd, sigh'd, and hung down her head;
Till conquer'd she fell on his breast,
And thus to the happy youth said:
"The bugle shall part us, love, never,
My bosom thy pillow shall be;
'Till death tears thee from me for ever
Still faithful I'll perish with thee!"
    Sweet Lady, dear Lady! I'm thine,
    I bend to the magic of beauty;
    Tho' the helmet and banner are mine,
    Yet love calls the soldier to duty.

John H. Hewitt, *Poems* (Baltimore: N. Hickman, 1838), 60, 143, 159–60.

But fame called the youth to the field,
His banner wav'd over his head;
He gave his guitar for a shield,
But soon he laid low with the dead:
While she o'er her young hero bending,
Received his expiring adieu;
"I die while my country defending,
With heart to my lady love true."
   "Oh, death!" then she sigh'd, "I am thine,
   I tear off the roses of beauty,
   For the grave of my hero is mine,
   He died true to love and to duty."

The Bridesmaid

THE last—the last sound I hear,
   Of groom and bride departing;
With lady bright and cavalier,
   And helms in sunlight darting.
Alone I sit and think of one,
   The noblest knight of all,
Who left his faithful love alone
   To bow to honor's call.
     He said he'd come at eventide
     And claim his lady for his bride.

They're gone—they're gone—now down the vale
   Their plumes are faintly streaming,
Their banners flap the evening gale,
   No sunlight on them gleaming.
The night bird now begins to sing,
   And star by star appears—
Each silent planet wondering,
   Why I should be in tears!
     Why comes he not at eventide,
     To claim his lady for his bride?

Be still—be still, my throbbing breast,
   I hear a bugle sounding;
I see a warrior's snowy crest—
   A war-steed proudly bounding.
He comes—I know his gallant mien,
   His helmet, sword and spear;
I know him by his doublet green,
   My own brave cavalier!
     True to his word—at eventide,
     He's come to claim me as his bride.

On Music

WHEN far from the scenes of my childhood I
   rov'd,
   Forgotten by those whom my bosom held dear,
I caught the mild strain of a song that I lov'd
   In the days of my youth, stealing soft on my ear.
How welcome, how blissful the feeling it gave!
   It told me of pleasures long, long past away;
And I questioned myself—if these numbers still
   live,
   Oh! why should remembrance so quickly decay?

Oh! music! what language can breathe so like thee,
   New life on the heart that is sinking in death?
How cold and how cheerless existence would be,
   Were our cares not appeased by thy life-giving
     breath.
When the strain of my boyhood passed slowly
   along,
   It brought me again to my own fireside;
And I caught every note of the soul-stealing song,
   To store in and cherish the dream ere it died.

38   🌿   The Hutchinson Family

The Hutchinson family was America's premiere singing group during the mid-nineteenth century. The thirteen children of Jesse and Mary Leavitt Hutchinson, from Milford, New Hampshire, were musically adept. By the autumn of 1841, three of the brothers, Judson, John, and Asa, had formed a trio. When their sister, Abby, just eleven years old, joined them the following year, they began to experience real success. Taking the name the Hutchinson Family Singers, they began to play before full houses in New England. They sang for President Tyler in 1844 and a year later toured the British Isles. Abby's marriage in 1849 and her decision not to continue touring brought the singers into troubled waters, but they continued performing, with some changes of cast, into the 1880s.

Activists by inclination, the Hutchinsons embraced a variety of causes. They championed abolition and their anti-slavery *Get Off the Track!* proved highly effective. Frequently they included in their concerts temperance songs like *King Alcohol*: "King Alcohol has many forms / By which he catches men." They sang about abuses in insane asylums in Henry Russell's *The Maniac*. They embraced utopian experiments in communal living, women's rights, dress reform, and universal suffrage. And although they remained true to their grass roots, the singing Hutchinsons were adopted more and more by adherents of high culture.

In true nineteenth-century tradition, the family kept journals. Asa Hutchinson (1823–1884) is mainly responsible for the writing. His misspellings are left intact.

John Wallace Hutchinson (1821–1908), who settled in Lynn, Massachusetts, toured well into the 1880s. He tells us that during his fifty-three years of public life he gave some eleven thousand concerts. John Hutchinson also left a memoir, published with an introduction by ex-slave and abolitionist Frederick Douglass, who writes:

> They sang for freedom, for temperance, for peace, for moral and social reform. In
> their earlier days they were well described as a "nest of brothers with a sister in
> it." Judson, John, Asa and Abby were their names. They brought to the various
> causes which they served, the divinest gift that heaven has bestowed upon man,
> the gift of music—the superb talent to touch the hearts and stir the souls of men to
> noble ends, even when such hearts were encased with the hardest pride and self-
> ishness.*

John Hutchinson tells us about the family's theme song, the "Old Granite State"—referring to New Hampshire. The text was frequently modified to suit particular occasions. A reference to the Bay State (Massachusetts) suggests that the version below may come from John Hutchinson's later career.

Story of The Hutchinsons, ed. Charles Mann (Boston: Lee and Shepard, 1896), 1: [xv]–xvi.

HUTCHINSON FAMILY SINGERS

Journal Entries (1843–1844)

Monday, May 8th 1843
We left Boston for New York, Monday afternoon at 4 o'clock in the Cars via of Wocester and Norwich. And from thence to N.Y. by the Means of— and of in the Steamboat Cleopatra. We rode in the car in company with Messrs. Garrison, Jackson, Foster, Douglass, Phillips, Quincy, Buffum, and many other gentlemen from Mass.[1] We arrived at Norwich at about 8 after a very pleasant ride of 80 or 90 miles. The weather was very fine—the Moon shining beautifully as we left the Cars for the Steamboat that lies in the clear stream of the River Tames. Many passengers joined us at Norwich and soon after going on board, the Bell rang and in a few minutes, the Splendid boat glided majesticly down the grand river. We traveled over the whole boat with a good share of verdancy, having never rode but a very short distance before. We were perfectly delighted with the foaming and appearance of the water as we glided swiftly on. The bright rays of the moon shining on the deep blue water gave a most sublime appearance to the whole crew. After Tea we went upon the upper deck where many congregated and there we sung several of our good pieces of music. The people were very enthusiastic. By request we went below into the cabin where we sung 5 or 6 pieces. James Buffum passed around his hat. Receipts—S6.50. At 10 we retired to our births where we passed a night of miselanious feelings. Arived in New York at 5 o'Clock Tuesday Morning, after a pleasant voyage.

* * *

Sunday morning, Washington—February 4, 1844
8 o'clock. Rather cloudy but pleasant.
Zephaniah, Judson, John and O. Nichols are arranging their apparel, washing, etc. Our concert last night at Carusi's Hall was a great triumph. The room was full. We did not sing so well as usual but the audience received the songs with warm applause. After "The Old Granite State" (the audience having responded by cheers) many of our friends rushed towards us, grasping us by the hand, arm, back, side, etc. I almost forgot myself when I saw so many crowding about us. Levi Woodbury and family first shaking hands with real Yankee feeling, telling Abby she must sing "The Nice Young Man" next time. Next—I do not know who, they come so thick. In the crowd shook hands with the President's daughter[2] and relatives. Mr. Coyle and family, Mr. Wickliffe, and his amiable daughter,[3] who says she is going to attend all our concerts while here, said she would call on us Monday and have us go to her house with her. Next was as true a representative as ever sat in Congress—J.R. Giddings, whose countenance beamed with love and humanity as he pressed my hand with the most cordial respect. I experienced more plesure in speaking to this friend of freedom last night than with all the others. Next our Parker Pillsbury friend, Mr. A.P. Hale. He was very much excited. Then there were a host of friends which I do not now recollect.

The bell is ringing. We will go and get some breakfast and then will write a little more.

I do rejoice that we are having a moral influence in this city. I am glad we came here. The curse of slavery in this land yet rests but soon we may look on this our country and see it is free. After the audience had dispersed, we retired to our little

---

Excelsior: Journals of the Hutchinson Family Singers, 1842–1846, ed. Dale Cockrell (Stuyvesant, N.Y.: Pendragon Press, 1989), 115, 218–20.

[1] Members of the Massachusetts Anti-slavery Society.

[2] According to Cockrell, probably Letitia Tyler Semple, who served as hostess at the White House after Robert and Priscilla Tyler moved to Philadelphia in March, and before President Tyler remarried in June.

[3] According to Cockrell, of the four daughters of Charles and Margaret Wickliffe, Mary, Nancy, and Margaret would all have been the right age to enjoy the company of the Hutchinsons.

room in company with Osgood Mussey[4] and two of his friends. Put on our clothes, and Osgood Mussey having agreed to call on us this morning,

we bid them good night. Took a coach and came home. Had a good supper and retired to rest. O. Nichols, who came all the way from Baltimore to have us promise to give more concerts in Baltimore on our return, slept with us, we having put the beds together so as to give ample room for five.

[4]Mussey, a boyhood friend of the Hutchinsons, was serving in 1844 as a secretary to Daniel Webster.

JOHN WALLACE HUTCHINSON

from *Story of the Hutchinsons* (1896)

We tried to do our rehearsing early in the day. Sometimes calling friends delayed us until after dinner. At about nine o'clock we would give an hour or two to practising. When we were so engaged, I never was quite satisfied. *Spero meliora*—"We hope for better things"—was my motto. We were not always agreed on this point. Judson, for instance, was usually satisfied when a thing was well done, without seeking for perfection, and when I suggested that we try it once more, would abruptly turn on his heel and leave the room.

For many years we sung to the music of two violins and a violoncello. We sought to have Abby use a guitar, and she did so to some extent. In my own company Henry often accompanied himself beautifully with this instrument.[5] Sometimes in our carriage, as we rode along we would sing, she or he thrumming the chords on the guitar.

In playing, Judson always kept the air, and I played second violin to him. In early times we interspersed orchestral selections, but were advised to give it up, as it did not seem to really add to our concerts. In those days, one of our sterling selections was "The Maniac." It did a great deal to make a sensation and help us. I bought this song in Boston in 1841, as I have elsewhere said. It was a cantata, but I sung it alone to the accompaniment of the brothers. Judson and Asa would commence

a prelude. Meanwhile, I would be in my chair behind them, with the fingers of each hand raising the hair on my head, and bringing it over in partial dishevelment. Then I would rise, with the expression of vacancy inseparable from mania, and commence:

"Hush! 'tis the night watch, he guards my lonely cell;
Hush! 'tis the night watch, he guards my lonely dell;—
'Tis the night watch,
        He comes, he comes this way,
        His glimmering lamp I see—
Softly!—he comes!
        Hush! Hush! Hush!"

This would be accompanied with appropriate gestures. Then, addressing the imaginary guard in most piteous tones, I would continue:

"No, by Heaven, I am not mad!
Oh, release me! Oh, release me!
No, by Heaven, I am not mad.
        I loved her sincerely,
        I loved her too dearly,
        In sorrow and pain.
Oh, this poor heart is broken

. . . .

Hush! I hear the music in the hall—
I see her dancing—she heeds me not—
No, by Heaven! I am not mad!"

And so the song would go on, to the conclusion. I presume the critics were correct in saying it froze their blood.

John Wallace Hutchinson, *Story of the Hutchinsons (Tribe of Jesse)*, compiled and edited by Charles E. Mann, 2 vols. (Boston: Lee and Shepard, 1896), 2:293–301.

[5]Henry Hutchinson, John's son, was born in 1844.

In the course of time I introduced the melodeon which was for so long a familiar sight in all our concerts. I saw this Prince melodeon, made at Buffalo, in a music store in Springfield. I at once concluded it was just what I wanted. We had of course seen the ancient style of melodeon, made to rest on a table or in one's lap, with round keys, the size and general appearance of those of a typewriter. The bellows were worked like an accordion, pressing down on the keyboard, with a "Rock me to Sleep, Mother" motion. The Springfield melodeon had a keyboard of the regular pattern, and rested on legs with pedals. One miscreant paper called it a "washing machine." The boys thought this instrument an innovation, and gave it a cold welcome. Abby was sure she never could sing with it. She loved the accompaniment of viols. Of course none of us knew how to play the new instrument. So I made no attempt to use it in any of our concerted pieces, but at first brought it in for an accompaniment to my own song, "Man the Life-Boat," getting an imitation of the sinking of the vessel and the roaring of the waters that was very effective. In time, when I got used to playing it, the objections to the instrument on the part of the others ceased.

We made up our programme, a miscellaneous one, from the best songs from hymn books and song books, and utilized anything that came in our path. If we heard a song and liked it, we would find a way to get hold of it ourselves. . . .

We found it better, in the course of time, to set songs to our own music. . . .

To return to the "Old Granite State." Jesse sang the solo and we came in on the refrain. The song seemed the essence of egotism to us, and we wondered that Jesse could have written it. We could not conceive that the public cared anything about the Hutchinson family names. But the fact was, Jesse saw better than we, that this song would make a hit, and we saw it too, after singing it once or twice. By the time we had sung it through Great Britain, we had ceased to think of it in the light of egotism. The song was somewhat changed by the addition of new verses on our trip to England, and as time wore on and conditions changed politically, other verses were modified and I added some to it. The song as it has been sung for many years is as follows:[6]

We have come from the mountains,
We've come down from the mountains,
Ho we've come from the mountains,
    Of the Old Granite State.
        We're a band of brothers,
        We're a band of brothers,
        We're a band of brothers,
            And we live among the hills.

We have left our aged parents,
We have left our aged parents,
We have left our aged parents,
    In the Old Granite State.
        We obtained their blessing,
        We obtained their blessing,
        We obtained their blessing,
            And we bless them in return.

We had ten other brothers,
And of sisters just another,
Besides our father and our mother,
    In the Old Granite State.
        With our present number,
        With our present number,
        With our present number,
            There are thirteen in the tribe.

We're the tribe of Jesse,
We're the tribe of Jesse,
We're the tribe of Jesse,
    And our several names we'll sing.

David, Noah, Andrew, Zephy, Caleb, Joshua,
    Jesse, Benny,
Judson, Rhoda, John and Asa and Abby
    are our names;
We're the sons of Mary, of the tribe of Jesse,
And we now address you
    in our native mountain song.

---

[6]First published in 1843. The tune was that of the revival hymn, *The Old Church Yard*; Jesse Hutchinson (1813–1853) wrote the text.

Hail! ye noble sons and daughters
Hail! ye noble sons and daughters,
Hail! ye noble sons and daughters,
 Of the Old Bay State;
  Here's a friendly greeting,
  Here's a friendly greeting,
  Here's a friendly greeting
   From New Hampshire's granite hills.

We are all real Yankees,
We are all real Yankees,
Real native Hampshire Yankees,
 From the Old Granite State.
  And by prudent guessing,
  And by prudent guessing,
  And by prudent guessing,
   We shall whittle through the world.

We're the friends of emancipation,
And we'll sing the proclamation
Till it echoes through the nation
 From the old Granite State.
  That the tribe of Jesse,
  That the tribe of Jesse,
  That the tribe of Jesse
   Are the friends of equal rights.

Party threats are not alarming,
For when music ceases charming,
We can earn our bread at farming
 In the Old Granite State.
  We're a band of farmers,
  We're a band of farmers,
  We're a band of farmers,
   And we love to till the soil.

Oh, we love the rocks and mountains,
Oh, we love the rocks and mountains,
Oh, we love the rocks and mountains
 Of the Old Granite State.
  Pointing up to heaven,
  Pointing up to heaven,
  Pointing up to heaven,
   They are beacon lights to man.

And we love our glorious nation,
Holding firm its lofty station,
'Tis the pride of all creation,
And our banner is unfurled.
  Men should love each other,
  Nor let hatred smother,
  Every man's a brother,
   And our country is the world.

We have labored for our nation,
For its life and preservation;
And we've sung our emancipation
 Since the good old days of yore.
  But our warfare soon is ended,
  Human rights are well defended,
  And our voices, once more blended.
   Shout "Free Suffrage" evermore.

Yes, the good time's drawing nigher,
And our nation, tried by fire
Shall proclaim the good Messiah,
 Second coming of the Lord.
  Heart and hand together,
  Every friend and neighbor,
  Let us live and labor
   For the good of all mankind.

Now, farewell, friends and brothers,
Fathers, sons, sisters, mothers,
Lynn people and all others,
 In the land we love the best;
  May the choicest blessings,
  May the choicest blessings,
  And may Heaven's blessings,
   Ever rest upon you all.

While the song was written to be sung by the quartet, it was Jesse's ambition to have the whole family of children appear together. He wanted us all to be united in music. I sympathized with this, and deprecated anything suggesting trading or bickering between one another.

Shouting the Jubilee
of Temperance

Nineteenth-century America had seen enough alcohol abuse to realize that the virtues of the "water of life" had been much overrated. In 1810, some fourteen thousand distilleries were producing twenty-five million gallons of spirits yearly, enough for about seven gallons of absolute alcohol for white men and women over fifteen years old; by 1830, that amount had increased to ten gallons.

The movement against alcohol consumption became increasingly institutionalized. The American Society for the Promotion of Temperance, later known as the American Temperance Society, was formed by Boston clergy in February 1826, as the church took the lead with missionary zeal. The society wanted people throughout the country to sign a pledge of abstinence from distilled liquor (but not from wine or beer). Those who did were asked to put a "T" beside their signature—the origin of our word "teetotaler." By the 1850s, temperance societies had multiplied and now called for total abstinence from *all* beverages containing alcohol.

Songs were prominently used at temperance meetings as participants bound themselves to "touch it not." The message was clothed in well-known tunes chosen from an ample repertoire of church hymns and popular songs.

Arba Lankton (1835–1905) of Hartford, Connecticut, identified in a local newspaper as a "well-known pop-corn vender," found his real calling within the temperance movement. On September 29, 1876, he organized Arba Lankton's Total Abstinence and Anti-Tobacco Society, taking for a motto, "The Sword of the Lord, and of Lankton." He published the book, *Incidents in the Life of Arba Lankton*, in Hartford in 1891 and followed it up eight years later with a collection of *Favorite Songs and Hymns*. By his own account, Lankton held a total of 589 meetings, obtained nearly five thousand total abstinence pledges and some three thousand anti-tobacco signatures.

ARBA LANKTON

from *Incidents in the Life of Arba Lankton* (1891)

Preface

The aim of the author in placing this volume before the public is to show the evil effects from the use of strong drink and tobacco, to enlighten and elevate the mind of the reader and help to save souls. Hundreds of books are printed annually, the moral tendency of which is downward. The Bible says, "No man liveth to himself," which means that we all have an influence upon others. Having been greatly benefited by reading good books, tracts and papers, I feel that it is my duty, with God's help, to distribute good reading, and thus use my influence on others to guide them to a port of virtue, safety and happiness. As the Quaker has said, "Let me do

Arba Lankton, *Incidents in the Life of Arba Lankton* . . . (Hartford, Conn. Arba Lankton's Total Abstinence and Anti-Tobacco Society, 1891), [Preface], 51–52, 57.

my work well, for I shall not pass this way again."

I desire by all good means to suppress the sale of strong drink and tobacco, and to reform those who have formed the habit of drinking, and to prevent as many children as possible from every learning to use strong drink or tobacco.

> "What good can it do
> To smoke and to chew,
> To swear and to drink,
> And never to think
> What will the end be?"
>
> The Author

* * *

As a large number of persons had signed my pledges, by my individual effort, it seemed a good plan to hold public meetings.

I hired Whittelsey's Hall, Hartford, and Sunday evening, March 31, 1878, Arba Lankton's Total Abstinence Society held its first meeting, President Arba Lankton presiding. There was singing, prayer, and six short addresses.

The Society held several good meetings in this hall and also at Hope Chapel.

It has been well said, "If you would have your business done, go, if not send."

April 28, 1878, I spoke to a man who had at-

tended one of my meetings in Whittelsey's hall, and asked him to inquire at Parkville, where he lived, and see if I could get a place to hold temperance meetings in. He told me in about a week that he had inquired, but could not find any place to hold meetings. But I went to Parkville myself and quite readily by inquiring of one person and another obtained the privilege to hold a meeting.

According to my journal, on the evening of May 19, 1878, Arba Lankton's Total Abstinence Society, held a meeting at the old school house, Parkville. Mr. S. Marslen presided. There were singing, prayer and a number of temperance speeches. Capt. Patrick O'Farrell remarked that they had long been talking about the need of temperance meetings, but they did not succeed in starting them until I came along like a God-sent messenger to set the ball in motion. The school house was full to overflowing, and a great interest was kept up to the end of the meeting. Thirteen signed the pledge.

* * *

But I felt it my duty to do good as I had opportunity, and I advertised the meetings, and if helpers come well, if not, I went on alone, yet not alone, for the Lord was with me. Praise His holy name.

ARBA LANKTON

Texts of Two Songs (1889)

Battle Cry of Temperance
Tune—"Battle Cry of Freedom"

We are gathering for a right cause,
    with earnest hearts and true,
    Shouting the battle cry of Temp'-rance;
Millions bless our onward progress,
    in the work we have to do,
    Shouting the battle cry of Temp'-rance.

Chorus

Cold water forever, hurrah! then hurrah!
Down with the wine glass; up with our star,
    As we gather for a right cause,
    With earnest hearts and true,
Shouting the battle cry of Temp'-rance.

We have signed the good old pledge,
    that our brothers signed before.
    Shouting the Jubilee of Temp'-rance:
And we'll number in our ranks a million signers
    more
    Shouting the Jubilee of Temp'-rance.

Lankton, Arba. *Favorite Songs and Hymns* (Hartford, Conn.: Arba Lankton's Total Abstinence and Anti-Tobacco Society, 1889), 14, 17.

Chorus

We are springing to the call, the young, the old
    and all,
    Shouting the Jubilee of Temp'-rance:
And we'll banish alcohol from parlor, shop and
    hall,
    Shouting the Jubilee of Temp'-rance.

Chorus

The Contrast.
Tune—"Yankee Doodle"

Time was when we were soaked in rum,
    Our work became neglected.
Our wives and children too at home,
    Were weeping and dejected.
Our bodies covered too with rags,
    Our system's out of order,
Our wood it came in little jags,
    Our cow, she low'd for fodder.

Our pig was squealing in the pen,
    With nothing could we feed him,

And nothing for the chick and hen,
    Until we ceased our drinking;
Our landlords too would warn us out,
    Our tailors wouldn't trust us,
Our merchants too would often pout,
    Relations too have curs'd us.

But now we see some brighter days,
    We're happy and respected,
We've joined the LODGE, repair'd the ways,
    And all are now collected.
Our happy spirits look ahead,
    Our path with splendor shining,
All sorrow from each bosom fled,
    And none are heard repining.

Our peaceful homes and firesides sweet,
    Again we are enjoying,
With wife and children all complete,
    In peace their time employing.
In conversation we can spend
    A winter evening gaily,
And never wanting a good friend,
    Or good employment daily.

40   The Dodworth Band

The Dodworth family, Patrick S. Gilmore, John Philip Sousa—these names represent the best in American band music from the 1830s well into the twentieth century. Allen Dodworth led the first all-brass bands in the United States, his renowned ensembles establishing new standards of excellence. The flamboyant Patrick Gilmore was a prime mover in the rise of the American symphonic band. John Philip Sousa, the most famous name of all, brought professional band music to new renown. Over the years, bands have played functional and concert music for a wide variety of occasions, particularly those held out of doors. For many Americans, band music has been their principal source of musical exposure.

Thomas Dodworth and his eldest son, Allen T. Dodworth (1817–1896), emigrated from England in 1828 and joined the Independent Band of New York. Thomas played trombone, while Allen was a fine piccolo player. The band soon changed its instrumentation, becoming one of the first all-brass bands in the country. Upon its demise, a number of its members formed the National Brass Band led by Allen Dodworth, which in 1836 became the Dodworth Band, considered for many years to be the finest in the United States. Allen continued with the band into the 1850s. The great era of the Dodworth Band itself extended into the 1870s.

The eccentric Patrick S. Gilmore wrote of the Dodworth ensemble that "brass instruments were never played with greater delicacy or refinement than by the Dodworth organization . . . to be a member" was to be "a star in the profession."*

In 1853 Allen Dodworth brought out an interesting instructor, *Dodworth's Brass Band School*, published by his musician son Harvey Dodworth, who had established a publishing company in New York City. The attention to professional standards is clear throughout the work. It assumes very little musical knowledge on the part of the players or would-be players to whom it is directed. The instructor emphasizes the military connection with band music, and in fact, the Dodworth Band routinely played under contract to a military regiment. The music is arranged for twelve instruments, plus drums and cymbals, but, we are told, it can be played by more than twelve (Dodworth is careful to say which parts may be doubled) or as few as six. Dodworth comments further about band size in *The Message Bird* of August 15, 1849, where he tells us that "most of the bands in existence at present, consist of from ten to fifteen members, from which number very fine effect can be produced, if the instruments are *well balanced*."† Dodworth prefers brass instrument bells to point in one direction. In his *Brass Band School*, he provides alternate formations for parading with bells "in front or upwards" or "with bells behind, over the shoulder." The latter would be particularly advantageous for throwing the sound backward toward troops marching behind.

---

*Quoted in Frank J. Cipolla, "Dodworth," *New Grove Dictionary of American Music* 1: 638.
†*The Message Bird* (New York), August 15, 1849: 9.

ALLEN DODWORTH

from *Dodworth's Brass Band School* (1853)

Practicing in Concert, or Band Playing

Each member of the Band, having practiced all that has been laid down, will next take his part of the first lesson, practice that until perfectly familiar with it, so that he may be able to play it without its absorbing the whole of his attention, for it often occurs, with beginners, that they are so engaged with the difficulties (or beauties) of their own part, that they are scarcely conscious that any but themselves have been playing; this should not be so; every member should be familiar enough with his own part to be able to pay some attention to what is doing about him, and although it is praiseworthy to play his part as if the whole effect depended upon the proper execution of that part, yet, at the same time, he should remember that band playing is not, simply a number of men playing certain notes with great correctness and precision, it is, in addition to all that, a number of instruments harmonizing and sympathizing with each other, as if the same sensitive soul governed all, as one; let every member *play his part* and *nothing more*; if this is not difficult enough to show his abilities, let him play a solo; do not mutilate the arrangement of the music. Before beginning a new piece, look closely to the signature, observing what notes are made flat or sharp, what time it is in, and how fast it is to be played. Attend closely to the *Pianos*; it is an old and very true saying, that "the fortes always take care of themselves;" there are many shades of *forte* and *piano*, which should be carefully attended to; then there are the *forzandos, crescendos, diminuendos, staccatos, slurs*, and all the other little marks connected with music, the attention to which evinces the excellence of a Band's training.

Do *not* attempt to lead the leader.

And finally, remember that *noise* is not music.

Rules for Band Practice

1st. Tune all the instruments by the 1st Soprano.
2d. First tune but two at a time.
3d. Finally tune in a body.
4th. No blowing or practicing between the pieces; that should be done at home.
5th. Begin together.
6th. Obey the leader or director, in every particular, in relation to the performance of the music; a Band to play well must be governed by one mind.
7th. Let the drums beat VERY softly, otherwise it will be impossible to hear the defects.

Formation for Parading

When instruments are used with bells in front or upwards, the following will be found the best formation:

Front rank. . . . . Basses.
2d do. . . . . Tenores and Baritones.
3d do. . . . . Sopranos and Altos.
4th do. . . . . Drums and Cymbals.
Leader on the right of the 3d rank.

When instruments are used with bells behind, over the shoulder:

Front rank. . . . . Altos-Sopranos.
2d do. . . . . Baritones and Tenores.
3d do. . . . . Basses.
4th do. . . . . Drums and Cymbals.
Leader on the right of the front rank.

Formation of Regiment

In camp, a signal is given half an hour before the time appointed for parade, notifying the companies to assemble.

Ten minutes after which the adjutant's call is given, by order of the adjutant.

The band, standing where the right of the line

Allen Dodworth, *Dodworth's Brass Band School* (New York: H. B. Dodworth, 1853), 23–[24], 32, [33].

is to be, will next play a quickstep, to which the companies march into line, the band continuing to play until the last company is in line.

The adjutant will then order the band to beat off.

The band will then execute the troop in the following manner.

Left wheel! Give three chords in the key of the piece intended to be played—which should be a waltz—play the first strain once through without moving—step off at the first bar of the repeat—march down the entire length of the line—when past the line counter-march, or wheel entirely round, halt, and finish the strain. Then the drums will give three rolls; the band then commences a quickstep or polka, playing the first strain as before without moving, and march at the repeat. March back to the right, and round into place; finish the strain, and then the drums conclude with three rolls.

The adjutant will then order, "shoulder arms!" "open order!" &c., &c.; and at the order, "present arms!" the drums give one roll to the colonel, who now takes command, he orders "shoulder arms!" &c., and at the order of "present arms!" the drums beat to the colors for half a minute, or give three rolls, on receiving the regimental colors. This concludes the formation.

* * *

Honors to Be Paid by the Troops

The President is to be saluted with the highest honors—all standards and colors dropping, officers saluting, drums beating, and trumpets sounding.

A Major-General commanding in chief is to be received—by cavalry, with swords drawn, trumpets sounding the march, and all the officers saluting, standards dropping—by infantry, with drums beating the march, colors dropping, officers saluting, and arms presented.

* * *

Remarks on Band Music

ALL the music is arranged for twelve instruments, but can be played by any number less than twelve, down to six; viz. 1st Soprano, 2d Soprano or 1st Alto, 2d Alto, 1st and 2d Tenores, and 1st Bass. It can also be played by more than twelve by doubling on some of the parts. If the Sopranos are doubled, it should be only on the second—the same with the Altos and Tenores; the Baritone may not be doubled, as this is a powerful instrument for the part it usually plays, consequently when there are two of them, the second should play with the 1st Bass. In the arrangement of the score, such instruments have been selected as will produce the best effect, as it is impossible to arrange one score to suit every band.

The author would take occasion to say here that the addition of trombones and trumpets is more in accordance with the public taste than with his own, for these fine instruments are so constantly abused, by those who mistake noise for music, that the appearance of one of them in a band, is an object of very considerable annoyance. For what reason, almost all who use these instruments think it necessary to blow them until they crack or snarl, is difficult to understand; that it is so, will be very generally admitted, for many players seem to imagine, that the more snarl and crack, or less tone they produce, the greater the effect,—this is a most unfortunate error, and is an error that has had a very mischievous effect upon the public mind, with regard to brass instruments and bands,—how unreasonable it is then to sacrifice so many sublime effects for the mere matter of making a noise, which appears to be the great object of many of our brass bands, as if it was necessary to make up in *quantity* what was lacking in *quality*, but noise is certainly but a sorry substitute for *music*.

This matter is not confined to brass bands only, the brass department of many of our finest orchestras, conducted by the most able directors, is used as if the only object of that portion of the orchestra was to alarm the audience occasionally. However, it is hoped that enough has been said to call the attention of the reader to this most lamentable abuse of a truly noble branch of music.

Review of Dodworth's Band Concert (1849)

Allen Dodworth's concert. The inimitable *Dodworth's Cornet Band* [will] give a concert, this evening at the Tabernacle, for the benefit of their talented founder and leader. It is to the exquisite skill and taste of Mr. Allen Dodworth that we are indebted for the surprising musical effects of this celebrated band. His skill and judgment in the selection and improvement of the instruments used, no less than the admirable arrangement of the music performed by this famous band, are as much the foundation and source of their celebrity as the individual ability of the performers.

The Message Bird (New York), December 15, 1849: 167.

41 Patrick S. Gilmore and His Magnificent Vision

The Boston *Post* of June 16, 1869, reported:

> The National Peace Jubilee began yesterday. The occasion was one of equal success, splendor, extent, and novelty. It was beyond all comparison the grandest musical scheme ever attempted on the American continent, and its initiatory performance fully justified the most sanguine expectations of its most ardent supporters and friends.

The organizer of this monumental event was America's premier bandmaster of the period, Patrick Sarsfield Gilmore (1829–1892). Born in Ireland, Gilmore always retained a bit of blarney in his personality. He emigrated to Boston in 1849 and within ten years had established his own ensemble, Gilmore's Band. Success followed. A gigantic event in New Orleans in 1864 enhanced his national reputation and served as a model for what he would achieve later in Boston.

Gilmore operated frequently on what he called his "visions." The one for Boston came to him in June 1867:

> A vast structure rose before me, filled with the loyal of the land, through whose lofty arches a chorus of ten thousand voices and the harmony of a thousand instruments rolled their sea of sound, accompanied by the chiming of bells and the booming of cannon, all pouring forth their praises and gratifications in loud hosannas with all the majesty and grandeur of which music seemed capable.*

The Boston Jubilee of 1869, which commemorated the return of peace after the Civil War, was a celebration indeed. A large, specially erected building seating 30,000 included a mammoth, newly built organ by Elias & George G. Hook of Boston. The orchestra and military band numbered one thousand, the chorus, ten thousand. Real cannons were fired electrically from the conductor's stand. The "Anvil Chorus," from Verdi's *Il Trovatore*, which Gilmore himself conducted, was made the more dramatic through the services of a hundred Boston firemen striking anvils.

Despite all the hoopla, first-rate musicians took part. These included conductors Eben Tourjee (director of the New England Conservatory); Carl Zerrahn (leader of the Handel and Haydn Society); Julius Eichberg (director of the Boston Conservatory and superintendent of music for the Boston public schools); the opera impresario Carl Rosa (who served as concertmaster); the famed and popular Norwegian violinist Ole Bull (a solo chair); composers John Knowles Paine and Dudley Buck, each conducting his

---

*Marwood Darlington, *Irish Orpheus: The Life of Patrick S. Gilmore* (Philadelphia: Olivier, Maney, Klein, 1950), 39.

own music; the remarkable cornetist Matthew Arbuckle; and excellent singers, such as the Scottish soprano Euphrosyne Parepa-Rosa and English contralto Adelaide Phillipps. Lowell Mason was honored, and President Grant made an appearance. Characteristically, Gilmore chronicled the entire five-day event in a large book of over 750 pages.

Gilmore brought band music to a new height of popularity. His work served as a significant model for his true successor, John Philip Sousa (1854–1932), who cherished the memory of Gilmore for promoting the interests of instrumental performers.

PATRICK S. GILMORE

from *History of the National Peace Jubilee* (1871)

The conception was an inspiration, which shed a lustre over one soul as bright and pure as if it were a light from heaven. When it came like a flash, filling the eye with the dazzling splendor of the scenes portrayed, and the ear with the enchanting harmony of its wonderful music, there was no thought of the scoffs, the ridicule, the derision which it would have to encounter, and the terrible struggle through which it would have to pass,—a struggle which threatened to strangle it at almost every step. O that it could come to pass in all the magnificence of the vision by which it was foreshadowed! How much more wonderful it would then be than it shall be even now, when its realization promises such thrilling and glorious scenes, effects, and results! He whose every thought has been devoted to it since the moment it first sank into his soul would have had the government of the nation say, "Let this feast of music and rejoicing take place, regardless of its cost; let all the people gather together and witness the marvellous beauties of an offering inspired by Peace!" The nation that expended hundreds of millions of treasure, and offered hundreds of thousands of lives to secure its own life, could well afford to have said this. Then, indeed, it might be called a "*National*

Peace Jubilee"; but it was soon discovered that it would need even the voice of an angel in the legislative halls of the nation to gain for it such recognition and support.

What could be done? It seemed to say to its chosen medium, "Go forth and proclaim that I *must* be heard! I *must* be realized! the nation *must* see and hear me in the name of Peace and Union!"

* * *

As has already been stated, the doors of the Coliseum were thrown open for the admission of the public at One o'clock on Tuesday, June 15, and from that hour the tide of humanity kept flowing into the great building until Three, the time announced for the inaugural exercises of the Jubilee to commence. The scene within the building when all was in place was the grandest and most impressive ever beheld upon the American continent; nay, we might go further, and say ever witnessed in the world beneath one roof. The band of a thousand performers were in their seats, each with his instrument in hand ready to perform his part. They occupied a platform which, having a slight descent from rear to front, brought every member of the orchestra into view from the floor, and from every part of the house.

From the right, left, and rear of the band platform the chorus seats, filled with ten thousand of the best singers in the land, ascended row above row, going up, up, up, up, higher and higher and higher, until they reached the very eaves; and the

Patrick S. Gilmore, *History of the National Peace Jubilee and Great Musical Festival, Held in the City of Boston, June, 1869* (Boston: Published by the Author and for sale by Lee and Shepard, 1871), 348–49; 443–44; 460–66.

sight of this great choir alone was a scene never to be forgotten.

The magnificent organ, which, without other voice or instrument, could fill the huge edifice with rich harmony, was all ready to pour out its marvellous tones under the artistic fingers of that true genius and gentlemen, Dr. John H. Willcox, who was already at his post.[1]

The big guns were in position, and together with all the bells of the city, were prepared to respond to the touch of the electrician, and lend their power and loftiness to the National Air.

But while the beautiful and picturesque musical scene within the building filled the eyes of the vast audience with wonder and admiration, the band and chorus looked in turn with kindred feelings of astonishment upon the sea of faces turned towards them. In fact, for the time being, each and all felt a new sensation, a thrill of joy, of inspiration, of exquisite pleasure, which in life they never felt before, and which cannot be explained.

"If the scene alone awakens such feelings, what will be the effect of the music when the flood-gates of such harmony as we shall soon hear are opened upon us?" was a question the solution of which thousands awaited with mingled feelings of joy and fear.

"Will it be frightfully loud, or will it be very beautiful?" "May not the first grand outburst of the organ, with that immense body of voices and instruments combined, create such a concussion in the air as to destroy our hearing, and perhaps shake down the building?" "Is it possible that such a multitude of voices and instruments can harmonize and make agreeable music?"

These questions would soon be solved, and solved to the *entire satisfaction* of all within and without,—ay, of hundreds of thousands throughout the country who anxiously awaited the result.

*   *   *

---

[1]John H. Willcox (1827–1875), extroverted and personable, was an organist and organ builder active around Boston.

The Musical Exercises of the Peace Jubilee

The first piece upon the programme was Luther's grand choral,

GOD IS A CASTLE AND DEFENCE.
For Full Chorus, Organ, Orchestra, and Military Bands.

The first peal of the organ was the signal to the chorus and orchestra to prepare; the ten thousand singers arose, and the thousand musicians placed their instruments in position. All eyes were now directed to the uplifted *baton*; chorus, organ, and orchestra were to come in *fortissimo* at its very first move. For a moment all seemed hushed into breathless silence. Then—"*In the name of God*"—the wand came down, and the grandest volume of song that ever filled human ear rolled like a sea of sound through the immense building; grander and grander came wave after wave, now loud as the roar of the ocean, now soft as the murmuring stream. O how beautiful, how pure, how heavenly! what sublime chords, what ravishing harmonies! Not a jarring note from first to last, but like the mingling of many waters, organ, voices, instruments, all blended together in one noble flood of music, sweeping away forever in its mighty and majestic flow every vestige of doubt and fear, and carrying upon its swelling tide joy to all hearts, and bearing the fact to the world abroad of a glorious triumph for art and for the musical people of America.

The instant the music ceased there was an immense outburst of applause; the question of "feasibility" was decided; the entire audience felt relieved of a great weight of anxiety; and, as if to heighten the glory of the occasion, the bright sun, which had been under a cloud all day, now shone upon the scene, its golden lustre streaming in through every aperture like rays from heaven, while upon the wings of lightning the news sped to all parts of the land that the "great experiment," the great Musical Festival, the great Peace Jubilee, had passed the threshold of doubt, and was most successfully and auspiciously inaugurated.

The second piece upon the programme was

WAGNER'S OVERTURE TO TANNHAUSER

This was played by a chosen band of Six Hundred performers, under the *baton* of Julius Eichberg; and his appearance upon the conductor's stand gave the greatest pleasure to all who admire modest merit, true musical genius, and genuine artistic ability.

The beauties of Wagner's magnificent overture were never developed with such fine effect before. The fulness of the instruments in all the parts enabled Mr. Eichberg to bring out every figure clear and bold; and in the *finale*, where the brass (which was largely increased for this grand climax) take up the principal theme *fortissimo* in unison, and the strings come in, rushing through the stately choral like a whirlwind through the forest, the effect was highly inspiring.

The performance was received with a storm of applause, and was a grand triumph for the orchestra, the conductor, and for Wagner.

The third piece was the

GLORIA, FROM MOZART'S TWELFTH MASS.
For Full Chorus, Organ, and Orchestra.[2]

The able and experienced conductor, Carl Zerrahn, assumed the *baton* in this piece, and his appearance created a *furor* as great as ever welcomed musical chieftain.

The Gloria was a severe test for the chorus. Ten Thousand voices could not move with the celerity of a church choir, and from an inclination on the part of some of the singers to hasten while others retarded the time, it seemed at one moment as if the chorus would go to pieces; but under the firm lead of Mr. Zerrahn, who marked the stately measure with force and inspiration, the whole body soon came under subjection, and the four parts moved along majestically to the close. The effect of this— one of the best choruses ever written—was grand, and elicited the warmest applause of the audience.

The fourth piece was

GOUNOD'S AVE MARIA.
For Voice, Violin Obbligato, Piano, Organ, and Orchestra.

At the proper moment the Queen of Song, Madame Parepa-Rosa, made her appearance[3]; and as she came down through the orchestra to the front of the platform, she received an ovation from band, chorus, and audience of which any queen might well feel proud.

When the applause subsided the *arpeggio* figure originally for piano, which runs through the whole piece, was taken up, *pizzicato*, by Thirty cellos and Thirty violas; then came the organ, leading into the theme, usually played by one instrument, but now by *Two Hundred Violinists*. The effect of this great body of strings in unison, playing the beautiful and plaintive melody, is indescribable; they reach the climax, the orchestra comes in with a full accord, and now the voice takes up the theme just played by the Two Hundred violins, while they perform the *obbligato*. How beautifully the crystal voice of Madame Rosa soars over all! how steadily she sustains every tone! hear the violins follow and repeat the measures she has just sung! with what expression and agitation she appeals to Maria, Maria, adding the fervor of inspired song to the beautiful prayer, while the violins are wailing beneath. Now they go together, the cellos and violas snap the *pizzicato* stronger, the organ and orchestra increase their *forte*; and with full power the voice and Two Hundred violins ascent to the upper B natural. O, what a magnificent effect! what heavenly music! what a superb voice! Now comes the *diminuendo*; what sweet sadness in every tone! Amen, Amen; it seems as if the music is weeping, when through the thrilling *tremolando* is heard the final Amen.

Never, never was there anything more beautiful than this; the vast audience and the Ten Thousand singers made the welkin ring again and again, while the waving of handkerchiefs from the remotest corner of the building testified that, according to measurement, the incomparable voice of Madame Parepa-Rosa was fully proven to be "five

[2]The Mass K. Anh. 232 in G major, which is regarded as spurious.

[3]Euphrosyne Parepa-Rosa (1836–1874), born in Scotland, first toured America in 1865 with violinist Carl Rosa, rehearsal conductor for the National Peace Jubilee, whom she subsequently married.

hundred feet long, three hundred feet wide, and a hundred feet high."

Next came the National Air,

THE STAR-SPANGLED BANNER.
For Full Chorus, with Organ, Orchestra, Military Band,
Drum-Corps, Chiming of Bells,
and Cannon Accompaniment.

After an introductory symphony the first stanza of the first verse was taken up by about Twenty-five Hundred bass voices in unison, next came all the tenors in the second stanza, and then the full chorus. In the rendering of this verse the orchestra got "mixed" for a few moments, and came near "smashing up." The parts had never been played from before, and in consequence of four measures, which by accident were marked repeat, and should not be so, the chorus went on all right, while the orchestra were four measures behind. This was a frightful moment for the writer, who was conducting at the time. However, it fortunately happened that the harmony was about the same, and with the exception of a few, nobody knew there was anything wrong, and the members of the Band discovering the error, avoided the repetition after the first verse. There was no time to run over the orchestra parts in the morning, but this was a proof that even the simplest thing should not be produced in public without a rehearsal of all the parts. The second verse went beautifully, and was sung by all the sopranos and altos in duet, ending with the full chorus. The first stanza of the last verse was sung by all the tenors and basses in unison, and the second stanza by the same voices in duet. Then came the full chorus with all the power of the organ, orchestra, military band, drum-corps, bells, and cannon accompaniment.

It would be impossible to describe the effect which the national air produced, rendered as above. No sooner had it closed than the entire audience arose, giving vent to a perfect storm of applause. Such enthusiasm never was known in any assemblage before. The piece had to be repeated, and its second hearing created another scene of wild delight.

The peculiar effect of such vast numbers singing in unison and in duet was wonderful, but when in the last chorus all the elements of sound were let loose, and the cannon came booming in at the touch of the electrician, as prompt as the sound of the bass-drum, the audience unanimously proclaimed that "Old Glory" was a wonderful institution set to music.

This being the end of the first part, a general stand-up fraternization and interchange of congratulations took place; the entire audience, chorus, and band were alike astonished and delighted with the result; those who had devoted all their days to the profession never experienced anything like it before. Even the old violinist who came three thousand miles to attend the Festival,—all the way from Germany,—opened his eyes with surprise and admiration, and enthusiastically declared that the Old World had never known anything to equal this fest of Young America. The telegraph office at the Press Headquarters was immediately besieged by parties sending private and public despatches to all parts of the country. One gentleman, in sending a message to his wife, said, "Come on immediately by first train. Will sacrifice anything to have you here. Nothing like it in a lifetime."

A New Vision of Concert Life: Boston's Handel and Haydn Society

During the early years of the nineteenth century, a musical reform movement sprang up in New England agitating for "improved" musical taste, particularly in the realm of sacred music. The aim was to cultivate appreciation for and performance of music from Europe by such composers as Handel, Haydn, Mozart, and Beethoven. Like its earlier cousins, the Middlesex Musical Society led by Nathaniel Gould (founded in 1805) and the Handel Society of Dartmouth College under John Hubbard founded in 1807, the Boston Handel and Haydn Society, which was established in 1815, espoused these aims. Its first program took place on Christmas night of that year in King's (Stone) Chapel with one hundred singers, mostly men, performing a concert that emphasized sacred music by the composers for which the Society was named. The concert was a new kind of undertaking for which the press was generally enthusiastic but somewhat mystified. One reviewer found the composers' styles "peculiar."

Seven years later, the Society published Lowell Mason's *Boston Handel and Haydn Society Collection of Church Music*. This highly popular book provided a big break for Mason, who moved to Boston and soon began a five-year term as president and music director of the Society. The publication ran to more than twenty editions. The title pages of early ones lacked the names of Mason and George K. Jackson, an English organist then in Boston who contributed much to the *Collection* and to whom the first edition was dedicated. A preface, letters of approbation, a dedication, an explanation of musical terms, and an introduction to the art of singing precede the music itself.

The success of the Handel and Haydn Society over many years established Boston as a citadel of musical excellence with a European bent. Seeking to educate America in its musical growth, this Society, along with others, continued to promote its ideas of fine music to large numbers of listeners and amateur participants.

Concert Advertisement (1815)

The Handel and Haydn Society, will perform an Oratorio, consisting of a selection of pieces of Sacred Music, chiefly from the works of Handel and Haydn, this evening, the 25th instant, in the *Stone Chapel*, in School street, to commence at six o'clock.

*   *   *

Tickets for admission may be obtained at the Bookstores of *Munroe, Francis & Parker*, and *West & Richardson*, Cornhill; of *David Francis*, Newbury-street, near Boylston Market; *Robert Fennelly*, Prince-street; and *G. Graupner*, Franklin-street. Price of tickets 1 dollar each.

N. B. Gentlemen who wish to take their families, are informed that on purchasing *four* tickets, they will be presented with a *fifth* gratis; and those purchasing *six*, will be entitled to *two* additional ones.

Boston Daily Advertiser and Repertory, December 25, 1815: [3].

Concert Review in the *Boston Patriot* (1816)

We were so highly gratified by the performance of the *Sacred Oratorio* by the Handel and Haydn Society, on Christmas evening, that we are truly happy to see it announced for repetition on Thursday evening next; not merely on account of a desire again to witness and enjoy the performance ourselves, but because it will afford many lovers of Sacred Music who were necessarily absent, an account of the usual engagements, on Christmas evening, an opportunity of indulging themselves in their favorite enjoyment.—We are informed that his Excellency the Governor and the Honorable council intend to be present, and have no doubt that many of the members of the Legislature will avail themselves of this opportunity of witnessing a performance, which we think will be at least equal if not superior to any thing of the kind they have ever had an opportunity of witnessing.—We think the public should duly appreciate the merits and exertions of the gentlemen who have instituted this Society, who must necessarily devote much of their time gratuitously for the attainment of its great object, which appears from the Constitution to be, to cultivate and improve a taste for *pure Sacred Music.*

Boston Patriot, January 17, 1816: [2].

Concert Review in the *Columbian Centinel* (1816)

It must have been pleasing to the friends and patrons of the *Handel and Haydn Society*, as well as all lovers of sacred song, to see the Oratorio by them repeated on Thursday evening, 18th inst, so honorably attended. The Governor, Lt. Governor, most of the Council, and many of the two branches of the Legislature, besides several of the neighboring Clergymen and other Gentlemen from the country, were among the numerous and respectable audience on that occasion. It is also gratifying to find so many gentlemen of character and respectability uniting their talents in this grand design of presenting to the public in an appropriate style, the works of eminent masters in this polite and delightful art. The selections on this occasion appear to have been made principally from the publications of the two distinguished authors, whose names the Society bears; and we are happy to say, that the execution and style of performance did great justice to the composition, and was calculated to give us a true idea of the talents and genius of those celebrated masters. These first attempts afford a happy presage of the future exertions of this society: and lead us to hope that we shall soon see performances of this nature in our metropolis bearing some comparison with those of Europe. The music on this occasion was certainly very well selected and judiciously arranged. The succession of recitative, solo, duet, and chorus, interspersed with beautiful overtures and symphonies completed one entire and delightful entertainment. By turns we had the eloquence, the expression, the melody and the majesty of music. Considering the lofty and difficult character of the composition in general the execution was remarkably correct both in time and tune. The performers had so perfectly studied their respective parts, and so generally acquitted themselves to the admiration of the audience, that it would seem invidious to attempt particular encomiums. The peculiar and respective provinces of the vocal and instrumental performers were perfectly observed. The former was not, as is too often the case, overpowered and rendered inaudible by the latter.—The instruments on the contrary were touched with

Columbian Centinel (Boston), January 31, 1816: [1].

great delicacy and taste, and accompanied the voice with such effect, that, while it was left perfectly audible and distinct, it was aided and rendered more melodious. The occasion also gave us an opportunity of discerning the respective merits of these two great composers; at least, so far as can be done by the effects on the ear of an audience. The style however of each is so peculiar, that, as in all other cases in which we attempt to judge of the talents of men, it is difficult so to compare them as to come at a satisfactory result as to the superiority.

Haydn is excessive in his modulations, and in the inversions and involutions of his harmony; indeed his combinations are often wonderful, and sometimes difficult to be resolved by any known and established rules of harmony.—Handel is more simple in his melodies, direct in his harmony, and therefore grand and majestic in his choruses.—The former continually displays his learning and skill in the science of harmony, the latter discovers his genius in this simplicity and unrivalled sublimity. Haydn will therefore continue to be the favorite with professors, while Handel will forever astonish and delight the Amateur.

This society certainly deserve and will undoubtedly receive the countenance and encouragement of an enlightened public.

From Preface to *The Boston Handel and Haydn Society Collection of Church Music* (1822)

The Handel and Haydn Society, having been instituted for the purpose of improving the style of Church Music, have felt it their duty to keep two objects continually in view; the first to acquire and diffuse that style and taste in performance without which even the most exquisite compositions lose their effect and influence; the second, what was indeed a necessary pre-requisite, to furnish the public with a selection of such compositions, both of ancient and modern authors, as are considered most excellent, and at the same time most useful.

With regard to the first of these objects, they reflect with great pleasure upon the success which has attended their efforts. A visible improvement has taken place in the style of singing, and consequently in the taste of the community. Not only the practice but the science and theory of music, have been the objects of great attention; the increase of patronage has been commensurate with the increase of knowledge and fondness for the art: and the various collections of psalmody, and the number of editions to which some of them have passed, are sure and certain indications of increasing refinement in the public taste.

These favourable appearances have animated the exertions of the Society with regard to what they have mentioned as the second object of their attention; and they have for some time been engaged with much labour, and at considerable expense, in collecting materials for the present work. . . .

While there has been in our country a great improvement in the taste for good melody, there has not been a correspondent attention to good harmony. To remedy this defect has been the special object of the Society in the present work.

Many of the oldest and best psalm tunes, as they were originally composed, were simple melodies; and as the practice of singing metre psalms in public worship was only allowed, not enjoined in England, and was confined to the parish churches, it was not much attended to by the principal masters, who were chiefly engaged in the composition of Cathedral Music. When therefore the other parts were added to these simple melodies, metre psalmody being considered of minor importance, the harmonies were mostly added by inferior composers. And even when the harmonies were original parts of the composition, a

---

The Boston Handel and Haydn Society Collection of Church Music (Boston: Richardson and Lord, 1822), [iii]–v.

beautiful air might be composed without any of that science which was necessary to direct with propriety the inferior movements.

Of late years, however, a great change has taken place in the public sentiment with regard to the importance of psalmody, and this has of course called the attention of the most eminent masters in England to the subject. Several of them have been recently employed in harmonizing anew many of the old standard airs, and also in selecting and adapting movements from the works of Handel, Haydn, Mozart, Beethoven and other great masters, whose mighty talents have been displayed and acknowledged throughout Europe.

These works are among the materials to which the Handel and Haydn Society have had access, and they have exercised their best judgment in making such selections from them as would most enrich the present work. They consider themselves as peculiarly fortunate in having had, for the accomplishment of their purpose, the assistance of Mr. Lowell Mason, one of their members now resident in Savannah, whose taste and science have well fitted him for the employment, and whose zeal for the improvement of Church Music, has led him to undertake an important part of the labour in selecting, arranging and harmonizing the several compositions. But what has most contributed to the confidence with which they offer the present collection to the public, the whole work has been finally and most carefully revised by Doctor G. K. Jackson. The obligations which the Society owe to that gentleman for his gratuitous and unwearied labours, they have endeavoured in some measure to express, by prefixing his name to their work.

The Society are fully aware of the cautious delicacy with which variations should be admitted into tunes that by long use have become familiar, and by the power of association with holy purposes have been in some measure sanctified. They have been careful, therefore to retain in general, the airs of the several tunes unaltered; but as the longest usage cannot reconcile science and correct taste with false harmony, it has been found indispensably necessary to introduce changes into the accompanying parts. The leading part, however, being unaltered the change will not be such as to shock even the most accustomed ear; while the increased richness of the harmony cannot fail to increase the delight of every lover of Sacred Music.

It is obvious that these improvements will create an additional interest in psalmody, both in schools and societies, and in congregations for public worship. If the inferior parts are tame and spiritless, there will be a reluctance in the scholars or members of societies, to take them. The consequence must be that very unsuitable voices will sing upon the principal part, and thus materially injure the effect of the whole. The same remark is equally applicable to congregations for public worship. With regard to private worship, the improvements in harmony which have now been introduced will operate as an incitement to family devotion. Where there are three or more voices to be found in the same family, capable of sustaining the different parts, a much more powerful effect will be produced by a noble and expressive harmony, than if all should be confined to the Air alone.

43   Henry Erben and His Splendid Organ

The power of music to inspire congregations is symbolized by the organ, often spoken of as the "king of instruments." Although present in America from the early days of Spanish and French settlements, it was not until the early eighteenth century that organs began to appear along the Eastern seaboard. A small religious colony that settled near Philadelphia in 1694 apparently brought a small instrument with them from Germany, and a small, four-stop English instrument was installed in King's Chapel, Boston, in 1713. Johann Gottlob Klemm, a Saxon from Dresden, Germany, was the first person known to build an organ in the colonies. His largest instrument was installed in Trinity Church, New York, in 1739. His successor, David Tannenberg, built a large number of instruments mainly for Moravian churches in Pennsylvania. In general, acceptance of organs in churches was slow, particularly in areas under Puritan influence, since Puritans preferred their worship unadorned.

Organ building came into its own in America during the nineteenth century. Congregations spent considerable sums in order to experience that majesty of sound that could hardly be replicated elsewhere. By the early 1800s, New York and Boston were both becoming influential centers of organ construction. Thomas Hall (1791–1874), a Philadelphian by birth, was responsible for generating much of the interest in organs in New York City after he went there about 1816. He trained his son-in-law, Henry Erben (1800–1884), as an apprentice, and the two worked as partners in the firm of Hall & Erben during the mid-1820s.

Henry Erben's career blossomed. He was responsible for many important organ installations in the New York area, in the South, and as far west as Cleveland and Chicago. His impressive installation at Trinity Church, New York, in 1846 was heralded by the *New-York Daily Tribune* on October 10, 1846, as "the largest Organ in the United States. . . . Its powers, combined with its sweetness of tone, astonished the professional gentlemen who were present" at the inaugural concerts, "as well as the audience." The *New York Morning Express* reported the same day that 17,939 persons had attended the inaugural concerts during the two days, October 7 and 8.

"Trinity Organ" (1846)

This splendid instrument was publicly exhibited yesterday before a large audience: it was performed on by Mr. Peter Erben, former Organist of Trinity, John Harrison, Organist of the Cathedral, Mr. William A. King, of St. Peters, Mr. Guatorex, of St. Pauls, Mr. Cornel of St. Johns, and Mr. Speissegger, from Charleston. The Organ gave great satisfaction, and is universally admitted to be the finest instrument of its kind in the United States.

The case is of solid oak in the Gothic style, richly carved, 53 feet high, 27 feet wide, and 32 feet deep, the largest wooden pipe is 36 inches wide, and 32 feet long, the longest metal pipe is 18 inches in diameter and 22 feet long; it contains about 2500 pipes. The reed stops are admirable, the Clarionets, Hautboys, Trumpets, Bassoons and Trumboons [*sic*] are excellent imitations; the Diapasons are very heavy and rich; when the four Organs[1] were united the power and effect was astonishing. The playing was very much admired, particularly that of Mr. King, who showed the vast powers of the instrument to the great delight of the numerous audience. This instrument is from the manufactory of Mr. Henry Erben of this city, and will for ages be a monument to his fame as an organ builder. The interest which the public take in this instrument may be estimated when we state that the number of tickets received at the Church door was 13,700.

To-Day.—The further exhibition of the Organ in this Church will be continued this afternoon. Mr. Geo. Loder, of Grace Church, Mr. Guatorex, of St. Paul's will perform at 2 o'clock. At 4 o'clock, Mr. W. A. King, of St. Peters, and Mr. H. C. Timm, of the Messiah, will perform a duet.

The Evening Post (New York), October 8, 1846: 2.

[1] Three manuals plus pedals.

44 John Sullivan Dwight and His *Journal of Music*

Utopian communities flourished in pre–Civil War America. The Ephrata Cloister, George Rapp's community of Lutherans in Pennsylvania, the Shakers founded by Ann Lee Stanley (Mother Ann), the Oneida Community in Vermont, Robert Owen's New Harmony in Indiana, and the "phalanxes" founded on the ideas of the French social theorist Charles Fourier, including Brook Farm in Massachusetts, all caught the climate of reform during the Jacksonian era.

John Sullivan Dwight (1813–1893) was a leading member of Brook Farm from its beginning. Trained as a minister, always interested in writing, well versed in languages, and with an overriding interest in music, he taught music at Brook Farm and contributed heavily to its weekly journal, the *Harbinger*. Upon the demise of this utopian experiment in 1847, Dwight moved back to Boston, continuing to edit, translate, and lecture. Supported by the Harvard Musical Association, with which he had a life-long connection, he launched his own *Journal of Music* on April 10, 1852.

In a circular written in February 1852 to elicit aid for his project, Dwight wrote that his periodical would represent "no school or class" but would simply be an organ for what he called the "Musical *Movement*" in America. The opening statement in the first issue of the *Journal* promised that the contents would relate mainly to music, but also would take into account the wider world of "Art and of polite Literature."

The *Journal* always sought to proclaim the highest in cultivated taste. For Dwight, this meant primarily music by European composers, principally Germans and Austrians. His ideals were Bach, Handel, Mozart, Beethoven—particularly Beethoven—and Schubert, in other words, the "old school." In his valedictory on September 3, 1881, he wrote, "We candidly confess that what now challenges the world as new in music fails to stir us to the same depths of soul and feeling that the old masters did and doubtless always will." Yet Dwight, the critic, placed standards above European bias as he tried to take a broad view: "Art soars above all narrow nationalities" (February 4, 1854).

Dwight provided his readers with an intellectual and aesthetic basis for good music as he drew audiences and performers to respond to it. In September 1870, he remarked in the *Atlantic Monthly* that, "the first real and deep interest in music awakened here in Boston was an interest in the greatest kind of music. Handel, and then more irresistibly Beethoven, were the first to take deep hold on thoughtful, earnest, infuential souls. . . . Music is the art and language of the feelings, the sentiments, the spiritual instincts of the soul, and so becomes a universal language, tending to unite and blend and harmonize all who may come within its sphere."*

---

*John S. Dwight, "Music as a Means of Culture," *The Atlantic Monthly*, September 1870: 321, 329.

Dwight's Journal of Music turned out to be the most important music magazine published in nineteenth-century America. It had a run of twenty-nine years, 1852–81, during three decades that saw the beginnings of some 138 other music magazines. It grew to a circulation of about 2,500 copies, high for its day.

Dwight held up a mirror to the exuberant Romanticism of the age, cautioning us to strive for high ideals and to see ourselves from an international perspective. His appeal resonated with the "elite," his voice epitomizing an important strand of thinking at that time. With missionary zeal, he wrote strong articles favoring that which he believed would grow to become the best tradition in the nation's evolving musical culture.

JOHN SULLIVAN DWIGHT

from a Statement on American Music (1854)

What we are most anxious to state here as our conviction is, that there is no very general prejudice, (certainly none on our part) against American composers as such. Art soars above all narrow nationalities; and there is of course no inherent *a priori* reason, as a correspondent in another column says, why this age and this country may not produce works of Art, in every kind, as great or greater than the famous masterpieces of the world. The creative soul and genius of human-

Dwight's Journal of Music, February 4, 1854: 141–42.

ity undoubtedly are not exhausted; but progress, growth, continual upward aspiration and achievement, we believe as strenuously as any one, are still the law of human history. But who shall foretell the coming of a genius in the world? Who shall anticipate its hour and birth-place? What patriotic faith in our New World's great destiny can ever make us feel the new spell of genius, until that genius convert us to itself by its own proper magnetism? If a new Beethoven was born in America this very morning, is not the world as sure to hear from him and own him, as if he had sprung up under the guardianship of Liszt at Weimar, or of Hauptmann, Moscheles & Co., at Leipsic?

Time will take care of all these questions.

JOHN SULLIVAN DWIGHT

"Native Musical Talent" (1854)

[First Article]

We have been so much accused of *foreign* leanings in our love for music, that we presume we shall fall under no suspicion of a vulgar and vain-boasting patriotism, if we dwell awhile on what this country has produced, or is producing,

Dwight's Journal of Music, May 20, 1854, 54, May 27, 1854: 61–62.

in the way of musical artists and composers. We are beginning to have our music-makers and our music-interpreters, who woo Music as an Art; with what depth of passion, or what genuine fire of genius, time alone can fully show. It is only when individuals of either class assume the attitude of musical Shakespeares, or of musical Siddonses and Garricks, that we find it so hard to suppress the smile of incredulity, even if a certain sort of sympathetic sense of what is due to our country's modesty does not cry out "For shame!"[1]

There are two ways of regarding the recent achievements of our countrymen in the field musical. One is the boastful, shallow patriotic, "manifest destiny," all-the-world-annexing, Yankee Doodle way, which keeps proclaiming our's the greatest country in the world; believes that Americans can do everything that any other people have done, only a great deal better; that the whole world—of Art, as of all other spheres—is our inheritance, and that we are the most capable of entering and occupying it, as we are the most capable of governing ourselves, brow-beating our neighbors, bullying the world, reconciling social and moral contradictions and enormities, "extending the area of freedom" (by which is meant slavery), and metamorphosing little mean men into great dangerous presidents. This boastful, bloated, vulgar parody of the American idea is not confined to politics; its contagion operates even in the peaceful sphere of Art and Music. It mistakes enterprise for genius; the large scale on which things are attempted, for sublimity; familiarity with means, tools, mechanism and forms, for Art; new combinations, for original ideas; and, in a word, bold "go-ahead-itativeness" for inspiration armed with divine right to conquer and to charm the world.

The other way is more modest and reasonable. It leaves the patriotic rant to filibustering demagogues, and looks at music musically and not as one more peacock's feather in the tail of strutting patriotism. It is not ashamed to see ourselves just where we are in music, a nation of beginners, who have had heretofore but little time for Art, and who are not sprung from a particularly musical race. And it allows us to take just pride and pleasure in considering how much these few last years have done to develop in our people an appreciation of the musical Art and artists of the old world, as well as to tempt forth native efforts, in many

---

[1] Sarah Siddon (1755–1831), one of a theatrical family, was a renowned Shakespearean actress, especially of tragic parts. David Garrick (1717–1779) was not only a famous actor, but also a writer and from 1747 in the management of the Drury Lane Theater producing Shakespeare's plays.

cases quite successful, to acquire the art of writing and interpreting (with voice or fingers) musical works in many of the higher forms.

From this safer stand-point let us cast a cursory glance over some of the prominent instances of American activity in music-making and interpreting, which have recently been topics in musical circles. Out enumeration aims at no completeness; we merely pass in review such cases as most readily occur to our own mind; these are texts enough for one article, and times enough remain for treatment of new texts. And if we naturally are most familiar with the doings of our townsmen, and point to instances of their achievement, think not that we are disposed in the slightest degree to echo or endorse the assertion with which one of our city dailies a short time ago prefaced its account of the doings of our musical students abroad; the assertion namely: "that Boston at this present time possesses more native musical talent than any other city in the world"!! (we quote from memory). Such assertions, backed by the longest inventory we could append, can only make us laughed at for our exquisite presumption.

* * *

Second Article

Last week we glanced at some of the more prominent and successful instances of young American aspiration to the character of *performing* artists, or interpreters of music. It remains to cast a like glance upon our beginnings, such as they may be, in the art of musical composition or creation. Here it becomes us to be very modest, and to remember that it is indeed our day of small things, though there be signs of promise stirring which it is a pleasure to enumerate.

Of "native compositions" and "composers," in one sense, it is true we have no lack. The country swarms with enterprising fellows who can *put together* notes and *make up* little pieces, that will sell. Inquire at the mills where all this grist is ground, inquire of the publishers who *snow* "sheet music" over all the land, as fast as it melts away, and they will tell you that the native crop is quite a vast affair, and pays the better as it is the more ephemeral. But these people would not be considered as *composers* in any other country; and why should they here? To have made or arranged psalm-tunes; to have drummed out a pretty waltz or polka in one's own way, (which is only a feeble following of Strauss's or Labitsky's) while yet under the tingling influence of Jullien's or the Germania band; to have tortured airs from *Norma* into a flashy set of finger variations for the piano, according to some hacknied Thalberg or De Meyer formula;[2] least of all, to have clothed some common-place feeling in a pretty, sentimental, namby-pamby little song, (which may have no fault but that it is like a thousand others, and that there was no sort of need for its existence)—such songs, for instance, as sentimental young men sing about their old arm chairs, or dedicate to their mothers, with a portrait of the author on the title-page, perusing, with sad or sparkling face, a letter from the dear old lady:—these things, we apprehend, and far better things than these, do not in any artistic sense entitle a person to the name of composer.

That amid all this superficial productivity there has been much that is good and useful, educationally, in the way of furnishing "milk for babes" in music, we have no disposition to deny. Moreover we can well imagine, and indeed we know, that among so many young Americans as have devoted themselves of late years to music, there is now and then produced a clever song, or four-part glee, or anthem, or something like a *notturno* or "Song without Words" for the piano. Mendelssohn wrote little pieces too; but whether any of their little pieces are likely to survive and become classical like his,—the treasured lyrics of the land and of the age,—is certainly a question that can hardly yet be settled in the affirmative.

And "taking them for all in all," has there been aught among them yet to "give the world assurance of a *Man*" in music? Can we point to an instance of unquestionable musical *genius* of the creative kind? to any name that bids fair to be classed with the great names of the composers? Who can point us to one American composition, great or small, with much assurance that it is destined to become clas-

sical and to be treasured in the world's musical repertory? Granting that creditable works have been produced, sometimes in difficult and lofty forms, yet which of them is or is likely to be held of much account, say in the musical countries of Europe, supposing the work to stand simply on its own merits and not claim hospitable regard as the firstling of a beginner from a new country on the map of music? Which of them can the world not perfectly well afford to do without, and feel that, even on the score of novelty, its programmes do not need it? Of course the question is not put to Yankee Doodle patriotism;—that will answer glibly enough and place you a Jubal Smith, a Handel Corydon Stebbins or some other heaven-scaling native Titan alongside of every Mozart and Beethoven that the old world boasts. Indeed the very man has had us by the button, who (live Yankee that he was) has mastered all of Handel's methods, and with his own hand has scored original oratorios as many and as grand as Handel's!

Without therefore flattering ourselves that the signs have yet appeared of anything like positive musical *genius* in our countrymen; and leaving to any individual self-persuasion of such genius the fullest benefit of the plea that it is perhaps in advance of the understanding whether of the many or of the "appreciative few;"—remembering too the divine prerogative of genius, of being limited to no age or place, but of shining forth, should it so please the All-Wise, from the obscurest corner of a Nazareth,—we proceed to notice some quite creditable and quite promising achievements of young Americans, who have devoted themselves to musical composition in the higher forms of Art. . . .

Let us add no new fuel to the famous Fry and Bristow controversy; it is enough simply to refer to the fact that here are Americans who have written operas and overtures, and symphonies for the grand orchestra, some after the classic models, and some in brave defiance of all models, following the eccentric course of genius real or imaginary. That great musical knowledge and skill were involved in these works,—great mastery of instrumentation, &c.,—no one will doubt, however opinions may differ about their real aesthetic value.

---

[2]Louis Moreau Gottschalk?

45 Louis Jullien and New York's Musical Congress

The conductor, impresario, and showman Louis Jullien (1812–1860) gave the first of a short series of farewell concerts at New York's Crystal Palace on June 15, 1854. The whole production involved 1,500 performers and was managed by America's master showman, P. T. Barnum. One newspaper reviewer wrote with enthusiasm about the extravaganza, which included excerpts from *Messiah, The Creation*, and *Tannhäuser*, as well as a free-for-all four-alarm *Fireman's Quadrille* orchestrated by Jullien himself. The hall was so unfavorable and the crowd so vast that all but the loud effects were lost. Jullien admitted to the audience that he would have to change his repertoire—and play even louder music. A second report comes from the diary of New York lawyer and musical amateur George Templeton Strong (1820–1875), president of the New York Philharmonic Society during the early 1870s. An educated observer of New York's musical scene, Strong approached Jullien's concert with a jaded eye, finding at least some of it "trash" and "humbug," yet commenting that the conductor "is a genius after all."

The anomaly that was Jullien embraced some humbug mixed with showmanship, a real ability to captivate large audiences, a keen knowledge of the orchestra, and respect from players and critics alike. Born in France, Jullien spent several years at the Paris Conservatory but was lured away by the popularity he achieved through his lively performances of dance music. He concertized in Europe, coming to New York in August 1853 for a ten-month stint that included six months of touring. He gave over two hundred concerts in the United States, willingly playing music by American composers. Even the irascible John Sullivan Dwight, while not necessarily applauding Jullien's standards, recognized his excellence:

That Jullien is a masterly conductor, a scientific, classically trained musician (for he had Cherubini for a master), a shrewd observer of men and feeler of the public pulse, a man of wonderful vivacity of temperament, alive to all outward impressions, and with much inventive faculty to render them in music, we cannot doubt. . . . [Jullien] is the creator of perhaps the world's finest orchestra.*

*John Sullivan Dwight, *Dwight's Journal of Music* (October 15, 1853): 14.

"The Musical Congress: Great Gathering at the Crystal Palace" (1854)

The first musical Reunion—or Congress—as it is more properly named—came off last evening at the Crystal Palace, and met with the success such an undertaking deserves and will always receive, when, as in the present case, it is organized in an efficient and praiseworthy manner. The attendance was most satisfactory. We have no recollection of an audience more brilliant or numerous. All the fashion and refinement of New-York were there, and the *coup d'oeil* was such as we can seldom expect to enjoy. In the reserved seats there were at least four thousand persons; while the aisles, galleries, and every available inch of standing room were crowded with some twenty thousand spectators. The orchestra erected for the occasion is at the foot of the fountain, under the dome, and rises like the quadrant of an amphitheatre, nearly to the ceiling of the east nave. It was constructed, we believe, to contain fifteen hundred performers, and as it was filled last evening, we presume that number was present—the majority of course being vocalists.

Precisely at 7 o'clock, M. Jullien made his appearance in the orchestra, and was greeted with loud bursts of applause. When this special enthusiasm had subsided, the selections from Handel's Oratorio of the "Messiah," were commenced. Nine pieces were selected from this work.

The constant agitation of the immense audience interfered materially with the enjoyment of the solos, and indeed the building itself is only favorable for combined sound—and that of the loudest. There are so many apertures and outlets, to say nothing of the dome which absorbs without much reverberation, that single sounds become faint and broken. M. Jullien was fully aware of this fact, and in the speech he addressed to the audience admitted that it would be necessary to change his repertoire—in other words, play louder music.

For these reasons we are unable to refer specif-

ically to the vocalists Mesdames Brainerd, Hawley, Bouchelle, and Messrs. Frazer and Conway.

But of the choruses, particularly the "Hallelujah" and the "Glory of the Lord," we can speak in the most unqualified terms of praise. In precision and nice observance of contrast, both these glorious works were rendered in an unequaled manner. The final chorus "Worthy is the Lamb," ending with the famous "Amen," was not taken with such gusto and certainty, but otherwise it was creditably executed.

The excellence of the Choral artistes was again fairly tested in the chorus from Haydn's "Creation," the "Heavens are Telling," and the Prayer from Rossini's "Mose in Egilo"[1] all of which were given in a masterly manner.

* * *

Jullien's Fireman's Quadrille, composed for this occasion, terminated the second part, prior to which Mr. Barnum addressed the audience, like *Snug*, the Joiner, to desire that they would not be alarmed at the frightful effects which would be introduced. The *chef* then raised his *bâton*, and all the brass instruments were kept steadily employed to the end.

It is not easy to write a better description of this Quadrille than has already appeared in our advertising columns. Like every descriptive work from the same composer, it realizes thoroughly the idea contemplated. M. Jullien has, for the sake of contrast, availed himself of the occasion of the annual parade. All the Fire Companies are out in their gala costume; we hear the bands, and, what is better, see them, as they pass along in steady line. Presently the alarm-bell is heard; bustle ensues, engines hurry to the scene of action; speaking-trumpets discourse harsh vocalism to the runners; the fire is reached, and all the excitement of a struggle with the mighty element is produced in its wildest mood.

To produce the necessary effects, M. Jullien has

"The Musical Congress: Great Gathering at the Crystal Palace," *New-York Daily Times*, June 16, 1854: 1.

---

[1] *Mosè in Egitto.*

had to invent a variety of instruments and machines, to imitate the working of the engines, the falling of the house, the hissing of the water on the flames, &c., &c. To heighten the illusion (and it is hardly necessary to heighten it, we think), red fire is burnt outside the building; the firemen's bands, first heard in the distance, approach nearer, and then actually march across the orchestra; and other devices, of a similar kind, not strictly legitimate, but good.

The Quadrille was certainly not heard to advantage last night, for the enthusiasm was frequently so great that whole passages were lost. When it can be listened to without such wild demonstrations of delight, we are persuaded it will be received as one of M. Jullien's happiest productions. The finale, introducing effects which frightened Mr. Barnum, is perfect of its kind, admirable.

Mr. Jullien was twice called before the audience, and on his second appearance made a sensible speech—telling them that after a few more rehearsals, he would be better able to please them. Then Mr. Barnum made a short speech, and wound up triumphantly by unfolding a mighty banner, on which was inscribed the tidings that the Congress would be continued at the reduced admission of twenty-five cents, standing, or one dollar reserved seats. We have seldom witnessed anything more enthusiastic than the reception of these gentlemen. It was an unmistakable demonstration of satisfaction.

The principal item in the third part of the programme was the dramatic symphony of the "Broken Heart," by Mr. W. H. Fry—a work equal to any of the evening. There is less effort and more true genius in this symphony than in any other we have yet heard of Mr. Fry's.

The lateness of the hour compels us to be brief with the Soloists. We shall scarcely do them injustice, for they are already well known to the public. Paul Jullien gave Hauman's *Romance du Someil de Masaniello*, with brilliant variations. Mad. Wallace and Mr. W. V. Wallace, played the duo on themes from the opera of "L'Eclair"[2] anent which we expressed ourselves warmly on the occasion of Mr. Wallace's Complimentary Concert at Castle Garden Mr. Aptomnease, the Harpist, executed one of Parish Alvar's best fantasias, "La dance des Fees," and with the skill and success that always attends his performances on the National Instrument.

In short, the Musical Congress, last night, was a triumph in every respect. The triumph extended even to the architects of the Palace, for, notwithstanding the enormous pressure on the building, there was no perceptible deflection in any important rod or support about it.

Consequently, it is a matter of pleasure to us to announce that such an entertainment will be repeated, and at reduced prices. The best of results may be anticipated if the public once familiarize themselves with such programmes as we have attempted to sketch.

The United German Musical Societies were announced to sing between the first and second parts, but for some reason were not forthcoming. Whilst we cannot help regretting the absence of so many artists, we are yet consoled, for the choral honors were all won by American voices.

---

[2]By Fromental Halévy.

GEORGE TEMPLETON STRONG

Diary Entry (1854)

*J*une 18, [1854] Sunday. The conjunction of Barnum and Jullien at the so-called "Musical Congress of 1,500 performers" naturally produced one of the grandest humbugs on record. Went with Ellie,[3] George Anthon,[4] and Miss Tote. The last-named two dined here, as did Jack Ehninger, but after sitting down with them, I had to retire to the library for a headachy nap. The crowd was enormous. It is estimated at fifteen thousand by some and forty thousand by others. I've no opinion at all as to the accuracy of either estimate. But for some time after taking our seats I was seriously exercised about the possibilities of falling galleries and panic-stricken multitudes, and was tempted to evacuate the building at once.

The building is most defective, acoustically. Sound passes off into dome and transepts and is not reverberated by its flimsy walls of sheet iron and glass. Solos were inaudible; an occasional emphatic note or two, or a phrase from the orchestra, kept one *au courant*. To those who did not know *The Messiah* and so on, the solo pieces must have been a great mystery. Beside the unfitness of the building, there was the great mass of muslin and broadcloth behind the solo singers (the orchestra and chorus) which absorbed instead of reflecting their voices. And the incessant shuffling in and out of the vast crowd that was marching into and about the building was sufficient to drown the voice of any but Stentor or Boanerges[5] Four choruses from *The Messiah* (including the Hallelujah,

which was encored!!!, and the first chorus, "All flesh shall see it together,") certainly gave to them all new power, and clearer expression of their meaning. That first chorus of *The Messiah*, it seems to me, may perhaps be the most awful embodiment of thought extant in music, with the possible exception of the "Hallelujah." The rest of the concert was mostly trash. Overture to *William Tell* was unheard except the sharply cut, martial finale. We watched Jullien leading its opening movement and wondered what he could be doing, till a familiar squeak or two very high up in the scale indicated that the orchestra was at work on this overture. Wagner's *Tannhäuser* Overture was rather better—audible, and seems nice. Of the Symphony in C minor[6] only the third movement and part of the finale were played, the former half audibly, the latter very vilely.

As to the grand "Fireman's Quadrille," words can't express its clap-trap. It's a pleasure to see humbug so consistently, extensively, and cleverly applied: military bands beginning to play in the distance, drawing nearer and finally marching into the orchestra; red and blue fire visible through the windows of the dome; a clamorous chorus shouting "Go it, 20," "Play away, 49," "hay-hay," and so on. The audacity of the imposition reconciled one to its grossness. But Jullien is a genius after all. There were taking points, even in this atrocious production; e.g., a very clever appropriation of phrases from the second movement of Beethoven's *devilish* A Symphony,[7] and some admirable pieces of instrumentation meant to imitate the thundering, quivering, shuddering rush and roar of falling walls. Friday and Saturday nights the performances have been less ambitious and the audiences much smaller, though the price was reduced. I doubt the

---

George Templeton Strong, *The Diary of George Templeton Strong*, ed. Allan Nevins and Milton Halsey Thomas (Seattle: University of Washington Press, 1952), 81–82.

[3]Ellen Ruggles Strong, his wife.

[4]George Anthon, nephew of Strong's Latin and Greek professor at Columbia, was a frequent companion.

[5]Stentor refers to a Greek herald in the Trojan War, described in the *Iliad* as having a very loud voice; Boanerges, in like vein, refers to thunder, after a passage in Mark 3:17.

[6]Beethoven's Fifth Symphony.

[7]Beethoven's Seventh Symphony.

success of the speculation. I doubt whether the stock ever struggles much above 21. I sympathize with those who bought at par and held on for a rise at 175. The building seems all but gutted. Its character has changed. It is now merely an extension of Barnum's Museum.

46 🌿 Theodore Thomas, Traveling Virtuoso

Theodore Thomas was at least an equal among the elite cadre of nineteenth-century orchestral conductors which included Anton Seidl, Leopold and Walter Damrosch, and Arthur Nikisch. Born in Germany, Thomas (1835–1905) emigrated with his family to New York in 1845. He began his career as a violinist, joining the Philharmonic Society of New York in 1854. He also established a series of chamber music concerts with noted pianist William Mason, son of Lowell Mason.

Thomas, however, found his real calling in conducting. By 1862, he had organized an orchestra of his own. Seven years later, the Thomas Orchestra began to tour over what his second wife, Rose Fay Thomas, called "the great musical highway of America, for it included all the large cities which Thomas thought might become musical centers in time."

In 1877, Thomas was appointed conductor of the New York Philharmonic and continued in that position, except for a short hiatus, until 1891. He was associated with the College of Music in Cincinnati and the 1893 World's Fair in Chicago. He played a major role in the founding of the Chicago Symphony Orchestra in 1891, an ensemble he conducted until his death. The orchestra was known as the Theodore Thomas Orchestra from 1906 until it became the Chicago Symphony in 1912.

In 1883, Thomas took his own orchestra on a transcontinental tour, which the *Chicago Tribune* called a "march from sea to sea." In just over two months, Thomas, his fifty-five musicians, and six soloists traveled about fourteen thousand miles, playing about seventy-four concerts in thirty cities.

What the tour meant to cities along the way is exemplified by press reports. The reviewer for the *Cleveland Plain Dealer* wrote on May 9, 1883, that audiences had been large and appreciative. The music "was received with manifestations of the highest satisfaction." The *Chicago Tribune* applauded the tour. The *San Francisco Chronicle* commented, "Thomas has done more to make good music popular in America than any man living."

Thomas's life's work, in his words, was "to endeavor always to form a refined musical taste among the people by the intelligent selection of music; to give, in order to accomplish the desired result, only standard works, both of the new and old masters, and to be thus conservative and not given to experimenting with the new musical sensations of the hour."* Although musical idealism and the business of music are often incompatible bedfellows, Thomas managed to combine them successfully. His high standards became a model for orchestras across the country.

---

*George P. Upton, *Theodore Thomas: A Musical Autobiography*, 2 vols. (Chicago: A. C. McClurg, 1905), 1: 152.

News Item on the March from Sea to Sea (1883)

The most extensive and extraordinary concert tour ever made in this country by a symphony orchestra will be begun by Theodore Thomas on April 26. His circuit includes thirty cities and seventy-four concerts, and reaches from Baltimore to San Francisco. On the route, festivals will be held in Baltimore, Pittsburgh, Louisville, Memphis, St. Louis, Kansas City, St. Paul, Minneapolis, San Francisco, Salt Lake City, Denver, and Omaha. For every one of these twelve festivals, a chorus has been organized and rehearsed, the smallest comprising 380 voices, at Minneapolis, and the largest, the great Mormon Choir at Salt Lake City, of three thousand. Besides these twelve festivals, there will be concerts in many intermediate cities. The final concert of this extraordinary tour, which stretches from ocean to ocean, will be at Burlington, Iowa, on July 7. . . . It is a remarkable fact that every one of these seventy-four concerts has been guaranteed and the money raised without the slightest difficulty. This shows a remarkable interest in music in these distant cities. Out of all this enthusiasm and zeal will result a decided, healthy impulse for music in this country. Having heard this splendid body of musicians under so great a leader, the people will not be so contented as heretofore with trash. They will demand a higher standard in their home performances, and in every direction music will advance to a higher and more dignified plane. There is only one cause for apprehension. The route is one of extraordinary length and duration. For three months Mr. Thomas cannot take a single day of rest. He will be traveling or conducting almost without an hour's intermission, from April 26 to July 9. His health has not been of the best of late, and this trip will require herculean powers of endurance. It would be appalling to almost any other musician. In what trim, therefore, will he be at the close of this march from sea to sea?

Announcement, *Chicago Tribune*, quoted in Rose Fay Thomas, *Memoirs of Theodore Thomas* (New York: Moffat, Yard, 1911), 245–46.

THEODORE THOMAS

from "The Methods of a Great Conductor" (1883)

With the broad back and denuded crown of Theodore Thomas music-loving and fashionable San Francisco is by this time thoroughly familiar. It has also caught an occasional glimpse of the bright face, drooping mustache and high forehead of the great leader and has seen the movement of an infrequent smile as the *chef* half-turned in response to some rattle of applause. It has seen, too, the well-drilled orchestra file like soldiers into their places; has noticed them, still like soldiers, come to attention at the single tap of a thin white baton, and has watched the precision of their movements with almost as much interest as it has listened to the correctness of their playing. With the *entente* that exists between Thomas and his men, however—with his character as a man and not as a musician and with the nature of the work that is required to bring about so high a state of perfection as the orchestra exhibits with these points the public is not so familiar, and, being at once unfamiliar and interested, it will be pleased to read something in the nature of a sketch of the man and his manner. . . .

Theodore Thomas, "The Methods of a Great Conductor. His Schedule of Reproof. A Disciplinarian Like a Prussian Marshall and a Musician Withal," *San Francisco Chronicle*, June 10, 1883.

Eye and Ear

The material[1] is younger, but that does not mean that it is not so good as the old. The shaping, directing hand of the same master is at work and the result is nightly before the people of San Francisco. The owner of this hand is not lax in the use of its shaping power and the high standard of excellence has not been attained without pain, hard work, incessant practice and the tension of patience and temper. Thomas is not contented that his orchestra should play well; he wants them to look well; that is, he holds it as a part of his professional credo that those on the stage must not only please the ear but must please the eye. To this end he directs especial attention to the bowing of the violin players. In the orchestra to which San Francisco has been accustomed to listen—and this is not written in a harshly discriminating spirit—the first and second violins and the violas have gone on at their own sweet will, one bowing up and the other bowing down, like a class of girls in its first lesson of calisthenics. In the Thomas orchestra the players upon stringed instruments take their strokes with the unity of a machine. This is accomplished in two ways. First, by making every player watch the "leader" or first player of the particular instrument and take the movement from him, as the crew of a racing boat takes its "stroke." Next, by doing what no other musician in the United States does, having all his music written with the down-stroke and up-stroke marks inserted. The leading first violin has also to drill his men once or twice a week, to see that the regularity of movement is not broken. Thomas never fails to notice the faintest deflection from this rhythm of movement and the offender is sure to be brought up with a round turn.

Grades of Reproof

Thomas' methods of reproof naturally vary with the subject and the object to which they are directed. A mistake that is a mistake, such as the best regulated families are said not to be exempt from, he will treat as lightly as a mother does an erring child, but if the error is one of willfulness, or stupidity, or laziness—and Thomas has not an idle bone in his body, the reprimand it meets with is sudden and severe. . . .

It has been said by the very plain spoken that Thomas owes his success as much to being a martinet as a musician. The fact of the matter is, his success is due to his being both. He is a disciplinarian of the strictest. No Prussian General could be more so. From what he says there is no appeal. His word is law and his baton a scepter. But these qualities would be of no use if they were not backed by those of a musician. That he is such there is no dispute, and if there were any lingering doubts they were swept away in the great Beethoven controversy which he victoriously waged against the critical press of New York some years since. Thomas gave up the old fly-away, semaphore-in-a-fit style when he assumed the baton; and he is conceded to be a model of all that is delicate and graceful in conducting. But better than this, Thomas has done more to make good music popular in America than any man living, and he is to be looked upon as an educator whose energetic mind and liberal hand have made him as useful as he is popular. His place could not be filled and his visit here should be marked *con spirito*.

---

[1]That is, his orchestra.

THEODORE THOMAS
from "Musical Possibilities in America" (1881)

The Americans are certainly a music-loving people. They are peculiarly susceptible to the sensuous charm of tone, they are enthusiastic and learn easily, and with the growth in general culture of recent years, there has sprung up a desire for something serious in its purpose in music, as in the other arts. The voices of the women although inclined to be sharp and nasal in speaking, are good in singing. Their small volume reveals the lack of proper training, but they are good in quality, extended in compass, and brilliant in color. The larger number are sopranos, but there are many altos, and there would be more and they would be better were it not for ruinous attempts to make sopranos of them. The men's voices do not compare favorably with those of the women. They lack strength and character, and a well-balanced chorus is hardly possible as yet without a mixture of English or German voices to give body to the tone. Of late years, probably because of the growing attention to physical training, there has been a marked improvement, and many good and beautiful voices have been developed, chiefly baritones or high basses. The incessant pressure of work which every American feels, prevents the men from paying much attention to music, but as the country advances in age and begins to acquire some of the repose which age brings, there will come possibilities of development which cannot now be estimated.

In considering, therefore, the present condition of musical development in this country, I am led naturally to speak first of vocal music. Although the contrary has been asserted, I think it is in the vocal direction, and not in the instrumental, that the present development of the art tends. We have no public instrumental performers of American birth who can rank with our singers in public

estimation, nor is there at present more than a very limited demand for instrumentalists. New York is the only city in the country in which an orchestral player can make a living, and even here he must give lessons or play at balls and parties, thereby losing or injuring the finer qualities of an orchestral player. Boston, in spite of many efforts, cannot support a large, well-balanced orchestra. Philadelphia has no standing orchestra, and in Cincinnati and Chicago the orchestral musician must eke out a living by playing in beer-gardens and saloons. The only demand for piano players, except of the highest order, is as teachers, and of those we have many and good ones, who do what may be called missionary work. Singing, on the other hand, appeals to almost every one, and there is a certain demand, even if limited, for singers in the churches.

When we consider that music is taught in the public schools throughout the country, we might expect some evidence or result of this teaching among the people. Much money is spent in our schools for instruction in this branch, and what does it amount to? Many of the children learn like parrots, and soon forget the little which they have learned. Those who retain this knowledge find it a drawback when wishing to go on in the study of music. The fault is not in them, but in the system taught. So faulty is that system that it would be better to abolish singing entirely from the schools than to retain it under the present method. It does more harm than good. . . .

At present, the musical standard of the American public, taken as a whole, must be pronounced a low one. If we should judge of what has been done in music by the programmes of concerts given in the larger cities, we might rightly claim for this country a high rank in cultivation. Those concerts, however, appeal not to the general public, but to one class only, and that a limited one, as any one who observes the audiences can easily see. This class is growing in numbers as well as in cultivation, but it is still far too small to support more

Theodore Thomas, "Musical Possibilities in America," *Scribner's Monthly* 21 (March 1881): 777–78, 780. Also reproduced in George P. Upton, *Theodore Thomas: A Musical Autobiography* (Chicago: A. C. McClurg, 1905), 2: 265–75.

than a limited number of concerts, as at present those of the New York and Brooklyn Philharmonic societies. The general public does not advance in music, partly from want of opportunity, partly from the habits of the people. The average American is so entirely absorbed in his work that when he goes out in the evening he looks for relaxation in some kind of amusement which makes little or no demand upon his intellect, and he has no difficulty in finding it.

*   *   *

[W]e have in this country the possibilities of a great musical future. We have the natural taste of the people for music, their strong desire to have only the best, and their readiness to recognize what is the best when it is presented to them. We have exceptional natural resources for the making of musical instruments. Nature has done her part of the work generously; it remains for us to do ours.

47   Anthony Philip Heinrich, the Beethoven of America

When he was in his mid-twenties, Anthony Philip Heinrich (1781–1861), came to America from Bohemia, his fortunes having failed in Europe. He took on the values of the American frontier, tinged with Romanticism. His career is one of the strangest in the annals of American music.

Heinrich walked from Philadelphia to Pittsburgh, then traveled by boat and on foot to Lexington, Kentucky. Although relatively unschooled in music, he was gifted and resourceful. Through single-minded devotion, he trained himself acceptably to perform on the violin, piano, and even the organ. He moved to a log cabin near Bardstown, Kentucky, in 1818. What better locale could there be for an American "original"?

It was as a composer that Heinrich made his mark. His *Dawning of Music in Kentucky; or, The Pleasures of Harmony in the Solitudes of Nature* was published in Philadelphia in 1820. This remarkable set of forty-six works contains vocal and instrumental music that is descriptive, full of originality, and harmonically daring. A supplement of seventeen pieces, titled *The Western Minstrel: A Collection of Original Moral, Patriotic, & Sentimental Songs for the Voice & Piano Forte*, dedicated to the citizens of Philadelphia, was published the same year.

As Heinrich's fortunes improved, he was hailed as a genius and became known both as "Father Heinrich" and "the Beethoven of America." As a violinist, he led the first known performance of a Beethoven symphony in America in Lexington, Kentucky, in 1817. He also helped organize the New York Philharmonic Society. In his later years, he wrote large orchestral scores, none of which were published.

Heinrich possessed a remarkable personality. By many standards he could be considered eccentric, yet in exciting ways he explored the American frontier, both in his life and in his work.

The author of the *Euterpeiad* article "Musical Diary" was probably either John Rowe Parker or Charles Dingley, both of whom served as editor of the publication.

ANTHONY PHILIP HEINRICH

Preface to *The Dawning of Music in Kentucky* (1820)

In presenting this work to the world, the Author observes, that he has been actuated much less by

Anthony Philip Heinrich, *The Dawning of Music in Kentucky; or, The Pleasure of Harmony in the Solitudes of Nature* (Philadelphia: Bacon and Hart, 1820).

any pecuniary interest, than zeal, in furnishing a Volume of various <u>Musical Compositions</u>, which, it is hoped, will prove both useful and entertaining.

The many and severe animadversions, so long and repeatedly cast on the talent for Music in this Country, has been one of the chief motives of the

Author, in the exercise of his abilities; and should he be able, by this effort, to create but one single Star in the West, no one would ever be more proud than himself, to be called an American Musician.—He however is fully aware of the dangers which, at the present day, attend talent on the crowded and difficult road of eminence; but fears of just criticism, by Competent Masters, should never retard the enthusiasm of genius, when ambitious of producing works more lasting than the too many Butterfly-effusions of the present age.—He, therefore, relying on the candour of the Public, will rest confident, that justice will be done, by due comparisons with the works of other Authors (celebrated for their merit, especially as regards Instrumental execution) but who have never, like him, been thrown, as it were, by discordant events, far from the emporiums of musical science, into the isolated wilds of nature, where he invoked his Muse, tutored only by Alma Mater.

A. P. Heinrich,
Kentucky

ANONYMOUS

"Musical Diary. A. P. Heinrich" (1823)

The life of man presents only a continual endeavor to augment his pleasurable sensations, and all that is included in what the world calls civilization, is that transition from enjoyments violently or rudely procured, through the indulgence of grosser appetites and stronger passions, to the refinements by which the intellect is made to minister to sense, and by which more varied, more extensive, and more exquisite gratifications are attained without force and with little apparent personal hazard or fatigue; courage, enterprize and hardihood being exchanged for knowledge, address and opulence. We are not prepared to say whether the estimation in which the fine arts are held is precisely proportioned to this advancement, or rather to distinguish between the adventitious circumstances which fit the inhabitants of one region for a higher capacity of enjoyment more than those of another, the progress of civilization being the same or nearly the same; we have not, we say, sufficiently attended to this matter to hazard a conjecture whether nature may not have given a temperament so sanguine and a genius so lively, to one people in comparison with another, as not to be compensated by any other advantages—we rather incline to believe such to be the fact. But perhaps more time is yet necessary to enable the philosopher to discover whether those fine intelligences which render the inhabitants of Middle Europe so sensible to the powers of the fine arts above their Northern and American neighbors, be the effect of physical structure or of any particular period in the progress of manners and society.

It is certain that the Americans do not approach to the animated interest which the natives of the Continent of Europe manifest for the arts and for artists. Of late eminent literary characters have been treated with so much personal distinction as to prove that mind is gradually rising to the predominance mind must rise to in a state so cultivated as our own. Whether we shall ever come to bestow laurel crowns, whether our cities will be ever eager to enjoy and to reward the works of living poets, painters, and musicians, is a point yet to be determined.

In music, however, the general and exalted estimation of arts gives the European professors such superbundant encouragement over our own, as no other benefit can balance. With genius, (we speak of it in all times and ages,) no reward will weigh against personal fame, public deference, and the private respect that usually accompanies them. Hence the incitements which are administered to a

"Musical Diary. A. P. Heinrich," *The Euterpeiad; or, Musical Intelligencer*, June 1823: 35.

musician of talent by the multiplied engagements the cities of Italy, Germany, France and lately England, immediately hold out to a man who rises to celebrity, complete what a regular education in science begins.—Hence these nations are the fertile parents of the arts and of artists. For ourselves, whilst we are indulging this train of thought, we long to cast an eye into the coming on of time, and to ascertain whether it be granted to our own country to emulate them—whether nature, in the distribution of qualities, denies to one race what she has so liberally granted to another, or whether these differences are no more than modifications of the same physical principles, wrought by natural and moral changes in the revolutions of ages?

These remarks are elicited in observing the current of public taste evinced and encouragement held out to the gentleman, whose name stands at the head of this article, author of *The Dawning of Music in Kentucky—The Western Minstrel, etc.—* works which abound in boldness, originality, science, and even sublimity; and embrace all styles of composition, from a waltz or song up to the acme of chromatic frenzy. He may be justly styled the *Beethoven of America,* as he is actually considered by the few who have taken the trouble to ascertain his merits.

This original genius is now in this city,—and has accepted the appointment of Organist in the Old South Church—an honorable and judicious choice. Our feelings, as lovers of genuine merit, and our pride as citizens of Boston, are highly gratified by the opportunity of announcing an arrangement so honorable to all parties concerned; and we cannot but indulge the hope, that the liberal public will cheerfully co-operate in vindicating neglected genius, and of securing new and valuable services to our circle of musical science.

Notable operas were produced in the mid-nineteenth century by two American-born colleagues and friends, William Henry Fry (1813–1864) and George Frederick Bristow (1825–1898). The musical styles were European, but the composers were homegrown.

William Henry Fry's opera *Leonora* was the first grand opera by a composer born in United States. Two earlier operas by the composer were never produced, but a third, *Notre Dame of Paris*, was given in 1864. *Leonora* was first mounted at the Chestnut Street Theatre, Philadelphia, on June 4, 1845, in English. The opera, which ran to sixteen performances, translates European techniques (particularly that of Bellini) to the American stage. Not only is the music suggestive of Italy, but the drama is based on Edward Bulwer-Lytton's successful play *The Lady of Lyons: or, Love and Pride*, produced at the Covent Garden Theatre, London, in 1838. The story, set in sixteenth-century Spain, deals with a love triangle that resolves happily when the young peasant Giulio, Leonora's true love, returns from a trip of exploration to the New World.

The production of the opera was a family affair. Fry's brother, Joseph, was responsible for the libretto, and other family members helped make it become a reality. Francis Courtney Wemyss, whose remarks appear below, was co-manager of the theater at that time. The opera was revived near the end of Fry's life, in March 1858, at the Academy of Music in New York. For this production, significantly altered, this first opera by an American featured an excellent Italian cast, singing the work in Italian!

George Bristow's *Rip Van Winkle* was produced at Niblo's Garden, New York, on September 27, 1855, by the Pyne-Harrison English Opera Company, the composer conducting. The work is notable as the first opera on an American subject to enjoy real success. The *New-York Daily Tribune* went to pains to point out that, although it had been advertised as "Grand Opera," this was not correct, "as much of the dialogue is spoken. A grand opera is one in which the words are set to music throughout, and the recitatives are accompanied by full orchestra." A popular production, it was given seventeen performances in two months. The opera was substantially revised in 1878, with a different librettist, J. W. Shannon. The plot, truly American, recounts Washington Irving's tale of a Dutch immigrant who sleeps inadvertently for twenty years. As if to emphasize its Americanness, the original production incorporated additional scenes based on the American Revolution.

Born in Brooklyn, New York, into a musical family, Bristow became an active performer, conductor, church organist, and teacher of music in the New York City public schools. He appeared in notable concerts with Jenny Lind, Marietta Alboni, Jullien's Orchestra, and conductor Theodore Thomas. He joined the New York Philharmonic Society in 1843, the year after its founding, beginning a thirty-six-year relationship with that organization.

WILLIAM HENRY FRY

from Prefatory Remarks to *Leonora* (1845)

This Lyrical Drama was produced on the stage with a view of presenting to the American public, *a grand opera,* originally adapted to English words. The class of opera technically so designated, is, on the continent of Europe, employed for works of a serious or tragic character. Its peculiarity lies in the absence of all spoken monologue or dialogue; every word being sung throughout, and accompanied by the orchestra. This is essentially the high, complete, and classic form to give to the opera; it imparts proper uniformity of style to the entire declamation; does not confound the strictly musical with the acting drama; and with an artistic performance confirms the interest of the representation.

It would seem, however, that in England, to which America should naturally look for such a union of art and literature, the theory and practice have been to preclude the grand opera from the language, in original works. . . .

The plot of *Leonora,* it will be seen, is identical with that of Bulwer's *Lady of Lyons*; which, as an acting drama, holds a first rank in public estimation. Certain modifications have been made in the scenes and characters for musical purposes: in the omission of some persons; in the increased prominence given to others; in the change of place, and of the time to a more distant and hence romantic era. This change of time and place was readily effected, as there was no imperative delineation of national characteristics or localities in a purely domestic plot, to prevent it. For this reason, too, there has been no attempt made to infuse any popular or patriotic temper into the melodies. The tone of polite society—of "cavaliers and ladies," is much the same the world over. The action and expression of pointedly national characters, however, might suggest local music. But composers are not,

and cannot always be, particular on this head. A scene laid in ancient Greece or Rome would preclude a national style of music, now lost, if it ever existed. The action of an opera laid in this country, also, could not be illustrated with national music, since the original type is wanting.

The success which attended the production of *Leonora* has been as great as I could desire. The public attention so given to the first American work of the kind, induces the trust that in this country, which has the accumulating wealth, taste, and knowledge conferred by freedom and peace, and a coincident prosperity, there may be a rapid, and at the same time, a vigorous growth of this branch of Art. But it will be requisite to have a lyrical drama free from whatever is gross, so that it become essentially moral in its character, and thus disarm all opposition to its progress. A sense of public justice should, at the same time, establish an international copyright law—a republic of letters—by which American authorship shall be rendered secure, and the rights of Intellect be regarded, even though it be of foreign birth and politics. The hope may be indulged, that the period is not far distant, when, as a people, we shall not reap where we have not sown; and we shall be too honorable to enjoy the fruits of European genius without rewarding it.

It is a clear proposition, that no Art can flourish in a country until it assume a genial character. It may be exotic, experimentally, for a time, but unless it becomes indigenous, taking root and growth in the hearts and understandings of the people generally, its existence will be forced and sickly, and its decay quick and certain. And it may be remarked, emphatically, that, as vocal music must ever take precedence in general estimation of other music, for the reason that no musical instrument equals the human voice in quality and expression, it will be necessary to render national the lyrical drama, as being the only means by which

William Henry Fry, "Prefatory Remarks" from the vocal score to *Leonora: A Lyrical Drama* (New York: E. Ferret, 1846).

great singers can be formed, and a school of music reared. Upon the stage alone can the expression of the master passions be adequately given; and the identification of music with action and character, being an artistical exhibition of man's nature, while it gives lyrical representation the strongest hold upon the common heart, renders it necessary for the singer to attain to the perfection of his art, and be pathetic, eloquent, great. The church has ever been obliged to call upon the theatre for its chief devotional singers; and it must ever be thus, while the drama covers a spiritual as well as a tangible ground. All times and places are subservient to the illustrations of the stage. The mists of antiquity and the divination of the future; the abodes of the gods, of fairies, and of demons, as well as of men; earth, air, sea, and sky are searched for the facts and imaginings of the dramatist. To fight against such a material and immaterial array, is like a war upon the seven prismatic colors, upon the seven essential sounds, upon the very spirit of ideality which clothes all visible things with romance and beauty. To destroy dramatic music is to endanger all music; to bring back monkish formality and abused mathematics in the science. The chief interest of all instrumental music, of the passion displayed in the modern Oratorio and the Mass, lies in the dramatic expression derived originally from the universal lyrical delineations of the stage. Composers of religious works have learned to avoid frigid calculation and to attain the expression of devotional fervor, by the study directly or indirectly of Humanity in the lyrical drama. . . .

William H. Fry
Philadelphia, 1845

FRANCIS COURTNEY WEMYSS

from *Theatrical Biography* (1848)

On the 4th of June, 1845, an opera, by Mr. Fry, was placed before the public, in a style of which Messrs. Pratt and Weymss have reason to be proud: every scene, every dress, every property, was perfect; sixty choristers, and forty-two musicians; the principal characters supported by Mr. Fraser, Mr. and Mrs. Segnin, Mr. Richings, Mrs. Breenton, and Miss Inge; the subject of the libretto, the "Lady of Lyons," the title of the opera, "Leonora." A great deal has been written and said about plagiarism, and want of originality of thought and execution; but I appeal to any musician, whether such an opera be not a creditable performance to a composer. Had Mr. Fry selected New York, instead of Philadelphia, for the first field of his operations, the whole United States would have teamed with praises—praises, long and loud, would have greeted the eye of the composer from all quarters. The sin he committed was daring to present the first lyrical drama ever composed in America to the citizens of Philadelphia for judgment, before the New Yorkers had an opportunity of passing upon the merits. Should it be played with success in Europe, how altered will be public opinion in its favour here! Mr. Fry may plume upon it as a work of art, to be proudly cherished. I know of no greater gratification, as a manager, than having been the means of placing it before his countrymen. It was acted sixteen nights, although the expense attending such a production, rendered it unproductive both to the author and the managers, the Seguines reaped both money and fame.

Of Mr. Seguin's performance of Leonora, I can only say it was the most perfect thing I have ever seen, since Miss M. Tree's Zaidé in Coleman's play

Francis Courtney Wemyss, *Theatrical Biography: or, The Life of an Actor and Manager* (Glasgow: R. Griffin, 1848), 322–23.

of the "Law of Java,"[1] and I can hardly magnify such unqualified praise. On the last night, she was presented with a silver pitcher, bearing a suitable inscription—a well deserved compliment; a similar one should have been made to Mr. Chubb, the leader of the orchestra of the Park Theatre, to whose aid much of its success was due.

Announcements and Reviews of
George Frederick Bristow's *Rip Van Winkle* (1855)

New-York Daily Tribune, September 27, 1855

New American Opera at Niblo's.—An event of particular significance in the lyrical art will take place tonight, being the production of an American Opera—the composer being Mr. Bristow, and the word-writer Mr. Wainwright. So many foreign operas have been produced, and so much attention and such large means given to them, that it is more than time that an American Opera should be heard.

The New York Herald, September 27, 1855

Niblo's Garden—The New American Opera.— Mr. Bristow's grand native opera of "Rip Van Winkle," upon which a great deal of money and preparation has been spent, is to be produced to-night at this theatre. No American composition has ever been brought out under fairer auspices. The troupe is the best English one in existence, and has added to its strength a new baritone, Mr. Stretton, of whose talents report speaks favorably. Those who have heard the music of the opera at rehearsal entertain confident expectations of its success. It is said to be light, sparkling and characteristic, and is allied to an excellent libretto. All friends of native art should rally in strength round the composer on this interesting occasion.

New-York Daily Tribune, September 29, 1855

Niblo's Theater, which holds more people than the grand Opera House, Paris, was densely filled on Thursday night to hear the new American Opera, Rip Van Winkle, the joint production of Mr. Bristow, composer of the music, and Mr. Wainwright, writer of the words, both New Yorkers, and young men. Every disposition was manifested by the audience to give the work a favorable hearing; and on the composer taking his seat in the orchestra, of which he is the leader, he was loudly cheered. The leading artists of the City were present, but the literary men were occupied at the Publisher's Festival held at the same time at the Crystal Palace.

The title of this opera, according to the published libretto and the play bills, is "Rip Van Winkle: *An original American Grand Opera in three Acts Music* by George F. Bristow. *The Libretto* by J. H. Wainwright."

Now this is not correct, as much of the dialogue is spoken. A grand opera is one in which the words are set to music throughout, and the recitatives are accompanied by full orchestra. Operas with spoken dialogue are termed comic, to distinguish them from grand operas.

The principal characters are, Rip Van Winkle (Mr. Stretton), Dame Van Winkle (Miss Pyne), Alice Van Winkle (Miss Louisa Pyne), Edward Gardenier (Mr. Harrison), Frederick Vilcoeur (Mr. Horncastle), Young Rip Van Winkle (Mr. Miller). The scene lies partly among the Catskill mountains and partly on Saratoga plains. The action extends over the space of twenty years. Time of the first act, 1763; of the second act, 1777; of the third act, 1783. The libretto states that "The scenery, by Messrs. Hillyard and Thorne, is all printed from Nature drawings for the express purpose having been taken on the spot. The tableaux in the first act are after the celebrated etchings of 'Rip Van Winkle,' by F. O. C. Darley. The costumes, by Mr. Taylor, and properties by Mr. Silvester are according to the

---

[1] *The Law of Java, or, The Poison Tree*, London (c. 1822).

best historical authorities of the period to which they refer."

The plot of the opera is in the main similar to Washington Irving's famous story, the principal variation being in the second act, in which are introduced some scenes and characters not found in Irving. . . .[2]

The music of this opera now claims our attention. As it is by an American, who depends on the verdict of his countrymen—there being no ready-made opinion from Europe to be adopted, parrot-like, we have great pleasure in stating that Mr. Bristow's debut as a dramatic composer was equally successful with those of the established composers of Europe, if we are to believe their biographers. On a first night there are of course more or less nervousness, incertitude and crudity in the execution; if the performers are not perfectly familiar with their parts, the public is not familiar at all, and beyond its most salient portions little interest is awarded to it, the quieter beauties and deeper dramatizations being reserved for later considerations, if at all. . . .

The occasion of the production of a new American opera, amid delays and difficulties enough to destroy the enthusiasm of the composer, and an all-sufficient indifference on the part of the public up to the time it was actually produced, induces us to call attention to the relations of dramatic and other composers to the public and to fame, and to detail the causes which lie in the way of the extension of the musical art, especially in this country. We believe in so doing we recite facts which have escaped the attention of every writer here, certainly of every musical critic.

Inventors or discoverers in every walk of Literature, Science and Art have usually great difficulties in bringing their first works before the public in a form to secure a just appreciation and adequate reward. The lives of almost all great authors, painters and inventors contain records of early struggles; records of years of poverty and obscu-rity—the best years of youth and health and mental vigor—fretted away in the seemingly hopeless search for a bookseller, connoisseur, or capitalist willing to purchase, and make patent to the world the first product of the unknown.

But whatever obstacles lie between inventors like these and the public, they are as little hillocks to the Alps of difficulty that plant themselves in the path of the operatic composer whose success lies at the mercy of go-betweens and interpreters. . . .

In view of the anomalous position which the English and American composer occupies; of the peculiar obstacles which obstruct his way to the public, and which he must usually labor half a lifetime to overcome; we deem it a critical duty when, as in the case of Mr. Bristow's opera, at last his work is presented, to give it extended notice, and to claim for it from the public that attention and recognition to which so unusual and important an event in the world of art is justly entitled.

Mr. Bristow's opera, *Rip Van Winkle*, produced at Niblo's on Thursday evening, is the second one composed in this country by an American. As musical intelligence, it is due to the reader that we should give the following historical facts on purely American operatic matters which have never yet been treated by the press. The first opera by an American was *Leonora*, composed by Mr. W. H. Fry, and produced in Philadelphia by the Seguin troupe about ten years ago, where it had a perfect success, and was performed sixteen nights. It was a grand opera in the technical sense of the term—that is, without spoken dialogue—and was the first grand opera of the modern school by either an English or American composer. Mr. Fry composed several other operas, which have not yet been produced. The managers of all the theaters in New-York, as is well known, are in utter fear of a journal whose editor has made war on Mr. Fry and all his productions from the moment *Leonora* appeared.[3] The public is sufficiently acquainted with the causes of this hostility, but is hardly aware that its exercise has up to this time, through the acknowl-

---

[2]Scenes of the American Revolution, inserted by Wainwright.

[3]*Musical World*, edited by Richard Storrs Willis.

edged subserviency of the managers of all the theaters, deprived Mr. Fry of a hearing in New York for any of his operas; though his symphonies through Mr. Jullien, who defied the wrath of the editor in question, have been frequently performed. These being the facts, the following statement of the Satanic Press in relation to the opera of *Rip Van Winkle*, which is the first American opera performed in New-York and the second only in America, may be taken for what they are worth:

If Mr. Bristow's opera succeeds he will have the credit of being the first American composer who has written anything that kept the stage beyond its first night. There is one American opera, so called, which has long been a bugbear to artists, as its composer never loses an opportunity to endeavor to bully them into playing it. We never heard of any who ever heard the whole of it. There may be survivors, but they cannot be found in the usual haunts of men. As 'Rip Van Winkle' is truly an American opera, on an American subject, by an American composer, we hope that it will succeed.

The New York Herald, October 1, 1855

At Niblo's Garden, the new American opera "Rip Van Winkle" has been played three nights to full houses, and it will be given again this evening and every night this week. The composer, Mr. Bristow, may now claim to be the first successful writer of this style of opera in America, and in many respects this work is superior to anything that has yet come from the pen of any English composer.

49

The American Perspective: Fry and Bristow Again

Ralph Waldo Emerson wrote in 1837 that "our day of independence, our long apprenticeship to the learning of other lands, draws to a close. . . . We have listened too long to the courtly muses of Europe. . . . We will walk on our own feet; we will work with our own hands; we will speak our own minds."* European influence in America remained strong in the nineteenth century, as it still does in many quarters even today. The issue of what makes music "American" has been debated throughout our musical history.

Between late November 1852, the month he returned from several years in Paris, and early February 1853, William Henry Fry presented an important series of illustrated lectures at Metropolitan Hall, New York. Since Fry did not speak from a written text, we have no exact record of what he said. However, the discussion was carried into print as Fry, music critic for the *New York Tribune,* argued with the influential editor of *The Musical World & Times,* Richard Storrs Willis. Boston's John Sullivan Dwight reprinted articles and correspondence and made comments from the sidelines.

Fry had originally planned a series of ten lectures but included an explosive eleventh, in which he reportedly urged independence and self-determination for American composers. Willis produced a summary of thirty-one propositions that he took to be Fry's "Americanisms" in *The Musical World & Times.* Fry's reply to Willis follows below.

Fry also stirred up a fuss about not being taken seriously enough with his large, descriptive orchestral work *Santa Claus: Christmas Symphony,* played in New York on Christmas Eve, 1853, by the famous Jullien orchestra. And, again, as an American composer, he challenged New York's Philharmonic Society when he wrote to Willis on January 10, 1854, "The Philharmonic Society of this city, consecrated to foreign music, is an incubus on Art, never having asked for or performed a single American instrumental composition during the eleven years of its existence, but which has greedily sought for and eagerly thrust before the public every pretentious emanation from the brain of Europeans"—an exaggerated though essentially true charge.†

George Bristow, Fry's friend, led the Philharmonic Orchestra and Harmonic Society as part of Fry's lectures. He also enjoyed a thirty-six year relationship with the New York Philharmonic Society, beginning in 1843. Bristow rushed to Fry's defense upon learning of Fry's remarks about the Philharmonic Society just quoted. Bristow clarified Fry's overstatement but fanned the fire with passion when he, in turn, wrote to the *Mu-*

---

*Ralph Waldo Emerson, *The American Scholar;* Phi Beta Kappa Address at Harvard, 1837, from Norman Foerster, ed., *American Poetry and Prose,* 4th ed. (Boston: Houghton Mifflin, 1957), 481, 489.

†*Dwight's Journal of Music,* Feb. 4, 1854: 138; quotations below from *The Musical World and Times,* March 4, 1854: 100, and March 18, 1854: 122.

sical World a month later (February 27, 1854) that actually the organization had once "either by mistake or accident," performed a single work of his. But that was hardly enough to disprove that the orchestra "has been as anti-American as if it had been located in London, during the revolutionary war, and composed of native born English Tories."

The surprised Philharmonic answered the charges levied at them by a supposedly trusted comrade on March 9, 1854. They cited other works played either in "public rehearsals" or in concerts by "native or adopted citizens of this country." They regretted that Bristow had not honestly and frankly laid his grievances, "if he had any, before the society . . . instead of writing and publicizing a letter full of vehemence and passion, condemnatory of a body of musicians of which he had been himself a member for many years."

By this time Bristow, had, in anger, resigned his position with the Philharmonic, including his post as a recently elected director. His successor was announced, a Mr. Brannes of the cello section. The animosity was not to last. Emotions settled back. Bristow rejoined the orchestra at the beginning of the fourteenth season in November 1855. Wishing to make amends on its part, the orchestra went on to play Bristow's *Jullien* Symphony at that season's third concert on March 1, 1856. Bristow was, however, essentially right: significant European bias had existed in the orchestra's repertoire and was to continue for the next thirty years of its history.

WILLIAM HENRY FRY

Open Letter to Richard Storrs Willis (1853)

New York, March 16, 1853
Messrs. Editors:—I regret to have to notice the remarks of your journal on my lectures,[1] because it involves a correction of the summary made of them. You have put under separate heads various positions, some of which are accurately stated and others not. As I spoke without notes, and there was no Report made of what I said at the eleventh lecture, I cannot turn to the very words, but must only say that there are various things attributed to me which if I have the humblest practical acquaintance with the apothegm, *gnothi seauton*,[2] I never said. You speak of me thus:

"Among other remarks on this point during his course, and which he summed up in his last lecture, were the following: That,

"1. There is no taste or love for, or appreciation of true Art in this country. That,

"2. The public, as a public, know nothing about Art—they have not a single enlightened or healthy idea on the subject. That,

"3. A sort of childish wonder is the only tribute paid in America to exhibitions of high art, and even this tribute is called forth by solo performances. That,

The Musical World & Times, March 26, 1853: 195–97; reprinted in *Dwight's Journal of Music*, April 2, 1853.

[1]Copied by J. S. Dwight in *Dwight's Journal of Music*, March 12, 1853: 180–82.

[2]"Know thyself."

"4. We pay enormous sums to hear a single voice, or a single instrument, the beauties and excellencies of which (if it have any) we cannot discover. But that,

"5. We will pay nothing to hear a sublime work of Art performed, because we do not know enough to appreciate it, and consequently such a performance bores us terribly." . . .

"The American public are too fond of quoting Handel, Mozart, Beethoven and European artists generally and decrying whatever is not modelled after their rules:" No. 12 of your list says so, but I did not. I stated that certain writers quote these constantly, who would fail to discover anything in the same authors if they were American, for the reason of pusillanimity in forming original judgments.

Nor do "the American *public* (No. 20) decry native compositions and sneer at native artists." Critics, so called, may ignore as they do the existence of American musical works, or, not knowing the science of dramatic composition, speak of them ignorantly; but *the public* do not. My experience as a composer has been the reverse; and it was impossible for any compositions to be better received or more strenuously encored by the public than were those of mine well-sung at the Eleventh Lecture in presence of three thousand people; and that was my experience in Philadelphia, where an opera I wrote[3] ran seventeen nights in the summer season to full houses—the size of the city considered at that time, equal to a run of at least forty nights in New York now,—a success which fully satisfies me when I reflect that the great artist Madame Sontag advertises a new opera every two nights.[4]

"In Europe (No. 30) an American artist is spit upon." I said no such thing. I said when there I tried to have an opera produced, and I was spit upon, because I was an American: this I repeat in opposition to your comments. I took the best pos-

sible introductions, and offered to pay the expenses of a rehearsal, according to my invariable custom to expect nothing as a favor. I wished the music to be heard simply: given book in hand without dress or decoration, and so pronounced upon—a frightful hazard but one which I was willing to abide by, in the same way that I had my works performed at my lectures in New York without the necessary aids of the Opera-house. Meyerbeer never would let a note of his operas be heard originally except on the stage: and so should all dramatic composers, in fact. When I asked for this simple rehearsal—so easily accorded and fairly required—the director of the opera in Paris said to me: In Europe we look upon America as an industrial country—excellent for electric telegraphs and railroads but not for Art. I ventured to hint, that although we had excelled in making electric telegraphs to carry ideas without persons, it was not a necessary consequence that we built railroads to carry persons without ideas, or that we had not ideas on every fruitful subject. "It cannot be done under any circumstances," rejoined he: "they would think me crazy to produce an opera by an American." *Soit* (so be it) said I, as he turned away. So he would not even look at the work, but rejected it solely on the ground of its being American, not knowing whether it was good, bad, or indifferent.

. . . I did most assuredly say (No. 29) that "an American composer cannot get his works brought out at home unless he has a fortune which will enable him to bear the expense himself," and that I spent thousands to produce one of my operas in Philadelphia; and I do say, myself apart, that it is disgraceful on the part of this public to let foreign singers rush through the land under a flying artillery of the most glaring of lurid quackery and never ask whether we can create an American Opera on our own soil, and by artists whose heads and hearts are with us. When we do so, we shall rewrite the History of Art: for the influence of our institutions upon the artist is of the last importance to Humanity. Instead of illustrating a sect or a caste, his work will be for Man. All that has been done for kings is a proper estimate set upon the

---

[3]*Leonora.*

[4]Henriette Sontag (1806–1854) was a German soprano of considerable reputation.

dignity which belongs to our race. Thus viewing it we shall adopt it for ourselves.—Beauty and Art will then become common property. It will then be discovered, even by our colleges, that the perceptions of the Eye and the Ear should be considered as one:—that our language has yet to be lyrically written, which it never will be under their present dispensations: that the culture of a gentleman indispensably includes a knowledge of these Indissoluble Arts of testing sound and color and form: that the operatic stage is the common altar on which music, painting and poetry are laid: that the great masters of esthetics, the Greeks, so considered it, and that the genius from which flashed for all time the Parthenon and the Apollo found its largest nutrition in the lyre.

GEORGE FREDERICK BRISTOW

Open Letter to Richard Storrs Willis (1854)

New York, Feb. 27th, 1854

Dear Sir:—I have observed that my name is used several times in the discussion just concluded between yourself and Mr. Fry.[5] What Mr. Fry stated about the spirit and action of the New York Philharmonic Society, is perfectly accurate, except in one particular; and that relates to myself, and induces me to write this letter. As it is possible to miss a needle in a hay-stack, I am not surprised that Mr. Fry has missed the fact, that during the eleven years the Philharmonic Society has been in operation in this city, it played once, either by mistake or accident, one single American composition, an overture of mine.[6] As one exception makes a rule stronger, so this single stray fact shows that the Philharmonic Society has been as anti-American as if it had been located in London during the revolutionary war, and composed of native born English Tories. Your anonymous correspondent who is not worthy of notice except that you endorse him, says that a symphony of mine, also, was rehearsed, and not played in public. So Uncle Toby says—"Our army swore terribly at Flanders"—but that army did not fight. It appears the Society's eleven years of promoting American Art, have embraced one whole performance of one whole American overture, one whole rehearsal of one whole American symphony, and the performance of an overture by an Englishman stopping here—Mr. Loder—(whom your beautiful correspondent would infer is an American) who, happening to be conductor of the Philharmonic here, had the influence to have it played.[7] Now, in the name of the nine Muses, what is the Philharmonic Society—or Harmony-lovers' Society—in this country? Is it to play exclusively the works of German masters, especially if they be dead, in order that our critics may translate their ready-made praises from German? Or, is it to stimulate original Art on the spot? Is there a Philharmonic Society in Germany for the encouragement solely of American music? Then why should there be a society here for the encouragement solely of German music, to the exclusion of American; unless, as Mr. Fry says, the object be to render us a Hessian Colony, which we most incontestably are? Who are the men who told you that Americans cannot "write up" to the standard of the New York Philharmonic Society? The same style of *illuminati* that in the London Philharmonic, after attempting to rehearse it, kicked Beethoven's C minor Symphony

---

The Musical World & Times, March 4, 1854: 100.

[5] *Dwight's Journal of Music*, February 4, 1854: 138.

[6] For a list of works performed by the Philharmonic Society to 1880, see Frederic Ritter, *Music in America* (New York: Scribner's, 1890), 362–67.

[7] George Loder (1816–1868), English conductor and composer, was in America from 1836 to 1859, first in Baltimore and then in New York. He conducted the Philharmonic occasionally.

under their desks and pronounced the composer a fool or a madman? Can any of these men, who so decry American music, read a score? Not one. And what right, then, have they to pre-judge, unread and unheard, everything American, simply because it is American.

You speak of "writing up" to the Philharmonic Society: better say write down to it. In what way does it compare with Jullien's band? In playing a pianissimo—in the strength and unity of a fortissimo it cannot compete with them. And yet Mr. Jullien, a stranger, a traveler, finds during a short visit to this country, American instrumental compositions that he adapts in his symphonic repertory, and will carry back for performance in Europe, although the members of the Philharmonic Society have never been able to discover any such works during eleven years, and under such fostering care as theirs, none would ever attain to existence in eleven hundred years. I would add that, although three seasons ago, the Philharmonic performers were, individually, not so good as now, their execution was better. In fact, the best disposed persons towards the Society could not find it in their consciences to praise the last concert.

To resume: from the commencement, there has been on the part of the performing members or the direction of the Philharmonic Society, little short of a conspiracy against the Art of a country to which they come for a living; and, it is very bad taste, to say the least, for men to bite the hand that feeds them. If all their artistic affections are unalterably German, let them pack back to Germany and enjoy the police and bayonets and aristocratic kicks and cuffs of that land, where an artist is a serf to a nobleman, as the history of all their great composers show. America has made the political revolution which illumines the world, while Germany is still beshrouded with a pall of feudal darkness. While America has been thus far able to do the chief things for the dignity of man, forsooth she must be denied the brains for original Art, and must stand like a beggar, deferentially cap in hand, when she comes to compete with the ability of any dirty German village. Mr. Fry has taken the right ground. Against fearful odds, he has, as a classical

composer, through you and your journal challenged all Germany to meet him before the audiences of the Philharmonic and Mr. Jullien; and the challenge has not been accepted.

Mr. Dwight, too, the editor of *Dwight's Journal of Music,* published in Boston, has found my "forms" in symphonic writing "odd":—I beg to tell him they are not quite so odd as his critical forms when he gave an opinion on my music, as he now acknowledges "hastily," and without having heard a note of it.

It seems that as about nine-tenths, to say the least, of the performers and critics are foreigners, that American composers must be forced into the position of asserting their rights to be heard in their own country unless they will submit to be denied any existence whatever, or to be trampled out of existence altogether, when they have begun the great work of building a national school of Art. To this they should find sympathy, at least, from all their countrymen, as they have to learn composition under circumstances, and against obstacles which have no parallel in the history of Art in Europe, ancient or modern; for there every country has protected its own artists through a national school supported by government. Here, however, the development of Art, as did the development of political liberty, depends solely upon the courageous and long-sustained efforts of individual men. There are but few American composers now, and there will be none at all if musical matters are exclusively controlled by foreigners, as at present.

I may have occasion, with your kind permission, to address you upon this subject again, and to show more particularly the systematized effort of the Philharmonic Society for the extinction of American music. I respectfully request Mr. Dwight to copy this and let America have one word to say in his paper where Germany has had ten thousand[8]

I remain, very respectfully yours,

Geo. F. Bristow

---

[8]Dwight declined to reprint the letter in its entirety but extracted some of it and made further comments of his own in *Dwight's Journal of Music,* March 11, 1854.

50

The Music of Slavery

The slaves brought with them from Africa a rich music tradition that adapted to local conditions on the west side of the Atlantic. Singing was ubiquitous, and instruments, particularly the banjo, were popular. In the words of ex-slave Solomon Northup, "The African race is a music-loving one, proverbially; and many there were among my fellow-bondsmen whose organs of tune were strikingly developed, and who could thumb the banjo with dexterity."* Music as religious expression, including spirituals and the ring-shout; plantation songs of work, recreation, and dance, including corn songs, field songs, music for holidays, and "patting juba"; music for the entertainment of the master; boat and waterfront songs; and "code" songs, which aided plans for escape, were all part of everyday life.

Included below are narratives and songs by two major figures who were brought up in slavery but eventually found their freedom, Frederick Douglass and William Wells Brown.

Frederick Augustus Washington Bailey (c. 1817–1895) found his way into lasting freedom in 1838 and changed his name to Frederick Douglass, in the interests of safety. He gained prominence after a speech in 1841 before the Massachusetts Anti-Slavery Society, which published his *Narrative*, one of three autobiographies, seven years later. Douglass became an avid abolitionist. In the 1840s, he carried the cause to England, a trip that also helped prevent his recapture. He started an abolitionist newspaper for blacks in Rochester, New York, the *North Star*, later called *Frederick Douglass's Paper.* He went on to became recorder of deeds for the District of Columbia and American minister and consul general in Haiti (from 1889 to 1891).

Another important voice from slavery was that of William Wells Brown (c. 1816–1884). His *Narrative*, published in Boston by the Anti-Slavery Society in 1847, and *My Southern Home*, published in that city in 1880, tell of his experiences. His mother, Elizabeth, was a field hand who bore seven children; his father, George Higgins, was white. He made his way into freedom, having been befriended in 1834 in Ohio by a Quaker, Wells Brown, whose name he adapted as his own and to whom he dedicated his *Narrative*.

Brown married, continued his education, lectured on behalf of abolition, studied medicine, and published numerous important works. His interests as a reformer grew to include temperance, women's suffrage, and prison reform, and he was welcomed in Europe as a champion of freedom.

In *My Southern Home*, Brown describes a yearly corn-shucking event, which was something of a social occasion as well. Corn songs as a category were widely known in the South, where corn was a staple crop. Brown also describes events in Congo Square, a traditional meeting place for blacks in New Orleans.

---

*Solomon Northup, Twelve Years a Slave, ed. Sue Eakin and Joseph Logsdon (Baton Rouge, La.: Louisiana State University Press, 1968), 165.

FREDERICK DOUGLASS

from *Narrative of the Life of Frederick Douglass* (1845)

The home plantation of Colonel Lloyd wore the appearance of a country village.[1] All the mechanical operations for all the farms were performed here. The shoemaking and mending, the blacksmithing, cartwrighting, coopering, weaving, and grain-grinding, were all performed by the slaves on the home plantation. The whole place wore a business-like aspect very unlike the neighboring farms. The number of houses, too, conspired to give it advantage over the neighboring farms. It was called by the slaves the *Great House Farm*. Few privileges were esteemed higher, by the slaves of the out-farms, than that of being selected to do errands at the Great House Farm. It was associated in their minds with greatness. A representative could not be prouder of his election to a seat in the American Congress, than a slave on one of the out-farms would be of his election to do errands at the Great House Farm. They regarded it as evidence of great confidence reposed in them by their overseers; and it was on this account, as well as a constant desire to be out of the field from under the driver's lash, that they esteemed it a high privilege, one worth careful living for. He was called the smartest and most trusty fellow, who had this honor conferred upon him the most frequently. The competitors for this office sought as diligently to please their overseers, as the office-seekers in the political parties seek to please and deceive the people. The same traits of character might be seen in Colonel Lloyd's slaves, as are seen in the slaves of the political parties.

The slaves selected to go to the Great House Farm, for the monthly allowance for themselves and their fellow-slaves, were peculiarly enthusiastic. While on their way, they would make the dense old woods, for miles around, reverberate with their wild songs, revealing at once the highest joy and the deepest sadness. They would compose and sing as they went along, consulting neither time nor tune. The thought that came up, came out—if not in the word, in the sound;—and as frequently in the one as in the other. They would sometimes sing the most pathetic sentiment in the most rapturous tone, and the most rapturous sentiment in the most pathetic tone. Into all of their songs they would manage to weave something of the Great House Farm. Especially would they do this, when leaving home. They would then sing most exultingly the following words:—

"I am going away to the Great House Farm!
O, yea! O, yea! O!"

This they would sing, as a chorus, to words which to many would seem unmeaning jargon, but which, nevertheless, were full of meaning to themselves. I have sometimes thought that the mere hearing of those songs would do more to impress some minds with the horrible character of slavery, than the reading of whole volumes of philosophy on the subject could do.

I did not, when a slave, understand the deep meaning of those rude and apparently incoherent songs. I was myself within the circle; so that I neither saw nor heard as those without might see and hear. They told a tale of woe which was then altogether beyond my feeble comprehension; they were tones loud, long and deep; they breathed the prayer and complaint of souls boiling over with the bitterest anguish. Every tone was a testimony against slavery, and a prayer to God for deliverance from chains. The hearing of those wild notes always depressed my spirit, and filled me with ineffable sadness. I have frequently found myself in tears while hearing them. The mere recurrence to those songs, even now, afflicts me; and while I am writing these

Frederick Douglass, *Narrative of the Life of Frederick Douglass, an American Slave, Written by Himself* (Boston: Anti-Slavery Office, 1845), 12–15.

[1]Col. Edward Lloyd's plantation was in Tuckahoe, Maryland.

lines, an expression of feeling has already found its way down my cheek. To those songs I trace my first glimmering conception of the dehumanizing character of slavery. I can never get rid of that conception. Those songs still follow me, to deepen my hatred of slavery, and quicken my sympathies for my brethren in bonds. If any one wishes to be impressed with the soul-killing effects of slavery, let him go to Colonel Lloyd's plantation, and, on allowance-day, place himself in the deep, pine woods, and there let him, in silence, analyze the sounds that shall pass through the chambers of his soul,—and if he is not thus impressed, it will only be because "there is no flesh in his obdurate heart."[2]

---

[2]A quote from "The Time-Piece," book 2, line 8, of William Cowper, *The Task* (1785): "There is no flesh in man's obdurate heart."

I have often been utterly astonished, since I came to the north, to find persons who could speak of the singing, among slaves, as evidence of their contentment and happiness. It is impossible to conceive of a greater mistake. Slaves sing most when they are most unhappy. The songs of the slave represent the sorrows of his heart; and he is relieved by them, only as an aching heart is relieved by its tears. At least, such is my experience. I have often sung to drown my sorrow, but seldom to express my happiness. Crying for joy, and singing for joy, were alike uncommon to me while in the jaws of slavery. The singing of a man cast away from a desolate island might be as appropriately considered as evidence of contentment and happiness, as the singing of a slave; the songs of the one and of the other are prompted by the same emotion.

WILLIAM WELLS BROWN

from *My Southern Home* (1880)

An old-fashioned corn-shucking took place once a year, on "Poplar Farm," which afforded pleasant amusement for the out-door negroes for miles around.[3] On these occasions, the servants, on all plantations, were allowed to attend by mere invitation of the blacks where the corn was to be shucked.

As the grain was brought in from the field, it was left in a pile near the corn-cribs. The night appointed, and invitations sent out, slaves from plantations five or six miles away, would assemble and join on the road, and in large bodies march along, singing their melodious plantation songs.

To hear three or four of these gangs coming from different directions, their leaders giving out the words, and the whole company joining in the chorus, would indeed surpass anything ever produced by "Haverly's Minstrels," and many of their jokes and witticisms were never equalled by Sam Lucas or Billy Kersands.[4]

A supper was always supplied by the planter on whose farm the shucking was to take place. Often when approaching the place, the singers would speculate on what they were going to have for supper. The following song was frequently sung:

"All dem puty gals will be dar,
    Shuck dat corn before you eat.
Dey will fix it fer us rare,
    Shuck dat corn before you eat.
I know dat supper will be big,

William Wells Brown, *My Southern Home; or, The South and Its People* (Boston: A. G. Brown, 1880), 91–95, 121–24.

[3]St. Louis County, Missouri.

---

[4]Jack Haverly (1837–1901) was an important minstrel show manager. Sam Lucas (1840–1916), a major minstrel performer, was the first black actor to play the title role in Uncle Tom's Cabin. Billy Kersands (1842–1915) was a brilliant minstrel comedian, singer, and dancer with the minstrel shows.

Shuck dat corn before you eat.
I think I smell a fine roast pig,
    Shuck dat corn before you eat.
A supper is provided, so dey said,
    Shuck dat corn before you eat.
I hope dey'll have some nice wheat bread,
    Shuck dat corn before you eat.
I hope dey'll have some coffee dar,
    Shuck dat corn before you eat.
I hope dey'll have some whisky dar,
    Shuck dat corn before you eat.
I think I'll fill my pockets full,
    Shuck dat corn before you eat.
Stuff dat coon an' bake him down,
    Shuck dat corn before you eat.
I speck some niggers dar from town,
    Shuck dat corn before you eat.
Please cook dat turkey nice an' brown.
    Shuck dat corn before you eat.
By de side of dat turkey I'll be foun,
    Shuck dat corn before you eat.
I smell de supper, dat I do,
    Shuck dat corn before you eat.
On de table will be a stew,
    Shuck dat corn, etc."

Burning pine knots, held by some of the boys, usually furnished light for the occasion. Two hours is generally sufficient time to finish up a large shucking; where five hundred bushels of corn is thrown into the cribs as the shuck is taken off. The work is made comparatively light by the singing, which never ceases till they go to the supper table. Something like the following is sung during the evening:

"De possum meat am good to eat,
    Carve him to de heart;
You'll always find him good and sweet,
    Carve him to de heart;
My dog did bark, and I went to see,
    Carve him to de heart;
And dar was a possum up dat tree,
    Carve him to de heart.

Chorus.—"Carve dat possum, carve dat possum children,
Carve dat possum, carve him to de heart;

Oh, carve dat possum, carve dat possum children,
Carve dat possum, carve him to de heart.

"I reached up for to pull him in,
    Carve him to de heart;
De possum he began to grin,
    Carve him to de heart;
I carried him home and dressed him off,
    Carve him to de heart;
I hung him dat night in de frost,
    Carve him to de heart.

Chorus.—"Carve dat possum, etc.

"De way to cook de possum sound,
    Carve him to de heart;
First par-bile him, den bake him brown,
    Carve him to de heart;
Lay sweet potatoes in de pan,
    Carve him to de heart;
De sweetest eatin' in de lan,'
    Carve him to de heart.

Chorus.—"Carve dat possum, etc."

Should a poor supper be furnished, on such an occasion, you would hear remarks from all parts of the table,

"Take dat rose pig 'way from dis table."
"What rose pig? you see any rose pig here?"

"Ha, ha, ha! Dis ain't de place to see rose pig."
"Pass up some dat turkey wid clam sauce."
"Don't talk about dat turkey; he was gone afore we
    come,"
"Dis is de las' time I shucks corn at dis farm."
"Dis is a cheap farm, cheap owner, an' a cheap supper."
"He's talkin' it, ain't he?"
"Dis is de tuffest meat dat I is been called upon to eat
    fer many a day;
you's got to have teeth sharp as a saw to eat dis meat."
"Spose you ain't got no teef, den what you gwine to do?"
"Why, ef you ain't got no teef you muss *gum it!*"
"Ha, ha, ha!" from the whole company, was heard.

On leaving the corn-shucking farm, each gang of men, headed by their leader, would sing during the entire journey home. Some few, however, having their dogs with them, would start on the trail of a coon, possum, or some other game, which might keep them out till nearly morning.

* * *

Throughout the Southern States, there are still to be found remnants of the old time Africans, who were stolen from their native land and sold in the Savannah, Mobile, and New Orleans markets, in defiance of all law. The last-named city, however, and its vacinity, had a larger portion of these people than any other section. New Orleans was their centre, and where their meetings were not uninteresting.

Congo Square takes its name, as is well known, from the Congo negroes who used to perform their dance on its sward every Sunday. They were a curious people, and brought over with them this remnant of their African jungles. In Louisiana there were six different tribes of negroes, named after the section of the country from which they came, and their representatives could be seen on the square, their teeth filed, and their cheeks still bearing tattoo marks. The majority of our city negroes came from the Kraels, a numerous tribe who dwell in stockades. We had here the Minahs, a proud, dignified, warlike race; the Congos, a treacherous, shrewd, relentless people; the Mandringas, a branch of the Congos; the Gangas, named after the river of that name, from which they had been taken; the Hiboas, called by the missionaries the "Owls," a sullen, intractable tribe, and the Foulas, the highest type of the African, with but few representatives here.

These were the people that one would meet on the square many years ago. It was a gala occasion, these Sundays in those years, and not less than two or three thousand people would congregate there to see the dusky dancers. A low fence enclosed the square, and on each street there was a little gate and turnstile. There were no trees then, and the ground was worn bare by the feet of the people. About three o'clock the negroes began to gather, each nation taking their places in different parts of the square. The Minahs would not dance near the Congos, nor the Mandringas near the Gangas. Presently the music would strike up, and the par-

ties would prepare for the sport. Each set had its own orchestra. The instruments were a peculiar kind of banjo, made of a Louisiana gourd, several drums made of a gum stump dug out, with a sheepskin head, and beaten with the fingers, and two jaw-bones of a horse, which when shaken would rattle the loose teeth, keeping time with the drums. About eight negroes, four male and four female, would make a set, and generally they were but scantily clad.

It took some little time before the tapping of the drums would arouse the dull and sluggish dancers, but when the point of excitement came, nothing can faithfully portray the wild and frenzied motions they go through. Backward and forward, this way and that, now together and now apart, every motion intended to convey the most sensual ideas. As the dance progressed, the drums were thrummed faster, the contortions became more grotesque, until sometimes, in frenzy, the women and men would fall fainting to the ground. All this was going on with a dense crowd looking on, and with a hot sun pouring its torrid rays on the infatuated actors of this curious ballet. After one set had become fatigued, they would drop out to be replaced by others, and then stroll off to the groups of some other tribe in a different portion of the square. Then it was that trouble would commence, and a regular set-to with short sticks followed, between the men, and broken heads ended the day's entertainment.

On the sidewalks, around the square, the old negresses, with their spruce-beer and peanuts, cocoa-nuts and pop-corn, did a thriving trade, and now and then, beneath petticoats, bottles of tafia, a kind of Louisiana rum, peeped out, of which the *gendarmes* were oblivious. When the sun went down, a stream of people poured out of the turnstiles, and the *gendarmes*, walking through the square, would order the dispersion of the negroes, and by gun-fire, at nine o'clock, the place was well-nigh deserted. These dances were kept up until within the memory of men still living, and many who believe in them, and who would gladly revive them, may be found in every State in the Union.

51   Let My People Go

The *National Anti-Slavery Standard* was a major Northern journal agitating for the abolition of slavery. During the closing months of 1861, the *Standard* gave particular attention to the plight of so-called contrabands, black slaves who had found their way to freedom behind Northern lines. They were considered contraband of war, rather than property to be returned to their former owners. Among them were emancipated blacks at Fort Monroe, Virginia, at Port Royal, South Carolina, and at other areas in the South under Northern control. In October 1861, there were probably about 1,500 free blacks at Fort Monroe.

The first report of the Reverend Lewis C. Lockwood, who had been sent to Fort Monroe by the American Missionary Association, was published by the *Standard* in its issue of October 12, 1861. It describes a "prime deliverance melody, that runs in this style: 'Go down to Egypt—Tell Pharaoh / Thus saith my servant, Moses,—Let my people go.' " Using Biblical imagery, this spiritual represented the longings of enslaved Africans. The whole "curious hymn" was published on December 21, although clearly the text had been sanitized into a version more familiar to whites and had been influenced by hymnody familiar to them. The February 15, 1962, issue of the *Standard* refers to the published sheet music then on sale—an even more curious version arranged by Thomas Baker. This first publication of a black spiritual, with its hymn-like text, was set as a nineteenth-century parlor song.

By comparison, *The Atlantic Monthly* published *Song of the Negro Boatmen* from Port Royal in February 1862 in which the language tries to approximate the dialect of the local black people. The same issue also included Julia Ward Howe's stirring *Battle Hymn of the Republic.* Howe (1819–1910), a prominent abolitionist, had written the poem the previous November after she visited a Union army camp near Washington. The fiery third stanza is frequently omitted in softened hymnal versions prevalent today.

The Contrabands' Freedom Hymn (1861)

The following curious hymn comes to us from the Secretary of the Young Men's Christian Association, who received it from the Missionary among the contrabands at Fortress Monroe. It will be seen that there is evidence in this hymn that the slaves in a considerable part of Virginia, at least, have had a superstitious faith in being freed some time in the future. The air to which the hymn is

National Anti-Slavery Standard, December 21, 1861: 4.

sung is in the minor key, and very plaintive.

To the Editor of the N.Y. Tribune:

Sir: I this evening received the accompanying song from the Rev. L. C. Lockwood, recently employed by the New York Men's Christian Association in its army work, and at present, laboring under the auspices of the American Missionary Association, among the slaves at Fortress Monroe.

Mr. Lockwood publicly referred to this song

during his late visit to this city, and upon his return to the Fortress took it down *verbatim* from the dictation of Carl Holloway, and other contrabands.

It is said to have been sung for at least fifteen or twenty years in Virginia and Maryland, and perhaps in all the slave States, though stealthily, for fear of the lash; and is now sung openly by the fugitives who are living under the protection of our government, and in the enjoyment of Mr. Lockwood's ministry.

The verses surely were not born from a love of bondage, and show that in a portion, if not in all of the South, the slaves are familiar with the history of the past, and are looking hopefully toward the future.

Yours respectfully,
Harwood Vernon
New York, Dec. 2, 1861

"*Let My People Go*"
A Song of the "Contrabands"

When Israel was in Egypt's land,
O let my people go!
Oppressed so hard they could not stand,
O let my people go!
Chorus—O go down, Moses,
Away down to Egypt's land,
And tell King Pharaoh
To let my people go!

Thus saith the Lord, bold Moses said,
O let my people go!
If not, I'll smite your first-born dead,
O let my people go!

No more shall they in bondage toil,
O let my people go!
Let them come out with Egypt's spoil,
O let my people go!

Then Israel out of Egypt came,
O let my people go!
And left the proud oppressive land,
O let my people go!

O 'twas a dark and dismal night,
O let my people go!

When Moses led the Israelites,
O let my people go!

'Twas good old Moses, and Aaron, too,
O let my people go!
'Twas they that led the armies through,
O let my people go!

The Lord told Moses what to do,
O let my people go!
To lead the children of Israel through,
O let my people go!

O come along Moses, you'll not get lost,
O let my people go!
Stretch out your rod and come across,
O let my people go!

As Israel stood by the water side,
O let my people go!
At the command of God it did divide,
O let my people go!

When they had reached the other shore,
O let my people go!
They sang a song of triumph o'er,
O let my people go!

Pharaoh said he would go across,
O let my people go!
But Pharaoh and his host were lost,
O let my people go!

O Moses, the Lord shall cleave the way,
O let my people go!
A fire by night, a shade by day,
O let my people go!

You'll not get lost in the wilderness,
O let my people go!
With a lighted candle in your breast,
O let my people go!

Jordan shall stand up like a wall,
O let my people go!
And the walls of Jericho shall fall,
O let my people go!

Your foe shall not before you stand,
O let my people go!
And you'll possess fair Canaan's land,
O let my people go!

'Twas just about in harvest time,
O let my people go!
When Joshua led his host Divine,
O let my people go!

O let us all from bondage flee,
O let my people go!
And let us all in Christ be free,
O let my people go!

We need not always weep and mourn,
O let my people go!

And wear these Slavery chains forlorn,
O let my people go!

This world's a wilderness of woe,
O let my people go!
O let us on to Canaan go,
O let my people go!

What a beautiful morning that will be!
O let my people go!
When time breaks up in eternity,
O let my people go!

News Item on the Contrabands' Freedom Hymn (1862)

Among the most interesting of the agencies now employed for the redemption of the slave is Mr. Davis, one of the men called "contrabands," who has come among us from Fortress Monroe, and who addressed a few words to the audience on this occasion[1] It is interesting to hear this intelligent man tell of his earnest longing to read the Bible, of the difficulties he had to surmount in the accomplishment of that object, and of the peace and joy that filled his heart when he was able to spell out the words of Jesus. For years, the sad song of these poor "contrabands" has ascended to the God of the oppressed with its supplicating chorus, "Oh let my people go!" From lowly cabins and rude congregations of the ignorant, year after year, this cry of souls in thraldom has arisen in tones of plaintive music, and the world heard it not. Now, this "Song of the Contrabands" is for sale in the music-stores of Broadway and Washington street.[2] The *nation* hears them now. Let us thank God, and renew our courage, in view of the wondrous changes that have come to pass in these days!

National Anti-Slavery Standard, February 15, 1862: 3.

[1] An anniversary celebration in Music Hall, Boston, on January 22, 1862.

[2] In New York and Boston, respectively.

Song of the Negro Boatmen (1862)

Oh, praise an' tanks! De Lord he come
To set de people free;
An' massa tink it day ob doom,
An' we ob jubilee.
De Lord dat heap de Red Sea waves
He jus' as 'trong as den;

He say de word; we las' night slaves;
To-day, de Lord's freemen.
 De yam will grow, de cotton blow,
 We'll hab de rice an' corn:
 Oh, nebber you fear, if nebber you hear
 De driver blow his horn!

Ole massa on he trabbels gone;
He leab de land behind:

The Atlantic Monthly, February 1862: 245–46.

De Lord's breff blow him furder on,
Like corn-shuck in de wind.
We owe de hoe, we own de plough,
We own de hands dat hold;
We sell de pig, we sell de cow.
But nebber chile be sold.
De yam will grow, de cotton blow,
We'll habe de rice an' corn:
Oh, nebber you fear, if nebber you hear
De driver blow his horn!

We pray de Lord: he gib us signs
Dat some day we be free;
De Norf-wind tell it to de pines,
De wild-duck to de sea;
We tink it when de church-bell ring,
We dream it in de dream;
De rice-bird mean it when he sing,

De eagle when he scream.
De yam will grow, de cotton blow,
We'll hab de rice an' corn:
Oh, nebber you fear, if nebber you hear
De driver blow his horn!

We know de promise nebber fail,
An' nebber lie de word;
So, like de 'postles in de jail,
We waited for de Lord:
An' now he open ebery door,
An' trow away de key;
He tink we lub him so before,
We lub him better free.
De yam will grow, de cotton blow,
He'll gib de rice an' corn:
So nebber you fear, if nebber you hear
De driver blow his horn!

JULIA WARD HOWE

Text of *Battle Hymn of the Republic* (1862)

Mine eyes have seen the glory of the coming of the
Lord:
He is trampling out the vintage where the grapes
of wrath are stored;
He hath loosed the fateful lightning of His terrible
swift sword:
His truth is marching on.

I have seen Him in the watch-fires of a hundred
circling camps;
They have builded Him an altar in the evening
dews and damps;
I have read His righteous sentence by the dim and
flaring lamps:
His day is marching on.

I have read a fiery gospel writ in burnished rows
of steel;

"As ye deal with my contemners, so with you my
grace shall deal;
Let the Hero, born of woman, crush the serpent
with his heel,
Since God is marching on."

He has sounded forth the trumpet that shall never
call retreat;
He is sifting out the hearts of men before His
judgment-seat;
Oh, be swift, my soul, to answer Him! be jubilant
my feet!
Our God is marching on.

In the beauty of the lilies Christ was born across
the sea,
With a glory in His bosom that transfigures you
and me:
As he died to make men holy, let us die to make
men free,
While God is marching on.

National Anti-Slavery Standard, February 1, 1862: [1]; also
The Atlantic Monthly, February 1862: 10.

Voices of Abolition

Anti-slavery publications appeared as early as 1817. Momentum increased as the anti-slavery movement gained strength: the New England Anti-Slavery Society was founded in 1831 and the American Anti-Slavery Society two years later.

Ex-slaves participated in the movement with zeal. William Wells Brown, who, like Frederick Douglass, left written memoirs, also left us *The Anti-Slavery Harp,* a collection of popular anti-slavery song texts first published in Boston in 1848. A well-received anthology, it immediately went through several editions. Suggested tunes came from a repertoire that, it was assumed, everybody knew.

Lucy McKim (1842–1877), a staunch abolitionist, visited Port Royal, off the coast of South Carolina, and wrote to *Dwight's Journal of Music* in 1862 describing what she found there. McKim, who lived a short life, was indoctrinated early into the abolitionist cause; her grandfather's farm was a regular stop on the Underground Railroad. In 1865, she married Wendell Phillips Garrison, the third son of a prominent abolitionist, William Lloyd Garrison. A pianist and teacher, who had also studied the violin, she brought a musician's training to her collecting activities.

Much of what she tells us found its way into the introduction to *Slave Songs of the United States* (1867), the first printed collection of such material. It provides the texts and melodies (without accompaniment) to 136 pieces, grouped by region. McKim, one of three coeditors, collected and edited transcriptions and followed the work through the press.

John Sullivan Dwight published Lucy McKim's letter in *Dwight's Journal of Music* under the title "Songs of the Port Royal 'Contrabands.' " He added a supportive introduction in which he noted that *Poor Rosy* has a melody of "simple and touching pathos, a flavor of individuality which makes one desire to know more of these things."

The other editors of *Slave Songs* were Charles Ware, who provided the largest number of transcriptions, and the scholar of the group, William Francis Allen (1830–1889). Allen, a classicist who was born at Northboro, Massachusetts, and graduated from Harvard College, wrote the preface. After studying in Europe, he settled in Boston, where he embarked on a teaching career. He spent eight months in 1863–64 on St. Helena Island, South Carolina, employed by the Freedman's Aid Commission to teach the freed slaves there.

Two Songs from *The Anti-Slavery Harp* (1854)

Freedom's Banner

Air: Freedom's Banner

My country, shall thy honored name,
Be as a by-word through the world?
Rouse! for, as if to blast thy fame,
This keen reproach is at thee hurled;
The banner that above thee waves,
Is floating over three millions slaves.

That flag, my country, I had thought,
From noble sires was given to thee,
By the best blood of patriots bought,
To wave alone above the Free!
Yet now, while to the breeze it waves,
It floats above three millions slaves.

The mighty dead that flag unrolled,
They bathed it in the heavens' own blue;
They sprinkled stars upon each fold,
And gave it as a trust to you;
And now that glorious banner waves
In shame above three millions slaves.

O, by the virtues of our sires,
And by the soil on which they trod,
And by the trust their name inspires,
And by the hope we have in God,
Arouse, my country, and agree
To set thy captive children free.

Arouse! and let each hill and glen
With prayer to the high heavens ring out,
Till all our land with freeborn men,
May join in one triumphant shout,
That freedom's banner does not wave
Its folds above a single slave!

Flight of the Bondman.
Dedicated to William W. Brown and Sung by the Hutchinsons.
By Elias Smith

Air: Silver Moon

From the crack of the rifle and baying of hound,
Takes the poor panting bondman his flight;
His couch through the day is the cold damp
        ground,
But northward he runs through the night.

Chorus.
O, God speed the flight of the desolate slave,
Let his heart never yield to despair;
There is room 'mong our hills for the true
        and the brave,
Let his lungs breathe our free northern air!

O, sweet to the storm-driven sailor the light,
Streaming far, o'er the dark swelling wave;
But sweeter by far, 'mong the lights of the night,
Is the star of the north to the slave.
        O, God speed, &c.

Cold and bleak are our mountains and chilling
        our winds,
But warm as the soft southern gales
Be the hands and the hearts which the hunted
        one finds,
'Mong our hills and our own winter vales.
        O, God speed, &c.

Then list to the 'plaint of the heart-broken thrall,
Ye blood-hounds, go back to your lair;
May a free northern soil soon give freedom to *all*
Who shall breathe in its pure mountain air.
        O, God speed, &c.

William W. Brown, ed., *The Anti-Slavery Harp*, 4th ed. (Boston: Bela Marsh, 1854), [3–4], 15.

LUCY McKIM

Open Letter to John Sullivan Dwight (1862)

Mr. Dwight,

Sir:—In a recent number of your journal there appeared an article relating to the music of the slaves of Port Royal, taken from an address delivered by my father before the members and friends of the Port Royal Freed-men's Association of this city. The extract included the words of one of their songs, beginning "Poor Rosy, poor gal!"

My chief object in writing to you, is to say, that having accompanied my father on his tour to Port Royal, and being much struck with the songs of its people, I reduced a number of them to paper; among them, the ballad referred to. I send you herewith a copy of it, hoping it may interest you. Whether to have the others printed, is as yet, a question with me.

It is difficult to express the entire character of these negro ballads by mere musical notes and signs. The odd turns made in the throat; and the curious rhythmic effect produced by single voices chiming in at different irregular intervals, seem almost as impossible to place on score, as the singing of birds, or the tones of an Aeolian Harp. The airs, however, can be reached. They are too decided not to be easily understood, and their striking originality would catch the ear of any musician. Besides this, they are valuable as an expression of the character and life of the race which is playing such a conspicuous part in our history. The wild, sad strains tell, as the sufferers themselves never could, of crushed hopes, keen sorrow, and a dull daily misery which covered them as hopelessly as the fog from the rice-swamps. On the other hand, the words breathe a trusting faith in rest in the future—in "Canaan's air and happy land," to which their eyes seem constantly turned.

A complaint might be made against these songs on the score of monotony. It is true there is a great deal of repetition of the music, but that is to ac-

commodate the *leader*, who, if he be a good one, is always an improvisator. For instance, on one occasion, the name of each of our party who was present, was dexterously introduced.

As the same songs are sung at every sort of work, of course the *tempo* is not always alike. On the water, the oars dip "Poor Rosy" to an even andante; a stout boy and girl at the hominy-mill will make the same "Poor Rosy" fly, to keep up with the whirling stone; and in the evening, after the day's work is done, "Heab'n shall-a be my home" peals up slowly and mournfully from the distant quarters. One woman,—a respectable house-servant, who had lost all but one of her twenty-two children, said to me:

"Pshaw! dont har to dese yer chil'en, misse. Dey just rattles it off,—dey dont know how for sing it. I likes "Poor Rosy" better dan all de songs, but it cant be sung widout *a full heart and a troubled sperrit!*"

All the songs make good barcaroles. Whittier "builded better than he knew" when he wrote his "Song of the Negro Boatman." It seemed wonderfully applicable as we were being rowed across Hilton Head Harbor among United States gunboats,—the Wabash and the Vermont towering on either side. I thought the crew *must* strike up

"And massa tink it day ob doom,
And we ob jubilee."

Perhaps the *grandest* singing we heard was at the Baptist Church on St. Helena Island, when a congregation of three hundred men and women joined in a hymn—

"Roll, Jordan, roll, Jordan!
Roll, Jordan, roll!"

It swelled forth like a triumphal anthem. That same hymn was sung by thousands of negroes on the 4th. of July last, when they marched in procession under the Stars and Stripes, cheering them for

Dwight's Journal of Music, November 8, 1862: 254–55.

the first time as the "flag of *our* country." A friend writing from there, says that the chorus was indescribably grand,—"that the whole woods and world seemed joining in that rolling sound."

There is much more in this new and curious music, of which it is a temptation to write, but I must remember that it can speak for itself better than any one for it.

Very respectfully,
Lucy McKim

WILLIAM FRANCIS ALLEN

from *Slave Songs of the United States* (1867)

Introduction

The musical capacity of the negro race has been recognized for so many years that it is hard to explain why no systematic effort has hitherto been made to collect and preserve their melodies. More than thirty years ago those plantation songs made their appearance which were so extraordinarily popular for a while; and if "Coal-black Rose," "Zip Coon" and "Ole Virginny nebber tire" have been succeeded by spurious imitations, manufactured to suit the somewhat sentimental taste of our community, the fact that these were called "negro melodies" was itself a tribute to the musical genius of the race.[1]

The public had well-nigh forgotten these genuine slave songs, and with them the creative power from which they sprung, when a fresh interest was excited through the educational mission to the Port Royal islands, in 1861. The agents of this mission were not long in discovering the rich vein of music that existed in these half-barbarous people, and when visitors from the North were on the islands, there was nothing that seemed better worth their while than to see a "shout" or hear the "people" sing their "sperichils." A few of these last, of special merit, soon became established favorites among the whites, and hardly a Sunday passed at the church on St. Helena without "Gabriel's Trumpet," "I hear from Heaven to-day," or "Jehovah Hallelujah." The last time I myself heard these was at the Fourth of July celebration, at the church, in 1864. All of them were sung, and then the glorious shout, "I can't stay behind, my Lord," was struck up, and sung by the entire multitude with a zest and spirit, a swaying of the bodies and nodding of the heads and lighting of the countenances and rhythmical movement of the hands, which I think no one present will ever forget.

Attention was, I believe, first publicly directed to these songs in a letter from Miss McKim, of Philadelphia, to *Dwight's Journal of Music*, Nov. 8, 1862, from which some extracts will presently be given. At about the same time, Miss McKim arranged and published two of them, "Roll, Jordan" (No. 1) and "Poor Rosy" (No. 8 [i.e., 9])—probably on all accounts the two best specimens that could be selected.

* * *

The best that we can do, however, with paper and types, or even with voices, will convey but a faint shadow of the original. The voices of the colored people have a peculiar quality that nothing can imitate; and the intonations and delicate variations of even one singer cannot be reproduced on paper. And I despair of conveying any notion of the effect of a number singing together, especially in a complicated shout, like "I can't stay behind, my Lord" (No. 8), or "Turn, sinner, turn O!"

William Francis Allen, Charles Pickard Ware, and Lucy McKim Garrison, eds., *Slaves Songs of the United States* (New York, 1867) [i]–ii, iv–vi, xxi–xxiii, 1, 7.

[1] It is not generally known that the beautiful air "Long time ago," or "Near the lake where drooped the willow," was borrowed from the negroes, by whom it was sung to words beginning, "Way down in Raccoon Hollow" [Allen's note].

(No. 48). There is no singing in *parts* as we understand it[2] and yet no two appear to be singing the same thing—the leading singer starts the words of each verse, often improvising, and the others, who "base" him, as it is called, strike in with the refrain, or even join in the solo, when the words are familiar. When the "base" begins, the leader often stops, leaving the rest of his words to be guessed at, or it may be they are taken up by one of the other singers. And the "basers" themselves seem to follow their own whims, beginning when they please and leaving off when they please, striking an octave above or below (in case they have pitched the tune too low or too high), or hitting some other note that chords, so as to produce the effect of a marvelous complication and variety, and yet with the most perfect time, and rarely with any discord. And what makes it all the harder to unravel a thread of melody out of this strange network is that, like birds, they seem not infrequently to strike sounds that cannot be precisely represented by the gamut, and abound in "slides from one note to another, and turns and cadences not in articulated notes." "It is difficult," writes Miss McKim, "to express the entire character of these negro ballads by mere musical notes and signs. . . . "

*   *   *

As the negroes have no part-singing, we have thought it best to print only the melody; what appears in some places as harmony is really variations in single notes. And in general, a succession of such notes turned in the same direction indicates a single longer variation. . . . In repeating, it may be observed that the custom at Port Royal is to repeat the first part of the tune over and over, it may be a dozen times, before passing to the "turn," and then to do the same with that. In the Virginia songs, on the other hand, the chorus is usually sung twice after each verse—often the second time with some such interjaculatory expression as "I say now," "God say you must," as given in No. 99.[3]

We had some thought of indicating with each the *tempo* of the different songs, but have concluded to print special directions for singing by themselves. It should be remarked, however, that the same tune varied in quickness on different occasions. . . .

The rests, by the way, do not indicate a cessation in the music, but only in part of the singers. They overlap in singing, as already described, in such a degree that at no time is there any complete pause. In "A House in Paradise" (No. 40) this overlapping is most marked.

It will be noticed that we have spoken chiefly of the negroes of the Port Royal islands, where most of our observations were made, and most of our materials collected. The remarks upon the dialect which follow have reference solely to these islands, and indeed almost exclusively to a few plantations at the northern end of St. Helena Island.

*   *   *

1. *Roll, Jordan, Roll*

1.

My brudder[4] sittin' on de tree of life,
An' he yearde when Jordan roll;
    Roll, Jordan,
    Roll, Jordan,
    Roll, Jordan, roll!

O march de angel march,
O march de angel march;
O my soul arise in Heaven, Lord,
For to yearde when Jordan roll.

---

[2]"The high voices, all in unison, and the admirable time and true accent with which their responses are made, always make me wish that some great musical composer could hear these semi-savage performances. With a very little skilful adaptation and instrumentation, I think one or two barbaric chants and choruses might be evoked from them that would make the fortune of an opera."—*Mrs. Kemble's 'Life on a Georgia Plantation,* p. 218 [Allen's note].

---

[3]*Let God's Saints Come In.*

[4]Parson Fuller, Deacon Haunch, Rudder Mosey, Massa Linkup, &c. [Authors' note; alternative wordings for "My brudder."]

2.

Little chil'en, learn to fear de Lord,
And let your days be long;
    Roll, Jordan, &c.

3.

O, let no false nor spiteful word
Be found upon your tongue;
    Roll, Jordan, &c.

This spiritual probably extends from South Carolina to Florida, and is one of the best known and noblest of the songs.

9. *Poor Rosy*

1.

Poor Rosy, poor gal;[5]
Poor Rosy, poor gal;
Rosy break my poor heart,
Heav'n shall-a be my home.

I cannot stay in hell one day,
Heav'n shall-a be my home;
I'll sing and pray my soul away,
Heav'n shall-a be my home.

2.

Got hard trial in my way,
Heav'n shall-a-be my home.
O when I talk, I talk[6] wid God,
Heav'n shall-a be my home.

3.

I dunno what de people[7] want of me,
Heav'n shall-a be my home.

This song ranks with "Roll, Jordan," in dignity and favor. The following variation of the second part was heard at "The Oaks":

Before I stay in hell one day,
Heaven shall-a be my home;
I sing and pray my soul away,
Heaven shall-a be my home.

---

[5]Poor Caeser, poor boy. [Authors' note.]

[6]Walk. [Authors' note.]

[7]Massa. [Authors' note.]

53   Rallying 'round the Flag: Songs of the Civil War

Our wars have defined us as a people, and for many, the Civil War became the defining period in their lives.

The vast song and instrumental literature of the Civil War period testifies to heroism in the field, fear of battle, bravery in facing death, thoughts of mother, and, on the home front, stoicism, devotion, and fears for those who have gone to fight in the war. In both the North and the South, music reflected the age in a unique way, providing a catharsis for the expression of basic human needs and desires.

Several decades after the war, the publishing house of S. Brainard's Sons in Cleveland brought out two collections of war songs. Although these anthologies arose out of nostalgia and remembrance, they reflected the passionate involvement of many who could still relive the experience.

In their discussion of specific songs in the introduction to *Our War Songs North and South* (1887), the editors focus on George F. Root's *Battle-Cry of Freedom*, describing its considerable effect on the populace (see No. 24, above).

Brainard's introduction also discusses *All Quiet along the Potomac To-night,* set by John Hill Hewitt to a poem by Ethel Lynn Beers. A caustic anti-war song, it refers to frequent press reports that all was well, despite the death of a lowly picket. *Maryland, My Maryland,* which the introduction mentions as well, was one of the earliest and best known songs to come out of the war. Its Southern text, written by James Ryder Randall, a professor of English from Baltimore then living in New Orleans, was sung to the tune of the German Christmas song *O Tannenbaum* (*O Christmas Tree*). The linkage of text and tune sparked some tongue-in-cheek comments in the *Cleveland Morning Leader* of September 26, 1862, attesting to the song's immense popularity:

> Everywhere in the mouldering old towns, from secluded houses, where dwelt fiery eyed dainty ladies, who say do' for door, and hi-ar for here, can be heard "Maryland, My Maryland," as though that unfortunate triangular bit of country needed especial compassion at their hands for not being a part of the Confederacy. . . . It is a great pity that a respectable tune, a tune to which so many fine scholars have got drunk in their day, should be impressed into so base a service.

The anonymous *Our Maryland* is a Northern parody of the song.

S. BRAINARD'S SONS
from *Our War Songs North and South* (1887)

The heated guns have ceased to belch forth their deadly fires; the civil war has long since ended; its wounds are healed, and every humane and patriotic heart hopes that never again will our country be engaged in fratricidal strife. The men that stood bravely side by side in many a heated contest, the comrades who have tented and messed and marched together, are all employed in peaceful avocations, and only the recollections of the terrible scenes and sufferings of "red-handed war" remain.

But when the boys in blue and the boys in gray meet at their frequent gatherings and talk over old scenes and events, there is always some one to call out, "Give us a song," and someone to respond, and the old war strains are sung with the same ardor as they were a quarter of a century ago, when the whole country was a vast camp of soldiers, eager "to do or die" for their countries and their flags.

How the people sang in those days, the people North as well as South, and what an immense stock of songs, with reference to the war, were called into existence! Music always was and always will be a great factor in National life and National warfare. . . .

The war was a fruitful theme for young poetic aspirants, and while under ordinary circumstances their productions would not have attracted attention, they were given places in our daily papers, and not unfrequently they were set to music by those gifted with the power of song. Though they often were mere doggerel, they were eagerly read, for the public never grew weary of reading concerning its own struggles, nor was it in the least particular as to the poetic nature of these patriotic and often very fiery effusions. If the lines contained a happy hit or two, if they were calculated to arouse sentiment, if they had a good jingle, the verses were usually welcomed and sometimes even enjoyed a temporary popularity.

Pianists were not forgotten. They were supplied with battle pieces, musical compositions designed to glorify the Nation's victories. Between the lines one could read the story of the advance, and the meeting of the armies. The sound of the first gun was distinctly heard, then came the rattle of the musketry and the firing of the cannon. The cries of the wounded of course were not to be forgotten, and finally was heard the shout of victory, and all this was to be pictured upon a piano! The Southern composer ended his battle pieces with "Dixie" or the "Bonnie Blue Flag," while he of the North very appropriately closed with the "Star Spangled Banner" and "Yankee Doodle."

It was but natural that at the time when the war-cry was heard throughout the land, such music should please best, for was not every heart engaged in the contest; were there not members of almost every household in the far-off camp, and were there not many empty sleeves and vacant chairs? When playing these pieces and singing these songs the heart poured out its love as much for the loved ones actively engaged in the contest, or for those resting in death, as for the cause itself. . . .

Mr. Root's most famous war song is the "Battle-Cry of Freedom." It became popular early in the war, and enjoyed its popularity over all other songs during that weary and hot contest. It was written in 1861, and its popularity originated at a public meeting held in Union Square, New York City, in the same year. It was sung on that occasion by the Hutchinson family, and struck fire, so to speak. It became at once a popular favorite, for its effect upon the masses was simply electrifying. The song was, on that memorial occasion, repeatedly called for, and the refrain being easily learned, the masses chimed in, fairly singing themselves hoarse.

Our War Songs North and South (Cleveland: S. Brainard's Sons, 1887), [5]–7, 10–11.

From that hour the "Battle-Cry of Freedom" was and remained the rallying song of the North. It was known by all soldiers and was heard in all the camps where the star spangled banner floated. Says a writer: "During the terrible Battle of the Wilderness on the 6th of May, 1864, a brigade of the Ninth Corps, having broken the enemy's line by an assault, became exposed to a flank attack, and was driven back in disorder with heavy loss. They retreated but a few hundred yards, however, reformed, and again confronted the enemy. Just then some gallant fellow in the ranks of the 45th Pennsylvania began to sing:

"We'll rally round the flag, boys,
Rally once again,
Shouting the Battle-Cry of Freedom."

The refrain was caught up instantly by the entire regiment and also by the 36th Massachusetts, next in line. There the grim ranks stood at bay in the deadly thicket. The air was filled with the crackle and smoke of the burning underbrush, the pitiful cries of the wounded, the battle of musketry and the shouts of command were heard, but above all, answering the exalted yells of the enemy, rose the inspiring chorus:

"The Union forever, hurrah boys, hurrah,
Down with the traitor, up with the star!
And we'll rally round the flag, boys,
Rally once again,
Shouting the Battle-Cry of Freedom!"

This is simply one instance to show what a power this song exerted in the army. . . .

It is a very strange fact, that while the two contesting sections of the country were so far apart in their sentiment, that there should be a song, the authorship of which is claimed on both sides. This song is entitled "All Quiet on the Potomac." For many a weary month the troops laid on the banks of this river. While there were no advances made, a good many brave boys were shot down on the picket post. Every day the newspapers came with these head lines: "All Quiet on the Potomac," until at last the expression became a by-word. . . .

One of the best liked Southern songs was "My Maryland." The words were produced by James Ryder Randall, of Baltimore. He was educated at Georgetown College, D. C., and when quite young went to Louisiana to edit a paper. It was in New Orleans in 1861 that he wrote this song, the object of which was to appeal to Maryland to join the Southern cause. The tune is an old German student melody, known as "O Pine Tree." This song was very popular throughout the South, and so pleasing was the melody that many people in the North even sung it perhaps, without knowing its meaning. Said a soldier: "We remember hearing it sung under circumstances that for the time made us fancy it was the sweetest song we ever listened to. Our command had just reached Frederick City, Md., after a distressing forced march, and going into bivouac the staff to which we were attached took up their quarters on the piazza of a lonely mansion, and there wrapping themselves in their blankets, with their saddles for pillows, sought needed repose. Sleep would not come to our eyelids. The night was a delicious one, it was warm, but a slight breeze was stirring, the sky was clear and the stars shone brilliantly. The stillness was profound, everyone around us was asleep, when suddenly there fell upon our ears the song 'The tyrant's heel is on thy neck, Maryland, my Maryland.' The voice was a mezzo-soprano, full, round and clear, and the charming melody was sung with infinite tenderness and delicacy of shading. We listened almost breathlessly for it was the first time we had heard the song, and as it was ended we arose for the purpose of ascertaining who it was that sang so sweetly. "We found her," said the soldier, "in the person of a plump negro girl of about sixteen years, with a face blacker than the smoke in Vulcan's smithy."[1]

---

[1]Vulcan was the Roman God of fire and metalworking.

ETHEL LYNN BEERS

Text of *All Quiet along the Potomac To-night* (1863)

"All quiet along the Potomac to-night,"
    Except here and there a stray picket
Is shot, as he walks on his beat to and fro,
    By a rifleman hid in the thicket;
'Tis nothing! a private or two now and then,
    Will not count in the news of the battle,
Not an officer lost! only one of the men
    Moaning out all alone the death rattle.
"All quiet along the Potomac to-night!"

"All quiet along the Potomac to-night,"
    Where the soldiers lie peacefully dreaming,
And their tents in the rays of the clear autumn
    moon,
    And the light of the camp fires are gleaming;
There's only the sound of the lone sentry's tread,
    As he tramps from the rock to the fountain,
And thinks of the two on the low trundle bed
    Far away in the cot on the mountain.

His musket falls slack—his face, dark and grim,
    Grows gentle with memories tender,
As he mutters a prayer for the children asleep,
    And their mother—"may Heaven defend her."
The moon seems to shine as brightly as then—
    That night, when the love yet unspoken
Leap'd to his lips, and when low murmur'd vows
    Were pledg'd, to be ever unbroken.

Then drawing his sleeve roughly over his eyes,
    He dashes off the tears that are welling,
And gathers his gun close up to his breast,
    As if to keep down his heart's swelling;
He passes the fountain, the blasted pine tree,
    And his footstep is lagging and weary,
Yet onward he goes, thro' the broad belt of light,
    Toward the shades of the forest so dreary.

Hark! was it the night-wind that rustles the leaves!
    Was it the moonlight so wond'rously flashing?
It looked like a rifle! "Ha! Mary good-bye!"
    And his life-blood is ebbing and plashing.
"All quiet along the Potomac to-night,"
    No sound save the rush of the river;
While soft falls the dew on the face of the dead,
    "The Picket's" off duty for ever.

Ethel Lynn Beers, *All Quiet along the Potomac To-night* (Baltimore: Miller & Beacham, 1863).

JAMES RYDER RANDALL

Text of *Maryland, My Maryland* (1861)

The despot's heel is on thy shore,
    Maryland, My Maryland!
His touch is at thy temple door,
    Maryland, My Maryland!
Avenge the patriotic gore
That fleck'd the streets of Baltimore,
And be the Battle-Queen of yore,
    Maryland! My Maryland!

Hark to a wand'ring Son's appeal!
    Maryland, My Maryland!
My Mother State! to thee I kneel,
    Maryland, My Maryland!
For life or death, for woe or weal,
Thy peerless chivalry reveal,
And gird thy beauteous limbs with steel,
    Maryland, My Maryland!

James Ryder Randall, *Maryland, My Maryland!* (Baltimore: Miller & Beacham, 1861).

Thou wilt not cower in the dust,
  Maryland! My Maryland!
Thy beaming sword shall never rust,
  Maryland! My Maryland!
Remember Carroll's sacred trust.
Remember Howard's warlike thrust—
And all thy slumberers with the just,
  Maryland! My Maryland!

Come! for thy shield is bright and strong,
  Maryland! My Maryland!
Come! for thy dalliance, does thee wrong,
  Maryland! My Maryland!
Come! to thine own heroic throng,
That stalks with Liberty along,
And give a new <u>Key</u> to thy song,
  Maryland! My Maryland!

Dear Mother! burst the tyrant's chain,
  Maryland! My Maryland!
Virginia should not call in vain!
  Maryland! My Maryland!
She meets her sisters on the plain—
"Sic semper" tis the proud refrain,
That baffles minions back amain,
  Maryland! My Maryland!

I see the blush upon thy cheek,
  Maryland! My Maryland!
But thou wast ever bravely meek,
  Maryland! My Maryland!
But lo! there surges forth a shriek,
From hill to hill, from creek to creek—
Potomac calls to Chesapeake,
  Maryland! My Maryland!

Thou wilt not yield the vandal toll,
  Maryland! My Maryland!
Thou wilt not crook to his control,
  Maryland! My Maryland!
Better the fire upon the roll,
Better the blade, the shot, the bowl,
Than crucifixion of the soul,
  Maryland! My Maryland!

I hear the distant thunder-hum,
  Maryland! My Maryland!
The Old Line's bugle, fife, and drum,
  Maryland! My Maryland!
She is not dead, nor deaf, nor dumb—
Huzza! she spurns the Northern scum!
She breathes—she burns! she'll come! she'll come!
  Maryland! My Maryland!

ANONYMOUS

Text of *Our Maryland* (c. 1862)

The rebel thieves were sure of thee,
  Maryland! our Maryland!
And boasted they would welcome be,
  Maryland! our Maryland!
But now they turn and now they flee,
With Stonewall Jackson and with Lee
And loyal souls once more are free!
  Maryland! our Maryland!

With plundered guns and stolen swords,
  Maryland! our Maryland!

Beadle's Dime Knapsack Songster (New York: Beadle & Co.,
1862?), 52.

On thee they came in ruffian hordes,
  Maryland! our Maryland!
With raving oaths and roaring words,
And pirates' knives and hangmen's cords,
They swarmed across the border fords,
  Maryland! our Maryland!

Through passways of the mountain crags,
  Maryland! our Maryland!
They bore their vile secession flags,
  Maryland! our Maryland!
Like beggar troops, in filthy rags,
Barefooted men and spavined nags,
Their voices hoarse with Southern brags,
  Maryland! our Maryland!

Like dogs all raving for a crumb,
  Maryland! our Maryland!
They madly rushed for bread and rum,
  Maryland! our Maryland!

But backward ran, with voices dumb,
  And drooping hands, and faces glum,
They ran from Union's rolling drum,
  Maryland! our Maryland!

Music Afloat

Music and the military have been affiliated in America since the seventeenth century. Fifes and snare drums provided marching cadences for both European and Colonial troops for decades. In the late eighteenth century, regimental bands gave town concerts, and European-style wind bands, consisting of paired oboes, bassoons, clarinets, and horns, were also prominent in the early Federal period, playing marches, dances, patriotic songs, and operatic and other airs.

The presence of military bands was hardly unusual in the early years of the United States, but these ensembles were not the awe-inspiring legions they became in the twentieth century. Growth and change in the manner of producing loud, attention-getting sounds was gradual. More durable and chromatically capable brass instruments supplemented or replaced some of the traditional woodwinds in the 1830s. And despite a decrease in the number of players assigned to an "official" United States army band between the 1780s and the 1830s, by the time of the Civil War, the Union Army maintained five hundred bands comprising some nine thousand players. Confederate forces probably had a comparable number of musicians, at least in 1861 and 1862, generally allowing up to sixteen privates to serve as musicians besides the "chief musician" in a single company.

Although soldiers' diaries and postwar accounts occasionally mention music, they rarely stress it, suggesting that while band music was not lacking, its presence was taken for granted on the field and aboard ship. In addition to providing the traditional support for marching, dancing, and periods of conviviality, bands could at times be used to send other messages, as we learn in Raphael Semmes's detailed account of his experiences as an admiral "of the late Confederate states navy," published in 1869. Far more than a mere nautical report, Semmes's 833 pages form an extended memoir, discussing such wide-ranging topics as the institution of slavery, the formation of the Confederate government, the international voyages of his ships, and the details of sieges, attacks, and blockades.

Semmes's account seems trustworthy, and some of his observations are borne out by other, separate sources. For example, he notes that seamen designated who would take the female role in dances by tying banners or scarves around their waists. A similar story in William Beven's 1861 Confederate army diary reports, "We also gave dances, and tied handkerchiefs on the arms of the smallest boys to take the part of ladies in square dances." Semmes, in contrast to other writers, provides details about instruments, popular dance names, and the placement of activities on the ship. Although he published his narrative some years after the war, the precision of his storytelling (based on diaries from the time) and his wit make his tale vivid and immediate.

—Thomas L. Riis

RAPHAEL SEMMES

from *Memoirs of Service Afloat during the War between the States* (1869)

But though I took good care to see that my men had plenty of employment, it was not all work with them. They had their pastimes and pleasures, as well as labors. After the duties of the day were over, they would generally assemble on the forecastle, and, with violin and tambourine—and I always kept them supplied with these and other musical instruments—they would extemporize a ball-room, by moving the shot-racks, coils of rope, and other impediments, out of the way, and, with handkerchiefs tied around the waists of some of them, to indicate who were to be the ladies of the party, they would get up a dance with all due form and ceremony; the ladies, in particular, endeavoring to imitate all the airs and graces of the sex—the only drawback being a little hoarseness of the voice, and now and then the use of an expletive, which would escape them when something went wrong in the dance, and they forgot they had the aprons on. The favorite dancing tunes were those of Wapping and Wide Water Street,[1] and when I speak of the airs and graces, I must be understood to mean those rather demonstrative airs and graces, of which Poll and Peggy would be likely to be mistresses of.[2] On these occasions, the discipline of the ship was wont to be purposely relaxed, and roars of laughter, and other evidences of the rapid flight of the jocund hours, at other times entirely inadmissible, would come resounding aft on the quarter-deck.

Sometimes the recreation of the dance would be varied, and songs and story telling would be the amusements of the evening. . . .

Among the amusing things that had occurred during my absence in the Jamaica mountains, was a flare-up, which Captain Blake, my prisoner, had had with the British Commodore.

The steamer *Greyhound* had a band of music on board, and as one of the young lieutenants was an old acquaintance of several of my officers, whom he had met at Nassau, he ordered the band on the evening after our arrival, and whilst Captain Blake was still on board the *Alabama*, to play "Dixie;" which, I may remark, by the way, had become a very popular air everywhere, as much on account of the air itself, perhaps, as because of its association with a weak and gallant people struggling for the right of self-government. Captain Blake chose to construe this little compliment to the *Alabama*, as an insult to Yankeedom, and made a formal protest to the British Commodore, in behalf of himself, and the "old flag." Commodore Dunlap must have smiled, when he read Blake's epistle. He was certainly a man of humor, for he hit upon the following mode of settling the grave international dispute. He ordered the offending *Greyhound*, when she should get up her band, on the following evening, first to play "Dixie," and then "Yankee Doodle."

When the evening, which was to salve the Yankee honor, arrived, great was the expectation of every one in the squadron. The band on board the *Jason*, flag-ship, led off by playing "God save the Queen," that glorious national anthem, which electrifies the Englishman, as the Marseilles' hymn does the Frenchman, the world over. The *Challenger*'s band followed and played a fine opera air. The evening was still and fine, and the poops of all the ships were filled with officers. It then came the *Greyhound*'s turn. She first played something un-

---

Raphael Semmes, *Memoirs of Service Afloat during the War between the States* (Baltimore: Kelly, Piet, 1869) 453–54, 461–62.

[1]Wapping was an unsavory London district, a "sailors'" district, filled with taverns and, presumably, brothels.

[2]"Poll" and "Peggy" probably suggest "loose" women given to obvious, broad, and flamboyant gestures, rather than the typically restrained "airs and graces" of ladies and gentlemen; in other words, the sailors were pretty wild party animals, according to Symmes.

usually solemn, then "Dixie" with slowness, sweetness, and pathos, and when the chorus

"In Dixie's land, I'll take my stand,
I'll live, and die in Dixie!"

had died away on the soft evening air, such an infernal dim, of drums, and fifes, and cymbals, and wind instruments, each after its fashion, going it strong upon

"Yankee Doodle Dandy!"

arose, as to defy all description! The effect was electric; the officers had to hold their sides to preserve their dignity, and—Captain Blake was avenged. There could be no protest made against this time-honored rogue's march. It was the favorite tune of the b'hoys,[3] and there the matter had to end. I have never learned whether Mr. Seward ever called Lord Palmerston to an account about it, in any one of his "Essays on English Composition."[4]

---

[3] A contraction of "bo-hoys," a mid-nineteenth century American dialect spelling for boys, presumably intended here as both patronizing and affectionate.

[4] William Henry Seward (1801–1872) was the secretary of state under Lincoln, who negotiated with the British prime minister and foreign affairs expert Lord Palmerston over the damages inflicted to Union shipping by Semmes's vessel, *Alabama*, which had been built, outfitted, and protected by the British. Reference to his "Essays" would seem to be a punning allusion to Seward's diplomatic notes to Palmerston.

55   James M. Trotter and the Music of Black Americans

James Monroe Trotter (1842–1892), an African American, wrote *Music and Some Highly Musical People* (1878), the first general survey of African-American music. Trotter offers chapters on the music of nature, the history of music from the beginning of time until his day, and the beauty, power, and uses of music, as well as chapters on the Colored American Opera Company, the Fisk Jubilee Singers, and the Georgia Minstrels. More black musicians are discussed in the second part of the book, along with musical activities in principal cities. The work includes the music for compositions by twelve composers.

Trotter himself was born at Grand Gulf, Mississippi, studied music in Cincinnati, Ohio, and took a teaching position in that state. Following a tour of duty in the Civil War, he worked at the Boston post office for thirteen years, during which time he published his book. He reached the pinnacle of his career when President Grover Cleveland appointed him recorder of deeds in Washington, then the highest federal position to which an African American might aspire.

The first excerpt from Trotter's book deals with the Jubilee Singers, who toured to raise money for Fisk University, a fledgling institution for black Americans. Fisk University, in Nashville, Tennessee, opened its doors in 1866, just two years after the close of the Civil War. The Jubilee Singers brought a new kind of music, "slave spirituals," before the American public and eventually to Europe as well. They were one of the choirs that participated in Patrick Gilmore's World Peace Jubilee held in Boston in 1872.

The second excerpt from Trotter's book concerns Francis "Frank" Johnson (1792–1844), the first African-American musician to win wide acclaim in the United States and in England. He was first to publish sheet music (1818), to develop a "school" of black musicians, to give formal band concerts, to tour widely, to appear in integrated concerts with white musicians, to take an American musical ensemble abroad to perform in Europe, and to introduce the promenade concert to the United States.

JAMES M. TROTTER

from *Music and Some Highly Musical People* (1881)

The Famous Jubilee Singers of Fisk University

Among the organizations (I cannot mention individual names: their number is too great) that early sought to build up the waste places of the South, and to carry there a higher religion and a much-needed education, was the American Missionary Association. This society has led all others in this greatly benevolent work, having reared no less than seven colleges and normal schools in various centres of the South. The work of education to be done there is vast, certainly; but what a very flood of light will these institutions throw over that land so long involved in moral and intellectual darkness!

The principal one of these schools is Fisk University, located at Nashville, Tenn.; the mention of which brings us to the immediate consideration of the famous "*Jubilee Singers*," and to perhaps the most picturesque achievement in all our history since the war. Indeed, I do not believe that anywhere in the history of the world can there be found an achievement like that made by these singers; for the institution just named, which has cost thus far nearly a hundred thousand dollars, has been built by the money which these former bond-people have earned since 1871 in an American and European campaign of song.

But what was the germ from which grew this remarkable concert-tour, and its splendid sequence, the noble Fisk University?

Shortly after the close of the war, a number of philanthropic persons from the North gathered into an old government-building that had been used for storage purposes, a number of freed children and some grown persons living in and near Nashville, and formed a school. This school, at first under the direction of Professor Ogden,[1] was ere long taken under the care of the American Missionary Association. The number of pupils rapidly increasing, it was soon found that better facilities for instruction were required. It was therefore decided to take steps to erect a better, a more permanent building than the one then occupied. Just how this was to be done, was, for a while, quite a knotty problem with this enterprising little band of teachers. Its solution was attempted finally by one of their number, Mr. George L. White[2] in this wise: he had often been struck with the charming melody of the "slave songs" that he had heard sung by the children of the school; had, moreover, been the director of several concerts given by them with much musical and financial success at Nashville and vicinity. Believing that these songs, so peculiarly beautiful and heart-touching, sung as they were by these scholars with such naturalness of manner and sweetness of voice, would fall with delightful novelty upon Northern ears, Mr. White conceived the idea of taking a company of the students on a concert-tour over the country, in order to thus obtain sufficient funds to build a college. This was a bold idea, seemingly visionary; but the sequel proved that it was a most practical one.

All arrangements were completed; and the Jubilee Singers, as they were called, left Nashville in the fall of 1871 for a concert-tour of the Northern States, to accomplish the worthy object just mentioned. Professor White, who was an educated and skilful musician, accompanied them as musical director. . . .

The songs they sang were generally of a religious character,—"slave *spirituals*,"—and such as have been sung by the American bondmen in the cruel days of the past. These had originated with the slave; had sprung spontaneously, so to speak, from souls naturally musical; and formed, as one eminent writer puts it, "*the only native American music.*"

James M. Trotter, *Music and Some Highly Musical People* (Boston: Lee and Shepard, 1881), 255–58, 306–8.

[1]John Ogden, Fisk's administrator.

[2]A young white teacher at the school.

The strange, weird melody of these songs, which burst upon the Northern States, and parts of Europe, as a revelation in vocal music, as a music most thrillingly sweet and soul-touching, sprang then, strange to say, from a state of slavery; and the habitually minor character of its tones may well be ascribed to the depression of feeling, the anguish, that must ever fill the hearts of those who are forced to lead a life so fraught with woe.

*   *   *

Frank Johnson

This city[3] enjoys the honor of having been the home of *Mr. Frank Johnson*, and the place of organization of the celebrated brass band that bore his name. It has been the intention of the writer to give a somewhat extended sketch in this book of this famous impresario and his talented body of performers; but as yet he has not succeeded in obtaining the necessary materials. He will mention, however, briefly, that Mr. Johnson was a well-educated musician, very talented and enthusiastic, with fine powers for organization and leadership. He was exceedingly skilful as a performer on the bugle. In his hand the instrument

"Became a trumpet, whence he blew
Soul-animating strains: alas! too few."

Besides, he played well several other instruments. He was very much esteemed, and was foremost in promoting in many ways the musical spirit: he was, in fact, the P. S. Gilmore of his day. His band attracted much attention all over the country for fine martial music.

Some time between the years 1839 and 1841 Mr. Johnson organized a select orchestra, with which he visited several of the principal cities of the country, "astonishing the natives" by a fine rendering of the best music in vogue at that time. Indeed, the novelty formed by such an organization,—all colored men,—its excellent playing, and the boldness of the enterprise, all combined to create a decided sensation wherever these sable troubadours appeared. It is said that sometimes, while the band was on this tour, many persons would doubt the ability of its members to read the music they were playing, believing that they performed "by ear," as it is called; nor could such persons be convinced of their error until a new piece of music—a piece not previously seen by them—was placed before the band, and by the same readily rendered from the printed page.

Mr. Johnson at one time visited England with his band, and gave concerts in all the principal cities, being received everywhere with the most demonstrative marks of favor. They were invited to play before Queen Victoria and her court. This noble-hearted sovereign was so highly pleased with the musical ability displayed by Mr. Johnson and the other members of the band, that she caused a handsome silver bugle to be presented to him in her name. Returning to this country with such a noble-won mark of honor, he became the centre of attraction, and thereafter, as a musician, easily maintained before the country a position of great popularity. At his funeral, which occurred in 1846 [i.e., 1844], the bugle just alluded to was placed upon the coffin, and so borne to the grave, as a fitting emblem of one of the important victories he had won, as well as of the music-loving life he had led.

The memory of this gifted musician and indefatigable worker should long be kept green in the hearts of all the members of his race, and in those of his countrymen in general. For the former he of course performed a specially noble service in demonstrating so powerfully its capability for musical comprehension and for the scientific performance of music,—points which, strange to say, were much in dispute when he began his career; while in his well-nigh matchless ability as a musician, displayed in no selfish manner, but in a way that promoted in a high degree a general love for the elevating art of music, Frank Johnson proved himself an honor to the whole country, and one who should be long and gratefully remembered by all.

The band continued in existence, and was much in demand, for many years after the great leader died, retaining its old and honorable name, "Frank Johnson's Band."

---

[3]Philadelphia.

56   Spirituals after the War: Improvising Troubles into Art Forms

After the appearance of *Slave Songs of the United States* in 1867, more collectors, folklorists, and audiences began to show a respectful and lively interest in the performance of spirituals. But the fears of commercial exploitation expressed by the *Slave Songs* singers proved to be justified. After the success of the Fisk University students, "Jubilee Singers" groups sprang up everywhere. George L. White, the director of the Fisk group, personally encouraged the Hampton Institute, another post–Civil War college established to benefit freed slaves, to copy Fisk's example. Accordingly, Hampton became a school that was built, like Fisk, on profits flowing from performances of African-American sacred music, choral versions of songs similar to those collected by Allen, Ware, and Garrison.

By the time R. Nathaniel Dett (1882–1943) came to direct the choir at Hampton in 1913, African-American spirituals in some form had been heard throughout the world, even in the large cities of Asia and the Pacific Islands, and, of course, in Europe and America. The Fisk Jubilee Singers had performed before English and German royalty, and the Hampton students would soon sing at the White House for the president of the United States. As a second-generation singer of spirituals and a conservatory-trained composer, Nathaniel Dett takes a high-minded, conservative attitude in the foreword to his 1927 collection, *Religious Folk-Songs of the Negro as Sung at Hampton Institute.* He expresses the belief, widely held by earlier generations and shared by many of his contemporary intellectuals, that spirituals should be sung in proper settings and without the corrupting influences of the (white) blackface minstrel shows and even the later all-black Broadway shows, which, in his opinion, cheapened the spiritual message through "the artificial flippant atmosphere of the extravaganza."

Dett's opinions carried weight because of his authority as a composer, teacher, and choral director. He had, in 1908, been the first African American to receive a Bachelor of Music degree from Oberlin Conservatory, and, in the same year, at age eighteen, he had his music published. By the time he issued his collection of spirituals, he had built the Hampton Institute Choir into a world-famous organization devoted to serious music of all kinds. He received many awards, and in 1919 he helped found the National Association of Negro Musicians.

Dett's wide-ranging foreword moves from a patronizing characterization of the old slave songs as "crudely fantastic" to a description of his own performance ideals for his choirs that implicitly justifies the concert singing of spirituals.

Dett's hope that spirituals would revive church singing and be a "heart-quickening note to give new life to hymnology" has not been completely in vain. Although the fervor of modern gospel music and the instrumental additions taken up since Dett's day would probably have offended his taste, the central place he sought for African-American religious music as an expression of black culture has been secured.

—Thomas L. Riis

R. NATHANIEL DETT
from *Religious Folk-Songs of the Negro* (1927)

Foreword

I

It is a well-known fact that humanity is most prayerful in the hour of need. Religion comes then as the reverberation of a great cry of soul; which explains in brief the Negro Spiritual, which more than almost any other folk-music in the world is a great cry of soul whose burden is of age-old promises of eternal freedom, of feasts of milk and honey, and of the divine glory of a love all-inclusive.

"Folk-songs," says the late Henry E. Krehbiel, "are the echoes of the heart-beats of the vast folk and in them are preserved feelings, beliefs, and habits of vast antiquity, not only in the words, but also in the music and perhaps more truthfully in the music than in the words. Music cannot lie, for the reason that the things which are at its base, the things without which it could not be, are unconscious, involitional human products."[1] Folk-songs, then, quite aside from their music value, are of inestimable worth because of the light which they throw upon those individualizing elements in the character of the race that produced them.

*   *   *

III

That the Negro as a race had, and still has, an outlook on life which is quite his own, and that his songs express moods born of his own peculiar experience, and which are quite original with him, may strike many as new. But how, otherwise, shall one explain the strong, unwavering note of hope of final recompense, and the assurance of the perfect-ness of another life to come, unless one is willing to admit that the slave brought with him from Africa a religious inheritance which, far from being shaken in any way, was strengthened by his American experience? Does it seem natural to suppose that there could be anything in slave life, not only as it existed in our Southern States, but even in slave life as it existed anywhere in the world, to inspire such an idea? It was nothing else, then, than this religious inheritance, this oriental regard for parable and prophecy, which made easy the incorporation into the spiritual of so much of Bible story; for in striving to give voice to his experiences the slave found in the Testaments, in the story of the children of Israel, for instance, much in the way of a text that was ready made; all of which was quite to his liking though, of course, unconsciously, for he could thus sing of one thing and mean another. This indirect mode of expression, it is well known, is one of the most characteristic earmarks by which the art of the East is distinguished from that of the West; it is characteristic of Negro music, often hiding, mask-like, its fundamental mood and not a little of its real meaning.

There are many songs, however, in which the Negro's soul sorrow is hidden by no mask. How poignantly it is revealed in "Farewell, farewell to my only child"; how prayerfully in "O Lord, O my Lord, keep me from sinking down"; how filled with longing in "Deep River! My home is over Jordan, Lord, I want to cross over into camp ground"; with what philosophical self-analysis in "Sometimes I feel like a motherless child" or in "I'm troubled in mind; if Jesus don't help me, I surely will die."

IV

What this ability of the black man to improvise his troubles into art-forms has fully meant to him will probably never be told. Very likely it served as a sort of safety valve for his pent feelings, saving the country from an even greater

---

Nathaniel Dett, *Religious Folk-Songs of the Negro As Sung at the Hampton Institute* (Hampton, Va.: Hampton Institute Press, 1927), xi, xiii–xviii, 167, 172, 228, 229, 236.

[1]Henry Krehbiel, *Afro-American Folksongs* (New York: G. Schirmer, 1914), 3; Krehbiel (1854–1923) was an influential music critic and writer.

tragedy than that precipitated by the Civil War, and himself from a disaster equally great.

"O glorious solace of immense distress
A conscience and a God,"

cries Dr. Watts, and his words are profoundly true.[2] But the worth of native Negro genius to America is paramount; for certainly it is most important that in a country given over to commercial enterprise, there should be at least one wellspring of spiritual issue.

To the world is brought a great message of goodwill, for one of the most outstanding characteristics of all the songs is that, free as the music is from cacophony and discord, just as free is its poetry from any word of bitterness, anger, or reproach. . . .

V

It is now generally conceded that this music is original to the Negro, insofar as any folk-music is original. Of those who sometimes still assert that the Negro folk idioms are derivations of revival hymns the question might pertinently be asked: Where is that wonderful matrix of hymnology out of which has grown these song jewels of Negro spirituals? It has long been accepted as scientifically true that the black man brought his musical idiom with him from his native land as he must have brought his susceptibility to religious suggestion. It would, of course, be unreasonable to suppose that this idiom was entirely unaffected by environment. But if it received, it also gave. In "Slave Songs of the United States" we read: "The words of the fine hymn 'Praise Member' (a Negro melody) are found with very little variation in 'Choral Hymns' (a standard hymnbook of the late sixties)." The editor of this collection[3] informs us, however, that "*many of his songs were learned from Negroes in Philadelphia,*" and Lt.-Colonel Trowbridge tells us

that he "*heard this hymn before the war among the colored people of Brooklyn.*"[4]

In an old Baptist hymnal in Kentucky the editor[5] once saw the words of "Not all the blood of beasts" set to a pentatonic tune which had all the characteristics of a Negro melody; and in a Methodist hymnal, recently in use in Tennessee, besides the familiar setting known to all, "How firm a foundation" appears to an alternative tune traditional with colored people.

William Francis Allen, one of the first to compile a collection of Negro folk-tunes, as early as 1867 writes, "The greater number of songs which have come into our possession seem to be the natural and original production of a race of remarkable musical capacity—imbued with the mode and spirit of European music, often nevertheless retaining a distinct tinge of their native Africa. The words are from Scripture and from hymns heard at church, expressions we find abundantly in Methodist hymnbooks, but with much searching I have been able to find hardly any trace of the tunes." Subsequent investigation by such authorities as H. E. Krehbiel, Henry T. Burleigh, Natalie Curtis (Burlin), Ballanta-Taylor, James Weldon Johnson, and others confirm this conclusion as to the original quality of Negro music.[6]

---

[2]Dr. Isaac Watts (1674–1748) and his many books of psalms and hymns were well known to African Americans even in the eighteenth century.

[3]William Francis Allen.

---

[4]William Allen, Charles Ware, and Lucy Garrison, *Slave Songs of the United States* (New York: Peter Smith, 1929, c. 1867), ix. Lt.-Colonel Charles Trowbridge, one of the minor contributors to *Slave Songs,* was a fellow officer, captain of Company A, with Colonel Thomas Wentworth Higginson, whose *Army Life in a Black Regiment* (pub. 1869) constitutes one of the most extensive reports of black culture in South Carolina during the Civil War.

[5]Allen.

[6]Krehbiel's *Afro-American Folksongs* (1914) was mentioned earlier. Harry Burleigh (1866–1949), who studied at the National Conservatory of Music in New York under Antonín Dvořák, became a well-known singer, composer, and music editor. His arrangement of *Deep River* (1917) did much to establish his fame. Natalie Curtis-Burlin, who published *Negro Folk-Songs* (1919), Nicholas George Julius Ballanta-Taylor, *Saint Helena Island Spirituals* (1925), and James Weldon Johnson and J. Rosamond Johnson, *The Book of American Negro Spirituals* (1925), were all active in Dett's day.

VI

The arrangements in this book are for unaccompanied choruses because practically all Negro folk-singing is unaccompanied group singing. A word on the manner of conducting, therefore, does not seem out of place.

For the most part, Negro music consists of a series of pulses, all of which are alike. That is, the secondary beats are as strong as the primary, or perhaps it would be still better to say that there are no secondary beats. The rhythm of the songs might very well be compared to that of the human pulse which is a series of throbs all of equal intensity.

When a song is once set in motion, its rhythm becomes immutable, the pause, especially in the refrain in which all join, being almost unknown. The singing sometimes begins a fraction slower than its regular tempo, but not markedly so. Sometimes there is, however, a feeling that a song is gaining in momentum until a certain rate is reached which is then maintained until the end.

Feeling for tempo is an inheritance with Negroes, as it is with most people, and if this natural feeling has not been disturbed by outside influences, it may be trusted to a large extent by the leader. It becomes the collector's chief duty, then, merely to set the chorus in motion, and by easy and natural beats, which need be only occasional, keep them going and up to time.

Expressive singing, especially of solo lines, should he encouraged, as this is one of the means of achieving much of interest and variety in a form of music which, regardless of race, is universally characterized by monotomy. Besides, it is an established tradition in the folk music of all peoples that the effect of any song depends largely on the way it is sung, but anything like mimicry or characterization should not for a moment be tolerated; the members of the chorus should be led to appreciate the idea that folk-music is essentially *soul music* which they, having made their own, are to help others enjoy and understand.

Dr. Robert R. Moton, principal of Tuskegee Institute, who for many years as the "Major" was the leader of the "plantation singing" at Hampton Institute, was in many ways ideal in this capacity, as

he has since proved himself to be in many others.[7] He sang many of the solo lines in a voice which, though uncultivated, was powerful and expressive. Often, after getting the chorus of a thousand voices going, he would place both hands behind his back, leaving the singers to carry on in their own way, and the resultant freedom and informality seemed never to fail in adding a certain zest to the singing. His beat was inconspicuous.

One must deplore much of the present-day singing of these songs on the concert platform. So few of the artists of either race seem willing to trust alone to the inherent beauty of the music to make its own appeal; still fewer seem to realize that music which has come from the heart of one people, will go by its own strength to the heart of another; that such music needs no mannerisms or stage tricks to help it on its way.

VIII

One of the most encouraging signs of our times is the apparent awakening of the mind of the public in regard to the true meaning of Negro folk-songs. The idea that the Negro spiritual has a message worthy of serious attention seems to be becoming more and more widespread. A recent protest of the press, both Negro and white, against the incorporation of these songs into some of the popular Broadway musical reviews, is indicative of an increasing regard for their religious significance which made the spirituals appear strikingly out of place in the artificial and flippant atmosphere of the extravaganza.

It may be that the religious music of the Negro will add a new note to ecclesiasticism, as the secu-

---

[7] Major Robert R. Moton (1867–1940) resided at the Hampton Institute for over twenty-five years, as student, faculty member, and most prominently as commandant of cadets. A beloved figure who served as an important administrative go-between for the predominantly white faculty and the African-American and Native American students, Moton was a musical enthusiast and avid supporter of the singers at Hampton. He left the Institute to succeed his friend Booker T. Washington (who was also a Hampton graduate) as the second president of the Tuskegee Institute in Tuskegee, Alabama.

lar music of the Negro has done to the affairs of everyday life. From the time of the plantation days to the present, the world has been cheered by the individual note of jocularity which has made unique the ragtime of America's minstrelsy and street songs and the jazz of her dance-halls and music comedies.

Even so, from the religious music of the Negro, from the aptly named "spirituals," may come as equally welcome a heart-quickening note to give new life to hymnology.

That it was an error, centuries ago, on the part of the church to divorce religious music from rhythmic utterance, no one will now deny; even so, the most popular hymns ever have been those with a more or less pronounced rhythm. The Negro spiritual, combining as it does religious feeling with a regular, almost irresistible beat, based on a scale in existence five hundred years before Christ, having its own simple harmonies and archaic cadences, presents in an elemental form the solution of one of the great problems of Christianity; how to evolve a style of music that will convey a religious message through a popular medium without at the same time suggesting things of the world.

In such a volume as this there is an opportunity, not only of experiencing the original psalms of suffering as born in the Negro breast, but also a greater opportunity of touching, as it were, the fringes of the robes of Grandeur, whose garments trail the dust but whose face, uplifted above the clouds, we are not yet permitted to see.

Deep River

[*Chorus:*]
Deep river, my home is over Jordan,
Deep river, Lord, I want to cross over into camp ground.
Lord, I want to cross over into camp ground,
Lord, I want to cross over into camp ground.
Lord, I want to cross over into camp ground.

1

Oh, don't you want to go to that Gospel feast,
That promised land where all is peace?

Lord, I want to cross over into camp ground.
Lord, I want to cross over into camp ground.
Lord, I want to cross over into camp ground.
[*Chorus*]

2

I'll go into heaven and take my seat,
Cast my crown at Jesus' feet.
[*Chorus*]

3

O when I get to heav'n I'll walk all about,
There's nobody there for to turn me out.
[*Chorus*]

Like a Rough and a Rolling Sea

Tutti__Farewell, farewell to my only child
               Like a rough and a rolling sea,
               Like a rough and rolling sea.

The lightnings flashed,
And the thunders rolled,
Like a rough and a rolling sea.

The storms beat high,
And the winds blew fierce,
Like a rough and a rolling sea.

Keep Me from Sinkin' Down

Refrain/Tutti
               Oh Lord, Oh, my Lord! Oh my good
                  Lord!
               Keep me from sinkin' down,
               Oh, my Lord! Oh my good Lord!
               Keep me from sinkin' down.

Solo	I tell you what I mean to do,
Tutti	Keep me from sinkin' down,
Solo	I mean to go to hebben too,
Tutti	Keep me from sinkin' down.

Solo	I bless de Lord I'm gwine to die,
Tutti	Keep me from sinkin' down,
Solo	I'm gwine to judgment by an' by,
Tutti	Keep me from sinkin' down.

Refrain

Sometimes I Feel Like a Motherless Child

Solo   Sometimes I feel like a motherless child,
Tutti   Sometimes I feel like a motherless child,
         Sometimes I feel like a motherless child,
         A long ways from home,
         A long ways from home.
Solo   True believer,
Tutti   A long ways from home,
         A long ways from home.

I'm Troubled in Mind

Refrain [*Chorus*]
   I'm troubled, I'm troubled, I'm troubled in
     mind,

If Jesus don't help me, I surely will die.
Oh Jesus, my Saviour, on thee I'll depend,
When troubles are near me, you'll be my true
   friend.
Chorus—I'm troubled, *etc.*

When ladened [*sic*] with troubles and burdened
   with grief,
To Jesus in secret I'll go for relief.
Chorus—I'm troubled, *etc.*

In dark days of bondage to Jesus I prayed,
To help me to bear it, and he gave his aid.
Chorus—I'm troubled, *etc.*

57 Louis Moreau Gottschalk, Our Quintessential Romantic

He has been called the "quintessentially Romantic musician of the New World" and "our first matinee idol." He was lauded in Europe, where Berlioz praised him as a "consummate pianist" and Chopin predicted he would become "the king of pianists." He was born in Louisiana, spoke French in preference to English, and was a prominent southerner who sympathized with the Union during the Civil War. He toured internationally carrying on a devastatingly busy concert life. He was Louis Moreau Gottschalk (1829–1869).

Gottschalk was born in New Orleans to well-to-do parents. His father, an intellectual of English origin, worked in the brokerage business, and his mother came from an aristocratic French Creole family. Their first-born son, Moreau, the oldest of eight, was a genuine child prodigy. Having shown remarkable promise in New Orleans, he was wafted off to France when he turned thirteen to study with the best teachers available. Though at first turned aside at the Paris Conservatoire, he was within a few years sitting at official functions, judging his fellow students. A remarkable debut concert in 1849 at the Salle Pleyel that was warmly praised by Chopin aided his acceptance by the public. The success of his compositions *Bamboula, La savane,* and *Le bananier* heightened his popularity.

After the death of his father in 1853, Gottschalk found himself without financial resources. The impresario Max Strakosch brought the pianist back to the United States for a lucrative grand tour. Gottschalk opened in New York on February 11, 1962, after a private audition on February 8. An intensive period of concertizing and composing followed. In December 1862, he reports:

> I have just finished (it is hardly two hours since I have arrived in New York) my
> last tour of concerts for this season. I have given eighty-five concerts in four
> months and a half. I have traveled fifteen thousand miles on the railroad. At St.
> Louis I gave seven concerts in six days; at Chicago, five in four days. A few weeks
> more in this way and I would have become an idiot!*

Gottschalk's programs relied heavily on his own music. Well-crafted and musicianly, his pieces were written to attract audiences and to please the crowd. It was not his playing, which was uniformly praised, but his repertoire that put Gottschalk at odds with certain critics.

Like many during the nineteenth century, Gottschalk kept a journal of his thoughts and activities. The diary, which was left in a confused state, covered the years 1857 to 1868, the year before his death. His sister, Clara Gottschalk, edited it for publication in

---

*Louis Moreau Gottschalk, *Notes of a Pianist* (Philadelphia: Lippincott, 1881), 174.

a translation from the French by Robert E. Peterson, her brother-in-law and later her husband. *Notes of a Pianist,* published in Philadelphia twelve years after Gottschalk's death, makes for interesting reading, although it is not entirely reliable.

Three articles submitted by Gottschalk to the *Atlantic Monthly* were, however, published during his lifetime, in early 1865. The third, dated February 1862, can be placed at the time Gottschalk returned to New York. These articles found their way in altered form into the published version of *Notes.* Since the *Atlantic Monthly* articles saw print while Gottschalk was still alive, they probably reflect his thinking more closely than the book.

William Mason (1829–1908), one of Lowell Mason's sons, became a fine pianist and piano teacher. He and Gottschalk were close personal friends.

WILLIAM MASON

from *Memories of a Musical Life* (1901)

I knew Gottschalk well, and was fascinated by his playing, which was full of brilliancy and bravura. His strong, rhythmic accent, his vigor and dash, were exciting and always aroused enthusiasm. He was the perfection of his school, and his effects had the sparkle and effervescence of champagne. He was as far as possible from being an interpreter of chamber or classical music, but, notwithstanding this, some of the best musicians of the strict style were frequently to be seen among his audience, among others Carl Bergmann,[1] who told me that he always heard Gottschalk with intense enjoyment. . . .

A funny thing happened one day. At the time of which I write, forty-five years ago, William Hall & Sons' music-store was in Broadway, corner of Park Place, and was a place of rendezvous for musicians. Going there one day, I met Gottschalk, who, holding up the proof-sheet of a title-page which he had just received from the printer, said: "Read that!" What I read was, "The Latest Hops," in big block letters after the fashion of an outside music title-page. "What does this mean?" I asked. "Well," he replied, "it ought to be 'The Last Hope,'[2] but the printer, either by way of joke or from stupidity, has expressed it in this way. There is to be a new edition of my 'Last Hope,' and I am revising it for that purpose."

William Mason, *Memories of a Musical Life* (New York: Century Co., 1901), 205–8.

[1]Carl Bergmann (1821–1876), born in Germany, emigrated to New York, where he made a fine name for himself as a conductor and cellist.

[2]The piously sentimental *The Last Hope* (1854), subtitled *Religious Meditation,* became one of Gottschalk's most popular piano pieces.

LOUIS MOREAU GOTTSCHALK
"Notes of a Pianist, III" (1865)

New York, *February*, 1862—One thing surprises me. It is to find New York, to say the least of it, as brilliant as when I took my departure for the Antilles in 1857. In general, the press abroad relates the events of our war[3] with such a predetermined pessimist spirit, that at a distance it is impossible to form a correct estimate of the state of the country. For the last year I have read in the papers statements to this effect:—"The theatres are closed; the terrorism of Robespierre sinks into insignificance, compared to the excesses of the Americans; the streets of New York are deluged with blood" (I very nearly had a duel in Puerto Rico for venturing to question the authenticity of this last assertion, propounded by a Spanish officer); "in short, the North is in a starving condition."

"How can you think of giving concerts to people who are in want of bread?" was the remark of my friends, on being apprised of my resolution to return to the United States; and, in all humility, I must acknowledge that the same question suggested itself not unfrequently to my mind, when I discussed within me the expediency of my voyage. I have still in my possession a newspaper in which a correspondent states the depreciation of our currency to be such that he actually saw a baker refuse to take a dollar from a famished laborer in exchange for a loaf of bread.

The number of these trustworthy correspondents has increased in the direct ratio of our prosperity, the development of our resources, and the umbrage these blessings give to the enemies of democratic principles. There are very few governments that would not deem it a matter of duty to exult over the ruin of our republican edifice. Fear actuates the less enlightened; jealousy is the motive of the more liberal. A celebrated statesman once said to me, "A republic is theoretically a very fine thing, but it is a Utopia," Like the man in antiquity, who, on hearing motion denied, refuted the assertion simply by rising and walking, we had hitherto put the "Utopia" into practice; and the *thing did* march on, and proved a reality. The argument was peremptory. A principle can be discussed; a fact is undeniable. Although refracted by the organs of the foreign press, the light of truth still flashed at times upon the people in Europe, and taught it to reflect. When our troubles broke out, I was in Martinique. In all the Antilles,—Spanish, French, Danish, English, Swedish, Dutch,—it was but one unanimous cry, "Did not we say so?" and the truthful and independent correspondents immediately embraced this opportunity to redouble their zeal, and forthwith began to multiply like mosquitoes in a tropical swamp after a summer shower.

But it is not my province to pronounce upon lofty political and moral questions. I would merely say that New York, for a deserted city, is singularly animated; that Broadway yesterday was thronged with pretty women, who, famished as they are, present, nevertheless, the delusive appearance of health, and brave with heroic indifference the bloody tumults of which our streets are daily the theatre; that Art is not so utterly dead among us but the Maretzek gives "Un Ballo in Maschera" to crowded houses, and Church sees his studio filled with amateurs desirous of admiring his magnificent and strange "Icebergs," which he has just finished.[4]

Louis Moreau Gottschalk, "Notes of a Pianist, III," *Atlantic Monthly* (May 1865): 573–75; equivalent passage in Gottschalk's *Notes of a Pianist* (Philadelphia: Lippincott, 1881), 122–31.

[3]The American Civil War.

[4]Max Maretzek (1822–1897) was an Austrian composer and conductor who came to the United States in 1848 and was active here as both a conductor and an opera impresario. Frederick E. Church (1826–1900) belonged to the Hudson River School of Romantic landscape painting.

It is difficult to account for the extreme ignorance of many foreigners with regard to the political and intellectual standing of the United States, when one considers the extent of our commerce, which covers the entire world like a vast net, or when one views the incessant tide of immigration which thins the population of Europe to our profit. A French admiral, Viscount Duquesne, inquired of me at Havana, in 1853, if it were possible to venture in the vicinity of St. Louis without apprehending being massacred by the Indians. The father of a talented French pianist who resides in this country wrote a few years since to his son to know if the furrier business in the city of New York was exclusively carried on by Indians. Her Imperial Highness the Grand-Duchess of Russia, on seeing Barnum's name in an American paper, requested me to tell her if he were not one of our prominent statesmen.[5] For very many individuals in Europe, the United States have remained just what they were when Châteaubriand wrote, "Les Natchez," and saw parrots (?) on the boughs of the trees which the majestic *Méchasébé* rolled down the current of its mighty waters.[6] All this may seem improbable, but I advance nothing that I am not fully prepared to prove. There is, assuredly, an intelligent class of people who read and know the truth; but, unfortunately, it is not the most numerous, nor the most inclined to render us justice. Proudhon himself—that bold, vast mind, ever struggling for the triumph of light and progress—regards the pioneer of the West merely as an heroic outlaw, and the Americans in general as half-civilized savages.[7] From Talleyrand, who said, "*L'Amérique est un pays de cochons sales et de sales cochons,*"[8] down to Zimmermann,[9] the director of the piano-classes at the Conservatory of Paris, who, without hearing me, gave as a reason for refusing to receive me in 1841, that "America was a country that could produce nothing but steam-engines," there is scarcely an eminent man abroad who has not made a thrust at the Americans.—It may not be irrelevant to say here that the little Louisianian who was refused as a pupil in 1841 was called upon in 1851 to sit as a judge on the same bench with Zimmermann, at the "*Concours*" of the Conservatory.

Unquestionably there are many blanks in certain branches of our civilization. Our appreciation of the fine arts is not always as enlightened, as discriminating, as elevated, as it might be. We look upon them somewhat as interlopers, parasites, occupying a place to which they have no legitimate right. Our manners, like the machinery of our government, are too new to be smooth and polished; they occasionally grate. We are more prone to worship the golden calf, in bowing down before the favorites of Fortune, then disposed to kill the fatted calf in honor of the elect of thought and mind. Each and every one of us thinks himself as good and better than any other man: an invaluable creed, when it engenders self-respect; but, alas! when we put it in practice, it is generally with a view of pulling down to our level those whose level we could never hope to reach. Fortunately, these little weaknesses are not national traits. They are inherent in all new societies, and will completely disappear when we shall attain the full development of our civilization with the maturity of age.

My *impresarios*, Strakosch and Grau, have made the important discovery, that my first concert in New York, on my return from Europe in 1853, took place the 11th of February, and conse-

---

[5]P. T. Barnum (1810–1891), circus proprietor, was the foremost showman of nineteenth-century America. He offered Gottschalk a lucrative tour through the United States in 1853 but Gottschalk turned him down on the advice of his father, who disapproved of the association.

[6]Vicomte de François René de Châteaubriand (1768–1818) was a Romantic writer and politician. *Les Natchez* (1826) was one of three novels resulting from his trip to the United States in 1791.

[7]Pierre Joseph Proudhon (1809–1865) was an important French moralist and advocate of social reform.

[8]The edition of 1882 translates: "America is a country of dirty hogs and filthy hogs." Charles Maurice Talleyrand-Périgord (1754–1838) was a French bishop who became a highly influential political leader and diplomat. He served in the top levels of French government throughout the first half of the nineteenth century.

[9]Pierre Zimmermann (1785–1853).

quently have decided to defer my reappearance for a few days in order that it may fall upon the 11th of February, 1862.[10] The public (which takes not the remotest interest in the thing) has been duly informed of this memorable coincidence by all the papers.

Query by some of my friends: "Why do you say such and such things in the advertisements? Why do you not eliminate such and such epithets from the bills?"

Answer: Alas! are you ignorant of the fact that the artist is a piece of merchandise, which the *impresario* has purchased, and which he sets off to the best advantage according to his own taste and views? You might as well upbraid certain pseudo-gold-mines for declaring dividends which they will never pay, as to render the artist responsible for the puffs of his managers. A poor old negress becomes, in the hands of the Jupiter of the Museum, the nurse of Washington[11]; after that, can you marvel at the magniloquent titles coupled with my name?

The artist is like the stock which is to be quoted at the board and thrown upon the market. The *impresario* and his agents, the broker and his clique, cry out that it is "excellent, superb, unparalleled,—the shares are being carried off as by magic,—there remain but very few reserved seats." (The house will perhaps be full of dead-heads, and the broker may be meditating a timely failure.) Nevertheless, the public rushes in, and the money follows a similar course. If the stock be really good, the founders of the enterprise become millionaires. If the artist has talent, the *impresario* occasionally makes his (the *impresario*'s) fortune. In case both stock and artist prove bad, they fall below par and vanish after having made (quite innocently) a certain number of victims. Now, in all sincerity, of the two humbugs, do you not prefer that of the *impresario*? At all events, it is less expensive.

---

[10]Jacob Grau and his nephew Maurice Grau (1849–1907) were also important impresarios. Gottschalk's mention of Jacob Grau along with Max Strakosch suggests that they both had a hand in managing Gottschalk in 1862.

[11]Gottschalk is referring to an elderly African-American woman promoted by Barnum as Washington's nurse.

I heard Brignoli yesterday evening in "Martha."[12] The favorite tenor has still his charming voice, and has retained, despite the progress of an *embonpoint*[13] that gives him some uneasiness, the aristocratic elegance which, added to his fine hair and "beautiful throat," has made him so successful with the fair sex.[14] Brignoli, notwithstanding the defects his detractors love to heap upon him, is an artist I sincerely admire. The reverse of vocalists, who, I am sorry to say, are for the most part vulgar ignoramuses, he is a thorough musician, and perfectly qualified to judge a musical work. His enemies would be surprised to learn that he knows by heart Hummel's Concerto in A minor. He learned it as a child when he contemplated becoming a pianist, and still plays it charmingly. Brignoli knows how to sing, and, were it not for the excessive fear that paralyzes all his faculties before an audience, he would rank among the best singers of the day.

I met Brignoli for the first time at Paris in 1849. He was then very young, and had just made his *début* at the Théâtre Italien, in "L'Elisire d'Amore" [*sic*], under the sentimental patronage of Mme. R., wife of the celebrated barytone.[15] In those days Brignoli was very thin, very awkward, and his timidity was rendered more apparent by the proximity of his protectress. Mme. R. was an Italian of commanding stature, impassioned and jealous. She sang badly, although possessed of a fine voice, which she was less skillful in showing to advantage than in displaying the luxuriant splendor of her raven hair. The public, initiated into the secret of the greenroom, used to be intensely amused at the piteous attitudes of Nemorino Brignoli, contrast-

---

[12]The Italian operatic tenor Pasquale (Pasquilino) Brignoli (1824–1884), born in Naples, was also under Strakosch management when he first came to America in 1855.

[13]Physical heaviness.

[14]Gottschalk was no slouch with them either, although he never mentions his love affairs in *Notes of a Pianist*. He left the United States in 1865 never to return, following a minor involvement with a student at Oakland Female Seminary.

[15]*Notes*, p. 131, likewise refers simply to the "beautiful Madame R."

ing, as they did, with the ardent pantomime of Adina R., who looked by his side like a wounded lioness. Poor woman! What has been your fate? The glossy tresses of which you were so proud in your scenes of insanity, those tresses that brought down the house when your talent might have failed to do so, are now frosted with the snow of years. Your husband has forsaken you. After a long career of success, he has buried his fame under the orange-groves of the Alhambra. There he directs, according to his own statement, (but I can scarce credit it,) the phantom of a Conservatory for singing. I am convinced he has too much taste to break in upon the poetical silence of the old Moorish palace with *portamenti*, trills, and scales, and I flatter myself that the plaintive song of the nightingales of the Generalife and soft murmur of the Fountain of the Lions are the only concerts that echo gives to the breeze that gently sighs at night from the mountains of the Sierra Nevada. Alas! poor woman, your locks are silvered, and Brignoli—has grown fat! "*Sic transit gloria mundi!*"

58 🌿 Arthur Foote and the Boston Group

At the end of the nineteenth century Boston became a center for a group of well-trained composers who were greatly influenced by music from Europe, particularly Germany. Dubbed variously as "the Second New England School," "the Boston Classicists," or "the Boston Academics," the group included John Knowles Paine, George W. Chadwick, Arthur Foote, Horatio Parker, Amy Beach (Mrs. H. H. A. Beach), Charles Martin Loeffler, Edward MacDowell, Arthur Whiting, and others. Several were also skilled pianists or organists. In intellectual Boston, these musicians found a conducive stimulus for musical creativity.

Arthur Foote (1853–1937) was unusual in that he received all of his training in the United States. He graduated in 1874 from Harvard University, where he studied with John Knowles Paine, and went on for his Master's degree there—the first M.A. in music granted by an American university. Except for eight summer forays to Europe and one to the University of California at Berkeley, Foote's entire career was spent in Boston, where he became a leading figure in the musical community.

In his *Autobiography*, printed privately in 1946, and in his article, "A Bostonian Remembers," published in the year he died, Foote speaks admiringly of his teacher, Paine, and relates other Boston experiences. He underscores the interaction among the Boston group:

> One of my cherished remembrances is of the meetings several times a year of Chadwick, Parker, Whiting, and myself, at which we each offered manuscript compositions for criticism, sometimes caustic, always helpful. The talk was honest and frank to a degree, and one was certainly up against the unadorned truth. I learned a lot from it.*

---

*Arthur Foote, "A Bostonian Remembers," *The Musical Quarterly*, January 1937: 41.

ARTHUR FOOTE

from *An Autobiography*[1]   (C. 1930; PUB. 1946)

In the early nineties there were a number of us in Boston writing music more or less worth while, some of which has lived (e.g., Parker's "Hora Novissima," Chadwick's "Melpomene"). They were Chadwick, Horatio Parker, Whiting, MacDowell, Nevin, John Paine, J. C. D. Parker, Mrs. Beach, Margaret Ruthven Lang, Mrs. H. M. Rogers; Converse and Hadley were to come a little later.[2] Parker was still in Boston weekly as organist of Trinity Church, and Whiting had not yet gone to New York. These two, with Chadwick and me, used sometimes to meet at the St. Botolph Club after dinner. We allowed ourselves frank discussion and the most out-spoken criticism I have ever heard. I got no end of good from it. As an example of what a few words can do in the way of opening one's eyes, I remember Parker saying, after I had ended the playing through of a movement from my orchestra Suite, "All in D minor, isn't it?" And that was the trouble; easily remedied by the simple alteration of some authentic cadences to deceptive ones. This pleasant association came to an end when Whiting went to New York, and Parker to New Haven as Professor at Yale.

It was not until 1877 that I attempted to write real music. I was late in this respect in comparison with Chadwick, Parker, and MacDowell; and of course I lacked their training. My first published music was three pieces for 'cello (reminiscent and rather of a stencil pattern, but melodious), which I played with Wulf Fries a good deal. This, as well as the three piano pieces referred to before, was published by Cranz of Hamburg, for whom Schmidt was agent, as he was for Litolff.[3] These pieces are all commonplace, but their composition gave me encouragement; and from that time until a few years ago I was very busy indeed putting notes on paper. The most significant things of this period are the first Trio (finished the summer we were at Neuilly,[4] in 1883, and played from MS. in one of my own chamber concerts), the little Serenade for strings, and an Overture, "In the Mountains." The latter two were produced by Gericke with the Boston Symphony Orchestra (at about the time when he brought out Chadwick's "Melpomene," that proved so successful).[5] Though I knew little about orchestration, the Overture is effective, if old-fashioned; and it is singular that, in spite of my not playing any stringed instrument, nor indeed knowing in detail about the technique of even the violin, everything for strings has been practical and

---

Arthur Foote, *An Autobiography* (Norwood, Mass.: privately printed at the Plimpton Press, 1946), 54–57.

[1]"My father wrote this autobiography at our farm in South Hampton, New Hampshire. It does not extend much beyond 1926, and was written primarily for me, with no thought of publication." [From the foreword by Katherine Foote Raffy.]

[2]George Whitefield Chadwick (1854–1931) became director of the New England Conservatory of Music in 1897; composers Horatio Parker (1863–1919) and Arthur Whiting (1861–1936) both studied with Chadwick; composer Edward MacDowell (1860–1908) lived in Boston from 1888 to 1896; Arthur Nevin (1871–1943) later taught at the University of Kansas; John Knowles Paine (1839–1906) organized the department of music at Harvard University; James Cutler Dunn Parker (1828–1916) taught at the New England Conservatory of Music and served as organist at Trinity Church, Boston; Amy Beach (1867–1944) was an important pianist and composer; Margaret Ruthven Lang (1867–1972) was the first woman to have a work played by a major symphony orchestra, the Boston Symphony, in 1893; Clara Kathleen Rogers (1844–1931) was a singer who composed mainly songs and became a professor at the New England Conservatory in 1902; composer Frederick Shepherd Converse (1871–1940), who studied with Paine and Chadwick, became dean of the faculty at the New England Conservatory; and Henry Kimball Hadley (1871–1937) was an excellent conductor who founded the Berkshire Music Festival in 1934.

[3]Another German music publisher.

[4]A suburb of Paris.

[5]Wilhelm Gericke was conductor of the Boston Symphony Orchestra, 1884–1889.

grateful. Much of my early reputation came from the Overture and from this Trio, which forty years afterwards is still sometimes on programs. At about this time came a setting of an extract from "Hiawatha" (Apollo Club, Boston) with orchestra, which is today still going strong, while the "Bedouin Song" for men's voices (afterwards arranged for mixed voices) is probably the most successful piece of the sort written by an American (1892). A Violin Sonata (1890), dedicated to Kneisel,[6] has had an unusual number of concert performances, as has also a Quartet for piano and strings in C major (written at the Alhambra, Mrs. Gardner's cottage at Pride's Crossing, in 1891). This last I have probably played myself in at least forty concerts. In 1884 my first song, "Go, Lovely Rose," written for Mrs. Henschel,[7] was published, to be followed by probably one hundred twenty-

five others. "I'm Wearing Awa'," written one Sunday morning before going to church, and the "Irish Folk Song," written to be sung at a reception given to Gilbert Parker, have been the most successful, still selling after thirty-five years. As a musician I prefer many of my later ones as being more original and of greater interest harmonically. As to this last point, my influences from the beginning, as well as my predilection, were ultra-conservative: as a boy, General Oliver, later Emery[8] and Paine, later still Dresel[9] were my mentors; and I formed myself, so to speak, on Mendelssohn (having none the less a love for Schumann and Chopin). Consecutive fifths, even cross-relations, were anathema to my teachers and to me. My harmony was correct but with little variety, the structure of my pieces conventional; and it was only much later that I absorbed harmonic finesse and became sensitive to it.

---

[6]Franz Kneisel was at this time concertmaster and assistant conductor of the Boston Symphony Orchestra.

[7]The American soprano Lillian Bailey married George Henschel, the first conductor of the Boston Symphony Orchestra.

[8]Boston composer and teacher Stephen Emery (1841–1891).

[9]Pianist and teacher Otto Dresel (1826–1890).

ARTHUR FOOTE

"A Bostonian Remembers" (1937)

These are reminiscences of a Bostonian who puts down mainly what he has known and experienced in his own town—a fragment only of what could be told of the country as a whole. But these happenings, in our little corner, nevertheless assume a certain importance with regard to the general musical development of these United States.

The town of Salem, Massachusetts, where I was born, March 5, 1853, was a quiet, prosperous, self-contained place, not dependent for music and theatre on Boston. It had tradition and cultivation;

life there was simple and easy, and is a pleasant thing to look back upon in these restless, anxious days. Salem had a picturesque and stirring history, the rotting wharves being reminders of its vanished merchant shipping, and of the privateers of 1812.

At thirteen I began to take notice and to find that music was to be a real thing in my life—my ambition having previously been to become a locomotive engineer! Lessons began with a pupil of B. J. Lang[10] (with whom I studied later). I must have made quick progress, for when my teacher

---

Arthur Foote, "A Bostonian Remembers," *The Musical Quarterly*, January 1937: 37–44.

[10]Benjamin Johnson Lang (1837–1909).

took me to Boston one day to play for Lang, the crack piece was the Chopin A-flat Ballade. A decisive result of this visit was that, on Lang's advice, I went to Stephen A. Emery for lessons in harmony, the textbook being Richter's, dry and with nothing but figured basses for exercises. It was a book so full of rules about what to do and what not to do as to make one giddy.

My father was editor of the Salem Gazette (founded in 1760); it was issued two days in the week, the other days being shared between two other newspapers. As was the custom then, the *Gazette* exchanged copies with other journals, one of them a New York musical paper, in which there were always music supplements. One day I found a piece with the odd name of "Kreisleriana," by a composer unknown to me, Schumann; I still remember my delight in it. Mendelssohn's fame had not begun to lessen, and it was naturally his "Songs Without Words" that I always chose for playing to people; today most likely it would be Brahms. In 1867 my father gave me a lot of music which he had bought in London; in it was the E-flat Nocturne (op. 9) of Chopin (which on the title-page was called *Murmures de la Seine*); there were also several Beethoven sonatas, among them Op. 10, No. 3, the slow movement of which made an impression that has lasted through the years. And how I did revel in the slow movement of the Fifth Symphony, when I discovered it a little later.

A good illustration of our standards at that time is the following: as a boy really interested in music and giving some promise, I attracted the attention of the composer of the well-known hymn-tune "Federal Street."[11] He wrote a great many such tunes, octavo books of them by him and by others being numerous and fairly representative of the type of music written here then. Lowell Mason's "Nearer, my God, to Thee" is today no doubt the best known of these tunes. There was little of harmonic interest in them (mostly I, IV, and V), but they still hold their own in our New England churches, and are from association dear to many;

of late years, however, it looks as if they would have to give way to more sophisticated music, as a comparison of the old hymnals with those of today will show.

There came a "great awakening" in the so-called Peace Jubilee of 1869. This was a monstrous affair, with its chorus of thousands, the orchestra of 1,000 (?), a "Bouquet of 40 Artists," with visiting German, French, and English bands, with Johann Strauss from Vienna to lead his waltzes. In certain compositions cannon were fired to emphasize rhythm, while one of the sights was to witness a group of red-shirted firemen in the street on their way to the "Coliseum," where they were later to strike their anvils, giving a final touch of sonority to the "Anvil Chorus" of *Il Trovatore*.

All the same, the music (mainly oratorio choruses) exerted its spell; and though we may smile at the occasion today, these concerts had a mighty influence, especially in New England. For choruses had been started at that time in many towns, later to be combined in forming this great one. Some of them are still in existence.

In 1870 I entered Harvard, where for further study in theoretical subjects it was my good luck to have as teacher John K. Paine, who the year before had been appointed instructor and college organist. Paine had only recently returned from studies in composition and organ at Berlin. He was beginning to be accepted as our most important composer. As a teacher he was helpful to one who wanted to learn, I owe much to him for having turned me in the right direction at a critical time. The lessons were usually at his house, I being the only student in advanced work; today there are eight or more teachers, classes, for example, of 96 in appreciation of music, an adequate building which houses recitation rooms, and a hall in which many chamber concerts are given. I was leader of the Harvard Glee Club, the membership of which did not exceed twenty; here again time has wrought great changes. Our programs were good of their kind, consisting mainly of light German part-songs. The Harvard Glee Club of today, with its average of 150 members, and with programs of the finest sort of music, has come to be what it is

---

[11]Henry Kemble Oliver (1800–1885).

because of Dr. Davison's[12] belief that the young men have but to be shown great music to enjoy and appreciate it.

After graduation, in 1874, another year was spent with Paine, at the end of which I received the A.M. degree, the first one given at Harvard for work in music. Meanwhile, in the summer of 1874, having a desire to know something of the organ, I took some lessons with Lang. This was the turning point in my life, for he spoke with such encouragement of the probability of success as a professional musician that I began serious work at the piano. Lang was an exceptionally fine organist, a pianist to whom Boston owed most of the first performances of the newer piano concertos and chamber music. He also conducted the Apollo Club and Cecilia Society. While my work at the piano was progressing without definite aim, my organ lessons led to the very practical result of my engagement as organist at the First (Unitarian) Church in Boston, in 1878; I occupied that post until 1910, for thirty-two years.

The quartet choir was at that time much more common in churches than a boys' or mixed chorus. For music we relied chiefly on the anthems of Stainer, Sullivan, and the others of that group, since those written by our own composers were as a rule inferior; today we can hold our own.

The founding, in 1896, of the American Guild of Organists marks an important date, for it has had as its object the raising of our standard of music in the churches as well as in organ playing. As to this latter, in the 90's we turned our steps towards Paris instead of Berlin, for Guilmant in his tours at that time had made such an impression that students from all parts of the country began to go to him, as they have since to Widor, Bonnet, Vierne, and others. The teaching they received was exacting and thorough in every detail, "getting by" being frowned upon. In piano playing, also, there has been extraordinary gain both with professionals and amateurs. Technique is now not an end but a means, being taken for granted. As to recitals or concerts in those early days, we had only a few by visiting pianists, e.g. from 1873 (when Rubinstein appeared) to 1890 I remember only Bülow, Essipoff, Rummel, and Scharwenka. In Boston, Mme. Essipoff[13] gave what was probably the first "American" program; I had the luck to be on it with a gavotte (now, thanks be, out of print). Very little in the way of decent piano music was composed here in those days, and a large part of the program consisted of transcriptions of pieces by Schubert, etc., the other numbers being by Gottschalk, William Mason, Sherwood, Paine, Brandeis, and Richard Hoffman.

As it is not probable that a new race of superpianists has come into the world, the inference is fair that progress is due chiefly to an improvement in teaching. When I was a youngster, training was generally not completed until one had gone to some celebrated teacher in Germany, in Leipzig or Berlin preferably. (By the way, William Mason's reminiscences and Amy Fay's "Music Study in Germany" are good reading for this generation, for they give a perfect picture.) At that time it was generally taught that the knuckles must be flattened, that the fingers should always be quite curved and should "strike" the keys as near the nail as possible; as a natural result, there was stiffness in wrist and arm, and we had high finger action almost exclusively, with little regard for beauty of tone. In teaching, I think three things have contributed to our better standard—(1) the abandonment of the foregoing for a more logical way of using arm, wrist, and fingers, with heed to the proper laws in relaxation; (2) the training of the student so that rhythm and accent are always present in his technical work, as well as in his general playing (Mason's "Touch and Technic" probably contains the first clear statement of this principle); and (3) the training of the hands so that they play comfortably in all sorts of positions among the black and white keys (as to this, Tausig's famous technical exercises opened our eyes).

---

[12]Archibald T. Davison (1883–1961).

[13]Russian pianist Annette Nikolayevna Essipoff (Essipov), 1851–1914.

* * *

In the 70's Paine was our foremost musical figure; important in his life were two dates: 1876, when his first symphony was produced by the Thomas orchestra; and 1881, when there was heard his choral music for the performances at Harvard of *Oedipus* in Greek. A few years later his Second Symphony was published by subscription by Arthur P. Schmidt, probably the first large score issued here. Schmidt later did great service to American composers by publishing every year at least one orchestral score or large piece of chamber music; he once said to me that this country had done so much for him that such was the least return he could make.

The year 1879 also was important: it saw Chadwick emerge as a full-fledged composer with his overture "Rip van Winkle." The succeeding years brought us Parker's "Hora Novissima," MacDowell's "Indian Suite," Mrs. Beach's "Gaelic" Symphony, Loeffler's first work for violin with orchestra, Hadley's "Salome," Kelley's "Pilgrim's Progress," Carpenter's "Adventures in a Perambulator."

In 1888, after visiting Bayreuth, I took a roundabout way of returning to Paris; I went to Wiesbaden to make the acquaintance of MacDowell and Templeton Strong. In Boston we were already familiar with their music, especially with the first Suite and first Concerto of MacDowell. A few months after our meeting he came to Boston, to stay there as a distinguished composer, pianist, and teacher until he joined the faculty of Columbia University.

While there were various orchestral concerts in Boston before the 80's, those of the Harvard Musical Association, in spite of its comparatively small orchestra, were the most ambitious.

After graduation I became a member of the Association, being also soon added to the program committee, and finding myself there in a very conservative atmosphere. The two most influential members were John S. Dwight, not a musician (editor of "Dwight's Journal of Music," which had a

great and deserved influence in its day), and Otto Dresel, a wise and very cultivated musician, both of them devoted to the classic masters. Although the programs consisted chiefly of works of the classic school, we nevertheless got a fair number of novelties, *e.g.*, the first two Brahms symphonies. Two or three of us used to fight like cats to get a performance of, say, a new symphony by Raff or Rubinstein (now gone with last year's snows); perhaps it is remembrance of this that makes me slower in reaching an opinion on the Hindemiths and Stravinskys of today. Because of these concerts the Boston Symphony Orchestra found an audience ready for it, when the time came. The history of this distinguished body of musicians and its several conductors is a matter of public record. Thanks to the initiative and munificence of Henry L. Higginson, Boston's musical renown very soon came to be not only national but international. The programs of the Boston Symphony Orchestra showed from the first a rightly hospitable attitude towards American compositions and have continued to do so (in the last five years, for example, there have been thirty-three performances). Not only first hearings have taken place; some works have retained their position in the repertoire. . . .

As one of the older generation, I should hardly be expected to feel in the same way [as innovating composers] about the happenings in the past twenty-five years—about polytonality, "linear" counterpoint, etc.

Dissonance and consonance seem to me to be complementary: while music entirely consonance soon becomes monotonous, that which is constantly dissonant without the relief of consonance is not only tiresome, but, worse than this, unpleasant. Dissonance is not undesirable in itself, but often becomes so because of the unskillful way in which it is used. It is rather "old hat" to bring logic into the question, but after all this does exist in music from Bach to Sibelius.

All in all, ours has been a great time in which to be living and to watch the development of music.

59 ❧ Amy Beach and the Gender Issue

Amy Marcy (Cheney) Beach (1867–1944), or as she preferred to be called, Mrs. H. H. A. Beach, was a woman of firsts. When the Handel and Haydn Society of Boston performed her Mass in E-flat, op. 5, in 1892, it was the first time they had sung a work by a woman. Likewise, when Walter Damrosch and the New York Symphony Orchestra performed her setting of *Eilende Wolken, Segler die Lüfte* in the same year, it was the first time that ensemble had played a work by a woman. As an American woman musician, Beach broke new ground.

The press was generally enthusiastic about her achievements as a pianist and composer, yet commentators often included in their statements remarks of surprise at her accomplishments because she was a woman. About her performance of the Chopin Concerto in F Minor in 1885, the critic from the *Boston Evening Transcript* wrote that her playing had "a totality of conception that one seldom finds in players of her sex." Julia Ward Howe commented in the *Women's Journal* in 1892 about Beach's Mass in E-flat, "Mrs. Beach is, so far as we know, the first of her sex who has given to the world a musical composition of the first order as to scope and conception. . . . [The performance] made evident that capacity of a woman's brain to plan and execute a work combining great seriousness with unquestioned beauty." The *New York Sun* called her "the first woman in America to compose a work of so much power and beauty," and she was welcomed by George Chadwick as "one of the boys." John Knowles Paine commented that "art knows no sex," and according to Percy Goetschius, "Those accustomed to proclaim the superiority of the male composer would possibly, without exception, fail to suspect they were listening to the artistic creations of a woman."

Amy Beach first acquired a reputation as a brilliant pianist. She made her debut at age sixteen playing Ignaz Moscheles's Piano Concerto in G Minor with full orchestra. Her performance of Chopin's Piano Concerto in F Minor with the Boston Symphony Orchestra under Wilhelm Gericke on March 28, 1885, was described in the *Boston Evening Transcript* as "thoroughly artistic, beautiful and brilliant."

In 1885, she married the noted Boston surgeon, Henry Harris Aubrey Beach, a man much her senior, after which she always called herself Mrs. H. H. A. Beach. She also turned more to composition, and by 1893, she had already scored a significant success with her Mass. In addition, she had written a recitative and aria based on Schiller's *Mary Stuart—Eilende Wolken, Segler die Lüfte*. That year also saw the performance of her *Festival Jubilate*, op. 17, commissioned for the World Columbian Exposition in Chicago and sung by a chorus of three hundred under the baton of Theodore Thomas. Three years later, in October 1896, the Boston Symphony Orchestra premiered her *Gaelic* Symphony, op. 32, an event that greatly enhanced her reputation.

There is no doubt that Beach had certain advantages over earlier female composers. She benefited from the strength of the women's movement during the latter years of the nineteenth century. She also gained from her high position in Boston's cultivated circles and from her marriage to a supportive husband. Yet her musicianship was really what set her apart. Her talent was even more remarkable because, unlike most of her colleagues, she had been trained entirely in this country and was largely self-taught. Indeed, by the turn of the century, many considered her the dean of American women composers.

RUPERT HUGHES

from "The Women Composers" (1896)

When an intimate friend of mine had attained the pomp of college Seniority he wrote a most exhaustive (not to say exhausting) thesis on the philosophical justification of the advanced woman. With Norn-like calm he denied all possibility of feminine genius in the Professions, the Sciences, and the Arts. He proved most conclusively that She could never attain any real, permanent, or high success. Especially in music did he ridicule Her pretensions.

In the usual course of post-graduate diminution the struggle of installing a little wisdom has dispossessed a vast amount of knowledge. Though less profound and content, he has come to see the error of his way, and now, with more appreciative humility, he admits that in the Arts as well as at home a woman will have whatever she sets her mind on, if you will only give her a little time.

While I must confess my blindness to the existence of any downright and exalted genius among the women who write music—unless Mlle. Chaminade and Miss Lang are to be excepted[1]—a few of them are doing so much better than the great majority of men, and most of them are so near the average, that it is simply old-fashioned bigotry and empty nonsense to deny the sex musical recognition.

'Tis pity, but 'tis true, that women still write too little from their own souls, too few love-songs in which the woman speaks, too few lullabies, and too few feminine moods. Yet Art knows no sex, and what they write in man-tone is at times surprisingly strong. The vast majority of our pianists and singers and music-teachers are women, and now they are flooding the market with a snow-storm of sheet-music. The time has evidently quite vanished when women, like Mendelssohn's sister,[2] deem it a brazen disgrace to publish their compositions under their own names.

The Atlanta Exposition has promulgated the woman composer with great thoroughness, and the number of those who have written music, either good enough or bad enough for publishers' approval, is astounding. I have neither the room nor the patience, nor yet the desire, to catalogue the fair legion. But among the few who write with evident ambition and cultivation the following are noteworthy: (As my praise would be accredited more than empty chivalry, may I beg that my blame be thought better than ungallant prejudice?)

To come down at once to the *argumentum ad hominem—de femina*—how many living men can point to a composition of more maturity, more dignity, and more inspiration than Mrs. H. H. A. Beach's piece of occasion, the *Jubilate* for the Dedication of the Woman's Building at the Columbian Exposition? The work is as big as its name; it is the best possible answer to sceptics of woman's musical ability. If it is a little too long, that is a common fault in the work of men along larger lines. It may be too sustainedly loud—curiously enough, this is

---

Rupert Hughes, "Music in America: IX.—The Women Composers," *Godey's Magazine*, January 1896: 30–31, 33.

[1]The French composer Cécile Chaminade and the Bostonian Margaret Ruthven Lang (daughter of the composer B. J. Lang).

[2]The German composer Fanny Mendelssohn.

a peculiarly feminine quality in music—and the infrequent and short passages *piano* are rather breathing-spells than contrasting awe. But women do not monopolize *fortissimo* cacophoneity. Frequently this work shows a very magnificence of power and exaltation. And the ending is simply superb—though I could wish that some of the terrific dissonances in the accompaniment had been put into the unisonal voices to widen the effect and strengthen the final grandeur.

Another work of force and daring is the Mass in E flat, for organ and small orchestra. It is conventionally ecclesiastic as a rule, and suffers from Mrs. Beach's besetting sin of over-elaboration, but it proclaims a great ripeness of technic. The "Qui Tollis" is especially perfect in its sombre depth and richness. The "Credo" works up the cry of "crucifixus" with a thrilling rage of grief and a dramatic feeling rare in Mrs. Beach's work; thence it breaks into a stirringly joyous "Et resurrexit." An example

of her undramatic nature is her ballade for chorus and orchestra, "The Minstrel and the King," which is uninteresting and loose-jointed.

* * *

Her works have been publicly performed by the best organizations, and her name is always the first to be mentioned when American women are mentioned as composers.

Though Mrs. Beach may stand at the head of American women for the largeness of her ambition, and the importance of her work, I seem to see a more perfect fire, enkindled not clogged by culture, and a more passionate inspiration, in the general quality of the music of Miss Margaret Ruthven Lang.[3]

[3]Boston composer Margaret Lang (1867–1972) was the first woman in America to have a work played by a major orchestra: her *Dramatic Overture* was performed by the Boston Symphony Orchestra on April 7, 1893.

ARTHUR ELSON

from *Woman's Work in Music* (1903)

If the term American be applied as is often the case, only to the United States, then the list of its women composers will still be found to include practically all who have done work in this line in the Western hemisphere. By far the larger part of these women are living now, for our musical growth has taken place in recent years. The record is already a worthy one, and will become still more extensive in the near future.

At the head of the list stands Mrs. H. H. A. Beach, the one great name to be found in our country. . . .

The question of allowing women to compose, if they wish to do so, is hardly one that needs any extended debate. Yet it is only in the last few decades that woman's inalienable right to compose

has been fully established. The trials of Carlotta Ferrari[1] in getting her first opera performed are an example in point. The opposition of Mendelssohn to the publication by his sister of even a few minor works is another instance of the attitude formerly taken by even the greatest composers. The life of Chaminade[2] affords still another case of this opposition. When Rubinstein[3] heard a few of her early compositions, upon which he was asked to pass an opinion, he could not gainsay their excellence, but

[1]Carlotta Ferrari (1837–1907) composed operas to her own libretti.

[2]Cécile Chaminade (1857–1944) was a French pianist and composer whose most successful works include songs, pianoforte pieces, and a *Concertstück* with orchestra, which she presented before the public on her many concert tours in France and England.

[3]Probably Anton Grigorevich Rubinstein (1830–1894), well-known Russian pianist and composer.

Arthur Elson, *Woman's Work in Music* (Boston: L. C. Page, 1903), 195, 234–35.

insisted on adding that he thought women ought not to compose. The time has gone by when men need fear that they will have to do the sewing if their wives devote themselves to higher pursuits. The cases of Clara Schumann, Alice Mary Smith (Mrs. Meadows-White), and Ingeborg von Bronsart afford ample proof, to say nothing of our own Mrs. Beach.

Edward MacDowell

Edward MacDowell (1861–1908) was widely recognized as the leading composer of his day. Born in New York in 1861 to a Quaker family of Scotch-Irish extraction, he spent the years 1876–87 in Europe, first in France, then in Germany—a country he found highly congenial. Returning to America in 1887, he settled in Boston. In 1896, however, he moved to New York to teach at Columbia University, a position that eventually embroiled him in conflicts. He resigned in 1904 and died five years later.

MacDowell founded the influential retreat for artists, the MacDowell Colony, in Peterborough, New Hampshire. Distinguished musicians such as Amy Beach carried out significant work there. It still functions as an important center for creative work.

An accomplished pianist, MacDowell appeared with the Kneisel Quartet soon after his arrival in Boston. Concerts with the Boston Symphony Orchestra and with the Theodore Thomas Orchestra in New York followed. As a composer, MacDowell was heir to the German Romantic tradition but was receptive to Native American elements, as in his *Indian Suite* first played by the Boston Symphony Orchestra in 1896. It was with his Second Piano Concerto (1889) that he particularly made his mark.

In a lecture given at Columbia University during the late 1890s and published after his death, MacDowell came as close as he ever did to describing his concept of music as a kind of "soul-language," based in "the power of suggestion."

EDWARD MacDOWELL

from "Suggestion in Music" (1890S; PUB. 1912)

In speaking of the power of suggestion in music I wish at the outset to make certain reservations. In the first place I speak for myself, and what I have to present is merely an expression of my personal opinion; if in any way these should incite to further investigation or discussion, my object will in part have been attained.

In the second place, in speaking of this art, one is seriously hampered by a certain difficulty in making oneself understood. To hear and to enjoy music seems sufficient to many persons, and an investigation as to the causes of this enjoyment seems to them superfluous. And yet, unless the

public comes into closer touch with the tone poet than that objective state which accepts with the ears what is intended for the spirit, which hears the sounds and is deaf to their import, unless the public can separate the physical pleasure of music from its ideal significance, our art, in my opinion, cannot stand on a sound basis.

The first step toward an appreciation of music should be taken in our preparatory schools. . . .

Mere beauty of sound is, in itself, purely sensuous. . . . For it to become music, it must possess some quality which will remove it from the purely sensuous. To my mind, it is in the power of suggestion that the vital spark of music lies.

Before speaking of this, however, I wish to touch upon two things: first, on what is called the science of music; and secondly, on one of the sen-

Edward MacDowell, *Critical and Historical Essays: Lectures Delivered at Columbia University* ed. W. J. Baltzell (Boston: Arthur P. Schmidt, 1912), 261–73.

suous elements of music which enters into and encroaches upon all suggestion.

If one were called upon to define what is called the intellectual side of music, he would probably speak of "form," contrapuntal design, and the like. Let us take up the matter of form. If by the word "form" our theorists meant the most poignant expression of poetic thought in music, if they meant by this word the art of arranging musical sounds into the most telling presentation of a musical idea, I should have nothing to say: for if this were admitted instead of the recognized forms of modern theorists for the proper utterance, we should possess a study of the power of musical sounds which might truly justify the title of musical intellectuality. As it is, the word "form" stands for what have been called "stoutly built periods," "subsidiary themes," and the like, a happy combination of which in certain prescribed keys was supposed to constitute good form. Such a device, originally based upon the necessities and fashions of the dance, and changing from time to time, is surely not worthy of the strange worship it has received. A form of so doubtful an identity that the first movement of a certain Beethoven sonata can be dubbed by one authority "sonata-form," and by another "free fantasia," certainly cannot lay claim to serious intellectual value.

Form should be a synonym for *coherence*. No idea, whether great or small, can find utterance without form, but that form will be inherent to the idea, and there will be as many forms as there are adequately expressed ideas. In the musical idea, *per se*, analysis will reveal form.

The term "contrapuntal development" is to most tone poets of the present day a synonym for the device of giving expression to a musically poetic idea. *Per se*, counterpoint is a puerile juggling with themes, which may be likened to high-school mathematics. Certainly the entire web and woof of this "science," as it is called, never sprang from the necessities of poetic musical utterance. The entire pre-Palestrina literature of music is a conclusive testimony as to the non-poetic and even uneuphonious character of the invention.

In my opinion, Johann Sebastian Bach, one of the world's mightiest tone poets, accomplished his mission, not by means of the contrapuntal fashion of his age, but in spite of it. The laws of canon and fugue are based upon as prosaic a foundation as those of the rondo and sonata form; I find it impossible to imagine their ever having been a spur or an incentive to poetic musical speech. Neither pure tonal beauty, so-called "form," nor what is termed the intellectual side of music (the art of counterpoint, canon, and fugue), constitutes a really vital factor in music. This narrows our analysis down to two things, namely, the physical effect of musical sound, and suggestion.

The simplest manifestations of the purely sensuous effect of sound are to be found in the savage's delight in noise. In the more civilized state, this becomes the sensation of mere pleasure in hearing pleasing sounds. It enters into folk song in the form of the "Scotch snap,"[1] which is first cousin to the Swiss *jodel*, and is undoubtedly the origin of the skips of the augmented and (to a lesser degree) diminished intervals to be found in the music of many nations. It consists of the trick of alternating chest tones with falsetto. It is a kind of quirk in the voice which pleases children and primitive folk alike, a simple thing which has puzzled folklorists the world over.

The other sensuous influence of sound is one of the most powerful elements of music, and all musical utterance is involved with the inseparable from it. It consists of repetition, recurrence, periodicity.

Now this repetition may be one of rhythm, tone tint, texture, or colour, a repetition of figure or of pitch. We know that savages, in their incantation ceremonies, keep up a continuous drum beating or chant which, gradually increasing in violence, drives the hearers into such a state of frenzy that physical pain seems no longer to exist for them.

The value of the recurring rhythms and phrases of the march is well recognized in the army. A body of men will instinctively move in cadence with such music. The ever recurring lilt of a waltz rhythm will set the feet moving unconsciously, and

---

[1] Dotted figures, short-long, with the short notes on the beat.

as the energy of the repetition increases and decreases, so will the involuntary accompanying physical sympathy increase or decrease.

Berlioz jokingly tells a story of a ballet dancer who objected to the high pitch in which the orchestra played, and insisted that the music be transposed to a lower key. Cradle songs are fashioned on the same principle.

This sensuous sympathy with recurring sounds, rhythm, and pitch has something in common with hypnotism, and leads up to what I have called suggestion in music.

This same element in a modified form is made use of it poetry, for instance, in Poe's "Raven,"

Quoth the raven, nevermore,

and the repetition of colour in the same author's "Scarlet Death." It is the mainspring (I will not call it the vital spark) of many so-called popular songs, the recipe for which is exceedingly simple. A strongly marked rhythmic figure is selected, and incessantly repeated until the hearer's body beats time to it. The well-known tunes "There'll Be a Hot Time," etc., and "Ta-ra-ra, Boom-de-ay" are good examples of this kind of music.

There are two kinds of suggestion in music: one has been called tone-painting, the other almost evades analysis.

The term tone-painting is somewhat unsatisfactory, and reminds one of the French critic who spoke of a poem as "beautiful painted music." I believe that music can suggest forcibly certain things and ideas as well as vague emotions encased in the so-called "form" and "science" of music.

If we wish to begin with the most primitive form of suggestion in music, we shall find it in the direct imitation of sounds in nature. We remember that Helmholtz, Hanslick, and their followers denied to music the power to suggest things in nature;[2] but it was somewhat grudgingly admitted

that music might express the emotions caused by them. In the face of this, to quote a well-known instance, we have the "Pastoral" symphony of Beethoven, with the thrush, cuckoo, and thunderstorm. The birds and the storm are very plainly indicated; but it is not possible for the music to be an expression of the emotions caused by them, for the very simple reason that no emotions are caused by the cuckoo and thrush, and those caused by thunderstorms range all the way from depression and fear to exhilaration, according to the personality of individuals.

That music may imitate any rhythmic sounds or melodic figure occurring in nature, hardly needs affirmation. Such devices may be accepted almost as quotations, and not be further considered here. The songs of birds, the sound made by galloping horses' feet, the moaning of the wind, etc., are all things which are part and parcel of the musical vocabulary, intelligible alike to people of every nationality. I need hardly say that increasing intensity of sound will suggest vehemence, approach, and its visual synonym, growth, as well as that decreasing intensity will suggest withdrawal, dwindling, and placidity.

The suggestion brought about by pattern is very familiar. It was one of the first signs of the breaking away from the conventional trammels of the contrapuntal style of the sixteenth and seventeenth centuries. The first madrigal of Thomas Weelkes (1590) begins with the words, "Sit down," and the musical pattern falls a fifth.[3] The suggestion was crude, but is was caused by the same impulse as that which supplied the material for Wagner's "Waldweben," Mendelssohn's "Lovely Melusina," and a host of other works.

The fact that the pattern of a musical phrase can suggest kinds of motion may seem strange; but could we, for example, imagine a spinning song with broken arpeggios? Should we see a spear thrown or an arrow shot on the stage and hear the orchestra playing a phrase of an undulating pat-

---

[2]Hermann von Helmholtz (1821–1894) was an important physiologist and physicist who wrote *The Sensations of Tone* in 1862; Eduard Hanslick (1825–1904) was a preeminent Austrian music critic who resisted the Wagner-Liszt movement.

[3]Thomas Weelkes, *Madrigals to 3. 4. 5. & 6. Voyces*, no. 1: "Sit down and sing, Amyntas joys, his little lambs rejoice to see the Spring."

tern, we should at once realize the contradiction. Mendelssohn, Schumann, Wagner, Liszt, and practically everyone who has written a spinning song, has used the same pattern to suggest the turning of a wheel. That such widely different men as Wagner and Mendelssohn should both have adopted the same pattern to suggest undulating waves is not a mere chance, but clearly shows the potency of the suggestion.

The suggestion conveyed by means of pitch is one of the strongest in music. Vibrations increasing beyond two hundred and fifty trillions a second become luminous. It is a curious coincidence that our highest vibrating musical sounds bring with them a well-defined suggestion of light, and that as the pitch is lowered we get the impression of ever increasing obscurity. To illustrate this, I have but to refer you to the Prelude to "Lohengrin." Had we no inkling as to its meaning, we should still receive the suggestion of glittering shapes in the blue ether.

Let us take the opening of the "Im Walde" symphony by Raff as an example; deep shadow is unmistakably suggested.[4] Herbert Spencer's theory of the influence of emotion on pitch is well known and needs no confirmation. This properly comes under the subject of musical speech, a matter not to be considered here. Suffice it to say that the upward tendency of a musical phrase can suggest exaltation, and that a downward trend may suggest depression, the intensity of which will depend upon the intervals used. As an instance we may quote the "Faust" overture of Wagner, in which the pitch is used emotionally as well as descriptively. If the meaning I have found in this phrase seems to you far-fetched, we have but to give a higher pitch to the motive to render the idea absolutely impossible.

The suggestion offered by movement is very obvious, for music admittedly may be stately, deliberate, hasty, or furious, it may march or dance, it may be grave or flippant.

Last of all I wish to speak of the suggestion conveyed by means of tone-tint, the blending of timbre and pitch. It is essentially a modern element in music, and in our delight in this marvelous and potent aid to expression we have carried it to a point of development at which it threatens to dethrone what has hitherto been our musical speech, melody, in favour of what corresponds to the shadow languages of speech, namely, gesture and facial expression. Just as these shadow languages of speech may distort or even absolutely reverse the meaning of the spoken word, so can tone colour and harmony change the meaning of a musical phrase. This is at once the glory and the danger of our modern music. Overwhelmed by the new-found powers of suggestion in tonal tint and the riot of hitherto undreamed of orchestral combinations, we are forgetting that permanence in music depends upon melodic speech.

In my opinion, it is the line, not the colour, that will last. That harmony is a potent factor in suggestion may be seen from the fact that Cornelius was able to write an entire song pitched upon one tone, the accompaniment being so varied in its harmonies that the listener is deceived into attributing to that one tone many shades of emotion.[5]

In all modern music this element is one of the most important. If we refer again to the "Faust" overture of Wagner, we will perceive that although the melodic trend and the pitch of the phrase carry their suggestion, the roll of the drum which accompanies it throws a sinister veil over the phrase, making it impressive in the extreme. . . .

Possibly Strauss's "Thus Spake Zarathustra" may be considered the apotheosis of this power of suggestion in tonal colour, and in it I believe we can see the tendency I allude to. This work stuns by its glorious magnificence of tonal texture; the suggestion, in the opening measures of the rising sun is a mighty example of the overwhelming power of tone colour. The upward sweep of the music to the highest regions of light has much of splendour about it; and yet I remember once hearing in Lon-

---

[4]Joachim Raff (1822–1882), Symphony no. 3 (1869).

[5]Peter Cornelius (1824–1874), *Ein Ton.*

don, sung in the street at night, a song that seemed to me to contain a truer germ of music.

For want of a better word I will call it ideal suggestion. It has to do with actual musical speech, and is difficult to define. The possession of it makes a man a poet. If we look for analogy, I may quote from Browning and Shakespeare.

Dearest, three months ago
When the mesmerizer, Snow,
With his hand's first sweep
Put the earth to sleep.
                    Browning, *A Lovers' Quarrel*

                    Daffodils,
That come before the swallow dares, and takes
The winds of March with beauty; Violets dim,
But sweeter than the lids of Juno's eyes.
                    Shakespeare, *Winter's Tale*

For me this defies analysis, and so it is with some things in music, the charm of which cannot be ascribed to physical or mental suggestion, and certainly not to any device of counterpoint or form, in the musical acceptance of the word.

61 Antonín Dvořák and the Development of National Music

Antonín Dvořák's American period ran from September 1892 to April 1895. During this brief time, the composer served as director of the National Conservatory in New York, having been lured there by its energetic president, Jeannette Thurber. While in the United States, he traveled across the upper Midwest and spent a fruitful summer in the Czech community of Spillville, Iowa.

Dvořák (1841–1904) clearly felt himself to be a foreigner on American shores, and in an 1895 *Harper's* article he notes that "many of my impressions therefore are those of a foreigner who has not been here long enough to overcome the feeling of strangeness and bewildered astonishment which must fill all European visitors upon their first arrival." Yet he was concerned with the development of a national music in America. "I came," he wrote in a *New York Herald* article of May 21, 1893," to discover what young Americans had in them and to help them to express it." He urged American composers to open their ears to the music around them and to their heritage, particularly from African-American and Native American sources.

Dvořák wanted American composers to look to their indigenous sources in order to build a valid American music. "Undoubtedly the germs for the best of music lie hidden among all the races that commingled in this great country," he wrote. That he actually knew very little about these sources is evident in his statement that he finds the music of African Americans and of Native Americans to be practically identical. Dvořák's knowledge basically came from a single source, his black student Henry T. Burleigh (1866–1949), who performed many spirituals as well as Stephen Foster songs for him.

Dvořák's most famous American work, his Symphony no. 9 *From the New World*, was premiered on December 16, 1893, with his friend Anton Seidl leading the New York Philharmonic in Carnegie Hall. The day before, the *New York Herald* printed an interview with Dvořák in which, after emphasizing his interest in "the national music of the negroes and the Indians," he provided an interesting program note. The passage makes explicit the influence of Native American music and of images from Longfellow's *Hiawatha*. "It is this spirit which I have tried to reproduce in my new symphony," Dvořák tells us. "I have simply written original themes embodying the peculiarities of the Indian music." The spirit of African-American song is clearly there as well.

Each of the following articles from the *New York Herald* results from interviews. An editorial voice is evident in the surrounding prose, and the quotations themselves may have been subject to distortion. The article from *Harper's* although printed without editorial comment, acknowledges the cooperation of Mr. Edwin Emerson Jr.* What

---

*Possibly Edwin Emerson (1823–1908), a journalist and professor of English literature, or, more probably, his son, Edwin Emerson (1869–1959?).

we may have here, at least in part, is some editorial magnification of statements put into Dvořák's mouth.

The fact remains clear, however, that Dvořák added fuel to the debate about American nationalism. The results were far ranging, and they influenced American music for some time to come.

ANTONÍN DVOŘÁK

from "Real Value of Negro Melodies" (1893)

I am now satisfied . . . that the future music of this country must be founded upon what are called the negro melodies. This must be the real foundation of any serious and original school of composition to be developed in the United States. When I first came here last year I was impressed with this idea and it has developed into a settled conviction. These beautiful and varied themes are the product of the soil. They are American. I would like to trace out the individual authorship of the negro melodies, for it would throw a great deal of light upon the question I am most deeply interested in at present.

These are the folk songs of America and your composers must turn to them. All of the great musicians have borrowed from the songs of the common people. Beethoven's most charming scherzo[1] is based upon what might now be considered a skillfully handled negro melody. I have myself gone to the simple, half forgotten tunes of the Bohemian peasants for hints in my most serious work. Only in this way can a musician express the true sentiment of his people. He gets into touch with the common humanity of his country.

Possibilities of Negro Melody

In the negro melodies of America I discover all that is needed for a great and noble school of music. They are pathetic, tender, passionate, melancholy, solemn, religious, bold, merry, gay or what you will. It is music that suits itself to any mood or any purpose. There is nothing in the whole range of composition that cannot be supplied with themes from this source. The American musician understands these tunes, and they move sentiment in him. They appeal to his imagination because of their associations.

When I was in England one of the ablest musical critics in London complained to me that there was no distinctively English school of music, nothing that appealed particularly to the British mind and heart. I replied to him that the composers of England had turned their backs upon the fine melodies of Ireland and Scotland instead of making them the essence of an English school. It is a great pity that English musicians have not profited out of this rich store. Somehow the old Irish and Scotch ballads have not seized upon or appealed to them.

I hope it will not be so in this country, and I intend to do all in my power to call attention to this splendid treasure of melody which you have.

Among my pupils in the National Conservatory of Music I have discovered strong talents. There is one young man upon whom I am building strong expectations.[2] His compositions are based upon negro melodies, and I have encouraged him in this direction. The other members of the composition class seem to think that it is not in good taste to get ideas from the old plantation songs, but they are wrong, and I have tried to impress upon their minds the fact that the greatest composers

New York Herald, May 21, 1893: 28.

[1]Possibly the scherzo from his Sixth Symphony.

[2]Henry T. Burleigh.

have not considered it beneath their dignity to go to the humble folk songs for motifs.

I did not come to America to interpret Beethoven or Wagner for the public. That is not my work and I would not waste any time on it. I came to discover what young Americans had in them and to help them to express it. When the negro minstrels are here again I intend to take my young composers with me and have them comment on the melodies.

ANTONÍN DVOŘÁK

from "An Interesting Talk about 'From the New World' Symphony" (1893)

Chattily at his residence, No. 327 East Nineteenth street, last evening Dr. Dvořák gave a few details regarding this his latest composition. "Since I have been in this country I have been deeply interested in the national music of the negroes and the Indians. The character, the very nature of a race is contained in its national music. For that reason my attention was at once turned in the direction of these native melodies. . . .

Now, I found that the music of the negroes and of the Indians was practically identical. I therefore carefully studied a certain number of Indian melodies which a friend gave me and became thoroughly imbued with their characteristics—with their spirit, in fact.

It is this spirit which I have tried to reproduce in my new symphony. I have not actually used any of the melodies. I have simply written original themes embodying the peculiarities of the Indian music, and, using these themes as subjects, have developed them with all the resources of modern rhythms, harmony, counterpoint and orchestral color.

The symphony is in E minor. It is written upon the classical models and is in four movements. It opens with a short introduction, an adagio, of about thirty bars in length. This leads directly into the allegro, which embodies the principles which I have already worked out in my Slavonic dances; that is, to preserve, to translate into music, the spirit of a race as distinct in its national melodies or folk songs.

The second movement is an adagio. But it is different to the classic works in this form. It is, in reality, a study, or sketch for a longer work, either a cantata or opera which I purpose writing, and which will be based upon Longfellow's "Hiawatha." I have long had the idea of some day utilizing that poem. I first became acquainted with it about thirty years ago through the medium of a Bohemian translation. It appealed very strongly to my imagination at the time, and the impression has only been strengthened by my residence here.

The scherzo of the symphony was suggested by the scene at the feast in "Hiawatha" where the Indians dance, and is also an essay which I made in the direction of imparting the local color of Indian character to music.

The Final Movement

The last movement is an allegro con feroce. All the previous themes reappear and are treated in a variety of ways. The instruments required are only those of what we call the "Beethoven orchestra," consisting of strings, four horns, three trombones, two trumpets, two flutes, two oboes, two clarinets, two bassoons and tympani. There is no harp, and I did not find it necessary to add any novel instrument in order to get the effect I wanted.

I have indeed been busy since I came to this country. I have finished a couple of compositions in chamber music, which will be played by the

New York Herald, December 15, 1893: 11.

Kneisel String Quartet, of Boston, next January, in Music Hall. They are both written upon the same lines as this symphony and both breathe this same Indian spirit. One is a string quartet in F major and the other a quintet in E flat for two violins, two violas and violoncello.

ANTONÍN DVOŘÁK

from "Music in America" (1895)

It is a difficult task at best for a foreigner to give a correct verdict of the affairs of another country. With the United States of America this is more than usually difficult, because they cover such a vast area of land that it would take many years to become properly acquainted with the various localities, separated by great distances, that would have to be considered when rendering a judgment concerning them all. It would ill become me, therefore, to express my views on so general and all-embracing a subject as music in America, were I not pressed to do so, for I have neither travelled extensively, nor have I been here long enough to gain an intimate knowledge of American affairs. I can only judge of it from what I have observed during my limited experience as a musician and teacher in America, and from what those whom I know here tell me about their own country. Many of my impressions therefore are those of a foreigner who has not been here long enough to overcome the feeling of strangeness and bewildered astonishment which must fill all European visitors upon their first arrival.

The two American traits which most impress the foreign observer, I find, are the unbounded patriotism and capacity for enthusiasm of most Americans. Unlike the more diffident inhabitants of other countries, who do not "wear their hearts upon their sleeves," the citizens of America are always patriotic, and no occasion seems to be too serious or too slight for them to give expression to this feeling. Thus nothing better pleases the average American, especially the American youth, than to be able to say that this or that building, this or that new patent appliance, is the finest or grandest in the world. This, of course, is due to that other trait—enthusiasm. The enthusiasm of most Americans for all things new is apparently without limit. It is the essence of what is called "push"—American push. Every day I meet with this quality in my pupils. They are unwilling to stop at anything. In the matters relating to their art they are inquisitive to a degree that they want to go to the bottom of all things at once. It is as if a boy wished to dive before he could swim.

At first, when my American pupils were new to me, this trait annoyed me, and I wished them to give more attention to the one matter in hand rather than to everything at once. But now I like it, for I have come to the conclusion that this youthful enthusiasm and eagerness to take up everything is the best promise for music in America. The same opinion, I remember, was expressed by the director of the conservatory in Berlin[3] who, from his experience with American students of music, predicted that America within twenty or thirty years would become the first musical country.

Only when the people in general, however, begin to take as lively an interest in music and art as they now take in more material matters will the arts come into their own. Let the enthusiasm of the people once be excited, and patriotic gifts and bequests must surely follow.

It is a matter of surprise to me that all this has not come long ago. When I see how much is done in every other field by public-spirited men in

Antonín Dvořák, "Music in America," *Harper's New Monthly Magazine*, February 1895: 429, 432–34.

---

[3]Joseph Joachim?

America—how schools, universities, libraries, museums, hospitals and parks spring up out of the ground and are maintained by generous gifts—I can only marvel that so little has been done for music. After two hundred years of almost unbroken prosperity and expansion, the net results for music are a number of public concert-halls of most recent growth; several musical societies with orchestras of noted excellence, such as the Philharmonic Society in New York, the orchestras of Mr. Thomas and Mr. Seidl[4] and the superb orchestra supported by a public-spirited citizen of Boston;[5] one opera company, which only the upper classes can hear or understand, and a national conservatory which owes its existence to the generous forethought of one indefatigable woman.[6]

It is true that music is the youngest of the arts, and must therefore be expected to be treated as Cinderella, but is it not time that she were lifted from the ashes and given a seat among the equally youthful sister arts in this land of youth, until the coming of the fairy godmother and the prince of the crystal slipper? . . .

A while ago I suggested that inspiration for truly national music might be derived from the Negro melodies or Indian chants. I was led to take this view partly by the fact that the so-called plantation songs are indeed the most striking and appealing melodies that have yet been found on this side of the water, but largely by the observation that this seems to be recognized, though often unconsciously, by most Americans. All races have their distinctively national songs, which they at once recognize as their own, even if they have never heard them before. When a Tsech,[7] a Pole, or a Magyar[8] in this country suddenly hears one of his folk-songs or dances, no matter if it is for the first

time in his life, his eye lights up at once, and his heart within him responds, and claims that music as its own. So it is with those of Teutonic or Celtic blood, or any other men, indeed, whose first lullaby maphap was a song wrung from the heart of the people.

It is a proper question to ask, what songs, then, belong to the American and appeal more strongly to him than any others? What melody could stop him on the street if he were in a strange land and make the home feeling well up within him, no matter how hardened he might be or how wretchedly the tune were played? Their number, to be sure, seems to be limited. The most potent as well as the most beautiful among them, according to my estimation, are certain of the so-called plantation melodies and slave songs, all of which are distinguished by unusual and subtle harmonies, the like of which I have found in no other songs but those of old Scotland and Ireland. The point has been urged that many of these touching songs, like those of Foster, have not been composed by the negroes themselves, but are the work of white men, while others did not originate on the plantation, but were imported from Africa. It seems to me that this matters but little. One might as well condemn the Hungarian Rhapsody because Liszt could not speak Hungarian. The important thing is that the inspiration for such music should come from the right source, and that the music itself should be a true expression of the people's real feelings. To read the right meaning the composer need not necessarily be of the same blood, though that, of course, makes it easier for him. Schubert was a thorough German, but when he wrote Hungarian music, as in the second movement of the C-Major Symphony, or in some of his piano pieces, like the Hungarian Divertissement, he struck the true Magyar note, to which all Magyar hearts, and with them our own, must forever respond. This is not a *tour de force,* but only an instance of how much can be comprehended by a sympathetic genius. The white composers who wrote the touching negro songs which dimmed Thackeray's spectacles so that he exclaimed, "Behold, a vagabond with a corked face and a banjo

---

[4]Theodore Thomas and Anton Seidl.

[5]Probably Henry Lee Higginson, founder of the Boston Symphony Orchestra.

[6]Jeannette M. Thurber, who arranged for Dvořák's sojourn in America.

[7]Czech.

[8]Hungarian.

sings a little song, strikes a wild note, which sets the whole heart thrilling with happy pity!" had a similarly sympathetic comprehension of the deep pathos of slave life. If, as I have been informed they were, these songs were adopted by the negroes on the plantations, they thus became true negro songs. Whether the original songs which must have inspired the composers came from Africa or originated on the plantations matters as little as whether Shakespeare invented his own plots or borrowed them from others. The thing to rejoice over is that such lovely songs exist and are sung at the present day. I, for one, am delighted by them. Just so it matters little whether the inspiration for the coming folk-songs of America is derived from the negro melodies, the songs of the creoles, the red man's chant, or the plaintive ditties of the homesick German or Norwegian. Undoubtedly the germs for the best of music lie hidden among all the races that are commingled in this great country. The music of the people is like a rare and lovely flower growing amidst encroaching weeds. Thousands pass it, while others trample it under foot, and thus the chances are that it will perish before it is seen by the one discriminating spirit who will prize it above all else. The fact that no one has as yet arisen to make the most of it does not prove that nothing is there. . . .

My own duty as a teacher, I conceive, is not so much to interpret Beethoven, Wagner, or other masters of the past, but to give what encouragement I can to the young musicians of America. I must give full expression to my firm conviction, and to the hope that just as this nation has already surpassed so many others in marvelous inventions and feats of engineering and commerce, and has made an honorable place for itself in literature in one short century, so it must assert itself in the other arts, and especially in the art of music. Already there are enough public-spirited lovers of music striving for the advancement of this their chosen art to give rise to the hope that the United States of America will soon emulate the older countries in smoothing the thorny path of the artist and musician. When that beginning has been made, when no large city is without its public opera-house and concert-hall, and without its school of music and endowed orchestra, where native musicians can be heard and judged, then those who hitherto have had no opportunity to reveal their talent will come forth and compete with one another, till a real genius emerges from their number, who will be as thoroughly representative of his country as Wagner and Weber are of Germany, or Chopin of Poland.

To bring about this result we must trust to the ever-youthful enthusiasm and patriotism of this country. When it is accomplished, and when music has been established as one of the reigning arts of the land, another wreath of fame and glory will be added to the country which earned its name, the "Land of Freedom," by unshackling her slaves at the price of her own blood.

62

Amy Beach
Replies to Antonín Dvořák

Amy Beach (Mrs. H. H. A. Beach) was one of the musicians caught up in the debate over nationalism. Beach, a northerner, questioned Dvořák's emphasis on African-American and Native American sources. Her feeling was echoed by Philip Hale, who wrote in the *Boston Herald* on June 30, 1907, "The great majority of Americans are neither Negro nor Indian, nor are they descendants of Negroes or Indians. How then can folk songs attributed to the Negro or Indians be distinctively, peculiarly American?" Beach held that material of English, Scottish, or Irish origin and Civil War songs of the North and South were more relevant.

Beach sought her identity as an *American* composer, as did others associated with her on the Boston scene, at a time when the question of American nationalism was of real artistic concern. She wrote a number of pieces based on native sources, including her *Gaelic* Symphony (1894), *Eskimos* (1906), *From Blackbird Hills: An Omaha Tribal Dance* (1922), and the *String Quartet in One Movement* (1929), based on Eskimo themes. (See also the Introduction to No. 59.)

AMY BEACH

from Letter to the Editor of *The Boston Herald* (1893)

In view of the great success attained by Dr. Dvořák in his treatment of the Slavonic folk-songs, it is, perhaps, only natural that he should be strongly inclined to suggest the use of the folk-songs of other nations, as a source from which their composers should draw inspiration for musical composition. He advises our young writers to employ the negro melodies because "they are American," "the folk-songs of America."

Without the slightest desire to question the beauty of the negro melodies of which he speaks so highly, or to disparage them on account of their source, I cannot help feeling justified in the belief that they are not fully typical of our country. The African population of the United States is far too small for its songs to be considered "American." It represents only one factor in the composition of our nation. Moreover, it is not native American. Were we to consult the native folk-songs of the continent, it would have to be those of the Indians or the Esquimaux, several of whose curious songs(?) are given in the publications of the Smithsonian Institute.[1] The Africans are no more native than the Italians, Swedes or Russians.

Dr Dvořák says: "The American musician understands these tunes and they move sentiment in him. They appeal to his imagination because of their associations."[2] This might be true of a musician born and brought up in the South, surrounded by Negro life, hearing from babyhood

Amy Cheney Beach, "From Mrs. H. H. A. Beach," *The Sunday Herald (Boston)*, May 28, 1893: 23.

[1]Beach refers here to Franz Boas's early study of Native Americans, *The Central Eskimo*, published by the Smithsonian Institution.

[2]Dvořák in the *New York Herald*. May 21, 1893.

their songs in the fields as well as in the homes of the people. But to those of the North and West there can be little, if any, "association" connected with negro melodies. In fact, excepting to those especially interested in folk-lore, only very few of the real negro melodies are even known. The songs with which we are familiar have been written by Stephen C. Foster and other song-composers of our own race, of whom (as well as of the genuine negro songs) interesting articles by Mr. Francis H. Jenks are published in Grove's dictionary.[3] We of the North should be far more likely to be influenced by old English, Scotch or Irish songs, inherited with our literature from our ancestors, than by the songs of a portion of our people who were kept for so long in bondage, and whose musical utterances were deeply rooted in the heart-breaking griefs attendant upon their condition.

It seems to me that, in order to make the best use of folk-songs of any nation as material for musical composition, the writer should be one of the people whose songs he chooses, or at least brought up among them. Of Grieg, for instance, it has been said by Edward Dannreuther[4] that "Danish, Swedish and Norwegian Volkslieder and dances absorbed his fancy more than the study of any great composer's works. His compositions are marked with the stamp of a particular nationality more clearly than that of any man, except perhaps Chopin." Is not this because Grieg is a Norwegian, and, by early surroundings as well as by inheritance, has assimilated the spirit of the northern folk-music and made it his own? Dr. Dvořák himself has used the songs of the Slavonic races

with a brilliancy and effectiveness that we all know and admire; he is a Bohemian. If a negro, the possessor of talent for musical composition, should perfect himself in its expression, then we might have the melodies which are his folk songs employed with fullest sympathy, for he would be working with the inherited feelings of his race. Of truly American songs, I think that any fair minded person will agree with me that the war songs and ballads of the North and South more fully represent the feeling of our entire country than those of any one of its component nationalities could possibly do, whether African, German or Chinese. . . .

That the negro melodies may be of influence in an indirect, suggestive way, "a potent inspirer and trainer," to our composers, is possible. They are of great beauty and variety, and it is easy to see how their quaint rhythms and curious devices of melody would interest a master like Dr. Dvořák. Of how much development, used as themes for symphonies or other works in strict classical form, they are capable, can only be decided by time and experience in the hands of native and other composers. Whatever success may accrue by their employment cannot be justly claimed as American, but should be impartially laid at the feet of a people whose sufferings and sorrows gave them birth.

Musical students will be interested in knowing that Saint-Saëns has already used negro melodies in his work, "Africa," for piano and orchestra, coloring the barbaric rhythms and unusual scales with the instrumentation for which he is famous.

(Mrs.) H. H. A. Beach

---

[3]The first edition of *Grove's Dictionary of Music and Musicians* appeared 1879–89.

[4]Edward Dannreuther (1844–1905) was an important pianist and writer.

63

Patronage by Notable
                            American Women

Jeannette M. Thurber (1850–1946) was the energetic impresaria who lured Antonín Dvořák to the United States. She was one of several important American women of commitment whose vision has exerted over the years an immeasurable, positive influence on the arts. Her contemporary Elizabeth Sprague Coolidge (1864–1953) also stands high on the list. She has been called the patron saint of chamber music in America.

Jeannette Thurber was educated privately in New York and Paris, studying music at the Paris Conservatory. Upon her return home and after her marriage in 1869, she began to support worthy musical ventures. She helped Theodore Thomas with his concerts for young people in 1883, and a year later she was behind the first festival in this country that produced full-scale productions of the works of Richard Wagner. She founded the American Opera Company in 1885, an unsuccessful venture led by Theodore Thomas, which nonetheless produced significant works in English. She sponsored the New York debut of the Boston Symphony Orchestra in 1888–89.

But most important, the National Conservatory of Music was created largely through her efforts. Located in New York City, it was incorporated by an act of Congress on March 3, 1891—to date the only music school acknowledged in this way. Students were admitted on the basis of talent, not on their ability to pay. "It stands apart from all commercialism," wrote James Creelman in 1894. "The 2,497 students it has educated, and the sincerity it has shown in discouraging unpromising pupils, compel both admiration and faith."* The Conservatory's proudest moment came when Antonín Dvořák became its director (1892–95). It was at Thurber's urging that the composer wrote his Symphony no. 9, *From the New World* (1893).

The National Conservatory was not to last. There was considerable public debate over whether or not a capitalist society should support a federally funded conservatory. Other music schools across the country were increasingly providing competition and did not want to serve as "feeders" to a national institution. Its demise, however, should not distract our attention from its significant vision.

The grande dame of American patronage undoubtedly was Elizabeth Sprague Coolidge (1864–1953). Her father, Albert Arnold Sprague, was a sponsor of the Chicago Orchestra. Elizabeth Sprague herself was a pianist and composer. She married the orthopedic surgeon Dr. Frederick Shurtleff Coolidge in 1891. They had one son, Albert Sprague Coolidge, who became a professor of chemistry at Harvard University.

Above all, Elizabeth Coolidge was interested in chamber music. In 1916, she heard a chamber ensemble that later became known as the Berkshire Quartet perform in

---

*James Creelman, "Does it Pay to Study Music?" *The Illustrated American*, August 4, 1894: 136–37.

Chicago. "How well I remember their exciting performance of the César Franck! It has never thrilled me more than on that unique occasion in 1916. Before I left Chicago I had signed with these artists a three-year contract. They were to play for and with me in Pittsfield, my summer home, and at my New York apartment in winter." So began the Berkshire Chamber Music Festival, held in a hall she built in Pittsfield, Massachusetts.

Coolidge sponsored music not only in the United States but also in Rome (1923) and in other European cities from London to Moscow. France awarded her the Legion of Honor and Belgium the Order of Leopold and the Order of the Crown.

But her major achievements came through her support of chamber music in Washington, D.C., and through her commissions. In 1925, Congress accepted her offer to build an auditorium in the Library of Congress. The Elizabeth Sprague Coolidge Foundation was established that same year. The Foundation championed modern music through the commissioning and performing of new works. A notable example was Aaron Copland's *Appalachian Spring,* choreographed by Martha Graham, which premiered in the Coolidge Auditorium in 1944. The eminent critic, Olin Downes, author of the article below, referred to Coolidge as the patron saint of chamber music in America. The testimony seems entirely appropriate.

From "The National Conservatory of Music of America" (1890)

Among the few music schools in this country which really merit the name of conservatory, the National Conservatory of Music of America in New York deserves special attention, because it was not organized as a money-making institution, but as a sort of musical high-school, where pupils could prepare themselves for the career of concert, church, or opera singers, of solo or orchestral players, or of teachers, for a merely nominal sum, or, if talented, without any charge for tuition. This institution was founded in 1885 by Mrs. Jeannette M. Thurber, whose name has become a household word in connection with the development of music in the United States, and who is always one of the first to help along a meritorious musical enterprise. Passionately fond of music, and a critical student of the art, she has for years devoted her means to helping talented struggling musicians to

help themselves; and when the demands outgrew her individual ability, she conceived the idea of establishing a National Conservatory of Music in the United States similar to those of European countries, where instruction of the highest class might be obtained at moderate cost, or free, if need be, where exceptional talent was found to exist without the means necessary for its cultivation. Like the most famous music schools in Europe, the National Conservatory was originally started with one branch (voice)—training young singers for the operatic stage. It was the desire to prove to the public what talent in a crude state really existed, and how necessary it was to found an institution in this country worthy of the name "National Conservatory of Music," that led Mrs. Thurber to organize the American Opera Company, which for the first time presented the master-works of grand opera in the English language in this country in a satisfactory manner: but owing to the bad financial management, through no fault of Mrs.

"The National Conservatory of Music of America," *Harper's Weekly*, December 13, 1890: 969–70.

Thurber's, it was impossible for the American Opera company to continue long in existence; yet, while it lasted, it was a revelation to many persons, showing the progress already made in musical art in this country, and indicating its possibilities for the future. It gathered and put in evidence before the American people some of the talent already in existence; it attracted public attention and stimulated interest in the development of the art; and in these respects great good was accomplished, and, as beautifully stated in Harper's Monthly by Mr. George William Curtis, "it seemed as if Brother Jonathan had become of age," and "that it was the first warble of the American Independence."

The National Conservatory was located at 126 and 128 East Seventeenth Street, New York, in 1885, and during the last two years Mrs. Thurber's time has been almost exclusively devoted to it. In its organization she showed the same intelligence as in the establishment of American opera. Just as, in starting the American opera, an unrivaled orchestra was secured, so, in making up the faculty of the National Conservatory, Mrs. Thurber endeavored to put specialists of national and in some cases international reputation at the head of each department of instruction. The faculty comprises forty odd names, there are only three or four which are not known through the country as those of competent specialists.

OLIN DOWNES

from "Servant of Music" (1953)

The conventional phraseology is perfectly correct—that the musical world "suffered an irreparable loss" in the passing of one of its most famous and influential patrons with the death of Mrs. Elizabeth Sprague Coolidge on Nov. 4, shortly after her eighty-ninth birthday. The companion fact is that the musical world and, what is more important, music itself experienced an incalculable gain and a new creative impulse in its cultivation in America—especially in the field of chamber music—which has no parallel in the modern period on either side of the Atlantic through her exceptionally sagacious and enlightened patronage.

Her principal philanthropies in this field are well known. They included the establishment of the Berkshire Festival of Chamber Music, in Pittsfield, Mass., in 1918; the gift the following year of $100,000 for a pension fund for the Chicago Symphony Orchestra; the presentation to Yale University, in memory of her father and mother, of Sprague Memorial Hall, with its superbly equipped auditorium and accessory accommodations for the study and performance of music. But Mrs. Coolidge's greatest accomplishment was her building and giving of the Coolidge Auditorium to the Library of Congress in 1925 and the establishment of a trust fund of $600,000 for its maintenance and functioning.

World Center

With the donation to the Library of Congress of the Coolidge Auditorium and the Elizabeth Sprague Coolidge Foundation, instituted in 1925, our national library becomes a world center of chamber music and has been responsible for the creation of some of the most outstanding compositions of the twentieth century.

This work has already carried so far and effectively that it would be difficult to name a composer of importance of the present day who has not benefited by Mrs. Coolidge's support. Among them are Samuel Barber, Béla Bartók, Ernest Bloch, Frank Bridge, Benjamin Britten, Alfredo Casella,

Olin Downes, "Servant of Music: Passing of Mrs. Coolidge Removes a Vital Force," *New York Times,* November 15, 1953: sect. 10, p. 7.

Aaron Copland, Paul Hindemith, Arthur Honegger, Charles Martin Loeffler, Gian Francesco Malipiero, Bohuslav Martinu, Darius Milhaud, Walter Piston, Ildebrando Pizzetti, Maurice Ravel, Ottorino Respighi, Arnold Schoenberg, Igor Stravinsky, Heitor Villa-Lobos, Anton von Webern. As an offshoot of the foundation's work there has accrued to the library a collection of autograph scores, letters and other memorabilia of the composers and compositions commissioned by the foundation, having a special value for reference and research.

Anonymous Aid

These are only the outstanding and generally known examples of Mrs. Coolidge's contributions to the cause of music and musicians. She also assisted unnumbered and unnamed composers and musical organizations in need of aid to exist and function. Nothing was said of these details by her or by those who executed her wishes.

She was always idealistic, but always foresighted and practical, in her undertakings. . . . She had the great advantage in this work of knowing music as a musician who had been trained in her youth in fundamentals of the art, with special study of the piano and composition. Mrs. Coolidge loved to play, and appeared as soloist in her youth with the Chicago Symphony Orchestra under Frederick Stock.[1] She composed, through her life, when she had the time and the opportunity to do so, with enthusiasm and without illusion about the value of her production. There were piano pieces, songs, a string quartet, an ensemble for oboe and strings, played at the most recent of the Pittsfield Festivals, held last Sept. 13 in her honor.

It was not that Mrs. Coolidge spent unprecedented sums of money for her purposes. The virtue of her undertaking was the sound thinking and artistic judgment with which she entered upon her engagements. She knew how to reach her objective without waste.

---

[1]Frederick Stock became conductor of the Chicago Symphony Orchestra in 1905 upon the death of Theodore Thomas.

Frank Mitchell (Olta'í Tsoh), Navajo Blessingway Singer

Outsiders who confronted Native American music often had difficulty bridging the gap between cultures so different from their own: the spectrum was wide, attitudes were divergent, and Native American music was passed down through oral transmission. No less a problem was writing down what they heard in a way that would reflect the unique sound of the music.

One Native American who was willing to open up concerning his heritage was Frank Mitchell (1881–1967), known to his own Navajo people as Olta'í Tsoh, or Big Schoolboy. As a Blessingway singer, Mitchell performed and led highly meaningful religious ceremonies, which form the backbone of his tribe's faith. These ceremonies take place over hours and even days in small groups, often to benefit particular individuals who need them because, for example, they are ill or expecting a child. They are also performed on other occasions, such as home blessings and natural events, for example, an eclipse of the sun or moon.

Mitchell lived on the Navajo reservation that spans parts of Arizona and New Mexico. He was one of the first to attend the government-established boarding school at Fort Defiance in the late 1800s. As he tells us, because of the authority bestowed on him through his leadership of the Blessingway ceremony and because others could understand him well, he became one of the first members of the tribal council on the reservation. He served also as a chapter officer in Chinle and a judge in the Courts of Indian Offenses. But above all, Mitchell was a much beloved family man.

In 1957, ethnomusicologist David McAllester began to study Navajo customs and soon encountered Mitchell, who became interested in his work. Thus commenced a long and fruitful relationship. Charlotte Frisbie joined the project in 1963. Later that same year, Mitchell was persuaded to tell his life story, which was recorded on tape without interruption. His words, as amplified in subsequent sessions, became the basis of a book.

During that period, there were about 140,000 Navajos living on the reservation, including an estimated three or four hundred singers.

Although McAllester and Frisbie's friendship with Mitchell began after the mid-century mark, when the Navajo singer was an old man, it is clear that he is speaking out of an oral tradition passed down through generations. And while interpretations and traditions change through time, such historical knowledge gives us insights into a culture that was well formed before the intervention of whites.

FRANK MITCHELL

from *Navajo Blessingway Singer* (1960s; PUB. 1978)

During the time I was going to school, my brother John was working at Fort Defiance,[1] and his family was living there with him. I already told about how he was married twice; that was his first wife he was living with when he was at Fort Defiance. I lived there with him during the time that I worked at the trader's place as a housekeeper and dishwasher. There was an old man who was some relation to my brother's wife. His name was He Who Seeks War, and he was a singer of the Blessingway.

He used to visit my brother's place a lot, and I guess John learned that he was a Blessingway singer and started picking up some of the songs, learning something about them. That man used to give me some instruction in Blessingway, too, telling me what goes on in the ceremony and how the Blessingway goes. At the same time I listened whenever I could, trying to pick up pieces of it. I began learning some of the songs from here and there in the ceremony, and I remembered them pretty well.

Later on I came back over here because my wife's parents were getting pretty old and sick. I gave up hauling freight and started tending their farm and livestock. Like I have said, my father-in-law was a well-to-do man: he had cattle and sheep and horses. Also, he was a Blessingway singer, and I went out with him whenever he performed his ceremony. I noticed that the songs I had learned from He Who Seeks War were the same as the ones my father-in-law was singing. . . .

It was mainly from Man Who Shouts[2] that I learned the Blessingway, by following him when-

ever he was asked to do some singing. I picked up most of his songs and prayers that way. Whenever he went to Fort Defiance we would go in a buggy. We would stop in Sawmill overnight where there lived He Who Seeks War and his younger brother, who knew the same Blessingway songs. They would practice them, and I would listen. After we would leave there he would explain things to me, and that is how I would learn.

We would spend the night there sitting around talking about the Blessingway until late at night, and then we would go on to Fort Defiance the next day. And then, coming back, we did the same thing. We always stopped there, and I learned a little more again. Just gradually like that I learned all about that ceremony from those two men.

*   *   *

As for the songs I use, I have told you how I learned one set from my own father and the other set from my father-in-law. Originally they belonged to two different persons: one was Man Who Speaks Often, my grandfather. He learned it from his father, and handed it down to his son, Water Edge Man, who was my father. The other was Kaya, and his son was named He Who Seeks War, who in turn passed it on to Man Who Shouts, my father-in-law. From there on it was handed down to me.

These songs were handed down originally to the Earth People by the beings who had returned to the sky and other places and were no longer visible on the earth. They had gone, just as in your church[3] where you teach about an afterlife. But still their songs and ceremonies are left here. Still, they are remembered; that is how our ceremonies were left to us.

This is the way we think about these things. These deities are living somewhere. They are aware of what we are doing, of how we are conducting

---

Frank Mitchell, *Navajo Blessingway Singer: The Autobiography of Frank Mitchell, 1881–1967*, ed. Charlotte J. Frisbie and David P. McAllester (Tucson: University of Arizona Press, 1978), 192–194, 204–206, 211–212, 219, 231–235, 238–239.

[1]Close to the Arizona–New Mexico border.

[2]His father-in-law.

[3]Catholic church.

ourselves here on earth: if we misuse the songs, that displeases them. It is the same way if we combine two songs that do not properly go together. They know about it there.

As we understand it, the songs were left here by different groups of holy beings. We are supposed to keep them intact and not mix them up. If we do start mixing them up, one with another, they know about it, and therefore, that ceremony is not recognized, it is not honored. It has no effect on the person that you are treating with it.[4] Those Holy People are displeased with you if you start acting like that, and they no longer want to accept your songs and prayers. Otherwise, if you are keeping it up as it should be practiced, it is always accepted. It is understood that the different ceremonials, like Shootingway, Windway and Mountaintopway, are distinctly separate and were left here by the Holy People for the People to use. So, if you are singing Shootingway, you cannot just take songs from the Mountaintopway and add them. That is forbidden.

*   *   *

There are special songs, Chief songs, that are sung during the time that they are making up [a] bundle for a new singer.[5] Nobody knows them but me; my father taught me those songs. As far as I know, around here none of the Blessingway singers know those songs. I am the only one. Those particular songs are for tying up the Mountain Earth bundle. There is another reason that most Blessingway bundles are not as properly made as mine: these younger men just ask the older singers a few questions, but they do not stop long enough to find out the real answers; they just want to do it their own way. I know a lot of them who have this mountain earth, but it is not put together the way it should be.

I learned how to prepare a bundle from my father, Water Edge Man; my grandfather, Man Who Speaks Often, was the one that knew it before my father did. It was carried down in the family to me.

Another generation back, Man Who Speaks Often's father, would be my great-grandfather. It was his ceremony in the beginning. His name was Thin Man. He was from the area of Wheatfields, and Man Who Speaks Often was from there, too. My father was from Pointed Red Rocks, somewhere over on the road to Keams Canyon.

Those special songs are kept very secret, and they cannot be sung just anywhere. The only time they should be used is when you are performing that particular ceremony. There are three or four different special songs, and each one is sung at a particular time when something is taking place during the making or the renewal of the Mountain Earth bundle.[6] Last of all there is a song after everything is all put together and the last cord is being wrapped around the whole bundle. Even that has a song to go with it.

After it is all put together, it is set in a basket on the floor. Then a pipe is smoked for it, too. We use a special dry herb and breathe out the smoke from it on the bundle while it is sitting there. Some singers make this pipe themselves out of a kind of hard rock, and some of them have found their pipes in the ruins where the early people lived. These pipes are usually small and in the shape of an L.

When the bundle is all tied up and set in the basket, the singer lights this pipe, and some of the smoke is blown on the person for whom the bundle is being made or renewed. Then smoke is also blown on the bundle, there in the basket. And then the pipe is passed from south of the door of the hogan all the way around to everybody there. Everyone takes a puff of that smoke. It is just the way they pass the pollen in a ceremony. The tobacco is made of special herbs, and when they use up what is in the pipe, it is just refilled, lit again and passed on. Matches are not used; instead there is a particular lighting stick.

The ashes in the pipe are saved; they are not thrown out. Some of them are put on the bundle and some on the person for whom the bundle is

---

[4]Ceremonies may be performed for an individual, the "one-sung-over."

[5]The bundle, which must be periodically renewed, is an essential part of Blessingway.

[6]A bundle of earth gathered from four sacred mountains.

being fixed. This is done just like a pollen blessing, starting with the feet and going on up to bless the other parts of the body. When that is finished, the singer gets up, takes the bundle and puts it in the hands of the new Blessingway singer. Then that person has what is needed to start giving this ceremony.

* * *

Blessingway is used for everything that is good for a person, or for the People. It has no use other than that. For instance, when a woman is pregnant she has the Blessingway in order to have a good delivery with no trouble. It is also done so that she and her child may have a happy life. In case of bad dreams, they are a kind of warning that there are some misfortunes ahead of you; in order to avoid that you have the Blessingway so that you will have happiness instead. Or if you are worried about something, your family will want to get you back, to get that out of your mind, out of your system, so that you may have a good life. It is the same for any other things that could cause you to worry, to feel uneasy about yourself. That is the sort of thing it is used for.

As for the prayers, you say, "Beauty shall be in front of me, beauty shall be in the back, beauty shall be below me, above me, all around me" On top of that you say about yourself, "I am everlasting, I may have an everlasting life. I may live on, and lead an everlasting life with beauty." You end your prayers that way.

* * *

This is the Twelve-Word song from my Blessingway.[7]

Haiya, naiya yana.
I have come upon it, *yo,* I have come upon
    blessing, *wo,*

People, my relatives, *yowo laŋa,* I have come
    upon blessing,
People, my relatives, *ya,* blessed, *na'eye laŋa
    heya 'eye.*

I have come upon it, *yo,* I have come upon
    blessing, *wo,*
People, my relatives, *yowo laŋa.* I have come
    upon blessing,
People, my relatives, *ya,* blessed, *na'eye laŋa
    heya 'eye, holaghei.*

Neya, now, Darkness, *'iya.*
    He comes upon me with blessing, *wo,*
    Behind him, from there, *ye, Sạ'ah naaghéi,*
    He comes upon me with blessing, *wo,*
    Before him, from there, *ye, Bik'eh hózhǫ́ǫ́,*
    He comes upon me with blessing, *wo,*
    Before him, it is blessed,
    Behind him, it is blessed, *neya'eye, laŋa heya
        'eye, holaghei.*

Neya, behind her, from there, *ye,* Dawn, *'iye,*
    She comes upon me with blessing, *wo,*
    Before her, from there, *ye, Bik'eh hózhǫ́ǫ́,*
    She comes upon me with blessing, *wo,*
    Behind her, from there, *ye, Sạ'ah naaghéi,*
    She comes upon me with blessing, *wo,*
    Behind her, it is blessed,
    Before her, it is blessed, *neya'eye, laŋa heya
        'eye,*
    I have come upon it, *yo,* I have come upon
        blessing, *wo,*
        People, my relatives, *yowo laŋa,* I have come
            upon blessing,
        People, my relatives, *ya,* blessed, *ya'eye, laŋa
            heya 'eye, holaghei.*

Neya, behind him, from there, *ye,* Afterglow, *woye,*
    She comes upon me with blessing, *wo,*
    Behind her, from there, *ye, Sạ'ah naaghéi*
    She comes upon me with blessing, *wo,*
    Before her, from there, *ye, Bik'eh hózhǫ́ǫ́,*
    She comes upon me with blessing, *wo,*
    Before her, it is blessed,
    Behind her, it is blessed, *neya'eye, laŋa heya
        'eye, holaghei.*

---

[7]"A Blessingway is usually attended by the immediate family and a few other relatives. There may be only a dozen participants. The women and children are seated on the north side of the hogan and the men face them from the south side." Also, "This is the (Twelve-Word) song with which Frank concluded his Blessingway. It was recorded by Frank for McAllester in 1957. There are the usual vocables with no lexical meaning." [Author's notes.]

Neya, behind him, from there, *ye*, Sun *'iye*,
   He comes upon me with blessing, *wo*,
   Before him, from there, *ye*, *Bik'eh hózhǫ́ǫ́*,
   He comes upon me with blessing, *wo*,
   Behind him, from there, *ye*, *Sǫ'ah naaghéi*,
   He comes upon me with blessing, *wo*,
   Behind him, it is blessed,
   Before him, it is blessed, *neya'eye, laṇa heya
      'eye,*

I have come upon it, *yo*, I have come upon
   blessing, *wo*,
      People, my relatives, *yowo laṇa*, I have come
         upon blessing,
      People, my relatives, *ya*, blessed, *na'eye, laṇa
         heya 'eye, holaghei.*

Neya, behind him, from there, *ye*, now Talking
   God, *'iye*,
   He comes upon me with blessing, *wo*,
   Behind him, from there, *ye*, *Sǫ'ah naaghéi*,
   He comes upon me with blessing, *wo*,
   Before him, from there, *ye*, *Bik'eh hózhǫ́ǫ́*,
   He comes upon me with blessing, *wo*,
   Before him, it is blessed,
   Behind him, it is blessed, *neya'eye, laṇa heya
      'eye, holaghei.*

Neya, behind him, from there, *ye*, now Calling
   God, *'iye*,
   He comes upon me with blessing, *wo*,
   Before him, from there, *ye*, *Bik'eh hózhǫ́ǫ́*,
   He comes upon me with blessing, *wo*,
   Behind him, from there, *ye*, *Sǫ'ah naaghéi*,
   He comes upon me with blessing, *wo*,
   Behind him, it is blessed,
      Before him, it is blessed, *neya'eye, laṇa heya
         'eye,*

I have come upon it, *yo*, I have come upon
   blessing, *wo*,
   People, my relatives, *yowo laṇa*, I have come
      upon blessing,
   People, my relatives, *ya*, blessed, *na'eye, laṇa
      heya 'eye, holaghei.*

Neya, behind him, from there, *ye*, Coming With A
   Turquoise Boy, *'iye*,

   He comes upon me with blessing, *wo*,
   Behind him, from there, *ye*, *Sǫ'ah naaghéi*,
   He comes upon me with blessing, *wo*,
   Before him, from there, *ye*, *Bik'eh hózhǫ́ǫ́*,
   He comes upon me with blessing, *wo*,
   Before him, it is blessed,
   Behind him, it is blessed, *neya'eye, laṇa heya
      'eye, holaghei.*

Neya, behind her, from there, *ye*, Coming With A
   Corn Kernel Girl, *'eye*,
   She comes upon me with a blessing, *wo*,
   Before her, from there, *ye*, *Bik'eh hózhǫ́ǫ́*,
   She comes upon me with a blessing, *wo*,
   Behind her, from there, *ye*, *Sǫ'ah naaghéi*,
   She comes upon me with a blessing, *wo*,
   Before her, it is blessed,
   Behind her, it is blessed, *neya'eye, laṇa heya'eye,*

I have come upon it, *yo*, I have come upon
   blessing, *wo*,
   People, my relatives, *yowo laṇa*, I have come
      upon blessing,
   People, my relatives, *ya*, blessed, *na'eye, laṇa
      heya 'eye, holaghei.*

Neya, behind him, from there, *ye*, White Corn
   Plant Boy, *'iye*,
   He comes upon me with blessing, *wo*,
   Behind him, from there, *ye*, *Sǫ'ah naaghéi*,
   He comes upon me with blessing, *wo*,
   Before him, from there, *ye*, *Bik'eh hózhǫ́ǫ́*,
   He comes upon me with blessing, *wo*,
   Before him, it is blessed,
   Behind him, it is blessed, *neya'eye, laṇa heya
      'eye.*

Neya, behind her, from there, *ye*, Yellow Corn
   Plant Girl, *'eye*,
   She comes upon me with blessing, *wo*,
   Before her, from there, *ye*, *Bik'eh hózhǫ́ǫ́*,
   She comes upon me with blessing, *wo*,
   Behind her, from there, *ye*, *Sǫ'ah naaghéi*,
   She comes upon me with blessing, *wo*,
   Behind her, it is blessed,
      Before her, it is blessed, *neya'eye, laṇa heya
         'eye,*

I have come upon it, *yo*, I have come upon
blessing, *wo*,
People, my relatives, *yowo laŋa*, I have come
upon blessing,
People, my relatives, *ya*, blessed, *na'eye laŋa
heya 'eye, holaghei.*

Neya, behind him, from there, *ye*, Pollen Boy, *'iye*,
He comes upon me with blessing, *wo*,
Behind him, from there, *ye*, Sǫ'ah naaghéi,
He comes upon me with blessing, *wo*,
Before him, from there, *ye*, Bik'eh hózhǫǫ,
He comes upon me with blessing, *wo*,
Before him, it is blessed,
Behind him, it is blessed, *neya'eye, laŋa heya
'eye, holaghei.*

Neya, behind her, from there, *ye*, Harvest Fly Girl,
'eye,
She comes upon me with blessing, *wo*,
Before her, from there, *ye*, Bik'eh hózhǫǫ,
She comes upon me with blessing, *wo*,
Behind her, from there, *ye*, Sǫ'ah naaghéi,
She comes upon me with blessing, *wo*,
Behind her, it is blessed,
Before her, it is blessed,
Beneath her, it is blessed,
Above her, it is blessed,
All around her, it is blessed,
Everywhere, it is blessed, *neya'eye, laŋa heya
'eye,*

I have come upon it, *yo*, I have come upon
blessing, *wo*,
People, my relatives, *yowo laŋa*, I have come
upon blessing,
People, my relatives, *ya*, blessed, *na'eye, laŋa
heya 'eye, holaghei.*

In the Twelve-Word song at the end of my Blessingway, I mention the Darkness coming to my relative. Right after that comes *Sǫ'ah naaghéi* and right after that *Bik'eh hózhǫǫ*. That has to do with the Darkness, not the singer, who only pronounces those words. It is what is in the song that is *Bik'eh hózhǫǫ*. But in another song, for example, the Returning Home song, you say, "I am Talking God." You say, "I am," you do not mention anyone else and you say "*Sǫ'ah naaghéi*, I am," and "*Bik'eh hózhǫǫ* I am." That is the way you say it. Then you are referring to yourself, not what is in the song. That is the difference between the songs: a lot of them are like that, you see.

So for each verse in the song, you say, "*Sǫ'ah naaghéi, Bik'eh hózhǫǫ.*" The phrase is a holy being. You see, these songs, when they were turned over to the Earth People, were to be used in a certain way. If you leave out those words, then the holy beings feel slighted. They know you are singing, they are aware of it. But if you omit those words, then they feel it and they are displeased. Then, even though you are singing, whatever you are doing over the one-sung-over has no effect.

If you forget to mention those holy words in one song, and in the next song you think of it, then you will mention them. That makes up, somewhat, for their having been left out before. That is the reason that at the conclusion of your songs, you will say a prayer in your own words. You ask the holy beings to help you and to go through these songs with you; that also helps to make up for what you may have left out.

65   Singing for Power and Wakaṇtaṇka

It is difficult to generalize about the music of Native Americans who lived for centuries on two large continents, North and South America. Comprising more than one thousand tribes speaking at least sixty languages, even the people who covered only the North American land mass cannot be thought of as a single entity. As we can best reconstruct them, the cultural styles of these northern Native American groups coincide with the large geographical boundaries of the continent: the East, the Great Plains, the Great Basin, California, the Pacific Northwest, and the Southwest, although even between different regions there are some shared traits. Overall, Native American music in precolonial time was used mostly to accompany dance or poetry recitations. It played an important role in the ritual expressions of belief and religion as these were variously understood among different tribes. Music professionals, if they existed in a tribe, were the shamans, priests, or doctors, occupations held primarily by men. But music was often broadly participatory, a communal activity that reinforced the basic values and myths of a family, clan, or tribe.

Even though the earliest accounts preserved in European records of Native American speakers are heavily mediated by the religious and moral views of the Europeans, clear outlines of widespread practices emerge. Accounts from the last hundred years are much more numerous and faithful to Indian worldviews, although many are still subject to problems of translation and reporter bias.

Sources of information about Indian cultures include sound recordings (some among the first ever made); ethnographic reports (including the pioneering work of Alice Fletcher and Frances Densmore); biographies; and collections of poetry and song texts. Examples from each of the last three categories are included below.

The motivation for the sudden recording of Indian lore in the late nineteenth century sprang from the mistaken belief that Indians would soon become extinct and that they possessed a wholly distinct and ancient culture uncontaminated by modern urban life. Despite this element of romanticization, the high level of sympathy for the lives of the people they were studying and occasionally the ability to listen carefully to the broader ideas held by the cultures, led the ethnographers and ethnomusicologists to provide—or, attempt to provide—interpretations of the complex Native American cultures.

Translated biographies are, of course, more idiosyncratic than ethnographic, but they have the virtue of representing the views of a single authoritative person (as opposed to a colorless norm) within a group or tribe. Usually, the biographical subject is speaking to a reporter who is knowledgeable in the language and concerned with presenting as complete and accurate a picture as possible.

The Sun Dance, a central ritual in the lives of the Teton Sioux before 1890, was associated with a variety of musical expressions. More than thirty songs from the Sun

Dance ritual are transcribed in Frances Densmore's 1918 book, *Teton Sioux Music,* most based on performances by three singers, Lone Man, Red Bird, and Śiya'ka. In explaining the significance of the Sun Dance, Red Bird has said,

> There is a great deal in what a man *believes*, and if a man's religion is changed for the better or for the worse he will know it. The Sun Dance was our first and only religion. We believed that there is a mysterious power greater than all others, which is represented in nature, one form of representation being the sun.*

Until it was discontinued late in the nineteenth century, the Sun Dance culminated with an annual midsummer gathering of all Teton Sioux bands. During the gathering, the chiefs transacted tribal business, long-separated friends greeted one another, and people related news and achievements from the past year. The days prior to the main dance were filled with preparatory activities, many highly charged. In times of battle and anxiety, warriors made vows to take part in the Sun Dance, during which they received gashes in their arms and were suspended from the ground by their flesh. By demonstrating such stoic endurance of pain, they gave thanks for success in battle, for life and health sustained by the Great Spirit, and for reunions with friends and loved ones.

Densmore's volume includes a quotation from Red Weasel:

> One of the first and most important things that I was taught was that I must have the greatest reverence for Wakaṇ'taṇka [Great Spirit]. Dreamer-of-the-Sun told me that if I would obey his instructions I would be a help to the Sioux nation, and that, if properly prepared for the highest office of the Sun Dance, I need have no anxiety when filling the office as the proper thing to do would come to my mind at the time. In regard to the songs, Dreamer-of-the-Sun told me that I may pray with my mouth and the prayer will be heard, but if *I sing* the prayer it will be heard *sooner* by Wakaṇ'taṇka.†

Red Weasel's statement testifies to the special efficacy of singing—as opposed to merely speaking words—among the Teton Sioux. All males could take part in music making, which was a communal activity rather than merely a personal statement. The musical power generated by a group was one means by which Native Americans held their culture together through the bleak years of the late nineteenth century.

Among the most poetically compelling of Native American accounts is the story of Black Elk (1863–1950), an Oglala Sioux shaman. In the book *Black Elk Speaks,* written down in 1931 by John G. Neidhardt (Flaming Rainbow), Black Elk relates his life story, including his recollections of Custer's last stand, the murder of Crazy Horse, his travels with "Buffalo" Bill Cody's Wild West Show, a visit to England and an audience with Queen Victoria, and the massacre at Wounded Knee. Most significant for Black Elk was his personal vision that led to his calling as a healer and servant of his people. Re-

---

*Frances Densmore, *Teton Sioux Music* (Washington, D.C.: Government Printing Office, 1918), 86.

†Ibid., 88.

ceived at the age of nine and reenacted with his tribesmen when he was eighteen years old, the vision interweaves the wondrous dancing and singing of animals with prophecy, speaking of nature's intimate and tender links with human beings.

The story of Black Elk's vision begins as he is ill and being cared for in the family *tipi.* He is summoned by spear-carrying men of angelic power and is whisked away on a cloud to the council of elders, six grandfathers. He is instructed by them and shown portents of the future on four horseback "ascents."

The Papago Indians in Southern Arizona had relatively little contact with European-Americans until the middle of the twentieth century. Their desert habitat was shunned by sixteenth-century Spaniards and westward-moving Americans alike. Even among their Aztec forebears, they lived on the periphery of civilization. As a consequence, their songs probably represent a relatively uncontaminated tradition, although of undated origins. Not surprisingly for a desert climate, the subjects of many of the traditional songs, recorded in 1931–33 by Ruth Murray Underhill, involve rain, water, and the act of drinking. The image and power of water is often invoked. In the following "Speech to Cleanse the Village of Sickness," the phrase "soft rain" is a gentle refrain, and "the moisture that lies above" signals the completion of the cure.

The images in the song are related to specific plants and to vivid actions used in the ritual to drive out evil. In the Papago cosmology, plants can be used for good or evil, and even found objects, such as feathers, are sometimes thought to contain contagious evil, which can be cultivated like a plant. Objects are buried like seeds, and evil shoots spring forth from the ground, spreading their new seeds like pollen in the air. The task of the good medicine man is to find and destroy the buried charm by uprooting or crushing it. The ocotillo is a plant with long-thorned branches that suggest animate danger. Single isolated lines of verse are not immediately repeated—as in many other regional styles of Indian poetry—although the refrain lines exemplify the Papago stress on the symbolic power of the number four: actions occur four times, the youth makes four steps, each ocotillo possesses the same four traits, and so on.

A more business-minded view of music but, nevertheless, one in which a song's magical properties are seen as highly potent is found in the autobiography of a Navajo man named Left Handed. In *Son of Old Man Hat,* Left Handed narrates his life story from his birth in 1868 until age twenty to anthropologist Walter Dyk. Left Handed refers to the importance of a song as a practical tool, a lesson he learned as a boy. He speaks of a scene in which Old Man Hat gives advice to an older cousin named Who Has Mules. Some years later, Left Handed himself receives similar advice. In describing his method of learning the songs—by noting that they fall into distinct groups with similar melodies—he reveals an important stylistic aspect of the repertoire and provides us with an insider's view of the music-making process.

—THOMAS L. RIIS

BLACK ELK

from *Black Elk Speaks* (1932)

And when we reached the summit of the third ascent and camped, the nation's hoop was broken like a ring of smoke that spreads and scatters and the holy tree seemed dying and all its birds were gone. And when I looked ahead I saw that the fourth ascent would be terrible.

Then when the people were getting ready to begin the fourth ascent, the Voice spoke like some one weeping, and it said: "Look there upon your nation." And when I looked down, the people were all changed back to human, and they were thin, their faces sharp, for they were starving. Their ponies were only hide and bones, and the holy tree was gone.

And as I looked and wept, I saw that there stood on the north side of the starving camp a sacred man who was painted red all over his body, and he held a spear as he walked into the center of the people, and there he lay down and rolled. And when he got up, it was a fat bison standing there, and where the bison stood a sacred herb sprang up right where the tree had been in the center of the nation's hoop. The herb grew and bore four blossoms on a single stem while I was looking—a blue, a white, a scarlet, and a yellow—and the bright rays of these flashed to the heavens.[1]

I know now what this meant, that the bison were the gift of a good spirit and were our strength, but we should lose them, and from the same good spirit we must find another strength. For the people all seemed better when the herb had grown and bloomed, and the horses raised their tails and neighed and pranced around, and I could see a light breeze going from the north among the people like a ghost; and suddenly the flowering tree was there again at the center of the nation's hoop where the four-rayed herb had blossomed.

I was still the spotted eagle floating, and I could see that I was already in the fourth ascent and the people were camping yonder at the top of the third long rise. It was dark and terrible about me, for all the winds of the world were fighting. It was like rapid gun-fire and like whirling smoke, and like women and children wailing and like horses screaming all over the world.

I could see my people yonder running about, setting the smoke-flap poles and fastening down their tepees against the wind, for the storm cloud was coming on them very fast and black, and there were frightened swallows without number fleeing before the cloud.

Then a song of power came to me and I sang it there in the midst of that terrible place where I was. It went like this:

A good nation I will make live.
This the nation above has said.
They have given me the power to make over.

And when I had sung this, a Voice said: "To the four quarters you shall run for help, and nothing shall be strong before you. Behold him!"

Now I was on my bay horse again, because the horse is of the earth, and it was there my power would be used. And as I obeyed the Voice and looked, there was a horse all skin and bones yonder in the west, a faded brownish black. And a Voice there said: "Take this and make him over; and it was the four-rayed herb that I was holding in my hand. So I rode above the poor horse in a circle, and as I did this I could hear the people yonder calling for spirit power, "A-hey! a-hey! a-hey! a-hey!" Then the poor horse neighed and rolled and got up, and he was a big, shiny, black stallion with dapples all over him and his mane about him like a cloud. He was the chief of all the horses; and when he snorted, it was a flash of lightning and his eyes

---

Black Elk, *Black Elk Speaks: Being the Life of a Holy Man of the Oglala Sioux*. As told through John G. Neidhardt (Flaming Rainbow) (New York: Morrow, 1932), 38–42.

[1]Blue as well as black may be used to represent the power of the west. [Neidhardt's note.]

were like the sunset start. He dashed to the west and neighed, and the west was filled with a dust of hoofs, and horses without number, shiny black, came plunging from the dust. Then he dashed toward the north and neighed, and to the east and to the south, and the dust clouds answered, giving forth their plunging horses without number—whites and sorrels and buckskins, fat, shiny, rejoicing in their fleetness and their strength. It was beautiful, but it was also terrible.

Then they all stopped short, rearing, and were standing in a great hoop about their black chief at the center, and were still. And as they stood, four virgins, more beautiful than women of the earth can be, came through the circle, dressed in scarlet, one from each of the four quarters, and stood the great black stallion in their places; and one held the wooden cup of water, and one the white wing, and one the pipe, and one the nation's hoop. All the universe was silent, listening; and then the great black stallion raised his voice and sang. The song he sang was this:

My horses, prancing they are coming.
My horses, neighing they are coming;
Prancing, they are coming.
All over the universe they come.
They will dance; may you behold them.
　　　　　(4 times)

A horse nation, they will dance.
May you behold them.
　　　　　(4 times)

His voice was not loud, but it went all over the universe and filled it. There was nothing that did not hear, and it was more beautiful than anything can be. It was so beautiful that nothing anywhere could keep from dancing. The virgins danced, and all the circled horses. The leaves on the trees, the grasses on the hills and in the valleys, the waters in the creeks and in the rivers and the lakes, the four-legged and the two-legged and the wings of the air—all danced together to the music of the stallion's song.

And when I looked down upon my people yonder, the cloud passed over, blessing them with friendly rain, and stood in the east with a flaming rainbow over it.

Then all the horses went singing back to their places beyond the summit of the fourth ascent, and all things sang along with them as they walked.

And a Voice said: "All over the universe they have finished a day of happiness." And looking down, I saw that the whole wide circle of the day was beautiful and green, with all fruits growing and all things kind and happy.

Then a Voice said: "Behold this day, for it is yours to make. Now you shall stand upon the center of the earth to see, for there they are taking you."

"Speech to Cleanse the Village of Sickness" (1938)

Ready!
There did I call by the kinship term
The youth whom I had reared.
Toward the west was a black road made and
　　finished.
Four stops made the youth and speedily did come

Ruth Murray Underhill, *Singing for Power: The Song Magic of the Papago Indians of Southern Arizona* (Berkeley: University of California Press, 1938), 147–50.

Where stood a black ocotillo.
Not slowly back to me he came and said:

"Within itself it rustles as it stands;
Within itself it thunders as it stands;
Within itself it roars as there it stands;
Within there is soft rain.
Around it four times did I circle
And toward the west a branch I broke with all my
　　force.
I took it and to you I brought it."

Therewith a part of the sickness
Did I pound into the earth and stake it down.

There was toward the ocean
A road of many hardships made and finished.
Four stops made the youth and speedily did come
Where stood an ocotillo most painful to the
    touch.
Not slowly back to me he came and said:

"Within itself it rustles as it stands;
Within itself it thunders as it stands;
Within itself it roars as there it stands;
Within it there is much soft rain.
Around it four times did I circle
And toward the sea a branch I broke with all my
    force.
I took it and to you I brought it"
Therewith a part of the sickness
Did I pound into the earth and stake it down.

There was toward the sunrise
A white road made and finished
Four stops made the youth and speedily did come
Where stood a white ocotillo.
Not slowly back to me he came and said:

"Within itself it rustles as it stands;
Within itself it thunders as it stands;
Within itself it roars as there it stands;
Within there is soft rain.
Around it four times did I circle
And toward the sunrise a branch I broke with all
    my force.
I took it and to you I brought it"
Therewith a part of the sickness
Did I pound into the ground and stake it down.

There was toward the north a red road made and
    finished.
Four stops made the youth and speedily did come
Where stood a red ocotillo.
Not slowly back to me he came and said:

"Within itself it rustles as it stands;
Within itself it thunders as it stands;
Within itself it roars as there it stands;
Within it there is much soft rain.
Four times around it did I circle
And toward the north a branch I broke with all
    my force.
I took it and to you I brought it"
Therewith a part of the sickness
Did I pound into the ground and stake it down.

Then forth came black tarantula magician.
In four places did he bite the earth and continue
    biting.
Some remaining shreds of sickness did he then
    fold up,
Did pound them into the earth and stake them
    down.
Then forth came the red wasp magicians.
In four places did they bite the earth and continue
    biting.
In four places did they make the earth into clay
    jars.
Into them did they pour some of the sickness,
Did pound them into the earth and stake them
    down.

From above descended mighty winged birds.
Their own wing feathers did they pull out
And therewith whipped and scattered some of the
    sickness.
All gone they thought it.

Then came forth the little sleeping people [ants].
Entering my house in ceaseless journeys,
The food [that caused my sickness] did they take
And yonder toward the north wind did they send
    it.

Then did the moisture that lies above begin to fall
And altogether did destroy the sickness.

Thus you also always think, all you my kinsmen.

LEFT HANDED

from *Son of Old Man Hat* (1938)

Then [Old Man Hat] said [to Who Has Mules], "When you learn about the stocks and properties you'll surely get them. If you go ahead and overcome all these hardships you'll soon have a big herd and property, and you'll have lots to eat. After you get all these things you won't have to go around and beg for them. You'll have everything for yourself. A lot of Indians may say you're stingy. You don't have to mind them, pay no attention to them, just keep on working. That's the way to become a rich man.

"Then, when you learn about all these things, there's a song for each one. Even though you know only one song for each of them everything of yours will be strong. Even if you have only one song for the sheep you'll raise them, nothing will bother them, nothing will happen to them, you'll have them for a long time, the rest of your life. You may live for a long time, you may die of old age, even though you're old you'll still have lots of sheep, horses and cattle. When you haven't a song for the sheep you may raise them for two or three years, maybe longer than that, and you may have a lot, but those sheep will not be strong. Something will bother them all the time. Something will happen to them. They'll get lost every day. Sickness will bother them, and they'll be dying off. Soon you'll have no more sheep. You'll raise them all right, for two or three years, but once it begins they'll go back and disappear, and you won't know what's happened to them. That is, when you haven't a song for them. . . ."

That was all he said to his nephew, and then [Old Man Hat] started singing. He started a song from here, from the earth, and went along up to the sun and around and back and came to earth again. There were four long songs. My father said, "You need learn only these four songs. If you learn

these four, fix them well in your mind, the rest will be easy." Towards midnight, or a little after, while they were working on the songs I fell over and went to sleep. From there on I don't know what they said, nor how long they sang. Early in the morning my mother woke me and told me to go out and get some wood and build up the fire. She had the fire started. They were still sitting up. They said, "It's morning now," and Who Has Mules said, "I'd better be going back." My father said, "All right," and he went home.

*   *   *

[Old Man Hat] got up and said [to me] "Get up, my boy, you mustn't lie." So I got up, and he said, "You haven't learned anything from me, and I'm going down all the time. You ought to learn something about the stocks, how to handle them. You ought to learn some songs and prayers about them, because if you don't know anything, if you don't know any songs, you won't have healthy stocks. As soon as the cold weather comes they'll get some kind of disease. Maybe they'll catch cold, maybe they'll get some kind of soreness, maybe they'll get bugs, or they may freeze to death. If you know some songs about them you'll have a good herd all the time. You'll be raising them year after year and get many lambs. The same with the horses. In the springtime you'll have colts, and they'll be looking fine. If you don't know any songs you'll soon lose all the stock. So you'd better start in right now and learn something, because you won't get a song from anyone else. You don't know any of the people of your clan, you don't know any of your clansmen, you just know your fathers, but I know they won't teach you anything. I know they don't want you to learn anything about these things. So you'd better go ahead and try it right now."

Then he started with the songs. He sang six and told me to repeat them. I repeated them, and he said, "Repeat them again." I repeated every one and he said, "Repeat once more." So I repeated

Left Handed, *Son of Old Man Hat: A Navaho Autobiography*, recorded by Walter Dyk (Lincoln: University of Nebraska Press, 1938), 76–78, 257–58.

every one again. Then he said, "That's right. Every one is correct. The rest can be counted." So I just counted the others, and there were twenty-eight altogether. After we'd put these songs away he started on another set. They were twelve in number. They were the same as the others, but with just a little different tune. "All these are called Driving Songs. When you're out with the herd you sing these songs, and while you're singing you take out your corn pollen and give it to the sheep." When we were through with the second set he started on another. They were twenty-eight. I learned four and just counted the rest again. They were all exactly alike in tune and words, but altogether different from the others.

When we were through it was morning. He said, "Now you've learned some songs about the stocks. I know you'll have good-looking stocks all the time. And you'll have strong stocks. None of them will be weak. They won't die off on you. They won't get any kind of disease. That's as far as I want you to learn from me. The rest of your fathers know all about these songs. There are more songs, but the other fathers of yours will teach you those. I know they will, when you ask them. A fellow shouldn't be stingy about the songs. So try and ask them. Don't be afraid to tell them you want to learn some songs about the stocks. If they're unkind to you they won't let you learn any; if they're kind enough, I'm pretty sure they'll teach you some."

That was all. That's as far as I learned some songs about the horses and sheep from him. That was the only time he sang songs for me, just that once, and no more. I never learned any from him again. He had a great many that he used on all different things, but I didn't get to learn any of them. If he'd lived longer I'd have learned more about the other things, but I never got the chance. That day, while I was out herding, I practiced and repeated all the songs I'd learned and got them fixed in my mind.

66 Songs from the Northwest Coast and the Far North

Haida and Eskimos are two of the groups that originally migrated to what is now Alaska over the land bridge connecting it with Siberia. The Haida, who worked their way down the coast, are typical North-Pacific-Coast Native Americans in physical type, language, and culture. Generally of a peaceful nature, their language is related to that of the more warlike Tlingit and to the Athabaskan family. Haida are renowned for their arts and crafts. Their lineages descended through maternal lines and formed two major divisions, Ravens and Eagles, with intermarriage prohibited. Histories are displayed on totem poles.

The Eskimos (called Inuit, in Canada) migrated later to the New World. They adapted and acclimated to the harsh conditions of a large territory in the far north, where the land lies frozen under snow and ice for six to nine months of the year. While daylight hours are long in summer, a considerable period passes in winter during which there is no visible sun.

Bear Song is a somewhat enigmatic Haida song that personalizes death; the Eskimo *Summer Song* has a cheerful text. Like most Native American poetry, these highly personal songs speak to particular occasions.

Haida and Eskimo Song Texts (PUB. 1934)

Bear Song (Haida)

Chief, chief, that I am,
Be careful how you pull your grandfather around.
Be careful how you pull around your grandfather
As you sit beside him.
I am too much of a boy for you.
Chief, chief that I am.

Chief, chief that I am,
I am already far away.
At the cliff, coming from my passage through the
    mountains,
I hold up my head grandly.
Chief, chief that I am.

I am already far away from it.
From my blue mountain I am now far away.
On the Island I travel, led about proudly.
From it I am far away.
Chief, chief that I am.

Chief, chief that I am,
They say that I have green mountains.
They say that I went into the creek I own
        which stretches its length afar.
Chief, chief that I am.

Chief, chief that I am,
When the sun rises I start traveling about.
Now I am lying under a deadfall.[1]
Chief, chief that I am.

George W. Cronyn, ed., *American Indian Poetry: An Anthology of Songs and Chants* (New York: Liveright, 1934), 159–61, 185–87. Trans. by John R. Swanton ("Bear Song") and Franz Boas ("Summer Song").

[1]Bear trap.

Chief, chief that I am,
My power is all taken away,
My power is all taken away.
Chief, chief that I am,
My power is all taken away,
Chief, chief that I am.

Chief, chief, whither did my great brother wander
    proudly?
My mind shakes as I go about.
Chief, chief.

Chief, chief,
Tell me where he fell.
I do not know the place.
Chief, chief, chief.

Summer Song (Eskimo)

Ajaja, it is pleasant,
    it is pleasant at last
    the great world
    when it is summer at last.

Ajaja, it is pleasant,
    it is pleasant at last
    the great world
    when our caribous begin to come.

Ajaja, they make great noise,
    they make great noise,

the brooks there in our country
    when it is summer.

Ajaja, this great water
    has spread over the ice;
    I cannot walk
    to the rock across there.

Ajaja, I feel sorry for them,
    I feel sorry for them,
    not being able to speak,
    these gulls.

Ajaja, I feel sorry for them,
    I feel sorry for them,
    not being able to speak,
    these ravens.

A great animal comes now;
    no one observes it;
    I keep it secret;
    the ravens do not tell.

Food like that I cannot obtain.
    but quickly I got
    little sculpins.[2]

Ajaja, he has found a smooth slope,
    he has found a smooth slope,
    to burrow into,
    the bad old fox.

---

[2]A sculpin is a spiny, large-headed, broad-mouthed, usually scaleless fish, like a scorpion fish.

Hawaii

Peoples from Asia first reached the Hawaiian Islands in the eighth century, probably by way of Tahiti. A long period followed during which the Asians and later arrivals developed their own customs and rituals. Captain James Cook, who landed on Kauai Island on January 20, 1778, is considered in the West to be the "discoverer" of Hawaii. He named the area the Sandwich Islands, in honor of his patron, the Earl of Sandwich. Fairly close on his heels came other travelers, two of whom, an explorer and a missionary, wrote journals quoted below.

Otto von Kotzebue (1787–1846), the second son of a popular German dramatist, August Friedrich Ferdinand von Kotzebue, commanded two voyages of circumnavigation. The first, from 1815 to 1818 aboard the brig *Rurick*, led him to discover a number of islands in the Pacific and to chart a significant portion of the coast of Alaska, where he discovered Kotzebue Sound. In 1816–17, he was in Hawaii. German writer and botanist Adelbert von Chamisso (1781–1838) accompanied him on this voyage.

William Ellis (1794–1872), a missionary, visited Hawaii in February 1822. A year later he returned to Oahu Island and journeyed from there to the islands of Hawaii and Maui, beginning on July 24, 1823. Like numerous other missionaries who arrived during the period, Ellis sought to bring religion and education to a sunny, friendly people eager to learn.

In his account, Chamisso mentions the "hurra." Ellis speaks of the "hura ka raau," as well as the "hura." The *hula* (hura, hurra), with its combination of the arts, was the typical and most highly esteemed artistic expression of these native people. Long training, devotion, and discipline were required to master the rituals involved.

ADELBERT VON CHAMISSO

from "Remarks and Opinions of the Naturalist of the Expedition" (1821)

Where we approached Owhyee,[1] doubling the north-west point, and sailing along the west coast to the southern foot of Woraray, near Titatua, the declivities appear bare and sun-burnt. Some parts are used for tillage, the most are covered with scanty grass. Amidst clouds, the region of the forests begins, and the eye scarcely reaches the naked crowns of this gigantic mountain. The strand presents to the view an uninterrupted row of settlements, which, as you approach further to the south, are surrounded with more luxuriant verdure, and more frequently relieved by cocoa-palms.

* * *

Poetry, music, and dancing, which, in the South Sea islands, appear hand in hand, in their original union, to adorn human life, deserve to be particularly attended to. The spectacle of the Hurra, the festive dances of the Owhyeeans filled us with admiration.

Otto von Kotzebue, *A Voyage of Discovery into the South Sea and Beering's Straits* (London: Longman, Hurst, Rees, Orme, and Brown, 1821), 3: 230, 253–55.

[1] Hawaii.

The words mostly celebrate, like the Pindaric Odes,[2] the fame of some prince. Our knowledge of the language was not sufficient to judge of their poetry. The song is in itself monotonous. With the accompanying beats of the drum, it measures the turns of the dance, bearing, as it were, upon its waves a superior harmony. In the varying dance, the human form develops itself to this measure, in the most admirable manner, representing itself in a constant flow of easy unconstrained motion, in every natural and graceful position. We fancy that we see the antique starting into life; the feet only bear the dancer. He moves forward with composure. His body, his arms, all his muscles, are expressive; his countenance is animated. We fix our eyes upon him as upon the Mime when his art transports us. The drummers sit in the back ground, the dancers stand before them in one or more rows; all join their voices in the chorus. The song is at first slow and piano, and is gradually and regularly quickened and strengthened, as the dancers advance, and their action becomes animated. All execute the same motions. It is as if the same dancer stood several times repeated before us. These festal games of Owhyee remind us of the chorus of the Greeks, of tragedy before the dialogue was introduced; and, if we cast a look upon ourselves, we perceive into what a wrong path we have absurdly strayed, by reducing the dance to a motion of mere pleasure. These games intoxicate the Owhyeeans with joy. Their usual songs are danced in the same spirit, standing or sitting; they are of very different characters, but always accompanied by graceful motions of the body and the arms. What a school is here opened to the artist! What an enjoyment is here offered to the amateur!

This fine art, the only one of these islanders, is the flower of their life, which is consecrated to enjoyment and to pleasure. They live for the present moment without calculation of time, and an old woman knows no more of her age than that she has lived beyond the first period of enjoyment, beyond the age of twelve years.

[2]Poetry written by, or in the style of, the Greek poet Pindar, c. 518–438 B.C.

WILLIAM ELLIS

from *Narrative of a Tour through Hawaii* (1823)

[Maui, probably July 5, 1823]. At sun-rise next morning, Mr. Stewart[3] and I walked down to Keopuolani's, and conducted the usual morning exercises, in the large house near the sea. About fifty persons were present. In the afternoon I accompanied the missionaries to their schools on the beach. The proficiency of many of the pupils in reading, spelling, and writing on slates, was pleasing.

Just as they had finished their afternoon instruction, a party of musicians and dancers arrived before the house of Keopuolani, and commenced a *hura ka raau* (dance to the beating of a stick). Five musicians advanced first, each with a staff in his left hand, five or six feet long, about three or four inches in diameter at one end, and tapering off to a point at the other. In his right hand he held a small stick of hard wood, six or nine inches long, with which he commenced his music, by striking the small stick on the larger one, beating time all the while with his right foot on a stone, placed on the ground beside him for that purpose. Six women, fantastically dressed in yellow tapa's,[4]

William Ellis, *Narrative of a Tour through Hawaii, or Owhyhee* (London: For the author by H. Fisher and P. Jackson, 1826), 48–49, 74–77.

[3] A missionary already on Maui.

[4]Coarse cloth made from pulverized bark of paper mulberry, breadfruit, and other plants, frequently decorated with geometric patterns.

crowned with garlands of flowers, having also wreathes of the sweet-scented flowers of the *gardenia* on their necks, and branches of the fragrant *mairi* (another native plant) bound round their ankles, now made their way by couples through the crowd, and, arriving at the area, on one side of which the musicians stood, began their dance. Their movements were slow, and though not always graceful, exhibited nothing offensive to modest propriety. Both musicians and dancers alternately chanted songs in honour of former gods and chiefs of the islands, apparently much to the gratification of the numerous spectators. After they had continued their *hura* (song and dance) for about half an hour, the queen, Keopuolani, requested them to leave off, as the time had arrived for conducting worship. The music ceased; the dancers sat down; and, after the missionaries and some of the people had sung one of the songs of Zion, I preached to the surrounding multitude with special reference to their former idolatrous dances, and the vicious customs connected therewith, from Acts xvii. 30. "The times of this ignorance God winked at, but now commandeth all men every where to repent." The audience was attentive; and when the service was finished, the people dispersed, and the dancers returned to their houses.

* * *

[Island of Hawaii, probably July 15, 1823]. About four o'clock in the afternoon, another party of musicians and dancers, followed by multitudes of people, took their station nearly on the spot occupied yesterday by those from Kaü. The musicians, seven in number, seated themselves on the sand; a curiously carved drum, made by hollowing out a solid piece of wood, and covering the top with shark's skin, was placed before each, which they beat with the palm or fingers of their right hand. A neat little drum, made of the shell of a large cocoa-nut, was also fixed on the knee, by the side of the large drum, and beat all the while with a small stick held in the left hand. When the musicians had arranged themselves in a line, across the beach, and a bustling man, who appeared to be master of ceremonies, had, with a large branch of a cocoa-nut tree, cleared a circle of considerable extent, two interesting little children (a boy and a girl), apparently about nine years of age, came forward, habited in the dancing costume of the country, with garlands of flowers on their heads, wreaths around their necks, bracelets on their wrists, and buskins on their ankles. When they had reached the centre of the ring, they commenced their dance to the music of the drums; cantilating all the while, alternately with the musicians, a song in honour of some ancient chief of Hawaii.

The governor of the island was present, accompanied, as it is customary for every chieftain of distinction to be on public occasions, by a retinue of favourite chiefs and attendants. Having almost entirely laid aside the native costume, and adopted that of the foreigners who visit the islands, he appeared on this occasion in a light European dress, and sat on a Canton-made arm chair, opposite the dancers, during the whole exhibition. A servant with a light *kihei* of painted native cloth thrown over his shoulder, stood behind his chair, holding a highly polished portable spittoon, made of the beautifully brown wood of the cordia in one hand, and in the other a handsome *kahiri*, an elastic rod, three or four feet long, having the shining feathers of the tropic-bird tastefully fastened round the upper end, with which he fanned away the flies from the person of his master.

The beach was crowded with spectators, and the exhibition kept up with great spirit, till the over-spreading shades of evening put an end to their mirth, and afforded a respite to the poor children, whose little limbs must have been very much fatigued by two hours of constant exercise. We were anxious to address the multitude on the subject of religion before they should disperse; but so intent were they on their amusement, that they could not have been diverted from it. I succeeded, however, in taking a sketch of the novel assemblage.

* * *

[July 16, 1823]

At four P.M. the musicians from Kaü again collected on the beach, and the dancer commenced a *hura*, similar to that exhibited on Monday evening. We had previously appointed a religious meeting for this evening, and, about an hour before sunset, proposed to the governor, to hold it on the beach, where the people were already assembled. He approved, and followed us to the edge of the circle, where we took our station, just opposite the musicians. At the governor's request the music ceased, and the dancer came and sat down just in front of us. We sang a hymn; I then offered up a short prayer, and afterwards addressed the people from Acts xiv.15: "And preach unto you, that ye should turn from these vanities unto the living God, which made heaven and earth, and the sea, and all things that are therein."

68   The Shakers

Hands to work,
Hearts to God.
—Shaker motto

In 1758, Ann Lee (1736–1786), whose four children had died in infancy, embraced a new religious doctrine that had spread from mainland Europe to England. Its outward manifestations of jumping, whirling, and shouting caused its practitioners to become known as Shakers, or Shaking Quakers.

Lee "Mother Ann" escaped persecution in 1774 to lead a few followers to America. In the spring of 1776 they settled at Niskayuna (Watervliet), near Troy, New York.

The Shakers, or the United Society of Believers in Christ's Second Appearing, grew rapidly in America. In the following century, their numbers greatly increased because they took in Civil War orphans. Other Shaker communities sprang up, from Maine, to Ohio, to Kentucky, but being a celibate population, the sect could not perpetuate itself.

The Shaker community at New Lebanon in Columbia County, New York, was founded in the early 1780s, on the heels of a religious revival there. The population there grew to 550 in 1869, divided into families of thirty to ninety members with men and women housed separately in dormitory buildings.

Worship on the Sabbath was a major event. Adults and children dressed alike. The sexes entered by separate doors, and remained separated during the long proceedings, which included song, dance, and sermonizing.

American historian Benson J. Lossing (1813–1891) visited New Lebanon in August 1856. He witnessed worship carried on by a family of "about sixty" on the Saturday of his visit. The following day, he attended worship of the whole community. He puts the number of worshipers at "four or five hundred"—a large number, but possible given the size of the community. He pegs the "audience" for the event at six hundred—possible but improbable.

The large number of worshipers on Sunday tended to formalize and stylize the event, while the presence of an audience inevitably gave it something of the atmosphere of a performance. Elder Evans took pains to address the audience and later to thank them for their attention. His discourse on "the peculiar doctrines of the Shakers" seems addressed more to the onlookers, the "World's People." The Shakers welcomed visitors, and they, in turn, colored community activities. In this light, the private family worship on Saturday must have been more personally meaningful.

Lossing's article, published in *Harper's New Monthly Magazine* in the year following his visit, was influential, not only because the journal was important but because it included excellent wood engravings that complemented the author's eyewitness account. The article met with the Shakers' approval.

BENSON J. LOSSING

from "The Shakers" (1857)

It was Saturday evening. The weekly toil of the community had ceased, and a Sabbath stillness brooded over the populous town. Immense dwellings filled with men and women, and extensive workshops supplied with choicest implements, lined the one broad street. Order and Neatness there held high court with a majesty I had never before seen. The very dust in the road seemed pure, and the virtue "next to godliness" was apparent upon every stone.

Near the centre of the village is a large brick building, painted a chocolate color, in the lower part of which is the Office and Store of the community. There I found several of the brethren and sisters, who received me kindly, and at my request they directed me to the dwelling of Elders Bushnell and Evans,[1] two of the principal men in the village. To them I frankly stated the object of my visit, and was cordially invited to partake of the hospitalities of the community, while I remained among them. An excellent supper was prepared for me, and early in the evening I returned to the family at the store, where I passed the night.

There I found Edward Fowler, the chief business-man of the Society, and had a long and instructive conversation with him respecting the temporalities of the Shakers. While thus engaged, I heard the sounds of music and dancing, and was told that the family (about sixty in number), on the opposite side of the street, were engaged in their usual evening worship. Curiosity at once led me thither. There, collected in a large room devoted to the purpose, were a large number of men and women, engaged in the peculiar religious rites of Shaker family worship. They sang hymns and lively spiritual songs, all of which were accompanied by dances and marches, conducted in an orderly, and, at times, very impressive manner. These exercises were interspersed with brief exhortations by both men and women; and in the general order of the ritual, it was not much unlike their public ceremonials on the Sabbath. There I saw what the eye of the stranger seldom sees. It was a physical "manifestation of the power of God," as they call it. One of the younger brethren, standing in the middle of the room, stretched out his arms and commenced whirling, not rapidly, but steadily, and continued to turn, as if upon a pivot, at least an hour, without cessation, the recipient of the "gift" being apparently unconscious of all that was passing around him. Except in costume, he strongly resembled a whirling Dervish, such as travelers frequently see in the East. This family worship continued about an hour and a half, when I retired to the room assigned me, filled with new emotions, for I was in the midst of social and religious novelties.

The Sabbath dawn was brilliant, and the beauty of the day was memorable. Opposite my lodgings was the house for public worship, a spacious frame building, painted white, with an arched roof. At its southern end is a smaller building, which they call the Porch, in which the chief ministers, two men and two women, reside. This edifice, built about thirty years ago, is a few yards from the first Shaker meeting-house erected in Lebanon, and which is yet standing.

The hour for the commencement of worship was half past ten. Half an hour earlier a long wagon arrived, in which were two brethren and several sisters from the "East Family," who reside partly over the mountain. At the same time vehicles came with visitors from Lebanon Springs, and soon the seats between the entrance doors, called the "lobby," were filled by "the Gentiles," the sexes being separated, the men on the left of the women. The floor, made of white pine, was as clean as

Benson J. Lossing, "The Shakers," *Harper's New Monthly Magazine*, July 1857: 166–69.

[1]Richard Bushnell and Frederick Evans were Elders of the North, or "Gathering," Family at New Lebanon.

a dining table. On the side of the room opposite the seats of the strangers were rows of movable benches, and upon them the sisters who came from a distance began to gather, after hanging their bonnets upon wooden pegs provided for the purpose. In the ante-rooms on the left, the brethren and sisters of the village were assembled, the sexes being separated. At the appointed hour they all came in in couples, stood a moment in silence, and then sat down, the men and women facing each other. Adults and children were dressed precisely alike. With the exception of the resident elders and some visiting brethren, the men were in their shirt sleeves. Their Sunday costume consists of pantaloons of blue linen, with a fine white stripe in it; vests of a much deeper blue, and plain, made of *linsey-woolsey* (woolen and linen); stout calf-skin shoes and gray stockings. Their shirt-collars and bosoms are made of cotton, like the body; the collar is fastened with three buttons and turned over. The women wear, on Sunday, some a pure white dress, and others a white dress with a delicate blue stripe in it. Over their necks and bosoms were pure white kerchiefs, and over the left arm of each was carried a large white pocket-handkerchief. Their heads were covered with lawn caps, the form of all, for both old and young, being alike. They project so as to fully conceal the cheeks in profile. Their shoes, sharp-toed and high-heeled, according to the fashion of the day when the Society was formed, were made of prunella,[2] of a brilliant ultramarine blue. Such was the appearance of the worshipers in the presence of at least six hundred strangers, attracted there by curiosity.

The worshipers soon arose, and approached from opposite ends of the room, until the two front rows were within two yards of each other, the women modestly casting their eyes to the floor. The benches were then instantly removed. There they stood in silence, in serried columns like platoons in military, while two rows of men and women stood along the wall, facing the audience. From these came a grave personage, and standing in the centre of the worshipers, addressed them

with a few words of exhortation. All stood in silence for a few minutes at the conclusion of his remarks, when they began to sing a hymn of several verses to a lively tune, and keeping time with their feet. In this, as in all of their songs and hymns, they did not pause at the end of each verse, but kept on without rest and with many repetitions until the whole hymn was completed. Elder Evans then came forward, and addressing a few words to the audience, asked them to regard the acts of worship before them with respectful attention. This request was unnecessary, for there was nothing in the entire performance calculated to elicit any other than feelings of deepest respect and serious contemplation.

After two other brethren had given brief "testimonies," the worshipers all turned their backs to the audience, except those of the two wall rows, and commenced a backward and forward march, or dance, in a regular springing step, keeping time to the music of their voices while their hands hung closely to their sides. The wall rows alone kept time with their hands moving up and down, the palms turned upward. The singing appeared like a simple refrain and a chorus of too-ral-loo, too-ral-loo, while all the movements with hand, foot, and limb were extremely graceful.

The worshipers now stood in silence a few moments, when they commenced singing another hymn, with chorus like the last. When it was ended they retired to each end of the room, the benches were replaced, and the men and women again sat down opposite each other. Elder Evans then came forward, and, in an able discourse of almost an hour, expounded the peculiar doctrines of the Shakers, especially that which relates to the duality of God as male and female, and the second advent of Christ upon earth in the person of Ann Lee, the founder of the Society. When he had ceased all the worshipers arose, the benches were removed, and they formed themselves into serried ranks as before. Then, with graceful motions, they gradually changed their position into circular form, all the while moving with springing step, in unison with a lively tune. In the centre stood twenty-four singers in a circle, twelve men and twelve women; and

---

[2]A heavy woollen fabric.

around them, in two concentric circles, marched and countermarched the remainder of the worshipers, the men three and the women two abreast. A brief pause and they commenced another lively tune and march, all keeping time with their hands moving up and down, and occasionally clapping them three or four times in concert. The women were now three and the men two abreast. When the hymn ceased, with a prolonged strain, they all turned their faces toward the inner circle of singers.

After another pause the worshipers commenced a hymn in slow and plaintive strain. The music was unlike any thing I had ever heard; beautiful, impressive, and deeply solemn. As it died away, the clear musical voice of a female was heard from the external circle, telling, in joyful cadence, how happy she felt as a member of that pure and holy community. To this many among the worshipers gave words of hearty concurrence. Another sweet female voice then commenced a hymn in which "Mother Ann" was celebrated. The entire body of worshipers formed into a single line, marched slowly around the central circle of singers, and as the strain ceased their hands fell gracefully to their sides, their bodies were inclined gently forward, and their thin hands were slowly raised and clasped over the waist.

After a brief pause they commenced singing a lively spiritual song. The worshipers now formed four circles, with the singers as the central one, and held each other by the hand, the men and women separately. These circles symbolized the four great Dispensations—the first from Adam to Abraham; the second from Abraham to Jesus, the third from Jesus to "Mother Ann;" and the fourth the present, which they hold to be the millennial period. In this hymn they sang of Union, as exhibited by their linked hands; and when it had ceased they all lifted up their hands, and gave a subdued shout—the shout of victory—the final victory of Christ in all the earth, and the triumphs of the Shaker, or Millennial Church.

Three or four more songs and hymns, with graceful dances or marches, and the ceremonials drew to a close. While singing the last sweet song, the men and women took their respective places at each end of the room, and stood facing each other. Elder Evans then addressed a few words of encouragement to them, and stepping forward, thanked the audience for their kind attention, and informed them that the meeting was closed.

From that house of strange worship every "Gentile" seemed to depart with serious feelings. Whatever may have been the scenes among the Shakers in former times or in other communities, of which many have spoken with contempt and ridicule, it can not be denied that their public worship at Lebanon is dignified, solemn, and deeply impressive. We may differ from them in opinion as to its propriety, but we must accord to them great earnestness and sincerity. Their songs and hymns breathe a pure and Christian spirit; and their music, unlike any to be heard elsewhere, captivates the ear because of its severe simplicity and perfect melody. Their movements in the dance or march, whether natural or studied, are all graceful and appropriate; and as I gazed upon that congregation of four or five hundred worshipers marching and countermarching in perfect time, I felt certain that, were it seen upon a stage as a theatrical exhibition, the involuntary exclamation of even the hypercritical would be, "How beautiful!" The women, clad in white, and moving gracefully, appeared ethereal; and among them were a few very beautiful faces. All appeared happy, and upon each face rested the light of dignified serenity, which always gives power to the features of woman.

On leaving the house of worship I was invited to the dwelling of the preacher,[3] and there I spent the afternoon and evening with him, and some of the brethren and sisters, in pleasant conversation, the chief topic of which was their doctrine and discipline.

---

[3]Probably Elder Frederick Evans.

Shaker Song Texts (PUB. 1940)

Come Life, Shaker Life

Come life, Shaker life!
Come life eternal!
Shake, shake out of me
All that is carnal.

I'll take nimble steps,
I'll be a David,
I'll show Michael twice
How he behaved!

Who Will Bow and Bend Like a Willow

Who will bow and bend like a willow,
Who will turn and twist and reel
In the gale of simple freedom,
From the bower of union flowing.

Who will drink the wine of power,
Dropping down like a shower,

Pride and bondage all forgetting,
Mother's wine is freely working.

Oh ho! I will have it,
I will bow and bend to get it,
I'll be reeling, turning, twisting,
Shake out all the starch and stiff'-ning.

Simple Gifts

'Tis the gift to be simple, 'tis the gift to be free,
'Tis the gift to come down where we ought to be,
And when we find ourselves in the place just right,
'Twill be in the valley of love and delight.

When true simplicity is gain'd,
To bow and to bend we shan't be asham'd.
To turn, turn will be our delight,
'Till by turning, turning we come round right.

Edward D. Andrews, *The Gift to Be Simple: Songs, Dances and Rituals of the American Shakers* (New York: J. J. Augustin, 1940), 102–3, 114, 136.

69   The Mormons: Long Live Brother Brigham Young

In John Stone's famous ballad about westward expansion, *Sweet Betsey from Pike,* Betsey and her lover, Ike, encounter the Mormons at Great Salt Lake in the Territory of Utah. The Mormons practice polygamy, and Betsey wants no part of becoming another of leader Brigham Young's wives:

> They stopped at Salt Lake to inquire the way,
> When Brigham declared that sweet Betsey should stay;
> But Betsey got frightened and ran like a deer,
> While Brigham stood pawing the ground like a steer.

The history of the Mormon Church in the United States—The Church of Jesus Christ of Latter-day Saints—is one of revelation, migration, bloodshed, and eventual harmony and peace. In 1827, in upstate New York, revelation came to Joseph Smith, Jr., who claimed to have received, from an angel, golden plates from which he translated the *Book of Mormon.* The Church accepts this book as holy scripture along with the Bible. Smith's persecuted followers settled in Kirtland, Ohio, in Missouri, and in Illinois. Illinois militiamen arrested and murdered Smith in 1844. Exodus followed, as well as confrontations with federal troops as Mormons defied federal authority. When the group eventually settled in the valley of the Great Salt Lake in 1847, they could finally establish a stable community, which continues as an important force to this day.

Brigham Young (1801–1877) rose from humble beginnings in upstate New York to a position of leadership. He led a small party of followers to the valley of the Great Salt Lake, arriving on July 24, 1847. Young promoted missionary work in Great Britain and Scandinavia, became governor of the Territory of Utah in 1850, and instituted polygamy a year later (it was relinquished in 1890 as a condition for Utah's statehood). He established community enterprises and sponsored the University of Utah.

Among the travelers to Salt Lake City who wrote about their experiences are the French botanist Jules Remy and the British naturalist Julius Brenchley, who visited in 1855; Mark Twain in 1861; and Ralph Waldo Emerson in 1871. Of all the accounts, the most detailed was provided by the English explorer, adventurer, journalist, and writer Richard Francis Burton (1821–1890). Burton crossed Indian territory to spend three weeks in Salt Lake City from August 25 to September 19, 1860, then returned to England via San Francisco and the Isthmus of Panama (his entire trip lasted close to five months).

Burton, who described Young as a remarkable leader of uncommon astuteness, himself enjoyed an extraordinary career, which he described extensively in his writings. His travels took him to India, Egypt, Saudi Arabia, Ethiopia, and Somaliland. On several occasions, he played the dangerous game of donning a disguise to help him penetrate a foreign society: in India, he masqueraded as a Bushiri merchant; in Egypt, as an Indian doctor; in Saudi Arabia, as a Pathan; and in Ethiopia, as a Muslim. In 1858, he traveled under harrowing circumstances as far as Lake Tanganyika to search for the source of the White Nile. His interest in the Mormons was quickened by their practice of polygamy.

RICHARD F. BURTON

from *The City of the Saints* (1862)

We returned homewards by the States Road, in which are two of the principal buildings. On the left is the Council Hall of the Seventies, an adobe tenement of the usual barn shape, fifty feet long by thirty internally, used for the various purposes of deliberation, preaching, and dancing; I looked through the windows and saw that it was hung with red. It is a provisional building, used until a larger can be erected. A little beyond the Seventies' Hall, and on the other side of the road, was the Social Hall, the usual scene of Mormon festivities; it resembled the former, but it was larger—73 × 33 feet—and better furnished. The gay season had not arrived; I lost, therefore, an opportunity of seeing the beauty and fashion of Great Salt Lake City in ballroom toilette, but I heard enough to convince me that the Saints, though grave and unjovial, are a highly sociable people. They delight in sleighing and in private theatricals, and boast of some good amateur actors, amongst whom Messrs. B. Snow, H. B. Clawson, and W. C. Dunbar are particularly mentioned. Sir E. L. Bulwer will perhaps be pleased to hear that the "Lady of Lyons" excited more furore here than even in Europe.[1] It is intended, as soon as funds can be collected, to build a theatre which will vie with those of the old country. Dancing seems to be considered an edifying exercise. The Prophet dances, the Apostles dance, the Bishops dance. A professor of this branch of the fine arts would thrive in Zion, where the most learned of pedagogues would require to eke out a living after the fashion of one Aristocles, surnamed the "broad-shouldered." The saltation is not in the languid, done-up style that polite Europe affects; as in the days of our grandparents, "positions" are maintained, steps are elaborately executed, and a somewhat severe muscular exercise is the result. I confess to a prejudice against dancing after the certain, which we are told is the uncertain, epoch of life, and have often joined in the merriment excited amongst French folks by the aspect of some bald-headed and stiff-jointed "Anglais," mingling crabbed age with joyful youth in a public ball. Yet there is high authority for perseverance in the practice; David danced, we are told, with all his might, and Scipio, according to Seneca, was wont thus to exercise his heroic limbs.

Besides the grand fêtes at the Social Hall and other subscription establishments, there are "Ward Parties," and "Elders' Weekly Cotillion Parties," where possibly the seniors dance together, as the Oxford dons did drill—in private. Polkas, as at the Court of St. James's, are disapproved of. It is generally asserted that to the New Faith Terpsichore owes a fresh form of worship, the Mormon cotillion—alias quadrille—in which the cavalier leads out, characteristically, two dames. May I not be allowed to recommend the importation of this decided improvement into Leamington and other watering-places, where the proportion of the sexes at "hops" rarely exceeds one to seven?

The balls at the Social Hall are highly select, and are conducted on an expensive scale: invita-

---

Richard F. Burton, *The City of the Saints* (New York: Harper & Brothers, 1862), 229–31.

[1]Edward Bulwer-Lytton's *The Lady of Lyons; or, Love and Pride* was first produced at Covent Garden Theatre, London, in 1838 (see No. 50).

tions are issued on embossed bordered and gilt-edged white paper, say to 75–80 of the *élite*, including a few of the chief Gentiles. The ticket is in this form and style:—

Party at Social Hall

————

Mr. _____ and ladies are respectfully invited to attend a Party at the Social Hall,

ON TUESDAY, FEBRUARY 7, 1860.

Tickets, $10 (£2) *per Couple*.

Mayor A. O. Smoot,⎱
Marshal J. C. Little, ⎰ Managers.

Committee of Arrangements.

William C. Staines,   William Eddington,   John T. Caine
H. B. Clawson,   Robert T. Burton,   David Candling.

Great Salt Lake City:
   Feb. 1, 1860.

The $10 tickets will admit only one lady with the gentleman; for all extra $2 each must be paid. In the less splendid fêtes $2.50 would be the total price. Premiums are offered when the time draws nigh, but space is limited, and many a Jacob is shorn of his glory by appearing with only Rachel for a follower, and without his train of Leahs, Zilpahs, and Billahs.

An account of the last ball may be abridged. The Hall was tastefully and elegantly decorated; the affecting motto "Our Mountain Home," conspicuously placed among hangings and evergreens, was highly effective. At 4 P.M. the Prophet and ex-President entered, and "order was called." (N.B. Might not this be tried to a purpose in a London ball-room?) Ascending a kind of platform, with uplifted hands he blessed those present. Further East I have heard of the reverse being done, espe-

cially by the *maître du logis*. He then descended to the boards and led off the first cotillion. At 8 P.M. supper was announced; covers for 250 persons had been laid by Mr. Candland, "mine host" of "The Globe." On the next page will be found the list of the somewhat substantial goodies that formed the *carte*.

It will be observed that the *cuisine* in Utah Territory has some novelties, such as bear and beaver. The former meat is a favorite throughout the West, especially when the animal is fresh from feeding; after hybernation it is hard and lean. In the Himalayas many a sportsman, after mastering an artificial aversion to eat bear's grease, has enjoyed a grill of "cuffy." The paws, which not a little resemble the human hand, are excellent—*experto crede*.[2] I cannot pronounce *ex cathedrâ* upon beavers' tails; there is no reason, however, why they should be inferior to the appendage of a Cape sheep. "Slaw,"—according to my informants —is synonymous with sauer-kraut. Mountain, Pioneer, and Snowballs are unknown to me, except by their names, which are certainly patriotic, if not descriptive.

After supper dancing was resumed with spirit, and in its intervals popular songs and duets were performed by the best musicians. The "finest party of the season" ended as it began, with prayer and benediction, at 5 A.M.—thirteen successive mortal hours—it shows a solid power of enduring enjoyments! And, probably, the revelers wended their way home chanting some kind of national hymn like this, to the tune of the "Ole Kentucky shore":

"Let the chorus still be sung
Long live Brother Brigham Young.
   And blessed be the Vale of Deserét—rét—rét!
   And blessed be the Vale of Deserét." . . .[3]

---

[2] According to expert belief.

[3] Deserét, meaning honeybee, became the Mormon symbol of industry and of the promised land of Utah. The University founded there in 1850, first called the University of Deserét, became what is now the University of Utah.

70 Ira D. Sankey and the Power of the Gospel

The urban religious revival movement, spurred on by the harsh conditions that resulted from industrialization in America, brought with it an upsurge in religious song. The revival was helped along by the singing of well-known hymns. The words were most important; tunes had to be of a popular sort, highly singable and harmonically simple. The result, as American music historian H. Wiley Hitchcock put it, "at its best, was a kind of religious pop art almost irresistible in its visceral appeal; at its worst, an embarrassingly trivial sacred counterpart of the sentimental 'songs of hearth and home' of the same era."*

The name of Ira D. Sankey (1840–1908) is nearly synonymous with gospel hymnody during the late nineteenth century. Reared in Pennsylvania as one of nine children, he was brought up in the gospel tradition. By his own account in *My Life and the Story of the Gospel Hymns*, he counted *The Ninety and Nine* and *There'll Be No Dark Valley* among his favorite hymns.

Sankey served as a Union soldier in the Civil War, returned home, married, and began assisting his father as a revenue collector. But his love of music, fine voice, and religious feelings (he experienced a spiritual conversion at age sixteen) became his primary focus, so that when he met evangelist Dwight L. Moody (1837–1899) in 1870, his fate was sealed. After settling briefly in Chicago, Moody and Sankey began to tour, at first throughout the United States and then, in 1873–75, in England and Scotland. At their mass meetings, Sankey would introduce the gospel hymns, which carried the evangelistic message. He sang solos and led the singing from a melodeon (pump organ) placed next to the pulpit.

On his return from his highly successful English tour, he collaborated with the singing evangelist Philip Bliss (1838–1876) to publish the well-known *Gospel Hymns and Sacred Songs* (1875), which was used heavily in subsequent mass revival meetings in America. Together with Bliss and other collaborators, he published other hymn books, all collected in *Gospel Hymns: Nos. 1 to 6 Complete* (1895).

---

*Ira D. Sankey and George C. Stebbins, *Gospel Hymns Nos. 1 to 6 Complete* (1895), ed. H. Wiley Hitchcock (New York: Da Capo, 1972), [iii].

Two Gospel Song Texts (1875)

The Ninety and Nine

There were ninety and nine that safely lay
In the shelter of the fold,
But one was out on the hills away,
Far off from the gates of gold—
Away on the mountains wild and bare,
Away from the tender Shepherd's care,
Away from the tender Shepherd's care.

"Lord, Thou hast here Thy ninety and nine:
Are they not enough for Thee?"
But the Shepherd made answer: "Tis of mine
Has wandered away from me:
And although the road be rough and steep
I go to the desert to find my sheep."

But none of the ransomed ever knew
How deep were the waters crossed;
Nor how dark was the night that the Lord passed
    through,
Ere He found His sheep that was lost.
Out in the desert He heard its cry—
Sick and helpless, and ready to die.

"Lord, whence are those blood-drops all the way
That mark out the mountains' track?"
"They were shed for one who had gone astray
Ere the Shepherd could bring him back."
"Lord, whence are Thy hands so rent and torn?"
"They are pierced to-night by many a thorn."

But all thro' the mountains, thunder-riven,
And up from the rocky steep,
There rose a cry to the gate of heaven,
"Rejoice! I have found my sheep!"
And the angels echoed around the throne,
"Rejoice, for the Lord brings back his own!"

P. P. Bliss and Ira D. Sankey, *Gospel Hymns and Sacred Songs* (New York: Biglow & Main, 1875), Nos. 6, 43.

The Cross of Jesus

Beneath the Cross of Jesus
I fain would take my stand—
The shadow of a mighty Rock,
Within a weary land.
A home within the wilderness,
A rest upon the way,
From the burning of the noon-tide heat,
And the burden of the day.

O safe and happy shelter,
O refuge tried and sweet,
O trysting place where Heaven's love,
And Heaven's justice meet!
As to the Holy Patriarch
That wondrous dream was given,
So seems my Saviour's Cross to me,
A ladder up to heaven.

There lies beneath its shadow,
But on the further side,
The darkness of an awful grave
That gapes both deep and wide;
And there between us stands the Cross,
Two arms outstretched to save,
Like a watchman set to guard the way
From that eternal grave.

Upon that Cross of Jesus,
Mine eye at times can see
The very dying form of One,
Who suffered there for me
And from my smitten heart with tears,
Two wonders I confess,—
The wonders of His glorious love,
And my own worthlessness.

I take, O Cross, Thy shadow,
For my abiding place;
I ask no other sunshine
Than the sunshine of His face:
Content to let the world go by,
To know no gain nor loss,—
My sinful self, my only shame,—
My glory all the Cross.

IRA D. SANKEY

from *My Life and the Story of the Gospel Hymns* (1907)

There'll Be No Dark Valley

There'll be no dark valley when Jesus comes,
There'll be no dark valley when Jesus comes;
There'll be no dark valley when Jesus comes
To gather His loved ones home.

Refrain.

> To gather His loved ones home,
>   safe home;
> To gather His loved ones home;
>   safe home;
> There'll be no dark valley when Jesus
>   comes
> To gather His loved ones home.

There'll be no more sorrow when Jesus comes,
There'll be no more sorrow when Jesus comes;
But a glorious morrow when Jesus comes
To gather His loved ones home.

Refrain.

There'll be no more weeping when Jesus comes,
There'll be no more weeping when Jesus comes;
But a blessed reaping when Jesus comes
To gather His loved ones home.

Refrain.

There'll be songs of greeting when Jesus comes,
There'll be songs of greeting when Jesus comes;
And a joyful meeting when Jesus comes
To gather His loved ones home.

Refrain.

＊   ＊   ＊

In 1870, with two or three others, I was appointed a delegate to the International Convention of the Association,[1] to be held at Indianapolis that year.

For several years I had read in the religious press about Mr. Moody, and I was therefore pleased when I learned that he would be at the convention, being a delegate from the Chicago Association. For a couple of days I was disappointed in neither seeing nor hearing him. At several of the annual conventions prior to this occasion, it had been the custom to select Moody as chairman, but now it was decided that some one else should occupy the chair, and Moody therefore took a seat among the other delegates on the floor. However, late on a Saturday afternoon, it was announced that Moody of Chicago would lead a six o'clock morning prayer-meeting in the Baptist Church. I was rather late, and therefore sat down near the door with a Presbyterian minister, the Rev. Robert McMillan, a delegate from my own county, who said to me, "Mr. Sankey, the singing here has been abominable; I wish you would start up something when that man stops praying, if he ever does." I promised to do so, and when opportunity offered I started the familiar hymn, "There is a fountain filled with blood." The congregation joined heartily and a brighter aspect seemed to be given to the meeting.

At the conclusion of the meeting Mr. McMillan said to me: "Let me introduce you to Mr. Moody." We joined the little procession of persons who were going up to shake hands with him, and thus I met for the first time the man with whom, in the providence of God, I was to be associated for the remainder of his life, or nearly thirty years.

Moody's first words to me, after my introduction, were, "Where are you from? Are you married? What is your business?" Upon telling him that I lived in Pennsylvania, was married, had two children, and was in the government employ, he said abruptly, "You will have to give that up."

I stood amazed, at a loss to understand why the man told me that I would have to give up what

---

Ira D. Sankey, *My Life and the Story of the Gospel Hymns and of Sacred Songs and Solos* (Philadelphia: Sunday School Times, 1907), 18–24, 320.

[1]Young Men's Christian Association.

---

[1]Young Men's Christian Association.

I considered a good position. "What for?" I exclaimed.

"To come to Chicago and help me in my work," was the answer.

When I told him that I could not leave my business, he retorted, "You must; I have been looking for you for the last eight years."

I answered that I would think the matter over; but as yet I had no thought of giving up my position. He told me about his religious work in Chicago, and closed by saying that the greatest trouble in connection with his meetings was the matter of the singing. He said he could not sing himself, and therefore had to depend upon all kinds of people to lead his service of song, and that sometimes when he had talked to a crowd of people, and was about to "pull the net," some one would strike up a long meter hymn to a short meter tune, and thereby upset the whole meeting. Mr. Moody then asked me if I would go with him and pray over the matter, and to this I consented—out of politeness. After the prayer we parted, and I returned to my room, much impressed by Mr. Moody's prayer, but still undecided.

The next day I received a card from Mr. Moody asking if I would meet him on a certain street corner that evening at six o'clock. At that hour I was at the place named, with a few of my friends. In a few minutes Moody came along.

Without stopping to speak, he passed on into a store near by, and asked permission to use a large store-box. The permission was granted; he rolled the box into the street, and, calling me aside, asked me to get up on the box and sing something.

"Am I a soldier of the cross?" soon gathered a considerable crowd. After the song, Mr. Moody climbed up on the box and began to talk. The workingmen were just going home from the mills and the factories, and in a short time a very large crowd had gathered. The people stood spellbound as the words fell from Moody's lips with wonderful force and rapidity. When he had spoken for some twenty-five minutes he announced that the meeting would be continued at the Opera House, and invited the people to accompany us there. He asked me to lead the way and with my friends sing some familiar hymn. This we did, singing as we marched down the street, "Shall we gather at the river." The men with the dinner pails followed closely on our heels instead of going home, so completely were they carried away by the sermon from the store-box.

The Opera House was packed to the doors, and Moody first saw that all the workingmen were seated before he ascended to the platform to speak. His second address was as captivating as the one delivered on the street corner, and it was not until the delegates had arrived for the evening session of the convention that Mr. Moody closed the meeting, saying, "Now we must close, as the brethren of the convention wish to come in to discuss the question, 'How to reach the masses.'" Here was a man who could successfully reach the masses while others were talking about it.

When Mr. Moody again brought up the question of our going into the work together, I was still undecided. After a delay of over six months, and much urging on Mr. Moody's part, I consented to spend a week with him.

71

John Philip Sousa

For many Americans, the name John Philip Sousa (1854–1932) connotes the epitome of band music. The son of a trombonist in the U.S. Marine Band, Sousa showed an early interest in music. Educated entirely in America, he played violin in theater orchestras, taught, arranged music, and composed. A formative experience was hearing Patrick S. Gilmore's Band at the Centennial Exposition in Philadelphia in 1876. The lineage of Sousa's band runs through his illustrious predecessors, Dodworth and Gilmore. Not only did Sousa admire Gilmore, but a number of Gilmore's players joined Sousa when he formed his first band in 1892, the year in which Gilmore died.

In October of 1880, at age twenty-five, Sousa became the conductor of the U.S. Marine Band, an ensemble he directed for the next twelve years. Sousa came to the tradition of the military band through his family background and catapulted the genre to huge success, far beyond the confines of the military. Yet to him, the military stance, served up with a dash of patriotism, continued to represent the high ground. His performances were characterized by precision for both eye and ear, combined with real showmanship. In addition, Sousa had an uncanny ability to tailor concerts, particularly encores, to audience tastes and the exigencies of the moment. A formidable composer and arranger, Sousa's output over his lifetime included 136 marches. Sousa's marches from his Marine Band period include *Semper Fidelis* (1888) and *The Thunderer* (1889). *The Washington Post* (1889) made his name a household word.

In 1892, Sousa went on to form his own band, which he conducted until his death. The ensemble, which toured nationally and internationally, became the most famous band of all time.

Sousa's autobiography, *Marching Along,* was written and published when the composer was in his seventies.

JOHN PHILIP SOUSA
from *Marching Along* (1928)

Sousa's Band was born back in the "gay nineties" when David Blakely called upon me in Chicago where the Marine Band was giving a concert.[1] Blakely had taken it for granted that I would eagerly accept his offer to leave Washington. On the contrary I refused it at first, held by familiar ties in the capital. But the idea pleased me and secretly I was always favorable to it. I had often dreamed of a real band of my own, composed of the most talented musicians, who would provide a perfect response to my aspiring baton. Besides, it meant a considerable financial advancement—six thousand dollars salary, twenty percent of the profits and a five-year contract. Mother told me, after I had made my decision, that Father, only two weeks before his death, on reading the April ninth newspaper report of my opportunity to leave the Marines and go on tour had said to her slowly, "Well, Philip *ought* to have his own organization. The time has come for him to go!"

At the end of July, 1892, I gave a farewell concert at the National Theater and left for New York, carrying with me hundreds of gratifying and encouraging messages. Then came the organization of my band. I had met one of the leading cornetists in London, Arthur Smith, a splendid musician who had been solo cornet with the Coldstream Guards and soloist at the promenade concerts at Covent Garden. I then engaged Staats, of Boston, a graduate of the Paris conservatory; Henry D. Koch, one of the finest French-horn players in the United States; Arthur Pryor, the talented trombonist; Frank Holton, another fine trombone player; Jam-bon, a bassoonist, also a graduate of the Paris conservatory; John S. Cox, the Scotch flutist who calmly faced myriad-noted cadenzas; Richard Messenger, oboe; and a glorious array of clarinets, tubas, saxophones, as well as a valiant bass drummer from the Garde du Corps of Berlin. I had good reason to be proud of this assemblage.

I strove in every way to improve the quality and variety of the instruments. Way back when I was with the Marines they used a Helicon tuba wound around the body. I disliked it for concert work because the tone would shoot ahead and be too violent. I suggested to a manufacturer that we have an upright bell of large size so that the sound would diffuse over the entire band like the frosting on a cake! He designed a horn after that description and it has been in use ever since, by many bands, under the name of the Sousaphone.

There are now eighty-four men in my band. It has become almost entirely American in personnel. Last year—1927—there was only one player who was born abroad and he is a naturalized American citizen. That is quite in contrast to the early days when nearly all of them were foreigners, and the dramatis personae reminded you of a concert in Berlin or Rome.

We have a familiar and beloved routine. Every man knows his duty and performs it. Perhaps that is why there is so seldom any display of jealousy—less than in any organization I have known. No man is ever called upon to do another's part. Similar tastes promote a great friendship among them, and if a vain man joins the band he very soon is brought down to earth!

About July first we start on our tour. Contracts have been made from six months to a year ahead by my manager, Mr. Harry Askin. We assemble in New York from every corner of the country—each man with his trunk and his suitcase. The instruments are stowed in specially-designed trunks under the care of the band baggage man. Arrived at our destination, the men go to their hotels, and the

John Philip Sousa, *Marching Along: Recollections of Men, Women and Music* (Boston: Hale, Cushman & Flint, 1928), 333–36, 337–40, 342, 361–64.

[1]Impresario David Blakely, who had previously managed the Gilmore Band and Sousa's Marine Band on tour, made the conductor a lucrative offer to establish his own, private band, with which Blakely was associated until his sudden death in 1896.

band luggage is sent to the hall where we are to appear. The band librarian lays out our music, the accumulation of which is, I believe, one of the greatest libraries of band music in the world. We carry our own music stands and my podium. The men arrive about three quarters of an hour before the concert to tune up, soften their lips, and make sure everything is in order. That is the prelude which the public rarely hears—a pleasant, busy crooning and tuning, plucking of strings and blowing of low, disconnected notes. It is not music—yet, but it is the sign of efficiency and activity to the conductor, and always gives me a satisfactory feeling of "things about to happen."

When the concert is about to begin, the librarian calls out, "All on!" and they file on the stage. Each man is provided with a list of encores which, nine times out of ten, are Sousa marches, for we generally have advance letters containing requests for many of them. It is my invariable rule to begin the encore almost immediately after the programme number. This habit has come in for its share of criticism.

* * *

There has been only one type of uniform for the men and we have not changed it in more than thirty years. Salaries are from seventy-four dollars to two hundred dollars a week, according to proficiency and experience. Everywhere there is manifest good will and impartiality in the entire organization. The human contacts established are, of course, many and interesting. Four years ago one of my original players, Joseph Norrito, a solo clarinetist who had been with me ever since the band was "born," retired and went back to Italy. Sometimes band members marry and settle down, forsaking our nomadic life, but of late many of the men have taken their wives along on tour. Last year half a dozen wives were with us.

We have had basketball and baseball teams of our own and the latter have played the Marine teams at Philadelphia and at various Expositions. In 1900 on our Paris tour, we played the American Guard. We usually make a goodly showing. Recently we have had two teams in the band itself—one of reed players, the other of brass; the average

is about equal, even though one might expect the brass to win by virtue of long-windedness!

The Band is unique in the number of concerts given and mileage covered. In the thirty-six years of its existence it has visited every part of the United States and Canada, has made five tours of Europe and one of the world. We have traveled, in all, one million two hundred thousand miles. And this was accomplished quite without subsidy, depending entirely on our own drawing-power. From the ranks of the band have arisen several men who are now conductors of their own bands; among them, Herbert L. Clarke, Arthur Pryor, Walter Rogers, Bohumir Kryl, Fred Gilliland, Frank Simons and others. I am proud to call them graduates of Sousa's Band.

To obtain the best musicians we choose those belonging to the American Federation of Musicians and I have found them unfailingly loyal to me. Every man gives of his best, at all times, uncomplainingly and with spirit and vigor. Their punctuality too, which is the politeness of kings, is admirable. I rejoice at their attitude and at our rehearsals in June, when we go over everything which we are to play for the coming season, I look them over with affection and pride.

I have often been asked the reason for some of my methods of conducting. Is it not the business of the conductor to convey to the public in its dramatic form the central idea of a composition; and how can he convey that idea successfully if he does not enter heart and soul into the life of the music and the tale it unfolds? The movements which I make I cannot possibly repress because, at the time, I *am* actually the idea I am interpreting, and naturally I picture my players and auditors as in accord with me. I know, of course, that my mannerisms have been widely discussed. They have even said, "He goes through the motions as if he were dancing one of his own twosteps." Now I never move my legs at all. Perhaps my hands dance; they certainly do not make really sweeping motions, for the slightest movement suffices to carry my meaning. In Germany one man said, "Your band is like oil." I knew what he meant. Instead of waving my arms vigorously, I had gone at it smoothly. It struck them as something different. Moreover, they liked the way we did the pianissimo passages.

To my men the raising of a thumb is significant. Whenever we introduce a new man into the band, he invariably stands out too much, particularly if he has been playing under an extremely vigorous conductor. Always I have to jump on him and press him back into the united whole. All organizations work the same way—they must be a unit, and since I strive to paint my melodies usually with a camel's hair brush instead of with the sweeping stroke of a whitewash brush, I must insist upon that delicate oneness of tone.

Very clever players, they are—all of them in the Band—but if their interpretation of a passage does not agree with mine they can and will subordinate their idea to mine. That is why the greatest generals would make the finest privates. These men know that the whole effect will be better if they submit to one dominating spirit—the leader. On the other hand, the leader who doesn't watch for outbursts of genius in his men, in the playing of a phrase, makes a sad mistake. For example: I would be rehearsing a piece and would stop for five minutes to rest. As I went out, I would hear some fellow going over a portion of the piece and playing with it—trying it this way and that, until finally I would hear him play it in a certain way and I would say to myself, "That's the way it *ought* to be done!" Invariably, continuing the rehearsal, I would say to the men, "I heard Jones playing this over a while ago, and his way is better than mine," and after Jones, beaming with delight, had demonstrated, I would lead it in that fashion. If I were not open-minded I could not improve as a director—I am a better director than I was last year, and I hope to be a better one next year!

*   *   *

Nowadays I allow myself a bit more of vacationing than formerly. Up to the time of the World War I toured with the Band practically the entire year, often following the road for fifty weeks, including both summer engagements and winter tours; but since the War I travel from July to December and then gather together my guns and

equipment and go south for the shooting season. Then to Pinehurst for golf, and back to Long Island to write and to enjoy my home and my family. When June comes, I turn to programme-arranging for the next tour, to determining the personnel of the Band and to rehearsals. Once the tour is mapped out by my business manager it is submitted to me. On long engagements, and on foreign tours, I have always had my family with me.

*   *   *

It is much easier to ridicule the taste of a nation than to improve or correct it. Foreigners laugh at our naive taste in the arts, and we, with equal thoughtlessness, journey abroad and find food for mirth in their obsolete customs. There are plenty of explanations for both. *Our* limitations are due to the fact that we have been developing an enormous territory in an astonishingly short time and have been trying simultaneously to absorb the literature, art and music of Europe.

We can afford the best in this country, and once convinced that we desire it, we shall achieve it; the desire is rapidly being implanted, therefore we are going to achieve the best in music. Of course our cousins across seas, like all affectionate relatives, persist in prolonging our infancy. Witness Williams of the English Grenadier Guards Band, who said, indulgently, upon his return to London after an American tour: "We did not try to force upon the American people too 'hifalutin' music—and that is no doubt the secret of our success."

If I could meet the rising army of young American composers face to face, I should say to them, speaking with a veteran's privilege of frankness, *"Be yourself and never be an imitator. Do not be obscure, and do not be a materialist*—it will ruin your work. Remember always that the composer's pen is still mightier than the bow of the violinist; in you lie all the possibilities of the *creation* of beauty. You need turn to the orchestra, the piano and the band only for the faithful interpretation of what *you* have envisioned."

The rest of the world has had a long start, but the American composer with his heritage of creative genius from a race which has produced thirteen out of twenty of the great inventions of the past three centuries, is well qualified to catch up! We require time but (to employ the American vernacular) "we'll get there!"

Today, if I were a young composer, I would rather submit my chances of success or failure to an American public than to any other public in the world. It is essentially music-loving. I have "laid my ear to it, to see if it be in tune" for these many years, and it has never discouraged or disappointed me. I can think of a thousand glorious and satisfying responses. Moreover, there is concrete evidence of musical interest all over the country. Looking over the field of the finest, I find some twenty-five orchestral societies giving series of concerts; some forty-five festival associations appearing before the public every year; some hundred choral groups and musical ensembles; some eight grand opera companies; at least a hundred and fifty pianists and an equal number of violinists and 'cellists; more than two hundred agencies, and a myriad of singers going up and down the highways and byways of this great land. All this confirms my assertion that ours *is* a musical nation.

As for myself, I began my apprenticeship as an orchestral player—a violinist, and I paid little attention to wind organizations until I led the Marine Band. Like most people who are, so to speak, brought up on the fiddle, I didn't have a proper respect for wind combinations. To me, band instrumentation in those early days left a void that cried out to be filled—I was never satisfied. Wholly lacking were the qualities I felt a band should and could possess—a tone as sustained as that of an organ and a brilliancy of execution similar to that of the piano. I began my career with the Marines determined to develop a musical body as important in its own field, as any orchestra. This determination was bound, of course, to deflect my sympathies and affection from orchestra to wind-band.

Since the day when I strove to lift the Marine Corps Band out of its narrow rut of polkas, grand opera cavatinas and national airs, the public has accepted my offerings graciously. The press too, has always treated me with the utmost consideration, and has ever shown a kindly spirit toward the work I produced. Whenever I look over my unwieldy tomes of clippings, I feel like saying, "Gentlemen of the press, I salute you!" Success is, after all, only the friendly fusion of the feelings of giver and receiver and I appreciate every cordial handclap and every printed word which has paved the way to the long continuation of my band appearances. Had I not received so overwhelming a reception thirty years ago I could not have proceeded with enthusiasm and confidence; in those days when the air resounded to the strains of Sullivan, Strauss and Sousa, I was warmed and delighted by this appreciation of my work.

72

The Business of Music

The "can do," "go get 'em" spirit of American enterprise hit the music business in a big way toward the end of the nineteenth century. Older firms, such as Boston-based Oliver Ditson & Co., tended to rely on general advertising, house publications, and the workings of the marketplace. But the newer world of popular sheet music publishing adopted more aggressive tactics. The center for sheet music publication became New York City, in lower Manhattan. Presumably because of the tinny sound of the upright pianos used constantly by song pluggers, the area around East 14th Street and Union Square became known as "Tin Pan Alley." The location shifted uptown, but the name "Tin Pan Alley" stuck, signifying a center for publishing and marketing until the 1940s.

Edward B. Marks (1865–1945), who knew the scene well, established a firm that became a leading publisher of American and Latin American popular music. From its beginning in 1894 until 1920, the firm bore the name of Marks's partner, composer Joseph Stern (1870–1934). Marks's book *They All Sang* (1934) gives us an insider's look at the popular-music world of his time. He describes the aggressive tactics of song plugging employed by him and his partner as they made the rounds of New York night spots in 1897. Marks, who claims he is not a musician himself, is under no delusions about the music business, nor is he really interested in the musical quality of the songs he plugs. His is a rugged, competitive view of the rough-and-tumble New York popular-music scene as he knew it.

Opportunities in the music business expanded greatly in the late nineteenth century as a result of the invention of sound recording technology. Thomas Alva Edison (1847–1931) spoke the first recorded words, "Mary had a little lamb," into his revolutionary new machine on August 12, 1877. Edison's sounds were captured on a tin or wax-covered cylinder and could be played back by reversing the recording process. Ten years later, a German immigrant, Emile Berliner, came up with the first version of the so-called "gramophone," which used a flat disc. As if in reply to Edison, Berliner's first recorded words were "Twinkle, twinkle, little star." An advantage to Berliner's machine was that copies of recordings could quickly and easily be made from master discs. An improved gramophone became the basis in 1898 for the Victor Talking Machine Company, which used the trade name "Victrola." The growth of the recording industry began in earnest around 1900.

EDWARD B. MARKS
from *They All Sang* (1934)

During our impressionable youth my partner and I had heartaches and headaches; we learned that an orchestra leader's word was water, and a soubrette's, lightest air. But during our nightly peregrinations we did hear our songs sung a great number of times. True, we didn't know how many copies any particular public performance helped us sell, but we found a rough relation between the number and variety of plugs we could get for a number, and its subsequent sale.

It was in this matter of plugs that the new music publishing houses in the nineties differed from the old firms like C. H. Ditson, Wm. A. Pond & Co., Willis Woodward, Frank Harding and Hamilton S. (Ham) Gordon, the impressive old codger who owned "Silver Threads among the Gold." These old timers of the game maintained the same Dickensian dignity as the book publishers of their era.

The song writers practiced still another brand of aloofness. Since they generally disposed of their work outright for ten or fifteen dollars a complete specimen, they were not interested in what happened subsequently. Sober, they acquiesced in the fate society decreed for Bohemians. Drunk, they gloried in it. Mostly they were drunk. "Look at Foster," they would say. Stephen Foster, their immediate predecessor, whom many of them could remember, had died in a cheap lodging house on the Bowery, hadn't he? They considered their mode of life a confirmation of their talents, which, truthfully, were sometimes slim. Let the publishers, drab souls, pick up the gold.

There was another type of song writer, like J. W. Kelly or Joe Casey, who was primarily a performer, and wrote songs for his own use. Sometimes the songs attained a general popularity. Then

a whole batch, perhaps written over a span of a decade, would be published in a collection: Harrigan songs, Scanlan songs, Gus Williams songs.

From the nineties on, the song writer became more of a business man, and the publisher perforce more of a Bohemian, so that they eventually met on common ground. Lyricists and composers even started their own publishing houses, and Tin Pan Alley, which received its name about that time, became a fairly homogeneous estate, like the stage.

What attracted me to this particularly insane business which had Joe Stern and myself prowling the streets at night, drinking aggregate reservoirs of beer, listening to the troubles of lady singers whose men had just given them a black eye, or bass fiddlers whose wives had eloped with cornetists, I do not know. Nor do I know what has held me in it for forty years, even after Stern's retirement. Nobody else in my family ever wrote a lyric. They were all respectable people. It isn't because I'm intensely musical, either. I don't play any instrument and I can carry a tune a little farther than Equipoise can carry the Empire State Building. Maybe it's because I was the family poet laureate. When there was a wedding or a birthday party, I used to write rhymes, and my mother always said they were good. Maybe it's because I was a member of the Puzzlers' League of America at old Pythagoras Hall when I was a kid, and W. W. Delaney, who signed his rebuses "Wille Wildwave," and was the president, presented me with prizes occasionally.

Delany, in after years, was to publish song books at 117 Park Row—just words, no music. He bought the privilege from the publisher of every successful song, and his presence at our office was always a sign that we had a hit. Delany had a remarkable habit of never coming directly to the point. He wouldn't walk in and ask what you'd take for the right to reprint some words. He would just hang around the office looking absentminded, as if he had wandered in by mistake, until

Edward B. Marks, *They All Sang: From Tony Pastor to Rudy Vallee*, as told to Abbott J. Liebling (New York: Viking Press, 1934), [22]–26, 59, 101–2.

you said, "Hello, Will, guess we rang the bell with that waltz, huh?" Then he would say, " 'Tain't so bad. How much do you want for it? Remember, I ain't got too much money." His song sheets went all over the country, wherever people wanted cheap, sentimental reading matter. Songs usually had from four to eight verses in those days, and they were quite edifying. We never objected to Delaney's use of our lyrics—if he paid for them—because lots of hinterlanders, after reading the words of a song, wrote to us for the music. Not so, the pirated song sheets illegally peddled along Broadway today. They are a curse of the publishing business. When an economical ukelele player has a sheet of words in front of him and gets the tune over the radio, the publisher makes nothing. This is all a digression, but life is full of them.

Puzzle competitions and rhyming contests being favorite newspaper devices to promote circulation in the late eighties, I won a number of handsome celluloid dresser sets and beautifully framed chromos of paintings by Sir Edward Landseer, featuring St. Bernard dogs and golden-haired female children. All this, in the opinion of my immediate relatives, indicated God-given talents. But it would be hard to live on celluloid shoe horns; so I became a notions salesman.

As for my life of cracked songs and cracked people, it was really inevitable, I guess, because I was stage-struck. I had no qualifications for the theater—I never could have doubled for Mr. Henry E. Dixey[1] in *Adonis*, and, as I have hinted, I could not sing. But with my cousin, Robert Spero, now "Uncle Robert," I liked to hang around Fourteenth Street and Third Avenue, which corresponds to Longacre Square today, and exchange wise conversation with the actors from Tony Pastor's.[2] Since the general level of literacy in the

"profesh" was not high, even such modest talents as mine got noised about. Polly Holmes, an Irish character comedienne playing Pastor's, asked me for a comedy number, and I obliged. The song was called, "Since McManus Went Down to the Track." It recounted the evil destiny of a prosperous bricklayer who imagined himself a judge of horseflesh, and it had a chorus that Polly could put over. For my music I went to the hole-in-the-wall shop of George M. Rosenberg, the arranger.

At that time publishers issued only a simple piano score for each song. To get a ten-piece orchestration, which fit the standard theater band of the era, an actor had to go to an arranger who would write it out by hand. If an actor played a theater with a smaller or larger orchestra, he needed a fresh arrangement. Competent musicians like Rosenberg and our old friend Schmalz, therefore, never lacked work, and would write a simple original melody as readily as an arrangement.[3] In such cases they never bothered about copyrights or demanded public credit for their work. They were musical cobblers and they would as soon put on a full sole and heel as a patch. In the same informal manner Yiddish singers on the East Side today buy a whole song, music and lyrics, for five dollars from a tea-sipping expatriate on Seventh Street.

Some years later, when Joe and I had founded our publishing house, I persuaded Rosenberg to abandon his anonymous song cobbling and appear as a full-fledged song shoe-maker with a trademark. I invented the euphonious name of George Rosey for the new composer, and he wrote us an immediate hit, "The Honeymoon March," a two-step in the Sousa style, to which Dave Reed, Jr., set several hundred gay and innocuous words. Joe and

---

[1]Comedian and singer Henry Dixey (1859–1943) achieved stardom as the statue brought to life in *Adonis* in 1884; the play was the first in Broadway's history to run for more than five hundred consecutive performances.

[2]Impresario and singer Tony Pastor (1837–1908), who as a boy performed in minstrel shows and circuses, opened theaters in various locations in New York City; In 1881, Pastor

---

opened a new theater on Fourteenth Street that Marks describes elsewhere as "an institution," and that Pastor himself described as "the first specialty and vaudeville theater of America."

[3]Elsewhere, Marks tells us that Schmalz, "an old German with a European musical background," was arranger for the Atlantic Gardens, a music hall and beer garden in lower Manhattan where Marks frequently plugged his songs.

I then read the announcements of wedding engagements in the *Herald*, which was the socially favored newspaper, and sent each future bride a copy gratis. A year later Rosey wrote an "Anniversary March," and we pulled the same stunt.

Rosey always was—and is today, happily—an honest man. Many a song have I seen brought to him by a one-key composer who thought he had a hit and wanted George to arrange it. He would promise five, ten, even fifteen dollars. George would look at the music, his derby on the back of his head, his cigar sticking up from the corner of his mouth. "No," he would say, "I don't see noddings in it. It's rodden." And the one-key guy would "take back his gold."

George left his mark on the song business. It was he who first suggested that publishers print professional copies, with orchestrations. This simple suggestion eliminated his own former trade overnight, and retail song cobblers no longer ply their trade so successfully.

*   *   *

If you wanted to put a song over in New York in the nineties, you had to make them sing it in the late joints; the tingel tangels, as we called the minor German beer halls on the East Side; the back rooms of saloons like O'Flaherty's Harp, where you were invited to join a quartet or put up your dukes. You had to make them play it at Terrace Gardens, where the athletic clubs and benevolent associations held their refined balls. You had to make friends with variety stars who would launch your numbers at Koster and Bial's, or Pastor's. Then in time the tune might rise from New York gutters to the New York first-floor front, and the piano trade would be yours.

*   *   *

The bicycle, ragtime, colored slides, pluggers, and now the phonograph. This succession of new developments in the song business fairly appalled the old-timers. And it is not surprising that they were unable to grasp the full significance of the phonograph. Here was the first step in the mechanization of music which would in time render the home piano semi-obsolete and ruin the sheet music game. But in the nineties the machines, known interchangeably as graphophones and phonographs, were so imperfect that nobody thought of them as a dangerous rival of the piano. No process existed for the quantity manufacture of records, which were all of the thick cylindrical wax type that you picked up a like a dog collar.

The Edison interests had patents on both the machine and the records, but they sold wax "blanks" to anybody who wanted to record. The same machine served for recording and reproduction. To record, you sang into the amplifying horn. Few voices reproduced well, and these, for some reason, were not always voices one should have wished to reproduce. The recording of a number was considered something of a plug, because ordinary human beings, who owned upright pianos but didn't go in for the new eccentricities, might hear your song and then buy the sheet music for their piano.

It was as a plug that Joe Stern and I saw the phonograph. As you have gathered by this time, we were strong on plugs. Since anybody could buy the blank cylinders, we opened our own recording studio in a loft at 21 East Twentieth Street, a couple of doors west of our publishing office. A staff paper folder, tan and brown, lies upon my desk as I write. It is the March (1897, I think) bulletin of the Universal Phonograph Company. That was us.

The first offering for the month was a series of records by the Diamond Quartette: A. C. Campell, S. C. Porter, J. K. Reynard, and Will C. Jones. They did an "Imitation Medley," with "imitations of the nightingale, pigs, baby cry, crows, etc., concluding with a most amusing cat fight." Their other numbers included "The Cornfield Medley," "with steamboat Imitation, bells, whistles, banjos, etc." I don't remember how the steamboat got in the cornfield.

THOMAS ALVA EDISON

from *The Diary and Sundry Observations of Thomas Alva Edison* (1920–1925; PUB. 1948)

[*April 1925.*] The phonograph never would have been what it now is and for a long time has been if I had not been deaf. Being deaf, my knowledge of sounds had been developed till it was extensive and I knew that I was not and no one else was getting overtones. Others working in the same field did not realize this imperfection, because they were not deaf. Deafness, pure and simple, was responsible for the experimentation which perfected the machine. It took me twenty years to make a perfect record of piano music because it is full of overtones. I now can do it—just because I'm deaf.

* * *

[*July 1920.*] The phonograph is the acid test of a voice, for it catches and reproduces the voice just as it is; in fact, it is nothing more nor less than a re-creation of the voice. If a singer can reproduce on the phonograph advantageously, then you may be sure that the voice can run the gamut of criticism on the concert stage. For while the phonograph is primarily a parlor or concert hall instrument, yet I have tested it out in the Metropolitan Opera House to good effect.

Indeed, we use large theatres for our "Tone Tests," as we call them, where the singer stands beside the phonograph and sings with a record he or she has previously made. Suddenly the singer stops, but the song goes on, and the audience cannot tell the difference except by noting that the singer's lips are closed. The singer takes up the song again at times, with the same result. These demonstrations have been given in theatres from Maine to California before hundreds of thousands of music lovers.

Again, it is here that the phonograph can be of infinite advantage to those desiring to book singers for their concerts, as they naturally should know just what they are getting before engaging their singers. For instance, the clubs in other cities, when wishing to engage talent, could very readily hear and judge not only the singer's voice but the entire repertoire of songs, and thus be able to select the music best suited to their own community.

* * *

[*January 1921.*] Which do I consider my greatest invention? Well, my reply to that would be that I like the phonograph best. Doubtless this is because I love music. And then it has brought so much joy into millions of homes all over this country, and, indeed, all over the world. Music is so helpful to the human mind that it is naturally a source of satisfaction to me that I have helped in some way to make the very finest music available to millions who could not afford to pay the price and take the time necessary to hear the greatest artists sing and play.

Thomas Alva Edison, *The Diary and Sundry Observations of Thomas Alva Edison*, ed. Dagobert D. Runes (Westport, Conn.: Greenwood Press, 1948), 53–54, 83–84, 169–70.

73

Cowboy Songs

The major symbol of the American West has always been the cowboy. The first cowboys were Texans, and their model was the Mexican *vaquero*. After the Civil War, Texas ranchers began moving their cattle to the Midwestern railheads for shipment to the cities of the industrial North. Cattle trails reached such places as Sedalia in Missouri, and Abilene, Dodge City, and Ellsworth in Kansas. The height of the cattle drives came in the 1870s and 1880s. By this time, cowboys were also dispersing north and west. By the 1890s, increased railroad activity and the use of barbed wire to fence in animals were bringing an end to the era. Yet freedom, independence, individuality, ruggedness, self-sufficiency, and closeness to nature remain part of the image of cowboy life—indeed, of the American dream.

The actual cowboy experience was anything but romantic. The life was hard. Working for months on end in all kinds of weather in a males-only society, often alone, bored, and dependent on one's horse for both transportation and company could be miserable. Dangers of all sorts abounded, sleep was scarce, and the food was poor.

Under such circumstances, singing brought levity and relief. Cowboy songs were often based on poems written and published by westerners, embellished in pick-up performances or made up on the spot. These words were sung to a small repertoire of known melodies, and performance quality varied. "I never did hear a cowboy with a real good voice. If he had one to start with, he always lost it bawling at cattle," commented one writer. A cowboy might sing to quiet the cattle, and he usually sang without accompaniment. If he used an instrument around a campfire, it was likely a violin or banjo (the guitar did not become a common folk instrument until after the turn of the century). This was music of the people, an art that grew and changed as songs were passed along orally.

The songs, usually ballads, tell of disasters, early death, tragedy, love, and adventure. The stories could extend to many stanzas, sometimes displaying awkward rhymes. They could incorporate yodeling, falsetto singing, and nonsense syllables. Many had refrains. Accompaniments, when they existed, were minimal, bland, and rather too upbeat to suit the mood of the text. The narrator sang in an objective, detached way, a kind of performance that oddly enhanced the drama.

If we wish to regain something of the authentic experience we must look to early singers such as Carl T. Sprague ("The Original Singing Cowboy," 1895–1978) and Jules Verne Allen ("The Singing Cowboy," 1883–1945) who, cowboys themselves, went on to preserve their heritage on recordings. We may also look to those who collected cowboy songs and preserved them early on—renegade easterner Nathan Howard "Jack" Thorp (1867–1940), who also was a cowboy and cowboy singer, and the legendary folklorist John A. Lomax (1867–1948). Thorp published an important collection in 1908, *Songs of the Cowboys.* Lomax's *Cowboy Songs and Other Frontier Ballads* followed two years later.

NATHAN HOWARD THORP

from "Banjo in the Cow Camps" (PUB. 1945)

Words and banjo-strumming floated soft and clear on the night. I reined up in the brush to listen. It was pitch dark where I was, Pecos River behind me, Roswell down that-a-way quite a piece, and somebody's chuck wagon just ahead, drawn up for the night in flat sand-dune country rich in grama grass and tabosa. The campfire flickered and fell. I knew there would be maybe half a dozen men sprawled around it, their day's riding done, supper over, and a banjo-pickin' cowboy to tell a story under the stars: a story in verse, about their own country and kind, in their lingo, home-grown and maybe as thorny as cactus. This one I was hearing now was about "a little steel dust the color of rust," the fastest cutting-horse in Texas—name of Dodgin' Joe. It was a new song to me. As the final words died away, I rode into the light of the campfire. . . .

Songs of the range had a special appeal for me. I was a singin' cowboy myself, by adoption, with a little mandolin-banjo that went where I went, and the songs I heard some cowboys sing were an authentic feature of the land and life that made it seem good to me. Sometimes on the trail or in camp I would think up a song of my own. . . .

Maybe cowboy singing was an answer to loneliness. Maybe it was just another way of expressing good fellowship. Maybe it was several things. Something happened in the day's work, funny or sad, and somebody with a knack for words made a jingle of it; if it was liked, others learned it and passed it on. A ballad like "The Old Chisholm Trail," with its catching *come ti yi youpy* refrain, seems to have just grown. It was sung from the Canadian line to Mexico, and there were thousands of verses; nobody ever collected them all. Every cowboy knew a few, and if he had a little whiskey in him, or was heading for town with wages in his pocket, he might make up a few. These weren't "cultured" songs. Sometimes the rhymes didn't match very well. Often the language was rough and had to be heavily expurgated for publication. But ballad-making and song-singing were living parts of cowboy life.

Nathan Howard (Jack) Thorp, "Banjo in the Cow Camps." *Pardner of the Wind* (Caldwell, Idaho: Caxton Printers, 1945), 21–22, 24.

NATHAN HOWARD THORP

The Old Chisholm Trail (PUB. 1921)

The origin of this song is unknown. There are several thousand verses to it—the more whiskey the more verses. Every puncher knows a few more verses. Sung from the Canadian line to Mexico.

Come along, boys, and listen to my tale,
I'll tell you of my trouble on the old Chisholm
    Trail.

Coma ti yi youpy, youpy ya, youpy ya,
Coma ti yi youpy, youpy ya.

I started up the trail October twenty-third,
I started up the trail with the 2-U herd.[1]

Oh, a ten-dollar hoss and a forty-dollar saddle,
And I'm goin' to punchin' Texas cattle.

Nathan Howard (Jack) Thorp, *Songs of the Cowboys* (New York: Houghton Mifflin, 1921), 109–12.

[1]The 2-U was a cattle brand.

I woke up one mornin' afore daylight,
And afore I sleep the moon shines bright.

Old Ben Bolt was a blamed good boss,
But he'd go to see the girls on a sore-backed hoss.

Old Ben Bolt was a fine old man,
And you'd know there was whiskey wherever he'd
    land.

My hoss throwed me off at the creek called Mud,
My hoss throwed me off round the 2-U herd.

Last time I saw him he was goin' cross the level
A-kickin' up his heels and a-runnin' like the devil.

It's cloudy in the west, a-lookin' like rain,
And my damned old slicker's in the wagon again.

Crippled my hoss, I don't know how,
Ropin' at the horns of a 2-U cow.

We hit Caldwell and we hit her on the fly,
We bedded down the cattle on the hill close by.

No chaps, no slicker, and it's pourin' down rain,
And I swear, by God, I'll never night-herd again.

Feet in the stirrups and seat in the saddle,
I hung and rattled with them longhorn cattle.

Last night I was on guard and the leader broke the
    ranks,
I hit my horse down the shoulders and I spurred
    him in the flanks.

The wind commenced to blow and the rain began
    to fall,
Hit looked, by grab, like we was goin' to lose 'em
    all.

I jumped in the saddle and grabbed holt the horn,
Best blamed cow-puncher ever was born.

I popped my foot in the stirrup and gave a little
    yell,
The tail cattle broke and the leaders went to hell.

I don't give a damn if they never do stop;
I'll ride as long as an eight-day clock.

Foot in the stirrup and hand on the horn,
Best damned cowboy ever was born.

I herded and hollered and I done very well,
Till the boss said, "Boys, just let 'em go to hell."

Stray in the herd, and the boss said kill it,
So I shot him in the rump with the handle of the
    skillet.

We rounded 'em up and put 'em on the cars,
And that was the last of the old Two Bars.

Oh, it's bacon and beans 'most every day,—
I'd as soon be eatin' prairie hay.

I'm on my horse and I'm goin' at a run,
I'm the quickest shootin' cowboy that ever pulled
    a gun.

I went to the wagon to get my roll,
To come back to Texas, dad-burn my soul.

I went to the boss to draw my roll,
He had it figgered out I was nine dollars in the
    hole.

I'll sell my outfit just as soon as I can,
I won't punch cattle for no damned man.

Goin' back to town to draw my money,
Goin' back home to see my honey.

With my knees in the saddle and my seat in the
    sky,
I'll quit punchin' cows in the sweet by and by.

    Coma ti yi youpy, youpy ya, youpy ya,
    Coma ti yi youpy, youpy ya.

JOHN A. LOMAX

"Collector's Note" and *Whoopee Ti Yi Yo* (1910)

Out in the wild, far-away places of the big and still unpeopled West—in the canyons along the Rocky Mountains, among the mining camps of Nevada and Montana, and on the remote cattle ranches of Texas, New Mexico, and Arizona—yet survives the Anglo-Saxon ballad spirit that was active in secluded districts in England and Scotland even after the coming of Tennyson and Browning. This spirit is manifested both in the preservation of the English ballad and in the creation of local songs. Illiterate people, and people cut off from newspapers and books, isolated and lonely— thrown back on primal resources for entertainment and for the expression of emotion—utter themselves through somewhat the same character of songs as did their forefathers of perhaps a thousand years ago. In some such way have been made and preserved the cowboy songs and other frontier ballads contained in this volume. The songs represent the operation of instinct and tradition. They are chiefly interesting to the present generation, however, because of the light they throw on the conditions of pioneer life, and more particularly because of the information they contain concerning that unique and romantic figure in modern civilization, the American cowboy.

The profession of cow-punching, not yet a lost art in a group of big Western states, reached its greatest prominence during the first two decades succeeding the Civil War. In Texas, for example, immense tracts of open range, covered with luxuriant grass, encouraged the raising of cattle. One person in many instances owned thousands. To care for the cattle during the winter season, to round them up in the spring and mark and brand the yearlings, and later to drive from Texas to Fort Dodge, Kansas, those ready for market, required

large forces of men. The drive from Texas to Kansas came to be known as "going up the trail," for the cattle really made permanent, deep-cut trails across the otherwise trackless hills and plains of the long way. It also became the custom to take large herds of young steers from Texas as far north as Montana, where grass at certain seasons grew more luxuriant than in the south. Texas was the best breeding ground, while the climate and grass of Montana developed young cattle for the market.

A trip up the trail made a distinct break in the monotonous life of the big ranches, often situated hundreds of miles from where the conventions of society were observed. The ranch community consisted usually of the boss, the straw-boss, the cowboys proper, the horse wrangler, and the cook—often a negro. These men lived on terms of practical equality. Except in the case of the boss, there was little difference in the amounts paid each for his services. Society, then, was here reduced to its lowest terms. The work of the men, their daily experiences, their thoughts, their interests, were all in common. Such a community had necessarily to turn to itself for entertainment. Songs sprang up naturally, some of them tender and familiar lays of childhood, others original compositions, all genuine, however crude and unpolished. Whatever the most gifted man could produce must bear the criticism of the entire camp, and agree with the ideas of a group of men. In this sense, therefore, any song that came from such a group would be the joint product of a number of them, telling perhaps the story of some stampede they had all fought to turn, some crime in which they had all shared equally, some comrade's tragic death which they had all witnessed. The song-making did not cease as the men went up the trail. Indeed the songs were here utilized for very practical ends. Not only were sharp, rhythmic yells—sometimes beaten into verse—employed to stir up lagging cattle, but also during the long watches the night-guards, as they

John Lomax and Alan Lomax, *Cowboy Songs and Other Frontier Ballads* (New York: Sturgis and Walton, 1910), xvii–xxii, 87–91.

rode round and round the herd, improvised cattle lullabies which quieted the animals and soothed them to sleep. Some of the best of the so-called "dogie songs" seem to have been created for the purpose of preventing cattle stampedes,—such songs coming straight from the heart of the cowboy, speaking familiarly to his herd in the stillness of the night.

The long drives up the trail occupied months, and called for sleepless vigilance and tireless activity both day and night. When at last a shipping point was reached, the cattle marketed or loaded on the cars, the cowboys were paid off. It is not surprising that the consequent relaxation led to reckless deeds. The music, the dancing, the click of the roulette ball in the saloons, invited; the lure of crimson lights was irresistible. Drunken orgies, reactions from months of toil, deprivation, and loneliness on the ranch and on the trail, brought to death many a temporarily crazed buckaroo. To match this dare-deviltry, a saloon man in one frontier town, as a sign for his business, with psychological ingenuity painted across the broad front of his building in big black letters this challenge to God, man, and the devil: *The Road to Ruin.* Down this road, with swift and eager footsteps, has trod many a pioneer viking of the West. Quick to resent an insult real or fancied, inflamed by unaccustomed drink, the ready pistol always at his side, the tricks of the professional gambler to provoke his sense of fair play, and finally his own wild recklessness to urge him on,—all these combined forces sometimes brought him into tragic conflict with another spirit equally heedless and daring. Not nearly so often, however, as one might suppose, did he die with his boots on. Many of the most wealthy and respected citizens now living in the border states served as cowboys before settling down to quiet domesticity.

A cow-camp in the seventies generally contained several types of men. It was not unusual to find a negro who, because of his ability to handle wild horses or because of his skill with a lasso, had been promoted from the chuck-wagon to a place in the ranks of the cowboys. Another familiar figure was the adventurous younger son of some British family, through whom perhaps became current the English ballads found in the West. Furthermore, so considerable was the number of men who had fled from the States because of grave imprudence or crime, it was bad form to inquire too closely about a person's real name or where he came from. Most cowboys, however, were bold young spirits who emigrated to the West for the same reason that their ancestors had come across the seas. They loved roving; they loved freedom; they were pioneers by instinct; an impulse set their faces from the East, put the tang for roaming in their veins, and sent them ever, ever westward.

That the cowboy was brave has come to be axiomatic. If his life of isolation made him taciturn, it at the same time created a spirit of hospitality, primitive and hearty as that found in the mead-halls of Beowulf. He faced the wind and the rain, the snow of winter, the fearful dust-storms of alkali desert wastes, with the same uncomplaining quiet. Not all his work was on the ranch and the trail. To the cowboy, more than to the goldseekers, more than to Uncle Sam's soldiers, is due the conquest of the West. Along his early winding cattle trails the Forty-niners found their way to California. The cowboy has fought back the Indians ever since ranching became a business and as long as Indians remained to be fought. He played his part in winning the great slice of territory that the United States took away from Mexico. He has always been on the skirmish line of civilization. Restless, fearless, chivalric, elemental, he lived hard, shot quick and true, and died with his face to the foe. Still much misunderstood, he is often slandered, nearly always caricatured, both by the press and by the stage. Perhaps these songs, coming direct from the cowboy's experience, giving vent to his careless and his tender emotions, will afford future generations a truer conception of what he really was than is now possessed by those who know him only through highly colored romances.

* * *

Whoopee Ti Yi Yo, Git Along Little Dogies

As I walked out one morning for pleasure,
I spied a cow-puncher all riding alone;

His hat was throwed back and his spurs was
               a-jinglin',
As he approached me a-singin' this song:

    Whoopee ti yi yo, git along little dogies,[2]
    It's your misfortune, and none of my own.
    Whoopee ti yi yo, git along little dogies,
    For you know Wyoming will be your new
       home.

Early in the spring we round up the dogies,
Mark and brand, and bob off their tails;
Round up our horses, load up the chuck wagon,
Then throw the dogies upon the trail.

It's whooping and yelling and driving the dogies,
Oh, how I wish you would go on;
It's whooping and punching and go on little
   dogies,
For you know Wyoming will be your new home.

Some boys goes up the trail for pleasure,
But that's where they get it most awfully wrong;
For you haven't any idea the trouble they give us
When we go driving them all along.

When the night comes on and we hold them on the
    bedground,
These little dogies that roll on so slow;
Roll up the herd and cut out the strays,
And roll the little dogies that never rolled before.

Your mother she was raised way down in Texas,
Where the jimson weed and sand-burrs grow;
Now we'll fill you up on prickly pear and cholla[3]
Till you are ready for the trail to Idaho.

Oh, you'll be soup for Uncle Sam's Injuns;
"It's beef, heap beef," I hear them cry.
Git along, git along, git along little dogies
You're going to be beef steers by and by.

---

[2]The meaning of *dogie* has been debated. The ranchers of the Southwest, according to Lomax, generally held that a "dogie" is a stunted calf that has had to "subsist at too tender an age on greass and so has grown pot-bellied, or 'dough-bellied.' "

---

[3]A spiny cactus.

PART III

The Twentieth Century

74   Arthur Farwell and Music for a Democracy

Arthur Farwell (1872–1952) wondered what it might mean to produce music of mass appeal in a democratic society. He explored American sources. Together with Charles F. Lummis, he wrote *Spanish Songs of Old California* (Los Angeles, 1923). He wanted to see music become a grassroots part of the American communal experience. Above all, he was drawn to Native American music.

Farwell's activity with Native American sources peaked in the first decade of this century when he ran the Wa-Wan Press, established in 1901 at Newton Centre, Massachusetts, a suburb of Boston. The press, which took its name from an Omaha Indian ceremony for peace, fellowship, and song, published songs and piano works by thirty-seven composers (including ten women) over an eleven year period to 1912, thereby providing a major impetus for the "Indianist movement" in music during the first three decades of the twentieth century.

Following his involvement with the Wa-Wan Press, Farwell broadened out to envision music of mass appeal, based on community singing. He hoped thereby to inspire a democratic society in a social and spiritual way.

A prolific composer, Farwell believed that a national music could evolve into a universal expression. He held that American composers must study American life and character and work for the good of all. By so doing, he believed they would find renewed relevance in society. He zealously envisioned the dawning of a new epoch in music. In an article titled "The Zero Hour in Musical Evolution," published in the *Musical Quarterly* in 1927, he wrote, "The movement has already established the chief principles held to be essential to a new epoch, corrective of the past and present, viz.; a new type of musical event of the people, with its doors open to all; the active participation of the people, and the restoration of the fundamental position of song."*

Farwell lived these ideals. He composed music for pageants, conducted community choruses, and experimented with musical forms as communal expression. As chief critic for *Musical America* from 1909 to 1914, he provided far-ranging coverage of the period's music scene.

---

*Arthur Farwell, "The Zero Hour in Musical Evolution," *The Musical Quarterly*, January 1927: 98.

ARTHUR FARWELL

from "Pioneering for American Music" (1935)

The story of the promotion of serious American musical composition, from its emergence out of the nocturnal mists of adolescence and provincialism into the present encouraging dawn of its artistic importance, covers a period of about thirty-five years. This story has by no means yet been written with all its implication of detail, human interest, personalities, incidents and historical significance, although excellent and important steps have recently been taken in that direction.[1] Within the limits of time and space permitted in a brief magazine article, I can myself set down only a few random observations out of my own experience in this general development.

When the Manuscript Societies of New York, Philadelphia and Chicago were organized, between 1889 and 1896, no broad awakening to contemporary world-developments in music had yet taken place in America. My own contact, a fugitive one, was with the New York society in the nineties. To those of us who were beginning to get a faint glimpse, a very faint one, of "modern" music and future American possibilities, this organization appeared hopelessly dilettante, though I now recognize that it had its place in the gradual evolution. Its founder, Addison Andrews, once took a printed song of mine from his desk drawer to show me with what he was accustomed to horrify musical visitors. The chiefly horrifying element was an altered major dominant ninth chord, with the ninth below the third.

It was in those days that MacDowell was living, obscurely enough, in Boston, and Paderewski was said to have scolded Arthur Nikisch into producing some of his works with the Boston Symphony.

I was present when Nikisch subsequently directed an orchestral suite by MacDowell and his second piano concerto with the composer as soloist. On the former occasion MacDowell made his nervous bow from his usual seat in the second balcony.

The American discovery of the real Wagner, and the staggering emergence of Tschaikowsky, Brahms and Strauss in the last decade of the nineteenth century drove many young American students of composition to Europe. There soon appeared a new generation of composers, who were aware of contemporary music. Not until such a generation should arise could there be any true awakening to the art of writing music in America. It was now, in this decade, that Anton Dvořák stepped into the scene, to teach students who could not go to Europe and to send out his call to American composers to strike into the musical folk-sources of their own soil. Dvořák came to this country, I was informed in Europe, against the scornful protests of Brahms, who urged him not to accept America's invitation, saying that Americans "cared for nothing but the dollar."

The result of these events appeared in the first decade of the present century, which I have termed the "Period of American Musical Awakening." For the first time American composers began to write music which showed that they were observing what France and Russia, as well as the more advanced Germany were doing to expand and modernize music. But the publishers would have none of it and would accept only the most conventional pieces from these men. I made a contact with this younger group in 1901, two years after my return from European study. During this latter experience I had particularly observed that the countries which were gaining a national individuality of their own, notably France, Russia, Norway, Bohemia, Spain, were doing so through the development of their own folk material. I had taken Dvorak's challenge deeply to heart, and worked in the field of Indian music, not with the idea that this or any other

---

"Pioneering for American Music," *Modern Music*, March–April 1935: 116–19, 122.

[1]Notably by John Tasker Howard in his book *Our American Music*, and in the survey, Altruistic Music Publishing in America, which Juliet Danziger contributed to the *Musical Mercury* of October, 1934. [Farwell's note.]

non-Caucasian folk music existing in America was the foundation of a national art, but because it existed only in America and its development was part of my program to further all unique and characteristic musical expressions that could come only from this country. By 1901 the degree of interest shown in some early recitals of my Indian developments, given in Boston, led me to believe that they should be printed. But I could find no publisher who was like-minded. So I had reached an impasse.

I went to Chadwick[2] with my troubles, and found him sympathetic. I said, "We go to Europe and spend a lot of money, or it is spent on us, to be trained as *composers*; we come back and they will have us as lecturers, writers, accompanists, teachers, or what not, but they won't have us as composers. Composers, they tell us, are Europeans." "True," said Chadwick, "but what are you going to do about it?"

I said, "I am going to fight," and received his approbation and blessing.

The issue, of course, was not for myself alone, but for the new generation of composers. My contact with the younger group, and my own impasse, led me immediately afterwards, in December, 1901, to the founding of the *Wa-Wan Press*, at Newton Centre, Massachusetts. Stillman-Kelley,[3] of somewhat more advanced years and experience, cautioned me about using this cryptic name, (that of an Omaha ceremonial of peace, fellowship and song), but I felt the moment demanded a striking and curiosity-provoking title. My capital was about ten dollars, which went for stationery and postage. With the first subscriptions to come in for an announced quarterly series of works, I paid for the circulars and the printing of the first issue.

The point which I wish to make here is that this was not a mere whimsical adventure on my part, but an inevitable event, forced by the condition and movement of the times. It is this which

gives it historical importance as the first of such ventures. There was no avoiding it; if I had not undertaken it, someone else soon would have.

In the eleven years of our existence we published works of some thirty composers, and the passage of time indicates that we did not fail to gather in a very good proportion of those then beginning their careers who have since come to national prominence. Among them were Edgar Stillman-Kelley (the only one among us who already enjoyed a considerable reputation), Frederic Ayres, Louis Campbell-Tipton, Arne Oldberg, Edward Burlingame Hill, Arthur Shepherd, Gena Branscombe, Henry Gilbert, and Noble Kreider, whose name has not carried as far as it will one day. Charles T. Griffes and John Alden Carpenter would have been with us, but at the time they knocked at the Wa-Wan doors I was compelled by force of affairs to terminate the enterprise, and was turning the catalog over to G. Schirmer, New York.

In the earliest days of the venture we gave numerous concerts in various places, usually under private auspices. One of the most memorable of these was held in the parlors of the Lafayette-Brevoort Hotel in New York, on February 16, 1903. Among various other offerings, Henry Gilbert played his *Negro Episode, a Tone-Poem on African Rhythms*, and *Verlaine: Sunset Colors and Reveries*, and characteristically made the affair unforgettable by removing his cuffs, which bothered him in playing, and placing them prominently on top of the piano.

Between 1903 and 1907, I made four trips to the Far West, stopping everywhere across the country, at towns large and small, drawing audiences by playing my Indian music, preaching the gospel of American music, and discovering new composers. The Indian music, because of its novelty, became a powerful weapon of propaganda; it enabled me to reach large numbers of people. Indeed I could not have made this national campaign without it.

* * *

Looking backward to the American musical awakening of the first years of the century, and even still farther to the apparently but really futile

---

[2]George W. Chadwick, then director of the New England Conservatory of Music in Boston.

[3]Composer Edgar Stillman-Kelley was then teaching at Yale.

efforts of an earlier time, we realize that the present status of composition in America, and the enterprises for its promotion, strike deep roots, in a continuous series, into the past. True, the present battle for new styles and more matured technic could not have been fought without our previous struggle for national recognition of the composer in America. But that earlier battle also could not have been fought without the basic effort for national musical education, with its attendant primitive creative efforts, in the Reconstruction period.

ARTHUR FARWELL

from "The New Gospel of Music" (1914)

The New Gospel of Music is this:

That the message of music at its greatest and highest is not for the few, but for all; not sometime, but now; that it is to be given to all, and can be received by all.

Let no one get the false impression that this is merely a pretty dream or a vague altruistic fancy. The New Gospel of Music stands upon established fact and principle, and its full meaning is a thing to be grappled with by everyone who sets out to lead in musical matters from this time forth. The fact upon which it rests is that its successful practice is arising and becoming established in many places, as will be shown; and the principle upon which it rests is that which I have called "mass-appreciation," the spontaneous response of the human mass to the substantive reality in all music, however great, without previous education in musical appreciation.

Fact and Principle

The *fact* is beginning to be somewhat broadly appreciated in America, as is witnessed by the emulation of the communities which have been most successful in their experiments, and the corresponding constant advance in the movement to bring the best music to the people through various channels. The immense significance of the *principle*—its potential capacity to give birth to the most stupendous developments of music in its relation to humanity in the future—has not as yet been dreamed of by our present civilization. Our method of growth by emulation and experiment in America is a healthy one, but nevertheless in a large measure blind. Many of our American cities set out to build a system of municipal music, or other means of bringing the great message of music to the people, very much as a child sets out to build a house of blocks. The child imitates and endeavors, without any thought of inquiring into the principles of construction, or its purposes. The time has come when we must improve on such primitive hit-or-miss methods, and proceed in accordance with understood principles, which cannot be violated without a diminution in the efficiency of the undertaking, or perhaps without actual failure. The principles of universal musical distribution which we are now discovering, such as "mass-appreciation," bear the same relation to our completed communal musical enterprises, as the electrical principles of resistance, induction, etc., bear to the completed dynamo. These principles ignored or violated, an impairment of the result necessarily follows; but the understanding and fulfillment of the conditions fixed by them brings the most complete possible efficiency which those principles, by their nature, are capable of yielding. . . .

"The New Gospel of Music," *Musical America* 19, (April 4, 1914): 32.

75 Henry Gilbert: Promoting American Music

During the early years of the twentieth century European influence ran strong, yet American nationalism was in the wind. The early repertoire of the New York Philharmonic consisted mainly of works by European composers. Since its opening in 1883, the repertoire of New York's Metropolitan Opera has also remained generally a Europe-based collection of classical works, usually those of wide appeal. German influence, particularly Wagner, prevailed throughout the nineteenth century and into the 1920s, when French currents began increasingly to be felt. Composer Henry F. Gilbert commented in *The New York Times* on March 24, 1918: "Musical America is in the grip of Europe. Europe dictates to us what music we shall hear, tells us the kind we should prefer, and, worst of all, insists upon dictating to our composers what kind they should write." Despite this European bias, however, the Metropolitan Opera did premiere seventeen new American works between 1908 and 1935, and on Broadway a rising tide of patriotism was apparent in such songs as George M. Cohan's *You're a Grand Old Flag.*

Henry Gilbert (1868–1928), Edward MacDowell's first pupil, later became close friends with Arthur Farwell. Gilbert lived a life of poverty, poor health, odd jobs, and travel. In the early teens, he became interested in ragtime and fascinated with jazz. He explored African-American and Native American traditions and music from New Orleans. His *Comedy Overture on Negro Themes*, premiered by the Boston Symphony Orchestra in 1911, includes ragtime in its opening theme and draws on riverboat songs and spirituals. *Negro Rhapsody, 'Shout'* (1915) includes spirituals. *The Dance in Place Congo* (1918) was based on New Orleans Creole dances by George W. Cable. His works also include *American Dances in Ragtime Rhythm* (1915) and *Jazz Study* (1924).

Gilbert was, as the *Boston Post* said in 1914, "genuinely American." Although better known in his own day than in ours, his works bubble with youthful American exuberance. Gilbert considered himself a "pioneer in American music," and his work presaged the Americanists of the twenties and thirties: George Gershwin, Aaron Copland, and Roy Harris.

HENRY GILBERT

from "The American Composer" (1915)

The position of the native composer of music in America is, to say the least, peculiar. The art of music plays a large and important part among the present day diversions of the American public, but it is in the nature of an imported toy and is not a significant part of the life of the people. We have much music, it is true; the greatest in the world; and probably a more catholic and broader view of the world's musical achievements than can be obtained in any other country. But the reverse side of the fact is, that the poor, struggling, and as yet not very individual native musical product has perhaps a harder time than it has had in other countries.

In America, Symphony Orchestras and Opera Companies spring up as it were over night. Beside which there is always an abundance of piano and vocal recitals. The members and directors of these opera companies, the conductors of the symphony orchestras, besides the vast majority of the players, and by far most of the recitalists, are Europeans. Even when they have not been born in Europe, all their training has been European, and all their mental bias is in accordance with European musical tradition. Naturally almost all the music performed is European and thus the public is educated to an ideal of musical beauty which though great and wonderful in itself is perforce exclusive of anything which differs from it.

The American composer, even one of the best and most earnest sort, in submitting a composition of his to one of our European-American symphony-orchestra conductors, must abide by his decision respecting its worthiness of performance. The decision of the orchestral conductor respecting the value of the work submitted is naturally influenced by the degree in which the new work approaches those great European models with which his life-training has made him familiar. It

therefore happens that many works which are not in the least significant, nor important to the development of an *American* school of composition, are given the high honor of a finished performance and a wide-spread publicity.

To this it should be added that the great body of our professional critics is likewise educated exclusively to European standards of musical beauty. There are of course a few brilliant exceptions who are doughty champions of the new note wherever it appears. But the vast majority proceed to judge the work performed in accordance with their Europe-derived standards of taste; to praise it wherever it coincides, however weakly, with these standards; and to condemn it whenever it departs, with no matter how much intrinsic justification, from these standards.

* * *

[O]ur composers are gradually beginning to realize that we cannot arrive at a distinctive adulthood in our music until we have left the home nest of European tradition and struck out for ourselves. Now these first steps are naturally somewhat blundering and unsure and can hardly give any true indication of what may be arrived at ultimately. But the main point, on which we should all congratulate ourselves, is, that the first step toward an American music has actually been taken. Its subsequent arrival is merely a question of time.

The foundations of culture in a new and only partially civilized country are always laid in imitation of the culture of a completely developed and civilized country. Thus, early Italy imitated Greece; France and Germany imitated Italy; Russia imitated Germany, and in the nineteenth century we have seen America imitating England in literature and Germany in music. All the European countries mentioned have eventually developed a fine, sturdy, and distinctive culture of their own. Something native to themselves and expressive of their own race consciousness. But what of America?

Henry Gilbert, "The American Composer," *The Musical Quarterly* (April 1915): 171–72, 179–80.

To the minds of all thinkers and the hearts of all who sincerely love our country and have a living faith in its future, this question must be big with interest. We have already, as has been said, struck a distinctive note in our literature. But the spirit of our music is still largely imitative. In the order of the development of the arts music usually comes last, and it is perhaps too early to look for a distinctive note in American music. Still I see here and there a gleam of something big and vital.

But it is the potentialities, the latent possibilities of American music which arouse my most earnest enthusiasm. Here we are in America with a population composed of all European racial stocks. Each having its own distinctive race consciousness, yet all bound together by a free, liberated and on-rushing national spirit. When the amalgam is complete— shall there not arise eventually a strong and beautiful music in whose texture is woven all those various strands of race consciousness? For all these threads shall be here gathered together and harmoniously blended, and I, for one, look with great interest to the ultimate development of an art of music, which, while containing these many elements, shall yet be superior in expressive power to any of the single elements from which it has been built.

If creativity is pushing the envelope, thinking beyond traditional boundaries, and making new connections, Charles Ives (1874–1954) had it in abundance. His bandmaster father, George Ives, was also an experimenter: he explored the mysteries of acoustics and quarter tones; he asked Charlie to sing in one key while he played in another, and he savored the results when two bands playing different music marched toward each other from the opposite ends of town.

Charles Ives was a Connecticut Yankee, born in Danbury. He subscribed to the transcendentalist philosophy of visionary idealism in the ultimate spiritual reality of hidden unities and mysteries of human existence. He was interested in music as human expression, no matter the amateur results that others might find awkward. By incorporating quotations from a wide variety of American sources, he employed a "collage" technique that made his music more universal and all-embracing.

At Yale University, Ives excelled in athletics; he was well-liked; and he immersed himself in music. He received rigorous training from the newly appointed Horatio Parker, whose conservative mastery, although frustrating for Ives, provided him with a solid foundation. So involved did he become in music that he neglected his other studies and nearly flunked out of Yale.

Although he held professional organist positions from 1889 to 1902 at the First Presbyterian Church in Bloomfield, New Jersey, and then at the Central Presbyterian Church in New York, Ives earned his living primarily as a businessman. He led a double life, composing at night and on weekends. He believed that a substantial art "comes directly out of the heart of experience and thinking about life and living life." He claimed that his music helped his business and vice versa.

In 1918, Ives suffered a severe heart attack, and by the 1920s, his creative flame was exhausted by his double life. He also suffered from a complete lack of recognition for his music. Other than his own performances, no work of Ives's appeared on any concert program between 1902 and 1920. He issued private printings of his Second Piano Sonata (*Concord*), *Essays before a Sonata*, and *114 Songs*—the first steps that would lead to recognition beyond a small coterie of admirers. It remained to composer Aaron Copland, pianist John Kirkpatrick, and a few other supporters to bring his music to a wider audience during the 1930s. Since then, Ives's status has grown to the point that many consider him America's foremost twentieth-century composer.

Winthrop Pitt Tryon (1870–1969), who wrote about a visit with Ives, was the music critic for *The Christian Science Monitor.*

WINTHROP P. TRYON

from "A Composer in Wall Street" (1924)

I called on a composer the other day down in the district of New York known as Wall Street. His name is Charles E. Ives, and I found him not greatly different from other men of business whom I have met, and not greatly different from other men of art, either. The only unusual circumstance was the man's surroundings. But they were typically enough American, being an office for the transaction of commercial affairs. Nor was I, for my part, surprised to find Mr. Ives as much a musician in the midst of desks, typing machines and filing cabinets, as other persons I have known were in their studios, with grand piano and all the other fixings.

In talk, I found Mr. Ives quite a conservative. If I knew nothing of his writing except what I could gather from our conversation, I should imagine his songs, sonatas and symphonies to be the straightforward, old-fashioned sort of production that university professors turn out. From hearing him tell of studying at Yale, I should imagine his notes would look the strict harmony and counterpoint of the treatises. But I had had the opportunity of actually listening to a violin sonata of his in a recital in Aeolian Hall. And more than that, I had read somewhat his book of "114 Songs," and his second piano sonata, entitled "Concord, Mass., 1840–60," which are privately printed.

The songs are full of American melody, some of it remembered, Mr. Ives told me, from camp-meeting services which he attended as a boy at Redding, Conn. But the themes are treated with anything but the ancient simplicity of the New England tune makers. A good many scores in modern style I have seen in the last few years, but scarcely anything so unsettling of traditional rules as these.

Winthrop P. Tryon, "A Composer in Wall Street," *The Christian Science Monitor*, August 16, 1924: 10.

CHARLES IVES

from *Memos* (1932; PUB. 1972)

I might add one more matter, as some ask me about [it] and apparently don't get it all right:—why and how a man who apparently likes music so much goes into business. Two things:— (1) As a boy [I was] partially ashamed of it—an entirely wrong attitude, but it was strong—most boys in American country towns, I think, felt the same. When other boys, Monday A.M. on vacation, were out driving grocery carts, or doing chores, or playing ball, I felt all wrong to stay in and play piano. And there may be something in it. Hasn't music always been too much an emasculated art? Mozart etc. helped.[1]

(2) Father felt that a man could keep his music-interest stronger, cleaner, bigger, and freer, if he didn't try to make a living out of it. Assuming a man lived by himself and with no dependents, no one to feed but himself, and willing to live as simply as Thoreau—[he] might write music that no one would play, publish, listen to, or buy. *But*—if

Charles Ives, *Memos*, ed. John Kirkpatrick (New York: W. W. Norton, 1972), 130–31.

[1] The editor, John Kirkpatrick, comments: "Ives's reaction to Mozart could very well be explained by the kind of Mozart performance that was fashionable when Ives was a young man—smoother and daintily smirking like Dresden china figurines. . . ."

he has a nice wife and some nice children, how can he let the children starve on his dissonances—answer that, Eddy! so he has to weaken (and as a man he should weaken for his children), but his music (some of it) more than weakens—it goes "ta ta" for money—bad for him, bad for music, but good for his boys!!

(3) If a man has, say, a certain ideal he's aiming at in his art, and has a wife and children whom he can't support (as his art products won't sell enough unless he lowers them to a more commercial basis), should he let his family starve and keep his ideals? No, I say—for if he did, his "art" would be dishonestly weakened, [and] his ideals would be but vanity.

(4) Also other reasons, from experience, that to be thrown with people of all conditions all day long, for a good part of a man's life, widens rather than cramps up his sensibilities, etc. (for instance, see Bellamann's *Musical Quarterly* article, January '33). But others (many) feel differently, [that] writing sellable music part of the time doesn't disturb their better music. The way I'm constituted, writing soft stuff makes me sore—I sort of hate all music.

HENRY BELLAMANN

from "Charles Ives: The Man and His Music" (1933)

It is not easy to interview Charles Ives. But when finally cornered on the question of his parallel system of life he said: "My business experience revealed life to me in many aspects that I might otherwise have missed. In it one sees tragedy, nobility, meanness, high aims, low aims, brave hopes, faint hopes, great ideals, no ideals, and one is able to watch these work inevitable destiny. And it has seemed to me that the finer sides of these traits were not only in the majority but in the ascendancy. I have seen men fight honorably and to a finish, solely for a matter of conviction or of principle—and where expediency, probable loss of business, prestige, or position had no part and threats no effect. It is my impression that there is more open-mindedness and willingness to examine carefully the premises underlying a new or unfamiliar thing, before condemning it, in the world of business than in the world of music. It is not even uncommon in business intercourse to sense a reflection of a philosophy—a depth of something fine—akin to a strong beauty in art. To assume that business is a material process, and only that, is to undervalue the average mind and heart. To an insurance man there *is* an 'average man' and he is humanity. I have experienced a great fullness of life in business. The fabric of existence weaves itself whole. You can not set an art off in the corner and hope for it to have vitality, reality and substance. There can be nothing '*exclusive*' about a substantial art. It comes directly out of the heart of experience of life and thinking about life and living life. My work in music helped my business and my work in business helped my music."

Henry Bellamann, "Charles Ives: The Man and His Music," *The Musical Quarterly*, January 1933: 47–48.

HENRY COWELL
from *American Composers on American Music* (1933)

His finding so many new musical resources is the result of his powerful musicality, which demands freedom of expression. He is not content, like many superficial radicals, with merely tearing down known standards. If Ives finds it necessary to reject an older standard, he never rests until he has created a new structure to take its place. Such cre-

Henry Cowell, "Charles E. Ives," *American Composers on American Music: A Symposium* (Stanford, Calif.: Stanford University Press, 1933), 144–45.

ations he has made and still makes in every field of music, and the result is a wonderfully universal, rounded-out whole, not technical, but deliciously and fascinatingly human and charming, and with an emotional but not a sentimental basis. . . .

[O]ne can predict that his work will come more and more into public favor. Public favor comes slowly to those great enough to be independent. Ives is independent, and is truly great; both in invention and in spirit he is one of the leading men America has produced in any field.

CHARLES IVES
from "Some 'Quarter-Tone' Impressions" (C. 1920; PUB. 1962)

Man now is a kind of melodic-harmonic-rhythmic feeling creature, and we are an occidental, equal-tempered race—sometimes. We like our melody not straight but blended. We like to sing our songs on the fence, but not in Greek modes with intervals out of gear with our close harmony. Old Pythagoras was strong on 5ths and 4ths but not on our swipe chords or even our perfect imperfect 5ths.[1]

It seems to me that a pure quarter-tone melody needs a pure quarter-tone harmony not only to back it up but to help generate it.

This idea may be due to a kind of family prejudice, for my father had a weakness for quarter-tones—in fact he didn't stop even with them. He rigged up a contrivance to stretch 24 or more violin strings and tuned them up to suit the dictates of his own curiosity. He would pick out quarter-tone

Charles Ives, "Some Quarter-Tone Impressions," *Essays Before a Sonata and Other Writings*, ed. Howard Boatwright (New York: W. W. Norton, 1962), 110–11.

[1]Diminished fifths, that is, "imperfect" fifths but "perfect" halves of the octave.

tunes and try to get the family to sing them, but I remember he gave that up except as a means of punishment—though we got to like some of the tunes which kept to the usual scale and had quarter-tone notes thrown in. But after working for some time he became sure that some quarter-tone chords must be learned before quarter-tone melodies would make much sense and become natural to the ear, and so for the voice. He started to apply a system of bows to be released by weights, which would sustain the chords, but in this process he was suppressed by the family and a few of the neighbors. A little later on he did some experimenting with glasses and bells, and got some sounds as beautiful, sometimes, as they were funny —a complex that only children are old enough to appreciate.

But I remember distinctly one impression (and this about 35 years ago). After getting used to hearing a piano piece when the upper melody, runs, etc., were filled out with quarter-tone notes (as a kind of ornamentation) when the piece was played on the piano alone there was a very keen sense of dissatisfaction—of something wanted but missing—a kind of sensation one has upon hearing a piano after a harpsichord.

As I've got into family affairs, I feel like keeping on. Father had "absolute pitch," as men say. But it seemed to disturb him; he seemed half ashamed of it. "Everything is relative," he said. "Nothing but fools and taxes are absolute."

A friend who was a "thorough musician"—he had graduated from the New England Conservatory at Boston—asked him why with his sensitive ear he liked to sit down and beat out dissonances on the piano. "Well," he answered, "I may have absolute pitch, but, thank God, that piano hasn't." One afternoon, in a pouring thunderstorm, we saw him standing without hat or coat in the back garden; the church bell next door was ringing. He would rush into the house to the piano, and then back again. "I've heard a chord I've never heard before—it comes over and over but I can't seem to catch it." He stayed up most of the night trying to find it in the piano. It was soon after this that he started his quarter-tone machine.

CHARLES IVES

from *Essays before a Sonata* (1920)

The humblest composer will not find true humility in aiming low—he must never be timid or afraid of trying to express that which he feels is far above his power to express, any more than he should be afraid of breaking away, when necessary, from easy first sounds, or afraid of admitting that those half-truths that come to him at rare intervals, are half true; for instance, that all art galleries contain masterpieces, which are nothing more than a history of art's beautiful mistakes. He should never fear of being called a highbrow—but not the kind in Prof. Brander Matthews' definition.[2] John L. Sullivan[3] was a "highbrow" in his art. A highbrow can always whip a low-brow.

If he "truly seeks," he will "surely find" many things to sustain him. He can go to a part of Alcott's philosophy: that all occupations of man's body and soul in their diversity come from but one mind and soul! If he feels that to subscribe to all of the foregoing and then submit, though not as evidence, the work of his own hands is presumptuous, let him remember that a man is not always responsible for the wart on his face, or a girl for the bloom on her cheek; and as they walk out of a Sunday for an airing, people will see them—but they must have the air. He can remember with Plotinus that in every human soul there is the ray of the celestial beauty; and therefore every human outburst may contain a partial ray. And he can believe that it is better to go to the plate and strike out than to hold the bench down—for by facing the pitcher he may then know the umpire better, and possibly see a new parabola.

Charles Ives, *Essays before a Sonata*, in *Essays before a Sonata and Other Writings* (New York: W. W. Norton, 1962), 96–97. Original ed.: *Essays before a Sonata* (New York: Knickerbocker Press), 1920.

[2]Probably in *The American of the Future and Other Essays*, according to John Kirkpatrick.

[3]The boxer.

CHARLES IVES
from "Music and Its Future" (1933)

The hope of all music—of the future, of the past, to say nothing of the present—will not lie with the partialist who raves about an ultramodern opera (if there is such a thing) but despises Schubert, or with the party man who viciously maintains the opposite assumption. Nor will it lie in any cult or any idiom or in any artist or any composer. "All things in their variety are of one essence and are limited only by themselves."

The future of music may not lie entirely with music itself, but rather in the way it encourages and extends, rather than limits, the aspirations and ideals of the people, in the way it makes itself a part with the finer things that humanity does and dreams of. Or to put it the other way around, what music is and is to be may lie somewhere in the belief of an unknown philospher of half a century ago who said: "How can there be any bad music? All music is from heaven. If there is anything bad in it, I put it there—by my implications and limitations. Nature builds the mountains and meadows and man puts in the fences and labels." He may have been nearer right than we think.

Charles Ives, "Music and Its Future," *American Composers on American Music: A Symposium*, ed. Henry Cowell, (Stanford, Calif.: Stanford University Press, 1933), 197–98.

AARON COPLAND
from *Music and Imagination* (1952)

[W]e wanted to find a music that would speak of universal things in a vernacular of American speech rhythms. We wanted to write music on a level that left popular music far behind—music with a largeness of utterance wholly representative of the country that Whitman had envisaged.

Through a curious quirk of musical history the man who was writing such a music—a music that came close to approximating our needs—was entirely unknown to us. I sometimes wonder whether the story of American music might have been different if Charles Ives and his work had been played at the time he was composing most of it—roughly the twenty years from 1900 to 1920. Perhaps not; perhaps he was too far in advance of his own generation. As it turned out, it was not until the thirties that he was discovered by the younger composers. As time goes on, Ives takes on a more and more legendary character, for his career as composer is surely unique not only in America but in musical history anywhere.

Aaron Copland, *Music and Imagination: The Charles Elliot Norton Lectures, 1951–52* (Cambridge, Mass.: Harvard University Press, 1952), 111.

77   W. C. Handy: Memphis, Mr. Crump, and the Blues

The term *blues* goes far back in history, connoting a mood of melancholy, depression, or longing, and as such, it plays a major role in the history of black culture in the United States. A personal expression on the part of the singer, who feigns humor through tears, the blues is a style, a type of performance, a musical form, a state of mind. In the words of W. C. Handy, composer of *St. Louis Blues*, "The blues is a thing deeper than what you'd call a mood today. Like the spirituals, it began with the Negro, it involves our history, where we came from, and what we experienced. . . . The blues came from the man farthest down. The blues came from nothingness, from want, from desire. And when a man sang or played the blues, a small part of the want was satisfied from the music."*

The blues has its roots in the musical traditions of Africa; these traditions were sustained and developed in the New World by Africans brought over as slaves. In the United States, southern black rural music—particularly from the Mississippi delta—and southern black theater were the progenitors of the now-familiar blues style. Through the performance traditions of the minstrel shows and other forms of traveling entertainment, the blues moved away from a rural environment into wider experience, aided by the northward exodus of African Americans from southern rural areas during the 1910s. Thus, the "classic" form of the blues became associated more fully with urban centers. Female blues singers, such as Mamie Smith, Ma Rainey, and Bessie Smith, became principal performers in place of the traditional, rural, male singers. The blues emanated from and existed alongside ragtime, and both fed into early jazz. As classic blues tended to follow (but not replace) country blues, so its descendants became urban blues, rhythm and blues, Motown, and soul music.

William Christopher Handy (1873–1958) was a cornetist, composer, and music publisher who was instrumental in bringing the blues into the American national consciousness. He recounts that his parents "were among the four million slaves who had been freed and left to shift for themselves." Although his father, a Methodist minister, was dead set against Handy's becoming a musician, the son prevailed, and succeeded. In the selection below, we catch a glimpse of Handy at work with his own ensembles. As a composer, he left a legacy of more than 150 songs and instrumental pieces in a variety of popular idioms. As a publisher, he celebrated the achievements of African Americans. He was involved in large-scale concerts of black music for Carnegie Hall (1928), the Chicago World's Fair (1933), the New York World's Fair (1939–40), and the Golden Gate Exposition in San Francisco (1939).

---

*W. C. Handy, *Hear Me Talkin' to Ya: The Story of Jazz As Told by the Men Who Made It,* ed. Nat Shapiro and Nat Hentoff (New York: Rinehart, 1955), 252.

Handy gave identity to the genre of the blues and helped crystallize its form. He may be forgiven for his statement that *Memphis Blues* was "the first of all the many published 'blues' "; at least two other blues titles were published or registered for copyright earlier, including Hart Wand's *Dallas Blues* and the vocal blues song *Baby Seals Blues* by Baby F. Seals [H. Franklin Seals]. But Handy's publication of *Memphis Blues* (1912), *Jogo Blues* (1913), *Joe Turner Blues* (1914), and, especially, *St. Louis Blues* (1914), solidified the genre.

W. C. HANDY
from *Father of the Blues: An Autobiography* (1941)

The band which I found in Clarksdale and the nine-man orchestra which grew out of it did yeoman duty in the Delta. We played for affairs of every description. I came to know by heart every foot of the Delta, even from Clarksdale to Lambert on the Dog and Yazoo City. I could call every flag stop, water tower and pig path on the Peavine with my eyes closed. It all became a familiar, monotonous round. Then one night at Tutwiler, as I nodded in the railroad station while waiting for a train that had been delayed nine hours, life suddenly took me by the shoulder and wakened me with a start.[1]

A lean, loose-jointed Negro had commenced plunking a guitar beside me while I slept. His clothes were rags; his feet peeped out of his shoes. His face had on it some of the sadness of the ages. As he played, he pressed a knife on the strings of the guitar in a manner popularized by Hawaiian guitarists who used steel bars. The effect was unforgettable. His song, too, struck me instantly.

Goin' where the Southern cross' the Dog.

The singer repeated the line three times, accompanying himself on the guitar with the weirdest music I had ever heard. The tune stayed in my mind. When the singer paused, I leaned over and asked him what the words meant. He rolled his eyes, showing a trace of mild amusement. Perhaps I should have known, but he didn't mind explaining. At Moorhead the eastbound and the westbound met and crossed the north and southbound trains four times a day. This fellow was going where the Southern cross' the Dog, and he didn't care who knew it. He was simply singing about Moorhead as he waited.

That was not unusual. Southern Negroes sang about everything. Trains, steamboats, steam whistles, sledge hammers, fast women, mean bosses, stubborn mules—all become subjects for their songs. They accompany themselves on anything from which they can extract a musical sound or rhythmical effect, anything from a harmonica to a washboard.

In this way, and from these materials, they set the mood for what we now call blues. My own fondness for this sort of thing really began in Florence, back in the days when we were not above serenading beneath the windows of our sweethearts and singing till we won a kiss in the shadows or perhaps a tumbler of good home-made wine. In the Delta, however, I suddenly saw the songs with the eye of a budding composer. The songs themselves, I now observed, consisted of simple declarations expressed usually in three lines and set to a kind of earth-born music that was familiar throughout the Southland half a century ago. Mississippi with its large plantations and small cities

William C. Handy, *Father of the Blues: An Autobiography*, ed. Arna Bontemps (New York: Macmillan, 1941), 73–76, 93–94, 99–100, 118–21.

[1] Clarksdale, Tutwiler, and Yazoo City are all along the Yazoo River in Mississippi, the heartland of the blues.

probably had more colored field hands than any other state. Consequently we heard many such song fragments as *Hurry Sundown, Let Tomorrow Come*, or

Boll Weevil, where you been so long?
Boll Weevil, where you been so long?
You stole my cotton, now you want my corn.

Clarksdale was eighteen miles from the river, but that was no distance for roustabouts. They came in the evenings and on days when they were not loading boats. With them they brought the legendary songs of the river.

Oh, the Kate's up the river, Stack O' Lee's in the
     ben',
Oh, the Kate's up the river, Stack O' Lee's in the
     ben',
And I ain't seen ma baby since I can't tell when.

Wheelbarrow Song

[music example:]

Prettiest gal I ever saw,
Stood on de banks of Arkansaw;
Ha-la-la ding ding ding,
Ha-la-la ding ding ding.

At first folk melodies like these were kept in the back rooms of my mind while the parlor was reserved for dressed-up music. Musical books continued to get much of my attention. There was still an old copy of Steiner's *First Lessons in Harmony*, purchased back in Henderson for fifty cents. While traveling with the minstrels I had bought from Lyon and Healy a copy of Moore's *Encyclopedia of Music*.[2] For a time books became a passion. I'm afraid I came to think that everything worth while was to be found in books. But the blues did not come from books. Suffering and hard luck were the midwives that birthed these songs. The blues were conceived in aching hearts.

*   *   *

Mr. Crump won't 'low no easy riders here
Mr. Crump won't 'low no easy riders here
We don't care what Mr. Crump don't 'low
We gon' to bar'l-house[3] anyhow—
Mr. Crump can go and catch hisself some air!

The city[4] was in the midst of a three-cornered campaign to elect a mayor, and our band was beating the drum for Mr. E. H. Crump, who was running on a strict reform platform. I had composed a special campaign tune for this purpose, but without words. We had played it, with success. Meanwhile I had heard various comments from the crowds around us, and even from my own men, which seemed to express their own feelings about reform. Most of these comments had been sung, impromptu, to my music. My lyric was based upon some of these spontaneous comments, with my own development and additions. Luckily for us, Mr. Crump himself didn't hear us singing these words. But we were hired[5] to help put over his campaign, and since I knew that reform was about as palatable to Beale Street voters as castor oil, I was sure those reassuring words would do him more good than harm.

I don't say that my campaign tune contributed to this result, but at any rate it has another claim. Its musical setting, which I afterwards published under the new title *Memphis Blues*, was the first of all the many published "blues," and it set a new fashion in American popular music and contributed to the rise of jazz, or, if you prefer, swing, and even boogie-woogie. The 1909 campaign is only part of the story of this piece, which began in the back room of Thornton's barber shop near the Poplar Street Station.

*   *   *

---

[3]The term "barrelhouse" refers to a kind of makeshift, rough saloon and also to a style of piano playing associated with ragtime and the blues.

[4]Memphis.

[5]Not by him personally. I have learned that Mr. E. H. Crump was and is quite unaware of my employment to play in connection with his 1909 campaign, and I am sure he would have been easily elected without me. [Handy's note.]

---

[2]John Weeks Moore (1807–1889) published his *Complete Encyclopedia of Music* with Oliver Ditson in Boston, 1852.

Since *Mr. Crump* was the first of the published blues compositions, the lyric that I have quoted demands an explanation. It was a five-line stanza, but the preceding strain and the strain that followed the refrain both called for three-line stanzas in the proper blues fashion (actually no words were written for these at this time). The three-line stanza had twelve instead of sixteen measures to the strain, another blues characteristic. The final strain in this piece had a spot for Osborne's tenor sax to do a haunting break just before the finish.

The melody of *Mr. Crump* was mine throughout. On the other hand, the twelve-bar, three-line form of the first and last strains, with its three-chord basic harmonic structure (tonic, subdominant, dominant seventh) was that already used by Negro roustabouts, honky-tonk piano players, wanderers and others of their underprivileged but undaunted class from Missouri to the Gulf, and had become a common medium through which any such individual might express his personal feelings in a sort of musical soliloquy. My part in their history was to introduce this, the "blues" form to the general public, as the medium for my own feelings and my own musical ideas. And the transitional flat thirds and sevenths in my melody, by which I was attempting to suggest the typical slurs of the Negro voice, were what have since become known as "blue notes."

Thoroughly rehearsed and intoxicated by the new melody, my musicians arrived at Main and Madison riding in a band wagon and got set to play the blues to the general public for the first time in America. It certainly did not occur to us that we were aiding or abetting any trend whatever, but subsequent events make it interesting to recall that the group that struck it up that afternoon consisted of Ed. Wyer, first violin; George Higgins, guitar; Archie Walls, string bass; Robert H. Young, clarinet; James Osborne, tenor saxophone; George Williams, trombone; and myself on the trumpet. We were all seated in chairs. I flashed the sign and the boys gave. Feet commenced to pat. A moment later there was dancing on the sidewalks below. Hands went into the air, bodies swayed like the reeds on the banks of the Congo.

Now and again one got happy and shouted, "Aw, do it, Mister Man." In the office buildings about, the white folks pricked up their ears. Stenographers danced with their bosses. Everybody shouted for more. We heard them on all sides demanding that we play the song again. One bystander came directly in front of us and insisted on knowing the name of the tune.

"That's *Mr. Crump*," Higgins told them, missing a beat on his guitar. Then he sang the words again.

* * *

I rented a room in the Beale Street section and went to work. Outside, the lights flickered. Chitterling joints were as crowded as the more fashionable resorts like the Iroquois. Piano thumpers tickled the ivories in the saloons to attract customers, furnishing a theme for the prayers at Beale Street Baptist Church and Avery Chapel (Methodist). Scores of powerfully built roustabouts from river boats sauntered along the pavement, elbowing fashionable browns in beautiful gowns. Pimps in boxback coats and undented Stetsons came out to get a breath of early evening air and to welcome the young night. The poolhall crowd grew livelier than they had been during the day. All that contributed to the color and spell of Beale Street mingled outside, but I neither saw nor heard it that night. I had a song to write.

My first decision was that my new song would be another blues, true to the soil and in the tradition of *Memphis Blues*. Ragtime, I had decided, was passing out. But this number would go beyond its predecessor and break new ground. I would begin with a down-home ditty fit to go with twanging banjos and yellow shoes. Songs of this sort could become tremendous hits sometimes. On the levee at St. Louis I had heard *Looking for the Bully* sung by roustabouts, which later was adopted and nationally popularized by May Irwin.[6] I had watched the joy-spreaders rarin' to go when it was played

---

[6]May Irwin (1862–1938) was an actress and singer who often appeared with her sister, Flo. May Irwin's biggest success came with *The Widow Jones* (1895), in which she sang her most famous song, *The Bully Song*.

by the bands on the *Gray Eagle*, or the *Spread Eagle*. I wanted such a success, but I was determined that my song would have an important difference. The emotions that it expressed were going to be real. Moreover, it was going to be cut to the native blues pattern.

A flood of memories filled my mind. First, there was the picture I had of myself, broke, unshaven, wanting even a decent meal, and standing before the lighted saloon in St. Louis without a shirt under my frayed coat. There was also from that same period a curious and dramatic little fragment that till now had seemed to have little or no importance. While occupied with my own miseries during that sojourn, I had seen a woman whose pain seemed even greater. She had tried to take the edge off her grief by heavy drinking, but it hadn't worked. Stumbling along the poorly lighted street, she muttered as she walked, "Ma man's got a heart like a rock cast in de sea."

The expression interested me, and I stopped another woman to inquire what she meant. She replied, "Lawd, man, it's hard and gone so far from her she can't reach it." Her language was the same down-home medium that conveyed the laughable woe of lamp-blacked lovers in hundreds of frothy songs, but her plight was much too real to provoke much laughter. My song was taking shape. I had now settled upon the mood.

Another recollection pressed in upon me. It was the memory of that odd gent who called figures for the Kentucky breakdown—the one who everlastingly pitched his tones in the key of *G* and moaned the calls like a presiding elder preaching at a revival meeting. Ah, there was my key—I'd do the song in *G*.

Well, that was the beginning. I was definitely on my way. But when I got started, I found that many other considerations also went into the composition. Ragtime had usually sacrificed melody for an exhilarating syncopation. My aim would be to combine ragtime syncopation with a real melody in the spiritual tradition. There was something from the tango that I wanted too. The dancers at Dixie Park had convinced me that there was something racial in their response to this

rhythm, and I had used it in a disguised form in the *Memphis Blues*. Indeed, the very word "tango," as I now know, was derived from the African "tangana," and signified this same tom-tom beat. This would figure in my introduction, as well as in the middle strain.

In the lyric I decided to use Negro phraseology and dialect. I felt then, as I feel now, that this often implies more than well-chosen English can briefly express. My plot centered around the wail of a lovesick woman for her lost man, but in the telling of it I resorted to the humorous spirit of the bygone coon songs. I used the folk blues' three-line stanza that created the twelve-measure strain.

The primitive Southern Negro as he sang was sure to bear down on the third and seventh tones of the scale, slurring between major and minor. Whether in the cotton fields of the Delta or on the levee up St. Louis way, it was always the same. Till then, however, I had never heard this slur used by a more sophisticated Negro, or by any white man. I had tried to convey this effect in *Memphis Blues* by introducing flat thirds and sevenths (now called "blue notes") into my song, although its prevailing key was the major; and I carried this device into my new melody as well. I also struck upon the idea of using the dominant seventh as the opening chord of the verse. This was a distinct departure, but as it turned out, it touched the spot.

In the folk blues the singer fills up occasional gaps with words like "Oh, lawdy" or "Oh, baby" and the like. This meant that in writing a melody to be sung in the blues manner one would have to provide gaps or waits. In my composition I decided to embellish the piano and orchestra score at these points. This kind of business is called a "break"; entire books of different "breaks" for a single song can be found on the music counters today, and the breaks become a fertile source of the orchestral improvisation which became the essence of jazz. In the chorus I used plagal chords to give spiritual effects in the harmony. Altogether, I aimed to use all that is characteristic of the Negro from Africa to Alabama. By the time I had done all this heavy thinking and remembering, I figured it was time to get something down on paper, so I wrote, "I hate to see de evenin' sun go down." And if you ever had to sleep on the cobbles down by the river in St. Louis, you'll understand that complaint.

St. Louis had come into the composition in more ways than one before the sun peeped through my window. So when the song was completed, I dedicated the new piece to Mr. Russell Gardner, the St. Louis man who had liked *Jogo*

Blues, and I proudly christened it the *St. Louis Blues*. The same day on Pee Wee's cigar stand I orchestrated the number and jotted down scores for the men of my band.

The song was off my chest, and secretly I was pleased with it, but I could scarcely wait for the public verdict. Blurry-eyed from loss of sleep, I went with the band to the evening's engagement on the Alaskan Roof.

78 Ragtime:
Joplin, Berlin, and J. R. Europe

The ragtime craze at the turn of the century and beyond involved music that incorporates "ragged rhythm," a constant collision of syncopations cutting across the regular accents of strong and weak beats. Its major practitioner was Scott Joplin (1868–1917), who became known as the King of Ragtime. In his pedagogical *School of Ragtime,* which he self-published in 1908, Joplin shows us that the essence of a "Joplin Rag" lies in this kind of syncopation. Monroe H. Rosenfeld (1861–1918), a Tin Pan Alley composer, wrote eloquently about Joplin and his music.

Ironically, though, it was Irving Berlin (1888–1989), a Jewish immigrant from Russia, who gained the reputation during the 1910s as America's chief ragtime composer. Berlin, who was then working his way up through Tin Pan Alley, wrote "Alexander's Ragtime Band" (1911), which became the landmark song of the era and bolstered his career immeasurably. The song created little stir until it was incorporated as a production number into a summer show called *The Merry Whirl. The New York Herald* reported on June 13, 1911, that

> Of eight or ten musical numbers 'Alexander's Ragtime Band,' with the clock, snowman and chorus, was the one that pleased the audience most, and when a Columbia [Theater] audience are pleased they show it in no uncertain way. They applaud and whistle and decline to let the show go on until they have had encores enough. They seemed to be endless for that number.

Three months later, *Variety* called it "the musical sensation of the decade." The song was soon taken up and reused numerous times in other settings, and a piano version appeared that September.

Berlin, who had the longest songwriting career in American history, had the knack of pleasing his public by giving them familiar material, which sometimes included quotations from other songs. "Our work," he explained, "is to connect the old phrases in a new way, so that they will sound like a new tune."

Ragtime was heard abroad when James Reese Europe (1880–1919) took his band to France during World War I to bring the troops a taste of home. Noble Sissle, who went along as the regimental drum major, described the scene for the *St. Louis Post-Dispatch* of June 10, 1918, under the headline "Ragtime by U.S. Army Band Gets Everyone 'Over There' ": "I sometimes think if the Kaiser ever heard a good syncopated melody he would not take himself so seriously!"

MONROE H. ROSENFELD

"The King of Ragtime Composers Is Scott Joplin" (1903)

St. Louis boasts of a composer of music, who, despite the ebony hue of his features and a retiring disposition, has written possibly more instrumental successes in the line of popular music than any other local composer. His name is Scott Joplin, and he is better known as "The King of Rag Time Writers," because of the many famous works in syncopated melodies which he has written. He has, however, also penned other classes of music and various vocal numbers of note.

One of the interesting characteristics of Scott Joplin's personality is his conservatism. He rarely refers to his productions and does not boast of his ability, despite the fact that he is possibly one out of threescore of composers who arranges his own compositions. This negro is a tutored student of harmony and an adept at bass and counterpoint; and, although his appearance would not indicate it, he is attractive socially, because of the refinement of his speech and demeanor.

Scott Joplin was reared and educated in St. Louis. His first notable success in instrumental music was "The Maple Leaf Rag," of which thousands upon thousands of copies have been sold. A year or two ago Mr. John Stark, a publisher of this city, and father of Miss Eleanor Stark, the well-known piano virtuoso, bought the manuscript of "The Maple Leaf" from Joplin for a nominal sum. Almost within a month from the date of its issue, this quaint creation became a byword with musicians, and within another half a twelve-month circulated itself throughout the Union in vast numbers. This composition was speedily followed by others of a like character, until now the Stark list embraces nearly a score of the Joplin effusions. Following is a list of some of the more pronounced pieces by this writer, embodying these oddly titled works:

"Elite Syncopations"
"The Strenuous Life"
"The Rag-Time Dance" (song)
"Sunflower Slow Drag"
"Swipesy Cake Walk"
"Peacherine Rag"
"Maple Leaf Rag"

Probably the best and most euphonious of his latter-day compositions is "The Entertainer," a few bars of which are herewith given. It is a jingling work of a very original character embracing various strains of a retentive character, which set the foot in spontaneous action and leave an indelible imprint upon the tympanum.

Joplin's ambition is to shine in other spheres. He affirms that it is only a pastime for him to compose syncopated music and he longs for more arduous work. To this end he is assiduously toiling upon an opera, nearly a score of the numbers of which he has already composed and which he hopes to give an early production in this city.[1]

Monroe H. Rosenfeld, "The King of Ragtime Composers Is Scott Joplin, a Colored St. Louisan" *St. Louis Globe-Democrat*, June 7, 1903, 5.

[1] *The Guest of Honor*, an unpublished opera that is now lost, was staged in St. Louis later in 1903; *Treemonisha* was published in 1911.

SCOTT JOPLIN
from *School of Ragtime* (1908)

Remarks—What is scurrilously called ragtime is an invention that is here to stay. That is now conceded by all classes of musicians. That all publications masquerading under the name of ragtime are not the genuine article will be better known when these exercises are studied. That real ragtime of the higher class is rather difficult to play is a painful truth which most pianists have discovered. Syncopations are no indication of light or trashy music, and to shy bricks at "hateful ragtime" no longer passes for musical culture. To assist amateur players in giving the "Joplin Rags" that weird and intoxicating effect intended by the composer is the object of this work.

Scott Joplin, *School of Ragtime: 6 Exercises for Piano* (New York: Scott Joplin, 1908).

Exercise No. 1

It is evident that, by giving each note its proper time and by scrupulously observing the ties, you will get the effect. So many are careless in these respects that we will specify each feature. . . . Play slowly until you catch the swing, and never play ragtime fast at any time. . . .

Exercise No. 6

. . . We wish to say here, that the "Joplin ragtime" is destroyed by careless or imperfect rendering, and very often good players lose the effect entirely, by playing too fast. They are harmonized with the supposition that each note will be played as it is written, as it takes this and also the proper time divisions to complete the sense intended.

From "Great Composers Get Little; Popular Writers Well Paid" (1911)

In speaking of "popular writers" Irving Berlin, the instigator really of the present craze for "rag" and Italian (or "Wop") songs, comes first to mind. Before turning out "Alexander's Rag Time Band" (of which he composed both lyrics and music) Mr. Berlin wrote "hits" faster than the singers could find time to use them on the stage. "Alexander" is probably the musical sensation of the decade. It is a "natural hit" (without the customary assistance of the publisher). On top of it the young composer has others. Last year he got "statements" from his publishers which netted him $35,000. This year it is expected that Mr. Berlin will go to $50,000, or perhaps over that amount. It is not so long ago this young man was peddling his compositions along "Tin Pan Alley," without securing a willing ear.

"Great Composers Get Little; Popular Writers Well Paid," *Variety* (September 9, 1911): 6.

"Ragtime by U. S. Army Band Gets Everyone 'Over There' " (1918)

With the American Army in France, June 10. —The first (and best) Afro-American contribution to the French fighting line is its band. Subsidized by D. G. Reid with a check for $10,000, and organized by "Jim" Europe, colored orchestra leader, now a Lieutenant in the regiment,[2] the dusky band is fast becoming celebrated throughout France. At the A. E. F.'s[3] chief recreation center a big silver cup and several golden palms were presented to the musicians by the municipality.

Sergt. Noble Sissle, the regimental drum major, has made a study of the effect of Yankee ragtime, as interpreted by his bandsmen, on French audiences. He has addressed the following summary of his impressions to the correspondent of the Post-Dispatch with the American forces:

"After reading so many articles about the American bands and real need of them in France, I thought I would write concerning some of our experiences 'over here.'

"We have quite an interesting time playing our homeland tunes for the amusement of every nationality under the sun. The one interesting thing—to our agreeable surprise—was the enjoyment that all seemed to get out of hearing our ragtime melodies.

"When our country was dance-mad a few years ago, we quite agreed with the popular Broadway song composer who wrote: 'Syncopation rules the nation. You can't get away from it.'

"But if you could see the effect our good, old 'jazz' melodies have on the people of every race and creed you would change the word 'Nation' quoted above to 'World.'

"Inasmuch as the press seems to have kept the public well informed of our band's effort to make the boys happy in this land where everybody speaks everything but English, I will assume that you know Lieut. James Reese Europe, its organizer and conductor. This Lieut. Europe is the same Europe whose orchestras are considered to have done a goodly share toward making syncopated music popular on Broadway. Having been associated with Lieut. Europe in civil life during his 'jazz bombardment' on the delicate, classical, musical ears of New York's critics, and having watched the 'walls of Jericho' come tumbling down, I was naturally curious to see what would be the effect of a 'real American tune' as Victor Herbert calls our Southern syncopated tunes, as played by a real American band.

The Jazz Introduced

"At last the opportunity came and it was a town in France where there were no American troops, and our audience, with the exception of an American General and his staff, was all French people. I am sure the greater part of the crowd had never heard a rag-time number. So what happened can be taken as a test of the success of our music in this country where all is sadness and sorrow. The occasion was at a concert given in a well packed opera house on Lincoln's Birthday, and after the opening address by the Mayor and the response by the American General our band began with its evening entertainment.

"The program started with a French march, followed by favorite overtures and vocal selections by our male quartet, all of which were heartily applauded. The second part of the program opened with 'The Stars and Stripes Forever,' the great Sousa march, and before the last note of the martial ending had been finished the house was ringing with applause. Next followed an arrangement of 'plantation melodies' and then came the fireworks, 'The Memphis Blues.'

"Lieut. Europe, before raising his baton twitched his shoulders apparently to be sure that his tight-fitting military coat would stand the strain, a musician shifted his feet, the players of

---

"Ragtime by U.S. Army Band Gets Everyone 'Over There,' " *St. Louis Post-Dispatch*, June 29, 1918: 2. The article is mostly by Sissle.

[2]The U.S. Fifteenth Infantry.

[3]American Expeditionary Force.

brass horns blew the saliva from their instruments, the drummers tightened their drumheads, everyone settled back in their seats, half closed their eyes, and when the baton came down with a swoop that brought forth a soul-rousing crash both director and musicians seemed to forget their surroundings: they were lost in scenes and memories. Cornet and clarinet players began to manipulate notes in that typical rhythm (that rhythm which no artist has ever been able to put down on paper), as the drummers struck their stride their shoulders began shaking in time to their syncopated raps.

Whole Audience Catching It

"Then, it seemed, the whole audience began to sway, dignified French officers began to pat their feet, along with the American General, who, temporarily, had lost his style and grace. Lieut. Europe was no longer the Lieut. Europe of a moment ago, but Jim Europe, who a few months ago rocked New York with his syncopated baton. His body swayed in willowy motions, and his head was bobbing as it did in days when terpsichorean festivities reigned supreme. He turned to the thrombone players who sat impatiently waiting for their cue to have a 'jazz spasm' and they drew their slides out to the extremity and jerked them back with that characteristic crack.

"The audience could stand it no longer, the 'jazz germ' hit them and it seemed to find the vital spot loosening all muscles and causing what is known in America as an 'eagle rocking it.' 'There, now,' I said to myself, 'Col. _____ has brought his band over here and started ragtimitis in France! Ain't this an awful thing to visit upon a nation with so many burdens?' But when the band had finished and the people were roaring with laughter, their faces wreathed in smiles, I was forced to say that this is just what France needs at this critical moment.

"All through France the same thing happened. Troop trains carrying allied soldiers from everywhere passed us en route, and every head came out of the window when we struck up a good old Dixie tune. Even German prisoners forgot they were prisoners, dropped their work to listen and pat their feet to the stirring American tunes.

"But the thing that capped the climax happened up in Northern France. We were playing our Colonel's favorite ragtime, 'The Army Blues,' in a little village where we were the first American troops there, and among the crowd listening to that band was an old woman about 60 years of age. To everyone's surprise, all of a sudden she started doing a dance that resembled 'Walking the Dog.' Then I was cured, and satisfied that American music would some day be the world's music. While at Aix-les-Bains other musicians from American bands said their experiences had been the same.

"Every musician we meet—and they all seem to be masters of their instruments—are always asking the boys to teach them how to play ragtime. I sometimes think if the Kaiser ever heard a good syncopated melody he would not take himself so seriously.

"If France was well supplied with American bands, playing their lively tunes, I'm sure it would help a good deal in bringing home entertainment to our boys, and at the same time make the heart of sorrow-stricken France beat a deal lighter."

79 ❧ Reminiscing with Sissle and Blake

Singer, lyricist, and composer Noble Sissle (1889–1975) met ragtime pianist and composer Eubie (James Hubert) Blake (1883–1983) in Baltimore in 1915. Their first songwriting collaboration was the successful *It's All Your Fault.* They joined James Reese Europe's Society Orchestra in New York and subsequently organized a regimental band during World War I. Following that they teamed up to perform in vaudeville. Their 1921 musical *Shuffle Along* established their reputation.

Sissle was a showman all his life. Having first gained attention as a singer in 1908 with Edward Thomas's Male Quartet, he later found himself organizing orchestras and working with other composers, especially Blake, in the creation of musical shows, all the while performing successfully as a singer. Blake, whose parents had been slaves, began to play professionally at the age of fifteen. A year later, in 1899, he wrote *Charlestown Rag,* his first piano rag. He continued to perform with much success but retired in 1946 to study composition at New York University and to notate his own compositions. A ragtime revival during the 1960s brought renewed attention to Blake, who had become a legendary figure. He embarked on a second career, performing widely in the U.S. and abroad. His more than three hundred songs and many piano rags show him as a wide ranging and skilled composer.

Shuffle Along was born from a chance meeting in Philadelphia of Sissle, Blake, and librettists Flournoy Miller and Aubrey Lyles. Operating on a shoestring, they mounted the show in New Jersey, Pennsylvania, and Washington, D.C., between late February and May 1921, and then moved on to New York. The musical opened there on May 23, 1921, caught hold, and became a smash hit, running for more than fourteen months on Broadway, with 504 performances, before going on tour.

The show's influence continued well beyond its closing. Two successful all-black musicals, *Strut Miss Lizzie* (1922) and *How Come?* (1923), were indebted to it, as were *Runnin' Wild* (1923) and the much later *Blackbirds of 1939.* Sissle and Blake's own *Chocolate Dandies* (1924), although well received, did not achieve the team's earlier success; *Keep Shufflin'* (1928) fared better, but *Shuffle Along of 1932,* with a new score by Sissle and Blake, failed to find an audience, and a 1952 revival, a botched rewrite of the original, was likewise unsuccessful.

ANONYMOUS ("IBEE")

"Shuffle Along" (1921)

The 63rd Street Theatre, acquired by John Cort interests some months ago, stepped into the theatre division Monday with the first all-colored show that has got close to Broadway since Williams and Walker.[1] "Shuffle Along" is programmed as presented by the Nikko Producing Co., of which Harry L. Cort is said to be one of the principals. The house was formerly used mostly for recitals and special performances, having practically no stage. For this attraction the apron has been extended outward, taking in the first box on either side. By use of drapings the stage can be closed in by pulley lines and a similar arrangement for "one" is provided. The orchestra takes up the space occupied by the first three rows, the first row now being D. This is supposed to be a temporary device. In the fall the house is to be given a regular stage. With the present extension the depth is under 20 feet.

"Shuffle Along" is a lively entertainment. It has an excellent score supplied by Eubie Blake and Noble Sissle, both members of the late Lieutenant Jim Europe's band that won admiration abroad during the war. The musical numbers are worthy of a real production, which "Shuffle Along" lacks entirely. Whatever book there is and the comedy business came from F. E. Miller and Aubrey Lyles. Both these players are from vaudeville, which field further contributed with the staging, done by Walter Brooks.

A private showing was given the piece Sunday night. Song writers who were not present then came Monday for the premiere, for there appears to be a hearty respect for Sissle's ability as a composer, and wiseacres predicted that some of the big shows downtown would receive a suggestion or two.

Broadway may not know it, but the fashion of wearing the feminine head with the bobbed hair effect has more fully invaded the high browns [sic] of the colored troupes than in the big musical shows. All the gals in "Shuffle Along" showed some sort of bobbed hair style, principals and chorus alike. It wasn't so successful with some, but they tried just the same. The feminine contingent was probably recruited from the colored organizations that have entertained the uptown colored populace in the shows at the Lafayette.

Miller and Lyles handled the comedy entirely and they worked up some laughs away from anything they offered in vaudeville. There was a grocery store bit, that suggested the old afterpiece idea. Both boys are partners and both are tapping the till. One of the richest lines came when Lyles was told that a detective was coming to catch his partner, the informant saying that he sure was done stealing now. Lyles inquired: "When did he die?" The humor of the situation was that neither wanted the "bull," fearing he would catch the wrong man first. The partners are rival candidates for mayor of Jimtown. Miller in making a speech to the citizens said he "had no idea there was going to be a dark horse, but you ain't going to be no black mayor." The team inserted their boxing bit in the second act, and it was the comedy hit of the show.

Dancing started in the second act, but there was comparatively little of it. The song numbers had the call all evening. Gertrude Saunders, the ingenue, and Lottie Gee, prima donna, together with Roger Matthews, juvenile, handled most of the songs, and all showed good voices. The show opened with "Simply Full of Jazz," handled by Miss Saunders, and it went for three encores. Miss Gee proved herself a few minutes later while the two girls and Matthews scored with "Gypsy Blues," a tricky melody that caught on quickly.

Anonymous "Ibee," "Shuffle Along," *Variety*, May 27, 1921: 28–29.

[1] Egbert Williams and George Walker created a breakthrough with *In Dahomey*, the first full-length musical written and played by blacks to be accorded a major Broadway production.

The melody hit came at the finale of the first act. It was "Love Will Find a Way," probably the same number first handled by Miss Gee. Repetition brought the air out to its true value. It is a peach. "Shuffle Along," from which the show takes its name, was led by Matthews, it opening the second act. Matthews is a neat worker, sings well and delivered in duets with Miss Gee several times. Miss Saunders was alone for "I am Craving That Kind of Love," another tricky number. She had a number called "Daddy" for encore, which was well liked. "Oriental Blues," sung by Sissle, was perhaps the only number where half a dozen show girls bloomed out in anything like a costume flash. The number was delivered in "one."

The actual song hit score came near the close. Here Blake, who directed the orchestra from the piano, went to the stage for a specialty with Sissle. Their first number was "Low Down Blues." The other songs were out of the team's vaudeville routine, taking in "Pickanniny's Shoes" and "Out in No Man's Land," Sissle announcing the number coming from "our benefactor, the late Jim Europe." But the playing of the "Love" melody won out so strong Sissle used it also to Blake's smiling accompaniment.

Immediately afterwards the show went into the finale with "Baltimore Buzz," another number that stood out and should have been earlier. For that song the only flash of "shimmy" was present.

"Shuffle Along" played Philadelphia for a week, repeated three weeks later, then came into New York to rehearse a week before opening. In Quaker Town the show had a $1 top, including war tax, and grossed around $8,000 for its first engagement there. At the 63rd Street the top is $2 for half the lower floor, the price for the other downstairs rows being $1.50. Colored patrons were noticed as far front as the fifth row on the opening night when the upper floors did not sell out. The house has a balcony and gallery, seating around 1,100.

The production cost looks close to the minimum. Costume outlay was not a heap more, some of the outfits appearing to have come from the wardrobe of another show, perhaps one of the elder Cort's productions. The show therefore stands a good chance to grab a tidy profit, unless the scale is too high. The 63rd Street is around the corner from the Century. A few blocks to the westward is a negro section known as "San Juan Hill." The Lenox Avenue colored section is but 20 minutes away on the subway, so that "Shuffle Along" ought to get all the colored support there is along with the white patrons who like that sort of entertainment.

Some day Sissle and Blake will be tendered a real production and they deserve it.

Louis Armstrong (1901–1971), also known as Dippermouth, Pops, Satchelmouth, and Satchmo, grew up as part of the early jazz scene in New Orleans. He was brought up in poverty, deprived both physically and emotionally. When he landed in the Home for Colored Waifs (read: reformatory) in 1913, he was handed a cornet and began to play. Soon he was determined to become a musician.

Armstrong held a variety of odd jobs but found his way around the Storyville honky-tonks. He was befriended by Joe "King" Oliver (1885–1938). When Oliver left for Chicago in 1918, Armstrong joined Edward "Kid" Ory's excellent band. He was also hired by bandleader Fate Marable to perform on river boats plying the Mississippi.

Oliver's invitation in 1922 to join his Creole Jazz Band in Chicago marked a pivotal step for Armstrong, and he made his first recordings with that group. A landmark series of recordings for Okeh Records occurred between 1925 and 1928 with his Hot Five, Hot Seven, and the imaginative pianist Earl Hines. *Heebie Jeebies*, the Hot Five's first big commercial success, featured Armstrong in an early example of scat singing. His instrumental virtuosity and velvety tone—plus his showmanship, imagination, and passion—marked him as a jazz soloist of the first rank. "Over the years you find you can't stay no longer where you are, you must go on a little higher now," he said.

As Armstrong evolved out of the fascinating decade of the twenties he increasingly became a stand-up soloist with big bands. Unlike some of his earlier colleagues, he survived the changing times, his technique sure and his career an immense success. When interest in big bands waned after World War II, he returned to a small-band format with his All Stars.

Duke Ellington called him "the epitome of jazz." By whatever name one may call his art and by any measure, Louis Armstrong was a pivotal figure in American music.

LOUIS ARMSTRONG

from *A Self-Portrait* (1966)

I'm always wondering if it would have been best in my life if I'd stayed like I was in New Orleans, having a ball. I was very much contented just to be around and play with the old timers. And the

Louis Armstrong, *A Self-Portrait: The Interview by Richard Meryman* (New York: Eakins Press, 1971), 7–13, 17–20, 23–25, 57. A major portion of this interview was first published in the April 15, 1966, issue of *Life* magazine.

money I made—I lived off of it. I wonder if I would have enjoyed that better than all this big mucky-muck traveling all over the world—which is nice, meeting all those people, being high on horse, all *grandioso*. All this life I have now—I didn't suggest it. I would say it was all wished on me. Over the years you find you can't stay no longer where you are, you must go on a little higher now—and that's the way it all come about. I couldn't get away from what's happened to me.

But man I sure had a ball there growing up in New Orleans as a kid. We were poor and everything like that, but music was all around you. Music kept you rolling.

When I was about 4 or 5, still wearing dresses, I lived with my mother in Jane's Alley in a place called Brick Row—a lot of cement, rented rooms sort of like a motel. And right in the middle of that on Perdido Street was the Funky Butt Hall—old, beat up, big cracks in the wall. On Saturday nights, Mama couldn't find us 'cause we wanted to hear that music. Before the dance the band would play out front about a half hour. And us little kids would all do little dances. If I ever heard Buddy Bolden play the cornet, I figure that's when.[1]

Then we'd go look through the big cracks in the wall of the Funky Butt. It wasn't no classyfied place, just a big old room with a bandstand. And to a tune like *The Bucket's Got a Hole in It*, some of them chicks would get way down, shake everything, slapping themselves on the cheek of their behind. Yeah! At the end of the night, they'd do the quadrille, beautiful to see, where everybody lined up, crossed over—if no fights hadn't started before that. Cats'd have to take their razors in with them, because they might have to scratch somebody before they left there. If any of them cats want to show respect for their chick—which they seldom did—they'd crook their left elbow out when they danced and lay their hat on it—a John B. Stetson they'd probably saved for six months to buy. When the dance was over, fellow would walk up and say, "Did you touch my hat, partner?" and if the cat say "yes"—Wop!—he hit him right in the chops.

Once a year, on a certain day, all the social clubs—the Broadway Swells, the Bulls, the Turtles—would have a parade. I eventually joined the Tammany Social Club. One was called the Moneywasters. They used to carry a big cabbage with cigars and paper dollars sticking out of it. And oh it was beautiful in the parades—you know? Everybody with silk shirts, white hats, black pants, streamers across their chests with the club's name, everybody shined up, the Grand Marshal always sharp and strutting, and some guys on horses. They always had stops where they go to dif-ferent members' houses, open a keg of beer, and they liable to end up at a big picnic at the fairgrounds.

And if they have a member that died, they all turn out. It'd be a beautiful thing. Night before a funeral they have a wake, everybody sitting all night around the body singing. You come in there, lead off a hymn and go right back in the kitchen and get cheese, crackers, whisky, beer. Boy, they shouting! Brother's rocking in that coffin. I know a guy who went to all wakes. He didn't care who it was, but he's right on time.

And in those early days, before embalming, some bodies used to come back to life. The body would raise up and sit there on that slab, and goddam, imagine all them people trying all at once to get out of one little bitty door.

Next morning at the funeral the musicians have to stand around outside waiting for the ceremonial to be over. The Catholics, their funerals were quick, but the Baptists, my God, look like they going to never come out of there. We had to do something. There was always a barroom on the corner. Ooooooh, boy!

After the sermon's over, they'd take the body to the cemetery with the band playing the funeral marches—maybe *Nearer My God to Thee*.

Them oldtime drummers, they just put a handkerchief under the snare on their drum and it go *tunk-a, tunk-a*, like a tom-tom effect. And when that body's in the ground, man, tighten up on them snares and he rolls that drum and everybody gets together and they march back to their hall playing *When the Saints* or *Didn't He Ramble*. They usually have a keg of beer back there and they rejoice, you know, for the dead.

Marching back, the funeral's going along one side of the street, and on the other side is the "second line"—guys just following the parade, one suspender down, all raggedy, no coat, enjoying the music. Course they had their little flasks, but when

---

[1] Charles Joseph "Buddy" Bolden (1877–1931), an early New Orleans jazz cornetist and bandleader and an important figure for Armstrong, whose lineage as a trumpet player stems from Bolden via King Oliver.

the parade stop to get a taste in a bar, the second line hold the horses or the instruments for the band and when the guys come back out, they give them their drinks.

In those days in New Orleans, there was always something that was nice and always with music. They used to advertise with them big long wagons they used during the week for hauling furniture. Be a big sign on the side of the wagon advertising a dance or boxing fight—Gunboat Smith was a big name down there. The band would sit in the wagon on chairs, with the trombone and bass at the end where the tailgate lets down. They'd stop at a corner and the band would play. People would come from all the neighborhood and be around the wagon. And here come another wagon and pull up too and that's where that bucking contest used to come—each band playing different tunes trying to outplay each other. King Oliver and Kid Ory used to cut them all. And devilish guys—them old hustlers and pimps—used to chain the wheels of those wagons together so they would have to stay there and play.

Joe Oliver in the Onward Brass Band fascinated me—he was the nearest thing to Buddy Bolden to me. When he went into a bar to yackety with the guys—he didn't drink—or when he'd be parading and not blowing, I'd hold his horn so all he had to do was wipe his brow and walk.

In the evening, people colored and white, used to give parties on the lawns in front of their houses—set up with lemonade and sandwiches and fried chicken and gumbo and the band sit down in front of the door on the porch and play. And people dance. And the musicians always have their uniforms on—a little music lyre on the collar around their neck, and the band's name on the hat. The bands wanted to be stipulated, you know— like the Crescent City Band, Robichaud's Band.[2]

Yeah, music all around you. The pie man and the waffle man, they all had a little hustle to attract the people. Pie man used to swing something on the bugle and the waffle man rang a big triangle. The junk man had one of them long tin horns they celebrate with at Christmas—could play the blues and everything on it. Called him Lonzo. I used to work with him and we'd go in all the rich neighborhoods and buy a lot of old clothes. And I'd be yelling "Old rags and bones, lady! Old rags and bones!" The banana man, he'd be hollering, "Yellow ripe bananas, lady, 15 cents a bunch! Yellow ripe bananas!" Oh, yeah, always had music all around me of some kind.

I worked on a coal wagon and, hell, I was singing selling coal. "Stone coal, lady! Nickel a water bucket! Stone coal, nickel a water bucket!" The bottoms of those buckets was all pounded up so maybe three or four big lumps would fill it. We was selling all through the red-light district—it was called Storyville. The women would be standing there in the doorways to their cribs wearing their "teddies"—that was a famous uniform they had, all silk, like baby bloomers only transparent. One of them would call, "Commere boy. Bring me three buckets." And it was fun for me to go in them cribs and for a quarter extra start them fires. And I'd take my little quick peek, you know, scared she'd catch me, slap me and shove me out of there. But they didn't pay me no mind. Just a stone-coal boy—breathing like a bitch, man.

Storyville was just for white people. Most of the whores were white or light creoles or mulattoes. Lulu White had the biggest house. All those rich men used to come there from all around. Only Negro who played there was Jelly Roll Morton on the piano.[3] That's how he got that gold tooth with a diamond in it. I don't think they had colored maids in Lulu White's. But she was colored. It was a crazy deal.

---

[2]Armstrong was a part of several New Orleans bands, with such names as the Silver Leaf Band and Oscar "Papa" Celestin's Tuxedo Brass Band. Of the two he mentions here, Robichaud's was the more important. John Robichaux (1866–1937), a black creole, frequently competed with Buddy Bolden.

[3]Ferdinand La Menthe "Jelly Roll" Morton (1890–1941), the highly influential jazz pianist, was born near New Orleans. Starting around 1904 he began to travel widely. Armstrong comments in *Satchmo* that he did not know him during the early years.

* * *

When I got my first job in New Orleans playing in a honky-tonk—Matranga's at Franklin and Perdido—I was 17, and it was same as Carnegie Hall to me. Yeah. Night I made my debut, I thought I was somebody. I took 15 cents home and I give it to my mother, and my sister woke up out of a sound sleep, say, "Huh, blowing your brains out for 15 cents." I wanted to kill her. Finally I got raised up to $1.25 a night—top money, man.

I played with a piano and a drum, two guys I only knew as Boogus and Garbee. We'd play from about 8 to daybreak, take little intermissions and go have a beer with some of the gamblers. And Mama would make a lunch—cabbage and rice, or something—to eat at the honky-tonk around midnight. I'd get a couple of hours sleep at home, then I had a job at the coal yard loading carts. I was getting 15 cents a load and made five loads a day. That shovel was as big as a table. Then I had to deliver that coal maybe across the city, and you make a little extra taste if you put the coal in the bin, maybe 40 cents and a sandwich. They call that "cakes throwed in."

Then I'd come home, put the mule up and sum up my coal money—75 cents. By the end of the week you get about $5.00. And I was young, full of fire, even with the shovel. So I try to get me an old lady on the money, too—and got to give her a couple little dollars.

When I wasn't down at the coal yard, I was unloading banana boats. And them bunches touch you on the shoulder and they both hanging to the ground. A big snake, big rat, anything might run out of them. I don't see why I got any strength left at all. But at that time I was enjoying it, being around the cats I wanted to be with, and as a kid I didn't know no better. I had to help Mama and sister. My stepfathers—you know stepfathers—they just going to do so much. Had to eat.

Once I was promised $50—more money than I'd ever seen all at once—for a tune I wrote I called *Get Off Katie's Head*. I sold it to A. J. Piron and Clarence Williams[4] to publish. Weren't no con- tracts or nothing. They wrote some words and called it, *I Wish I Could Shimmy Like My Sister Kate*. They never did pay me for it, never even put my name on it. I didn't bother about it. You can't get everything that's coming to you in this life.

Every corner in my neighborhood had a honky-tonk. There was Spano's and Kid Brown's and Matranga's and Henry Ponce. The first room in a honky-tonk was the saloon, and there'd be two rooms in back. Just throw everybody back there and they have a ball. One was for gambling, playing cotch. You deal three cards from the bottom of the deck and the highest cards win. I never did play much. I was too glad when I got a good hand so that everybody could tell.

The other room was for dancing—doing that slow drag, close together, humping up one shoulder—maybe throw a little wiggle into it. Had a little bandstand catty-cornered, benches around the walls. Drinks were cheap—and strong. Used to get beer in tin lard buckets and it was *cold*—liked to see that sweat on the outside—and you could get as high on that as regular whisky now. Whisky then was 100 proof and raw, too. Real rough. Us kids couldn't take it.

Around four or five in the morning, that's when all them whores would come in to the tonk—big stockings full of dollars—and give us a tip to play the blues. I was just a little fellow and they used to sit me on their knees behind their bottle of beer. And all the gals had their little perfume. They'd get a little box of powdered chalk, buy 15 cents worth of perfume, pour it over the chalk and powder themselves with it. It was pink chalk. Couldn't stand white chalk—looked like you scratch your leg in wintertime. So everybody was

---

[4]Violinist and composer Armand J. Piron (1888–1943) led his own band and played in various others, including those fronted by such notables as W. C. Handy and Papa Celestin. Pianist, vocalist, composer, and band leader Clarence Williams (1898–1965) moved with his family to New Orleans in 1906 and was later active in Chicago and New York City as performer, music publisher, and store owner. During the second decade, he toured extensively with Piron. They founded a short-lived publishing venture together in New Orleans, to which Armstrong refers. Williams's path crossed Armstrong's again in the 1920s, when he became race-recording judge for Okeh records.

smelling. And they'd wear their little calico dresses, show them cute shapes. I'll tell you one thing, they was attractive and very encouraging to look at. There wasn't no problem for them to do business. I thought the women in those days looked a lot more inviting than chicks today wearing all those damn tight-butted pants.

* * *

All this time I was living with Mama and we always poured our troubles into each other. She was a stocky woman—dark, lovely expression and a beautiful soul. And she instilled in me the idea that what you can't get—to hell with it. Don't worry what the other fellow has. Everybody loved her for that, because if you lived next door and you got the world, that's all right. Just don't mess with her little world. I think I had a *great* mother. She didn't have much power, but she did all she could for me—grabbing little knickknacks here and there and everything, and we put it all together.

Big event for me then was buying a wind-up victrola. Most of my records were the Original Dixieland Jazz Band—Larry Shields and his bunch. They were the first to record the music I played. I had Caruso records too, and Henry Burr, Galli-Curci, Tettrazini—they were all my favorites. Then there was the Irish tenor, McCormack—beautiful phrasing.

When I was 18, I got married to my first wife, Daisy, and left home. Everybody wanted to know, was Mama satisfied that her son's marrying a prostitute 21 years old. She say, "I can't live his life.

He's my boy and if that's what he wants to do, that's that." But Daisy had an awful temper, was awful jealous. One time she saw me with another gal, and I saw her coming. She was getting ready to cut me with that razor, and I jumped that ditch and my hat fell off. So she picked it up and started cutting it all up. It was a John B. Stetson and I'd saved a long time to get that hat. Hurt me to my heart, man. Rather lose her than that hat.

In 1917 they closed down the district and all the honky-tonks and in 1918, when Joe Oliver left New Orleans with Jimmy Noone to play in Chicago, they put me in his place in Kid Ory's band playing at Tom Anderson's restaurant. That was a place the horse race crowd hung out, and when those big steaks, half eaten, would go back to the kitchen past the bandstand, we'd tell the waiter–"That's us." And what with all the cats dying and having funerals, I did all right.

* * *

Jazz is all the same—isn't anything new. At one time they was calling it levee camp music, then in my day it was ragtime. When I got up North I commenced to hear about jazz, Chicago style, Dixieland, swing. All refinements of what we played in New Orleans. But every time they change the name, they got a bigger check. And all these different kinds of fantastic music you hear today—course it's all guitars now—used to hear that way back in the old sanctified churches where the sisters used to shout till their petticoats fell down. There ain't nothing new. Old soup used over.

81 George Gershwin: Stretching the Boundaries

When Paul Whiteman premiered George Gershwin's *Rhapsody in Blue* on February 12, 1924, the program notes indicated it was part of an "Experiment in Modern Music." Imbued with jazz, the work sought new ground: its composer was staking out his claim for jazz's acceptance on a "serious" level, with complex, extended works. More than that, he was challenging boundaries in attempting to synthesize American jazz and modern classical traditions. The performance, which was extensively hyped, provoked understanding, misunderstanding, and strong public comment.

This boundary stretching continued when Gershwin (1898–1937) premiered his Piano Concerto in F in 1925, commissioned by Walter Damrosch for performance by the New York Philharmonic at Carnegie Hall. It extended also to his symphonic poem, *An American in Paris* (1928), also premiered by Damrosch.

Boundaries were stretched on the operatic stage when Gershwin produced *Porgy and Bess*, in 1936, a work that has become one of the best-loved pieces of this century. Gershwin called it a folk opera that "brings to the operatic form elements that have never before appeared in opera." But the results confounded the critics. Virgil Thomson, writing in the December 1935 issue of *Modern Music*, commented that "Mr. Gershwin has . . . for some time been leading a double musical life . . . His gift and his charm are greater than the gifts or the charms of almost any of the other American composers . . . [but] he hasn't learned the business of being a serious composer." *Porgy and Bess*, "with a libretto that should never have been accepted on a subject that should never have been chosen" was written by "a man who should never have attempted it." Weighing in on the other side, *Time* reported that the composer "had written the score for what may prove to be the finest attempt yet at a real U.S. opera." Leonard Liebling, writing in the *New York American*, called it "the first authentic American opera."

At the heart of the matter is a gifted composer's attempt to write music of length and of value that really can be called "American." "I believe," Gershwin wrote, "American music should be based on American material." Here, the composer echos sentiments expressed earlier in the century by Antonín Dvořák. He also sympathizes with the point of view expressed by Henry Gilbert: "Shall there not arise eventually a strong and beautiful music in whose texture is woven all those various strands of race consciousness?" And he aligns himself with the "nationalists," including the earliest, William Henry Fry and George Bristow, through the latest, including Arthur Farwell, Roy Harris, and Aaron Copland.

Gershwin appreciated that a composer is rooted in place. In his work, Gershwin combined the best aspects of the American musical scene as he knew it.

GEORGE GERSHWIN

from "The Relation of Jazz to American Music" (1933)

The great music of the past in other countries has always been built on folk-music. This is the strongest source of musical fecundity. America is no exception among the countries. The best music being written today is music which comes from folk-sources. It is not always recognized that America has folk-music; yet it really has not only one but many different folk-musics. It is a vast land, and different sorts of folk-music have sprung up in different parts, all having validity, and all being a possible foundation for development into an art-music. For this reason, I believe that it is possible for a number of distinctive styles to develop in America, all legitimately born of folk-song from different localities. Jazz, ragtime, Negro spirituals and blues, Southern mountain songs, country fiddling, and cowboy songs can all be employed in the creation of American art-music, and are actually used by many composers now. . . .

Jazz I regard as an American folk-music; not the only one, but a very powerful one which is probably in the blood and feeling of the American people more than any other style of folk-music. I believe that it can be made the basis of serious symphonic works of lasting value, in the hands of a composer with talent for both jazz and symphonic music.

George Gershwin, "The Relation of Jazz to American Music," *American Composers on American Music: A Symposium* ed. Henry Cowell (Stanford, Calif.: Stanford University Press, 1933), 186–87.

GEORGE GERSHWIN

"Rhapsody in Catfish Row" (1935)

Since the opening of "Porgy and Bess" I have been asked frequently why it is called a folk opera. The explanation is a simple one. "Porgy and Bess" is a folk tale. Its people naturally would sing folk music. When I first began work on the music I decided against the use of original folk material because I wanted the music to be all of one piece. Therefore I wrote my own spirituals and folksongs. But they are still folk music—and therefore, being in operatic form, "Porgy and Bess" becomes a folk opera.

However, because "Porgy and Bess" deals with Negro life in America it brings to the operatic form elements that have never before appeared in opera and I have adapted my method to utilize the drama, the humor, the superstition, the religious fervor, the dancing and the irrepressible high spirits of the race. If, in doing this, I have created a new form, which combines opera with theatre, this new form has come quite naturally out of the material.

The reason I did not submit this work to the usual sponsors of opera in America was that I hoped to have developed something in American music that would appeal to the many rather than to the cultured few.

It was my idea that opera should be entertaining—that it should contain all the elements of entertainment. Therefore, when I chose "Porgy and Bess," a tale of Charleston Negroes, for a subject, I made sure that it would enable me to write light as well as serious music and that it would enable me to include humor as well as tragedy—in fact, all of the elements of entertainment for the eye as well as the ear, because the Negros, as a race, have all these

George Gershwin, "Rhapsody in Catfish Row," *New York Times*, October 20, 1935: sect. 10, pp. [1]–2.

qualities inherent in them. They are ideal for my purpose because they express themselves not only by the spoken word but quite naturally by song and dance.

Humor is an important part of American life, and an American opera without humor could not possibly run the gamut of American expression. In "Porgy and Bess" there are ample opportunities for humorous songs and dances. This humor is natural humor—not "gags" superimposed upon the story but humor flowing from the story itself.

For instance, the character of Sportin' Life, instead of being a sinister dope-peddler, is a humorous, dancing villain, who is likable and believable and at the same time evil. We were fortunate in finding for that role a young man whose abilities suit it perfectly. John W. Bubbles, or, as he is known to followers of vaudeville, just plain Bubbles, of Buck and Bubbles. We were equally fortunate in finding Todd Duncan for the role of Porgy and Anne Brown for the role of Bess, both of whom give to the score intense dramatic value. We were able to find these people because what we wanted from them lies in their race. And thus it lies in our story of their race. Many people questioned my choice of a vaudeville performer for an operatic role but on the opening night they cheered Bubbles.

We were fortunate, too, in being able to lure Rouben Mamoulian, a great director, back from Hollywood to stage the production. It was Mr. Mamoulian who staged the original production of "Porgy" as a play. He knew all of its value. What was even more valuable, he knew opera as well as he knew the theatre and he was able to bring his knowledge of both to this new form. In my opinion, he has left nothing to be desired in the direction. To match the stage in the pit we obtained Alexander Smallens, who has directed the Philadelphia and Philharmonic-Symphony Orchestras and who has conducted more than 150 operas and who has been invaluable to us.

I chose the form I have used for "Porgy and Bess" because I believe that music lives only when it is in serious form. When I wrote the "Rhapsody in Blue" I took "blues" and put them in a larger and more serious form. That was twelve years ago

and the "Rhapsody in Blue" is still very much alive, whereas if I had taken the same themes and put them in songs they would have been gone years ago.

No story could have been more ideal for the serious form I needed than "Porgy and Bess." First of all, it is American, and I believe that American music should be based on American material. I felt when I read "Porgy" in novel form that it had 100 per cent dramatic intensity in addition to humor. It was then that I wrote to Du Bose Heyward suggesting that we make an opera of it.

My feelings about it, gained from that first reading of the novel, were confirmed when it was produced as a play, for audiences crowded the theatre where it played for two years. Mr. Heyward and I, in our collaboration on "Porgy and Bess," have attempted to heighten the emotional values of the story without losing any of its original quality. I have written my music to be an integral part of that story.

It is true that I have written songs for "Porgy and Bess." I am not ashamed of writing songs at any time so long as they are good songs. In "Porgy and Bess" I realized I was writing an opera for the theatre and without songs it could be neither of the theatre nor entertaining, from my viewpoint.

But songs are entirely within the operatic tradition. Many of the most successful operas of the past have had songs. Nearly all of Verdi's operas contain what are known as "song hits." "Carmen" is almost a collection of song hits. And what about "The Last Rose of Summer," perhaps one of the most widely known songs of the generation? How many of those who sing it know that it is from an opera?

Of course, the songs in "Porgy and Bess" are only a part of the whole. The recitative I have tried to make as close to the Negro inflection in speech as possible, and I believe my song-writing apprenticeship has served invaluably in this respect, because the song writers of America have the best conception of how to set words to music so that the music gives added expression to the words.

I have used sustained symphonic music to unify entire scenes, and I prepared myself for that task by further study in counterpoint and modern harmony.

In the lyrics for "Porgy and Bess" I believe that Mr. Heyward and my brother, Ira, have achieved a fine synchronization of diversified moods—Mr. Heyward writing most of the native material and Ira doing most of the sophisticated songs. To demonstrate the range of mood their task covers, let me cite a few examples.

There is the prayer in the storm scene written by Mr. Heyward:

Oh, de Lawd shake de Heavens
   an' de Lawd rock de groun',
An' where you goin' stand, my brudder
   an' my sister,
When de sky come a-tumblin' down.

Oh, de sun goin' to rise in de wes,
An' de moon goin' to set in de sea
An' de stars goin' to bow befo' my Lawd,
Who died on Calvarie.

And in contrast there is Ira's song for "Sportin' Life" in the picnic scene:

It ain't necessarily so,
It ain't necessarily so,
De t'ings dat yo' li'ble
To read in de Bible,
It ain't necessarily so.

Li'l David was small, but oh my
Li'l David was small, but oh my
He fought big Goliath
Who lay down an' dieth.
Li'l David was small, but oh my

Then there is Mr. Heyward's lullaby that opens the opera:

Summer time, an' the livin' is easy,
Fish are jumpin', an' the cotton is high.
Oh, yo' daddy's rich an' yo' ma is good-lookin',
So hush, little baby, don't yo' cry.

One of these mornin's you goin'
   to rise up singin',
Then you'll spread yo' wings
   an' you'll take the sky.
But 'til that mornin' there's a
   nothin' can harm you
With Daddy an' Mammy standin' by.

And, again, Ira's song for Sportin' Life in the last act:

There's a boat dat's leavin' soon for New York.
Come wid me, dat's where we belong, sister.
You an' me kin live dat high life in New York.
Come wid me, dere you can't go wrong, sister.

I'll buy you de swellest mansion
Up on upper Fi'th Avenue,
An' through Harlem we'll go struttin',
We'll go a-struttin',
And dere'll be nuttin'
Too good for you.

All of these are, I believe, lines that come naturally from the Negro. They make for folk music. Thus "Porgy and Bess" becomes a folk opera—opera for the theatre, with drama, humor, song and dance.

82

Darius Milhaud:
A European Composer Looks at Jazz

Darius Milhaud (1892–1974), a prolific composer, was born in Aix-en-Provence, France. In 1916, after studies at the Paris Conservatory, he traveled to Rio de Janeiro as secretary to the French minister to Brazil, the writer Paul Claudel, whom he had come to know in Paris. On his return to Paris, Milhaud joined a loosely-knit group of musicians known as "Les Six." His ballet, *Le boeuf sur le toit* ("The Nothing-Doing Bar," 1920) captures the flippancy of the post–World War I era typical of Les Six and resonates as well with Brazilian influences.

American jazz was something of a hot item with European composers at the time— witness, for example, the dances in Stravinsky's *L'histoire du soldat*. Milhaud visited Harlem in 1922 and was fascinated by what he heard there. He described the music as "a revelation." After he returned to France, he composed his well-known jazz ballet *La création du monde* (The Creation of the World), on a book by Blaise Cendrars. The piece, which depicts an African creation myth, is a kind of rondo that incorporates a jazz fugue. Its small orchestration, for eighteen instruments, emphasizes winds and includes a saxophone. Here is American jazz interpreted through the eyes of a European musician. Successful though the work is, it is still an interpretation by one reared in another culture.

The composer, forced in 1940 to leave France in the face of German occupation because he was Jewish, moved to California, where he taught for many years at Mills College.

DARIUS MILHAUD

from *Notes without Music* (1953)

When I arrived in New York, I had told the newspapermen interviewing me that European music was considerably influenced by American music. "But whose music?" they asked me, "MacDowell's or Carpenter's?" "Neither the one nor the other," I answered, "I mean jazz." They were filled with consternation, for at that time most American musicians had not realized the importance of jazz as an art form and relegated it to the dance hall. The headlines given to my interviews prove the astonishment caused by my statements: "Milhaud admires jazz" or "Jazz dictates the future of European music." Of course, my opinions won me the sympathy of Negro music-lovers, who flocked to my concerts. The chairman of the Negro musicians' union even wrote me a touching letter of thanks. Little suspecting what complications this would cause, I immediately invited him to lunch; no restaurant would serve us, but at last Germaine Schmitz solved this delicate

Darius Milhaud, *Notes without Music*, (New York: Knopf, 1953), 135–37.

problem by asking the manager of the Hotel Lafayette to receive us. I was also called upon by Harry Burleigh, the famous arranger of Negro spirituals, who played me Negro folk tunes and hymns, which interested me keenly, for I wished to take advantage of my stay to find out all I could about Negro music. The jazz orchestra of the Hotel Brunswick was conducted by a young violinist called Reissmann, who got from his instrumentalists an extreme refinement of pianissimo tones, murmured notes, and glancing chords, whisperings from the muted brass, and barely formulated moans from the saxophone, which had a highly individual flavor. The regular rhythm was conveyed by the muffled beat of the percussion, and above it he spun the frail filigree of sound from the other instruments, to which the high notes of the violin lent an added poignancy. It made a great contrast to Paul Whiteman's lively orchestra, which I had heard a few days before in New York and which had the precision of an elegant, well-oiled machine, a sort of Rolls-Royce of dance music, but whose atmosphere remained entirely of this world.

I owe to Yvonne George my introduction to the pure tradition of New Orleans jazz. In the course of a little reception that followed a lecture I gave at the Alliance Française, she came up to me and said: "You look bored, come and have dinner with me, and afterwards I'll take you to Harlem when I've done my number." She lived in the Hotel Lafayette. In the next room to hers Isadora Duncan and her Russian poet Essenin used to quarrel and chase one another right out on the fire escape. Yvonne introduced me to Marcel Duchamp, an old friend of Satie and Picabia, whose paintings were closely associated with the beginnings of cubism and had played a dominant part in its development. After dinner I heard Yvonne George give her number. She was on Broadway, singing French songs of an intensely realistic character in a style that was both plain and charged with desperate feeling.

Harlem had not yet been discovered by the snobs and aesthetes: we were the only white folk there. The music I heard was absolutely different from anything I had ever heard before and was a revelation to me. Against the beat of the drums the melodic lines crisscrossed in a breathless pattern of broken and twisted rhythms. A Negress whose grating voice seemed to come from the depths of the centuries sang in front of the various tables. With despairing pathos and dramatic feeling she sang over and over again, to the point of exhaustion, the same refrain, to which the constantly changing melodic pattern of the orchestra wove a kaleidoscopic background. This authentic music had its roots in the darkest corners of the Negro soul, the vestigial traces of Africa, no doubt. Its effect on me was so overwhelming that I could not tear myself away. From then on I frequented other Negro theaters and dance halls. In some of their shows the singers were accompanied by a flute, a clarinet, two trumpets, a trombone, a complicated percussion section played by one man, a piano, and a string quintet. I was living in the French House of Columbia University, enjoying the charming hospitality of Mlle Blanche Prenez; the Schmitzes were my close neighbors. As I never missed the slightest opportunity of visiting Harlem, I persuaded my friends to accompany me, as well as Casella and Mengelberg, who were in New York at the time.[1]

When I went back to France, I never wearied of playing over and over, on a little portable phonograph shaped like a camera, Black Swan records I had purchased in a little shop in Harlem. More than ever I was resolved to use jazz for a chamber work.[2]

---

[1] Composer Alfredo Casella (1883–1947) and conductor Willem Mengelberg (1871–1951).

[2] *La création du monde*, 1923.

Composers from Europe who came to America between World Wars I and II greatly enriched culture in the United States. Both Schoenberg and Stravinsky settled in Los Angeles. Ernst Krenek moved there also, after holding academic appointments at Vassar College in Poughkeepsie, New York, and Hamline University in St. Paul, Minnesota.

In the selections below, Krenek writes about what it means to be a "transplanted composer," Schoenberg depicts his own situation, and Stravinsky describes his experiences in setting *The Star-Spangled Banner*.

ERNST KRENEK

from "The Transplanted Composer" (1938)

Since the migrations of composers these days are apt to be non-voluntary, their spiritual luggage may carry a heavy burden of resentment. This piece of baggage is often supremely cherished by the unhappy travelers as they set out on their dismal journeys, for anger is the only link with the homeland which they are willing to recognize. Obviously it is a device set up to counteract unconfessed home-sickness.

It would of course be well to throw overboard these sterile emotions before submitting to examination by the customs officers of the New World. First, for a very practical reason. Whereas in Europe the right to self-complaint is generally conceded to an artist (indeed he often furthers his cause by some display of misery), the New World, on the contrary, abhors such aspects of gloom. It prefers to bestow success on those who seem already possessed of it. More important of course is the fact that a mind oriented to the past is impeded in planning for the future.

There are, however, many positive convictions which the immigrant can bring with him to this New World. It would indeed be foolhardy and fu-

tile to attempt the abandon of all former mental equipment although the delicate psychological situation may tempt him to such desperate resolutions. He feels that he is hardly an invited guest, that no one awaits his arrival, and that, perhaps, to fit into strange surroundings, it would be best to remodel himself entirely. But no greater mistake could be made, for only time itself can accomplish such a metamorphosis.

The European composer preparing to settle in America is exposed to two very different sets of impressions. Between the musical cultures of the Old and the New Worlds, he observes at times a much closer relationship than he had expected. This is largely because many musicians established in America, especially the conductors and instrumentalists, are native Europeans trained in the schools and orchestras of the old continent. The program material of leading musical institutions resembles, with slight modifications, what is used for similar purposes in Europe. On the other hand, he meets situations which awaken doubts that there is any basis whatever for a common point of view. Thus he alternately overrates or underestimates the differences between his former and his new environment. . . .

And just as America builds the best highways and bridges, and not specifically American high-

Ernst Krenek, "The Transplanted Composer," *Modern Music* November–December 1938: 23–24, 27.

ways and bridges in some pseudo-mystical sense, so her aim should be to produce the best music. Toward this end she can be assisted by the newly arrived composers. They have left their native countries because their musical language does not conform to those opinions about the "national" qualities of art that have grown up everywhere in Europe during recent years. This curse of nationalism has fallen on all that is best in modern music, that is, music which reaches the highest artistic and spiritual levels, and sets forth new and original ideas in the greatest technical perfection. Music so dedicated is always endowed with a universal all-human significance, and can never be restricted to a local clan living in the shadow of its own church steeple. Such a goal should be especially adequate to the spirit of America where the idea of a culture embracing all humanity is more deeply rooted than anywhere else. The common denominator of America's ultimate contribution to the development of music should read "the good and the new."

ARNOLD SCHOENBERG

Lecture (1934)

Ladies and Gentlemen:

There are among you certainly many who know about my person only the fact of my so-called expatriation and probably some who know this fact for not much longer than a few minutes.

They fear—I can understand it—to hear now some of those nightmare-tales which cause an agreeable kind of shuddering and give the speaker the feeling of having deeply affected his hearers, and, in that regard, are very satisfactory. But unfortunately they are not in the slightest degree as satisfactory if you regard their influence on the state of German Jewry or on World Jewry.

I must disappoint this part of my hearers, for from the very beginning it was my opinion that the state of Jewry cannot be bettered by such nightmare-tales or by fighting against Germany. But I want to abstain from politics and, preferring other subjects, I must disappoint also another group of my hearers. Namely, those who know a little more about me: who have learned from all the musical misdeeds attributed to my person—that I am the so-called "father of modern music," that I have broken the eternal rules of musical art and aesthetics, that I have spoiled not only my own music, but also that of the classics and of the past, present and future times, that I am a sort of musical gangster who has forced men who know how to distinguish between Beethoven and Gershwin to protect themselves only by being conservatives, opposed to the terror of atonality—this terrible atonality!

I must disappoint them.

It is not at all my intention to speak about terrors—neither about the one which made me suffer myself, nor about the one by which, as I have stated, I made others suffer. I did not come into this marvellous country to speak about terrors—but to forget them.

Let us leave them!

As the snake was expatriated, as it was driven out of paradise, as it was sentenced to go on its belly and to eat dust all the days of its life—this was another kind of expatriation. For the snake came out of paradise and, going on its belly, symbolized, I fear, a certain lack of freedom. And, I fear further, the dust it had to eat, this poor food, was rationed out as in war-time so that the animal could not get enough to appease its hunger and was forced to eat ersatz-dust, surrogate-dust.

I, on the contrary, came from one country into

Arnold Schoenberg, "Two Speeches on the Jewish Situation," in *Style and Idea: Selected Writings of Arnold Schoenberg*, ed. Leonard Stein (New York: St. Martin's Press, 1975), 501–2. This speech was given in Hollywood on October 9, 1934.

another, where neither dust nor better food is rationed and where I am allowed to go on my feet, where my head can be erect, where kindness and cheerfulness is dominating, and where to live is a joy and to be an expatriate of another country is the grace of God. I was driven into paradise!

ROBERT CRAFT

Igor Stravinsky and *The Star-Spangled Banner* (1960)

R.C. What prompted you to arrange *The Star-Spangled Banner*?

I.S. I undertook the arrangement at the suggestion of a pupil—a composer, rather, who visited me twice a week to have his works recomposed —and partly because I was obliged to begin my concerts during the war with *The Star-Spangled Banner*, the existing arrangements of which seemed to me very poor. My version was composed in Los Angeles on 4th July, 1941, and performed shortly after that by an orchestra and Negro chorus conducted by my pupil's son-in-law. After this performance I sent the manuscript to Mrs. F. D. Roosevelt for a war-fund auction, but my major seventh chord in the second strain of the piece, the part patriotic ladies like best, must have embarrassed some high official, for my score was returned with an apology. I then gave it to Klaus Mann, who soon succeeded in selling it for a similar purpose. I performed it myself for the first time with the Boston Symphony Orchestra in the winter of 1944. I stood with my back to the orchestra and conducted the audience, who were supposed to sing but didn't. Though no one seemed to notice that my arrangement differed from the standard offering, the next day, just before the second concert, a police commissioner appeared in my dressing room and informed me of a Massachusetts law forbidding any "tampering" with national property. He said that policemen had already been instructed to remove my arrangement from the music stands. I argued that if an *Urtext* of *The Star-Spangled Banner* existed, it was certainly infrequently played in Massachusetts—but to no avail. I do not know if my version has been performed since. It ought to be, for it makes the linear and harmonic best of the material, and is certainly superior to any other version I have heard. (The compliment to myself in this comparison is very small indeed.)

Igor Stravinsky and Robert Craft, *Memories and Commentaries* (Garden City, N.Y.: Doubleday, 1960), 93–94.

84   Virgil Thomson: The Lure of France

Virgil Thomson (1896–1989) made his way to Harvard in 1918 after a local education in his hometown of Kansas City, Missouri, and service in the military. At Harvard, his principal teachers were the dedicated educator, organist, and choral conductor Archibald T. Davison (1883–1961) and the influential composer Edward Burlingame Hill (1872–1960).

Thomson participated in the pathbreaking European tour by the Harvard Glee Club in the summer of 1921 and remained in Paris for the 1921–22 season with the aid of a Harvard fellowship. As he tells us in his autobiography, he fell in love with the city. He studied with renowned teacher Nadia Boulanger (1887–1960), whose studio was beginning to attract a whole generation of American composers. Melville Smith, Aaron Copland, and Virgil Thomson were her first three American students. Thomson found her "an astounding combination of learning and spirit. . . . Her influence on me consisted of some excellent training in counterpoint, harmony, and organ-playing and in having put me at ease with regard to the act of composition." The French composers he admired particularly were Claude Debussy and Erik Satie. Thomson remarked of Satie, "I knew his music as the test, almost, of any composer's really inside twentieth centuryness."

In Paris in the autumn of 1926, Thomson met expatriate Gertrude Stein (1874–1946) and laid plans with her for a new opera that was to become his most famous work, *Four Saints in Three Acts*. It received a reading at Harvard in 1929 and was premiered at the Atheneum in Hartford, Connecticut, in 1934. *Four Saints* represents a new simplicity in American music, yet simplicity with a contemporary twist, since Thomson utilizes traditional triadic harmony in innovative ways.

Thomson moved to New York in 1940, becoming music critic for the *New York Herald Tribune*, a post he carried on with distinction (and no little bias) to 1954. He continued to compose music of all types, to guest conduct, and to work for the welfare of American music and his fellow composers.

Thomson represented the cultivated East-Coast musician, equally at home in letters as in composition. His refined taste, honed in Europe, reinforced rather than depleted his commitment to American musical values.

VIRGIL THOMSON
Letter to Victor Yellin (1949)

March 23, 1949

Dear Mr. Yellin:[1]

My early musical education was made in Kansas City, where I had piano lessons from the age of five and organ lessons at twelve. My best piano teacher I encountered when I was fifteen. Her name was Geneve Lichtenwalter, and she is still alive though partly blind. My organ teacher was Clarence D. Sears, also still alive, at that time organist at Grace Church (Episcopal), now the Cathedral of Grace and Holy Trinity. I was his assistant at twelve. I played the organ professionally in churches from that time till I was twenty-eight. I largely put myself through college by that means. Before the days of radio, children were not influenced by symphony orchestras; during my teens there was one in Kansas City, however. Brought up in a Southern Baptist family, and being a church organist myself quite early, I naturally became acquainted with American church music and hymn lore in all forms. If you look carefully, you will find as much of Gregorian and Anglican chant in my operas as of Protestant gospel hymns. Another valuable experience of my youth was playing accompaniments for singers, both in the studio and in public concerts. I was thoroughly trained in this technique and earned money by it from the time I was twelve till I went off to war at twenty. I learned about amateur choral singing from Dr. Davison at Harvard, but knew already almost all there was to know about the professional voice, which is after all what one deals with in the opera. I had also read all the opera scores used in current repertory and had heard most of them on the stage. All this means that I went to college as an experienced professional (though not necessarily first-class) accompanist, concert pianist, organist, and conductor. In Boston I had more piano and organ lessons and learned a great deal more about conducting, particularly choral. It was in Paris that my music started going American. Trained at Harvard and by Nadia Boulanger in the impressionist and neo-classic styles current around 1920, it was not till 1926 that I began fishing up out of my subconscious mind musical memories of the old South and the Middle West. This was the result of a working method I had little by little invented for myself, which was to write down the music I heard in my mind, instead of writing music by formula and then trying to hear it, which is the procedure one usually learns from one's teachers. I do not wish to deny the value of that education. I am merely telling you, since you ask, how it happens that I have not employed it systematically in my more mature years.

Most sincerely yours,
[Virgil Thomson]

Virgil Thomson, *Selected Letters*, ed. Tim Page and Vanessa Weeks Page (New York: Summit Books, 1988), 233–34.

[1]American musicologist and composer Victor Yellin.

VIRGIL THOMSON

from *Virgil Thomson* (1966)

In 1921, Europe itself had been my objective. That was where the good teachers lived and all the best composers—Stravinsky, Ravel, Schoenberg, Strauss, Satie, and masses of ingenious other ones, especially among the French, from the aged Fauré, Saint-Saëns, and d'Indy through the middle-aged Florent Schmitt and Paul Dukas down to Darius Milhaud, not thirty, and Francis Poulenc, just eighteen. Already twenty-four myself, I had then been needing to finish learning before I could get on with music writing. In 1925, four years later, only the musical pouring out was urgent; everything else I did got in its way. Organ playing, teaching, and conducting I had practiced successfully; but I did not want to go on doing any of them. They filled up my waking mind with others' music. When I remarked this to E. B. Hill, he declined to press me, like my father on the subject of going to war, pointing out that if I cared about such things I could easily have a professor's career at Harvard, with no doubt a composing and performing life as well, but that if I needed just then to compose only, I had every right to follow my impulse. It had never been my habit to relinquish a thing while learning to do it, but rather to give up only that which I had proved I could do. (A mastered branch could be picked up again.) In quitting at that time teaching and performance, I set for all time my precedent, incorrigibly to be followed in later life, of walking out on success every time it occurred.

My return to Europe in 1925 was therefore both a coming to and a going from. I was coming to the place where music bloomed. I was leaving a career that was beginning to enclose me. I was leaving also an America that was beginning to enclose us all, at least those among us who needed to ripen unpushed. America was impatient with us, trying always to take us in hand and make us a success, or else squeezing us dry for exhibiting in an institution. America loved art but suspected distinction, stripped it off you every day for your own good. In Paris even the police were kind to artists. As Gertrude Stein was to observe, "It was not so much what France gave you as what she did not take away."

* * *

As an American I had to keep contact with Europe. The new music growing up in my country was being pushed by German-trained musicians and German-culture patronage groups into paths I thought quite wrong for it. By keeping away from these Germanic pressures (and Paris was the only major center where one could do that) I could perhaps through my own music remind my country that it was not obliged to serve another country's power setup.

* * *

Now the *Four Saints* accompaniment is as odd as its text, so odd, indeed, that it has sometimes been taken for childish. In fact, many persons not closely involved with either poetry or music but mildly attached to all contemporary artwork by the conviction that it is thrifty to be stylish have for more than thirty years now been worried by my use of what seems to them a backward-looking music idiom in connection with a forward-looking literary one. That worry can only be argued against by denying the assumption that discord is advanced and harmoniousness old-fashioned. Not even the contrary is true, though the production of complete discord through musical sounds (the only kind of discord that is not just noise) has been practiced since before World War I. The truth is that only artists greedy for quick fame choose musical materials for their modishness. In setting Stein texts to music I had in mind the acoustical support of a trajectory, of a verbal volubility that would brook no braking. My skill was to be employed not for pro-

Virgil Thomson, *Virgil Thomson* (New York: Knopf, 1966), 73–74, 106–7, 118.

tecting such composers as had invested in the dissonant manner but for avoiding all those interval frictions and contrapuntal viscosities which are built into the dissonant style and which if indulged unduly might trip up my verbal speeds. Not to have skirted standard modernism would have been to fall into a booby trap. On the contrary, I built up my accompaniments by selecting chords for their tensile strength and by employing in a vast majority of cases only those melodic elements from the liturgical vernacular of Christendom, both Catholic and Protestant, that had for centuries borne the weight of long prayers and praises and of that even longer fastidiously fine-printed and foot-noted contract that we called the Creed.

I set all of Stein's text to music, every word of it, including the stage directions, which were so clearly a part of the poetic continuity that I did not think it proper to excise them. And for distributing all these parts among the singers I assumed a double chorus of participating saints and two Saint Teresas (not alter egos, just identical twins): and I added as nonsaintly commentators, or "end men," a *compère* and a *commère*. Though I had Gertrude's permission to repeat things if I wished, I no more took this freedom than I did that of cutting. She was a specialist of repetition; why should I compete? I simply set everything, exactly in the order of its writing down, from beginning to end.

Act Two was composed and written out by the end of February;[2] and Acts Three and Four (for

Four Saints in Three Acts is merely a title; actually there are thirty or more saints and four acts) were finished by summer and written out in July. Generally I worked mornings, sometimes also in the late afternoon. Always I went out for lunch and usually for dinner, unless I had a guest or two, in which case I had *cordon bleu* food sent in from the Hôtel de l'Université. This was a good quarter of a mile from door to door; but a dainty waitress would trip it twice, bearing her platter up five flights with soup and roast, a second time with dessert. When I had grippe a nearer restaurant would send a waiter up four times a day, twice to take the order and twice to deliver it. Otherwise, once out of the house and down my stairs, I usually stayed out till five or so on errands or walks.

Lunch was likely to be at a bistro on the rue Jacob called La Quatrième République, its title an irony left over from immediate postwar idealism. There one encountered almost always the singer Victor Prahl, usually Janet Flanner and her novelist companion Solita Solano, sometimes the reporter Vincent Sheean. The food, excellent and very cheap, was served downstairs by a portly *patron*, upstairs by a domineering waitress who had no fatigue in her as she ran up the circular staircase, or patience in her busy life for Americans who dallied over menus. *"Yvonne la terrible,"* Janet would call her. When one young man, mixing his salad, put in a whole teaspoonful of mustard, she teased him harshly, "You must be in love."

[2]1928.

85

Aaron Copland
and the American Artist

Aaron Copland (1900–1990), son of immigrant parents, grew up in the unlikely environment (for a composer) of Brooklyn, New York. He studied in France with the renowned teacher Nadia Boulanger and returned to the United States to become, for many, the dean of American composers.

Copland's styles reflect his universality. While he wrote abstract music, he also wrote music in a simpler vein with wide appeal. His search for an "American style" that incorporated folk and popular material resulted in masterworks such as his ballet *Appalachian Spring* (1944) and his Third Symphony (1946).

In his prose writings, Copland spoke for his American colleagues by arguing for a valid place for the arts in American culture. "The creative act," he wrote, ". . . gives value to the individual, and through him to the nation of which he is a part." He maintained that art of value must take its place alongside science and technology in order to "justify" our civilization, and that the government must play its part in helping it do so. These views are expressed in Copland's talk, "Creativity in America," given before the American Academy and National Institute of Arts and Letters in May 1952.

AARON COPLAND

from "The Composer and His Critic" (1932)

[It] is a truism that so long as a country cannot create its own music—and recognize it once it is created—just so long will its musical culture be in a hybrid and unhealthy condition. A true musical culture never has been and never can be solely based upon the importation of foreign artists and foreign music, and the art of music in America will always be essentially a museum art until we are to develop a school of composers who can speak directly to the American public in a musical language which expresses fully the deepest reactions of the American consciousness to the American scene. It is the elementary duty of every critic who recognizes this fact—and they all do—to realize that the time has come when he is expected to take more than a passive part in the encouragement and development of an indigenous American music, when he must be prepared to exert himself in its behalf.

Aaron Copland, "The Composer and His Critic," *Modern Music* May–June 1932: 144–45.

AARON COPLAND

"Creativity in America" (1952)

The creative spirit, as it manifests itself in our America, is assuredly an appropriate subject to bring before this academy and institute, dedicated as they are to the "furtherance of literature and the fine arts in the United States." We here know that the creative act is central to the life process. The creative act goes far back in time, it has functioned and continues to function in every human community and on every level of mankind's development, so that by now it possesses an almost hieratic significance—a significance akin to that of the religious experience. A civilization that produces no creative artists is either wholly provincial or wholly dead. A mature people senses the need to leave traces of its essential character in works of art, otherwise a powerful incentive is lacking in the will to live.

What, precisely, does creativity mean in the life of a man and of a nation? For one thing, the creative act affirms the individual, and gives value to the individual, and through him to the nation of which he is a part. The creative person makes evident his deepest experience—summarizes that experience and sets up a chain of communication with his fellow-man on a level far more profound than anything known to the workaday world. The experience of art cleanses the emotions; through it we touch the wildness of life, and its basic intractability, and through it we come closest to shaping an essentially intractable material into some degree of permanence and of beauty.

The man who lives the creative life in today's world is, in spite of himself, a symbolic figure. Wherever he may be or whatever he may say, he is in his own mind the embodiment of the free man. He must feel free in order to function creatively,

for only in so far as he functions as he pleases will he create significant work. He must have the right to protest or even to revile his own time if he sees fit to do so, as well as the possibility of sounding its praises. Above all he must never give up the right to be wrong, for the creator must forever be instinctive and spontaneous in his impulses, which means that he may learn as much from his miscalculations as from his successful achievements. I am not suggesting that the artist is without restraint of any kind. But the artist's discipline is a mature discipline because it is self-imposed, acting as a stimulus to the creative mind.

Creative persons, when they gather together, seldom speak of these matters as I speak of them now. They take them for granted, for they are quite simply the "facts of life" to the practicing artist. Actually, the creator lives in a more intuitive world than the consciously ordered one that I have pictured here. He is aware not so much of the human and aesthetic implications of the rounded and finished work as he is of the imperfections of the work in progress. Paul Valéry used to say that an artist never finishes a work, he merely abandons it. But of course, when he abandons it, it is in order to begin anew with still another work. Thus the artist lives in a continual state of self-discovery, believing both in the value of his own work and in its perfectability. As a free man he sets an example of persistence and belief that other men would do well to ponder, especially in a world distracted and ridden with self-doubts.

All this is very probably elementary stuff to the members of this distinguished community of creators. But the question in my mind is whether it is correct to assume that it is also "baby stuff" for the generality of our fellow citizens. Does the average American really grasp the concept included in the word "creativity"? Have the artists of America succeeded in impressing themselves—that is to say, in the deepest sense—on the mind of America?

Aaron Copland, "Blashfield Address: Creativity in America Part One," *Proceedings of the American Academy of Arts and Letters and the National Institute of Arts and Letters*, 2nd. ser., No. 3, May 1952, 33–40.

Frankly, I seriously doubt it. Some of my friends tell me that there are no special circumstances that surround the idea of creativity in our country, and that my theme—creativity in America—makes no sense, because creativity is the same everywhere. But my observation and experience convince me of two things: first, that the notion of the creative man plays a less important role here than is true in other countries; and second, that it is especially necessary that we, the artists of America, make clear to our countrymen the value attached in all lands to the idea of the creative personality.

The origins of the American attitude toward creativity are understandable enough. We are the heirs of a colonial people, and because for so long we imported cultural riches from overseas, it became traditional for Americans to think of art as something purchased abroad. Fortunately there are signs that the notion is slowly dissolving, probably forever, along with other nineteenth-century preconceptions about art in America. Europeans, however, seem intent upon perpetuating that myth. When I was abroad in 1951 I was aware of a certain reluctance on the part of the ordinary music-lover to believe that America might be capable of producing first-rate work in the field of music. The inference seemed to be that it was unfair for a country to have industrial and scientific power and, at the same time, the potentiality of developing cultural power also. At every opportunity I pointed out that it is just because commercial and scientific know-how alone are insufficient to justify a civilization that it is doubly necessary for countries like the United States to prove that it is possible, at the same time, to produce, along with men of commerce and of science, creative artists who can carry on the cultural tradition of mankind.

The British music critic Wilfrid Mellers dramatized the crucial role America must play in this regard by writing that "the creation of a vital American music [he might have written American poetry or American painting] . . . is inseparable from the continuance of civilization." One might, I suppose, use a less grandiose phrase and put it this way: to create a work of art in a non-industrial community and in an unsophisticated environment is comparatively unproblematical. Thus the impoverished peon with none of the distractions of modern urban life carves something out of a piece of wood, or weaves a design in cloth. Subsequently someone comes along and says: "Why, this is art; we must put it into a museum." A contrasted though analogous situation obtains in a country like France. There a long tradition of cultural achievement has been established for many centuries; hence it is not surprising that a young generation can carry that tradition forward through the creation of new works of art. Creativity in such an environment does not take *too* much imagination. But in a civilization like our own, with few traditional concepts, and with many conflicting drives, each generation must reaffirm the possibility of the coexistence of industrialism and creative activity. It is as if each creative artist had to reinvent the creative process for himself alone, and then venture forth to find an audience responsive enough to have some inkling of what he was up to in the first instance.

I say this with a certain amount of personal feeling, as a native from across the East River, who grew up in an environment that could hardly have been described as artistic. My discovery of music and the allied arts was the natural unfolding of an inner compulsion. I realize that not all lovers of art can be expected to have the kind of immediacy of contact that is typical of the practicing artist. What seems important to me is not that all our citizens understand art in general, or even the art that we ourselves make, but that they become fully cognizant of the civilizing force that the work of art represents—a civilizing force that is urgently needed in our time. My fear is not that art will be crushed in America, but that it won't be noticed sufficiently to matter.

Whose fault is it that the artist counts for so little in the public mind? Has it always been thus? Is there something wrong, perhaps, with the nature of the art work being created in America? Is our system of education lacking in its attitude toward the art product? Should our state and federal governments take a more positive stand toward the cultural development of their citizens?

I realize that I am raising more questions than can possibly be discussed in so brief an address. No doubt the most controversial of these questions is that of the involvement of government in the arts. Central to this issue is the problem as to whether the arts and artists ought to be nurtured in the first place, or whether it is more healthy to let them fend for themselves. One might deduce cogent arguments for both sides of this question. In America nurturing of the arts has traditionally come from private rather than public funds. The kind of free-lance patronage that served the country fairly well in previous times is now becoming more inadequate each year, for reasons that are obvious to all of us. The growing trend toward government involvement is clear, also. Everything points to the eventual admission of the principle at issue, namely, the principle that our government ought actively to concern itself with the welfare of art and professional artists in the United States. Actually the federal government does expend a certain part of its budget for cultural projects, but unfortunately these must always be camouflaged under the heading of education, or of information, or even of national defense—but never as outright support of the arts. That should be changed.

Please don't misconstrue me. I am not asking for a handout for the artists of America. Even on that level the Works Progress Administration proved that artists who were government employees often did valuable work. My belief is that the future will prove that the government needs artists just as badly as artists require government interest. Here is an instance that comes to mind. Our State Department, in a comparatively recent development, has set up more than a hundred fifty cultural centers throughout the world and deposited therein American books, musical scores, phonograph recordings, and paintings as well as educational and scientific materials. (It is a stimulating sight, by the way, to observe one of these cultural centers in action, as I have, in Rome or Tel-Aviv or Rio de Janeiro; to watch a crowded room of young people making contact with intellectual America through its books and music and paintings.) The government purchases the materials necessary for these centers and distributes them abroad. It is only one step further, is it not, to hope to convince the government that since the end product is needed, and worth purchasing, something should be done to stimulate the creation of the product itself, instead of leaving this entirely to the fortuitous chance that some artist will supply what is needed.

I have no doubt that some of you are thinking: "What of the obvious dangers of bureaucratic control of the arts? Is it worth the risk?" Personally, I think it is. The experience of European and Latin American countries in this regard is surely worth something. Subsidies for the arts in those countries are often of an astonishing generosity. These have persisted through periods of economic stress, through wars and violent changes of regime. On more than one occasion I have heard complaints about the dictatorial behavior of a ministry of fine arts, or objections to the academic dud produced by a state-sponsored opera house. But I have never heard anyone in foreign lands hold that the system of state subsidy for the arts should be abandoned because of the dangers it entails. Quite the contrary. They look on us as odd fish for permitting a *laissez-aller*[1] policy in relation to American art. Surely, in a democracy, where each elected government official is a "calculated risk," we ought to be willing to hope for at least as happy a solution as is achieved abroad. Bureaucratic control of the artist in a totalitarian regime is a frightening thing; but in a democracy it should be possible to envisage a liberal encouragement of the arts through allocation of government funds without any permanently dire results.

All this is not unrelated to my main contention that the artist and his work do not count sufficiently in twentieth-century America. People often tend to reflect attitudes of constituted authority. Our people will show more concern for their artists as soon as the government shows more concern for the welfare of art in America. This has been admirably demonstrated in our educational

[1] Let alone.

system in regard to the musical training of our youth. In one generation, with a change of attitude on the part of the teachers, the entire picture of music in the schools has altered, so that today we have symphony orchestras and choral ensembles of youngsters that would astonish our European colleagues, if only they knew about them. I cannot honestly report, however, that the young people who sing and play so well have been led to take any but the most conventional attitude to the musical creators whose works they perform. There is a vital link missing here, a link that should enable us to transform a purely perfunctory respect into a living understanding of the idea that surrounds creativity. Somehow, sooner or later, it is that gap in understanding that must be bridged, not only as regards music, but in all the arts. Somehow the reality of the creative man as a person made meaningful for the entire community must be fostered. Creativity in our country depends, in part, on the understanding of all our people. When it is understood as the activity of free and independent men, intent upon the reflection and summation of our own time in beautiful works, art in America will have entered on its most important phase.

86

Roy Harris and the
American Composer

During the 1930s, America lay in the depths of the Great Depression. The onslaught of World War II coupled with Franklin Roosevelt's New Deal policies awakened the nation once again to prosperity. The 1940s saw a new wave of patriotism, inspiring American composers to incorporate into their works features that might identify them as American. This was the period of Aaron Copland's "American" works, of Virgil Thomson's *The Plow That Broke the Plains*, and Roy Harris's Third Symphony.

Roy Harris (1898–1979) was born in a log cabin in Oklahoma on Lincoln's birthday. He did not begin composing until he was twenty-four. Success followed quickly, however, and soon, with the encouragement of Aaron Copland, Harris found himself studying in Paris with Nadia Boulanger. Back in America, he answered the call from Serge Koussevitzky, conductor of the Boston Symphony Orchestra, to write a "great symphony from the West," which turned out to be Harris's First Symphony (1933). His Third and Fifth Symphonies were also championed by Koussevitzky.

Harris taught at the Juilliard School from 1932 to 1940 and at half a dozen other institutions. He served as music director for the Office of War Information, organized music festivals, and became an advocate for American music both here and abroad.

ROY HARRIS

from "Problems of American Composers" (1933)

America is vast and elemental; America is desperately struggling to wrest social balance from her omnivorous industrialism. America is rolling plains, wind-swept prairies, gaunt deserts, rugged mountains, forests of giant redwoods and pines, lonely rockbound shores, seas of wheat and corn stretching on to the elastic horizon, cotton and tobacco fields, fruit orchards, little bare mining towns huddled on the sides of mountains, lumber camps, oil fields, and New England mill towns. America is smoking, jostling, clamorous cities of steel and glass and electricity dominating human destinies.

America is a nightmare of feverish struggling, a graveyard of suppressed human impulses; America waits calmly between the Pacific and the Atlantic while the tide of the Mississippi rises and falls with the seasons. Our land waits for us clothed in the elements and the vegetation which rises to meet them; our people, our society, are as spiritually naked as the pastoral Indian society which we conquered.

Wonderful, young, sinewy, timorous, browbeaten, eager, gullible American society, living in a land of grandeur, dignity, and untold beauty, is slowly kneading consistent racial character from the sifted flour of experience and the sweat of

Roy Harris, "Problems of American Composers," *American Composers on American Music: A Symposium*, ed. Henry Cowell (Stanford, Calif.: Stanford University Press, 1933), 149–54, 166.

racial destiny. Slowly, surely, there are emerging American types, with characteristic statures, facial expressions, and temperament.

Those of you who have been in Europe know that the characteristic American cannot avoid identification. It makes little difference whether he came from the Western plains or from an Atlantic seaboard city; on the Parisian boulevards or among the Swiss Alps, in the English theaters or in Florentine galleries, he is immediately recognizable as an American. He has no poise, he is searching for something, he is concerned about his destiny and the appraisal of his people and his country, he is willing and eager to discuss homely social philosophy with you, he is naïvely receptive and easily browbeaten and yet he radiates a fresh vitality, an unlimited reserve of energy; one feels within him a reticent ego which dares not emerge yet. Our climate plus our social, political, and economic customs have produced this characteristic American by the same biological process that characteristic Frenchmen, Germans, and Englishmen were molded from the same Aryan race-stream.

Our subjective moods are naturally being developed to meet the exigencies of our intensely concentrated mechanistic civilization. Our dignity is not pompous, nor are our profoundest feelings suppliant; our gayety is not graceful nor our humor whimsical. Our dignity lies in direct driving force; our deeper feelings are stark and reticent; our gayety is ribald and our humor ironic. These are moods which young indigenous American composers are born and surrounded with, and from these moods come a unique valuation of beauty and a different feeling for rhythm, melody, and form. It is precisely this spontaneous native feeling for distinctly different musical values which makes the problem of the serious American composer so especially difficult. His moods are not warmed-over moods of eighteenth- and nineteenth-century European society, nor is his musical material rearranged and retinted formulas of the standard classics which our audiences, teachers, and critics and our imported conductors and performers have been trained to think of as the only possible music.

To be more specific: Our rhythmic impulses are fundamentally different from the rhythmic impulses of Europeans; and from this unique rhythmic sense are generated different melodic and form values. Our sense of rhythm is less symmetrical than the European rhythmic sense. European musicians are trained to think of rhythm in its largest common denominator, while we are born with a feeling for its smallest units. That is why the jazz boys, chained to an unimaginative commercial routine which serves only crystallized symmetrical dance rhythms, are continually breaking out into superimposed rhythmic variations which were not written in the music. This asymmetrical balancing of rhythmic phrases is in our blood; it is not in the European blood. Anyone who has heard the contrast between a European dance orchestra and an American dance orchestra playing in the same dance hall cannot have failed to notice how monotonous the European orchestra sounds. The Hungarian and Spanish gypsies have a vital rhythmic sense, but it is much more conventional in its metric accents than the native American feeling for rhythm. When Ravel attempted to incorporate our rhythmic sense into his violin sonata, it sounded studied; it was studied, because he did not feel the rhythm in terms of musical phraseology. We do not employ unconventional rhythms as a sophistical gesture; we cannot avoid them. To cut them out of our music would be to gainsay the source of our spontaneous musical impulses. The rhythms come to us first as musical phraseology, and then we struggle to define them on paper. Our struggle is not to invent new rhythms and melodies and forms; our problem is to put down into translatable symbols and rhythms and consequent melodies and form those that assert themselves within us.

For instance: given a 4/4 meter, the European will generally think

♩ ♩ ♩ ♩ (in quarters),

or in eighths

1 2 3 4 + 5 6 7 8

or in sixteenths

1 2 3 4 + 5 6 7 8 + 9 10 11 12 + 13 14 15 16

but the American is very apt to feel spontaneously

1 + 2 3 4 (in quarters)

or in eighths

1 2 3 + 4 5 + 6 7 8

or in sixteenths

1 2 3 + 4 5 6 + 7 8 9 10 + 11 12 13 + 14 15 16

And moreover I repeat that the American does not think these rhythms out first as mathematical problems; they come as spontaneous musical ideas. Time and again I have heard my American associates play rhythmic-melodic phrases which sounded natural and spontaneous but which were very difficult to define on paper. In lecturing to groups I have repeatedly played rhythmic melodies before writing the melody. Invariably some musician in the audience will venture the comment that "it does not look as it sounds." Out of this unique rhythmic sense is developing a different feeling and taste for phrase balancing.

There is nothing strange about this American rhythmic talent. Children skip and walk that way—our conversation would be strained and monotonous without such rhythmic nuances, much like a child's first attempts at reading; nature abounds in these freer rhythms. The strange phenomenon is the power of repetition in accustoming our ears to the labored symmetrical rhythms which predominate in eighteenth- and nineteenth-century European music. Serious European composers have recognized for a long time that all the possible gamut of expression has been wrung

out of conventional rhythms and the consequent melodies and form, but they were born with conventional rhythmic impulses, and when they write complicated rhythms they sound as they look on paper, i.e., unnatural. Stravinsky's "Les Noces," for example, sounds like an embroglio of rhythmic patterns. To quote Arthur Lourie, an authority on Stravinsky and his friend and champion: ". . . Stravinsky's 'Les Noces' is so constructed as to prevent the hearing of the music itself. Here rhythm is driven to the maximum of its development and action; melody is totally submerged." Melody can be totally submerged by rhythmic action only when the rhythms are not an organic part of the melodic content and resulting form. His "Sacre du Printemps" changes its meter-signature so many times that it is extremely difficult to perform, but underneath it all is a steady reiteration of ultra-conventional rhythmic pulse. In fact the tympani player for the Los Angeles Philharmonic Orchestra told me that he rewrote his whole part into conventional meter-signatures. He could not have done that with an authentic American work in which the changing meter-signatures were necessary to the spontaneous musical phraseology.

American composers have not as yet developed any predominant type of harmonic idiom, but I have noticed two tendencies that are becoming increasingly prevalent both with our commercial jazz writers and with our more serious composers: (1) the avoidance of definite cadence which can be traced to our unsymmetrically balanced melodies (difficult to harmonize with prepared cadences) and our national aversion to anything final, our hope and search for more satisfying conclusions; (2) the use of modal harmony which probably comes from ennui of the worn-out conventions of the major and minor scales and our adventurous love of the exotic.

I am as confident that a national taste and talent for harmonic balance and nuance is developing as I am sure that we have already developed a national talent for unique rhythmic impulses and the spontaneous melodies and form which come from them. The American composer's problem is not one of inherent talent and authentic musical ideas;

it is rather the problem of being assured adequate performances, receptive audiences, intelligent appraisals from commercial critics, and an unprejudiced analytic attitude from teachers and music schools. . . .

America is developing a distinctly different civilization from Europe, Asia, or the Orient, and our percentage of musical creativeness is high. There can be no question of stifling the ultimate musical expression of America. The only question which is under consideration is how soon we as a people will become intelligent enough to lend ourselves willingly and gracefully to the processes of time as they unfold our musical destiny.

87 Edgard Varèse and Musical Modernism

During the 1910s and 1920s, audiences in New York City were increasingly being exposed to "serious" modern music. Audiences could savor new works by such European composers as Arnold Schoenberg and Igor Stravinsky. One well-known, avant-garde French composer on the scene, who spent more time in the United States than they, was Edgard Varèse. Born in France, but residing in America from 1915, Varèse (1883–1965) possessed one of the most highly original minds of the twentieth century. As a composer, conductor, and influential teacher, he became absorbed with Ferruccio Busoni's prophetic *Sketch of a New Esthetic of Music*. First published in German in 1907, this work examined redivisions of the octave and anticipated electronic music.

Varèse explored new sounds throughout his life: *Intégrales* (1925), for winds and percussion, develops sound-mass material; *Ionisation* (1931) explores the realms of unpitched sounds. He was one of the first to work with early electronic instruments. He used the ondes martenot in his large orchestral work *Amériques* (1921) and in the printed score of *Ecuatorial* (1934). In *Déserts* (1954), traditional instruments alternate with "organized sound" on magnetic tape. *Poème electronique*, also a spatial piece, is early electronic music devised for the Philips Pavilion of the Brussels Exposition in 1958, with four hundred loudspeakers placed within a structure designed by the architect Le Corbusier. Varèse, however, denied writing experimental music. "My experimenting," he commented in *A Looking-Glass Diary*, "is done before I write the music. Afterward it is the listener who must experiment."

Varèse, the visionary, repudiated what he regarded as the backward-looking stance of neoclassicism. Likewise he decried twelve-tone music which he described as "a sort of hardening of the arteries." As a performer, he championed new music through the International Composers' Guild, which he began with Carlos Salzedo in 1921. Its programs during the next six years presented works by leading composers of the avant garde, as well as premieres of Varèse's own compositions. After its discontinuance, he founded the visionary Pan-American Association of Composers, which was dedicated to performances of new American music.

Varèse spoke of music as an "art-science," and his affinity for science is borne out in the very titles he chose for some of his works. He presaged new machines that might allow him to write music as he conceived it—technology that was hardly possible until the advent of the electronic age after World War I. "I decided to call my music 'organized sound,'" he tells us, "and myself not a musician, but a worker in rhythms, frequencies and intensities." Continually he fought for what he called the "liberation of sound."

EDGARD VARÈSE

"Statements by Edgard Varèse" (PUB. 1976)

VARÈSE ON ELECTRICAL INSTRUMENTS, FROM A LECTURE IN THE 1930S: Liberation from the arbitrary, paralyzing tempered system; the possibility of obtaining any number of sub-divisions of the octave, consequently the formation of any desired scale, unsuspected range in low and high registers, new harmonic splendors obtainable from the now impossible use of subharmonic combinations, the possibility of obtaining any differentiation of timbre, sound combinations, dynamics far beyond the present human-power orchestra; a sense of projection into space by means of emission of sound in many parts of the hall, cross rhythms unrelated to each other treated simultaneously since the machine would be able to beat any number of desired notes, subdivisions of them, omission of a fraction of them, all in a given unit of measure or time which is not humanly possible.

* * *

ON FUTURISM AND DADAISM, IN A LETTER TO PROFESSOR THOMAS GREER: I have been called, erroneously, both a Futurist and a Dadaist composer.

I have always avoided groups and isms . . .

The futurists believed in reproducing sounds and noises literally; I believe in the metamorphosis of sounds into music. As for the Dada movement: though I have had good and very clever Dadaist friends, Tzara, Duchamp, Picabia, I was not interested in tearing down but in finding new means by which I could compose with sounds outside the tempered system, which existing instruments could not play. Unlike the Dadaists I am not an iconoclast.

* * *

ON NEO-CLASSICISM: Neo-classicism is a comfortable trend; one need only lie down in beds that have been made up for centuries. The timorous and the wily take advantage of it, since it gives them not only comfort but security, never thinking that it is only a kind of musical Maginot Line. With neo-classicism, tradition is lowered to the level of bad habits.

* * *

ON INTÉGRALES: I conceived *Intégrales* for spatial projection—that is, for certain acoustical media not yet available but which I knew could be built and would be available sooner or later.

While in our musical system we deal with quantities whose values are fixed, in the realization that I conceived the values would be continually changing in relation to a constant. In other words, this would be like a series of variations, the changes resulting from slight alterations of the form of a function or by the transposition of one function into another. A visual illustration may make clear what I mean: Imagine the projection of a geometrical figure on a plane with both figure and plane moving in space, each with its own arbitrary and varying speeds of translation and rotation. The immediate form of the projection is determined by the relative orientation between the figure and the plane to have motions of their own. A highly complex and seemingly unpredictable image will result. Further variations are possible by having the form of the geometrical figure change as well as the speeds.

* * *

In art an excess of reason is mortal.
It is imagination that gives form to dreams.

The joy of the artist is in the pursuit.

Truth and beauty must always come as a surprise just beyond our expectation.

Louise Varèse, ed. "Statements by Edgard Varèse," *Soundings* (Summer 1976): [6–9].

EDGARD VARÈSE

"Freedom for Music" (1939)

The raw material of music is sound. That is what the "reverent approach" has made most people forget—even composers. Today when science is equipped to help the composer realize what was never before possible—all that Beethoven dreamed, all that Berlioz gropingly imagined possible the composer continues to be obsessed by traditions which are nothing but the limitations of his predecessors. Composers like anyone else today are delighted to use the many gadgets continually put on the market for our daily comfort. But when they hear sounds that no violins, wind instruments, or percussions of the orchestra can produce, it does not occur to them to demand those sounds of science. Yet science is even now equipped to give them everything they may require.

Personally, for my conceptions, I need an entirely new medium of expression: a sound-producing machine (not a sound-reproducing one). Today it is possible to build such a machine with only a certain amount of additional research.

If you are curious to know what such a machine could do that the orchestra with its man-powered instruments cannot do, I shall try briefly to tell you: whatever I write, whatever my message, it will reach the listener unadulterated by "interpretation." It will work something like this: after a composer has set down his score on paper by means of a new graphic, similar in principle to a seismographic or oscilographic notation, he will then, with the collaboration of a sound engineer, transfer the score directly to this electric machine. After that anyone will be able to press a button to release the music exactly as the composer wrote it—exactly like opening a book.

And here are the advantages I anticipate from such a machine: liberation from the arbitrary, paralyzing, tempered system; the possibility of obtaining any number of cycles or if still desired, subdivisions of the octave, and consequently the formation of any desired scale; unsuspected range in low and high registers; new harmonic splendors obtainable from the use of subharmonic combinations, now impossible; the possibility of obtaining any differentiation of timbre, of sound-combinations, new dynamics far beyond the present human-powered orchestra; a sense of sound projection in space by means of the emission of sound in any part or in many parts of the hall as may be required by the score; cross rhythms unrelated to each other, treated simultaneously, or to use the old word, "counterpuntally," since the machine would be able to beat any number of desired notes, any subdivision of them, omission or fraction of them—all these in a given unit of measure or time which is humanly impossible to attain.

Edgard Varèse, "Freedom for Music," quoted in Gilbert Chase, *The American Composer Speaks* (Baton Rouge: Louisiana State University Press, 1966), 191–92. The essay originated as a talk at the University of Southern California, Los Angeles.

Evenings on the Roof

Evenings on the Roof, later "Monday Evening Concerts," was a chamber music concert series that brought Los Angeles to musical maturity and challenged musical establishments elsewhere with its adventurous programming and high standards of performance. Peter Yates and his wife, the pianist Frances Mullen, founded the concerts in 1939 to give distinguished Los Angeles performers, isolated by geography and frustrated by the limitations of playing for film studios and women's clubs, opportunities to explore their art to their own satisfaction. At the time the Yateses conceived this idea, Los Angeles audiences had little exposure to chamber music, although the cream of Europe's performing and creative musicians were settling in Los Angeles, having fled from Nazi persecution. The times demanded cultural growth. Peter Yates, a stubbornly courageous Canadian of Dutch and Scottish extraction, had developed a philosophy that "the idea of community begins with the individual" largely from discovering Charles Ives's *Essays before a Sonata* and, through Ives, reading Ralph Waldo Emerson. Furthermore, he felt strongly that "art is a part of the morality of any civilization," and that "to grow in culture a city must stimulate and encourage its own creative life, not import it."

Peter set out to establish a close community of musicians and to educate an audience. His own musical education came largely from Depression-era radio broadcasts of live concerts. With Frances, who had extraordinary sight-reading ability, he explored works of the moderns and rarely heard works by masters of the Classical and Romantic eras. He found musicians knowledgeable in Renaissance and early Baroque music and believed that "what is too easily received wears out easily." That their series would be "tough" for listeners was evident from the first concert, which offered an all-Bartók program to a small audience, many of whose members may never have heard of the composer. Initially, the programs were performed on Sunday and again on Tuesday so that the audience could hear the same works a second time. When the audience grew in sophistication, Monday evenings were adopted as more successful, and repeat performances were dropped.

Yates fostered new ensembles—string quartets, a piano trio, a wind quintet, a string trio, a piano quartet—and helped them endure. He became particularly enamored of early music and encouraged the formation of the New Friends of Old Music. By 1945, the concerts had become known nationwide, both for their high quality and for their programming of new and old music rarely heard elsewhere. Los Angeles's astonishing émigré community took part (including composers Arnold Schoenberg, Igor Stravinsky, Ernst Toch, Ernst Krenek, Ingolf Dahl, Eric Zeisl, Erich Wolfgang Korngold, and Mario Castelnuovo-Tedesco). Violinist Joseph Szigeti gave a benefit concert for the series in 1950, in which he played three of J. S. Bach's unaccompanied sonatas for violin. American composers flocked to the concerts to learn and to have their works performed. The finest performers from the Philharmonic and the film studios freed themselves from orchestral assignments to play chamber music for a pittance. Peter

Yates crowed to a friend in 1946 that "Los Angeles no longer eats anybody's dust. You can credit the best part of that to the Roof."*

The *Fourth Report,* which summarized the first eight seasons (in seven years), appeared in the periodical *Arts and Architecture.* The Yateses sent 4,200 copies to major musical organizations, periodicals, and critics in the United States and Europe.

—DOROTHY LAMB CRAWFORD

*Peter Yates, letter to Peyton Huston, March 27, 1946 (original at the University of California, San Diego). Other quotes, above, from an unpublished essay and from articles in *Arts and Architecture,* April 1941 and October 1944, and *Musical Digest,* May 1948.

PETER YATES

from *Evenings on the Roof: Fourth Report* (1946)

Evenings on the Roof is a unique musical organization, created to help a number of Los Angeles musicians prepare and play good music under better conditions and at less expense than would be possible in separate recitals; to relieve them of any feeling that music should condescend to or try to entertain a merely well-wishing majority of ticket-buyers; and to provide a collaborative means by which individual performers may be guarded against the fruitless spending of the impresario while standing together to meet the competition of imported big-name virtuosos.

Evenings on the Roof began during the winter of 1938–39, when Frances Mullen, a pianist, and her husband Peter Yates bought and remodeled a five-room bungalow on the Micheltorena Street hill overlooking Los Angeles. For several years, hampered by the inadequacies of the standard entertainment recital, they had been trying to find or to create an audience for that class of music which is always contemporary, whether written by the sixteenth-century composers Byrd and Gibbons or by the twentieth-century composers Hindemith and Ives. They had become convinced that an audience for such music does not exist in a fireside vacuum but must be created; that listeners who use

the radio or buy recordings are more likely to prefer the relatively small number of commonly played "famous" or "great" or "popular box-office" items than to explore on their own initiative the further reaches of the musical cosmos. But they knew that this great body of stalled inertia must contain isolated within it many persons of more eager and more curious interest who actively resent the limitations of the ordinary standard concert and recital programs. Hoping to bring into focus some portion of this diverse interest they added to their new home a studio large enough to contain a small audience. This plyboard room with its steeply sloping ceiling behind the piano like a sounding-board, its eighteen-foot peak and the long slow run of the stringers over the audience outwards through broad glass panels into the trees overlooking Los Angeles became "the Roof." Here Frances Mullen played for the first time in Los Angeles the *Concord Sonata* by Charles Ives, the Beethoven *Diabelli* Variations and with Leonard Stein and Emil Danenberg the piano works of Schoenberg. . . .

The studio was completed in March; the first concert, an all-Bartók program, was played in April 1939. The works selected, which established the standard of future Evenings on the Roof programming, were the Second Violin Sonata, the Piano Sonata, the *Rumanian Dances,* a group of the piano

Peter Yates, *Evenings on the Roof: Fourth Report* (Los Angeles: published privately, 1946), 1–11.

pieces, *For Children* and a song group. There was an audience of nineteen. The first schedule of six programs, to be played the fourth Sunday evening of each month and repeated Tuesday evening of the same week, included entire programs of music by Busoni and Ives, and a group of Tudor and seventeenth century German and French keyboard pieces. At the bottom of the printed announcement appeared the statement which has determined the character of all Evenings on the Roof activites: "The concerts are for the pleasure of the performers and will be played regardless of audience."

Los Angeles is a widely dispersed city containing an unusually large proportion of musicians, many of whom work in the radio and motion picture studios. . . . Although from the first the money taken in, at fifty cents a head, went to the performers, the amounts could not in themselves be an incentive. . . . The worth of the opportunity would be simply whatever [the artist] could make of it. From the beginning it was determined that these should be tough programs, put together out of the best compositions of all periods, to enlarge the repertoire and increase the playing skill of the performers, while bringing to focus an articulate and worthwhile audience. . . .

The third season[1] on the Roof featured a series of fourteen Beethoven recitals including all the piano works with opus numbers and the fifteen violin [and cello] sonatas. These alternated semimonthly with a series of more varied programs. By this time a nucleus of [thirteen] regular performers and a small dependable audience had been built up. Newspaper critics began mentioning the programs. It became evident that the next season of concerts should be presented in a more public and a more accessible location. . . . With the fourth season[2] Evenings on the Roof became a going public concert enterprise. The name itself . . . was retained and firmly affixed to the enterprise by action of the critics. The [fifth] season . . . was distinguished by the increasing participation of Philharmonic Orchestra members . . . playing such works as the Mozart *Divertimenti* for wind instruments, the Beethoven Septet, and the Schubert Octet. The chief problem at that time was to overcome the constant unpredictable changing of programs caused by motion picture calls and other better-paid coincidental opportunities. The Roof audience had not yet become large or interesting enough to encourage a [film studio] musician to sacrifice a business call for the privilege of playing. . . . [In January 1944] the concerts were moved to a former sound stage rebuilt as a broadcasting concert hall at KFWB, the Warner Bros. studio. Here Evenings on the Roof at last became established as a major concert series. . . . Greater musical variety made the first concert of [this sixth] season an event perhaps unique in musical history. The program was presented simultaneously in two halls . . . the first half of the program being played for the audience in Studio 3, while the second half was being played in Studio 4,[3] members of the audience occasionally following them to hear a repeat performance of a favorite work. The final program of this season included the first Roof appearance of the internationally known harpsichordist Alice Ehlers, assisted by Virginia Majewski on viola d'amore and Rebecca Hathaway on viola da gamba. During intermission the audience flooded the stage to examine the mechanics of the three unusual instruments. The seventh season[4] was dedicated jointly to the composers Arnold Schoenberg and Charles Ives, in honor of their seventieth anniversaries. During the season a special effort was made to present the work of twentieth-century composers. . . . Interest [in Schoenberg's *Pierrot lunaire*] was so great that more than half of the twenty-one songs were repeated after the formal ending of the concert. . . . This season also produced . . . two distinct readings of the Bach *Gold-*

---

[1]1940–41.

[2]1943–44.

[3]Ensembles scuttled between audiences to repeat performances of Schubert and Brahms string quartets, and premieres of works of California composers Charles Wakefield Cadman and Lou Harrison.

[4]1944–45.

berg Variations, played first in the registration for two pianos by Wesley Kuhnle and later by Alice Ehlers in the original version for two-manual harpsichord. . . . The eighth season[5] began with an evening of music by members of the Philharmonic Orchestra. . . . Only one scheduled composition had to be canceled because of studio commitments. The season concluded with two complete programs of music by the late composer Béla Bartók . . . played with unrivaled understanding. . . . Thus the cycle of eight seasons ended as it began with the music of Bartók. . . .

During the years the permanent Roof audience has increased in size without sacrificing its original vitality and cohesion. Many musicians, critics, and visitors have praised the unusual quietness and attention of the Roof audiences, their ability to receive the largest and the most concentrated works in classic and contemporary music with equal enthusiasm and without concession. Bach, Beethoven, Schoenberg, and Bartók programs have received ovations. . . . Except during the later war years a slight majority of the audience has usually been male. At the beginning of the eighth season members of the audience responded to a call for assistance in meeting the enlarging responsibilities of Evenings on the Roof by setting up under direction of the Coordinator, Peter Yates, a group of executive and assistance committees. These committees do not manage the concerts but assist the Coordinator and musicians in all operations [and] have divided the labor of presenting the Roof programs. It is now planned to issue Evenings on the Roof recordings and to offer programs from the Roof repertory for engagement by musical organizations in other communities.

---

[5]1945–46.

American socialist parties date back as far as the 1870s. But the Great Depression encouraged radicalism. The American Communist Party, which had been founded in 1919 and was essentially Russian-controlled, took on new life in the 1930s.

The Workers Music League (W.M.L.) became the major music association connected with the American Communist Party. The introduction to the *Red Song Book* (1932) had this to say: "The W.M.L., as the music section of the Workers Cultural Federation, is the cultural organization of all music forces connected with the American revolutionary working class movement. Its aim is to coordinate, strengthen, and give both ideological and musical guidance to these forces."

The musicologist, composer, conductor, and critic Charles Seeger (1886–1939)—under the pseudonym "Carl Sands"—helped lead the way. In 1932, he formed the New York Composers' Collective, whose purpose was to encourage the creation of proletarian songs. The Collective was affiliated with the Pierre Degeyter Club of New York, the official musical organization of the American Communist Party, named after the composer of the *Internationale*. Seeger's 1934 article in *Modern Music* was especially important because it appeared at the height of socialist activities and because it was published in a non-communist magazine.

CHARLES SEEGER

"On Proletarian Music" (1934)

Art, then, is always and inevitably a social function. It has social significance. It is a social force. It is propaganda: explicit, positive; implied, negative. The better the art, the better propaganda it makes: the better the propaganda, the better art it is. The propaganda element in recent bourgeois music has been ignored. It has ceased to have positive social value. The liberal composer who has sat in his ivory tower and said, "whether or not there is a class struggle, music has nothing to do with it," is broadcasting negative propaganda (tacit approval) for the social system that gives him a tower and allows him to sit in it. On the other hand, the art element in the proletariat's propaganda for a better life has been slighted. Too servile acceptance of a debased bourgeois musical idiom has constituted a negative approval in music of the social system against which it must revolt.

Composers have three possible paths ahead of them: fascism, which means positive propaganda for the older order; isolation, which means negative propaganda for it; and proletarianism, which means propaganda for the new order. Whether composers know it, admit it or not, the fact remains—they most of them belong to the proletariat. Let them withhold themselves from it and they will live lives of equivocation, opportunism and frustration. Let them join it openly and their talent will be strengthened, their technic purified, a content given to it and they will have a wider hearing—not of sophisticated individualists who half disdainfully tolerate them, but of the great masses who welcome them with hungry ears—not an audience of hundreds, but of millions.

Charles Seeger, "On Proletarian Music," *Modern Music*, March–April, 1934: 126–27.

From *Workers Song Book* (1934)

Foreword

The music front of the revolutionary movement in America has been advanced so far by two distinct types of song: first, well known and popular bourgeois tunes to which revolutionary words have been set; second, original tunes by proletarian composers. Both have done good service. But it is being increasingly felt that as regards the former type, some part—perhaps a large part—of what has been accomplished by the words has been offset by the persistence of certain undesirable bourgeois associations inherent in the melody, as, for instance, in the tune of "Solidarity Forever," which is the same as that of the "Battle Hymn of the Republic," and carries with it the jingoism of its traditional use. In respect to the second type, the original compositions, it is observable that resemblance to religious, patriotic and sentimental conventions has been studiously avoided. Free from defeatist melancholy, morbidity, hysteria and triviality, it shows a healthy and militant spirit that has been welcomed by America's workers in their more recent struggles, and promises much for the bitterer conflict of the immediate future.

The working class of America is developing a new, revolutionary music of its own. It cannot be made over night or out of whole cloth. It is at once a demand of the new, proletarian culture and an inevitable outgrowth of the old, bourgeois art-music. We shall have to use, for some time to come, the basic elements of the old idiom. We can, however, and must subject these basic elements to revolutionary scrutiny with a view of finding which of them we cannot help but use, which must be discarded as unsuitable and which must be given a leftward turn that will yield us a recognizably revolutionary music for recognizably revolutionary words. For more than a decade this scrutiny has been given to the needs of the workers in the Soviet Union, in Germany, France, China, Japan and the United States. Hundreds of new mass, choral and solo songs, composed by such well-known musicians as Eisler, Wolpe, Shekhter, Davidenko, Biely, Shostakovitch, Szabo, Schaefer, Adomian and others, have established distinct and characteristic musical trends that are gradually building up the revolutionary musical front. These songs are sung everywhere by huge masses of class-conscious workers. They represent marked departures from the older type of song. But the workers prefer them to the older type. The "catchy" quality is liked, but no less liked is the musical novelty often present which sets off to advantage that desirable quality. Though without special theoretical musical training, the workers instinctively appreciate, too, the sound theoretical grounding of this music. They sense the consistency of tune with verse and feel that at last they are getting hold of a music that is their own.

In this volume, with the exception of the Internationale, is presented the first collection exclusively of original revolutionary mass, choral and solo songs with English texts to be made in America. The composers represented are members of the Composers' Collective of the Pierre Degeyter Club of New York City, an affiliate of the Workers Music League. With four exceptions, the songs were all composed in 1933 as part of the work of the Collective—a group in which conservative and radical musical thought and taste meet in free and vigorous clash upon the question of the definition of a musical style "national in form, proletarian in content." Hardly a work comes through this critical fire without bearing the mark of modifications or alterations, proposed by colleagues and accepted by the composer. All of the works have been tested in rehearsals and most of them, in performance by mass organizations in New York City. The increase in number, size and competence of these workers' singing groups during the last two years has been amazing. Their gargantuan appetite for new music, their delight in attacking technical difficulties that cause their bourgeois contempo-

Workers Song Book No. 1 (New York: Workers Music League; U.S.A. Section of International Music Bureau, 1934), [iv–v], 4–6, 21–22.

raries no end of trouble, make composing for them the highest kind of calling. The composers, one and all in the Collective, take as a basic criterion of their work the following adaptation of the words of Joseph Stalin, viz.: that they must cultivate above all things "a good ear for the voice of the masses, must pay close attention to their revolutionary instinct, must study the actualities of their struggle, must carefully enquire whether their policy is sound—and must, therefore, be ready, not only to teach the masses, but also to learn from them."

Workers! Comrades! To you who sing and to you who hear these songs we dedicate this our first volume. We, and others who will join us in this great enterprise, will do ever better and better work. But we shall not do it without your criticism. We bear in mind and we ask you always to remember this: the composer is the hand that writes; the audience sings and decides what shall be sung. A great audience calls forth great song. You are a great audience—the greatest that has even been. As your call becomes clearer, stronger and more persistent by united mass action, great things will come forth—the greatest that have ever been. Individual men will write them down, but YOU will make them!

The Internationale

Arise, you pris'ners of starvation!
Arise, you wretched of the earth,
For justice thunders condemnation,
A better world's in birth.
No more tradition's chains shall bind us,
Arise you slaves; no more in thrall!
The earth shall rise on new foundations,
We have been naught, we shall be all.

> [*Refrain*]
> 'Tis the final conflict,
> Let each stand in his place,
> The International Soviet
> Shall be the human race!
> 'Tis the final conflict,
> Let each stand in his place,
> The International Soviet
> Shall be the human race!

We want no condescending saviors
To rule us from a judgment hall;
We workers ask not for their favors,
Let us consult for all.
To make the thief disgorge his booty,
To free the spirit from the cell,
We must ourselves decide our duty,
We must decide and do it well.
> *Refrain*

Toilers from shops and fields united,
The union we of all who work
The earth belongs to us, the workers,
No room here for those who shirk.
How many on our flesh have fattened!
But if the noisome birds of prey
Shall vanish from the sky some morning
The blessed sunlight still will stay.
> *Refrain*

Mount the Barricades

We are fighting with a host of foes,
We do not fear the guns or cannon.
Mount the barricades!
Mount the barricades
For the workers' cause,
Carry on the fight for freedom. . . .

Song of the Builders

We are the builders, we build the future,
The future world is in our hands.
We swing our hammers, we use our weapons,
Against our foes in many lands.

We are the builders, we build the future
And he who hinders us must fall.
Come join us comrades, our task is mighty,
We need your help you workers all.

Each day of struggle, each hour of battle,
Each blow we strike breaks yokes and chains
From limbs and shoulders, it frees the workers
In city factries, fields and plains.

And we, the workers, who are the builders,
We fight, we do not fear to die.
"All power and freedom into the workers!"
Is our defiant battle cry.

Cecil Sharp and English
Folk Song in America

The tendency of ethnic groups in the United States to maintain an identity with the old country through music has given a pluralistic cast to the American music scene, reminding us that we are, indeed, all part of the global community. An excellent example of European tradition preserved in the United States comes from the Appalachian Mountains, where songs of English and Scottish traditions continued to live even after their disappearance from the British Isles.

Cecil Sharp (1859–1924) came to America from England to study this repertoire. Sharp made three trips to the United States between 1916 and 1918, spending a total of forty-six weeks in the southern Appalachians of Kentucky, West Virginia, Virginia, Tennessee, and North Carolina. He was urged to visit this area by Massachusetts collector Olive Dame Campbell. Traveling with his assistant, Maud Karpeles, he visited remote communities where country singers welcomed them and readily shared their songs, particularly when they realized that the visitors had come to learn rather than to teach and "talk down" to them. Sharp and Karpeles recorded some 1,612 tunes, representing about 500 different songs performed by 281 different singers.

Karpeles quotes one singer as saying: "Singing is a great power in the world, and you are doing a noble work." She sums up the collection by observing,

> Thus, a song, originating in England and carried to America, lives there by oral tradition for some hundreds of years; it is written down and taken back to England by Cecil Sharp; then some thirty years later the song is carried back in printed form to the country of its adoption and takes on a new lease of life. Such are the devious ways of tradition.*

---

*Prefatory note to Cecil Sharp, *English Folk Songs from the Southern Appalachians*, 2nd ed. [rev.] (London: Oxford University Press, 1952), 1: xx.

CECIL SHARP

from *English Folk Songs from the Southern Appalachians* (1917)

I spent nine weeks only in the mountains, accompanied throughout by Miss Maud Karpeles, who took down, usually in shorthand, the words of the songs we heard, while I noted the tunes. Mr. John C. Campbell, Director of the Southern Highland Division of the Russell Sage Foundation, went with us on our first expedition and afterwards directed our journeyings and, in general, gave us the benefit of his very full knowledge of the country and its people. Our usual procedure was to stay at one or another of the Presbyterian Missionary Settlements and to make it our centre for a week or ten days while we visited the singers who lived within a walking radius. In this way we successively visited White Rock, Allanstand, Alleghany and Carmen, Big Laurel and Hot Springs, in North Carolina, and thus succeeded in exploring the major portion of what is known as the Laurel Country. Afterwards we spent ten days at Rocky Fork, Tenn., and a similar period at Charlottesville, Va. I should add that had it not been for the generous hospitality extended to us by the heads of the Missionary Settlements at which we sojourned, it would have been quite impossible to prosecute our work.

The present inhabitants of the Laurel Country are the direct descendants of the original settlers who were emigrants from England and, I suspect, the lowlands of Scotland. I was able to ascertain with some degree of certainty that the settlement of this particular section began about three or four generations ago, i.e. in the latter part of the eighteenth century or early years of the nineteenth. How many years prior to this the original emigration from England had taken place, I am unable to say; but it is fairly safe, I think, to conclude that the present-day residents of this section of the mountains are the descendants of those who left the shores of Britain some time in the eighteenth century.

The region is from its inaccessibility a very secluded one. There are but few roads—most of them little better than mountain tracks—and practically no railroads. Indeed, so remote and shut off from outside influence were, until quite recently, these sequestered mountain valleys that the inhabitants have for a hundred years or more been completely isolated and cut off from all traffic with the rest of the world. Their speech is English, not American, and, from the number of expressions they use which have long been obsolete elsewhere, and the old-fashioned way in which they pronounce many of their words, it is clear that they are talking the language of a past day, though exactly of what period I am not competent to decide. . . .

We found little or no difficulty in persuading those we visited to sing to us. To prove our interest in the subject and to arouse their memories, we would ourselves sometimes sing folk-songs that I had collected in England, choosing, for preference, those with which they were unacquainted. Very often they misunderstood our requirements and would give us hymns instead of the secular songs and ballads which we wanted; but that was before we had learned to ask for "love-songs," which is their name for these ditties. It was evident, too, that it was often assumed that strangers like ourselves could have but one object and that to "improve," and their relief was obvious when they found that we came not to give but to receive.

It is no exaggeration to say that some of the hours I passed sitting on the porch (i.e. verandah) of a log-cabin, talking and listening to songs were amongst the pleasantest I have ever spent. Very often we would call upon some of our friends early in the morning and remain till dusk, sharing the mid-day meal with the family, and I would go away in the evening with the feeling that I had never before been in a more musical atmosphere,

Cecil Sharp, "Introduction to the First Edition," *English Folk Songs from the Southern Appalachians*, 2nd ed., ed. Maud Karpeles (London: Oxford University Press, 1932), 1: xxi–xxii, xxvi–xxix, xxxiv, xxxvi–xxxvii. First ed. by Olive D. Campbell and Cecil Sharp (N.Y.: G. P. Putnam's Sons, 1917).

nor benefitted more greatly by the exchange of musical confidences.

The singers displayed much interest in watching me take down their music in my note-book, and when at the conclusion of a song I hummed over the tune to test the accuracy of my transcription they were as delighted as though I had successfully performed a conjuring trick.

The mountain singers sing in very much the same way as English folk-singers, in the same straightforward, direct manner, without any conscious effort at expression, and with the even tone and clarity of enunciation with which all folk-song collectors are familiar. Perhaps, however, they are less unselfconscious and sing rather more freely and with somewhat less restraint than the English peasant; I certainly never saw any one of them close the eyes when he sang nor assume that rigid, passive expression to which collectors in England have so often called attention.

They have one vocal peculiarity, however, which I have never noticed amongst English folk-singers, namely, the habit of dwelling arbitrarily upon certain notes of the melody, generally the weaker accents. This practice, which is almost universal, by disguising the rhythm and breaking up the monotonous regularity of the phrases, produces an effect of improvisation and freedom from rule which is very pleasing. The effect is most characteristic in 6/8 tunes, as, for example, No. 19 G, in which in the course of the tune pauses are made on each of the three notes of the subsidiary triplets.[1]

The wonderful charm, fascinating and well-nigh magical, which the folk-singer produces upon those who are fortunate enough to hear him is to be attributed very largely to his method of singing, and this, it should be understood, is quite as traditional as the song itself. The genuine folk-singer is never conscious of his audience—indeed, as often as not, he has none—and he never, therefore, strives after effect, nor endeavours in this or in any other way to attract the attention, much less the admiration of his hearers. So far as I have been able to comprehend his mental attitude, I gather that,

when singing a ballad, for instance, he is merely relating a story in a peculiarly effective way which he has learned from his elders, his conscious attention being wholly concentrated upon what he is singing and not upon the effect which he himself is producing. This is more true, perhaps, of the English than of the American singers, some of whom I found were able mentally to separate the tune from the text—which English singers can rarely do— and even in some cases to discuss the musical points of the former with considerable intelligence.

I came across but one singer who sang to an instrumental accompaniment, the guitar, and that was in Charlottesville, Va. (No. 12 B).[2] Mrs. Campbell, however, tells me that in Kentucky, where I have not yet collected, singers occasionally play an instrument called a dulcimer, a shallow, wooden box, with four sound-holes, in shape somewhat like a flat, elongated violin, over which are strung three (sometimes four) metal strings, the two (or three) lower of which are tonic-drones, the melody being played upon the remaining and uppermost string, which is fretted. As the strings are plucked with the fingers and not struck with a hammer, the instrument would, I suppose, be more correctly called a psaltery.

The only instrumental music I heard were jig tunes played on the fiddle. I took down several of these from the two fiddlers, Mr. Reuben Hensley and Mr. Michael Wallin, who were good enough to play to me. Wherever possible they used the open strings as drones, tuning the strings—which, by the way, were of metal—in a particular way for each air they were about to perform. I have not included any of these in this collection, but I hope, later on, to publish some of them when I have had further opportunities of examining this peculiar and unusual method of performance.

Many of the singers whose songs are recorded in the following pages had very large repertories. Mrs. Reuben Hensley, with the assistance of her husband and her daughter Emma, sang me thirty-five songs; while Mrs. Sands of Allanstand gave me twenty-five; Mr. Jeff Stockton of Flag Pond, Tenn.,

---

[1] No. 19 in the collection is *Lord Thomas and Fair Ellinor*.

[2] No. 12 in the collection is *The Two Brothers*.

seventeen; Mr. N. B. Chisholm of Woodridge, Va., twenty-four; Mrs. Tom Rice of Big Laurel, twenty-six; and Mrs. Jane Gentry of Hot Springs, no less than sixty-four. Attention has often been called to the wonderful and retentive memories of folk-singers in England, and I can vouch for it that these American singers are, in this respect, in no way inferior to their English contemporaries.

None of the singers whom I visited possessed any printed song-sheets, but some of them produced written copies, usually made by children, which they called "ballets," a term which the English singer reserves for the printed broadside. . . . No two singers ever sing the same song in identically the same way. . . .

THE BALLADS. The distinction between the ballad and the song is more or less arbitrary and is not easy to define with precision. Broadly speaking, however, the ballad is a narrative song, romantic in character and, above all, impersonal, that is to say, the singer is merely the narrator of events with which he personally has no connexion and for which he has no responsibility. The song, on the other hand, is a far more emotional and passionate utterance, and is usually the record of a personal experience—very frequently of an amatory nature. The ballads have, probably, the longer history behind them; at any rate, they attracted the attention of collectors earlier than the songs—the reason, perhaps, why the ballads have suffered, far more than the songs, from the unscrupulous editing of literary meddlers.

The ballad air is necessarily of a straightforward type, as it is sung indifferently to verses often varying very widely in emotional character. Nevertheless, many of the ballad tunes are very lovely, as the musician who studies the contents of this volume will readily perceive. . . . The most perfect type of ballad, however, is that in which the tune, whilst serving its purpose as an ideal vehicle for the words, is of comparatively little value when divorced from its text. . . .

THE SONGS. The song-melodies differ in many respects from those of the ballads. Structurally, many of them are built upon larger and more elaborate lines, while emotionally, for rea-

sons already given, they are far more intense and more heavily charged with sentiment. . . .

If the prevalence of the gapped scale[3] in the mountain tunes is any indication of the ethnological origin of the singers, it seems to point to the North of England, or to the Lowlands, rather than the Highlands, of Scotland, as the country from which they originally migrated. . . .

That culture is primarily a matter of inheritance and not of education is, perhaps, a mere truism, but it is one, nevertheless, which educationists often forget. My knowledge of American life may be too slender for an opinion of mine to carry much weight, but I cannot withhold the criticism—advanced with the greatest diffidence—that the educational authorities of some of the larger cities in the United States are too ready to ignore the educational and cultural value of that national heritage which every immigrant brings with him to his new home, and to rest too confidently upon their educational system, which is often almost wholly utilitarian and vocational, to create the ideal American citizen. I admit that the problem which faces the educationist in American is a peculiarly difficult one, but it will, I am convinced, never be satisfactorily solved until the education given to every foreign colonist is directly based upon, and closely related to, his or her national inheritance of culture. . . .

When [a folk-singer] sings his aim is to forget himself and everything that reminds him of his everyday life; and so it is that he has come to create an imaginary world of his own and to people it with characters quite as wonderful, in their way, as the elfish creations of Spenser.

We have in the following pages printed the songs exactly as we took them down from the lips of the singers, without any editing or "adornments" whatsoever, and we have done so because we are convinced that this is the only way in which work of this kind should be presented, at any rate in the first instance. Later on, we may harmonize and publish a certain number of the songs and so make a wider and more popular appeal.

---

[3]Five or six notes to the octave.

91   Alan Lomax: The Map Sings

Alan Lomax (b. 1915) began collecting songs with his father at the age of eighteen. They recorded what they found on a five-hundred pound Edison cylinder machine given to them as a gift by Edison's widow. He spent the rest of his life in what he calls "a deep river of song," collecting music in Great Britain, Haiti, Italy, and Spain, as well as in America. His recordings, radio programs, writing, teaching, and lecturing greatly aided the movement for folk-song preservation and promoted interest and scholarship in the field.

The Folk Songs of North America is a remarkable collection of more than three hundred folk song texts with their melodies, organized by geographical region. Lomax describes a folk song as

> actually a continuum of performances, each one varying in great or slight degree, and thus it grows as it lives, acquiring fresh material or losing bits of the old, and spawning variant forms, which continue to evolve. . . .

> So, slowly, our folk songs grew, part dream and part reality, part past and part present. Each phrase rose from the deeps of the heart or was carved out of the rock of experience. Each line was sung smooth by many singers, who tested it against the American reality, until the language became apt and truthful and as tough as cured hickory. Here lies the secret of their beauty.*

His aim, as he put it, was to give a voice to the voiceless and put neglected cultures and silenced people back into the communication chain.

Lomax was the first to record such influential folk singers as Leadbelly, Woody Guthrie, Muddy Waters, and Fred McDowell. He was a prime mover in the folk revival of the 1930s and 1940s, and an early advocate of World Music. His discoveries influenced musicians like Bob Dylan, the Rolling Stones, Eric Clapton, and Miles Davis.

---

*Alan Lomax, ed., *The Folk Songs of North America, in the English Language* (Garden City, N.Y.: Doubleday, 1960), xxv, xxviii.

ALAN LOMAX

from Introduction to *The Folk Songs of North America* (1960)

A Folk Song Map

The map sings. The chanteys surge along the rocky Atlantic seaboard, across the Great Lakes and round the moon-curve of the Gulf of Mexico. The paddling songs of the French-Canadians ring out along the Saint Lawrence and west past the Rockies. Beside them, from Newfoundland, Nova Scotia, and New England, the ballads, straight and tall as spruce, march towards the West.

Inland from the Sea Islands, slave melodies sweep across the whole South from the Carolinas to Texas. And out on the shadows of the Smoky and Blue Ridge mountains the old ballads, lonesome love songs, and hoedowns echo through the upland South into the hills of Arkansas and Oklahoma. There in the Ozarks the Northern and Southern song families swap tunes and make a marriage.

The Texas cowboys roll the little doughies north to Montana, singing Northern ballads with a Southern accent. New roads and steel rails lace the Southern backwoods to the growl and thunder of Negro chants of labour—the axe songs, the hammer songs, and the railroad songs. These blend with the lonesome hollers of levee-camp muleskinners to create the blues, and the blues, America's *cante hondo* [deeply felt folk song], uncoils its subtle, sensual melancholy in the ear of all the states, then all the world.

The blues roll down the Mississippi to New Orleans, where the Creoles mix the musical gumbo of jazz—once a dirty word, but now a symbol of musical freedom for the West. The Creoles add Spanish pepper and French sauce and blue notes to the rowdy tantara of their reconstruction-happy brass bands, stir up the hot music of New Orleans and warm the weary heart of humanity. . . . These are the broad outlines of America's folk-song map. The saga of American folk song, the story of the complex forces that shaped these traditions, follows presently.

The Melting Pot

The first function of music, especially of folk music, is to produce a feeling of security for the listener by voicing the particular quality of a land and the life of its people. To the traveller, a line from a familiar song may bring back all the familiar emotions of home, for music is a magical summing-up of the patterns of family, of love, of conflict, and of work which give a community its special feel and which shape the personalities of its members. Folk song calls the native back to his roots and prepares him emotionally to dance, worship, work, fight, or make love in ways normal to his place.

Each group of settlers in the New World tried to establish a musical community like the one they had left in Europe. They dotted the map with little Swedens, little Lithuanias, little Italies, and so on, while the music of Spain, Portugal, France, Great Britain, and West Africa spread over domains in the western hemisphere. Everywhere in the New World we find songs that were popular in the days when the colonists set sail from their homelands. Thus American folk song is, in one aspect, a museum of musical antiques from many lands. On the other hand, some European folk traditions, particularly those rooted in village ceremonial, did not long survive in the American melting pot. More will be said of this, but first a word about a tendency for which America is particularly notable—the mixing and blending of various folk-strains to produce new forms.

The isolation of colonial and frontier life sometimes had a benign effect upon the traditional arts, which are normally slow to ripen. Here and there in the wilderness circumstances permitted a cultural pocket to form, where regional or tribal song

Alan Lomax, ed., *The Folk Songs of North America, in the English Language* (Garden City, N.Y.: Doubleday, 1960), xv–xx.

families could slowly combine to produce a sturdy new breed. The music of Haiti, for instance, shows the mingling of several West African tribal strains; the music of the Southern Appalachians is an Anglo-Scots-Irish synthesis, more British than anything to be heard on those for ever disparate isles. Indeed, the pedant may search in vain for a "pure" American folk song. "There just ain't no such animal." Our best songs and dances are hybrids of hybrids, mixtures of mixtures, and this may be the source of their great appeal to a cosmopolitan age and the cause for their extremely rapid development. Folk music, like other arts and sciences, blooms hard by the crossroads.

Singing Democrats

On the American frontier men worked and sang together on terms of amity and equality impossible in the Old World. A man was judged not by his accent or his origins, but by his character and capacities. A song was treasured for its suitability to frontier life. Inherited regional patterns of speech and song broke down beneath this pragmatic, democratic pressure. However, the materials for new folk-song traditions were at hand. The mass of the colonists were poor country folk, carriers of traditional melodies. Many were rebels, fleeing from political persecution and longing to express their feelings openly. Thus a note of social protest rang through native American balladry, and the lives and problems of the common people became its main concern. What in Britain had been a tendency to heroize the sailor lad and the kitchen-maid became the dominant theme of the American ballad maker.

"A man ain't nothin' but a man . . ." sings John Henry for all these free-born workingmen, busy with the job of taming a continent. In the ballads the men bawl out their complaints about bad working conditions, and in the love songs the women keen their discontent with patriarchal conventions of love and marriage.

The common man, the individual, is everything in American folk song. The folk spirituals—in contrast to older types of hymns—sing mainly of personal salvation, while in the worldly ballads

and lyrics, the first person singular steadily replaces the impersonal narrator. What cantankerous individualists were these frontiersmen!

I'll buy my own whiskey, I'll drink my own dram,
And for them that don't like me I don't give a
damn!

Not only personal eccentricity, but musical non-conformity was relished. An historian tells of a Rocky Mountain hunter on his yearly spree in St. Louis, who lay on the bar-room floor and drummed out an accompaniment to his song on his bare belly. The stubby little Kentucky farmer bragged, "When I was a-singin' in my cornfield, my folks could hear me on the front porch a mile and a half down the holler." Southern hymn composers deliberately broke the rules of conventional harmony by writing series of parallel fourth and fifth chords. The New Orleans jazz men brought new sounds out of the trumpet by playing "dirty," that is, with as much of the forbidden vibrato as possible. . . . From the time of the "nigger minstrels" to the pelvic beat of rock and roll, Americans have welcomed every musical innovation of the Negro.

The saying was "It's a big country." If a man failed in one town, he could make a fresh start in a new one. Social and geographical mobility became a main feature of American life, and moving to new pastures or to a new apartment, a fixed national habit. . . .

I think I'll settle down, and I says, says I,
I'll never wander further till the day I die.
But the wind it sorta chuckles—Why of course
you will,
For once you git the habit, you just can't keep
still . . .

These restless Americans scattered certain folk songs from Maine to California, while others were left behind, half-finished, like so many ghost towns, when the work camps moved west or "culture" invaded frontier outposts. We are fortunate that the collectors have rescued these "ghost-songs" from oblivion. Their very rawness lends them the impact of truth, for they speak in the unvarnished language of the pioneer worker. Yet the "moving habit" gave Americans a rootless, lonesome feeling. Where the freedom of the wilderness was the breath of life to such bold spirits as Boone and Crockett, gentler folk were sometimes troubled by the vast landscapes and the awesome solitudes that surrounded their little cabins. The mountaineer speaks of his old songs as "lonesome tunes"; the pioneer sings of himself as a poor, wayfaring stranger—a poor, lonesome cowboy—a poor boy lookin' for a home—travellin' down a "lonesome road."

"Every jug stood on its own bottom" in America. In Europe the established churches had imposed an official code of conduct on a population which often had a pagan tradition. When this churchly authority was finally broken by the American Revolution and every man won the freedom to live according to the dictates of his own conscience, a new situation prevailed. The church was no longer a buffer between man and God. Calvinist morality became a self-imposed creed. Thus the religious freedom won by fighting Protestants in the Revolution left every man naked and alone, to come to terms with an angry and demanding God and with his own alerted, sin-ridden conscience. The American Protestant burdened his heart with the ethical and moral conflicts which had riven church and state in Europe for many centuries. The gains for the human spirit were magnificent, but the cost has been great, as our history and our folk songs show. . . .

White Solo—Black Chorus

Two principal traditions gave rise to our hybrid music—the British and the West African. The folk-song map shows dark and fertile islands of Afro-American songs rising out of a sea of Anglo-American music. Today these islands are slowly subsiding, but they have indelibly coloured the surrounding ocean.

For centuries, most British folk songs have been sung in solo with occasional unison choruses, although in remoter parts of the islands there are clear traces of an older choral style. The pioneer white in America retained scarcely any ability to make music in groups. When he and his fellows sang together in church, there was little blending and no harmony unless a singing teacher was there to instruct them. White pioneers sang long ballads, slow lyric pieces with highly decorated melodies, or lilting dance tunes—largely in solo, often in a high-pitched, sometimes "womanish" nasal tone. A tense throat allowed little variation in vocal colour, but great delicacy in ornamentation. The effect was a mournful wailing sound, like an oriental oboe, suitable to the inner melancholy and conflict of the songs. A singer sat stiffly erect, his body rigid, the muscles of his throat and face tense, gazing into the distance or with his eyes closed—an impersonal, though highly charged story-teller. For him the words and tune were separate entities and the words more important than the tune. Song rhythm conformed, normally, to the demands of the text; in the older pieces it wandered and wavered and gathered pace again as the verse demanded. The fiddle was the most widely used instrument and, as played, it was another high-pitched, reedy, wailing voice, seconding and matching the singer or lilting the dance tunes. Such were the characteristics of white folk music, North, South, and West during the pioneer period. Indeed, the modern crooner still sings in this style—with a trace of Neapolitan and a touch of the tarbrush.

The sounds that came from the dark islands of Negro song were a stimulating contrast. Most of the American Negro slaves came from West Africa, where music-making was largely a group activity, the creation of a many-voiced, dancing throng. Typically, a leader raised the song and was answered by a chorus of blended voices, often singing simple chords, the whole accompanied in polyrhythm by an orchestra of drums, shakers, hand clapping, etc. (Soloists singing highly decorated melodies were more characteristic of Arab-influenced cultures in the north near the Sahara.)

Few African instruments survived in North America, but African musical habits did. The slaves continued to sing in leader-chorus style, with a more relaxed throat than the whites, and in deeper-pitched, mellower voices, which blended richly. The faces of the singers were animated and expressive; the voices playful. They used simple European chords to create harmony of a distinctive colour. If not actually dancing as they sang, they patted their feet, swayed their bodies, and clapped out the subtle rhythms of their songs. A strong, surging beat underlay most of their American creations, and this was accompanied in an increasingly complex style as they improvised or acquired instruments. Words and tunes were intimately and playfully united, and "sense" was often subordinated to the demands of rhythm and melody. Community songs of labour and worship and dance songs far outnumbered narrative pieces, and the emotion of the songs was, on the whole, joyfully erotic, deeply tragic, allusive, playful, or ironic rather than nostalgic, withdrawn, factual, or aggressively comic—as among white folk singers.

For more than two hundred years these two contrasting musical cultures dwelt side by side in America in a state of continually stimulating exchange and competition. Song material passed back and forth across the racial line so that it becomes increasingly difficult to say which group has contributed most to a song. As in the West Indies and parts of South America, true Afro-European songs, and especially dances, developed, which gained continental, then world-wide popularity. Indeed, it seems very likely that one day all American music will be *café-au-lait* in colour. . . .

92   Jelly Roll Morton: The Diamond King

Like Louis Armstrong, Jelly Roll Morton came out of the New Orleans experience. Interviewer Alan Lomax recounts that, "Down in New Orleans they remember 'Jelly Roll used to play piano all day and practice all night. . . . We used to ask him when do he sleep?—he fool at the piano so much."* Christened Ferdinand Joseph La Menthe (Lemott; La Mothe; 1890–1941) sometimes referred to as Ferd, Morton made himself into a remarkable musician. The year 1923 found him in Chicago, where he made his first recordings. An astute arranger and composer, he published his music in Chicago, through the Melrose Brothers Music Company.

In 1926, he organized the Red Hot Peppers (cornet, clarinet, trombone, piano, banjo, bass, and drums). The group included mostly black musicians from New Orleans and had Edward "Kid" Ory on trombone, Omer Simeon on clarinet, and Johnny St. Cyr on banjo and guitar. Morton's careful work with this group produced a remarkable set of recordings—a high point of his career—in which he proved that meticulous rehearsal and attention to a score could enhance rather than detract from the spirit of improvised jazz. When Morton moved to New York in 1928, the Red Hot Peppers soon became a thing of the past. The Depression was on. Morton's New Orleans–based music seemed out of date as the big band swing era took hold.

The voice in the material that follows is basically that of Morton's wife, Mabel, whom he married in 1928 and who appreciated his genius and admired him despite high-living ways. It has been edited and incorporated into a book by folklorist Alan Lomax, who also recorded Morton in a remarkable set of interviews at the Library of Congress.

---

*Alan Lomax, *Mister Jelly Roll: The Fortunes of Jelly Roll Morton* (New York: Duell, Sloan and Pearce, 1950), 67.

MABEL MORTON

On Her Husband, Jelly Roll Morton (1949)

That was in November, 1928, at the sign of Justice McGuire on the highway.[1] Just me and the judge and Jelly Roll. Afterwards we drove to Kansas City and took in the night spots and different things and I saw that everybody knew him there in K.C. We stayed there a month (Bennie Moten was playing there, I remember, at the time) and then drove on into New York, and stayed with friends on 135th street in Harlem.

In 1929 and 1930 I lived on the road with him. He had a beautiful bus for the band with a sign on the outside—JELLY ROLL MORTON AND HIS RED HOT PEPPERS—but he and I traveled in the Lincoln. I guess the only trouble we ever had was over him going sixty-five around all those curves. That made me very nervous. He used to kid me and say, "May, I'm gonna leave you at home. . . . Don't you *know* I love myself better than anybody else in the world and I ain't never gonna have an accident when I'm driving the car?" Of course, he never did have an accident; and if a cop stopped him he could smooth-talk his way right out of it just like they were relatives.

Ferd did all his own bookings by letter or in person. Fifteen-hundred and sixteen-hundred dollars was about an average night's pay for the band and lots of time they would stay a whole week one place. He had his records; he showed them where he was Number One hot band with Victor. And when they heard that band, they wanted him back. He had Barney Bigard, Albert Nicholas, Red Allen, Wellman Braud, and other great men long before Ellington and those other bands was ever heard of. They broke all records in Pennsylvania, Indiana, Ohio, the interior of Canada, and all up through the New England States, playing the best places

such as Narragansett Pier. In the time I was with him he never went South, I don't know why.

The band all wore black tuxedos, but Jelly Roll wore a wine-red jacket and tie to match, white pants and white shoes. He directed the band himself, used to cut a lot of capers, then sit down at that piano with that great big smile of his, and, I'm telling you, he was a sensation. He never carried a singer with his band. He took the solos on piano and then the rest of the band didn't mean anything. They would just stop dead and all the people would gather around the stand to look and to hear. Jelly had two perfect hands for the piano—not like some players, one hand good and the other weak—he was just as good in the bass clef as in the treble. It was a wonderful thing to listen to him every night.

You see, I was right with him on the bandstand at every date. He was very jealous, didn't like anybody to speak to me—in fact he would get mad at his best friends if they so much as pass the time of day with me, but he wanted me there, dressed my best, so everybody could see me. Sometimes the boys in the band would ask him to let me sing, but he would never allow that. He used to tell me, "After all, I'm the big thing here and it would be bad for me if I shared with you my popularity." To tell you the truth, he was a little too jealous in that way, because after a while I began to want to go on with my professional career.[2]

He was Number One hot band then. All the others, like Ellington and Calloway and Basie and those, came up after. Jelly was first. Just like when you plant a seed, the others came along up, but Jelly was first. And he was so well liked by the white people that he never had to play a colored engagement; the colored places couldn't afford him. Only time colored people saw him was when he dropped into a cabaret for a drink, an announcement would

---

Mabel Morton as reported in Alan Lomax, *Mister Jelly Roll: The Fortunes of Jelly Roll Morton* (New York: Duell, Sloan and Pearce, 1949), 207–11, 216–17.

[1]In Gary, Indiana.

[2]Mabel Morton had been in the theater.

be made and everybody would stand up to get a look at him. Really, Jelly Roll didn't like Negroes. He always said they would mess up your business. And Negroes didn't like him. I guess they were jealous.

He was all in diamonds, those days. He wore a ring with a diamond as big as a dime and a diamond horseshoe in his tie. He carried a locket with diamonds set all around it. His watch was circled in diamonds. His belt buckle was in gold and studded with diamonds. He even had sock-supporters of solid gold set with diamonds. Then you could see that big half-carat diamond sparkling in his teeth. That year they called him the diamond king. . . .

He used to tell his band, "You'd please me if you'd just play those little black dots—just those little black dots that I put down there. If you play them, you'll please me. You don't have to make a lot of noise and ad-lib. All I want you to play is what's written. That's all I ask."

Jelly always kept the same band, but along in 1930 he began to have trouble with his men. They thought they were great and knew their instruments and how to make jazz without him. They began getting drunk and wouldn't behave.

Jelly, he was very strict about that. Any man that drank on his stand, he didn't want because of his reputation. And he told them, "If this don't stop, I'm giving up the band, because you can spoil my name and reputation by getting drunk and trying to mingle with the guests on the dance floor. Because I pay higher than any other leader—ninety and one hundred dollars a week, you think you're in demand; but I can get along without you, because I can always play plenty of piano and get good men for recording dates . . . so come on, boys, and stick to those black dots." . . .

All during these years, from 1930 to 1933, after his regular band broke up, Jelly kept busy and made good money playing gigs up through the New England states. But he began to have more and more trouble getting the cooperation of the colored musicians. They wanted to play everything but what he had dotted down. They thought they could bring a bottle of whiskey to the job in their back pockets. All that hurt him. Jelly spoke and preached and did everything he could.

"I want to tell you one thing," he used to say to the boys around the Rhythm Club, "you cannot play around, just because you think you're so great. I'm telling you those white boys are not playing corny any more. They're coming up right along. I hear them playing my tunes. They're getting the *idea* of how to play hot. Once they get it, they're going to use it. Then they're gonna sell *you* for five cents a dozen. If I ask you now to go out on a gig, it's thirty-five or forty dollars for that night. But it won't be long till you'll be around the club, standing on the corner, with your instruments under your arm and glad to get a five-dollar job."

And that's what happened, just the way he told them. Once the white boys got the idea of it, they went to town. Like Benny Goodman. To get the idea, he taken Fletcher Henderson with him as his arranger. Then Goodman got the idea and he branched off, because then *he* knew what to do with the hot idea. . . . Artie Shaw, he taken Billie Holliday [sic] with him, but when he began playing the New England states, he said to Billie, "You're marvelous. You're wonderful. Nobody can compare with your style, but they will not book me in the New England states with a colored entertainer."

Now, my husband didn't feel there was prejudice involved in the white bands taking jazz over; he felt it was all through the Negro musicians thinking they were so great, getting drunk on the job and not cooperating.

93 ASCAP: Protection of Performing Rights

Although the notion of copyright has existed since the beginnings of the United States as a country, its extension to include musical works came slowly. The first copyright law, passed in 1790, protected maps, charts, and books for a term of fourteen years. It underwent general revisions in 1831, 1870, and 1909. Musical compositions were mentioned for the first time in the 1831 revision, and original musical works were duly registered for copyright from then on, although a real attempt to clarify the complicated situation regarding music had to wait until an entirely new statute was adopted in 1976.

A performing right—that is, the right of public performance—was not addressed legally until 1897, and it was not until 1914 that the first performing rights society, the American Society of Composers, Authors and Publishers (ASCAP), was founded. "The object of the society," reads one report of its organizational meeting, included below, "is to prevent the playing of any copyrighted music by any orchestra or at any public performance unless a royalty is paid."

Overseeing the numerous performances around the country was an enormous task, especially since the beginnings of radio broadcasting in the 1920s had created an upsurge in performances, particularly of popular music. While radio opened up new worlds in the American music marketplace, it also complicated ASCAP's situation. The organization had to fight to establish its position, and the stakes were high.

Copyright protection for music is still imperfectly understood, and the quick rise of distributing and downloading songs via the World Wide Web has complicated things further. The notion behind ASCAP is generally recognized as beneficial, and ASCAP has helped the world of music enormously through its award programs and distribution of revenues. Yet many Americans feel a tug of independence that leads them to resist control.

NEWS ARTICLE

"Trust for Control of Music Business" (1914)

At a meeting yesterday afternoon in Claridge's Hotel, at which every big music-publishing concern and most of the authors and composers of all kinds and conditions of songs were represented, the American Society of Authors, Composers, and Publishers was organized. The society is expected by its founders to become the most powerful organization in the world for the control of the music business, and within the next year, according to its President elected yesterday, will collect more than $1,000,000 in New York City alone for its members.

The object of the society is to prevent the play-

"Trust for Control of Music Business," *New York Times*, February 14, 1914: [1].

ing of any copyrighted music by any orchestra or at any public performance unless a royalty is paid. Theatre orchestras, cabaret shows, and the phonograph records will be the principal music fields in which the tolls will be collected.

Every class of song writer and composer, from Victor Herbert to Irving Berlin, was represented at the meeting. Rag time writers joined hands with publishers of chamber music, and the President of the organization is George Maxwell, the head, in this country, of G. Ricordi & Co., the largest publishers of operatic music in the world. . . .

"The Society of Authors, Composers, and Publishers," said Mr. Maxwell, "is built on the lines of the same organization which has ruled the music field in France, Germany, and Italy for many years. In France the society collects more than $1,000,000 from public performances each year, and this is divided among its members. We will be able to collect more than that every year right here in New York, and the amount collected around the country will run into many millions.

"The society has not been formed to make a fight upon any one or to stir up any trouble. The writers and publishers are given protection under the copyright laws of the United States, and until now that protection has never been carefully brought into use. When orchestras play the music of our members they will have to pay for the right to do so. That is only fair, and the laws of the country make it possible for us to see that the collections are made.

"There is really nothing new in our plans, except the getting together of the men interested to protect their rights. The rights have always been there, and now we are going to enforce them."

NEWS ARTICLE

"Radio's Battle of Music" (1940)

Now that the election is over, about the hardest fight raging in the United States is radio's battle of music. It started last spring and is rising in intensity to an expected crescendo Jan. 1.[1] On one side, in a strongly fortified position, is the American Society of Composers, Authors, and Publishers (ASCAP), copyright holder of a majority of the best American popular music of the past twenty years. In the opposing trenches are the radio networks and most of the nation's independent stations.

When the war broke out over a new five-year contract at higher rates asked by ASCAP, few in the radio industry thought the conflict would last long. But by last week it was increasingly apparent that the radio forces would not retreat and that, barring an ASCAP surrender or a quiet word from the Federal Communications Commission (both unlikely), the works of Herbert, Berlin, Porter, Kern, Romberg, Gershwin, and other ASCAP greats would go off the network air at the turn of the year. . . .

The innocent neutrals in this music war are band leaders, and, as usual, they are feeling the pinch worse than the belligerents themselves. Theme songs are being junked by the score, and arrangers are working overtime on backlogs of non-ASCAP music.

Some shows—such as the Lucky Strike Hit Parade—probably will be crippled. Last week Frank Hummert of the Blackett-Sample-Hummert advertising agency, which runs the hard-hit American Album of Familiar Music program, took steps to bring Washington into the fight. As a private citizen and user of "familiar music," he instructed his attorneys to file a protest with the FCC on the ground that "the music the American people love is about to be driven off the air."

"Radio's Battle of Music," *Newsweek*, November 18, 1940: 69–70.

[1]January 1, 1941, when ASCAP refused permission for its music to be played on the air.

NEWS ARTICLE

"Peace on the Air" (1941)

The air waves used by NBC and CBS were opened again last week to old-timers like "Dinah," "Sweet Adeline," and "God Bless America," and to new tunes aborning in composers' imaginations. Such songs, along with 1,500,000 others controlled by the American Society of Composers, Authors, and Publishers, came back to dialers[2] in a compromise agreement which ended the two networks' ten-month blackout of them over a dispute on fees. As MBS[3] already had reached a settlement with the ASCAP, thus was concluded radio's great "Battle of Music," which had etched an epic chapter in American entertainment history.

ASCAP—an organization of 1,166 tunesmiths and 140 music publishers holding royalty rights to about 90 percent of popular songs—had opened the fight by demanding for the first time that the three webs pay 7 1/2 percent of their revenue for use of its catalogues. Hitherto, ASCAP had collected a fee—amounting to 5 percent—only from the individual stations. The networks refused—they branded ASCAP a monopoly and assailed its blanket charge on music whether one song or a hundred were played a month. In reply, the society on last Jan. 1 yanked its lists from the air.

The effect was startling. Big musical programs were at first imperiled. Virtually all theme songs, from Amos 'n' Andy's to Edgar Bergen's, had to be deleted of ASCAP-copyrighted phrases or junked entirely. College songs copyrighted by ASCAP could not be picked up at football and other games.

What saved the day completely for the networks was the formation the year before, in anticipation of the battle, of Broadcast Music, Inc., an independent clearing and publishing house, which took over dissident ASCAP members and encour-

aged new writers to compose works. It also took over some independent music catalogues which featured Latin-American songs, with the result that the air presently was filled with south-of-the-border tunes. In the early dearth of available music the networks loosed a deluge of Stephen Foster classics and other music out of copyright.

By early spring it became apparent that ASCAP was losing. The Federal government cracked down in an antitrust action which stopped the mandatory-charge practice. The society reached its agreement with MBS, always a lukewarm member to the fight. And BMI suddenly came through with a number of hit tunes—"My Sister and I," "Amapola," "Wise Old Owl," and others—which did much to tip the scales in favor of the broadcasters.

As it turned out in the final settlement, ASCAP took a beating. On the financial side, the society lost $4,000,000 from loss of revenue alone during the year; income in future from radio also will be some $3,000,000, in contrast to about $5,100,000 earned in 1940. It lost its monopoly over both stations and networks (BMI will continue as a permanent concern), as well as its old blanket-paying policy. Public opinion compelled the society's controlling officers to liberalize its practices to help outside song writers. However, it did gain a victory in the settlement when the networks agreed to pay fees at the source of programs rather than on the basis of individual stations. The contract signed last week runs to Dec. 31, 1949, and these fees will be 2 3/4 per cent of net receipts from network commercial business and 2 1/4 per cent of intake from network-managed and network-operated stations.

Despite the network peace, discord continued to reign in Tin Pan Alley. Nearly 100 song writers, some associated with ASCAP, decided to form the American Federation of Songsmiths. Organizers were Al Lewis, who wrote "Blueberry Hill," Nelson

---

"Peace on the Air," *Newsweek*, November 10, 1941: 72–73.

[2] Radio listeners.

[3] The Mutual Broadcasting System.

Cogane, who composed "We Three," and Robert Daru, who represents fourteen tunesmiths in a suit against the broadcasters in connection with the settled ASCAP row. Charging that ASCAP was "no union but just a collection agency," Daru said the new group would join the AFL or CIO.

94

William Grant Still,
African-American Composer

Following military service in World War I, William Grant Still (1895–1978) moved to New York, where he joined W. C. Handy's publishing company, played oboe in theater orchestras (in 1921, he was in the pit for Eubie Blake's *Shuffle Along*), composed and arranged music (for Donald Voorhees, Sophie Tucker, Artie Shaw, Willard Robison, Paul Whiteman, and others), and studied composition with George Chadwick and Edgard Varèse. Chadwick held Still to traditional values; Varèse, the avantgardist, expanded his horizons.

During these years, important artistic efforts were taking place in New York in the cultural movement known as the Harlem Renaissance. Still was aware of it but tells us he was not a part of it.

The combination of popular and classical activity gave Still considerable breadth of outlook and experience. Always conscious of his race and the needs of African-American musicians, he championed their cause, although his humanistic view made him an integrationist who fought against racial stereotypes. He believed that money should be incidental to a career in music, that particular obstacles faced black musicians but there is always "room at the top," and that African Americans could contribute much to racial advancement and interracial understanding through music.

Still's *Afro-American Symphony* provides an excellent example of his humanitarianism. It is rooted in African American traditions—the blues and the banjo, which it uses for the first time in a major symphony—yet speaks to us in universal terms. A significant four-movement work, it was premiered in 1931 by the Rochester Philharmonic Orchestra under the direction of Howard Hanson and was performed shortly thereafter in Europe. It was heralded as the first major work written by an African-American composer to be played by a leading orchestra.

Other milestones followed. In 1936, Still became the first African American to conduct a major orchestra—the Los Angeles Philharmonic in the Hollywood Bowl—in an evening of his own works. He was commissioned to write a piece for a Jewish service, at the Park Avenue Synagogue in New York. His opera, *Troubled Island,* was produced by the New York City Opera Company in 1949. And in 1955, he became the first African American to conduct a major all-white orchestra—the New Orleans Philharmonic Orchestra—in the deep South.

Still's catalog grew to include about 150 works, including operas, ballets, symphonies, symphonic poems, and many smaller pieces. He ranks among the preeminent African-American composers of classical music.

WILLIAM GRANT STILL

from "Can Music Make a Career?" (1948)

To keep going, a Negro must be better prepared than anyone else. The day when things will be accepted because they are "pretty good for a colored man" is past. To reach the very top, a Negro has to fight not only the battles fought by everyone else in his profession (professional jealousy, and so on) but also the subtle barriers set up by prejudice. . . .

Here are the circumstances of my life, as far as music is concerned:

My parents were teachers. The stepfather who came into my life in my boyhood was a postal clerk. Therefore my family was comfortable from the standpoint of finances. The public schools of Little Rock, Arkansas, gave me my elementary and high school education, while violin lessons with a private teacher were provided by my mother. My stepfather took me to musical shows and bought the phonograph and the library of Red Seal records which inspired me and made me want to compose serious music. My mother spent much of her income on good books, which I was willing and eager to read.

Because the colored musicians of that day were not accepted in the best social circles, my mother had decided that I should become a doctor. Accordingly, my courses at Wilberforce University were chosen with a B.S. degree in mind. I, on the other hand, had made up my mind that I would go into music as a profession, so that most of my activities at Wilberforce were slanted toward that end. I played in the string quartet, joined the band, made arrangements for the musical ensembles, led the band. I trained new members of the band to play musical instruments I had only just learned to play myself so that my arrangements would sound all right when they were performed. I wrote little compositions of my own which were presented in

concert at Wilberforce. When I came home on vacation I spent most of the time writing music, some of it for contests in which I had not the ghost of a chance of winning due to my inexperience. Almost all of this musical activity was done without guidance and amounted to learning by doing.

My mother still refused to go along with me on the idea of a musical career. Then, Fate took a hand and brought me to a violent disagreement with my mother when I left Wilberforce after four years of study and just two months before I was scheduled to graduate. All support from home stopped. I was thrown out on my own. Instinctively I sought—and got—work in musical circles. For many years after that, I made a living playing various instruments in orchestras, orchestrating for shows, radio, and so on—sometimes for colored employers and sometimes for white—making friends and contacts wherever I could and living as precariously as a free lance usually does. This work was interrupted only by service in the U.S. Navy, and even there I eventually became an entertainer, playing the violin for the officers at mealtimes.

It would have been easy to have been deluded by this life, but I refused to let it conquer me. I determined to learn from it everything possible, to help myself in the work I really meant to do in the future. What a wonderful thing it turned out to be for me, musically speaking! Had I stayed at home, well supplied with funds from my family, I might have steeped myself in the academic lore of music and missed the outside contacts that meant equally as much.

As it was, the life I adopted of necessity gave me a first-hand experience with American music. It let me understand music from the players' points of view. It made me teach myself to orchestrate, evolving new techniques and effects not found in textbooks. Finally, when the day came that I conducted the "Deep River" program on radio station WOR after having made orchestrations

William Grant Still, "Can Music Make a Career?" *Negro Digest* (December 1948): 79–84.

for it for many months, it was the men in the orchestra who had asked for me to conduct them and the men who showed me how to do it. All this practical experience later blended with the things I had learned from serious study on the side, and made something a little different from the things other composers and orchestrators were turning out.

Naturally, I had done as much serious studying as possible all during this commercial career. At first, shortly after leaving Wilberforce, a delayed legacy from my father made it possible for me to study at Oberlin. When that fund was exhausted, I worked to pay my tuition. Then one day our instructor, Professor F. J. Lehmann, gave the class Dunbar's poem *Good Night* to set to music.[1] When he saw my setting, he called me aside and asked me why I did not go on to study composition. On learning that I could not afford it, he called a meeting of the theory committee which created for me a scholarship that had not existed before.

Later, when playing oboe in the *Shuffle Along* orchestra, I took advantage of the visit of the show to Boston to go to the New England Conservatory of Music and ask to study with the pioneer American composer, George W. Chadwick. Mr. Chadwick looked at some of my work and sent word that he wished to teach me for nothing. I sent back word that at last I could afford to pay for my lessons and that I wished to do so, but he would not accept pay. So here again, I was fortunate in coming in contact with a new musical influence— a man who was forging ahead to help build a new culture for a young nation.

The third teaching influence was that of Edgar Varèse, the noted French ultra-modernist, who was so impressed by Col. Charles Young, whom he had met on a voyage, that he wanted to help a young Negro composer. A letter was sent to the Black Swan Phonograph Company, where I was employed at the time, asking if they could suggest a worthy young Negro composer to take advantage of this free scholarship. The man who received the letter sat down to write back that he knew of no one suitable, when I happened to look over his shoulder.

"You can just tear your letter up," I said, "because I want that scholarship." Then began an inspiring period of study during which Mr. Varèse opened new musical worlds to me, both as regards the creation of music and in opportunities to get my symphonic works performed by important organizations. He, like Mr. Chadwick and the professors at Oberlin, asked in return for this nothing but my willingness to work hard and to be worthy of the help.

For the most part, the past fifteen years have been spent on my own, developing and integrating the things I learned during the many years of preparation. Guggenheim and Rosenwald Fellowships made it possible to live for four years of this time without the need of doing commercial work. Today, I no longer need to accept commercial work. I am not, and never expect to be, wealthy. But the satisfaction that has come from doing exactly the work I enjoy doing is worth more than material wealth.

That brings up one of the most essential points of all. All along the way, decisions will have to be made by the aspirant for musical fame. One must do one thing or the other, and there can be little "middle-of-the-roading." In my opinion, the first question an aspiring musician should ask himself is, "Do I want to make music, or do I want to make money?" For you can make money in the entertainment world—far more than you can make in serious music—sometimes with a very small amount of preparation and a great amount of personal magnetism. One reason for this is that the American public patronizes popular music more than serious music. Another reason is that a Negro in this field conforms to many people's idea of where a Negro ought to stay.

In serious music, a Negro can still be a pioneer and thus contribute to racial advancement and to inter-racial understanding, and he can have the satisfaction of doing something eminently worthwhile. My view is that the glory or money that may

---

[1] Paul Laurence Dunbar (1872–1906) was a leading African American poet and lyricist.

come from one's profession should be an incidental aim rather than a major consideration.

For the sincere musician, this last should be one of the most important of all thoughts. No one should adopt music as a profession unless he enjoys it, unless it comes from his heart, and unless he loves it so much that he can't be happy doing anything else. Also, one of the first requisites for a good musician is that he be *musical*. So many people who create or perform music nowadays are really cut out for other professions! . . .

As a colored person advances in the field of serious music he will have to face not only the obstacles mentioned previously but in addition the apathy of a large percentage of colored people who aren't educated musically and who think that the coming of a Negro bandleader (with blatant, paid advance publicity) to a local dance hall is far more important than the playing of a piece of symphonic music by a Negro composer by a great symphony orchestra under a distinguished conductor.

To compensate, if one is fortunate enough to establish contact, he will have the friendship and sympathy of the really important people—both colored and white—who will understand his aspirations and be working along with him toward success.

I do not urge young colored people to adopt music as a profession unless they are meant for that work and for none other, and unless they are willing to work, to starve if need be, to struggle and to use their success wisely when it is won. To those who are sincere in their musical ambitions, I would say, "Come on along. The teaching field is no longer the only one. Negro singers have made names for themselves. Soon Negro instrumentalists will do the same. A few symphony conductors now are willing to take a chance on having capable colored players in their orchestras. More will follow. The compositions of Negroes are performed by soloists and by ensembles. In time this will become a matter of course rather than a novelty. Negro conductors are few, but at least they are getting a hearing today, when there was no hope for them in the past at all. Negro songwriters have been successful since the days of minstrel shows. Quite a few Negro orchestrators have been successful during the past thirty years. There now even is one Negro impresario, who books concerts by artists of such stature as Marian Anderson and Yehudi Menuhin, when they come to his city. Slowly, but surely, opportunities are here for the alert, prepared individual. In short, come on along! There is, as the saying goes, always room at the top!

95

Count Basie

William "Count" Basie (1904–1984), born in Red Bank, New Jersey, knew early that he wanted to follow a career in music. His formal schooling was slim. He didn't see any point in finishing school "so one day I just got up and walked on out of there." But he played the piano from the beginning, first studying with his mother. Later he went to New York, where he encountered James P. Johnson, Thomas "Fats" Waller, and other pianists of the Harlem stride school. He began to tour on the show circuits. In 1927, he found himself stranded in Kansas City, at the time a hotbed of activity and a hub for touring in the Midwest. The following year, he joined bass player Walter Page's Blue Devils. He tells us that after playing with them, "being a musician was where it was really at for me." Shortly thereafter, he made his way into the city's premiere band, led by Bennie Moten, who was himself pianist for the group. Soon the Count was spelling Moten regularly on piano.

The selections below follow Basie through a good portion of his Kansas City years and beyond, through Moten's death, to the organization of his own groups: Three, Three, and Three; the Barons of Rhythm; and, by the late 1930s, the Count Basie Orchestra, which became one of the leading big bands of the swing era. The voice is Basie's, although filtered through his "co-writer," Albert Murray.

COUNT BASIE

from *Good Morning Blues* (1985)

By the time I started to pick up on all of the talk about Bennie and his band that I was beginning to hear once I was settled back in Kansas City, the name was not really new to me. But then the more I heard, the more impressed I was. Then I also heard some of his records, and I found out he was the top recording band in that part of the country, and I was very impressed all over again. So then I really became very interested in what they were doing, and I can actually remember talking to somebody one day, and Bennie Moten's name came up, and I remember myself saying how much I liked that band. I said I would really like to

play with that band, and whoever it was that I was talking to looked at me and asked me what I meant. I said I sure would like to play with that band. And he said, "What you talking about? *Bennie Moten himself is the piano player.*" Which was true. Bennie was a hell of a good piano player. He could play all kinds of stuff that I wasn't even about to try to tackle. But I have always been a conniver and began saying to myself, I got to see how I can connive my way into that band. I like that band. I got to play with that band.

I don't know why the fact that Bennie Moten himself was such a good piano player didn't faze me. All I know is that I just had to play with them, and I was going to do everything I could to get myself in there. I kept watching for my first chance. . . .

William Basie, *Good Morning Blues: The Autobiography of Count Basie*, as told to Albert Murray (New York: Random House, 1985), 113–15, 120–21, 170–71, 199.

I went to a couple of dances that they played in around town following that first night,[1] and I met a few of the fellows, and I also got a chance to chat with Bennie himself. But the main contact I made was with Eddie Durham.[2] That was a real piece of good luck. I think he and I must have turned up at a few of the same sessions, probably somewhere like the Subway or the Yellow Front or somewhere like that, and I got on more and more familiar terms with him. Then I found out from somebody that he could write music and that he was one of Bennie's arrangers, and that was when I saw my chance to make my first move.

The very next time I saw him, I asked him whether, if I played something on the piano, could he write it. He said sure. And it also turned out that he was always on the lookout for new things to arrange for the band. So we got together some-where, and I began playing something on the piano that I wanted the band to play, and he wrote it down. I would play the parts for each section, and he would make the sheets for the trumpets and reeds and trombone and so on like that, and we worked up a couple of arrangements. I knew exactly how I wanted the band to sound, and Eddie picked right up on it. So I was ready for my next move.

I got Eddie to take me and the sheets along with him to Bennie's next rehearsal. I sat there and listened and then, when Eddie got a chance, he had them run down our two things, and both of them sparked old Bennie up a bit. It's a peculiar thing, but for the life of me I can't remember the names of those two charts. I don't think they were origi-nals; I think they were something we did on a cou-ple of standards or something like that.

But anyway, Bennie liked the way they went down and said he wanted to talk to me, and he asked me a few little things and then said the very thing I had been waiting to hear. He asked me if I would like to go along on the trip that the band was getting ready to make out to Wichita for a few days.

He wanted me to listen to the band and work with Eddie on some more arrangements. And right away I said I'd love to go down there with them, and I said we had already been thinking about some more things we'd like to work up for the book.

So Bennie said okay, and I went and told Jap Eblon,[3] and I went to Wichita on my first trip with Bennie Moten. I want along as a staff arranger, and I couldn't have written a tune on my own or worked up a chart if my life depended on it. But the understanding was that I was to be working with Eddie. So everything was fine, because the main thing for me was that I was getting that much closer to actually playing with that band. That was what I was conniving for, and I got a chance to sit in that very first trip.

Maybe Bennie had heard me playing. I don't really remember much about that. But I probably sat in on the piano at some point while the band was rehearsing the two numbers that Eddie and I had brought in, or something like that. Or maybe he just took Eddie's word for it. Anyway, after a couple of sets at that dance in Wichita, he wanted to take a break to look into some business matters, and he called me and told me to come on up and sit in for him. That's how I got my chance to per-form with that band, and right then I could tell that he liked the way I sounded in there. Because he took his time about coming back, and when he did, he just played a few things and turned it back over to me again until just before the last number.

*   *   *

I really don't know how you would define stomp in strict musical terms. But it was a real thing.[4] What I would say is if you were on the first floor, and the dance hall was upstairs, that was what you would hear, that steady *rump, rump, rump, rump* in that medium tempo. It was never fast. And you could also feel it. Of course, the band[5] used to have to play other kinds of things

---

[1]After he heard Moten's band play at a dance at Paseo Hall.

[2]Trombonist, guitarist, and arranger Eddie Durham (1906–1987) worked with Moten from 1929 to 1933.

[3]Kansas City theater owner.

[4]"Stomp" was a common term in jazz titles of the 1920s and 1930s. Such pieces often had energetic, sharp rhythms.

[5]Moten's band.

too. Sometimes we'd be playing somewhere and there would be those little cardboard signs that somebody would put up on a rack by the bandstand to announce that the next dance would be a one-step, foxtrot, waltz, and those other little steps that called for different rhythms and tempos. When we were playing that kind of dance, most likely Bennie himself would take over at the piano. Naturally, he could play the stomps too, because that was the band's thing. But anytime they played anything, the floor was full of dancers. *That* told you something.

But it was not the kind of jump band or swing band that the Blue Devils band was. The Blue Devils' style was snappier. They were two different things, and we wanted some of that bluesy hot stuff in there too. So we needed Lips, and Bennie brought him in for us.[6] We didn't get rid of anybody to bring him in. Eddie[7] wrote special parts for him.

Here are a few bars that Eddie ran down for my co-writer[8] about what was happening musicwise: "When some of the guys in the band heard that Lips was coming, they came and asked me whose place he was taking and what notes he was going to play. 'I'm playing second and so-and-so is playing lead and what's his name is playing third on the trombone.' So I said, 'I'll find a note for him. I'll add another part to the harmony.' Because they were just playing three-part harmony all the time. And when Lips came, I started writing four-part harmony, and I added a sixth tone in there. And I found out that those guys couldn't play a sixth. They couldn't hear a sixth. It would hurt their ears. So I gave it to Lips because he was a hot man, and he was hitting them sixes as solo work.

"Now, the way all that got started was with the things that Basie was playing for me to work up arrangements on. I told him, 'Man, this stuff you got here will stand four- and five-part harmony.

The way you're carrying this, let's get away from all these triads and add another man.' So he said, 'Get Lips.' That's the way it was, and then I was writing ninth chords, which is a five-part harmony, and they could hear the ninth a little better than the sixth. I gave that to Lips. They didn't know how to blend it. So that's how Basie and I got it going. The others thought it was out of tune. But Bennie went along with us, and when the rest of them heard it on the next records, they began to understand what was happening."

* * *

By the time we first started getting the band together at the Reno,[9] I already had some pretty clear ideas about how I wanted a band to sound like. I knew how I wanted each section to sound. So I also knew what each one of the guys should sound like. I knew what I wanted them there for. Even back when I was dictating those arrangements to Eddie Durham for Bennie Moten's band, I could actually hear the band playing those passages while we were working on them. And that's the way Eddie wrote. We could write just like I heard it. He could voice each section just the way I wanted it.

I have my own little ideas about how to get certain guys into certain numbers and how to get them out. I had my own way of opening the door for them to let them come in and sit around awhile. Then I would exit them. And that has really been the formula of the band all down through the years. It's been more or less the same patterns, and all of our arrangers know what I like to hear and how I like to do things. . . .

Sometimes I like to play loud. And fast too, Sometimes you need to do it with a little volume, and I hear some numbers with the tempo way up. But I also like the band when the guys are just swinging their cans off down easy, like a number called "Softly, With Feeling." Then I also like to bust it out when we have to. That's the sort of thing I already hear in my head before the band plays it. I always did hear things like that. And of course, I always did like good shouting brass.

[6]Oran Thaddeus "Hot Lips" Page, a trumpeter and singer who played with the Blue Devils before joining Moten's band.

[7]Eddie Durham.

[8]Albert Murray.

[9]The Reno Club in Kansas City, after Moten's death.

Shouting brass choruses. And we used to do it. And I'm gradually getting back to that a little bit. Good shouting brass choruses, boy . . . that's something. When you have a good shouting brass section, you got yourself something.

When we started working out the arrangements for the full-size band I was getting ready at the Reno, I knew just where I wanted those two tenors. After certain modulations and certain breaks, I knew exactly which one I wanted to come in, and sometimes it would be one and sometimes the other. Because each one had his own thing. But it was not really in my mind to battle them. Not at first. It was just a matter of using two different styles to the best advantage of the band.

The band was called the Barons of Rhythm. So we were advertised as Count Basie and His Barons of Rhythm. That was the name somebody thought up as a gimmick for those radio broadcasts over W9XBY. So the announcer could say, "And now here is Count Basie and his fourteen Barons of Rhythm." Something like that. I don't know, maybe that is what somebody got mixed up with how I got the name Count Basie. But as I have said before, I was already billed as Count Basie a few years before those broadcasts. There were no Barons of Rhythm before those broadcasts, but there was Count Basie.

*   *   *

Anyway, we had an awful lot of time to rehearse, and that was what we did, right down there in the basement at the Woodside.[10] We got together down there at least three times a week, and we made some great head arrangements[11] down

there during those sessions, and those guys in each section remembered everything. I don't know how the hell they did it, but they really did. So by the time we got through with a tune, it was an arrangement. People thought it was written out.

It was like the Blue Devils. We always had somebody in those sections who was a leader, who could start something and get those ensembles going. I mean, while somebody would be soloing in the reed section, the brasses would have something going in the background, and the reed section would have something to go with that. And while the brass section had something going, somebody in the reed section might be playing a solo. When a trumpet player would have something going, the band would have something. While he's playing the first chorus, they'd be getting something going down there in the reeds. That's all they needed, and the next chorus just followed.

That's where we were at. That's the way it went down. Those guys knew just where to come in and they came in. And the thing about it that was so fantastic was this: *Once those guys played something, they could damn near play it exactly the same the next night.* That's what really happened. Of course, I'm sitting there at the piano catching notes and all, and I knew just how I wanted to use the different things they used to come up with. So I'd say something like "Okay, take that one a half tone down; go ahead down with it and then go for something." We'd do that, and they would remember their notes, and a lot of times the heads that we made down there in that basement were a lot better than things that were written out.

---

[10]On Seventh Avenue in New York City.

[11]Arrangements that were not notated.

96   Duke Ellington

*M*usic Is My Mistress was published by Edward Kennedy "Duke" Ellington (1899–1974) several months before his death. Ellington had agreed to do the book on condition that Stanley Dance, his chronicler and confidant, would work on it with him. According to Mercer Ellington, Duke's son and manager,

> Stanley had expected that it would be done with a tape recorder, following the same method they had used for articles, so he was surprised to find that Pop intended to write it himself. The manuscript that eventually materialized was undoubtedly unique. It was written on hotel stationery, table napkins, and menus from all over the world.*

The result, which Ellington called "the Good Book," is a retrospective of a long life in music. Parallels with Scott Joplin and George Gershwin, who bridged jazz and conventional forms, suggest themselves, but Ellington was unique. He resisted the notion of categories and even found the term *jazz* meaningless: "We stopped using the word in 1943, and we much prefer to call it the American Idiom, or the Music of Freedom of Expression." He absorbed the music of both black and white cultures and built on them. He deepened as a composer, both harmonically and conceptually, and gradually, he broadened his approach to include large-scale productions, fulfilling numerous commissions from major symphonic and ecclesiastical organizations. Eventually, he became an emissary for American musical culture, receiving some two hundred awards, citations, and decorations from governments and organizations around the world and fifteen honorary doctorates.

The organization of *Music Is My Mistress* reflects Ellington's belief that "The story of jazz is a long list of great names." Its eight short essays, or "acts," are interspersed with his recollections of individual musicians, which he groups under the heading *Dramatis Felidae* (cast of cats).

---

*Mercer Ellington, with Stanley Dance, *Duke Ellington in Person* (Boston: Houghton Mifflin, 1978), 171–72.

DUKE ELLINGTON

from *Music Is My Mistress* (1973)

Q. Which of all your tunes is your favorite?
A. The next one. The one I'm writing tonight or tomorrow, the new baby is always the favorite.

* * *

Roaming through the jungle, the jungle of "oohs" and "ahs," searching for a more agreeable noise, I live a life of primitivity with the mind of a child and an unquenchable thirst for sharps and flats. The more consonant, the more appetizing and delectable they are. Cacophony is hard to swallow. Living in a cave, I am almost a hermit, but there is a difference, for I have a mistress. Lovers have come and gone, but only my mistress stays. She is beautiful and gentle. She waits on me hand and foot. She is a swinger. She has grace. To hear her speak, you can't believe your ears. She is ten thousand years old. She is as modern as tomorrow, a brand-new woman every day, and as endless as time mathematics. Living with her is a labyrinth of ramifications. I look forward to her every gesture.

Music is my mistress, and she plays second fiddle to no one.

* * *

What Is Music?

What is music to you?
What would you be without music?

Music is everything.
Nature is music (cicadas in the tropical night).

The sea is music,
The wind is music,
Primitive elements are music, agreeable or
    discordant.

The rain drumming on the roof,
And the storm raging in the sky are music.

Every country in the world has its own music,
And the music becomes an ambassador;
The tango in Argentina and calypso in Antilles.

Music is the oldest entity.

A baby is born, and music puts him to sleep.
He can't read, he can't understand a picture,
But he will listen to music.

Music is marriage.

Music is death.

The scope of music is immense and infinite.
It is the "esperanto" of the world.

Music arouses courage and leads you to war.
The Romans used to have drums rolling before
    they attacked.
We have the bugle to sound reveille and pay
    homage to the brave warrior.

The Marseillaise has led many generations to
    victories or revolutions;
It is a chant of wild excitement, and delirium, and
    pride.

Music is eternal,
Music is divine.

You pray to your God with music.

Music can dictate moods,
It can ennerve or subdue,
Subjugate, exhaust, astound the heart.

Music is a cedar,
An evergreen tree of fragrant, durable wood.

Music is like honor and pride,
Free from defect, damage, or decay.

Without music I may feel blind, atrophied,
    incomplete, *inexistent.*

* * *

Edward Kennedy Ellington, *Music Is My Mistress* (Garden City, N.Y.: Doubleday, 1973), 463, 447, 212–13, 298–99, 411–12.

Hooked

Much of the adventure in one-nighters is in the anticipation of approaching confrontations with one's self. When face to face with one's self, or looking one's self in the eye, there is no cop-out. It is the moment of truth. I cannot lie to me, or vice versa.

So the question is, was, and always will be: have we been true to ourselves? Did we compromise for the sake of monetary or material gain? Have we been too idealistic, as when we blew an opportunity that included bonus bundles? Just how far or how much should we bend in the interest of holding our position or an advantageous edge?

This is the kind of counterbanter we must contend with—no ifs, ands, or buts. The next time, of course, it will be different. The audience will have matured and we can allow our true artistic selves to come to the fore.

The cats all showed,
The gig was blowed.
Now that we've played,
Goodbyes are bade.
Oh, how we grieve
That we must leave!
Sorry we have to go-go-go!

Are we leaving now to duck the responsibility of reacting sympathetically to the action whipped up in reaction to the action we have just laid down? Or to go in pursuit of our constant compulsion? Is this not a merry-go-round?

The constant chase, or being chased . . . the constant reaching for the melody that's right up there, so close you can almost see it . . . you grab at it, and think you've got it, only to find later that all you've got is a little piece of the tail!

So you're hooked on music. You think and anticipate music. You write music, play music, and listen to music. Your joy is music. You are lucky to be hooked on something you make a living by playing—and playing with—day after day, play after play, fifty-two weeks a year, in possibly the only band that doesn't take time off. This is probably the only group of people doing anything fifty-two weeks a year without weekends, holidays, or vacations, here and now in an age where most people who work a five-day week are talking about a four-day week, and four-day workers are demanding three-day weeks. You are most fortunate not to be one of those who do not enjoy what they do for a living. Don't you know that money is important to most people, and everything to some? And isn't it true when they say that anyone who makes a living doing what he doesn't enjoy is actually indulging in a form of prostitution?

Music to me is a sound sensation, assimilation, anticipation, adulation, and reputation. It takes me to new places and experiences. It brings me invitations to the most interesting occasions in North and South America, in Europe, Africa, Asia, and Australia. I get to smell things in India I couldn't smell anywhere else. I see skies in Sweden I could see nowhere else. I hear distant drums in Africa. I get a compelling urge from the *cuíca*[1] in Brazil. I see a flying saucer in Phoenix; a moonbow in Reno; snow and fog together in Toronto; snow and lightning accompanied by thunder in Chicago; four rainbows at once in Stockholm; and at precisely the hour and minute one year after Billy Strayhorn's demise, a celebration in the sky—a cloudburst on the New Jersey Turnpike like a testimonial to grief in the heavens.[2]

Music is thus a key to great rewards in terms of experience. But when someone has to be told that he should study or specialize in music for the purpose of making a career—then I think more harm than good is done. Anyone who loves to make music knows that study is necessary. There are periods when music is a lucrative pursuit, but if money is

---

[1] A barrel-like percussion instrument.

[2] Elsewhere in his book, Ellington writes about his relationship with composer, arranger, and pianist William Thomas (Billy) Strayhorn (1915–1967): "I am indebted to him for so much of my courage since 1939," when Strayhorn joined the Ellington band. "Our rapport was the closest. Many people are indebted to Billy Strayhorn, and I more than anybody." Strayhorn collaborated with Ellington on a large number of works and is now credited with composing many of them, including the band's theme song, *Take the A Train.*

the only reason for participating in it, then money can be more of a distraction than anything else. And I think this is true of every art form. Music—love it or leave it!

* * *

Music and the Future

I am an optimist. From where I sit, music is mostly all right, or at least in a healthy state for the future, in spite of the fact that it may sound as though it is being held hostage.

Opera, for instance, has its audience (and its union problems!). Many ballet companies are obviously doing very well. The symphonies manage to keep themselves well subsidized and to do concert tours with itineraries that encircle the world. Chamber music retains its loyal following, and nobody is more enthusiastic than a chamber music aficionado. There is enough new cultural concrete and steel in the major cities of the world to build a bridge all the way to Mars and back.

This, I think you'll agree, promises well for the future.

The sound, of course, will be dependent on the good taste of everyone involved, from the symphony's Chairman of the Board down to the fourth triangle player.

As I said, I am an optimist. I do not think those in charge will ever demand that everything played in their elite edifices of culture must be Top Forty or Pseudo-Rock. Nor do I believe that the *prima ballerina assoluta* will be choreographed with ten thousand repetitions of a limp to fit the syncopation of a broken-down space tractor. Neither do I think that the contrabassoonist will become the virtuoso of the blew-fuse or the blue fugue—or is it Frug?

I am an optimist, although the big band, for example, is a hazardous gamble. Sideman demand enormous salaries, and there are heavy overheads like transportation, orchestrations, copying, commission, and uniforms. Nevertheless, Wayne King still has his waltz audience. Benny Goodman, when he feels like working, gets more money than ever before. Count Basie is the most imitated piano player around, and his band swings like crazy. Woody Herman, Harry James, Buddy Rich, Charlie Barnet, Gerald Wilson, Ray Charles, Thad Jones, Mel Lewis, Guy Lombardo, Freddy Martin, Sammy Kaye, Buddy De Franco, Les and Larry Elgart—they all have bands and they all sound great. They have the courage of their convictions and they are true to their own tonal personalities. George Wein's Newport Jazz Festival and Jimmy Lyon's Monterey Jazz Festival draw SRO audiences. The guys in Hollywood are writing wonderful music. Every country in Europe has great musicians, too, but they're not the kind that get the *big* play.

Maybe I have reason to be an optimist, for our band works fifty-two weeks a year, in Europe, North America, Africa, and the Orient.

A lot of people say the kids dictate the tone of the music today. This is not true. They are told what to listen to, from many directions. "If you want to be In," they're told by other kids who have been brainwashed musicwise, "get with the Big Beat, man!" The policy of most of the radio stations has gone Top Forty, whatever that means. Maybe it has something to do with the record you are complaining about at home, the one the kids keep playing all day.

It just isn't fashionable not to worship the Scorpions, the Ants, or the Ogres. The girl around the corner, whom the boy likes, thinks that the Scorpions, the Ants, and the Ogres are divine. She too has been told what to like. So the boy says to himself, "What difference does it make, so long as I get to hold her hand?" The disc jockey says, "Crazy, baby!" And that settles it.

Yet I have reason to be optimistic, for with all those good musicians graduating from the conservatories, the future has got to be bright. Of course, the same people who say they don't like electrically amplified guitars and basses will often add that they "just love a string section." The basic concern should not be the instrument, but the taste and skill of the person who plays it.

I know a guy who sells a trashy kind of music but wouldn't dream of missing Bernstein's winter season or Fiedler's Tanglewood season.[3] The American listening audience is actually growing more mature every day. I believe the brainwashing will soon subside, because all the brainwashers have become wealthy. Their problem now is that their children, too, have been brainwashed.

So if you're annoyed by the music of today, watch the man who sells it. Follow him. For his kicks, he more than likely goes to listen to the music *you* like. Good music is just around the corner.

[3]Leonard Bernstein (1918–1993), who conducted the Boston Symphony Orchestra, and Arthur Fiedler (1894–1979), who conducted the Boston Pops Orchestra. Tanglewood, in Lenox, Massachusetts, is the Boston Symphony's summer home, where the Boston Pops, which comprises mostly the same players, also performs.

During the 1920s and into the 1930s, the growing importance of phonograph records, the rapid growth of radio, and the advent of talking pictures meant a widely expanded and changing marketplace for popular music. As these formats involved the dissemination of music through performance, not first of all through the printed page, this also transformed the basic ways in which music was introduced into American homes.

Techniques for adding sound to films were developed during the 1920s. *Don Juan*, a pioneering film with operatic music, was put on in New York in 1926. When talking pictures began in ernest the following year, the introduction of popular music was not far behind. *The Broadway Melody*, released in February of 1929 by Metro-Goldwyn-Mayer, was the first "all-talking, all-singing, all-dancing musical."

Reviews in *Variety* (1929)

Grauman's Chinese[1] opened Friday night with "The Broadway Melody" and a Sid Grauman stage presentation of around 80 people that clicked heavily. The premiere take was $5[2] and business was unusually heavy for first five performances, the Saturday midnight show doing close to $3,000. Looks like this one is in for unusually long stay.

*   *   *

"Broadway Melody". . . Trade unanimous in admitting this one a pip; heavy campaign aided send off which beat "Big Parade" in money but not on attendance, due to a slightly higher scale; opened Friday night.[3]

*   *   *

If "Broadway Melody" had a tune there wouldn't be anything to stop it from being another cinema "Fool." As is, there isn't very much that's going to impede it from being a big box-office picture either for $2 in the keys or on a grind. It's the first flash New York has had as to how the studios are going after musical comedy numbers and there's no question of the potent threat to the stage producers. The boys had better lift the body over to this 45th street corner and take a peek at the latest Hollywood menace.

Paradoxically enough, "Broadway Melody," the initial screen musical, is basically going to draw on its story, the performances of its two lead girls and simply the novelty rather than the quality of the interpolated numbers. In the sticks the three-minute inclusion of a natural color first act finale, cameraed through a proscenium arch, may bowl them over. But New York first saw this jazz dancing wedding idea as far back as '14 in "Watch Your Step," maybe before that. They can't startle Manhattan by moving the camera up on a couple of mediocre adagio teams and a tap toe dancer.

The possibilities are what jolt the imagination. This particular interlude classes as just a hint at what's coming. If the talker studios can top the production efforts of the stage and get the camera close enough to make the ensemble seem to be in the same theatre, what's going to happen in Boston between a musical comedy stage at $4.40 and screen at 75¢. . . .

Variety, February 6, 1929: 8; February 13, 1929: 9, 13.

[1]Grauman's Chinese theater in Hollywood.

[2]That is, $5 per ticket.

[3]At the Astor Theater, New York.

"Broadway Melody" has everything a silent picture should have outside of its dialog. A basic story with some sense to it, action, excellent direction, laughs, a tear, a couple of great performances and plenty of sex. It's the fastest moving talker that's come in, regardless of an anti-climax, with some of the stuff so flip and quick that when the capacity gets over 2,000 they may not catch everything. It's perfectly set at the Astor. And will it get dough around the country. Plenty.

Oklahoma! opened on March 31, 1943, during a season that saw business booming on Broadway despite the fighting in World War II. *Variety* predicted that the show would become one of the best moneymakers in the musical field in a generation. The libretto, by Oscar Hammerstein II, featured simple and direct lyrics that were matched by the poignant music of Richard Rodgers as together they told a sentimental tale of a bygone America. The production, which won high critical praise, ran for 2,248 performances in New York, yielding its backers a rich return on their investment. It also enhanced dramatically the careers of several artists, including Celeste Holm, Alfred Drake, and the choreographer Agnes de Mille.

Oklahoma! changed the course of American musical theater. Instead of a string of interchangeable songs loosely hung on a threadbare plot, the show offered a new cohesiveness and seriousness of purpose as it presented three-dimensional characters more typical of plays than of musicals. It also started a tradition of original-cast recordings.

Oklahoma! tapped into the American psyche at a critical point when the world was suffering under the horrors of war. Its open-air, back-to-our-roots spirit, its homey sentimentality, its view of America from the wide-open western spaces as seen through the eyes of common folk, and above all, its optimistic outlook, provided a comforting and much-needed vision of America.

LEWIS NICHOLS

Review of *Oklahoma!* (1943)

For years they have been saying the Theatre Guild is dead, words that obviously will have to be eaten with breakfast this morning. Forsaking the sometimes somber tenor of her ways, the little lady of Fifty-second Street last evening danced off into new paths and brought to the St. James a truly delightful musical play called "Oklahoma!" Wonderful is the nearest adjective, for this excursion of the Guild combines a fresh and infectious gayety, a

charm of manner, beautiful acting, singing and dancing, and a score by Richard Rodgers which doesn't do any harm either, since it is one of his best.

"Oklahoma!" is based on Lynn Riggs's saga of the Indian Territory at the turn of the century, "Green Grow the Lilacs," and, like its predecessor, it is simple and warm. It relies not for a moment on Broadway gags to stimulate an appearance of comedy, but goes winningly on its way with Rouben Mamoulian's best direction to point up its sly humor, and with some of Agnes de Mille's most

Lewis Nichols, "Oklahoma!" *New York Times*, April 1, 1943:
27.

inspired dances to do so further.[1] There is more comedy in one of Miss de Mille's gay little passages than in many of the other Broadway tom-tom beats together. The Guild has known what it is about in pursuing talent for its new departure.

Mr. Rodgers's scores never lack grace, but seldom have they been so well integrated as this for "Oklahoma!" He has turned out waltzes, love songs, comic songs and a title number which the State in question would do well to seize as an anthem forthwith.[2] "Oh, What a Beautiful Morning," and "People Will Say" are headed for countless juke-boxes across the land, and a dirge called "Pore Jud"—in which the hero of the fable tries to persuade his rival to hang himself—is amazingly comic. "The Farmer and the Cowman" and "The Surry with the Fringe on the Top" also deserve mention only because they quite clearly approach perfection; no number of the score is out of place or badly handled. The orchestrations are by Russell Bennett, who knows his humor and has on this occasion let himself go with all the laughter he can command.[3]

To speak and sing the words—Oscar Hammerstein 2d contributed the book and lyrics—the play has an excellent collection of players, none of whom yet is world-famous. Alfred Drake and Joan Roberts as the two leading singers are fresh and engaging; they have clear voices and the thought that the audience might also like to hear Mr. Hammerstein's poetry. Joseph Buloff is marvelous as the peddler who ambles through the evening selling wares from French cards to Asiatic perfume—and avoiding matrimony. Howard da Silva, Lee Dixon, Celeste Holm and Ralph Riggs are some of the others, and Katharine Sergava and Mark Platt are two of the important dancers. Possibly in addition to being a musical play, "Oklahoma!" could be called a folk operetta; whatever it is, it is very good.

---

[1]Mamoulian also directed *Porgy and Bess* in 1935; choreographer Agnes de Mille (1905–1993) also created the ballet *Rodeo*, with music by Aaron Copland.

[2]*Oklahoma!* became the Oklahoma state song in 1953.

---

[3]Robert Russell Bennett (1894–1981) was a popular composer, arranger, orchestrator, and conductor.

Elliott Carter, born in New York City in 1908, was educated at Harvard University and in Paris. His background emphasized mathematics and the humanities, particularly Latin and Greek, as well as music. His teaching career took him to St. John's College in Annapolis, the Peabody Conservatory in Baltimore, Columbia, Yale, Juilliard, and Cornell. His numerous awards and prizes brought him Pulitzer Prizes for both his Second and Third String Quartets. In 1985, President Reagan awarded him the National Medal of Arts.

Carter began his compositional life as a neoclassicist and then gravitated toward more complex atonal structures. Like many of his contemporaries, he absorbed the principles of serial technique but moved beyond them in his own particular way, following his own logical necessity as he conceived it and drawing frequent inspiration from his wide knowledge of classic literature. This part led him to write complex scores of real individuality. He developed what he called "metric modulation," which frees speed from regular meter in complex but smooth and logical ways. Instruments in his larger works, such as the *Variations for Orchestra* (1955) and the *Double Concerto for Harpsichord and Piano with Two Chamber Orchestras* (1961), assume their own personalities, characters, and rhythmic independence while presenting their special material alone or simultaneously. In his Second and Fourth String Quartets (1959 and 1986), each instrument likewise assumes its own individual profile.

Carter regards his scores as scenarios, with the players individual participants in the ensemble. A statement of his in *Newsweek*, January 16, 1967, is reminiscent of Milton Babbitt's article "Who Cares If You Listen?" (See No. 100): "I harbored the Populist idea of writing for the public. I learned the public didn't care. So I decided to write for myself." He added ironically that "since then people have gotten interested."

ALLEN EDWARDS

from *Flawed Words and Stubborn Sounds: A Conversation with Elliott Carter* (1971)

Was there a specific instance that decided you on composing?

I can't give a date, but certainly *The Rite of Spring* was a very important and meaningful work, as were several of the works of Varèse like *Intégrales* and *Octandre*, and certainly the later works of Scriabin, particularly *Le Poème de l'extase*, *Prométhée*, and the last preludes and sonatas, as well as Ives's *Concord Sonata* and some of his songs.[1] They were all very exciting and beautiful to me, and it was as a result of hearing and thinking about them that I decided to try composing.

Allen Edwards, *Flawed Words and Stubborn Sounds: A Conversation with Elliott Carter* (New York: W. W. Norton, 1971), 45, 77, 80–81, 83, 90–92, 100–101, 102, 121–122.

[1]Carter knew Ives well.

*   *   *

. . . [I]t would be interesting to know how you feel about your own relation to what is called "musical tradition." . . .

It seems to me that tradition provides not only a way of carrying on but also a way of turning away. People not basically aware of the tradition by which they are automatically conditioned are always the most acutely traditional—in just the pejorative sense they are so painfully anxious to avoid. I realize that what I am trying to do in music always remains in a "restricted frame," in that I try to write music that will appeal to an intelligent listener's ear and will be a strong enough expression so that the listener will be drawn to hear and grasp this music when it is presented by a performer who finds it gratifying enough to play effectively. It may take many years for the listener to be convinced, but I believe that my training and experience as a composer enable me to prejudge a possible future listener. In my opinion, the idea of writing a piece of music that no listener would ever be able to understand or enjoy is utterly incomprehensible. I sometimes hear others' music that I think to be of this sort, but later come to understand it; in other cases I continue to be mystified even after many hearings. And finally in these cases I begin to wonder what kind of composer is behind this, since there seems to be a willful desire to be unintelligible forever. And though this is to some degree understandable in terms of the "literary" movements that surround us, I find it utterly alien to my own conception of the nature and purpose of music, whether one wants to call this purpose traditional or something else.

*   *   *

What you are talking about has to do with a long historical debate on the nature of order and meaning in works of musical art in particular, one side of which insists on essentially mechanical criteria, the other on what might be called "psychological" or "dramatic" criteria, for lack of better terms. . . .

It's obvious that the real order and meaning of music is the one the listener *hears* with his ears. Whatever occult mathematical orders may exist on paper are not necessarily relevant to this in the

least. Now it's true that in writing my own works I sometimes try quasi-"geometric" things in order to cut myself off from habitual ways of thinking about particular technical problems and to place myself in, so to speak, new terrain, which forces me to look around and find new kinds of ideas and solutions I might not have thought of otherwise. Nonetheless, if what I come up with by these methods is unsatisfactory from the point of view of what I think is interesting to *hear*, I throw it out without a second thought.

Now in the case of certain types of serialism one is clearly dealing with an essentially visual-mechanical kind of "logic," which does not insure its being audibly perceptible or its conveying any musical meaning through its structure. And it is certainly a question whether the "logic" of a mechanically-ordered system of pitch and durational successions can be made to produce a psychological effect on the listener consistent in detail with the composer's expressive intentions. It thus seems to me that the serial system requires a great deal more manipulation than is often realized if a composer is to write a more or less consistently effective piece. What happens is that the system itself gets to be so intricate that it begins to usurp the attention that should be spent on making musical statements and devising whole continuities of these. On this matter of continuity, serialism gives only the simplest kind of schematic information.

*   *   *

Total serialism . . . invades every dimension of the musical rhetoric and predictably produces disastrous results, from any artistic standpoint, in the vast majority of cases. It's as if one were to make a statistical abstract of meteorological data over a certain period and proceed to construct a building on the basis of the figures thus obtained—and then attempt to justify a particularly chaotic jutting of the wall of the building on the grounds that the wind velocity was over 150 miles per hour on February 23, or some such nonsense. This kind of thing may *by chance* occasionally produce an interesting event or texture in music, but the musical interest of this event or texture will be independent of the method by which it was cooked up, just as the vast majority of textures and events concocted by these methods are musically null, though products of equally ingenious number games.

Thus the only thing to be said for total serialism is that, as a method of producing sound patterns that were never heard or thought of before, it has occasionally contributed to the expansion of the composers' available vocabulary. However, the criteria of musical sense, according to which such material can be effectively put to work in an actual piece, have nothing to do with the kind of mechanical thinking and procedure by which this kind of material is often first arrived at. In my opinion many composers have not been sufficiently aware of this.

*   *   *

In pointing here, as you do, to the role of "the sense of musical motion" in constituting the coherence of a musical continuity, you raise questions about the relation of music to time. . . .
Any technical or esthetic consideration of music really must *start* with the matter of time. The basic problem has always been that analysts of music tend to treat its elements as static rather than as what they are—that is, *transitive* steps from one formation in time to another. All the materials of music have to be considered in relation to their projection in time, and by time, of course, I mean not visually measured "clock-time," but the medium through which (or way in which) we perceive, understand, and experience events. Music deals with this experiential kind of time, and its vocabulary must be organized by a musical syntax that takes direct account of, and thus can play on, the listener's "time-sense" (which in my opinion is a more illuminating way of referring to the "psychology of musical hearing).

This began to seem important to me around 1944, when I suddenly realized that, at least in my own education, people had always been consciously concerned only with this or that peculiar local rhythmic combination or sound-texture or novel harmony and had forgotten that the really interesting thing about music is the time of it—the way it all goes along. Moreover, it struck me that, despite the newness and variety of the post-tonal

musical vocabulary, most modern pieces generally "went along" in an all-too-uniform way on their higher architectonic levels. That is, it seemed to me that, while we had heard every imaginable kind of harmonic and timbral combination, and while there had been a degree of rhythmic innovation on the *local* level in the music of Stravinsky, Bartók, Varèse, and Ives particularly, nonetheless the way all this went together at the next higher and succeeding higher rhythmic levels remained in the orbit of what had begun to seem to me the rather limited rhythmic routine of previous Western music. This fact began to bother me enough so that I tried to think in larger-scale time-continuities of a kind that would be still convincing and yet at the same time *new* in a way commensurate with, and appropriate to, the richness of the modern musical vocabulary. This aim led me to question all the familiar methods of musical presentation and continuation—the whole so-called musical logic based on the statement of themes and their development. In considering constant change-process-evolution as music's prime factor, I found myself in direct opposition to the static repetitiveness of much early twentieth-century music, the squared-off articulation of the neoclassics, and indeed much of what is written today in which "first you do this for a while, then you do that." I wanted to mix up the "this" and the "that" and make them interact in other ways than by linear succession. Too, I questioned the inner shape of the "this" and the "that"—of local musical ideas—as well as their degree of linking and non-linking. Musical discourse, it became obvious to me, required as thorough a rethinking as harmony had been subjected to at the beginning of the century.

Now concretely, in the course of thinking about all of this, I once again—after many years' hiatus—took up interest in Indian *talas*, the Arabic *durub*, the "tempi" of Balinese *gamelans* (especially the accelerating *gangsar* and *rangkep*), and studied newer recordings of African music, that of the Watusi people in particular. At the same time the music of the early *quattrocento*, of Scriabin, and Ives, and the "hypothetical" techniques described in Cowell's *New Musical Resources* also furnished me with many ideas. The result in my own music was, first of all, the way of evolving rhythms and continuities now called "metric modulation," which I worked out during the composition of my Cello Sonata of 1948.[2] Now while, as I say, my thinking about musical time was stimulated by a consideration of, among other things, different kinds of rhythmic devices found in non-Western music such as I have mentioned. I feel it is important to point out that these devices interested me as suggestions of many syntactical possibilities that would participate in a very rich and varied large-scale rhythmic continuity such as is *never* found in non-Western music, but *is* suggested by some aspects of Western classical music, starting with Haydn especially. This aim of mine is something very different from that of many European composers who have been influenced by non-Western music and who have tended to be interested in exotic rhythmic devices as "things in themselves" —as local ideas more or less immediately transposable into a (usually) extremely conventional and uninteresting overall rhythmic framework derived from the simplest aspects of older Western music and only slightly more varied than that of the exotic music from which the local ideas have been borrowed. As far as I am concerned, on the contrary, what contemporary music needs is not just

raw materials of every kind but a way of relating these—of having them evolve during the course of a work in a sharply meaningful way; that is, what is needed is never just a string of "interesting passages," but works whose central interest is constituted by the way everything that happens in them happens *as* and *when* it does in relation to everything else.

* * *

What began to interest me was the possibility of a texture in which, say, massive vertical sounds would be entirely composed of simultaneous elements having a direct and individual horizontal relation to the whole progress or history of the piece—that is, simultaneous elements, each of which has its own way of leading from the previous moment to the following one, maintaining its identity as part of one of a number of distinct, simultaneously evolving, contributory thought-processes or musical characters. Hence I began as early as 1944, in works like my *Holiday Overture*, to think in terms of simultaneous streams of different things going on together, rather than in terms of the usual categories of counterpoint and harmony.

In trying to deal with this idea in a viable way I've used many different methods—such as producing a texture of musical layers or streams in which the progression of one is slow and another fast, or in which one is very spasmodic and another very continuous, and so on; sometimes, in fact, the total motion of the piece is derived directly from this idea of simultaneously interacting heterogeneous character-continuities, as in my Second String Quartet.

* * *

[I]n my Concerto for Orchestra there is a vertical division into four main character-movements, which are all going on simultaneously, each one successively fading in and out of prominence relative to the others. This fading into and out of highlight provides a kind of "close-up" of elements that contribute to a total effect, and which are thus, as it were, picked out of a welter of things and contemplated carefully while the welter continues to press in on them, and gives them, "dialectically," a special new meaning.

---

[2]There is nothing new about metric modulation but the name. To limit brief mention of its derivations to notated Western music: it is implicit in the rhythmic procedures of late fourteenth-century French music, as it is in music of the fifteenth and sixteenth centuries that uses hemiola and other ways of alternating meters, especially duple and triple. From then on, since early sets of variations like those of Byrd and Bull started a tradition of establishing tempo relationships between movements, metric modulation began to relate movements of one piece together, as can be seen in many works of Beethoven, not only in the variations of Op. 111, but in many places where *doppio movimento* and other terms are used to indicate tempo relationships. In fact, at that very time, the metronome was invented, which establishes relationships between all tempi. In our time, Stravinsky, following Satie, perhaps, wrote a few works around 1920 whose movements were closely linked by a very narrow range of tempo relationships, and much later Webern did the same. [Carter's note.]

*   *   *

As has often been said, modern composition often seems to be no longer a public art, since in most places—certainly in America—the public is no longer held together by a consensus about what culture is or what its value can be unless it is "sold" this continually by the mass media, which rarely happens for serious music since it is commercially unprofitable. So the composer is left to his private world more than ever before, to follow whatever seems important to him. His music is highly unlikely to seem very important to many others—perhaps to some colleagues and some of a small public. If he is lucky like Bartók or Ives, he will be recognized by a larger group posthumously, but who can count on the future? But it is just because of these things that the field of composition is so interesting and such an adventure today, since it puts such a special burden on the composer alone. He is freer to write what he likes here at present than he has been in many centuries or even at the present time in Europe, let alone the Soviet Union, and freer than in any Oriental country, where patterns of each traditional music are so constricting and the new is often accepted uncritically as part of the march forward toward "modern civilization." Of course, as I have said several times, the social and economic censorship of serious, new American musical efforts prevents these from ever reaching a large public, unless a newsworthy gimmick is found.

Viewed in another way, music does have one advantage over almost all other human activities that may be important for the future. It keeps people active, busy, productive, and stimulated imaginatively, without harmful or especially wearing physical effects on them, and it produces no physical residue or pollution. It passes the time, rewarding with a wealth of civilizing (sometimes not so civilizing) experiences, helping us to envision qualities of life and social cooperation that seem to many worth striving for. When machines put us all out of work and we are all on welfare with nothing to do, it may come in handy for those who like to be active.

100   Milton Babbitt and the American Avant-Garde

Traditionally, the American concert hall has favored music that could be characterized as conservative. The academic world and certain innovative concert series that avoided commercial restraints, could pursue the avant-garde and indeed have provided a home for its composers and advocates. The middle decades of the twentieth century proved no different, as avant-garde works were still being ignored in the concert world, to the dismay of many composers and theorists.

Milton Babbitt addressed this concern head-on in a 1958 article—titled, it must be stressed, by the magazine in which the piece first appeared—"Who Cares If You Listen?" Babbitt's suggested titles, "The Composer as Specialist" and "The Composer as Anachronism," would have fit perfectly well, and neither would have led to the kind of angry response that the supplied title still provokes some two generations later.

Babbitt, born in 1916, has spent most of his career in academic positions, primarily at Princeton University, where he taught mathematics before switching to music in 1948. He has also taught at Columbia University and the Juilliard School. He was awarded a special citation from the Pulitzer Committee in 1982 for "his life's work as a distinguished and seminal American composer."

In his compositions, he moved away from the twelve-tone serialism of Schoenberg, Berg, and Webern to explore a new world of total serialism, wherein not only pitch but note values, time intervals, dynamic levels, and even instrumental timbres are brought under serial control. The scene was right for this innovation in the 1940s, when Babbitt wrote his *Three Compositions for Piano* (1947). Composers in Europe were experimenting along the same lines: Olivier Messiaen in his *Quatre Études de Rhythme*, No. 2 and his *Mode de valeurs et d'intensités* (1949), and Pierre Boulez in his Second Piano Sonata (1948).

As Babbitt moved increasingly toward total composer control, it seems only logical that he would be drawn to the music technology being developed after World War II. New works in Europe and America explored electronics during the 1950s: Edgard Varèse's *Déserts* (1954), probably the earliest major composition created on tape; Karlheinz Stockhausen's *Gesang der Jünglinge* (1956); and John Cage's *Fontana Mix* (1958). Babbitt's work at the Columbia-Princeton Electronic Music Center soon resulted in his *Composition for Synthesizer* (1961), *Vision and Prayer*, song for soprano (Bethany Beardslee) and synthesized magnetic tape (1961), *Ensembles for Synthesizer* (1964), and *Philomel* for voice and magnetic tape (1964). During the 1980s, Babbitt veered away from the use of electronics.

MILTON BABBITT

"Who Cares If You Listen?" (1958)

This article might have been entitled "The Composer as Specialist" or, alternatively, and perhaps less contentiously, "The Composer as Anachronism." For I am concerned with stating an attitude towards the indisputable facts of the status and condition of the composer of what we will, for the moment, designate as "serious," "advanced," contemporary music. This composer expends an enormous amount of time and energy—and, usually, considerable money—on the creation of a commodity which has little, no, or negative commodity value. He is, in essence, a "vanity" composer. The general public is largely unaware of and uninterested in his music. The majority of performers shun it and resent it. Consequently, the music is little performed, and then primarily at poorly attended concerts before an audience consisting in the main of fellow professionals. At best, the music would appear to be for, of, and by specialists.

Towards this condition of musical and societal "isolation," a variety of attitudes has been expressed, usually with the purpose of assigning blame, often to the music itself, occasionally to critics or performers, and very occasionally to the public. But to assign blame is to imply that this isolation is unnecessary and undesirable. It is my contention that, on the contrary, this condition is not only inevitable, but potentially advantageous for the composer and his music. From my point of view, the composer would do well to consider means of realizing, consolidating, and extending the advantages.

The unprecedented divergence between contemporary serious music and its listeners, on the one hand, and traditional music and its following, on the other, is not accidental and—most probably—not transitory. Rather, it is a result of a half-

century of revolution in musical thought, a revolution whose nature and consequences can be compared only with, and in many respects are closely analogous to, those of the mid-nineteenth-century revolution in mathematics and the twentieth-century revolution in theoretical physics. The immediate and profound effect has been the necessity for the informed musician to reexamine and probe the very foundations of his art. He has been obliged to recognize the possibility, and actuality, of alternatives to what were once regarded as musical absolutes. He lives no longer in a unitary musical universe of "common practice," but in a variety of universes of diverse practice.

This fall from musical innocence is, understandably, as disquieting to some as it is challenging to others, but in any event the process is irreversible; and the music that reflects the full impact of this revolution is, in many significant respects, a truly "new" music. Apart from the often highly sophisticated and complex constructive methods of any one composition, or group of compositions, the very minimal properties characterizing this body of music are the sources of its "difficulty, "unintelligibility," and—isolation. In indicating the most general of these properties, I shall make reference to no specific works, since I wish to avoid the independent issue of evaluation. The reader is at liberty to supply his own instances; if he cannot (and, granted the condition under discussion, this is a very real possibility), let him be assured that such music does exist.

First. This music employs a tonal vocabulary which is more "efficient" than that of the music of the past, or its derivatives. This is not necessarily a virtue in itself, but it does make possible a greatly increased number of pitch simultaneities, successions, and relationships. This increase in efficiency necessarily reduces the "redundancy" of the language, and as a result the intelligible communication of the work demands increased accuracy from

Milton Babbitt, "Who Cares If You Listen?" *High Fidelity Magazine*, (February 1958): 38–40, 126–27.

the transmitter (the performer) and activity from the receiver (the listener). Incidentally, it is this circumstance, among many others, that has created the need for purely electronic media of "performance." More importantly for us, it makes ever heavier demands upon the training of the listener's perceptual capacities.

Second. Along with this increase of meaningful pitch materials, the number of functions associated with each component of the musical event also has been multiplied. In the simplest possible terms, each such "atomic" event is located in a five-dimensional musical space determined by pitch-class, register, dynamic, duration, and timbre. These five components not only together define the single event, but, in the course of a work, the successive values of each component create an individually coherent structure, frequently in parallel with the corresponding structures created by each of the other components. Inability to perceive and remember precisely the values of any of these components results in a dislocation of the event in the work's musical space, an alteration of its relation to all other events in the work, and—thus—a falsification of the composition's total structure. For example, an incorrectly performed or perceived dynamic value results in destruction of the work's dynamic pattern, but also in false identification of other components of the event (of which this dynamic value is a part) with corresponding components of other events, so creating incorrect pitch, registral, timbral, and durational associations. It is this high degree of "determinacy" that most strikingly differentiates such music from, for example, a popular song. A popular song is only very partially determined, since it would appear to retain its germane characteristics under considerable alteration of register, rhythmic texture, dynamics, harmonic structure, timbre, and other qualities.

The preliminary differentiation of musical categories by means of this reasonable and usable criterion of "degree of determinacy" offends those who take it to be a definition of qualitative categories, which—of course—it need not always be. Curiously, their demurrers usually take the familiar form of some such "democratic" counterdefinition as: "There is no such thing as 'serious' and 'popular' music. There is only 'good' and 'bad' music." As a public service, let me offer those who still patiently await the revelation of the criteria of Absolute Good an alternative criterion which possesses, at least, the virtue of immediate and irrefutable applicability: "There is no such thing as 'serious' and 'popular' music. There is only music whose title begins with the letter 'X,' and music whose title does not."

Third. Musical compositions of the kind under discussion possess a high degree of contextuality and autonomy. That is, the structural characteristics of a given work are less representative of a general class of characteristics than they are unique to the individual work itself. Particularly, principles of relatedness, upon which depends immediate coherence of continuity, are more likely to evolve in the course of the work than to be derived from generalized assumptions. Here again greater and new demands are made upon the perceptual and conceptual abilities of the listener.

Fourth, and finally. Although in many fundamental respects this music is "new," it often also represents a vast extension of the methods of other musics, derived from a considered and extensive knowledge of their dynamic principles. For, concomitant with the "revolution in music," perhaps even an integral aspect thereof, has been the development of analytical theory, concerned with the systematic formulation of such principles to the end of greater efficiency, economy, and understanding. Compositions so rooted necessarily ask comparable knowledge and experience from the listener. Like all communication, this music presupposes a suitably equipped receptor. I am aware that "tradition" has it that the lay listener, by virtue of some undefined, transcendental faculty, always is able to arrive at a musical judgment absolute in its wisdom if not always permanent in its validity. I regret my inability to accord this declaration of faith the respect due its advanced age.

Deviation from this tradition is bound to dismiss the contemporary music of which I have been talking into "isolation." Nor do I see how or why the situation should be otherwise. Why should the layman be other than bored and puzzled by what he is unable to understand, music or anything else? It is only the translation of this boredom and puzzlement into resentment and denunciation that seems to me indefensible. After all, the public does have its own music, its ubiquitous music: music to eat by, to read by, to dance by, and to be impressed by. Why refuse to recognize the possibility that contemporary music has reached a stage long since attained by other forms of activity? The time has passed when the normally well-educated man without special preparation could understand the most advanced work in, for example, mathematics, philosophy, and physics. Advanced music, to the extent that it reflects the knowledge and originality of the informed composer, scarcely can be expected to appear more intelligible than these arts and sciences to the person whose musical education usually has been even less extensive than his background in other fields. But to this, a double standard is invoked, with the words "music is music," implying also that "music is *just* music." Why not, then, equate the activities of the radio repairman with those of the theoretical physicist, on the basis of the dictum that "physics is physics"? It is not difficult to find statements like the following, from the *New York Times* of September 8, 1957: "The scientific level of the conference is so high . . . that there are in the world only 120 mathematicians specializing in the field who could contribute." Specialized music on the other hand, far from signifying "height" of musical level, has been charged with "decadence," even as evidence of an insidious "conspiracy."

It often has been remarked that only in politics and the "arts" does the layman regard himself as an expert, with the right to have his opinion heard. In the realm of politics he knows that this right, in the form of a vote, is guaranteed by fiat. Comparably, in the realm of public music, the concertgoer is secure in the knowledge that the amenities of concert going protect his firmly stated "I didn't like it" from further scrutiny. Imagine, if you can, a layman chancing upon a lecture on "Pointwise Periodic Homeomorphisms." At the conclusion, he announces: "I didn't like it." Social conventions

being what they are in such circles, someone might dare inquire: "Why not?" Under duress, our layman discloses precise reasons for his failure to enjoy himself; he found the hall chilly, the lecturer's voice unpleasant, and he was suffering the digestive aftermath of a poor dinner. His interlocutor understandably disqualifies these reasons as irrelevant to the content and value of the lecture, and the development of mathematics is left undisturbed. If the concertgoer is at all versed in the ways of musical lifesmanship, he also will offer reasons for his "I didn't like it"—in the form of assertions that the work in question is "inexpressive," "undramatic," "lacking in poetry," etc., etc., tapping that store of vacuous equivalents hallowed by time for: "I don't like it, and I cannot or will not state why." The concertgoer's critical authority is established beyond the possibility of further inquiry. Certainly he is not responsible for the circumstance that musical discourse is a never-never land of semantic confusion, the last resting place of all those verbal and formal fallacies, those hoary dualisms that have been banished from rational discourse. Perhaps he has read, in a widely consulted and respected book on the history of music, the following: "to call him (Tchaikovsky) the 'modern Russian Beethoven' is footless, Beethoven being patently neither modern nor Russian. . . ." Or, the following, by an eminent "nonanalytic" philosopher: "The music of Lourié is an ontological music. . . . It is born in the singular roots of being, the nearest possible juncture of the soul and the spirit. . . ." How unexceptionable the verbal peccadilloes of the average concertgoer appear beside these masterful models. Or, perhaps, in search of "real" authority, he has acquired his critical vocabulary from the pronouncements of officially "eminent" composers, whose eminence, in turn, is founded largely upon just such assertions as the concertgoer has learned to regurgitate. This cycle is of slight moment in a world where circularity is one of the norms of criticism. Composers (and performers), wittingly or unwittingly assuming the character of "talented children" and "inspired idiots" generally ascribed to them, are singularly adept at the conversion of personal tastes into general principles. Music they do not like is "not music," composers whose music they do not like are "not composers."

In search of what to think and how to say it, the layman may turn to newspapers and magazines. Here he finds conclusive evidence for the proposition that "music is music." The science editor of such publications contents himself with straightforward reporting, usually news of the "factual" sciences; books and articles not intended for popular consumption are not reviewed. Whatever the reason, such matters are left to professional journals. The music critic admits no comparable differentiation. He may feel, with some justice, that music which presents itself in the market place of the concert hall automatically offers itself to public approval or disapproval. He may feel, again with some justice, that to omit the expected criticism of the "advanced" work would be to do the composer an injustice in his assumed quest for, if nothing else, public notice and "professional recognition." The critic, at least to this extent, is himself a victim of the leveling of categories.

Here, then, are some of the factors determining the climate of the public world of music. Perhaps we should not have overlooked those pockets of "power" where prizes, awards, and commissions are dispensed, where music is adjudged guilty, not only without the right to be confronted by its accuser, but without the right to be confronted by the accusations. Or those well-meaning souls who exhort the public "just to *listen* to more contemporary music," apparently on the theory that familiarity breeds passive acceptance. Or those, often the same well-meaning souls, who remind the composer of his "obligation to the public," while the public's obligation to the composer is fulfilled, manifestly, by mere physical presence in the concert hall or before a loudspeaker or—more authoritatively—by committing to memory the numbers of phonograph records and amplifier models. Or the intricate social world within this musical world, where the salon becomes bazaar, and music itself becomes an ingredient of verbal canapes for cocktail conversation.

I say all this is not to present a picture of a vir-

tuous music in a sinful world, but to point up the problems of a special music in an alien and inapposite world. And so, I dare suggest that the composer would do himself and his music an immediate and eventual service by total, resolute and voluntary withdrawal from this public world to one of private performance and electronic media, with its very real possibility of complete elimination of the public and social aspects of musical composition. By so doing, the separation between the domains would be defined beyond any possibility of confusion of categories, and the composer would be free to pursue a private life of professional achievement, as opposed to a public life of unprofessional compromise and exhibitionism.

But how, it may be asked, will this serve to secure the means of survival for the composer and his music? One answer is that after all such a private life is what the university provides the scholar and the scientist. It is only proper that the university, which—significantly—has provided so many contemporary composers with their professional training and general education, would provide a home for the "complex," "difficult," and "problematical" in music. Indeed, the process has begun; and if it appears to proceed too slowly, I take consolation in the knowledge that in this respect, too, music seems to be in historically retarded parallel with now sacrosanct fields of endeavor. In E. T. Bell's *Men of Mathematics*,[1] we read: "In the eighteenth century the universities were not the principal centers of research in Europe. They might have become such sooner than they did but for the classical tradition and its understandable hostility to science. Mathematics was close enough to antiquity to be respectable, but physics, being more recent, was suspect. Further, a mathematician in a university of the time would have been expected to put much of his effort on elementary teaching; his research, if any, would have been an unprofitable luxury . . ." A simple substitution of "musical composition" for "research," of "academic" for "classi-

---

[1]Eric Temple Bell, *Men of Mathematics* (New York: Simon and Schuster, 1937), p. 141.

cal," of "music" for "physics," and of "composer" for "mathematician," provides a strikingly accurate picture of the current situation. And as long as the confusion I have described continues to exist, how can the university and its community assume other than that the composer welcomes and courts public competition with the historically certified products of the past, and the commercially certified products of the present?

Perhaps for the same reason, the various institutes of advanced research and the large majority of foundations have disregarded this music's need for means of survival. I do not wish to appear to obscure the obvious differences between musical composition and scholarly research, although it can be contended that these differences are no more fundamental than the differences among the various fields of study. I do question whether these differences, by their nature, justify the denial to music's development of assistance granted these other fields. Immediate "practical" applicability (which may be said to have its musical analogue in "immediate extensibility of a compositional technique") is certainly not a necessary condition for the support of scientific research. And if it be contended that such research is so supported because in the past it has yielded eventual applications, one

can counter with, for example, the music of Anton Webern, which during the composer's lifetime was regarded (to the very limited extent that it was regarded at all) as the ultimate in hermetic, specialized, and idiosyncratic composition; today, some dozen years after the composer's death, his complete works have been recorded by a major record company,[2] primarily—I suspect—as a result of the enormous influence this music has had on the postwar, nonpopular, musical world. I doubt that scientific research is any more secure against predictions of ultimate significance than is musical composition. Finally, if it be contended that research, even in its least "practical" phases, contributes to the sum of knowledge in the particular realm, what possibly can contribute more to our knowledge of music than a genuinely original composition?

Granting to music the position accorded other arts and sciences promises the sole substantial means of survival for the music I have been describing. Admittedly, if this music is not supported, the whistling repertory of the man in the street will be little affected, the concert-going activity of the conspicuous consumer of musical culture will be little disturbed. But music will cease to evolve, and, in that important sense, will cease to live.

---

[2] *Webern: The Complete Music,* recorded under the direction of Robert Craft. Columbia Records K4L-232, c. 1957.

101 John Cage: The Perpetual Process of Artistic Discovery

Poet, philosopher, painter, writer, composer, and mushroom collector John Cage (1912–1992) sought to wake up our minds and ears "to the very life we're living, which is so excellent once one gets one's mind and one's desires out of its way." A great friend of the painter Marcel Duchamp, whose *Nude Descending a Staircase* he greatly admired, a longtime collaborator with the dancer Merce Cunningham whom he met in Seattle in 1938, and an inventor of extraordinary imagination, Cage became a leader of the American avant-garde in music. His works include pieces for conventional instruments, prepared piano, electronic music, and amplified sounds resulting in live electronics. The notation for his music is inventive.

Above all, Cage was associated with the creation and performance of music created through chance operations. His interest in indeterminacy, first pervasive in his *Music of Changes* (1951) for piano, resulted from his study of Indian music, Zen philosophy, and the Chinese oracle book *I Ching*. Works may be aleatoric in composition but determinate in performance, vice versa, or both.

Cage admired an all-white painting by the American artist Robert Rauschenberg, with whom he collaborated on a theatrical event in August 1952 at Black Mountain College in North Carolina. Rauschenberg's painting was an inspiration for Cage's most famous piece, *4'33"*, which was premiered at Woodstock, New York, later that month. The work is divided into movements of specific duration determined by chance operations. The performer sits at a piano (or other instrument) for the duration of the piece but does not play. The "music" thus becomes the ambient sounds of the space in which it is performed.

Indeterminacy, Cage maintained, is an invitation not to anarchy but to freedom. In this regard, his biggest problem was finding "a way to let people be free without their becoming foolish."*

---

*Quoted by Margaret Leng Tan, "John Cage Poses a Few Last Questions," *The New York Times*, August 1, 1993: sec. 2, 34.

JOHN CAGE

"The Future of Music: Credo" (1937; PUB. 1961)

I BELIEVE THAT THE USE OF NOISE
                    Wherever we are, what we hear is mostly noise. When we ignore it, it disturbs us. When we listen to it, we find it fascinating. The sound of a truck at fifty miles per hour. Static between the stations. Rain. We want to capture and control these sounds, to use them not as sound effects but as musical instruments. Every film studio has a library of "sound effects" recorded on film. With a film phonograph it is now possible to control the amplitude and frequency of any one of these sounds and to give to it rhythms within or beyond the reach of the imagination. Given four film phonographs, we can compose and perform a quartet for explosive motor, wind, heartbeat, and landslide.

TO MAKE MUSIC
                    If this word "music" is sacred and reserved for eighteenth- and nineteenth-century instruments, we can substitute a more meaningful term: organization of sound.

WILL CONTINUE AND IN-CREASE UNTIL WE REACH A MUSIC PRODUCED THROUGH THE AID OF ELECTRICAL INSTRUMENTS
                    Most inventors of electrical musical instruments have attempted to imitate eighteenth- and nineteenth-century instruments, just as early automobile designers copied the carriage. The Novachord and the Solovox are examples of this desire to imitate the past rather than construct the future. When Theremin provided an instrument with genuinely new possibilities, Thereminists did their utmost to make the instrument sound like some old instrument, giving it a sickeningly sweet vibrato, and performing upon it; with difficulty, masterpieces from the past. Although the instrument is capable of a wide variety of sound qualities, obtained by the turning of a dial. Thereminists act as censors, giving the public those sounds they think the public will like. We are shielded from new sound experiences.

The special function of electrical instruments will be to provide complete control of the overtone structure of tones (as opposed to noises) and to make these tones available in any frequency, amplitude, and duration.

WHICH WILL MAKE AVAILABLE FOR MUSICAL PURPOSES ANY AND ALL SOUNDS THAT CAN BE HEARD, PHOTOELECTRIC, FILM, AND MECHANICAL MEDIUMS FOR THE SYNTHETIC PRODUCTION OF MUSIC
                    It is now possible for composers to make music directly, without the assistance of intermediary performers. Any design repeated often enough on a sound track is audible. Two hundred and eighty circles per second on a sound track will produce one sound, whereas a portrait of Beethoven repeated fifty times per second on a sound track will have not only a different pitch but a different sound quality.

WILL BE EXPLORED. WHEREAS, IN THE PAST, THE POINT OF DISAGREEMENT HAS BEEN BETWEEN DISSONANCE AND CONSONANCE, IT WILL BE, IN THE IMMEDIATE FUTURE, BETWEEN NOISE AND SO-CALLED MUSICAL SOUNDS.

THE PRESENT METHODS OF WRITING MUSIC, PRINCIPALLY THOSE WHICH EMPLOY HARMONY AND ITS REFERENCE TO PARTICULAR STEPS IN THE FIELD OF SOUND, WILL BE INADEQUATE FOR THE COMPOSER, WHO WILL BE FACED WITH THE ENTIRE FIELD OF SOUND.

John Cage, "The Future of Music: Credo" in *Silence* (Middletown, Conn.: Wesleyan University Press, 1961), 3–6.

The composer (organizer of sound) will be faced not only with the entire field of sound but also with the entire field of time. The "frame" or fraction of a second, following established film technique, will probably be the basic unit in the measurement of time. No rhythm will be beyond the composer's reach.

NEW METHODS WILL BE DISCOVERED, BEARING A DEFINITE RELATION TO SCHOENBERG'S TWELVE-TONE SYSTEM

Schoenberg's method assigns to each material, in a group of equal materials, its function with respect to the group. (Harmony assigned to each material, in a group of unequal materials, its function with respect to the fundamental or most important material in the group.) Schoenberg's method is analogous to a society in which the emphasis is on the group and the integration of the individual in the group.

AND PRESENT METHODS OF WRITING PERCUSSION MUSIC

Percussion music is a contemporary transition from keyboard-influenced music to the all-sound music of the future. Any sound is acceptable to the composer of percussion music; he explores the academically forbidden "non-musical" field of sound insofar as is manually possible.

Methods of writing percussion music have as their goal the rhythmic structure of a composition. As soon as these methods are crystallized into one or several widely accepted methods, the means will exist for group improvisations of unwritten but culturally important music. This has already taken place in Oriental cultures and in hot jazz.

AND ANY OTHER METHODS WHICH ARE FREE FROM THE CONCEPT OF A FUNDAMENTAL TONE.

THE PRINCIPLE OF FORM WILL BE OUR ONLY CONSTANT CONNECTION WITH THE PAST. ALTHOUGH THE GREAT FORM OF THE FUTURE WILL NOT BE AS IT WAS IN THE PAST, AT ONE TIME THE FUGUE AND AT ANOTHER THE SONATA, IT WILL BE RELATED TO THESE AS THEY ARE TO EACH OTHER:

Before this happens, centers of experimental music must be established. In these centers, the new materials, oscillators, turntables, generators, means for amplifying small sounds, film phonographs, etc., available for use. Composers at work using twentieth-century means for making music. Performances of results. Organization of sound for extra-musical purposes (theatre, dance, radio, film).

THROUGH THE PRINCIPLE OF ORGANIZATION OR MAN'S COMMON ABILITY TO THINK.

JOHN CAGE

from "Composition" (1952)

Value judgments are not in the nature of this work[1] as regards either composition, performance, or listening. The idea of relation (the idea:

2) being absent, anything (the idea: 1) may happen. A "mistake" is beside the point, for once anything happens it authentically is.

* * *

And what is the purpose of writing music? One is, of course, not dealing with purposes but dealing with sounds. Or the answer must take the form of paradox: a purposeful purposelessness or a purposeless play. This play, however, is an affirmation

John Cage, from "Composition," part of "Four Musicians at Work," *trans/formation* 1 (1952). Reprinted in *Silence* (Middletown, Conn.: Wesleyan University Press, 1961), 59, 12.

[1] *Music of Changes* and *Imaginary Landscape No. 4.*

of life—not an attempt to bring order out of chaos nor to suggest improvements in creation, but simply a way of waking up to the very life we're living, which is so excellent once one gets one's mind and one's desires out of its way and lets it act of its own accord. . . .

JOHN CAGE

from *Silence* (1961)

THERE IS NO SUCH THING AS SILENCE, GET THEE TO AN ANECHOIC CHAMBER[2] AND HEAR THERE THY NERVOUS SYSTEM IN OPERATION AND HEAR THERE THY BLOOD IN CIRCULATION.

I HAVE NOTHING TO SAY AND I AM SAYING IT.

John Cage, *Silence* (Middletown, Conn.: Wesleyan University Press, 1961), 51.

[2]A room without echoes or reverberations.

STEVEN MONTAGUE

"John Cage at Seventy: An Interview" (1985)

Montague: Most composers like some of their own works better than others or at least feel some are more important than others. Which piece or pieces of yours would you consider the most important?
Cage: Well the most important piece is my silent piece, *4' 33"*.
Montague: That's very interesting. Why?
Cage: Because you don't need it in order to hear it.
Montague: Just a minute, let me think about that a moment.
Cage: You have it all the time. And it can change your mind, making it open to things outside it. It is continually changing. It's never the same twice. In fact, and Thoreau knew this, and it's been known traditionally in India, it is the statement that music is continuous. In India they say: "Music is continuous, it is we who turn away." So whenever you feel in need of a little music, all you have to do is to pay close attention to the sounds around you. I always

think of my silent piece before I write the next piece.
Montague: Where was it first performed?
Cage: In Woodstock, New York, 1952, in a hall quite suitably called the Maverick Hall, which was out in the woods. The back of the hall was open to the forest, and it was performed on a program of piano music given by David Tudor.
Montague: How did you come to compose a piece which is silence?
Cage: I had thought of it already in 1948 and gave a lecture which is not published, and which won't be, called: "A Composer's Confessions." And it was given as a lecture at Vassar College in a course of a festival involving artists and thinkers in all fields. Among those was Paul Weiss, who taught philosophy at Yale University. I was just then in the flush of my early contact with oriental philosophy. It was out of that that my interest in silence naturally developed. I mean it's almost transparent. If you have, as you do in India, nine permanent emotions, and the center one is the one without color—the others are white or black—and tranquility is in the center: freedom from likes and dis-

Steven Montague, "John Cage at Seventy: an Interview," *American Music*, (Summer 1985): 213–14.

likes. It stands to reason the absence of activity, which is also characteristically Buddhist . . . well, if you want the wheel to stop, and the wheel is the Four Noble Truths: the first is "Life is Activity," sometimes translated "Life is Pain." If the wheel is to be brought to a stop, the activity must stop. The marvelous thing about it is when activity comes to a stop, what is immediately seen is that the rest of the world has not stopped. There is no place without activity. Oh there are so many ways to say it. Say I die as a person. I continue to live as a landscape for smaller animals. I just never stop. Just put me in the ground, and I become part and par-cel of another life, another activity. So the only difference between activity and inactivity is in the mind. And the mind that becomes free of desire, Joyce would agree here, free of desire and loathing—that's why he said he was so involved with comedy, because tragedy is not free from these two. So when the mind has become in that way free, even though there continues some kind of activity, it can be said to be inactivity. And that's what I have been doing, and that's why the critics are so annoyed with my work. Because they see that I am denying the things to which they are devoted.

102   An Underground Look
at Rock

The 1960s were born amid high unemployment and great turmoil over civil rights. The aborted Bay of Pigs invasion was followed by a brutal escalation of the conflict in Vietnam. It was a time of campus protests, draft card burnings, and the assassination in 1963 of John F. Kennedy, which galvanized the nation and brought his New Frontier to an abrupt end. Lyndon Johnson's Great Society, though it declared a "war on poverty" and enacted civil rights legislation and school desegregation, did not calm the unrest. Young people across the nation were disillusioned with the world they were inheriting from their parents.

On March 11, 1966, the *Berkeley Barb* published what amounted to an obituary for rock and roll. On its coattails, new styles were struggling to life: rock, folk rock, acid rock. The Haight-Ashbury district in San Francisco, a center of the rock scene, was born out of the reemergence of the beat poets, coupled with new "hippie" values. Handbills for a big, three-day Trips Festival in January 1966 proclaimed, "Maybe this is the rock revolution!"* As the news spread across the country, the movement's ranks began to swell. "Like, Wow! There was an explosion. People began coming in from all over," said Jay Thelin, co-owner with his brother Ron of the Psychedelic Shop, a hive of activity. These were alienated young people, not so much playing out a scene of active protest, but searching for values through community. Community pads, love, sex, drugs, and acid rock were all part of the scene.

The community sought to live out Ken Kesey's philosophy of social protest. "The true meaning of psychedelics," said Kesey, "is to know all the conditioned responses of men and then to prank them. This is the surest way to get them to ask questions, and until they ask questions they are going to remain conditioned robots."

Musically, the district was represented by a variety of groups, sporting such names as Jefferson Airplane, the Doors, Quicksilver Messenger Service, and Big Brother and the Holding Company. Jerry Garcia of the Grateful Dead commented, "I hope that humanity survives the incredibly stupid hassles that we've gotten ourselves into."

The heyday of Haight-Ashbury proved short; the revolution faltered and moved away. Contributing to the breakup of the movement were business exploitation and gangsterism in the district, the disastrous effects of drug use, record companies' marketing of the psychedelic sound, and the blending of sexual openness into the American mainstream. When the Psychedelic Shop closed on October 4, 1967, the sign on the door read, "Be Free—Nebraska Needs You More."

---

*This quotation and the next are from David Szatmary, *Rockin' in Time: A Social History of Rock and Roll* (Englewood Cliffs, N.J.: Prentice-Hall, 1987), 112–24; Jerry Garcia is quoted from Jonathan Eisen, ed., *The Age of Rock* (New York: Random House, 1969), 34.

CHESTER ANDERSON

"Notes for the New Geology" (1967)

I

Rock's the first head music we've had since the end of the baroque. By itself, without the aid of strobe lights, day-glo paints & other subimaginative copouts, it engages the entire sensorium, appealing to the intelligence with no interference from the intellect. Extremely typographic people are unable to experience it, which—because TV didn't approach universality till 1950—is why the rock folk are so young, generally. (Most of the astounding exceptions are people, like the poet Walter Lowenfels,[1] who have lived a long time but have not become old.)

II

SOME PRINCIPLES

• That rock is essentially head (or even psychedelic) music.

• That rock is a legitimate avant garde art form, with deep roots in the music of the past (especially the baroque & before), great vitality, and vast potential for growth & development, adaptation, experiment, etcetera.

• That rock shares most of its formal/structural principles with baroque music (wherein lie its most recent cultural roots), and that it & baroque can be judged by the same broad standards (the governing principles being that of mosaic structure of tonal & textural contrast: tactility, collage).

• That rock is evolving Sturgeonesque *homo gestalt*[2] configurations:

- the groups themselves, far more intimately

interrelated & integrated than any comparable ensembles in the past;

- super-families, like Kerista & the more informal communal pads;

- and pre-initiate tribal groups, like the teenyboppers; all in evident & nostalgic response to technological & population pressures.

• That rock is an intensely participational & nontypographic art form, forerunner of something much like McLuhan's covertly projected spherical society.[3]

• That far from being degenerate or decadent, rock is a regenerative & revolutionary art, offering us our first real hope for the future (indeed, for the present) since August 6, 1945,[4] and that its effects on the younger population, especially those effects most deplored by typeheads, have all been essentially good & healthy so far.

• That rock principles are not limited to music, and that much of the shape of the future can be seen in its aspirations today (these being mainly total freedom, total experience, total love, peace & mutual affection).

• That today's teenyboppers will be voting tomorrow and running for office the day after.

• That rock is an intensely synthesizing art, an art of amazing relationships (collage is rock & roll), able to absorb (maybe) all of society into itself as an organizing force, transmuting & reintegrating what it absorbs (as it has so far); and that its practitioners & audience are learning to perceive & manipulate reality in wholly new ways, quite alien to typeheads.

• That rock has reinstated the ancient truth that art is fun.

• That rock is a way of life, international &

Chester Anderson, "Notes for the New Geology," *The San Francisco Oracle*, Vol. 1, February 1967.

[1]Poet, journalist, and anthologist who had been persecuted as a left-wing political activist in the McCarthy era of the early 1950s.

[2]A being described by science fiction writer Theodore Sturgeon (1918–1985) that is made up of many lesser beings.

[3]Marshall McLuhan (1911–1980), Canadian author of *The Medium Is the Message*.

[4]The date the atomic bomb was dropped on Hiroshima, Japan.

verging in this decade on universal; and can't be stopped, retarded, put down, muted, modified or successfully controlled by typeheads, whose arguments don't apply & whose machinations don't mesh because they can't perceive (dig) what rock really is & does.

• That rock is a tribal phenomenon, immune to definition & other typographical operations, and constitutes what might be called a 20th century magic.

• That rock seems to have synthesized most of the intellectual & artistic movements of our time & culture, cross-fertilizing them & forcing them rapidly toward fruition & function.

• That rock is a vital agent in breaking down absolute & arbitrary distinctions.

• That any artistic activity not allied to rock is doomed to preciousness & sterility.

• That group participation, total experience & complete involvement are rock's minimal desiderata and those as well of a world that has too many people.

• That rock is creating the social rituals of the future.

• That the medium is indeed the message, & rock knows what that means.

• That no arbitrary limitations of rock are valid (i.e., that a rock symphony or opera, for example, is possible).

• That rock is handmade, and only the fakes are standardized.

• That rock presents an aesthetic of discovery.

III

Marshall McLuhan makes no sense at all, not as I was taught to define *sense* in my inadequately cynical youth. He's plainly no Aquinas. And yet, somehow, he embarrassingly manages to explain to perfection an overwhelming array of things that used to make even less sense than he does and were somewhat threatening as well: things like pop, op & camp (which sounds like a breakfast food); the psychedelic revolution, the pot & acid explosion; the Haight-Ashbury community, and especially what we'll keep on calling Rock & Roll until we can find some name more appropri-

ate for it. (I nominate Head Music, but I don't expect it to catch on.)

Not that McLuhan mentions any of these things. He simply gives the clues. Synthesis & synaesthesia; non-typographic, non-linear, basically mosaic & mythic modes of perception; involvement of the whole sensorium; roles instead of jobs; participation in depth; extended awareness; preoccupation with textures, with tactility, with multisensory experiences—put 'em all together & you have a weekend on Haight Street.

The electronic extension of the central nervous system, the evolutionary storm that's happening right now (which is having, slowly, exactly the same effect on the whole world as acid has had on us), makes everything else make sense, and McLuhan taught us how to see it. He doesn't *have* to make sense.

IV

We're still so hooked on mainly visual perception that the possibilities of our other senses are almost unimaginable. We still interpret highs in visual terms, for instance: though acid is mainly tactile, spatial, visceral & integrative; whilst pot affects mostly hearing & touch. It's all a matter of conditioning: we'll learn.

The things a really imaginative engineer could accomplish by working on our many senses, singly & in orchestrated combinations, are staggering. Imagine: sensory counterpoint—the senses registering contradictory stimuli & the brain having fun trying to integrate them. Imagine *tasting* G-minor! The incredible synaesthesiae!

Rock & Roll is toying with this notion.

Though we've been brought up to think of music as a purely auditory art, we actually perceive it with the whole body in a complex pattern of sympathetic tensions & interacting stimuli.

Melodies, and especially vocal melodies or tunes in the vocal range, affect the larynx. It follows the tune, subvocalizing. As the line ascends, the larynx tightens, and as the line descends, it relaxes, responding sympathetically to the tension of the tones. (The larynx also tightens in response to strong emotion, just before the tears begin.) That's what makes an unexpected high note such an emotional event, because the part of the brain in charge of such things can't tell one kind of tension from the other. That's also much of what makes melodies work. Whether you want to or not, you participate.

Meanwhile, low notes—especially on the bass, and most acutely if it's plucked & amplified—are experienced in the abdomen as localized vibrations, an amazingly private sensation impossible to resist. The deeper the note, furthermore, the lower down on the trunk it seems to be felt. A properly organized R&R[5] bass line is experienced as a pattern of incredibly intimate caresses: still more unavoidable participation.

(The same visceral perception yields a sense of musical space.)

A steady bass line in scales induces something like confidence and/or well-being. A jagged, syncopated bass can range you from nervous exhilaration to utter frenzy. (Old Bach knew all about this.) The possibilities are next to endless.

Rhythms, meanwhile, affect the heart, skeletal muscles & motor nerves, and can be used to play games with these pretty much at will. Repeated patterns (ostinati) & drones induce an almost instant light hypnosis (just like grass), locking the mind on the music at hand & intensifying all the other reactions. Long, open chords lower the blood pressure: crisp, repeated chords raise it.

And this is only the beginning, the barest outline of our physical response to music, but data enough for me to make my point. An arranger/composer who knew all this, especially if he had electronic instruments to work with, could play a listener's body like a soft guitar. He could score the listener's body as part of the arrangement, creating an intensity of participation many people don't even achieve in sex. (So far this seems to have happened mainly by accident.) And there's no defense but flight: not even the deaf are completely immune.

---

[5]Rock and roll.

103

Rock Criticism:
Lester Bangs and Greil Marcus

Lester (born Leslie) Bangs (1948–1982) started writing for *Rolling Stone* in 1969. Since then, his reviews have appeared in a wide variety of newspapers and magazines, including Detroit's *Creem* and New York's *Village Voice*. After moving to New York in 1976, he began performing as a singer/songwriter with his own groups, and he made two recordings—*Let It Blurt* (1979) and *Jook Savages on the Brazos* (1981). He wrote two "fan" books as well, one in 1980 about the group Blondie and one the following year, *Rod Stewart*, with Paul Nelson. *Psychotic Reactions and Carburetor Dung*, edited by Greil Marcus, was published in 1987. His *Rock Gomorrah: Tales from beyond the Grooves*, completed just before his untimely death, remains in manuscript.

Greil Marcus (1945–) has written frequently for such journals as *Interview* and *Artforum*. A particular devotee of Bob Dylan and Elvis Presley, his books include *Mystery Train: Images of America in Rock 'n' Roll Music* (1975), *Lipstick Traces: A Secret History of the Twentieth Century* (1989), *Dead Elvis: A Chronicle of a Cultural Obsession* (1991), and *Invisible Republic: Bob Dylan's Basement Tapes* (1997).

Rock music in the 1960s made strong, disillusioning statements about social and political issues. Although the musical styles of the genre became more diverse, rock remained true to its inherent rebellious nature. Lester Bangs agrees with Chester Anderson (see No. 102) in believing that rock is "a way of living your life, a way of going about things." Greil Marcus discusses the relationship between rock and politics. The segment picks up with the Nixon presidency, which began in 1969.

LESTER BANGS

from "A Final Chat with Lester Bangs,"
Interview by Jim DeRogatis (PUB. 1999)

Just for posterity, can I have your definition of good rock 'n' roll?

Good rock 'n' roll . . . [Long pause] I don't know. I guess it's just something that makes you feel alive. It's just like, it's something that's human, and I think that most music today isn't. And it's like

Lester Bangs, Interview by Jim DeRogatis, "A Final Chat with Lester Bangs," *Perfect Sound Forever*, parts 2 and 3, November 1999. http://www.furious.com/perfect/lesterbangs.html

anything that I would want to listen to is made by human beings instead of computers and machines. To me, good rock 'n' roll also encompasses other things, like Hank Williams and Charlie Mingus and a lot of things that aren't strictly defined as rock 'n' roll. Rock 'n' roll is like an attitude, it's not a musical form of a strict sort. It's a way of doing things, of approaching things. Like anything can be rock 'n' roll.

It's just like that piece in the liner notes to Velvet

Underground Live 1969, *some of the greatest rock stars were Beethoven, Albert Einstein.*[1]
I don't know about Beethoven or Einstein, but I mean, you just know it when you see it. I mean, writing can be rock 'n' roll or a movie can be rock 'n' roll. It doesn't necessarily have to have anything to do with music. It's just a way of living your life, a way of going about things.

* * *

What do you think about radio today?
I never listen to it. I don't even have any opinion of it, because it's so bad that I don't even bother. I will say this, when Michael [Ochs][2] and I were traveling across country, we traveled like for six weeks to Detroit, Chicago, Nashville, Memphis, Muscle Shoals, and New Orleans, then drove back here. And it feels real weird to be working on a book about rock 'n' roll at a time when radio is so bad that we kept it off most of the time. There was no rock 'n' roll on the trip.
You don't think it's as important a force as it was in the '60s.
I don't think rock 'n' roll is as important a force as it was in the '60s. Rock 'n' roll is getting like jazz used to be—it's big in Europe. Those kids out there, they're concerned about getting good jobs and stuff. They'll go to see Styx and it's like spectacle. It's very much leisure-time activity right now. It's just something to consume.
Do you think there's a danger of rock 'n' roll becoming extinct?
Yeah, sure. Definitely.
What would there be to take its place?
Video games. A lot of things we don't like to think about. . . .

I think that even right now it's like rock 'n' roll doesn't exist. On the one side you have this utterly homogenized margarine, and on the other side you have a bunch of people celebrating total incompetence. The idea of New Wave originally was like do it yourself, and because there's no rules, you come up with something really inventive and creative and good and interesting. Not just saying, "I can't play." Like Brian Eno[3] gets these tapes from assholes that say, "Hi. We can't play our instruments either. Listen to this." He writes them back and says, "Listen, that's not the point." It's not that you're good because you can't play. So I don't know. These days, there's so little that is rock 'n' roll or that has any kind of vitality to it. It's almost like it doesn't exist right now. Don't you feel that way? Are you playing a lot of current stuff? What do you listen to?
New York Dolls and old stuff, I suppose. But I'm a Pink Floyd fan, too.
They're all right. Everybody wants to be so hip and they won't like . . . I had a Grateful Dead album out that I was playing for a while, and people would come in here like this writer from the NME[4] and they'd be like, "Are you listening to the Grateful Dead?" You know what I mean, you're not supposed to say you like something by the Grateful Dead, you're only supposed to like Public Image, Ltd., until somebody else tells you you're not supposed to like that anymore. And that's just shit. I hate that kind of stuff. The NME is like the king of that. They were political for like a year and a half when it was correct to be, and then they were into fashion. Fuck that. You have to go by what you believe in, what you feel. That's the only way anybody ever accomplished anything. I'm sure there'll be some kind of renaissance of rock 'n' roll again as a backlash if anything against all this electronic computer stuff. There'll probably be a backlash of people doing things with acoustic instruments or just the human voice unadorned, a cappella and stuff like that.
I hope not. I'm a drummer and I like loud stuff. Um, what do you think of rock video?

---

[1]The liner note is by Elliott Murphy. Actually, Beethoven is not mentioned as a rock 'n' roll star, but Einstein and others are.

[2]Proprietor of the Michael Ochs Archives, Venice, California.

[3]English-born rock artist Brian Eno (1948–) was a founder-member of Roxy Music. He went on to an important career as a record producer and performing musician. He is an experimenter interested in such cutting edge techniques as tape-looping, the ideas of John Cage, and video installations.

[4]*New Musical Express*, a weekly English journal.

I think it's shit. I was out West not long ago, and I was stuck in Yuma, Arizona, where my sister lives, and I had nothing to do but sit in a trailer all day watch this Music-on-TV, this music station on cable. I sat there and there's Elvis Costello and Styx and Echo and the Bunnymen and Pat Benatar, all the New Wave stuff mixed in with all the Styx and R.E.O.–type stuff and it sucked. It all sucked dogs equally. No good! It's just, also I think there's something about video tape that's intrinsically cold, it lends itself to stuff like soap operas and *Mary Hartman, Mary Hartman.*[5] It's sort of anti–rock 'n' roll right there.

* * *

That's some record collection.

That's the thing. How did I become a rock critic? I started amassing these things in 1958. And you just get more and more of them. More and more and more. It's like all I've ever thought about is music

---

[5] A television series of the 1970s that parodied soap operas.

writing for at least twenty years now. That's what I think about all the time.

When you first started playing, you were a fan of rock 'n' roll and you just thought, "I can do that"? You were self-taught?

I'll say I was self-taught! Sure.

Do you want to imitate your favorite musicians?

Initially, it was sort of like a lark. And then . . . I had things I wanted to do. There are certain ideas that the best way to get them across is in a song. And you can do things with songs, like a lot of my songs are little short stories. I've always been really excited by the whole idea that a song can tell a story and have dialog and all that kind of stuff. Description and set the scene. And that's what I try to do. It's just a matter of finding the right people to do it with.

Yeah, I know. I'm always trying to put together a band.

See one of the advantages of doing the way I do it is that if somebody doesn't feel like they're committed for the rest of their life, you can get somebody that's real good.

GREIL MARCUS

from "Do Politics Rock?" Interview by Billy Bob Hargus (1997)

How do you see that the radical movement, along with the music, changed once the Nixon administration came into power?

The Nixon administration saw as one of its missions to wipe out and destroy dissent in whatever form it occurred. It affected music in two ways. First, it made some people more combative (i.e. the Jefferson Airplane, the Byrds, David Crosby). Ultimately, the world of pop music responded like the rest of the world, which is to say that after Jackson State and Kent State, people got really scared. They found out that you could really get killed by doing this stuff at any time. They began to back off and they began to shut up. What broke the anti-

war movement was that. That was a self-betrayal analogous (in my mind) to teenagers waking up one day and saying "we really do like Tammy better than Arlene Smith (the Chantels)." When people found out that you could die from this, they backed off. It was a lack of a sense of history, intelligence and nerve for people to go into a battle against their own government with the illusion that nobody was going to get hurt.

A few years after this disillusion, the punk movement came along. What do you see as its legacy and how it also became a unique youth movement?

I don't know how to put it or position it. I don't know if punk started out as a rejection of pop music or life in the UK at that time. Certainly, as soon as it started, as soon as the Sex Pistols began to perform as a public outrage and even before they released their first record, a whole conflict of sym-

Greil Marcus, Interview by Billy Bob Hargus, "Greil Marcus: Do Politics Rock?" *Perfect Sound Forever*, June 1997. http://www.furious.com/perfect/marcus.html

bolism immediately gathered and was drawn to what they were doing.[6] None of this was accidental because Malcolm McLaren and Jamie Reid, who were the real college-educated Col. Parkers of this movement, had a Situationist background and were schooled in a haphazard way in nihilist European art politics going all the way back to the nineteenth century. They knew that architecture could be as repressive as a law (that would) put people in jail for criticizing the government. They believed that the music that people heard every day had as much of an effect on how people thought of themselves as anything people learned in school. They saw records as a way to disrupt the assumptions that people didn't question, that people used to hold themselves together. This is to say that these were the assumptions that held society together. I don't think they saw records, performances and songs as a way to change the world as such. It was more of a theft—"let's set off a bomb and see what happens."

Within that perspective, everything was a target. Pink Floyd are no more or no less the enemy than the government. That's the mindset here. This was utterly true for Johnny Rotten as someone who really schooled himself on James Joyce and Graham Greene and his sense of being an outsider because he was Irish and being just astonishingly smart and vehement and impatient. For the other people in the band, I don't think it was ever anything more than a chance to be in a band in the beginning and later what an absolute thrill it was to tell society to go fuck itself. By the time the band was really making records, they were all understanding (except maybe Sid Vicious) what it's about and what it's for. It was a chance, if not to change society, to live a life that you would never expect to live within society. That's not a life of money and fame and girls. That's a life of feeling free and complete and alive. From that, anything can flow.

From that, you get the Clash, an ideological band which really did have political positions. They went out and named the villains and wore political slogans on their clothes (which I think is hilarious in a way but they were great looking costumes). The funny thing about the Clash is that they turned lines that Johnny Rotten threw out in interviews into songs. They worked with received ideas and they were authentically changed by those second-hand ideas. Joe Strummer might have started out mouthing ideological slogans because it seemed like a good idea. But he began to think about the things he was singing and I think he actually decided they were true and they actually got him thinking.

Then of course by the time you get to the mid-'70s in England, the Beats are really a pervasive influence, William Burroughs and [Jack] Kerouac in particular. That sense of autonomy and nihilist rebellion, saying "the dominant society is a bunch of boring old shits and we are true and virile," is really strong. The angelization of the heroin addict is very strong. There's a lot of parallel with that scene.

How did the UK punk scene compare with the one that was going on in the States? Didn't it have any significance itself as a movement?

With the exception of Pere Ubu, I never found the U.S. punk movement all that interesting. I think X was a great band but if they came out of any tradition at all, if they tell a story, it's an L.A. story. In a way, it's a story that's already been told. You find all of X in film noir and Raymond Chandler.[7]

* * *

So you don't see the New York punk scene as having any significance then?

I don't think there's any question that for over twenty years the Ramones have inspired countless people to do all kinds of things. They inspired the Sex Pistols and the Clash. I didn't like them. I always thought they were a bunch of twits. As one of the guys in Gang of Four put it "these guys must be really thick." Gang of Four LOVED the Ramones. They just actually believed that you get past the parody/stupidity and find the real stupidity. Tele-

---

[6]The punk rock movement started in London in about 1975. The Sex Pistols established the new style, which soon merged into New Wave.

[7]American crime fiction writer Raymond Chandler (1888–1959) was influential in developing the film noir genre.

vision was an arty version of the Grateful Dead. To me, it was just a new form of rock and roll. It was all just a downtown New York bohemian scene. It was a local story. I still believe that. This was local music as far as I was concerned. I don't believe that the reason that punk came to life again and again all over the world is due to anything that happened in New York. It was because of the glimpse of possibility that people got out of the Sex Pistols or the Adverts or X-Ray Spex. These were bands where the most unlikely people suddenly appeared in public and said "I can say anything I want," which is the most liberating thing in the world to do. I don't think you ever saw that in New York. What New York said was "you can become a heroin addict and become cooler than anybody else and you can play guitar and be a real poet, and we obviously know that being a poet is the best thing in the world to be."

After the first wave of punk died out, did you find that there were other political movements building up around music or rock in particular?

I don't see a literal connection between bands and youth movements or songs and political activity. Both are forms of discourse, both are different forms of conversation. They inform each other but in ways that are not obvious and in ways that can only be teased out or imagined or churned into stories. I don't have anything to say about, for instance, the connection between the Gang of Four or the Mekons and what they were doing and their effect on what people might be doing politically. If anything, the effect is the other way around because these bands came out of a tremendously politicized milieu where feminism, gay rights, skinheads beating up and killing non-whites was their frame of reference, their everyday life. To make music that in some way didn't incorporate that would be to deny your own experience and knowledge and the things that got you excited, angry or happy or allowed you to make friends. The lines between what you could say in a song and what you said to people you cared about had long since been smashed by Bob Dylan. If you look at the most politicized music that the Mekons made, like *Fear and Whiskey* or *Edge of the World*, the music is

a lament for a battle that's been lost. This is not rallying troops or defining good. This is the kind of art that's often been made after the defeat of a revolt or a rebellion. This is music made as the Mekons understood it in the shadow of fascism. The same with Elvis Costello's music.[8]

Now if that music goes out into the world and hits people's hearts or makes people think the political situation that they perceive isn't as locked in as it appears to be, or if it just makes them think more deeply, the consequences of that can lead in any direction. The Weathermen actually used pop songs as part of their metaphors (they named themselves after a Dylan song). They went underground and set off bombs in strategic places to make sure people wouldn't get killed and they got publicity and made people see that the government is really not in control. Then a few of them got killed making bombs and they thought that maybe their strategy wasn't good after all because "gosh, you can get hurt making bombs." This is the same with "Tammy" and Kent State—this is the naivete that beggars all understanding. It had nothing to do with the validity of the strategy—it was "golly, we can get hurt. Better change our strategy." Their manifesto announcing their new strategy was called NEW MORNING, after a Dylan album. One of the songs in their songbook was an adaption of "Bad Moon Rising"—the only change was "better get your shit together" instead of "better get your things together." You can say that there's a connection between the Weathermen and pop music but I don't think there's a connection at all. I think the connection is utterly meaningless, trivial and exploitive on the part of the Weathermen. It was just a way to look "with it." It's a direct connection but, I think, a meaningless one. The connections between Elvis Presley, Jim Jones and David Koresh are much more interesting.

Do you see that a lot of rock has lost its rebellious nature as it's been used so much in commercials and elsewhere?

---

[8]English rock singer/songwriter Elvis Costello (Declan MacManus, 1954–) has toured and recorded widely.

That depends on your point of view. I think in those places where real rock and roll persists, it might be just as much a threat as it ever was in a way that's mysterious and hard to track. Sleater-Kinney is as inspiring, dangerous and troublesome as any band we've ever seen. What the consequences of their music are going to be is impossible to say.

You're talking about a perception where you say "this doesn't seem like a threat—it's part of mainstream culture." Bill Clinton gets inaugurated and Bob Dylan and Aretha Franklin show up to perform. Every old roclk and roll song is turned into a commercial and rewritten. It's everywhere you look. I don't believe that for a minute. I don't believe that any bite has gone out of "Gimmie Shelter" or "Ready Teddy." I don't believe that "Whole Lotta Shakin' Goin' On" has any less power to change anyone who's heard it for the first time today than it did in 1957.

104

Bill Monroe and
the Blue Grass Boys

Although within the long-standing tradition of southern folk music, bluegrass itself dates back only to 1938, the year in which Kentuckian Bill Monroe (1911–1996) established a new group, the Blue Grass Boys. At that time, Monroe first recorded his trademark song, *The Mule Skinner Blues*. Monroe and his players joined the Grand Ole Opry in Nashville, Tennessee, the following year and made the Opry their base of operations. They made numerous recordings. In 1945, when the Monroe style was flying high, the group was joined by banjo player Earl Scruggs (b. 1924), known for his three-finger style of playing (thumb and first two fingers), and Lester Flatt (1914–1979), guitarist, singer, and master of ceremonies. The musicians played country folk music on acoustic string instruments: guitar, string bass, mandolin, banjo, and fiddle. They also sang (Monroe in a high countertenor). Three years later, Scruggs and Flatt left to start their own group, the Foggy Mountain Boys. Such spread of the Monroe bluegrass style, plus the recordings, served to identify it further in the public consciousness as a new musical genre. Monroe went on to become a central figure in bluegrass festivals of the 1960s.

The two selections below inform us about bluegrass. Folklorist Alan Lomax included bluegrass music in a 1959 concert at Carnegie Hall, New York, called "Folksong '59." Lomax identifies bluegrass as part of a long-standing British-American folk tradition. Ralph Rinzler (1935–1994), an important promoter of bluegrass, was Monroe's manager and agent in the mid-1960s and subsequently founded and directed the Smithsonian Institution's Festival of American Folklife. Rinzler tells us what it was like to travel on the road with Bill Monroe in the mid-1960s and quotes him directly.

ALAN LOMAX

"Bluegrass Background: Folk Music with Overdrive" (1959)

While the aging voices along Tin Pan Alley grow every day more querulous, and jazzmen wander through the harmonic jungles of Schoenberg and Stravinsky, grass-roots guitar and banjo pickers are playing on the heartstrings of America. Out of the torrent of folk music that is the backbone of the record business today, the freshest sound comes from the so-called Bluegrass band—a sort of mountain Dixieland combo in which the five-string banjo, America's only indigenous folk instrument, carries the lead like a hot clarinet. The mandolin plays bursts reminiscent of jazz trumpet choruses; a heavily bowed fiddle supplies trombone-like hoedown solos; while a framed guitar and slapped base [*sic*] make up the rhythm section. Everything goes at top volume, with harmonized choruses behind a lead singer who hollers

Alan Lomax, "Bluegrass Background: Folk Music with Overdrive," *Esquire*, October 1959: 108.

in the high, lonesome style beloved in the American backwoods. The result is folk music in overdrive with a silvery, rippling, pinging sound; the State Department should note that for virtuosity, fire and speed our best Bluegrass bands can match any Slavic folk orchestra.

Bluegrass style began in 1945 when Bill Monroe, of the Monroe Brothers, recruited a quintet that included Earl Scruggs (who had perfected a three-finger banjo style now known as "picking scruggs") and Lester Flatt (a Tennessee guitar picker and singer); Bill led the group with mandolin and a countertenor voice that hits high notes with the impact of a Louis Armstrong trumpet. Playing the old-time mountain tunes, which most hillbilly pros had abandoned, he orchestrated them so brilliantly that the name of the outfit, "Bill Monroe and his Bluegrass Boys," became the permanent hallmark of this field. When Scruggs and Flatt left to form a powerful group of their own, Don Reno joined Monroe, learned Bluegrass, departed to found his own fine orchestra, too. Most of the Bluegrass outfits on Southern radio and TV today have played with Monroe or one of his disciples—with the noteworthy exception of the Stanley Brothers, who play and sing in a more relaxed and gentle style.

Bluegrass is the first clear-cut orchestral style to appear in the British-American folk tradition in five hundred years; and entirely on its own it is turning back to the great heritage of older tunes that our ancestors brought into the mountains before the American Revolution. A century of isolation in the lonesome hollows of the Appalachians gave them time to combine strains from Scottish and English folk songs and to produce a vigorous pioneer music of their own. The hot Negro square-dance fiddle went early up the creek-bed roads into the hills; then in the mid-nineteenth century came the five-string banjo; early in the twentieth century the guitar was absorbed into the developing tradition. By the time folk-song collectors headed into the mountains looking for ancient ballads, they found a husky, hard-to-kill musical culture as well. Finally, railroads and highways snaked into the backwoods, and mountain folk moved out into urban, industrialized, shook-up America; they were the last among us to experience the breakdown of traditional family patterns, and there ensued an endless stream of sad songs, from *On Top of Old Smoky* to *The Birmingham Jail.* Next in popularity were sacred songs and homiletic pieces warning listeners against drink and fast company; and in the late Thirties, the favorite theme for displaced hillbillies was *No Letter Today.*

Talented mountaineers who wanted to turn professional have had a guaranteed income since the day in 1923 when Ralph Peer skeptically waxed an Atlanta fiddler playing *The Old Hen Cackled and the Rooster's Going to Crow*, and Victor sold half-a-million copies to the ready-made white rural audience. Recording companies sent off field crews and made stars of such singers as Jimmie Rodgers, Uncle Dave Macon, Gid Tanner, the Carter family and Roy Acuff.

Countless combinations of hillbillies have coalesced and dispersed before radio microphones since WSB in Atlanta began beaming out mountainy music on its opening day. *Grand Ole Opry* has been broadcasting from Nashville for thirty-three years; the WWVA Jamboree has gone on for twenty-seven. In the beginning, performers sang solo or with one accompanying instrument; but before microphones they felt the need of orchestras, which, while originally crude, developed with the uncritical encouragement of local audiences.

By now there has grown up a generation of hillbilly musicians who can play anything in any key, and their crowning accomplishment is Bluegrass. When the fresh sound of New Orleans Dixieland combos hit the cities some fifty years ago, it made a musical revolution first in America, then the world. Today we have a new kind of orchestra suitable for accompanying the frontier tunes with which America has fallen in love. And now anything can happen.

RALPH RINZLER
from "A Visit to Rosine[1] and Other Observations" (1993)

Monroe has a deep and complex philosophy of music which he shared with me in a number of interviews conducted over several years. They are excerpted here:

"I was going to be sure through my life I played some blues, because I always loved it that well. I was going to play the blues in my way of playing them. I use the stuff that I heard as a little boy and notes that just sunk in my mind and I kept. If you'll listen to my work you'll see that there's blues in it. . . ."

"Singing the blues, there's not everybody that can sing them. There's people that can go through them, but they don't really put in there what's really there. The notes and things will work same as the words; they'll tell you lots of things, if you want to put yourself in there and be just thinking like the music goes."

"If you study music deep enough, old time music, why you get to learn what's good for it and what's not good for it. You just can't play it now and not pay any attention to it and do that. You've got to be thinking about it, maybe when you're working doing other things; you've got to keep your mind on that music to really get deep in it. I think I've studied old time music deeper than anybody in the country. It all leads to where I know what was the foundation of a number in old time music. I know what's back there and you can get it out or you cannot get it out; but if it's not brought out, why I don't care nothing about really listening to it."

"And it's the same thing about a song . . . just to get in there and run through the words and not make them stand out. There's places in a song that some words should mean more than others and

most times it's on the end of a line where they mean something. Just a voice that runs straight, that don't vary either way, why it doesn't do me any good. I like to hear up and down . . . what I mean I like to ease up, and then, you know, pick it back up here . . . you need some volume. And that's the kind of way with a fiddle piece or any kind of number. I like to break on any number if you'll get down and pick out the stuff that's really in that song."

Observations like these by Bill Monroe would emerge with unpredictable periodicity. If you were driving him a long distance at night and he was concerned about the driver staying awake, he would draw on his extensive body of philosophical thought and historical incident, recounting stories that he knew would keep you from falling asleep at the wheel. In contrast, on many occasions when the Blue Grass Boys were on the road with Bill and Bessie, the 1958 station wagon, which had already traveled about 250,000 miles, was loaded with string bass, all the other instruments, six people and their baggage. Under these conditions, Bill could withdraw into a pensive silence that might last two or more days. He was never unpleasant or glum, one never knew if he was composing tunes or studying on the past or planning some aspect of his musical development, but not a word was spoken by Bill and consequently anyone else in the car. Occasionally Bill or Bessie would instruct the driver to pull into a gas station or restaurant. On entering the restaurant the band would take a table, Bill would either go to the telephone booth or the washroom and on emerging would sit alone at a table at the opposite end of the room. The days of silence did create mild tension under the circumstances . . . particularly when days of travel were sparsely dotted with performances but the long distances required that we drive all night and never sleep in a bed for as many as three days at a stretch. Sometimes after a few days of silence, Bill

Ralph Rinzler, brochure notes for *Bill Monroe and the Blue-grass [sic] Boys: Live Recordings* 1956–1969, vol. 1 (Smithsonian/Folkways compact disc CD SF 40063, 1993), 20–22.
[1]Bill Monroe's home town of Rosine, Kentucky.

would come up with a melody which he'd either sing or pick out on the mandolin. Sometimes he might have a refrain to go with it, or would ask the group in the car to help him set words to the refrain. He would then teach the vocal lead to his singer and they would rehearse the song without any verses as a means of honing it and establishing it in memory. Thus, life on the road was fascinating, exhausting, and worth everything it took out of you.

105

Mahalia Jackson and
Gospel Songs of Hope

Mahalia Jackson (1911–1972) was born under shanty-town conditions in New Orleans. At age seventeen, she moved to Chicago and joined the choir of the Greater Salem Baptist Church on the city's South Side. The move, she believed, gave her life direction and commitment.

Untrained, but with a beautiful, natural contralto voice, Jackson was destined to sing gospel. In 1930, she helped form a gospel trio, the Johnson Gospel Singers. "Prince Johnson worked out our arrangement on the piano," she recalls. "With Prince at the piano, we had a bounce that made us popular from the start." This was ecstatic music of praise, full of emotion and bodily movement, and it suited Jackson perfectly.

Jackson's popularity propelled her into a major career. She toured the United States, Europe, and the Middle East, and she sang at a gala for John F. Kennedy's inauguration. Throughout, she remained true to the church and her background, seeing herself as an evangelist. "In the old Hebrew of the Bible," she tells us, "my name, Mahalia, means 'Blessed by the Lord.' " Widely regarded as the greatest gospel singer of her time, Jackson carried the genre to audiences around the world through performances and recordings.

The title of Jackson's autobiography, *Movin' On Up* is the title of her trademark song; she had known it since she was little and, she tells us, it came to be known as "my song." In the excerpt below, Jackson describes the early days of her career.

MAHALIA JACKSON

from *Movin' On Up* (1966)

Gospel music in those days of the early 1930s was really taking wing. It was the kind of music colored people had left behind them down South and they liked it because it was just like a letter from home.

Jazz sometimes seems like gospel music, but it isn't. Gospel singing is an expression of the way people feel and it's older than jazz or the blues. The Negro had his rhythm and his beat while he was still a slave in the cotton and rice fields long before he had a dime to buy a horn and learn to play jazz.

The nickel-a-night and dime-a-ticket programs of gospel music kept me traveling away from Chicago a lot of the time. The little churches would send for me and then pass me along from one to another. The minister's family would give me a room and something to eat and then we would divide the admission money, part for the church and part for my carfare and pocket money. I had to sit up in trains night after night, but sometimes I made as much as fifty dollars in one week. That was really good in those Depression days and much more than I could make ironing shirts in the white folks' homes on the North Side, or working in a factory....

Mahalia Jackson, with Evan McLeod Wylie, *Movin' On Up* (New York: Hawthorn Books, 1966), 60–68, 86–87.

I had met Professor A. Dorsey,[1] the great writer of gospel songs—he is to gospel music what W. C. Handy is to the blues—and we used to travel together to the same church meetings and conventions.

A lot of folks don't know that gospel songs have not been handed down like spirituals. Most gospel songs have been composed and written by Negro musicians like Professor Dorsey.

Before he got saved by the Lord and went into the church, Professor Dorsey was a piano player for Ma Rainey, one of the first of the blues singers. His nickname in those days was "Georgia Tom" and everybody who went to the tent shows used to know him for the rocking, syncopated beat he had on his piano.

When he began to write gospel music he still had a happy beat in his songs. They're sung by thousands of people like myself who believe religion is a joy.

There are still some Negro churches that don't have gospel singers or choirs and only sing the old hymns and anthems, but among Baptists and the Methodists and the Sanctified church people you will always hear gospel music.

Professor Dorsey would have copies of his wonderful songs like "Precious Lord" and "Peace in the Valley" along with him when we traveled together and he would sell these for ten cents a piece to the folks who wanted to own them. Sometimes he would sell five thousand copies a day. But I was still what you call a "fish and bread" singer in those days. I was still singing for my supper as well as for the Lord.

The more gospel singing took hold in Chicago and around the country, the more some of the colored ministers objected to it. They were cold to it. They didn't like the hand-clapping and the stomping and they said we were bringing jazz into the church and it wasn't dignified. Once at church one of the preachers got up in the pulpit and spoke out against me.

I got right up, too. I told him I was born to sing gospel music. Nobody had to teach me. I was serving God. I told him I had been reading the Bible every day most of my life and there was a Psalm that said: "Oh, clap your hands, all ye people! Shout unto the Lord with the voice of a trumpet!"[2] If it was undignified, it was what the Bible told me to do.

The European hymns they wanted me to sing are beautiful songs, but they're not Negro music. I believe most Negroes—unless they are trained concert artists or so educated they're self-conscious—don't feel at home singing them. Like me, they like to use their hands and their feet. How can you sing of Amazing Grace? How can you sing prayerfully of heaven and earth and all God's wonders without using your hands?

I want my hands . . . my feet . . . my whole body to say all that is in me. I say, "Don't let the devil steal the beat from the Lord! The Lord doesn't like us to act dead. If you feel it, tap your feet a little—dance to the glory of the Lord!"

When I'm singing at concerts, sometimes I whisper . . . sometimes I exclaim and drive the rhythm real hard and sometimes I get right down off the stage on my knees and sing with the folks and keep right on singing afterward in my dressing room before I've said all that I feel inside of me.

Most of the criticism of my songs in the early days came from the high-up society Negroes. There were many who were wealthy, but they did nothing to help me. The first big Negro in Chicago to help me was an undertaker and a politician. His name was Bob Miller. He was the first to present me in a concert in a high school and to raise my admission price from a dime to forty cents. He didn't criticize my simple songs or laugh because I nailed up my own cardboard signs on fences and telephone posts and got in my car and drove around town asking storekeepers to put them in their windows.

In those days the big colored churches didn't want me and they didn't let me in. I had to make it my business to pack the little basement-hall con-

---

[1]Thomas A. Dorsey (1899–1993).

[2]Psalm 47:1.

gregations and store-front churches and get their respect that way. When they began to see the crowds I drew, the big churches began to sit up and take notice because even inside the church there are people who are greedy for money.

Another reason I was so strongly drawn to gospel music was that I had a feeling by this time deep down inside me that it was what God wanted me to do. I'd felt closer than ever to God ever since he'd heard my prayers about my grandfather Paul during that long week in the hot summer of 1934.[3]

* * *

I had begun to make records of my gospel songs, too. One day in 1946 I was in the recording studio practicing. To limber up my voice I sang just to myself an old spiritual song that I had known since I was a little child:

One of these mornings I'm going to lay down my cross
and get my crown
As soon as my feet strike Zion, I'm going to lay down
my heavy burden
I'm gonna put on my robes in glory and move on up a
little higher . . .

A man from Decca Records named Ink Williams was in the studio and happened to hear me.

"What's that you're singing, Mahalia?" he asked.

"Why it's just an old song we used to call 'Movin' On Up,' Ink," I said.

"But who wrote it?" Ink asked.

"Don't anybody know who wrote it, honey," I said. "I've always sung it, since I was a little child down in New Orleans. I like to sing it my own way."

"You sing it just right," Ink said. "Why don't you make a record of it for us?"

I did and a few weeks later "I Will Move On Up a Little Higher" began to move so fast we couldn't keep track of it. Colored folks were buying it in New York, in Chicago, way out West and all over down South. They've kept on buying it until it's sold close to two million copies.

"Movin' On Up" got to be known as my song.

---

[3]Jackson's grandfather had had a stroke, an incident for which she felt partially responsible. She prayed that if God would cure her grandfather, she would lead a pure life and never go to the theater again. He recovered. "And since I made God that promise I have never set foot in a picture theater or vaudeville house again."

106 Innovators in Jazz: Charlie Parker and John Coltrane

Charlie "Bird" Parker (1920–1955), born in Kansas City, was a highly important improvising soloist who was central to the development of bop during the 1940s. He led his own group for the first time in New York, starting in late 1945. Two years later, during his most productive period, he formed a quintet that also included Miles Davis on trumpet, Duke Jordan on piano, Tommy Potter on double bass, and Max Roach on drums. He died young, badly in debt and suffering the ravages of alcohol and narcotics.

The interview below makes clear his relationship with bop but downplays the debt he owed to his inherited traditions, especially blues, which account for much of Parker's recorded legacy. What it does make clear, however, is Parker's acquaintance with the classical sphere and his love for its music. When asked to identify a music example, he replied, "Is it by Stravinsky? That's music at its best. I like all of Stravinsky—and Prokofiev, Hindemith, Ravel, Debussy—and, of course, Wagner and Bach. Give that all the stars you've got!" Parker's musical esthetic come through clearly in his oft-quoted statement: "Music is your own experience, your thoughts, your wisdom. If you don't live it, it won't come out of your horn."

Like Parker, tenor saxophonist and composer John Coltrane (1926–1967) worked closely with Dizzy Gillespie, Miles Davis, and other jazz greats. By 1960, "Trane" had emerged as a leading figure in jazz. His celebrated quartet, which premiered at New York's Jazz Gallery in May of that year, also included McCoy Tyner on piano, Jimmy Garrison on bass, and Elvin Jones on drums. Jones commented, "There was a basic life force in Coltrane's solos, and when he came out of them you suddenly discovered you had learned a great deal." Coltrane explained, "It's more than beauty I feel in music—that I think musicians feel in music. What we know we feel we'd like to convey to the listener. We hope that this can be shared by all."* Deeply religious, Coltrane expressed his beliefs in such highly personal, intense, and cathartic albums as the popular *A Love Supreme* (1964).

An experimenter at heart, Coltrane turned increasingly to radical musical styles. His music attracted large audiences and his recordings sold widely. However, like Parker, he was afflicted by drugs and alcohol, and died young.

---

*Don DeMichael, "John Coltrane and Eric Dolphy Answer the Jazz Critics," *Down Beat*, April 12, 1962: 22.

MICHAEL LEVIN AND JOHN S. WILSON

from "The Chili Parlor Interview" (1949)

"Bop is no love-child of jazz," says Charlie Parker. The creator of bop, in a series of interviews that took more than two weeks, told us he felt that "bop is something entirely separate and apart" from the older tradition, that it drew little from jazz, has no roots in it. The chubby little alto man, who has made himself an international music name in the last five years, added that bop, for the most part, had to be played by small bands.

"[Dizzy] Gillespie's[1] playing has changed from being stuck in front of a big band," he says. "Anybody's does. He's a fine musician. The leopard coat and wild hats are just another part of the managers' routines to make him box office. The same thing happened a couple of years ago when they stuck his name on some tunes of mine to give him a better commercial reputation."

Asked to define bop, after several evenings of arguing, Charlie still was not precise in his definition.

"It's just music," he said. "It's trying to play clean and looking for the pretty notes."

Pushed further, he said that a distinctive feature of bop is its strong feeling for beat.

"The beat in a bop band is with the music, against it, behind it," Charlie said. "It pushes it. It helps it. Help is the big thing. It has no continuity of beat, no steady chugging. Jazz has, and that's why bop is more flexible."

He admits the music eventually may be atonal. Parker himself is a devout admirer of Paul Hindemith, the German neo-classicist, and raves about his *Kammermusik* and *Sonata for Viola and Cello*. He insists, however, that bop is not moving in the same direction as modern classical. He feels that it will be more flexible, more emotional, more colorful. . . .

The closest Parker will come to an exact, technical description of what may happen is to say that he would like to emulate the precise, complex harmonic structures of Hindemith, but with an emotional coloring and dynamic shading that he feels modern classical lacks.

Parker's indifference to the revered jazz tradition certainly will leave some of his own devotees in a state of surprise. But, actually, he himself has no roots in traditional jazz. . . . His first musical idol, the musician who so moved and inspired him that he went out and bought his first saxophone at the age of 11, was Rudy Vallee.[2]

Tossed into the jazz world of the mid-'30s with this kind of background, he had no familiar ground on which to stand. For three years he fumbled unhappily until he suddenly stumbled on the music which appealed to him, which had meaning to him. For Charlie insists, "Music is your own experience, your thoughts, your wisdom. If you don't live it, it won't come out of your horn."

Michael Levin and John S. Wilson, "The Chili Parlor Interview [with Charlie Parker]," *Down Beat* (March 11, 1965): 13; revised from the original article published in *Down Beat* (September 9, 1949).

[1]Trumpeter John Birks "Dizzy" Gillespie (1917–1993) helped create bebop.

---

[2]Band-leader, singer, saxophonist, actor, and publisher Rudy Vallée (1901–1986) found considerable success, particularly during the 1930s and 40s.

JOHN COLTRANE

"Coltrane on Coltrane" (1960)

I've been listening to jazzmen, especially saxophonists, since the time of the early Count Basie records, which featured Lester Young.[4] Pres was my first real influence, but the first horn I got was an alto, not a tenor. I wanted a tenor, but some friends of my mother advised her to buy me an alto because it was a smaller horn and easier for a youngster to handle. This was 1943.

Johnny Hodges became my first main influence on alto, and he still kills me. I stayed with alto through 1947, and by then I'd come under the influence of Charlie Parker. The first time I heard Bird play, it hit me right between the eyes. Before I switched from alto in that year, it had been strictly a Bird thing with me, but when I bought a tenor to go with Eddie Vinson's band, a wider area of listening opened up for me.

I found I was able to be more varied in my musical interests. On alto, Bird had been my whole influence, but on tenor I found there was no one man whose ideas were so dominant as Charlie's were on alto. Therefore, I drew from all the men I heard during this period. I have listened to about all the good tenor men, beginning with Lester, and believe me, I've picked up something from them all, including several who have never recorded.

The reason I liked Lester so was that I could feel that line, that simplicity. My phrasing was very much in Lester's vein at this time.

I found out about Coleman Hawkins after I learned of Lester. There were a lot of things that Hawkins was doing that I knew I'd have to learn somewhere along the line. I felt the same way about Ben Webster. There were many things that people like Hawk, Ben, and Tab Smith were doing

in the '40s that I didn't understand but that I felt emotionally.

The first time I heard Hawk, I was fascinated by his arpeggios and the way he played. I got a copy of his *Body and Soul* and listened real hard to what he was doing. And even though I dug Pres, as I grew musically, I appreciated Hawk more and more.

As far as musical influences, aside from saxophonists, are concerned, I think I was first awakened to musical exploration by Dizzy Gillespie and Bird. It was through their work that I began to learn about musical structures and the more theoretical aspects of music.

Also, I had met Jimmy Heath, who, besides being a wonderful saxophonist, understood a lot about musical construction. I joined his group in Philadelphia in 1948. We were very much alike in our feeling, phrasing, and a whole lot of ways. Our musical appetites were the same. We used to practice together, and he would write out some of the things we were interested in. We would take things from records and digest them. In this way we learned about the techniques being used by writers and arrangers.

Another friend and I learned together in Philly—Calvin Massey, a trumpeter and composer who now lives in Brooklyn. His musical ideas and mine often run parallel, and we've collaborated quite often. We helped each other advance musically by exchanging knowledge and ideas.

I first met Miles Davis about 1947 and played a few jobs with him and Sonny Rollins at the Audubon ballroom in Manhattan. During this period he was coming into his own, and I could see him extending the boundaries of jazz even further. I felt I wanted to work with him. But for the time being, we went our separate ways.

I went with Dizzy's big band in 1949. I stayed with Diz through the breakup of the big band and played in the small group he organized later.

Afterwards, I went with Earl Bostic, who I con-

John Coltrane, with Don DeMichael, "Coltrane on Coltrane," *Down Beat*, September 29, 1960: 26–27.

[4]Lester "Pres" Young (1909–1959) first joined the Count Basie Band in 1934, an association that eventually led him to national recognition.

sider a very gifted musician. He showed me a lot of things on my horn. He has fabulous technical facilities on his instrument and knows many a trick.

Then I worked with one of my first loves, Johnny Hodges.[5] I really enjoyed that job. I liked every tune in the book. Nothing was superficial. It all had meaning, and it all swung. And the confidence with which Rabbit plays! I wish I could play with the confidence that he does.

But besides enjoying my stay with Johnny musically, I also enjoyed it because I was getting first-hand information about things that happened 'way before my time. I'm very interested in the past, and even though there's a lot I don't know about it, I intend to go back and find out. I'm back to Sidney Bechet already.

Take Art Tatum, for instance. When I was coming up, the musicians I ran around with were listening to Bud Powell, and I didn't listen too much to Tatum. That is, until one night I happened to run into him in Cleveland. There were Art and Slam Stewart and Oscar Peterson and Ray Brown at a private session in some lady's attic. They played from 2:30 in the morning to 8:30—just whatever they felt like playing. I've never heard so much music.

In 1955, I joined Miles on a regular basis and worked with him till the middle of 1957. I went with Thelonious Monk for the remainder of that year.

Working with Monk brought me close to a musical architect of the highest order. I felt I learned from him in every way—through the senses, theoretically, technically. I would talk to Monk about musical problems, and he would sit at the piano and show me the answers just by playing them. I could watch him play and find out the things I wanted to know. Also, I could see a lot of things that I didn't know about at all.

Monk was one of the first to show me how to make two or three notes at one time on tenor.

(John Glenn, a tenor man in Philly, also showed me how to do this. He can play a triad and move notes inside it—like passing tones!) It's done by false fingering and adjusting your lip. If everything goes right, you can get triads. Monk just looked at my horn and "felt" the mechanics of what had to be done to get this effect.

I think Monk is one of the true greats of all time. He's a real musical thinker—there're not many like him. I feel myself fortunate to have had the opportunity to work with him. If a guy needs a little spark, a boost, he can just be around Monk, and Monk will give it to him.

After leaving Monk, I went back to another great musical artist, Miles.

On returning, this time to stay until I formed my own group a few months ago, I found Miles in the midst of another stage of his musical development. There was one time in his past that he devoted to multichorded structures. He was interested in chords for their own sake. But now it seemed that he was moving in the opposite direction to the use of fewer and fewer chord changes in songs. He used tunes with free-flowing lines and chordal direction. This approach allowed the soloist the choice of playing chordally (vertically) or melodically (horizontally).

In fact, due to the direct and free-flowing lines in his music, I found it easy to apply the harmonic ideas that I had. I could stack up chords—say, on a C7, I sometimes superimposed an E♭7, up to an F♯7, down to an F. That way I could play three chords on one. But on the other hand, if I wanted to, I could play melodically. Miles' music gave me plenty of freedom. It's a beautiful approach.

About this time, I was trying for a sweeping sound. I started experimenting because I was striving for more individual development. I even tried long, rapid lines that Ira Gitler termed "sheets of sound" at the time. But actually, I was beginning to apply the three-on-one chord approach, and at that time the tendency was to play the entire scale of each chord. Therefore, they were usually played fast and sometimes sounded like glisses.

I found there were a certain number of chord progressions to play in a given time, and some-

---

[5]Johnny "Rabbit" Hodges (1907–1970), regarded as the most influential alto saxophonist prior to Charlie Parker, was a soloist and section leader with Duke Ellington for nearly four decades.

times what I played didn't work out in eighth notes, 16th notes, or triplets. I had to put the notes in uneven groups like fives and sevens in order to get them all in.

I thought in groups of notes, not of one note at a time. I tried to place these groups on the accents and emphasize the strong beats—maybe on 2 here and on 4 over at the end. I would set up the line and drop groups of notes—a long line with accents dropped as I moved along. Sometimes what I was doing clashed harmonically with the piano—especially if the pianist wasn't familiar with what I was doing—so a lot of times I just strolled with bass and drums.

I haven't completely abandoned this approach, but it wasn't broad enough. I'm trying to play these progressions in a more flexible manner now.

Last February, I bought a soprano saxophone. I like the sound of it, but I'm not playing with the body, the bigness of tone, that I want yet. I haven't had too much trouble playing it in tune, but I've had a lot of trouble getting a good quality of tone in the upper register. It comes out sort of puny sometimes. I've had to adopt a slightly different approach than the one I use for tenor, but it helps me get away—let's me take another look at improvisation. It's like having another hand.

I'm using it with my present group, McCoy Tyner, piano; Steve Davis, bass, and Pete LaRoca, drums. The quartet is coming along nicely. We know basically what we're trying for, and we leave room for individual development. Individual contributions are put in night by night.

One of my aims is to build as good a repertoire as I can for a band. What size, I couldn't say, but it'll probably be a quartet or quintet. I want to get the material first. Right now, I'm on a material search.

From a technical viewpoint, I have certain things I'd like to present in my solos. To do this, I have to get the right material. It has to swing, and it has to be varied. (I'm inclined not to be too varied.) I want it to cover as many forms of music as I can put into a jazz context and play on my instruments. I like Eastern music; Yusef Lateef has been using this in his playing for some time. And Ornette Coleman sometimes plays music with a Spanish content as well as other exotic-flavored music. In these approaches there's something I can draw on and use in the way I like to play.

I've been writing some things for the quartet—if you call lines and sketches writing. I'd like to write more after I learn more—after I find out what kind of material I can present best, what kind will carry my musical techniques best. Then I'll know better what kind of writing is best for me.

I've been devoting quite a bit of my time to harmonic studies on my own, in libraries and places like that. I've found you've got to look back at the old things and see them in a new light. I'm not finished with these studies because I haven't assimilated everything into my playing. I want to progress, but I don't want to go so far out that I can't see what others are doing.

I want to broaden my outlook in order to come out with a fuller means of expression. I want to be more flexible where rhythm is concerned. I feel I have to study rhythm some more. I haven't experimented too much with time; most of my experimenting has been in a harmonic form. I put time and rhythms to one side, in the past.

But I've got to keep experimenting. I feel that I'm just beginning. I have part of what I'm looking for in my grasp but not all.

I'm very happy devoting all my time to music, and I'm glad to be one of the many who are striving for fuller development as musicians. Considering the great heritage in music that we have, the work of giants of the past, the present, and the promise of those who are to come, I feel that we have every reason to face the future optimistically.

"Leonard Bernstein meant so many things to America that any description of him must resign itself to incompleteness, probably to distortion," began an obituary in *The New Yorker*. For Bernstein (1918–1990), versatility was key: he could play, talk, write, compose, conduct, and teach, all with consummate skill, and he moved easily between Broadway, the television studio, and the concert stage.

Bernstein might be described as the Great Communicator of the music world, exciting audiences young and old about music and helping them feel its emotional content. His ability to involve his listeners and musicians served particularly well amidst the mechanistic pulls and pushes of the twentieth century. His music found resonant chords in our own emotions, drawing us together. One of his passionate beliefs, expressed in a 1970 address, was that "it's the artists of the world, the feelers and the thinkers, who will ultimately save us; who can articulate, educate, defy, insist, sing and shout the big dreams. Only the artists can turn the 'Not-Yet' into reality."*

---

*Leonard Bernstein, "The Principle of Hope," *Sennets & Tuckets* (Boston: The Boston Symphony Orchestra and David Godine, 1988), 90. Welcoming address to participants at the Berkshire Music Center, July 8, 1970.

LEONARD BERNSTEIN

"The Mountain Disappears" (1954)

I believe in people. I feel, love, need and respect people above all else, including the arts, natural scenery, organized piety, or nationalistic super-structures. One human figure on the slope of a mountain can make the whole mountain disappear for me. One person fighting for the truth can disqualify for me the platitudes of centuries. And one human being who meets with injustice can render invalid the entire system which has dispensed it.

I believe that man's noblest endowment is his capacity to change. Armed with reason, he can see two sides and choose: he can be divinely wrong. I believe in man's right to be wrong. Out of this right he has built, laboriously and lovingly, something we reverently call democracy. He has done it the hard way and continues to do it the hard way—by reason, by choosing, by error and rectification, by the difficult, slow method in which the dignity of A is acknowledged by B, without impairing the dignity of C. Man cannot have dignity without loving the dignity of his fellow.

I believe in the potential of people. I cannot rest passively with those who give up in the name of "human nature." Human nature is only animal nature if it is obliged to remain static. Without growth, without metamorphosis, there is no godhead. If we believe that man can never achieve a society without wars, then we are condemned to

---

Leonard Bernstein, "The Mountain Disappears," in Edward R. Murrow, ed., *This I Believe: 2*, ed. Raymond Swing (New York: Simon and Schuster, 1954), 14–15.

wars forever. This is the easy way. But the laborious, loving way, the way of dignity and divinity, presupposes a belief in people and in their capacity to change, grow, communicate, and love.

I believe in man's unconscious mind, the deep spring from which comes his power to communicate and to love. For me, all art is a combination of these powers; for if love is the way we have of communicating personally in the deepest way, then what art can do is to extend this communication, magnify it, and carry it to vastly greater numbers of people. Therefore art is valid for the warmth and love it carries within it, even if it be the lightest entertainment, or the bitterest satire, or the most shattering tragedy.

I believe that my country is the place where all these things I have been speaking of are happening in the most manifest way. America is at the beginning of her greatest period in history—a period of leadership in science, art and human progress toward the democratic ideal. I believe that she is at the critical point in this moment, and that she needs us to believe more strongly than ever before, in her and in one another, in our ability to grow and change, in our mutual dignity, in our democratic method. We must encourage thought, free and creative. We must respect privacy. We must observe taste by not exploiting our sorrows, successes, or passions. We must learn to know ourselves better through art. We must rely more on the unconscious, inspirational side of man. We must not enslave ourselves to dogma. We must believe in the attainability of good. We must believe, without fear, in people.

LEONARD BERNSTEIN

from "Speaking of Music" (1957)

Ever since I can remember I have talked about music, with friends, colleagues, teachers, students, and just plain simple citizens. But in the last few years I have found myself talking about it publicly, thus joining the long line of well-meaning but generally doomed folk who have tried to explain the unique phenomenon of human reaction to organized sound.

It is almost like trying to explain a freak of nature (whatever that may be); ultimately one must simply accept the loving fact that people enjoy listening to organized sound (certain organized sounds, anyway); that this enjoyment can take the form of all kinds of responses from animal excitement to spiritual exaltation; and that people who can organize sounds so as to evoke the most exalted responses are commonly called geniuses. These axioms can be neither denied nor explained.

But, in the great tradition of man burrowing through the darkness with his mind, hitting his head on cave walls, and sometimes perceiving a pin point of light, we can at least try to explain; in fact, there's no stopping us.

There have been many more words written about the *Eroica* Symphony than there are notes in it; in fact, I should imagine that the proportion of words to notes, if anyone could get an accurate count, would be flabbergasting. And yet, has anyone ever successfully "explained" the *Eroica*? Can anyone explain in mere prose the wonder of one note following or coinciding with another so that we feel that it is exactly how those notes had to be? Of course not. No matter what rationalists we may profess to be, we are stopped cold at the border of this mystic area. It is not too much to say *mystic* or even *magic*; no art lover can be an agnostic when the chips are down. If you love music, you are a believer, however dialectically you try to wiggle out of it. . . .

Leonard Bernstein, "Speaking of Music, *Atlantic Monthly*, December 1957: 104–6.

We bumble. We imitate scientific method in our attempts to explain magic phenomena by fact, forces, mass, energy. But we simply can't explain human reaction to these phenomena. Science can explain thunderstorms, but can it explain the fear with which people react to them? And even if it can, somehow, how does science explain the sense of glory we feel in a thunderstorm, break down this sense of glory into its parts? Three parts electrical stimulation, one part aural excitement, one part visual excitement, four parts identification-feelings with the beyond, two parts adoration of almighty forces—an impossible cocktail.

But some people *have* explained the glory of a thunderstorm, and such people are called poets. Only artists can explain magic; only art can substitute for nature. By the same token, only art can substitute for art. And so the only way one can really say anything about music is to write music. . . .

If we are to try to explain music, we must explain the *music*, not the whole array of extramusical notions which have grown like parasites around it. . . .

There is a happy medium somewhere between the music-appreciation racket and purely technical discussion; it is hard to find, but it can be found.

It is with this certainty that it can be found that I have made so bold as to discuss music on television, on records, and in public lectures. Whenever I feel that I have done it successfully, it is because I may have found that happy medium. And finding it is impossible without the conviction that the public is not a great beast but an intelligent organism, more often than not longing for insight and knowledge. Wherever possible, therefore, I try to talk about music—the *notes* of music; and wherever extramusical concepts are needed for referential or clarifying purposes, I try to choose concepts that are musically relevant, such as nationalistic tendencies or spiritual development, which may even have been part of the composer's own thinking.

For example, in explaining jazz I have avoided the usual pseudohistorical discussions (up the river from New Orleans) and concentrated on those aspects of melody, harmony, rhythm, which make jazz different from all other music. In talking of Bach I have had to make references to his religious and spiritual convictions, but always in terms of the notes he produced. In analyzing Dvořák's *New World* Symphony for a lay audience listening to a recording, I have displayed all the thematic material, as music appreciation would demand, but in terms of Dvořák's attempt at nationalistic results.

In other words, music appreciation doesn't have to be a racket. The extramusical kind of reference can be useful if it is put in the service of explaining the *notes*; and the road-map variety can also be serviceable if it functions along with some central idea that can engage the intelligence of the listener. Therein lies the happy medium.

But, in the end, we can never really interpret music through words, or give even a shadowy equivalent. If it were possible for words to "tell" a Chopin mazurka—its sad-gay quality, the abundance of its brevity, the polish of its detail—why, then, would Chopin have had to write it in the first place?

ROBERT CHESTERMAN

from "Leonard Bernstein in Conversation" (1976)

Do you ever worry that in the end you might feel that you could have achieved more if you had just conducted or more if you had just been a composer?

No, because that is an inconceivable state of being. I can't think of myself as existing just as a composer, or just as a performer, because there are these two sides to my nature. I'm cursed with them, if you wish; call it not a blessing, call it a drawback. The truth of it is I have a side that likes to withdraw and be alone for long continuous periods, and I have a side that wants to be with people, a gregarious side, and that wants to share everything with people. I think that's a key word in everything I do, "share." I love to teach so much and I love to make these television programmes, both for young people and for adults, because the minute I know something, or recognize something, or enjoy something, that very second I have to share it. I can't bear keeping it to myself. This is true, strangely enough, even when I write music. If I happen to write something suddenly that I know is good, that's a real *trouvaille*.[1] I can't wait to run to my wife, or child, or friend, or whoever is around, to play it to them. I can't keep it to myself. I think that conducting is born from that in me, anyway—from that impulse to share what I feel, the excitement, the enthusiasm, the mystery, whatever insights I have about all music with as many people as possible.

Robert Chesterman, "Leonard Bernstein in Conversation with Robert Chesterman," *Conversations with Conductors* (Totowa, N. J.: Rowman and Littlefield, 1976), 71.

[1] A real effort.

108

Gunther Schuller and the Third Stream

Gunther Schuller (b. 1925) coined the adjective *third-stream* in the late 1950s to describe a kind of music formed from the combination of two existing "streams," classical music and jazz. The term, as a noun, has come to include a great variety of crossover styles.

The music reflects Schuller's wide-ranging talent, versatility, and interests. During his long career, Schuller has performed as a horn player with the Cincinnati Symphony and the Metropolitan Opera Orchestra and as an accomplished jazz performer, playing and recording with such artists as Dizzy Gillespie and Miles Davis. He is a prolific composer, credited with more than 160 compositions that encompass virtually every musical genre. He won the 1994 Pulitzer Prize for *Of Reminiscences and Reflections*, commissioned for the Louisville Orchestra, and composed works for the Modern Jazz Quartet. His extensive writings include a monumental history of jazz. He taught at the Manhattan School of Music and at Yale. As an administrator, he has served as president of the New England Conservatory of Music and as artistic director of the Berkshire Music Center at Tanglewood. He has also been the guiding force behind several publishing and recording companies.

Schuller describes third stream as "the music of rapprochement" and as "the quintessential American music."

GUNTHER SCHULLER

" 'Third Stream' Redefined" (1961)

About a year ago the term "Third Stream," describing a new genre of music located about halfway between jazz and classical music, attained official sanction by use in a headline of the *New York Times*. Since that day, almost everybody has had his say about this music and its practitioners, and, not surprisingly, much nonsense about it has found its way into print. I suppose this is inevitable. If we consider how much confusion and prejudice are attached to jazz and contemporary music as *separate* fields of musical activity, we can then imagine how existing misunderstandings are likely to be compounded when we speak of a *fusion* of these two forces.

I first used the term "Third Stream" in a lecture three or four years ago, in an attempt to describe a music that was beginning to evolve with growing consistency. For lack of a precise name, one was forced at the time to describe it either in a lengthy definition or in descriptive phrases comprising several sentences. I used the term as an adjective, not as a noun. I did not envision its use as a name, a slogan, or a catchword (one thinks back with horror to the indignities visited upon the modern jazz movement in the late forties by the banal commercialization of the catchword "Bop"); nor did

Gunther Schuller, "Third Stream Redefined," *Saturday Review*, May 13, 1961: 54–55.

this imply a sort of "canonization," as one critic facetiously put it; nor, least of all, did I intend the term as a commercial gimmick. Such a thought evidently comes most readily to some people's minds in a society in which commercial gimmickry is an accepted way of life. Ultimately, I don't care whether the term Third Stream survives. In the interim it is no more than a handy descriptive term. It should be obvious that a piece of Third Stream music is first of all *music*, and its quality cannot be determined solely by categorization. Basically I don't care what category music belongs to; I only care whether it is good or bad. As one fellow musician put it: "I like jazz, not because it's jazz, but because it's good music."

After a year of watching the confusion mount and the increasing commercial exploitation of the phrase "Third Stream" (often incorrectly used, to boot), and after reading numerous reviews revealing the writers' calloused misunderstanding of the music involved, I somehow feel obligated—since I may have indirectly instigated all this nonsense—finally to have *my* say about it, and in the process I hope to bring some clarity to the whole issue.

I am fully aware that, individually, jazz and classical music have long, separate traditions that many people want to keep separate and sacred. I also recognize the right of musicians in either field to focus their attention entirely on preserving the idiomatic purity of these traditions. It is precisely for these reasons that I thought it best to separate from these two traditions the new genre that attempts to fuse "the improvisational spontaneity and rhythmic vitality of jazz with the compositional procedures and techniques acquired in Western music during 700 years of musical development." I felt that by designating this music as a *separate, third* stream, the two other mainstreams could go their way unaffected by attempts at fusion. I had hoped that in this way the old prejudices, old worries about the purity of the two main streams that have greeted attempts to bring jazz and "classical" music together could, for once, be avoided. This, however, has not been the case. Musicians and critics in both fields have considered this Third Stream a frontal attack on their own tra-

ditions. My attempts to make important and precise distinctions have only created greater confusion.

Characteristically, the jazz side has protested against the intruder more vigorously than its opposite partner. And since my music in this genre has by now been accused of everything from "opportunism" to "racial callousness," I had better make some points unequivocally clear. I can best clarify my intentions by some straightforward categorical statements: (1) I am not interested in *improving* jazz (jazz is a healthy young music, and I would not presume to be capable of improving it); (2) I am not interested in *replacing* jazz (a thought like this could only emanate from some confused believer in the basic inferiority of jazz); (3) I am not interested in "bringing jazz into classical music," nor in "making a lady out of jazz," in the immortal words of the erstwhile "symphonic jazz" proponents (Paul Whiteman, Ferde Grofe *et al.*, come to mind).

I am simply exercising my prerogative as a creative artist to draw upon those experiences in my life as a musician that have a vital meaning for me. It is inevitable that the creative individual will in some way reflect in his creative activity that which he loves, respects, and understands; my concern, therefore, is precisely to preserve as much of the essence of both elements as is possible.

Yet, with disturbing consistency, "jazz critics" keep appraising the Third Streamers solely on the basis of jazz. The producers of this music are also equally at fault. One recently issued recording describes itself as "Third Stream Jazz," and I suppose before long we will have some "Third Stream Classics"—whatever that might turn out to be. This is analogous to calling a nectarine a nectarine-plum. The standards of jazz, per se, are not applicable to Third Stream, any more than one can expect a nectarine to taste like a peach. A Third Stream work does not wish to be heard as jazz alone; it does not *necessarily* expect to "swing like Basie" (few can, even within the jazz field); it does not expect to seduce the listener with ready-made blue-noted formulas of "soul" and "funk"; and it certainly does not expect to generate easy acceptance among those whose musical criteria are determined only on the basis of whether one can snap one's fingers to the music. And, I might add, it is not an attempt to find a niche in the hearts of the American public by capitalizing on the brash, racy "jazziness" of some recent Broadway musicals.

In *my* understanding of the term, Third Stream music must be born out of respect for and full dedication to both the musics it attempts to fuse. (This is more than one can say for the pop song or rock-'n'-roll commercializers of jazz, about whom, ironically, I have heard no serious complaints.) The lifting of external elements from one area into the other is happily a matter of the past. At its best it can be an extremely subtle music, defying the kind of easy categorization most people seem to need before they can make up their minds whether they should like something or not. As John Lewis[1] once put it to me in a conversation: "It isn't so much what we see (and hear) in the music of each idiom; it is more what we do *not* see in the one that already exists in the other."

Certainly both musics can benefit from this kind of cross-fertilization, in the hands of gifted people. For example, the state of performance in classical music at the professional level today is, despite all we hear about our skilled instrumentalists, rather low. Most performances touch only the surface of a work, not its essence; and this is most true of the performance of contemporary music. If virtuosic perfection at least were achieved, one could—in a forgetful moment—be satisfied with that. But one cannot even claim this, since the leisurely attitude of the majority of classical players toward rhythmic accuracy is simply appalling, and would seem so to more people were it not so widespread as to be generally accepted. There is no question in my mind that the classical world can learn much about timing, rhythmic accuracy, and subtlety from jazz musicians, as jazz musicians can in dynamics, structure, and contrast from the classical musicians.

It is this kind of mutual fructifying that will, I believe, be one of the benefits of Third Stream. It seems, therefore, unfair for critics to blame a piece of Third Stream music because "the symphony orchestras can't swing." Of course they can't swing; even in their own music they barely manage. But perhaps they will learn; and, when they do, will the compositions involved then be intrinsically better? It is this kind of confusion of levels that I am deploring. It happens, needless to say, on both sides of the fence.

It is not a lame apology, but rather a statement of fact, to say that this movement is still in its beginnings. The performance problems are still enormous, and much musical adjustment will have to be made by both sides before the compositional ideals of the composers can be realized on the performance level. However, if a symphony orchestra can be made to swing just a little, and if a compositional structure that makes jazz musicians push beyond the thirty-two-bar song forms of conventional jazz can be achieved, are not these already important achievements in breaking the stalemate artificially enforced by people who wish tenaciously to keep the two idioms separate? (That there are not only musical problems involved here, but also deep-rooted racial issues, need hardly be emphasized.)

If historical confirmation is needed, it is easy to point to many precedents, which undoubtedly were met with as much scoffing as Third Stream has encountered. The next time someone invokes the old saw about oil and water not mixing, just tell him that the most sacred and rigorously organized music of all time, the Flemish contrapuntal masses, was more often than not based on what once had been semi-improvised lighthearted secular troubadour ballads. Or tell him that the minuet, at first a simple and often crude popular dance, became a sophisticated classical form in the hands of Haydn and Mozart. Or if examples be needed from our own time, Bartók's music—originally compounded of Debussyan and Straussian elements—rose to its greatest heights *after* he was able to fuse his style with the idiomatic inflections of Eastern European folk music. Many more examples exist.

---

[1]Pianist in the Modern Jazz Quartet.

It seems to me that the kind of fusion which Third Stream attempts is not only interesting but inevitable. We are undergoing a tremendous process of musical synthesis, in which the many radical innovations of the earliest decades of our century are being finally assimilated. Whenever I read one of the "it-can't-be-done" reviews, I think of Wagner's line in *Die Meistersinger*, addressing Beckmesser:

Wollt ihr nach Regeln messen,
was nicht nach eurer Regeln Lauf,
sucht davon erst die Regeln auf!
Eu'r Urtheil, dünkt mich, wäre reifer,
hörtet ihr besser zu.

Freely translated: "Would you judge by conventional rules that which does not follow those rules? Your judgment, it seems to me, would be more mature if you listened more carefully."

It would seem that the Beckmessers of today are equally incapable of listening to music in terms of a *total* musical experience. When confronted with passages thoroughly fusing the worlds of jazz and classical music, they insist on hearing them in their separate categories, most likely because they can hear well only in one or the other. I am not by nature a polemicist or a crusader, and I would not, in any case, crusade for Third Stream music. I simply would hope for critics (amateur and professional) who could appraise the music on *its* terms, not *theirs*.

GUNTHER SCHULLER

from "Third Stream Revisited" (1981)

THIRD STREAM is a way of composing, improvising, and performing that brings musics together rather than segregating them. It is a way of making music which holds that *all musics are created equal*, coexisting in a beautiful brotherhood/sisterhood of musics that complement and fructify each other. It is a global concept which allows the world's musics—written, improvised, handed-down, traditional, experimental—to come together, to learn from one another, to reflect human diversity and pluralism. It is the music of rapprochement, of *entente*—not of competition and confrontation. And it is the logical outcome of the American melting pot: *E pluribus unum*. . . . It is in effect *the quintessential American music*.

Gunther Schuller, *Musings: The Musical Worlds of Gunther Schuller* (New York: Oxford University Press, 1986), 119–20; reprint from a brochure published by the New England Conservatory of Music, 1981.

109

Pauline Oliveros and Performance Art

Like musicians less than half her age, Pauline Oliveros (b. 1932), composer, accordionist, and teacher, maintains a Web site containing information about her current activities. Among them are retreats she runs to teach Deep Listening, which she describes online:

> As a musician, I am interested in the sensual nature of sound, its power of synchronization, coordination, release and change. Hearing represents the primary sense organ—hearing happens involuntarily. Listening is cultured and represents our experience and training. Deep Listening is listening in every possible way to everything possible to hear no matter what you are doing. Such intense listening includes the sounds of daily life, of nature, or one's own thoughts as well as musical sounds. Deep Listening represents a heightened state of awareness and connects to all that there is. As a composer I strive to make my music through Deep Listening.

Oliveros was an early member of the 1950s and 60s avant-garde, composing, for example, *Seven Passages* (1963), for dancer, mobile, and two-channel tape. Her series of *Sonic Meditations* (1971–72) call for audience improvisations. She practices performance art, mixed-media presentations, and meditation, creating sound environments intended to build community between participants. Her composition *Deep Listening* (1971–90) is a collection of thirty pieces "for vocal solo and group performances by anyone willing to try."

Oliveros also seeks to raise our consciousness concerning the role of women in music. The following article, written for *The New York Times* in 1970, speaks directly to that issue. She may not have been called "one of the boys," as Amy Beach once was, but Oliveros's article demonstrates that gender issues were as unresolved in the late twentieth century as they were in Beach's late nineteenth century.

PAULINE OLIVEROS

from "And Don't Call Them 'Lady' Composers" (1970)

Why have there been no "great" women composers? The question is often asked. The answer is no mystery. In the past, talent, education, ability, interests, motivation were irrelevant because being female was a unique qualification for domestic work and for continual obedience to and dependence upon men.

This is no less true today. Women have been taught to despise activity outside of the domestic realm as unfeminine, just as men have been taught

Pauline Oliveros, "And Don't Call Them 'Lady' Composers," *New York Times*, September 13, 1970: sect. 2, 23, 30.

to despise domestic duties. For men, independence, mobility and creative action are imperative. Society has perpetuated an unnatural atmosphere which encourages distortions such as "girl" used as a bad word by little boys from the age of nine or ten. From infancy, boys are wrapped in blue blankets and continually directed against what is considered feminine activity. What kind of self-image can little girls have, then, with half their peers despising them because they have been discouraged from so-called masculine activity and wrapped in pink blankets?

The distortion continues when puberty arrives and boys turn to girls as sex objects but do not understand how to relate on other important levels. Consider the divorce rate! No matter what her achievements might be, when the time comes, a woman is expected to knuckle under, pay attention to her feminine duties and obediently follow her husband wherever his endeavor or inclination takes him—no matter how detrimental it might be to her own.

A well-known contemporary composer has a wife who is also a competent composer. They travel together extensively and often return to the same places for performances of his work. She is rarely if ever solicited for her own work and no one seems to see anything wrong with constantly ignoring her output while continually seeking out her husband's work.

Many critics and professors cannot refer to women who are also composers without using cute or condescending language. She is a "lady composer." Rightly, this expression is anathema to many self-respecting women composers. It effectively separates women's efforts from the mainstream. According to the Dictionary of American Slang, "lady" used in such a context is almost always insulting or sarcastic. What critic today speaks of a "gentleman composer"?

It is still true that unless she is super-excellent, the woman in music will always be subjugated, while men of the same or lesser talent will find places for themselves. It is not enough that a woman chooses to be a composer, conductor or to play instruments formerly played exclusively by

men; she cannot escape being squashed in her efforts—if not directly, then by subtle and insidious exclusion by her male counterparts.

And yet some women do break through. The current Schwann Catalog lists over one thousand different composers. Clara Schumann of the Romantic Period and Elizabeth J. de la Guerre[1] of the Baroque are the sole representatives for women composers of the past. But on the positive side, over 75 percent of the almost 1,000 are composers of the present and 24 of these are women. These approximate statistics point to two happy trends: (1) that composers of our time are no longer ignored, and (2) that women could be emerging from musical subjugation. (It is significant that in a biography of Schumann that I have read, Clara is always talked about as a pianist, not a composer, and she is quoted as saying "I'd give my life for Robert.")

The first of the two trends is developing even though the majority of performers do not include contemporary music in their repertoire and private teachers seldom encourage their students to try new music or even to become acquainted with their local composers. Agencies such as the Rockefeller and Ford Foundations have helped establish centers for new music in universities across the country, and independent organizations such as the Once Group of Ann Arbor and the San Francisco Tape Music Center promoted lively programs of new music throughout the 1960's. Isolated individual efforts throughout the country have gradually created an active, new music network.

At last, the dying symphony and opera organizations may have to wake up to the fact that music of our time is necessary to draw audiences from the people under 30. The mass media, radio, TV and the press could have greater influence in encouraging American music by ending the competition between music of the past and music of the present.

---

[1]Elisabeth-Claude Jacquet de La Guerre (1665–1729), a renowned French Baroque harpsichordist and composer, was the first woman in France to compose an opera and to publish violin sonatas.

Many composers of today are not interested in the criteria applied by critics to their work and it is up to the critic to discern new criteria by going to the composer. With more performances of new works at which the composers are present, and with the greater mobility of our society, critics have a unique opportunity—a duty—to converse directly with the composer. Since performers are often irresponsible with new works because of disrespect for or lack of established models, works with which the critics have familiarized themselves would escape some scathing misjudgments due to poor performances. The ideal critic could not only interpret technically and encourage an atmosphere which is sympathetic to the phenomenon of new music, but present the composer as a real and reasonable person to audiences. Certainly, no "great" composer, especially a woman, has a chance to emerge in a society which believes that all "great" music has been written by those long departed.

The second trend is, of course, dependent on the first because of the cultural deprivation of women in the past. Critics do a great deal of damage by wishing to discover "greatness." It does not matter that not all composers are great composers; it matters that this activity be encouraged among all the population, that we communicate with each other in non-destructive ways. Women composers are very often dismissed as minor or light-weight talents on the basis of one work by critics who have never examined their scores or waited for later developments.

Men do not have to commit sexual suicide in order to encourage their sisters in music. Since they have been on top for so long, they could seek out women and encourage them in all professional fields. Libraries of women's music should be established. Women need to know what they can achieve. Critics can quit being cute and start studying scores. . . .

Near the beginning of this century, Nikola Tesla, electrical engineer and inventor of A.C. power,[2] predicted that women will some day unleash their enormous creative potential and for a time will excel men in all fields because they have been so long dormant. Certainly the greatest problems of society will never be solved until an egalitarian atmosphere utilizing the total creative energies exists among all men and women.

---

[2] Electrical power from alternating current.

110   Minimalism and Beyond

Minimalism, a movement of the late 1950s and 60s, began in San Francisco, spread to New York, and diffused out from there. Its antecedents lie in the music of Erik Satie, early works by John Cage, and music of non-Western peoples. It is characterized generally by a radical reduction in compositional materials; much repetition of short melodic fragments; diatonic, static harmony; rhythmic drive based on an eighth-note pulse; and rhythmic phasing. Seminal works include La Monte Young's *Trio for Strings* (1958), Terry Riley's *In C* (1964) and *Poppy Nogood and the Phantom Band* (1967); Steve Reich's *Come Out* (1966), *Drumming* (1971), and *Music for 18 Musicians* (1976); and Philip Glass's *Music in Contrary Motion* (1969) and *Music in Fifths* (1969).

Steve Reich (b. 1936) tours the world with his own ensemble, a group he founded with three members in 1966 and that has grown to eighteen or more. His recent compositions include *Different Trains* (1988), in which speech recordings and realistic sirens and train noises generate musical material that juxtaposes train trips across America and Europe during World War II. *The Cave* (1993) is a large production that includes documentary video footage. A full-length music theater piece, *Three Tales*, is slated to premiere in its complete form in 2002.

Philip Glass (b. 1937) began applying Eastern techniques to his own work after becoming acquainted with Indian music performed by Ravi Shankar during the early 1960s. Like Reich, he went on to establish his own performing group, the Philip Glass Ensemble. Glass has collaborated with major dance figures, among them Twyla Tharp and Lucinda Childs. He also has received commissions from major orchestras, including the Cleveland Orchestra, Atlanta Symphony Orchestra, and Rotterdam Philharmonic. Most of his works since 1975 have been written for dance, film, or theater, including his operatic trilogy *Einstein on the Beach* (1976), *Satyagraha* (1980), and *Akhnaten* (1984). Other recent operas and theater works include *The Fall of the House of Usher* (1988), *The Voyage* (1992), and a chamber opera, *Orphée* (1993), based on a film by Jean Cocteau.

John Adams (b. 1947) came under the spell of minimalism following a performance by Steve Reich of *Drumming* in 1974. This influence is reflected in a number of his works, including *Phrygian Gates* (1977), *Shaker Loops* (1978), and *Common Tones in Simple Time* (1979). He has written operas that have gained some measure of success, among them the topical *Nixon in China* (1987) and *The Death of Klinghoffer* (1991). In some compositions, such as *The Wound-Dresser* (1988), he embraces what has been called the New Romanticism. Although a native of New England, Adams has spent most of his career in San Francisco. Like Steve Reich and Philip Glass, Adams eschews compositional labels.

STEVE REICH

from Interview by William Duckworth (1995)

How do you define minimalism?
I don't. I steer away from that whole thing. Minimalism is not a word that I made up, I believe it was first used by Michael Nyman in about 1971.[1] Terms like impressionism—which is a nice parallel because it was taken from painting to apply to music—are useful in that they denote a group of composers. If you say minimalism, I know you're talking about me, Phil Glass, Terry Riley, La Monte Young, and maybe John Adams. But as a descriptive term, I'd say it becomes more pejorative than descriptive starting about 1973 with *Music for Mallet Instruments, Voices, and Organ*. As my pieces extend orchestration and harmony, the term becomes less descriptive, until by the time you get to *Tehillim* and *The Desert Music*, it's only called minimalism because I wrote it. But the larger issue is this: that kind of classification has traditionally not been the province of composers, even when they wanted it to be. Schoenberg was famous for loathing the word "atonal." He said there was no such thing and wanted to have his music called "pantonal." And nobody could give a tinker's damn what he wanted—the words *twelve-tone* and *atonal* have stuck to this day. And I think that that decision is correctly the province of journalists and music historians. I understand the reason for having it, but I don't get involved. My job is composing the next piece and not putting myself in some kind of theoretical box.

Are you sorry the term stuck? Is it useful, or has it boxed you in?
I leave it for you to judge. Nobody seems to accuse me of writing the same piece over and over again.

Do you find that people are disappointed when you don't write the same piece again and again?
I'm sure there are some who wish I'd write *Drumming* or *Music for Eighteen Musicians* for the rest of my life, but I'm just not that kind of composer; I move on.

William Duckworth, *Talking Music* (New York: Schirmer Books, 1995), 293.

[1]An English composer, author of *Experimental Music* (1981).

PHILIP GLASS

from Interview by William Duckworth (1995)

Are you comfortable being known as a minimalist?
Well, I haven't written any minimal music in twelve years. The difficulty is that the word doesn't describe the music that people are going to hear. I don't think "minimalism" adequately describes it. I think it describes a very reductive, quasirepetitive style of the late sixties. But by 1975 or '76, everyone had begun to do something a little bit different. Actually, the last holdouts are the Europeans. There are still minimalists in Europe, but not in America. So I think the term doesn't describe the music well. And if it doesn't prepare you at all for what you're going to hear, it's not a useful description.

Is there a term you like better?
Not particularly. Fortunately, it's not needed so much anymore. Usually people will say it's my music, *or* they will say, "Did you hear *Koyaanisqatsi*?"[2] The style is easily described in terms of the music it-

---

William Duckworth, *Talking Music* (New York: Schirmer Books, 1995), 342.

[2]Glass's 1982 film score.

self. It is concert music. I don't use bass drums or guitars. And it's in the tradition of notated music. It's basically chamber music that's amplified. I think that the diversity of contemporary music stands on its own in a certain way. I just did a solo concert—something I rarely do. No one in the audience seemed to think it needed any particular description.

JOHN ADAMS

from Interview by Reinder Pols (1991)

Your two operas, Nixon in China *and* The Death of Klinghoffer, *use recent historical events for their themes, but beyond this they seem very different. Can you describe these differences and explain how you arrived at your decisions?*

Both *Nixon* and *Klinghoffer* are superficially about highly publicized political events that occurred within narrowly defined dates. The Peking[3] leg of Nixon's trip to China in 1972 took only three days; the Achille Lauro hijacking was over in less than four days. Each was a kind of signal event, brief but loaded with implication, and as such seemed perfect for a dramatic treatment. Of course the isolated events themselves are only tips of the icebergs. In the case of *Nixon in China*, all that official protocol was little more than a cardboard covering, an attempt to conceal the deep and long-standing misunderstandings between cultures and their leaders. In *Klinghoffer* the story behind the story is one of millennia. The conflicts are not personal, but rather national, religious, and economic.

I felt I could best address the Nixon story by means of irony and sentimentality. The whole trip to China was a piece of puffery, and I wanted to utilize the sense of the absurd that comes about when very vain individuals think they are doing something important. That's why the *verismo* elements in that opera and its employment of operatic conventions (Madame Mao's coloratura *da capo* aria, Mrs. Nixon's "Countess" scene at the start of Act 2, the grand divertissement of "The Red Detachment of Women," etc.) add what I feel is an appropriate ironic distance to the story, not to mention bringing out the obvious absurdity of the whole event.

The difference between *Nixon* and *Klinghoffer* lies in the fact that the Achille Lauro story is a real tragedy made even more tragic by the way it was revealed to the world. There was no question of using the dramatic and musical techniques of *Nixon* to deal with the events of this particular story. A different tack altogether was needed. There was a story to be told, but exactly how it would be told was crucial.

With that in mind, how did you proceed?

Well, the models were not from the operatic tradition at all, but rather from those pieces of sacred music that tell a story, usually the Crucifixion, in a much more erratic tone. The Bach Passions were certainly a critical starting point for me. I think that Beethoven's extremely graphic use of the liturgy in the *Missa Solemnis* had a huge effect on Peter Sellars.

Finding the right tone was the challenge, and I think the breakthrough came when I saw Alice Goodman's choruses.[4] These choruses seem to stand apart from the more mundane and often desperate actions of the characters. Many of them focus on the natural world—the desert, the ocean, night, day, creation, and decay, and they are full of sacred artifacts. These choruses not only serve to

---

John Adams; Interview by Reinder Pols. *Severance Hall (Cleveland) Bulletin* 22 (April 1991): 33–39.
[3]Beijing.

[4]Alice Goodman was the librettist for both *The Death of Klinghoffer* and *Nixon in China*.

put a frame around the "story," they also remind us that this event, this hijacking and assassination, so seemingly lurid and "newsworthy" in our minds, was in fact played out in the very womb of Western civilization. For me they are a constant reminder that Judaism, Christianity, and Islam all originated within a small distance from each other and, to this day, bitter battles are being fought over this relatively small plot of earth.

Aside from the choruses, the actual story seems to be told by means of arias. There are very few instances of vocal ensemble or dialogue. Was this a conscious choice?

The only really conventional use of operatic dialogue is in the Prologue, what we refer to as "the New Jersey scene." This scene is meant to be a kind of comic presaging of the impending tragedy. Alice's text is a mine field of allusions, and I responded to this by doing a similar thing musically.

Otherwise, the story is told largely by individual utterance. The Captain, the Swiss Grandmother, the Austrian Woman, the First Officer, and the British Dancing Girl all recall the event as if they were doing so from the comfort of their own living rooms. The Palestinians and the Klinghoffers speak in the present tense. Add to this the "timeless" tone of the choruses, and you have a constantly shifting scale of closeness and distance from the actual event. At one moment you feel as though you're right there on the deck under the blistering sun with the rest of the passengers, and a moment later you feel like you're reading about it in some very ancient text.

How do you feel about characters? Did you find yourself liking some more than others?

As with the characters in *Nixon in China,* each has something interesting and intensely important to say. Obviously each of us—composer, librettist, stage director, and choreographer—has a different take on them. I think the Captain, for instance, tends to overrate his own ability to control the events that are unfolding before him. On this level he must have reminded me faintly of Nixon. Certainly the knowledge that I was writing this role for James Maddelena (our first Nixon) must have colored my perceptions as well. I also think the figure

of the Captain is heavily indebted to Joseph Conrad. He reminds me of Marlow (the Conradian mouthpiece in *Lord Jim* and several other tales) in the way he likes to spin out a good yarn and intertwine events with his own psychological and philosophical musing.

Alice, on the other hand, never lost sight of the fact that, in addition to everything else, this is a sea story. The sound of the radio, for example, whether it's the short-wave transmissions everyone is hoping to hear from Syria, or the unlicensed broadcasts of Arabic songs that Mamoud listens to at night, is always colored by the fact that it's all happening over water.

Each character has at least one moment of revelation. Even the British Dancing Girl, who appears on the surface to be little more than a supernumerary, has something acute to say. She has no political agenda. She's only interested in staying alive, and she is able to size up the other people with devastating accuracy.

Did you have any particular musical influences when writing for individual characters? The Palestinians, for example?

There's always danger when musically treating someone from another culture. Music is alarmingly precise in this sense, and one has to be on guard about any kind of exoticisms creeping into the work. On the other hand, I wanted at times to convey a sense of "otherness" to these Palestinians if only to point up the fear of the unknown that must have gripped these American and European tourists. At no point did I try to imitate Arabic music. That would have been completely wrong. What I did instead was to develop certain harmonic and melodic modes that were dedicated to one group and not shared by another.

Beyond that, the only specific influence I could name would be the music of Abed Azrié, a Palestinian composer and singer whose songs I was listening to while composing the long scene in Act 1 between Mamoud and the Captain.

How would you describe your musical style in this opera? Do you feel that it differs significantly from the style of your other works?

I think we are experiencing a period in all the arts

when stylistic purity is giving way to a freer, less constricted attitude toward making art. I've always been encouraged by the example of those artists who draw from the vernacular of everyday life, the quotidian, the ordinary, even the banal, and who are able to synthesize their experience into something that is at once familiar yet radically new.

I came of age as a composer during a time when the European post-war esthetic (composers such as Boulez, Berio, Stockhausen, etc.) had immense influence among the university music community in the United States. The question of one's adherence to a particular system or method of procedure became a matter of morality. Composers wished fervently to be treated with the deference we treat scientists.

But this was thirty to forty years ago, and the esthetic philosophies of the early '50s don't answer our present needs. Nevertheless, the prestige and influence of the older "avant garde" still exert a strangle-hold on a lot of young composers. It's like rigor mortis. Fortunately though, I detect now a certain unbending of attitudes, especially in America among the younger generation of composers. They don't seem to make such a great distinction between "serious" and "popular" art. I myself try not to worry about these categories. I prefer to think like a movie director . . . as if I were working in a totally new medium that didn't have such a long and over-powering historical precedent, one in which issues of "high" and "low" culture didn't exist.

But what about your own style?

Well, that's just the point. . . . I don't think style is the issue right now. I was formerly placed in the "minimalist" camp, but I don't think that's a helpful distinction any more. Certainly, some of the techniques of minimalism are at work here in this opera, but it's not a severe and pure example of the style such as you would find in the operas of Philip Glass, for example. I am inclined to think that many of the best works of musical theatre came about during periods of stylistic heterogeny.

111　　　　The Music Business

People in the music business learned in the nineteenth century that theirs was an enterprise that could turn a profit. Publishers such as S. Brainard's Sons in Cleveland and Oliver Ditson in Boston, instrument makers such as the Brothers Chickering in Boston and Henry Erben in New York and performers such as singer Jenny Lind, pianist Louis Moreau Gottschalk, and conductor Theodore Thomas shaped America's entrepreneurial attitudes. Music became a saleable commodity.

During the twentieth century, the music business expanded greatly. In the late 1920s, radio, records, and the advent of talking pictures exploded the market picture. Television followed in the 1940s, and by the late 1990s, new technology had rushed us into downloading digital music from the World Wide Web. The causes may change, but Americans' thirst for music and their willingness to pay for it continues.

Below, interviews with the presidents of two companies reveal how they dealt successfully with music in the marketplace. Osmun Music is a relatively new company that serves high-level players of brass and woodwind instruments. The roots of the old-line Holtkamp Organ Company, which manufactures fine organs, extend back to the 1850s.

Osmun Music sells and repairs professional-grade brass and wind instruments. Founded in 1976 in Cambridge, Massachusetts, the company has grown steadily and has become nationally renowned through its sales of instruments to the professional market and the excellence of its repair department. As its home page states, it is a business "run by musicians for musicians." The firm employs ten people at its spacious quarters in Arlington, Massachusetts. It publishes an international newsletter which it distributes by e-mail, and it sponsors master classes by prestigious performers at its headquarters.

Responsible for this growth is the company's president, Robert Osmun, a horn player who moved to Boston to study at the New England Conservatory. Starting originally as an instrument repair business, Osmun's fledgling company soon began selling new brass instruments as well, later expanding into woodwinds. Osmun points out that although the music instrument business has recently been under stress, good opportunities will continue to be available to those who serve committed players well.

The Holtkamp Organ Company of Cleveland, Ohio, continues a long tradition in America begun in the mid-eighteenth century by the Moravians Johann Gottlob Klemm and David Tannenberg, and by the Bostonian Thomas Johnston. The company began as a small, regional firm founded in 1855 by Gottlieb F. Votteler. The Holtkamp name has been associated with it for four generations, starting in 1903.

The firm gained international prominence in the 1930s by rejecting the popular orchestral organ and advocating a return to the kinds of instruments better suited for playing the music of Bach and other Baroque composers. Holtkamp incorporated a freestanding, unenclosed *Rückpositiv* (pipes behind the player's back) into the Skinner organ at the Cleveland Museum of Art, an installation then in its Garden Court. The instrument was then used in a remarkable series of twenty recitals by Melville Smith and Arthur Quinby. Carleton Bullis, writing in *The Diapason* of December 1933, commented, "One was able to listen attentively to a whole program of Bach music without feeling bored, so delightfully sparkling and incisive and alive was the effect of the music." The renowned physician and organist Albert Schweitzer journeyed to Cleveland in 1949 specifically to see the instrument.

Holtkamp's ideas gave impetus to the so-called organ reform movement in the 1930s, which aimed to allow older music to be heard as it was intended. The resulting instruments used slider chests and tracker (mechanical) action. At present, about half of the eight or so new organs built by the company yearly are tracker organs. The firm employs about two dozen people at its shop on Cleveland's west side, a site it has occupied since 1922.

ROBERT OSMUN

Interview by J. Heywood Alexander (1996)

Mr. Osmun, you are the president of a company serving the international needs for professional brasses and woodwinds. Would you briefly describe the nature of your business?

We sell, service, repair, and modify professional-grade wind instruments and provide a wide assortment of accessories and other music-related items to our customers. We try to serve the high end of the market, professional players, advanced amateurs, conservatory students. Many of our product lines are products that are difficult or impossible to get from other places. So we call ourselves pretty much a "niche" market or a "niche" business.

The business was known initially as Osmun Brass Instruments. When did you change the name to Osmun Music, and why?

We changed the name shortly before our move from Belmont to Arlington in 1995, and we decided to change from Osmun Brass Instruments to Osmun Music for two reasons: (1) because the name Osmun Brass Instruments was just too long and too big a mouthful to handle; and (2) because

we felt there was a lot of opportunity in the woodwind side of the business that we had been pretty much ignoring. Changing the name to Osmun Music just made it less specific and gave us the potential of branching out into the woodwind areas or any other music areas we wanted to get into.

How has your business grown from its inception until now?

It began in 1976 simply as a repair business in a loft in Cambridge that I shared with two flute makers. It continued in that way for several years in Cambridge, later in Foxboro, later still in Belmont specifically as a repair business. Then about 1982 or thereabouts I decided to start selling some instruments. I started with Paxman horns and gradually increased other lines until the sales became an important part of the business.

How many employees do you have at present and what do they do; i.e., how is your organization structured?

Currently we have ten employees. Of those, counting myself, we have four people in the repair department. We have four people in sales and we have a bookkeeper and we have my wife who is the treasurer of the company. My wife and I essentially

Robert Osmun, Interview by J. Heywood Alexander, September 1996.

run it as a partnership. The sales and repair operations report to us.

Is it true that you have opted to direct your attention first and foremost to professional instrumentalists, but that you also work with schools?

The school business is a very crowded business which is well served by a lot of different companies in our area. By concentrating on professional instruments and on service we have a knowledge component which other businesses have a hard time offering. We tend to confine ourselves to those schools which are interested in a kind of higher quality service that we can offer and try also to extend our reach to the students through private music teachers.

You have had ties to Japan through being one of the largest professional Yamaha dealers in the country. You also have represented other non-American concerns, such as Paxman in England. What problems and opportunities do you see in positioning yourself internationally?

Our relationship with the Yamaha Corporation of America differs from that with our other foreign suppliers in that we are dealing with an American subsidiary rather than with the Japanese parent company. Yamaha USA will buy its product from Japan, and we buy a product from them, much the same way the large Japanese car companies have American subsidiaries that actually run their American operations. We're the sole U.S. distributor of German-made Schmid horns and one of two distributors of Paxman and Alexander horns. In these cases we deal directly with the parent companies.

I think there are really unlimited possibilities in the export market, both in Japan and the Far East generally and in Europe. Right now the pricing structure in the United States is substantially lower than that in the Far East and Europe, so our instruments, even at prices that are in the U.S. double or more what competing instruments are selling for, are directly competitive in Japan. The Japanese appreciate high quality and they're willing to pay for it, and they also appreciate exclusivity. The notion of the high quality product that's available in limited quantities is appealing to them.

The Korean and Taiwanese markets are very strong. Those are countries where education is very highly valued and people have high incomes. They're a natural market for the kind of products that we sell.

The same is true to a lesser extent in Europe. The price disparity isn't as much and the access to the international market is greater. And, again, we haven't had enough product to seriously investigate selling it in Europe, but I think that it will sell there very well, too.

You represent the company personally at a number of conventions and other types of meetings in this country and abroad. How important is such personal exposure?

I think it's very important. I think that the basic product we have to sell is knowledge, and I think that by presenting myself as a knowledgeable person who's interested in the same musical things that the performers are interested in I build my own credibility. Also, I think it's really important to be out there and see what people are interested in and see where they're going so that we can meet their needs and hopefully position ourselves a little bit ahead of the curve.

Besides personal word of mouth, you also put out a national newsletter and have a home page on the Internet. How do you see this kind of written advertising, if we may call it that, developing in the future?

We're hoping very much that the Internet becomes a viable medium for getting out our message, primarily because it's much less expensive than efforts like the newsletter. It reaches potentially a wider variety of people and it can be updated and added to on a continuous basis. Furthermore, it will essentially involve a dialogue between us presenting things that we have to offer and want to sell and customers asking questions and asking for products. I think it is very mutually beneficial.

The newsletter, of course, we've been doing that for years, and it's fun to do. A lot of people look forward to it. However, I think we're going to be doing a lot less of that in the future primarily because of cost. Also, the sort of topical stuff we like to put into it tends to be out of date by the time the newsletter goes out to print. The newsletter is now distributed by E-mail. It's much less expensive and more timely that way.

You recently expanded and moved the business into new quarters in Arlington. Your beautiful new facilities will serve you well for the foreseeable future. Do you have any comments about your recent move?

Yes, I wish we'd done it five years ago, or ten. We now have enough space to do what we want to do. We have a nice display area that helps sell things just because the stuff is out where people can see it in pleasant surroundings. We have a large room we can use for recitals and master classes and we have a large workshop where we can spread out and where we can set up the machinery we need and the things we need to do the work the way we want to do it.

One of the things you have instigated is a series of master classes with highly respected players who come through Boston, often to play with the Boston Symphony Orchestra. How are these working out, and will you expand upon this series in the future?

Yes, the master classes are working out very nicely. I do it as a labor of love, really; there are no financial rewards in doing it. We've had some very good people who have come primarily because of my personal contacts with them, and, after a year of doing that, we're now at the stage where we're starting to have people asking us to come and play here, which is very pleasant. I think it builds credibility.

What major opportunities do you see down the road? How will your company continue to expand and grow? Do you want it to expand?

Our Internet Sales have become a major part of our business. We will continue to develop this area.

What characteristics are you looking for when recruiting employees?

We find that the single most important characteristic is the ability to get along with coworkers and to contribute as part of a team. So we look for people who will get along and work to build the operation as opposed to protecting their own turf, people who have agile minds, who think on their feet and can roll with the punches. Most musicians tend to be smart people.

Obviously, in the repair shop the skills are very specific, and it's always been our policy that when somebody came along and had what I thought were the requisite skills, to hire them. We're looking for people who are going to be with us for the long term.

What is your own assessment about the market you serve? What changes do you see on the horizon and how will they affect your business?

I think that it's true that the professional music business is a shrinking business and, as the level of educational attainment in the country continues to drop, the interest of people in supporting music organizations continues to dwindle. [Music] as an avocation is still very strong. I think you're going to see more and more of these amateur musicians, who are a great market for us because they've got stable, well paying jobs, a lot of disposable income, and a strong interest.

I think in the times since I've been in business I've seen the type of people involved in the music business change. Their wants and needs and aspirations are different from what they were a generation ago. And, again, I think we need to serve them on the upper edge with quality products, quality service, and well-chosen, thoughtful accessory products. [We will continue to serve a] top-level market with really fine products, backing it up with detailed knowledge and dedicated support. That's what our business is about.

WALTER HOLTKAMP, JR.

Interview by J. Heywood Alexander (1994)

Your company was founded in Cleveland in 1855 by Gottlieb Votteler. Why was an organ company begun in that city at that time?

Gottlieb Votteler had come to this country in the 1840s. He had trained as a piano maker in Germany. In this country he found work in organ shops and learned the trade. I am guessing that he came to Cleveland because it was a center of commerce and he was able to ship instruments via the Great Lakes or through the canal system to the interior of Ohio.

How did the Holtkamp name come into the business?

Gottlieb Votteler formed the firm. He was then succeeded by his son, Henry B. Votteler. By the turn of the century Henry B. wanted out of the business. He called upon my grandfather, Henry Holtkamp, who had a piano and organ store in St. Mary's, Ohio. Henry's father was Wilhelm Holtkamp, who had come to this country from Ladbergen, Germany. Wilhelm was quite musical. In the 1840s in western Ohio there were no instruments, so each church had a song leader. Wilhelm was that song leader for his church. His son Henry was also quite musical. He became an organist and choir director at the Reformed Church in Knoxville. He decided that his future did not lie in the church, but in selling musical instruments. So he set up a shop in St. Mary's where he did very well. When he would sell an organ, he would send the order to Votteler, who, in turn, would build the instrument and ship it to Holtkamp to be installed. And he did well enough that Votteler said, "Why don't you come to Cleveland and take over this shop?" You can pay me rent for the building and the machinery. The turn of the century, about 1903, was when my grandfather brought his family to Cleveland.

Walter Holtkamp, Jr., Interview by J. Heywood Alexander, January 1994.

When did your father start in the business?

All organ builders' sons grow up working in the shop. However, my father came into the business in a permanent way following his service in World War I. He did not muster out from the army immediately at the armistice in 1918, so I would say he came into the shop about 1920. He went to Minnesota, where he was a salesman for the company. Actually, he intended to make his life in Minnesota. But, around 1927 or 1928, he was down here [in Cleveland] and was introduced to a young woman named Margaret McClure, who turned out to be my mother. He decided he would make his life in Cleveland. He was active in the firm from about 1920.

It was really your father who raised the firm to international prominence. He led the organ movement towards bringing the organ into the room, towards the better realization of sound—the so-called Orgelbewegung. *When did that start?*

I would say roughly in the early 1930s. My father and my grandfather in the 1920s built very much the instruments of the day. They built orchestrally oriented instruments. They built theater organs. When they built a church organ, it was very much like a theater organ.

My grandfather died in 1931, and my father was left in charge of the firm. He had met at the Cleveland Museum of Art, Arthur Quinby; and from Western Reserve University, Melville Smith. They were fresh from Europe, having studied with Nadia Boulanger, and were very eager to perform the full works of Bach at the Cleveland Museum of Art. They felt, by virtue of their attitude toward the music of Bach, that this very orchestral instrument at the museum would not play that music as they wished to hear it and perform it. So they looked up this young organ builder in Cleveland named Holtkamp. They went to see him. And they said, "We would like to change the Skinner organ at the

Cleveland Museum." He thought they were nuts. He thought they were hippies, a bunch of cuckoos, because Ernest M. Skinner instruments were the highest flower of American organ building.

But a number of things had come together: the depression had hit, and my father was ripe for a change. He threw in his lot with these harum-scarum organ players. That was the beginning of the end of the orchestral organ era when people played transcriptions of *The Ride of the Valkyries* and instead were playing Bach and Buxtehude and Franck.

At the same time this was happening in the United States it was also happening in Europe, initially under the aegis of Albert Schweitzer. There was correspondence between my father and various Europeans interested in the pipe organ reform movement. Among them was Schweitzer. At the same time that my father was pushing this idea of a new instrument, a new kind of literature—this Bach and Buxtehude—there were in this country conservative groups who were trying to hang on to the orchestral instrument. It made a very interesting dichotomy in American organ music between these two camps. Organists and organ builders chose up sides to see which camp they would be in. That was the beginning of organ music as we know it today in this country, and in Europe for that matter.

You mentioned the Cleveland Museum of Art. One of the major achievements was the free-standing Rückpositiv *in the Garden Court.*

Yes. When Arthur Quinby and Melville Smith began to work with my father, they said what they needed, in order to play the works of Bach, was a new division for the instrument, which was a *Positiv* division. They put it over the rail in the traditional *Rückpositiv* position—*Rück* meaning [*at*] *your back*—and they experimented with various sets of pipes over a period of months to determine what sounds would cohere best. The Cleveland Museum organ became a laboratory for my father and Arthur Quinby and Melville Smith. Later, when Arthur Quinby left Cleveland, he was succeeded by Walter Blodgett. That experimentation

went on over a period of twenty years. Then that instrument was used in the construction of the new instrument that I built in Gartner Auditorium at the museum.

When did you enter the business?

I came into the organ business full time in 1956 when I came home from a tour of duty in the U.S. Navy. During four years in the Navy I was an operations officer on a destroyer. I had a lot of time to think about what I wanted to do with my life. I realized that organ building offered me everything that I wanted—it dealt in music, it dealt in visual design, it gave me a great deal of independence. I elected to come to work in the family shop, and my father and I worked together for about six years, until his death.

That was in 1962?

Yes. He died in February of 1962, very suddenly. At that point I became the president of the Holtkamp Organ Company.

You inherited a significant legacy of international achievement. What do you consider your own major achievements?

That's a hard question, perhaps better answered by someone else. However, I carried the firm from doing simply electro-pneumatic instruments into doing mechanical action instruments. Probably I carried the firm further in a variety of visual designs in the pipe organ. We achieved a certain [reputation] as visual designers. Tonally, I sought an amalgam of sounds that could support a wide range of the organ literature. I suppose those are the areas in which I have prospered.

Let's move on to consider organ building in today's world. We live in a highly technological society. What has been the impact of advancing technology on the organ building business?

There have been various technological advances in our world. One such is solid-state systems for instrument control. Each time new technology comes on the scene, there is a long period when organ builders look at it. Some people leap into it immediately; others, later. But, in general, the solid-state systems have come into use for control in the pipe organ. At the same time, we have had builders become very interested in getting away from any modern technology and going back to the simplest, most primitive kind of mechanical action systems. These two schools of thought regarding the organ have co-existed. There are a number of builders, such as myself, who have gone into mechanical action for the key action and the advantages that provides to the player—advantages of control, advantages of nuances of touch—but, at the same time have utilized the solid-state systems for stop control and registration, because [for] that particular part you don't need nuances of control.

Plastics have come into our world, and there are a number of builders who have utilized plastic in various forms, rather than using wood. A good example is that, in our tracker instruments, we have used fiberglass trackers, rather than thin strips of wood. Wood tends to suffer through changes in humidity and temperature, whereas the fiberglass is stable.

An organ builder really has to evaluate each of these things. A number of builders were badly burned in utilizing some plastic for pouch valves rather than using leather. It seemed like a natural thing to use. It was highly touted by the plastics [industry]. But, in fact, it was easily degraded by ultraviolet light, and builders had to go back and replace all the plastic they used.

So, some things work; some things don't work.

Organ builders have a particular problem in that we look at a time frame of more than a hundred years as to whether a material is a success. Most industry looks at a one-to-five-year time frame. If it lasts five years, it's adequate. We need things to last a hundred years.

What might you see as the opportunities and problems that face a builder of fine instruments in today's world?

Probably the biggest problem that faces a pipe organ builder today is that pipe organs are incredibly labor intensive, and there is less and less money to pay for highly labor-intensive artifacts in our world. We as builders cannot really avoid the labor-intensive quality. Each instrument is a unique instrument.

Where do you see all of this leading?

It seems to me within the United States, and probably internationally, the very large pipe organ firms—those that employ one hundred or two hundred people—will gradually lose their place; they will fail. The smaller firms of anything from ten to twenty people will carry the brunt of the organ building. People are interested in the craftsmanship aspect of the pipe organ. Hence, they seek out smaller, craft-oriented firms. People would rather talk with the designer of the instrument than a local sales rep. So I think there will always be a place for the smaller, craft-oriented builder.

Wynton Marsalis,
Spokesperson for Jazz

Wynton Marsalis (b. 1961), trumpet player, composer, and impresario, leads the Lincoln Center Jazz Orchestra and has been artistic director of Jazz at Lincoln Center since its beginning in 1991. Working with a program steered by director Rob Gibson and artistic consultants Stanley Crouch and Albert Murray, Marsalis is trying to create a jazz canon. In describing how the program started, Gibson remarked, "In 1987 there was a guy who could play on a trumpet a Haydn concerto with a symphony orchestra as well as anyone else could, then take a cab to a club and play with Art Blakey. So Wynton has had a whole lot to do with making something like Jazz at Lincoln Center possible."* This new emphasis on jazz at Lincoln Center gave it a base alongside the other arts at one of the most prestigious performing arts institutions in the nation. The canon being built by Marsalis comes out of a tradition rooted in New Orleans and the blues.

Born in New Orleans, the second of six sons, Marsalis counts among his teachers his father, jazz educator and pianist Ellis Marsalis. Wynton came to New York at age eighteen and attended the Juilliard School for one year. He emerged as a performer and composer during the 1980s. He won a Grammy award in 1982 for his recording of trumpet concertos by Haydn, Hummel, and Leopold Mozart, but his interest in jazz has gained the upper hand.

Among his compositions is a three-hour oratorio, *Blood on the Fields* (1994), a parable of love and freedom within slavery. The recording won a Pulitzer Prize in 1997. In its subject matter, the piece is related to Duke Ellington's *Black, Brown and Beige* (1943), which depicts the history of African Americans in the United States.

Aware that audiences of the future must be cultivated, Marsalis has followed in the footsteps of Leonard Bernstein's path-breaking televised broadcasts with the New York Philharmonic. He has been a frequent host on National Public Radio and PBS-TV and produced *Marsalis on Music* (1995), a four part television series for young people that compares a jazz orchestra with a symphony orchestra and teaches elements of musical form. He was also a featured commentator in *Jazz,* the ten-part television documentary produced by Ken Burns, which first aired in January 2001.

The interviews that follow were conducted by Ted Panken, who has broadcast regularly over New York's WKCR-FM since 1985 and has written articles for jazz periodicals and liner notes for jazz recordings. The excerpt from *Sweet Swing Blues on the Road* comes from a session Marsalis presented for Professor James Ketch and students at the University of North Carolina.

---

*Howard Reich, "Wynton's Decade: Creating a Canon," *Down Beat*, December 1992: 18.

WYNTON MARSALIS

Two Interviews by Ted Panken (1993–94; PUB. 1997)

December 1993

TP: Why is the New Orleans connection so important to you in terms of the musicians you perform with? It sounds like sort of a naive question, but I just would like to hear how you see it.

WM: Well, you know, it just has worked out that way. I didn't plan it that way, really. It's not like I went to New Orleans to find musicians, because I've been in New York for twelve years. But Herlin Riley and Reginald Veal with the drums and the bass, are from New Orleans, and they give us the ability to really play some New Orleans music. When you don't have New Orleans musicians in those two positions, it's difficult to get the authentic sound of the music. But you can always distill that sound, like the way that Duke played. He got that type of sound out of Jimmy Woode and Sam Woodyard. It's just that it was transformed. It didn't sound like the New Orleans beat.

TP: Of course Ellington got that sound out of Wellman Braud in the 1920's.

WM: Well, he's from New Orleans. As a matter of fact, Wellman Braud is in my family. You expect that New Orleans musicians will play like that. In Duke's early bands, he had Sidney Bechet, he had Wellman Braud, he had Barney Bigard—he had access to New Orleans musicians. He had Bubber Miley, who even though he wasn't from New Orleans, he was the closest thing you could find to King Oliver outside of Louis Armstrong.

TP: What type of repertoire does the band play in performance? You've accumulated such a diverse body of work in your recent recordings. Do you play the whole spectrum of material?

WM: We play all of it. Even the stuff we used to play, like "Black Codes from the Underground" or "Knozz-Mo-King." We play Duke's music, Monk,

Wayne Shorter—anything really. We haven't played that much of Wayne's music recently, but we'll really play pretty much anything. Some cats will play ballads. Or we try to play some of Trane's[1] music. . . .

TP: Why did you decide to get serious about the trumpet? What was it that inspired you?

WM: Well, then I went through puberty, and I wanted to have something that would distinguish me so that I could be able to rap to the ladies and they would have some respect for what I was saying.

TP: A lot of musicians say that about it!

WM: Oh, man, that's a motivating factor, now. And also just the competition of being in high school; a lot of people could play. And then I actually started listening to music. I started listening to Coltrane's music first, and then later on Clifford Brown and Miles Davis.

TP: Who turned you on to that?

WM: Well, my father always had the records sitting around. I just had never taken the time to listen to any of them. Mainly before that I was just listening to like James Brown or the Isley Brothers, whatever was popular—Earth, Wind & Fire then was becoming popular. We'd go to those little house parties that they have. Once again, it was still in the country. We weren't living in New Orleans yet.

In the summer that I was twelve, I was working, cleaning up a school. That's when I started listening to Trane.[1] I would come home from doing that, and then I would listen to "Giant Steps," and then I'd listen to Clifford Brown and *Max Roach on Basin Street*, and then *Clifford Brown with Strings*, and then a Miles Davis album entitled *Someday My Prince Will Come*, and then a Freddie Hubbard record entitled *Red Clay*. That got me into jazz.

Ted Panken, "Wynton Marsalis Interview[s]," published online, 1997. http://jazzhouse.org/files/panken1.html

---

[1]Saxophonist John Coltrane.

TP: How about jazz education? Your father, Ellis, along with Alvin Batiste, was one of the major educators in jazz really in the country in the 1970s.

WM: [*chuckles*] Well, I always hear that, and it makes me laugh. At most, my father never had more than five students in a class. We had the raggediest room in the school.

TP: Look who came out of it! . . .

TP: Do the words "classic" or "classicism" have a different meaning when applied to the jazz aesthetic as opposed to, say, European music?

WM: Well, you know, I never really know what they're talking about. Some people say "classic jazz," and they mean the 1930's. Some say New Orleans music. Some call Coltrane's group the classic quartet.

TP: What do you mean by it, though?

WM: Well, personally, a term like "classic jazz" really has never meant anything to me. You know, that's the title that was used for the Lincoln Center series that we do in the summertime. Jazz in Lincoln Center is what I believe in.

My feeling is to call it "real jazz." Because real jazz means that you are trying to swing. And when I say "swing," that means that you are dealing with the rhythmic environment that allows for the thematic development, consistent thematic development, in the context of a jazz groove. Which means that you don't have to be going *ting-tinkading-tinkading-tinkading*. A jazz musician will take this same groove, *doomp-dum-dum, doomp-dum-dum*. That will be repeated, but all of the instruments will be improvising and the soloists will be constructing solos that develop thematically.

So it's a matter of development, whenever you want to distinguish whether something is jazz or not, and the range that is played on the groove. A jazz drummer like Elvin Jones will take a groove like that, and he'll play many different things on it. Whereas people who are not playing in the style of jazz might take that same groove, and they will still be improvising, but what they will be playing will be more proscribed. They can improvise, too, but it will be off of the clav or off of a certain thing that's set, whereas a jazz drummer also

includes that into his vocabulary. Which is not to say that jazz is more sophisticated. It's just different. Because the other way is very, very sophisticated.

But when the horn players play and the soloists play, we deal with interaction. The key to jazz music is the interaction of the voices. And the way you can tell whether a piece of jazz is being played is if it's being rendered with some blues feeling, blues melodies, rhythms and harmonies, in the context of some type of form. That means that you're always addressing syncopation, some rhythms are being set up and they're being resolved. If it has the blues in it and also if it's swinging, then it has that sound that we identify with jazz. . . .

TP: When did you first hear Duke Ellington?

WM: I was eighteen or nineteen. Stanley Crouch played some Duke for me. He said, "Check this Duke out." I was like, "Yeah, yeah, just some old ballroom music for people. I mean, I was so steeped in the philosophy of my generation. . . . Then gradually I would start to listen to it, and hear all kinds of different forms, and people playing in different times, and the harmonic sophistication coming out of the blues. Then I got in touch with Jelly Roll Morton through the concert we did at Lincoln Center, the Jelly Roll Morton concert, and that gave me an understanding of how to construct these forms.

I mean, there's nothing really you can say about Duke. His genius speaks for itself. I went to the Smithsonian to see his scores, and there's walls full of large cabinets packed with Ellington's music written in his own hand. Anybody who is ever in Washington, it's really a great education to go in there and look at some of the volumes of music that this man wrote. The things that's most amazing about Ellington's music is that when he wrote it down the first time, he really didn't change it that much, apart from structural changes he would make. You will see pieces of music with people's phone numbers on it, and it will be "The Harlem Suite," and the whole suite will be written out. His conception is very, very clear, and his penmanship is very neat. He writes the notes very small. It doesn't mean that much, but for someone who wrote that much music it's very neat.

June 1994

* * *

TP: It seems to me that you've effectively used the opportunities of the different presentations of Jazz at Lincoln Center to engage in a dialogue with the different genres of music in performance situations, and that you've assimilated the vocabularies in a very personal way.

WM: Well, that was always what I wanted to do. But that was my intention from the beginning of playing music, from my first album. Even though I didn't know a range of music, I still would try to use Charleston rhythms, I would try to change times, use stuff with modes on it, play standards. Whatever information I knew about, I was always trying to include it. Play stuff that had, like, a New Orleans call-and-response, play standard forms like "rhythm" changes, and try to transform them.

My thing is to not cut myself off from my own tradition. That tradition can be anything from John Philip Sousa marches to Beethoven's symphonies, to the blues, to whatever. Because I grew up playing all of that different type of music. I didn't understand it, but that is what I grew up doing. I played in a waltz orchestra. I played in the marching band. I played in a funk band. I played in a jazz band. I played in a circus band. Played on a Broadway show. Played salsa music. All of these musics are part of my experience as a musician. So I don't feel that I should cut myself off from the

traditions I come out of to create a narrow style that's easily identifiable.

TP: To the contrary, I think it's very expansive. But I think the point I was making is that it seems to me that you have assimilated everything you've been working on from the inside-out, more or less, and that it's coming out in your writing in a very natural way.

WM: Well, it is very natural to me. First, I only went to school for a year—to Juilliard. I went for one year. And there really was no jazz class. I remember the first band we had, my brother had gone to Berklee, so he knew more about jazz music, because they have all these exercises and stuff that they had done. So I would always be saying, "Man, what is this and what is that?"

A lot of what I have learned about jazz music, I have learned from the musicians. I learned stuff from Art Blakey.[3] I had the opportunity to play and talk with Elvin Jones, and I learned a lot from him. Sweets Edison. Clark Terry. Whenever I'm around the musicians, I'm always really checking out what they're playing, and listening very carefully to what they are saying. Roy Eldridge taught me how to growl on the trumpet, then I started trying to learn how to do that. How to use the plunger. Joe Wilder gave me lessons on how to play with the hat. I mean, these things I just learned. To me they are all techniques that are important to know, because the expression of jazz music is something that you have to just be familiar with.

---

[3]Soon after he arrived in New York, Marsalis cut his teeth with drummer Art Blakey's Jazz Messengers.

WYNTON MARSALIS

from *Sweet Swing Blues on the Road* (1994)

[Q.] Why do you play Dixieland?
[A.] We don't play Dixieland. We play New Or-

leans music. This music puts us in closer contact with the spirit and meaning of jazz. New Orleans music uses all the idiomatic devices of jazz: riffs, breaks, call and response, vamps, solos, grooves, polyphonic improvisation, and chorus format. It

---

Wynton Marsalis, *Sweet Swing Blues on the Road* (New York: W. W. Norton, 1994), 146–49.

remains the most modern extension of the Western music tradition because you can hear whole groups negotiate with each other, making intelligent and unintelligent decisions while grooving.

Group improvisation means that everyone takes chances, dancing rhythms against the hardwood floor of the form, together attempting to step elegantly through the obstacles of bad musical judgment. One must be forgiving and resilient, have good ears and quick reflexes. That suits the modern world; find an interesting idea, but be ready to change if fresh evidence disproves it or elevates it.

You have to play this music with soul, and that's fun. It's fun to listen to another person stretching out and to go right on out on the limb yourself. Or to push them out. Way out on a limb with music is a hip place to be. And people like this music because it's joyous. The groove is happy and Herlin[2] knows how to play it. Swing is a collective decision. That is why we play New Orleans music.

[Q.] What do you like better, jazz or classical music?

[A.] Jazz.

[Q.] Because jazz has more feeling?

[A.] No. Classical music conveys a wide range of deeply felt experiences. But jazz is more modern and ancient. Jazz is harmony through conflict, like a good, hot discussion.

[Q.] You talk about technique, but not about feeling.

[A.] You know how you feel. To express your feelings, just don't be shy. Sometimes the discussion of feeling is used to cloak laziness. As Paul Hindemith said, "The impulse or feeling of an artist must be very small if it is manifest in such little knowledge." But, of course, I know that doesn't apply to you.

[Q.] Young musicians today have a lot of technique, but they haven't picked up the feeling of jazz in the streets or in the clubs like the older ones, isn't that so?

[A.] Not at all. If anything, the older musicians were much more technical. Clifford Brown, Clark Terry, Freddie Webster, Booker Little, Lee Morgan had highly developed technique. Not to mention Dizzy or Pops.[3] Miles and Monk[4] went to Juilliard. Jimmy Blanton took lessons from symphony bassists all around the world. Wayne Shorter went to New York University. Coleman Hawkins studied the cello. Jazz musicians have always respected scholarship.

The greatest lesson was the chance to take a master class by hearing a practicing virtuoso on the bandstand. Louis Armstrong sat at the feet of Joe Oliver, Charlie Parker at the feet of Lester Young, Buster Smith, and Chu Berry. Johnny Hodges learned from Sidney Bechet. Sweets Edison, Rex Stewart, Ray Nance, Cootie Williams, and Bunny Berrigan learned from Louis Armstrong, and so on.

The lives of young musicians are not less confused or painful or emotional than those of older musicians. It is just that the means of expressing their lives has been corrupted by cultural celebration of the insignificant. There have always been many types of jazzmen from the hellraisers like Sidney Bechet and Fats Waller to the pious like Lawrence Brown, the humorous like Dizzy Gillespie, the intellectual like Coleman Hawkins, the drug addicted like Charlie Parker, and the downright nice like Clifford Brown.

Today's musicians are equally diverse. The problem is not their technique or emotion, but the impoverished cultural soil in which they must grow. They are trying hard, but get very little help. Play the blues and swing, if you want to play jazz. Please don't go looking to pay dues and think it will make your playing soulful. Soul is honest expression, with warmth. Soul is a spiritual proposition. Soul means you make other people feel good.

[Q.] Play something for us.

[A.] With pleasure.

The blues has a twelve-bar form.

---

[2]Drummer Herlin Riley.

[3]Dizzy Gillespie, Louis Armstrong.

[4]Miles Davis, Thelonious Monk.

To improvise means attempting to improve and working with whatever is available.

Swing is a matter of ongoing coordination and participation.

The ultimate achievement in jazz soloing in the expression of a distinctive personality.

The ultimate achievement in jazz music is the interplay of distinctive personalities through some type of musical form. The group establishes its identity with this interplay while swinging.

Jazz is musical interplay on blues-based melodies, harmonies, rhythms, and textures in the motion of an improvised groove. A groove is the successful coordination of differing parts—like as clock. That's a vamp.

[Q.] Why do you all wear suits? Is that some kind of statement?

[A.] It looks good. That's the only reason. That's a tag.

The sound of human feeling has a power and intensity of its own. The power in jazz comes from the passionate intelligence of a group of musicians playing together. Musical freedom of speech. This has a timeless quality. The technology of the human soul does not change like an automobile or computer. That's why loud, overamplified sound defeats the main purpose of jazz, to invite the audience into a group's emotion, not to impose it on them. Volume gives the illusion of a power you have not earned and cannot control. That's a coda.

113   Supporting New Music

Jane Alexander, an actress who served a term as chairman of the National Endowment for the Arts, or NEA, expressed one side of a controversy about support for the arts in a 1997 statement:

> What future do we want for ourselves and for our nation? Our non-profit arts and the means by which they are funded are at a crossroads. In an age of diminishing resources in the public sector and no dedicated expansion in the private sector, we need to find ways to ensure that the arts are sustained and flourish at the community level. . . .*

The position on the other side, advanced by conservative members of Congress, can be guessed from their attempts to cut off all the Endowment's funding.

Support systems for musicians who write and perform "new music" are quite limited, primarily because the very term *new music* embraces twentieth-century compositions that general audiences neither like nor understand. Even so, some individuals and institutions, especially colleges and universities, have encouraged new creativity. Arts centers, which have sprung up in many communities, represent a new kind of venue for the arts. A 1998 *New York Times* survey paints a scene of growing enthusiasm for the arts across the United States, much of it outside the traditional, large city centers.

One organization that has supported music since early in the twentieth century is the American Society of Composers, Authors and Publishers, or ASCAP. The organization, which now numbers more than sixty-eight thousand composers, lyricists, and music publishers, collects royalties for its members from radio and television stations and performances venues.

Other organizations include the American Composers Alliance, which has published some fourteen thousand of its members' works through its American Composers Editions, and the American Symphony Orchestra League, which strives to further the cause of orchestral music.

The American Music Center was founded in 1939 by six classical-music composers: Marion Bauer, Aaron Copland, Howard Hanson, Otto Luening, Harrison Kerr, and Quincy Porter. The Center maintains a library of scores and recordings and serves as an information gathering and distribution service. Its Meet The Composer Fund, which became an independent organization in 1976, enables composers to participate actively in performances of their work by performing, conducting, speaking with the audience, presenting workshops, giving interviews, or coaching rehearsals. Meet The Composer, administered from its central office in New York as well as by a coalition of

---

*Jane Alexander, Remarks at the American Canvas Meeting, Washington, D.C., January 30, 1997.

regional arts organizations that comprise the National Affiliate Network, helps both emerging and established composers. Its commissioning, residency, and education programs have served as catalysts in the creation of thousands of new works in many styles across the United States and around the world.

The founder and president emeritus of Meet The Composer is John Duffy (b. 1928), a composer who has won Emmy, ASCAP, and other awards. A New Yorker by birth, he found early success with theater music and went on, in his twenties, to become music director, composer, and conductor of Shakespeare under the Stars in Yellow Springs, Ohio, followed by similar posts at the American Shakespeare Festival in Stratford, Connecticut, and the Guthrie, Long Wharf, and Vivian Beaumont Theaters. He has more than three hundred works for orchestra, opera, theater, television, and film to his credit.

The American Composers Forum was founded in the Twin Cities in 1973 by Libby Larsen and Stephen Paulus under the name Minnesota Composers Forum. Its mission is to unite individual artists, encourage musical creativity, provide services, and facilitate performances. From small beginnings it has grown significantly, particularly during the 1990s, taking on its present name in 1995.

The Forum hosts programs that (1) reach new audiences through commissions, performance incentives, radio, and recording and residency programs; (2) nurture creativity through outreach, including reading sessions and fellowship programs; and (3) seek new concert venues. It remains headquartered in Saint Paul but has established regional chapters around the country.

Composer Libby Larsen (b. 1950) has produced a significant body of work in a variety of media. Her *Sonnets from the Portuguese* was featured on a 1994 Grammy Award-winning CD with Arleen Auger. Other recordings include an all-Larsen release by the London Symphony Orchestra (1997). Her opera, *Frankenstein, the Modern Prometheus*, about which she speaks below, received high praise. Her next opera, *Eric Hermannson's Soul*, was premiered in November 1998, and her *String Symphony* was performed by the Minnesota Orchestra a month later.

Larsen served as composer-in-residence with the Minnesota Orchestra, becoming the first woman to serve as resident composer with a major orchestra. She used this and other posts, such as her service as a board member of the American Symphony Orchestra League and as an adviser to the NEA and ASCAP, to help lessen the gap between classical music and its audiences.

JOHN DUFFY

Interview by J. Heywood Alexander (1998)

When was Meet The Composer founded?

Meet The Composer actually opened its doors on July 1, 1974, in a corner of the American Music Center. I was hired by a group of composers representing non-American Music Center people and some members of the American Music Center. I named the organization and set out its mission and I ran it from that day forward.[1] I had been until that time the music director and composer at the American Shakespeare Festival but I wanted to be more involved with composers. The composers who were outside of the American Music Center, who were very keen to have me run this organization and who helped organize it with the American Music Center board, included Steve Reich, Milton Babbitt, Leroy Jenkins, Charles Dodge, and Cecil Taylor. The New York State Council on the Arts got us started with a generous grant.

We began the first year by making grants to New York organizations for all kinds of music. There is such diversity in this country—symphonic, chamber, jazz, theater and all the rest. The grants were for composers to present their music in communities throughout New York State. We introduced the works in workshops, lecture demonstrations, on radio, etc. The whole idea was to introduce the music to audiences and to break down some of the barriers that separate composers from concert goers.

Since then the organization has increased greatly in scope.

We began to get more and more attention because of the high quality of work that we were doing. But the central idea of the organization remained the same—to help composers earn a living composing. We worked for several years on a commissioning handbook to give composers and people who were

interested in commissioning composers an idea of how to go about it. The emphasis was to focus on integrating composers into society. We left the selection of the composer to the organization that would apply to us. Those organizations could be libraries, symphony orchestras, jazz ensembles, municipal organizations and the like. As we became more and more well known, foundations and corporations came to us with programs that focused on composers and the creation of new works. This led to our orchestral residency programs which at one time gave composers residencies with about thirty-two orchestras across the country. Many new works were created which received Pulitzer and other prizes. All were recorded.

Then we set up a dance program to foster the collaboration of composers and choreographers in creating new works; also education programs where composers created music for kids in school and their particular combinations of instruments. In general in the time I was involved commissions numbered about twenty-five thousand.

What about the National Affiliates?

The National Affiliates were established over a period from 1976 to 1980. The whole idea was to start affiliates where people in the community ran their own programs according to what the needs and means of the community were and to carry through the mission of Meet The Composer as it pertained to that particular community. That evolved into Meet The Composer: Midwest, Meet The Composer: Mid-America, Meet The Composer: New England, and the others. What we did in the first year was to provide 75 percent of the support for composer fees; 50 percent the second year; and 25 percent the third year. We encouraged local organizations to go out and raise their own matching funds.

What do you see as future directions for Meet The Composer?

Addressing issues that have to do with new generations of composers and their needs. Many young

John Duffy, Interview by J. Heywood Alexander, October 1998.

[1]Until 1995.

composers are now working in theater and film as a means of honing their craft, and many are working with advanced technology. Also, there is a great need for education in the arts. Meet The Composer seeks to respond to the needs of the community to provide composers a chance to serve our musical lives and earn a living doing so—like with Bach and Duke Ellington, an integral part of society.

LIBBY LARSEN

Interview by J. Heywood Alexander (1998)

You founded the Minnesota Composers Forum in 1973 together with Stephen Paulus when you were still a graduate student at the University of Minnesota. What led you to this innovative step?

From the outset of our graduate studies at the University of Minnesota, Steve and I deeply felt that the purpose of music is to communicate with individual auditors (the audience) through the best interpretive powers and spirit of performers. Not an innovative concept, to be sure. However, we both noticed that for many, in fact for most composers, an essential part of their process was missing or available only sporadically—that being the audience. There was no regular outlet for the work of young composers at the University of Minnesota. We were relegated to working in small groups, playing our pieces for each other on a piano. The best listening opportunity we could hope for our music was a laboratory situation consisting of a composition teacher and four or five composition students. This left the audience completely out of the creative process. That and an occasional performance (maybe one per year) of our pieces on a student concert was the creative process available to us.

Simply, the situation we found ourselves in as student composers at the University of Minnesota was only half the process we felt composers needed in order to develop their music and ultimately their lives' work as composers. We just naturally felt passionately that composers are a community and that that community was in need of a forum which existed beyond the academic definition. We suspected but didn't really know that the state of the composer in which we found ourselves was the state of the composer all over the country.

I remember very clearly when we formed the Forum. We were having coffee at Shevlin Hall on the University of Minnesota campus. We'd been talking seriously about making the group. That day we formulated our first mission statement: "To provide a platform and audience for the creation and performance of new music by Minnesota Composers." Also that day, we decided that the first thing to do administratively was to hire a friend, John Low, to create a letterhead. Steve and I paid for it ourselves. We knew that with a letterhead and our own logo we could meet on a professional footing with potential board members, concert producers, and funders. And from the very beginning, Steve and I wanted to create an organization in which the composer defined him/herself stylistically.

There was to be no stylistic bias. Each composer was to take responsibility for their own musical language, purpose and intent. The Forum was to act as a practical home for each composer's artistic journey. In addition, we knew that we wanted to found an organization which would survive well beyond the time that we were involved in its administration.

The increased outreach by the Forum, particularly during the 1990s, must validate your vision.

My father always said that "he who names it claims it." Within the first five years of the Forum's activity the Forum listed among its initiative a four-

Libby Larsen, Online interview by J. Heywood Alexander, November 1998.

concert series in varying locations, including a park series, the Walker Art Center, the Landmark Center series, our own choir (The Forum Chorale), a church series, a radio series with Minnesota Public Radio, the Composers Commissioning program, the McKnight Fellowships, the newsletter, and basically all the structure which it now enjoys. We acted as the sponsoring institution to bring Meet The Composer to the Upper Midwest. We spun Meet The Composer off into its present Midwest home after two years. We were, in fact, open to national membership after the first two years. And we received national funding (NEA, Rockefeller Foundation) early on.

What is very exciting about the activity of the 1990s is that what we young composers felt so passionately in the early 1970s—*that composers are vital to the musical spirit of a culture and that composers' work exists and belongs everywhere—from the smallest local park to the most abstract intellectual concert.* What Steve and I knew to be the truth in our lives as composers is felt deeply and passionately throughout the lives of composers across time, national boundaries, and stylistic investigations.

I remember when you and Stephen Paulus were in Cleveland in the late 1980s upon the occasion of the premiere of Bain Murray's new opera, The Legend. *One of the things you spoke about in your talk was creating/producing opera that could be performed from the back of a truck, and hence taken easily to rural locations. Is this the kind of thinking that lies behind the Forum?*

Your question concerning my comment that "opera can (and often should) be created to be performed from the back of a truck" is a very good one. Yes, I believe that the music itself is the thing that makes the music great. If the music is great, it will inspire greatness in all the other aspects brought to it. In opera, the music will inspire great singers, conductors, instrumentalists, directors, and designers to be even greater. But it is the music—the alpha and omega—which must be deeply strong and truthful.

Do you watch the television show *M*A*S*H*? In one of the final episodes Dr. Winchester teaches

Mozart to local Korean musicians. They leave the camp seated in the back of a jeep playing Mozart. It is truly touching and it illustrates, I think, what I meant with my statement.

The only thing that is truly universal and deeply moving about music is the music. All of the other parts are cultural, contextual, and over time, fleeting. Yes, of course, many musical works demand extra musical context to make them more communicative but what lives on in that part of us which *is* universal and perhaps timeless is the *music*. It's not for us to say at the time a piece of music is created and heard in an unsophisticated context if it is any more or less meaningful than a piece created in and for a sophisticated context. It it were, I wager to say that we would not have Bach, Duke Ellington, or many of the Mozart operas.

How have the concepts which lie behind the American Composers Forum influenced your own style?

I am not certain that I could separate the concepts of the first seventeen years of the Composers Forum from my own beliefs about music. For myself, there is an infinitely complicated balance between my own ability to truly create and the perceived needs of the audience and community for which I immediately create a piece of music. I can't [write] music based solely on other people's needs. I think this is because the creative process is an intricate dialogue between instinct and practical demands mediated by experience and technique. I want always to compose music which will be absorbed in its immediate hearing and retained in the heart through time and life experience.

What can you tell us about style in your opera. Frankenstein, the Modern Prometheus?

The musical style is based in free-ranging tonality which I chose as a deliberate metaphor for Victor's state of being. He is never at rest. He can never fully hear or take in those around him who are grounded in tonality. I made a deliberate choice to mix the sound of the entire opera. A recording engineer is needed as a member of the orchestra to mix the sound in real time throughout the opera.

Added to the orchestra is a bank of synthesizers. I use them in many ways but chiefly to make endless electronic droning—so crucial to a contemporary audience's ability to connect to the tension of Victor's moral dilemma. The mixed sound is both a metaphor and a reality. It is a metaphor for the theme of technology for its own sake. And of course, mixed sound is a reality in our musical world—one with which we classically trained musicians must deal whether we like it or not. I like it.

The vocal lines in the opera are often deliberately disjunct and truncated. I did this to heighten the sense of each character's inability to fully comprehend, much less deal with the events of the story. My goal was to create an overall atmosphere of gothic horror and Hieronymus Bosch.[2]

You have enjoyed several appointments as composer-in-residence with important orchestras. What has been your experience with these in terms of the orchestras' outreach and audience?

Each of the three orchestras with which I have been associated perceives itself as having trouble cultivating audiences. In fact, after serving on the Board of Directors of the American Symphony Orchestra League nearly a decade, I cannot think of an orchestra in the country that feels it is secure in its future or its audience. It seems to me that especially in the last half of this century in which classical music has become, by its own wish, an industry, the issues surrounding the question of audience have changed drastically. As I listen to orchestras' administrators and Boards of Directors wrestle with the problems of not enough audience to monetarily support entirely too much product I am struck with how easily, and I think naively, the conversation focuses on the repertoire as the "answer" to the "problem."

While accessibility of the music is a central issue, it is certainly and potentially also a central problem. Why? Because the passion, dedication, and spirit of the conductor and musicians absolutely *must be there, in the hall, in the music,* on fire and consuming the air. Without it any efforts to bring people into the hall are wasted.

When the musicians are asked to perform too often (which I think they are) and they are asked to perform a prescribed repertoire over and over again (which they most certainly are) and they are asked to perform music for which they have little or no passion (which they often are) it does not matter how the music is packaged and promoted much less what music is being programmed. The audience will have a very hard time feeling the value of the music in their lives if the performers themselves do not feel it.

We still seem to be reacting to a "gap" between composer and audience exacerbated by certain trends in composition particularly after World War I. To what extent do you feel our younger composers are "audience conscious"?

I like John Cage's definition of music as "any sound is potentially music, even silence." So in my music, any sound is a candidate to be part of my composition. I believe that my instrument is the air and that all sound sources are available to it. I believe that composition is the art of arranging sound in time and space. I believe that each composition of mine should communicate something of what it is like to be alive in this particular culture—a culture which is more percussive than lyrical, more unformed than formed, bound together by its belief in variety, confused by its own enormous energy, and deeply committed to find its own way as a culture in the face of having no one way. I believe that people listen uniquely and individually to music but that music can at the same time communicate its universals. I believe that a new song can be as new as a piece of new abstract music. That is why I list Duke Ellington and J. S. Bach in the same sentence above. What is "new" about a piece of new music is the composer's ability to deeply communicate something about what it is like to be alive through his/her sense of the order of sound in time and space.

There still does seem to be a gap. On the other hand, the number and definition of "audiences" has grown exponentially with the industrialization and market driven categorization of music in our culture. Still, in the contemporary concert hall

---

[2]Renowned Netherlandish artist (c. 1450–1516) of religious subjects, often fantastic and demonic.

where composers like myself want to find our audiences, I've seen composers over the last twenty-five years deal more and more with the questions of audience.

Twenty-five years ago, when abstract expressionism was the dominant trend, young composers were encouraged to disregard, even disdain, the audience. At the time Milton Babbitt wrote his famous essay "Who Cares If You Listen?" the academicians misinterpreted the intent of his article and adopted it almost as a battle cry to disregard the audience *for the sake of the future of music*. It wasn't until years later that I learned the intent of his article. It was written as a proposal to the faculty at Princeton to establish a Ph.D. in Music Theory. It had a different title. When it became widely published it was retitled, not by Babbitt. I remember that the article evoked a passion in me. I thought "I care" and then I set about figuring out what that meant.

Today, young composers care if an audience listens. I believe their challenge is to determine which audience they wish to embrace, even if it is an instinctual audience not defined by marketplace, academic or otherwise. So yes, I feel that our younger composers are "audience conscious." I dearly hope that the consciousness is a challenge to them as artists.

CREDITS

Chester Anderson: "Notes for the New Geology" from *San Francisco Oracle,* edited by Allen Cohen.

Edward Andrews: Shaker song texts from *The Gift to be Simple, Dances and Rituals of the American Shakers.* Reprinted by permission of Dover Publications.

Louis Armstrong: *A Self-Portrait.* Text is reproduced with permission, and copyright is held by Eakins Press Foundation, 1971.

Count Basie: *Good Morning Blues* by Count Basie, as told to Albert Murray, copyright © 1985 by Albert Murray and Count Basie Enterprises, Inc. Reprinted by permission of Random House, Inc.

Henry Bellamann: "Charles Ives: The Man and His Music," from *The Musical Quarterly,* January 1933. Reprinted by permission of Oxford University Press.

Leonard Bernstein: "Speaking of Music." Copyright © renewed 1985 by Leonard Bernstein. Used by permission of Amberson Holdings LLC.

Leonard Bernstein: Quote from "Tanglewood, Koussevitzky, and Hope" in *Findings* by Leonard Bernstein. Copyright © 1982 by Leonard Bernstein. Used by permission of Amberson Holdings LLC.

Leonard Bernstein: "The Mountain Disappears" by Leonard Bernstein. Copyright © Leonard Bernstein, 1954. Renewed. Used by permission of Amberson Holdings LLC.

John Cage: *Silence* © 1961 by John Cage. Reprinted by permission of Wesleyan University Press.

Robert Chesterman: "Leonard Bernstein in conversation with Robert Chesterman" from *Conversations with Conductors.* Reprinted by permission of Chrystalis Books, Ltd.

Dale Cockrell: *Excelsior: Journals of the Hutchinson Family Singers.* Reprinted courtesy of Pendragon Press.

Aaron Copland: Blashfield Address delivered at the American Academy of Arts and Letters, New York City, May 25, 1952. Published with permission of AAAL.

George W. Cronyn: Excerpt from *American Indian Poetry* by George Cronyn, editor. Copyright © 1918, 1934 and renewed 1962 by George Cronyn. Used by permission of Ballantine Books, a division of Random House, Inc.

Alonso de Benavides: *Fray Alfonso de Benavides' Revised Memorial of 1634,* ed. Frederick Hodge, George Hammond, and Agapito Rey. Copyright © 1945. Reprinted with permission of University of New Mexico Press.

R. Nathaniel Dett: *Religious Folk-Songs of the Negro as Sung at the Hampton Institute.* Courtesy of Hampton University Archives.

William Duckworth: Interviews with Steve Reich and Phillip Glass from *Talking Music.* Reprinted by permission of Schirmer Books.

Thomas A. Edison: *The Diary and Sundry Observations of Thomas Alva Edison.* Philosophical Library, New York.

Allen Edwards: *Flawed Words and Stubborn Sounds: A Conversation with Elliot Carter* by Allen Edwards. Copyright © 1971 by W. W. Norton & Company, Inc. Used by permission of W. W. Norton & Company, Inc.

Duke Ellington: *Music Is My Mistress* by Duke Ellington, copyright ©1973 by Duke Ellington, Inc. Used by permission of Doubleday, a division of Random House, Inc.

Benjamin Franklin: *The Autobiography of Benjamin Franklin* by Leonard W. Labaree. Copyright © 1964 by Yale University Press. Reprinted by permission of Yale University Press.

George Gershwin: "Rhapsody in Catfish Row" from the *New York Times,* October 20, 1935: sect 10. Reprinted by permission of the *New York Times.*

Left Handed: *Son of Old Man Hat: A Navaho Autobiography,* recorded by Walter Dyk. Rights held by the University of Nebraska Press.

Roy Harris: "Problems of American Composers" from *American Composers on American Music: A Symposium,* ed. Henry Cowell. Copyright © Stanford University Press, 1933. Reprinted by permission of the Continuum International Publishing Company, Inc.

Charles Ives: "Essays before a Sonata" from *Essays before a Sonata, the Majority, and Other Writings by Charles Ives* by Charles Ives, edited by Howard Boatright. Copyright © 1961, 1962 by W. W. Norton & Company, Inc., renewed 1990. Used by permission of W. W. Norton & Company, Inc.

Charles Ives: "Some Quarter Tone Impressions" from *Essays before a Sonata, the Majority, and Other Writings by Charles Ives* by Charles Ives, edited by Howard Boatright. Copyright © 1961, 1962 by W. W. Norton & Company, Inc., renewed 1990. Used by permission of W. W. Norton & Company, Inc.

Charles Ives: From *Memos* by Charles Ives. Copyright © 1972 by the National Institute of Arts and Letters. Used by permission of W. W. Norton & Company, Inc.

George Pullen Jackson: Excerpt from *White Spirituals in the Southern Uplands* by George P. Jackson. Copyright © 1933 by the University of North Carolina Press. Used by permission of the publisher.

Alan Lomax: From *The Folk Songs of North America* by Alan Lomax, copyright © 1960 by Alan Lomax. Used by permission of Doubleday, a division of Random House, Inc.

John A. Lomax and Alan Lomax: *Whoopee Ti Yi Yo, Git Along Little Dogies.* Collected, adapted, and arranged by John A.

INDEX